22nd Nordic Conference of Computational Linguistics (NoDaLiDa 2019)

NEALT Proceedings Series Volume 42

Turku, Finland
30 September – 2 October 2019

Editors:

Mareike Hartmann
Barbara Plank

ISBN: 978-1-5108-9444-0

NEALT

Northern European Association for
Language Technology

NEALT Proceedings Series No. 42

Proceedings of the
22nd Nordic Conference
on Computational Linguistics
(NoDaLiDa)

photo by Patrick Selin on Unsplash

September 30 - October 2, 2019
University of Turku
Turku, Finland

Editors: Mareike Hartmann and Barbara Plank

NoDaLiDa 2019

22nd Nordic Conference on Computational Linguistics (NoDaLiDa)

Proceedings of the Conference

September 30–October 2, 2019
University of Turku
Turku, Finland

Published by
Linköping University Electronic Press, Sweden
Linköping Electronic Conference Proceedings, No. 167
NEALT Proceedings Series, No. 42
Indexed in the ACL anthology

Introduction

Welcome to the 22nd Nordic Conference on Computational Linguistics (NoDaLiDa 2019) held at the University of Turku in the beautiful city of Turku in Finland, on September 30-October 2, 2019. The aim of NoDaLiDa is to bring together researchers in the Nordic countries interested in any aspect related to human language and speech technologies. It is a great honor for me to serve as the general chair of NoDaLiDa 2019.

NoDaLiDa has a very long tradition. It stems from a working group initiative led by Sture Allèn, Kolbjörn Heggstad, Baldur Jönsson, Viljo Kohonen and Bente Maegaard (as the preface of the oldest workshop proceedings in the ACL anthology reveals).[1] They organized the first NoDaLiDa ("Nordiska datalingvistikdagar") in Gothenburg on October 10-11, 1977. In 2006, NEALT, the Northern European Association for Language Technology was founded. We are very honored to bring this bi-annual conference after 42 years to Turku this fall.

We solicited three different types of papers (long, short, demo papers) and received 78 valid submissions. In total, we accepted 50 papers, which will be presented as 34 oral presentations, 10 posters and 5 demo papers. A total of 4 submissions were withdrawn in the process. Each paper was reviewed by three experts. We are extremely grateful to the Programme Committee members for their detailed and helpful reviews. Overall, there are 10 oral sessions with talks and one poster session organized into themes over the two days, starting each day with a keynote talk.

We would like to thank our two keynote speakers for travel to Turku and sharing their work. Marie-Catherine de Marneffe from Ohio State University will talk about "Do you know that there's still a chance? Identifying speaker commitment for natural language understanding". Grzegorz Chrupała from Tilburg University will talk about "Investigating neural representations of speech and language". We are also very grateful to Fred Karlsson, who accepted to share his insights into the Finnish language in the traditional NoDaLiDa language tutorial.

The conference is preceded by 5 workshops on a diverse set of topics: deep learning for natural language processing, NLP for Computer-Assisted Language Learning, Constraint Grammar Methods, Tools and Applications, NLP and pseudonymisation and Financial Narrative Processing. This shows the breadth of topics that can be found in language technology these days, and we are extremely happy and grateful to the workshop organizers for complementing the main program this way.

There will be two social events. A reception which is sponsored by the City of Turku and held at the Old Town Hall in Turku. A conference dinner will be held in the Turku Castle in the King's hall. Two fantastic evenings are awaiting.

I would like to thank the entire team that made NoDaLiDa 2019 possible in the first place. First of all, I would like to thank Beáta Megyesi for inviting me to take up this exciting (and admittedly at times demanding) role and all her valuable input regarding NEALT and previous editions of NoDaLiDa. Jörg Tiedemann, for the smooth transition from the previous NoDaLiDa edition and his input and work as program chair; the program chair committee Jurgita Kapočiūtė-Dzikienė, Hrafn Loftsson, Patrizia Paggio, and Erik Velldal, for working hard on putting the program together. I am particularly grateful to Jörg Tiedemann, Jurgita Kapočiūtė-Dzikienė, Kairit Sirts and Patrizia Paggio for leading the reviewing process. Special thanks goes to the workshop chairs Richard Johansson and Kairit Sirts, who have done an invaluable job with leading the workshop selection and organization. A big thanks also to Miryam

---

[1] https://www.aclweb.org/anthology/events/ws-1977/

de Lhoneux for her work as social media chair and Mareike Hartmann for leading the publication efforts that led to this volume, as well as the coordination of the workshop proceedings. Thank you! Finally, my ultimate thanks goes to the amazing local organization committee and team. Thank you, Filip Ginter and Jenna Kanerva. With your infinite support and pro-active engagement in organizing NoDaLiDa you are the ones that make NoDaLiDa possible and surely an unforgettable experience. Thanks also to the entire local team (with special thanks to Hans Moen for help with the program): Li-Hsin Chang, Rami Ilo, Suwisa Kaewphan, Kai Hakala, Roosa Kyllönen, Veronika Laippala, Akseli Leino, Juhani Luotolahti, Farrokh Mehryary, Hans Moen, Maria Pyykönen, Sampo Pyysalo, Samuel Rönnqvist, Antti Saloranta, Antti Virtanen, Sanna Volanen. NoDaLiDa 2019 has received financial support from our generous sponsors, which we would also like to thank here.

This is the usual place for the greetings from the local organizers, but as we set out to write it, it turns out that Barbara already said it all. So we really only need to add one thing: huge thanks to Barbara for all the hard work she put into NoDaLiDa. We can only wonder where you found the time for all this. We hope the Turku edition of NoDaLiDa will be a success, at least we tried our best to make it so. In two weeks we will know. — Filip, Jenna, and the local team

Danke - kiitos!

We very much hope that you will have an enjoyable and inspiring time at NoDaLiDa 2019 in Turku.

Barbara Plank

København

September 2019

General Chair

Barbara Plank, IT University of Copenhagen, Denmark

Program Committee

Jurgita Kapočiūtė-Dzikienė, Vytautas Magnus University, Lithuania
Hrafn Loftsson, Reykjavík University, Iceland
Patrizia Paggio, University of Copenhagen, Denmark
Jörg Tiedemann, University of Helsinki, Finland
Erik Velldal, University of Oslo, Norway

Organizing Committee

Publication Chair: Mareike Hartmann, University of Copenhagen, Denmark
Social Media Chair: Miryam de Lhoneux, Uppsala University, Sweden
Workshop Chair: Richard Johansson, Chalmers Technical University and University of Gothenburg, Sweden
Workshop Chair: Kairit Sirts, University of Tartu, Estonia
Local Chair: Filip Ginter, University of Turku, Finland
Local Chair: Jenna Kanerva, University of Turku, Finland

Invited Speakers

Marie-Catherine de Marneffe, Ohio State University
Grzegorz Chrupała, Tilburg University

Reviewers

Mostafa Abdou, University of Copenhagen
Yvonne Adesam, Department of Swedish, University of Gothenburg
Lars Ahrenberg, Linköping University
Laura Aina, Pompeu Fabra University
Eivind Alexander Bergem, UiO
Krasimir Angelov, University of Gothenburg and Chalmers University of Technology
Maria Barrett, University of Copenhagen
Valerio Basile, University of Turin
Joachim Bingel, University of Copenhagen
Arianna Bisazza, University of Amsterdam
Kristín Bjarnadóttir, HI.is
Anna Björk Nikulásdóttir, Grammatek ehf
Marcel Bollmann, University of Copenhagen
Gerlof Bouma, University of Gothenburg
Gosse Bouma, Rijksuniversiteit Groningen
Hande Celikkanat, University of Helsinki
Lin Chen, UIC
Jeremy Claude Barnes, University of Oslo
Mathias Creutz, University of Helsinki
Hercules Dalianis, DSV-Stockholm University
Miryam de Lhoneux, Uppsala University
Koenraad De Smedt, University of Bergen
Rodolfo Delmonte, Universita' Ca' Foscari
Leon Derczynski, ITU Copenhagen
Stefanie Dipper, Bochum University
Senka Drobac, University of Helsinki
Jens Edlund, KTH Royal Institute of Technology
Raquel Fernández, University of Amsterdam
Björn Gambäck, Norwegian University of Science and Technology
Filip Ginter, University of Turku
Jon Gudnason, Reykjavik University
Mika Hämäläinen, University of Helsinki
Daniel Hardt, Copenhagen Business School
Petter Haugereid, Western Norway University of Applied Sciences
Daniel Hershcovich, University of Copenhagen
Angelina Ivanova, University of Oslo
Tommi Jauhiainen, University of Helsinki
Anders Johannsen, Apple Inc
Sofie Johansson, Institutionen för svenska språket
Jenna Kanerva, University of Turku
Jussi Karlgren, Gavagai and KTH Royal Institute of Technology
Roman Klinger, University of Stuttgart
Mare Koit, University of Tartu
Artur Kulmizev, Uppsala University

Andrey Kutuzov, University of Oslo
Veronika Laippala, University of Turku
Krister Lindén, University of Helsinki
Nikola Ljubešić, Faculty of Humanities and Social Sciences
Jan Tore Loenning, University of Oslo
Hrafn Loftsson, Reykjavik University
Diego Marcheggiani, Amazon
Bruno Martins, IST and INESC-ID - Instituto Superior Técnico, University of Lisbon
Hans Moen, University of Turku
Costanza Navarretta, University of Copenhagen
Mattias Nilsson, Karolinska Institutet, Department of Clinical Neuroscience
Joakim Nivre, Uppsala University
Farhad Nooralahzadeh, UiO
Pierre Nugues, Lund University, Department of Computer Science Lund, Sweden
Emily Öhman, University of Helsinki
Robert Östling, Department of Linguistics, Stockholm University
Lilja Øvrelid, University of Oslo
Viviana Patti, University of Torino
Eva Pettersson, Uppsala University
Ildikó Pilán, University of Gothenburg
Tommi A Pirinen, University of Hamburg
Alessandro Raganato, University of Helsinki
Taraka Rama, University of Oslo
Vinit Ravishankar, University of Oslo
Marek Rei, University of Cambridge
Nils Rethmeier, DFKI LT-Lab
Corentin Ribeyre, Etermind
Fabio Rinaldi, University of Zurich
Samuel Rönnqvist, University of Turku
Jack Rueter, University of Helsinki
Rune Sætre, Dep. of Computer Science (IDI), Norwegian University of Science and Technology (NTNU) in Trondheim
Magnus Sahlgren, RISE AI
Marina Santini, SICS East ICT
Yves Scherrer, University of Helsinki
Natalie Schluter, IT University of Copenhagen
Ravi Shekhar, University of Trento
Miikka Silfverberg, University of Colorado Boulder
Raivis Skadiņš, Tilde
Aaron Smith, Google
Steinþór Steingrímsson, The Árni Magnússon Institute for Icelandic Studies
Torbjørn Svendsen, Norwegian University of Science and Technology
Nina Tahmasebi, University of Gothenburg
Aarne Talman, University of Helsinki
Samia Touileb, University of Oslo
Francis M. Tyers, Indiana University Bloomington

Martti Vainio, University of Helsinki, Institute of Behavioural Sciences
Rob van der Goot, RuG
Raul Vazquez, University of Helsinki
Erik Velldal, University of Oslo
Sumithra Velupillai, TCS, School of Computer Science and Communication, KTH Royal Institute
of Technology
Martin Volk, University of Zurich
Atro Voutilainen, University of Helsinki
Jürgen Wedekind, University of Copenhagen
Mats Wirén, Stockholm University
Anssi Yli-Jyrä, University of Helsinki
Marcos Zampieri, University of Wolverhampton
Heike Zinsmeister, University of Hamburg

Invited Talks

Marie-Catherine de Marneffe: Do you know that there's still a chance? Identifying speaker commitment for natural language understanding.

When we communicate, we infer a lot beyond the literal meaning of the words we hear or read. In particular, our understanding of an utterance depends on assessing the extent to which the speaker stands by the event she describes. An unadorned declarative like "The cancer has spread" conveys firm speaker commitment of the cancer having spread, whereas "There are some indicators that the cancer has spread" imbues the claim with uncertainty. It is not only the absence vs. presence of embedding material that determines whether or not a speaker is committed to the event described: from (1) we will infer that the speaker is committed to there *being* war, whereas in (2) we will infer the speaker is committed to relocating species *not being* a panacea, even though the clauses that describe the events in (1) and (2) are both embedded under "(s)he doesn't believe".

    (1) The problem, I'm afraid, with my colleague here, he really doesn't believe that it's war.

    (2) Transplanting an ecosystem can be risky, as history shows. Hellmann doesn't believe that relocating species threatened by climate change is a panacea.

In this talk, I will first illustrate how looking at pragmatic information of what speakers are committed to can improve NLP applications. Previous work has tried to predict the outcome of contests (such as the Oscars or elections) from tweets. I will show that by distinguishing tweets that convey firm speaker commitment toward a given outcome (e.g., "Dunkirk will win Best Picture in 2018") from ones that only suggest the outcome (e.g., "Dunkirk might have a shot at the 2018 Oscars") or tweets that convey the negation of the event ("Dunkirk is good but not academy level good for the Oscars"), we can outperform previous methods. Second, I will evaluate current models of speaker commitment, using the CommitmentBank, a dataset of naturally occurring discourses developed to deepen our understanding of the factors at play in identifying speaker commitment. We found that a linguistically informed model outperforms a LSTM-based one, suggesting that linguistic knowledge is needed to achieve robust language understanding. Both models however fail to generalize to the diverse linguistic constructions present in natural language, highlighting directions for improvement.

Grzegorz Chrupała: Investigating Neural Representations of Speech and Language

Learning to communicate in natural language is one of the unique human abilities which are at the same time extraordinarily important and extraordinarily difficult to reproduce in silico. Substantial progress has been achieved in some specific data-rich and constrained cases such as automatic speech recognition or machine translation. However the general problem of learning to use natural language with weak and noisy supervision in a grounded setting is still open. In this talk, I will present recent work which addresses this challenge using deep recurrent neural network models. I will then focus on analytical methods which allow us to better understand the nature and localization of representations emerging in such architectures.

Table of Contents

Long Papers

Short Papers

Demo Papers

Conference Program

Monday, September 30, 2019 Workshops

08:00- **Registration**

09:00-17:00 **The First NLPL Workshop on Deep Learning for Natural Language Processing**
Location: PUB2

09:00-17:30 **The 8th Workshop on Natural Language Processing for Computer-Assisted Language Learning (NLP4CALL)**
Location: PUB5

09:00-15:30 **Constraint Grammar - Methods, Tools and Applications**
Location: PUB 209

14:00-17:00 **The Workshop on NLP and Pseudonymisation**
Location: PUB4

09:00-15:30 **The Second Financial Narrative Processing Workshop (FNP 2019)**
Location: PUB 126

10:00-10:30 *Coffee break*

12:00-14:00 *Lunch break*
Location: Holiday Club Caribia

15:00-15:30 *Coffee break*

19:00 *Welcome Reception*
Location: Turku City Hall

09:00-09:15   **Opening**
Location: PUB1

09:15-10:05   **Keynote by Marie-Catherine de Marneffe: Do you know that there's still a chance? Identifying speaker commitment for natural language understanding**
Chair: Joakim Nivre
Location: PUB1

10:05-10:35   *Coffee break*

10:35-12:15   **Parallel session A: Multilinguality and Machine Translation**
Chair: Jörg Tiedemann
Location: PUB1

10:35-11:00   Comparison between NMT and PBSMT Performance for Translating Noisy User-Generated Content
José Carlos Rosales Nuñez, Djamé Seddah and Guillaume Wisniewski

11:00-11:25   Bootstrapping UD treebanks for Delexicalized Parsing
Prasanth Kolachina and Aarne Ranta

11:25-11:50   Lexical Resources for Low-Resource PoS Tagging in Neural Times
Barbara Plank and Sigrid Klerke

11:50-12:15   Toward Multilingual Identification of Online Registers
Veronika Laippala, Roosa Kyllönen, Jesse Egbert, Douglas Biber and Sampo Pyysalo

10:35-12:15   **Parallel session B: Embeddings, Biases and Language Change**
Chair: Richard Johansson
Location: PUB3

10:35-11:00   Gender Bias in Pretrained Swedish Embeddings
Magnus Sahlgren and Fredrik Olsson

11:00-11:25   A larger-scale evaluation resource of terms and their shift direction for diachronic lexical semantics
Astrid van Aggelen, Antske Fokkens, Laura Hollink and Jacco van Ossenbruggen

11:25-11:50   Some steps towards the generation of diachronic WordNets
Yuri Bizzoni, Marius Mosbach, Dietrich Klakow and Stefania Degaetano-Ortlieb

11:50-12:15	An evaluation of Czech word embeddings *Karolína Hořeňovská*

12:15-13:45	*Lunch break* Location: Holiday Club Caribia

13:45-15:00 Parallel session A: Semantics
Chair: Marianna Apidianaki
Location: PUB1

13:45-14:10	Language Modeling with Syntactic and Semantic Representation for Sentence Acceptability Predictions *Adam Ek, Jean-Philippe Bernardy and Shalom Lappin*
14:10-14:35	Comparing linear and neural models for competitive MWE identification *Hazem Al Saied, Marie Candito and Mathieu Constant*
14:35-15:00	A Wide-Coverage Symbolic Natural Language Inference System *Stergios Chatzikyriakidis and Jean-Philippe Bernardy*

13:45-15:00 Parallel session B: Morphology and Syntax
Chair: Kairit Sirts
Location: PUB3

13:45-14:10	Ensembles of Neural Morphological Inflection Models *Ilmari Kylliäinen and Miikka Silfverberg*
14:10-14:35	Nefnir: A high accuracy lemmatizer for Icelandic *Svanhvít Lilja Ingólfsdóttir, Hrafn Loftsson, Jón Friðrik Daðason and Kristín Bjarnadóttir*
14:35-15:00	Syntax-based identification of light-verb constructions *Silvio Ricardo Cordeiro and Marie Candito*

15:00-15:30	*Coffee Break*

15:30-16:45 Parallel session A: Machine Learning Applications, Text Classification
Chair: Jenna Kanerva
Location: PUB1

15:30-15:55	Natural Language Processing in Policy Evaluation: Extracting Policy Conditions from IMF Loan Agreements *Joakim Åkerström, Adel Daoud and Richard Johansson*
15:55-16:20	Comparing the Performance of Feature Representations for the Categorization of the Easy-to-Read Variety vs Standard Language *Marina Santini, Benjamin Danielsson and Arne Jönsson*

16:20-16:45   Unsupervised Inference of Object Affordance from Text Corpora
                     Michele Persiani and Thomas Hellström

15:30-16:45   **Parallel session B: Language Resources and Applications**
                     Chair: Elena Volodina
                     Location: PUB3

15:30-15:55   Annotating evaluative sentences for sentiment analysis: a dataset for Norwegian
                     Petter Mæhlum, Jeremy Barnes, Lilja Øvrelid and Erik Velldal

15:55-16:20   Interconnecting lexical resources and word alignment: How do learners get on with particle verbs?
                     David Alfter and Johannes Graën

16:20-16:45   An Unsupervised Query Rewriting Approach Using N-gram Co-occurrence Statistics to Find Similar Phrases in Large Text Corpora
                     Hans Moen, Laura-Maria Peltonen, Henry Suhonen, Hanna-Maria Matinolli, Riitta Mieronkoski, Kirsi Telen, Kirsi Terho, Tapio Salakoski and Sanna Salanterä

16:45-17:45   **Poster and demo session**
                     Location: Entrance hall

16:45-17:45   **Posters:**
                     Compiling and Filtering ParIce: An English-Icelandic Parallel Corpus
                     Starkaður Barkarson and Steinþór Steingrímsson

                     May I Check Again? ——A simple but efficient way to generate and use contextual dictionaries for Named Entity Recognition. Application to French Legal Texts.
                     Valentin Barriere and Amaury Fouret

                     Predicates as Boxes in Bayesian Semantics for Natural Language
                     Jean-Philippe Bernardy, Rasmus Blanck, Stergios Chatzikyriakidis, Shalom Lappin and Aleksandre Maskharashvili

                     DIM: The Database of Icelandic Morphology
                     Kristín Bjarnadóttir, Kristín Ingibjörg Hlynsdóttir and Steinþór Steingrímsson

                     Bornholmsk Natural Language Processing: Resources and Tools
                     Leon Derczynski and Alex Speed Kjeldsen

                     Morphosyntactic Disambiguation in an Endangered Language Setting
                     Jeff Ens, Mika Hämäläinen, Jack Rueter and Philippe Pasquier

                     Tagging a Norwegian Dialect Corpus
                     Andre Kåsen, Anders Nøklestad, Kristin Hagen and Joel Priestley

The Lacunae of Danish Natural Language Processing
Andreas Kirkedal, Barbara Plank, Leon Derczynski and Natalie Schluter

Tools for supporting language learning for Sakha
Sardana Ivanova, Anisia Katinskaia and Roman Yangarber

Inferring morphological rules from small examples using 0/1 linear programming
Ann Lillieström, Koen Claessen and Nicholas Smallbone

16:45-17:45 **Demos:**

LEGATO: A flexible lexicographic annotation tool
David Alfter, Therese Lindström Tiedemann and Elena Volodina

The OPUS Resource Repository: An Open Package for Creating Parallel Corpora and Machine Translation Services
Mikko Aulamo and Jörg Tiedemann

Garnishing a phonetic dictionary for ASR intake
Iben Nyholm Debess, Sandra Saxov Lamhauge and Peter Juel Henrichsen

Docria: Processing and Storing Linguistic Data with Wikipedia
Marcus Klang and Pierre Nugues

UniParse: A universal graph-based parsing toolkit
Daniel Varab and Natalie Schluter

19:30-23:59 *Conference Dinner*
Location: Turku Castle

Wednesday, October 2, 2019

09:00-09:50 **Keynote by Grzegorz Chrupała: Investigating Neural Representations of Speech and Language**
Chair: Lilja Øvrelid
Location: PUB1

09:50-10:20 *Coffee break*

10:20-12:00 **Parallel session A: Sentiment Analysis and Stance**
Chair: Mathias Creutz
Location: PUB1

10:20-10:45 Lexicon information in neural sentiment analysis: a multi-task learning approach
Jeremy Barnes, Samia Touileb, Lilja Øvrelid and Erik Velldal

10:45-11:10 Aspect-Based Sentiment Analysis using BERT
Mickel Hoang, Oskar Alija Bihorac and Jacobo Rouces

11:10-11:35 Political Stance Detection for Danish
Rasmus Lehmann and Leon Derczynski

11:35-12:00 Joint Rumour Stance and Veracity Prediction
Anders Edelbo Lillie, Emil Refsgaard Middelboe and Leon Derczynski

10:20-12:00 **Parallel session B: Named Entity Recognition**
Chair: Manex Agirrezabal
Location: PUB3

10:20-10:45 Towards High Accuracy Named Entity Recognition for Icelandic
Svanhvít Lilja Ingólfsdóttir, Sigurjón Þorsteinsson and Hrafn Loftsson

10:45-11:10 Named-Entity Recognition for Norwegian
Bjarte Johansen

11:10-11:35 Neural Cross-Lingual Transfer and Limited Annotated Data for Named Entity Recognition in Danish
Barbara Plank

11:35-12:00 Projecting named entity recognizers without annotated or parallel corpora
Jue Hou, Maximilian Koppatz, José María Hoya Quecedo and Roman Yangarber

12:00-13:00 *Lunch break*
Location: Holiday Club Caribia

13:00-14:00   **NEALT business meeting**
Location: PUB1

14:00-15:15   **Parallel session A: Text Generation and Language Model Applications**
Chair: Leon Derczynski
Location: PUB1

14:00-14:25   Template-free Data-to-Text Generation of Finnish Sports News
Jenna Kanerva, Samuel Rönnqvist, Riina Kekki, Tapio Salakoski and Filip Ginter

14:25-14:50   Matching Keys and Encrypted Manuscripts
Eva Pettersson and Beata Megyesi

14:50-15:15   The Seemingly (Un)systematic Linking Element in Danish
Sidsel Boldsen and Manex Agirrezabal

14:00-15:15   **Parallel session B: Speech**
Chair: Grzegorz Chrupała
Location: PUB3

14:00-14:25   Perceptual and acoustic analysis of voice similarities between parents and young children
Evgeniia Rykova and Stefan Werner

14:25-14:50   Enhancing Natural Language Understanding through Cross-Modal Interaction: Meaning Recovery from Acoustically Noisy Speech
Ozge Alacam

14:50-15:15   Predicting Prosodic Prominence from Text with Pre-trained Contextualized Word Representations
Aarne Talman, Antti Suni, Hande Celikkanat, Sofoklis Kakouros, Jörg Tiedemann and Martti Vainio

15:15-15:45   *Coffee Break*

15:45-16:25   **Tutorial on Finnish by Fred Karlsson**
Chair: Filip Ginter
Location: PUB1

16:25-16:35   **Closing**
Location: PUB1

Long Papers

A Comparison between NMT and PBSMT Performance for Translating Noisy User-Generated Content

José Carlos Rosales Núñez[1,2,3]   Djamé Seddah[3]   Guillaume Wisniewski[1,2]

[1]Université Paris Sud, LIMSI
[2] Université Paris Saclay
[3] INRIA Paris

{jose.rosales,guillaume.wisniewski}@limsi.fr   djame.seddah@inria.fr

Abstract

This work compares the performances achieved by Phrase-Based Statistical Machine Translation systems (PBSMT) and attention-based Neural Machine Translation systems (NMT) when translating User Generated Content (UGC), as encountered in social medias, from French to English. We show that, contrary to what could be expected, PBSMT outperforms NMT when translating non-canonical inputs. Our error analysis uncovers the specificities of UGC that are problematic for sequential NMT architectures and suggests new avenue for improving NMT models.

1   Introduction[1]

Neural Machine Translation (Kalchbrenner and Blunsom, 2013; Sutskever et al., 2014a; Cho et al., 2014) and, more specifically, attention-based models (Bahdanau et al., 2015; Jean et al., 2015; Luong et al., 2015; Mi et al., 2016) have recently become the method of choice for machine translation: many works have shown that Neural Machine Translation (NMT) outperforms classic Phrase-Based Statistical Machine Translation (PBSMT) approaches over a wide array of datasets (Bentivogli et al., 2016; Dowling et al., 2018; Koehn and Knowles, 2017). Indeed, NMT provides better generalization and accuracy capabilities (Bojar et al., 2016; Bentivogli et al., 2016; Castilho et al., 2017) even if it has well-identified limits such as over-translating and dropping translations (Mi et al., 2016; Koehn and Knowles, 2017; Le et al., 2017).

This work aims at studying how these interactions impact machine translation of noisy texts as generally found in social media and web forums and often denoted as User Generated Content (UGC). Given the increasing importance of social medias, this type of texts has been extensively studied over the years, *e.g.* (Foster, 2010; Seddah et al., 2012; Eisenstein, 2013).

In this work we focus on UGC in which no grammatical, orthographic or coherence rules are respected, other than those considered by the writer. Such rule-free environment promotes a plethora of vocabulary and grammar variations, which account for the large increase of out-of-vocabulary tokens (OOVs) in UGC corpora with respect to canonical parallel training data.

Translating UGC raises several challenges as it corresponds to both a low-resource scenario — producing parallel UGC corpora is very costly and often problematic due to inconsistencies between translators — and a domain adaptation scenario — only canonical parallel corpora are widely available to train MT systems and they must be adapted to the specificities of UGC. We therefore believe that translating UGC provides a challenging testbed to identify the limits of NMT approaches and to better understand how they are working.

Our contributions are fourfold:

- we compare the performance of PBSMT and NMT systems when translating either canonical or non-canonical corpora;
- we analyze both quantitatively and qualitatively several cases in which PBSMT translations outperform NMT on highly noisy UGC and we discuss the advantages, in terms of robustness, that PBSMT offers over NMT approaches;
- we explain how these findings highlight the limits of seq2seq (Sutskever et al., 2014b) and Transformer (Vaswani et al., 2017) NMT architectures, by studying cases in which, as opposed to the PBSMT system, the attention

---

[1]We thank our anonymous reviewers for their insightful comments. This work was funded by the ANR ParSiTi project (ANR-16-CE33-0021).

mechanism fails to provide a correct translation;

- we introduce the `Cr#pbank` a new French-English parallel corpus made of UGC content built on the French Social Media Bank (Seddah et al., 2012). This corpus is much noisier than existing UGC corpora.

All our data sets are available at https://gitlab.inria.fr/seddah/parsiti.

2 Related Work

The comparison between NMT and PBSMT translation quality has been documented and revisited many times in the literature. Several works, such as (Bentivogli et al., 2016) and (Bojar et al., 2016), conclude that the former outperforms the latter as NMT translations require less post-editing to produce a correct translation. For instance, Castilho et al. (2017) present a detailed comparison of NMT and PBSMT and show that NMT outperforms PBSMT in terms of both fluency and translation accuracy, even if there is no improvement in terms of post-editing needs.

However, other case studies, such as Koehn and Knowles (2017), have defended the idea that NMT was still outperformed by PBSMT in cross-domain and low-resource scenarios. For instance, Negri et al. (2017) showed that, when translating English to French, PBSMT outperforms NMT by a great margin in multi-domain data realistic conditions (heterogeneous training sets with different sizes). Dowling et al. (2018) also demonstrated a significant gap of performance in favor of their PBSMT system's over an out-of-the-box NMT system in a low-resource setting (English-Irish). These conclusions have recently been questioned by Sennrich and Zhang (2019) who showed NMT could achieve good performance in low-resource scenario *when* all hyper-parameters (size of the byte-pair encoding (BPE) vocabulary, number of hidden units, batch size, ...) are correctly tuned and a proper NMT architecture is selected.

The situation for other NMT approaches, such as character-based NMT, is also confusing: Wu et al. (2016) have shown that character-based methods achieve state-of-the-art performance for different language pairs; Belinkov et al. (2017) and Durrani et al. (2019) have demonstrated their systems respective abilities to retrieve good amount of morphological information leveraging on subword level features. However, Belinkov and Bisk (2018) found that these approaches are not robust to noise (both synthetic and natural) when trained only with *clean* corpora. On the other hand, Durrani et al. (2019) concluded that character-based representations were more robust to synthetic and natural noise than word-based approaches. However, they did not find a substantial improvement over BPE tokenization, their BPE MT system even slightly outperforming the character-based one on 3 out of 4 of their test sets, including the one with the highest OOV rate.

Similarly to all these works, we also aim at comparing the performance of PBSMT and NMT approaches, hoping that the peculiarities of UGC will help us to better understand the pros and cons of these two methods. Our approach shares several similarity with the work of Anastasopoulos (2019) that described different experiments to determine how source-side errors can impact the translation quality of NMT models.

3 Experimental Setup

As the goal of this work is to compare the output of NMT and PBSMT when translating UGC corpora. Because of the lack of manually translated UGC, we consider a out-domain scenario in which our systems are trained on the canonical corpora generally used in MT evaluation campaigns and tested on UGC data. We will first describe the datasets used in this work (§3.1), then the different systems we have considered (§3.2) and finally the pre- and post-processing applied (§3.3).

3.1 Data Sets

Parallel corpora We train our models on two different corpora. We first consider the traditional corpus for training MT systems, namely the WMT data made of the `europarl` (v7) corpus[2] and the `newscommentaries` (v10) corpus[3]. We use the `newsdiscussdev2015` corpus as a development set. This is exactly the setup used to train the system described in (Michel and Neubig, 2018) which will be used as a baseline throughout this work.

We also consider, as a second training set, the French-English parallel portion of `OpenSubtitles'18` (Lison et al., 2018), a collection of crowd-sourced peer-reviewed subtitles for movies. We assume that, because it is made of informal dialogs, such as those found in popular *sitcoms*, sentences from `OpenSubtitles` will be much more similar to UGC data than WMT data,

---

[2]www.statmt.org/europarl/
[3]www.statmt.org/wmt15/training-parallel-nc-v10.tgz

in part because most of it originates from social media and consists in streams of conversation. It must however be noted that UGC differs significantly from subtitles in many aspects: emotion denoted with repetitions, typographical and spelling errors, emojis, etc.

To enable a fair comparison between systems trained on WMT and on OpenSubtitles, we consider a small version of the OpenSubtitles that has nearly the same number of tokens as the WMT training set and a large version that contains all OpenSubtitles parallel data.

To evaluate our system on in-domain data, we use the newstest'14 as a test set as well as 11,000 sentences extracted from OpenSubtitles.

Non-canonical UGC To evaluate our models, we consider two data sets of manually translated UGC.

The first one is a collection of French-English parallel sentences manually translated from an extension of the French Social Media Bank (Seddah et al., 2012) which contains texts collected on Facebook, Twitter, as well as from the forums of JeuxVideos.com and Doctissimo.fr.[4]

This corpus, called Cr#pbank, consists of 1,554 comments in French annotated with different kind of linguistic information: Part-of-Speech tags, surface syntactic representations, as well as a normalized form whenever necessary. Comments have been translated from French to English by a native French speaker and extremely fluent, near-native, English speaker. Typographic and grammatical error were corrected in the gold translations but the language register was kept. For instance, idiomatic expressions were mapped directly to the corresponding ones in English (e.g. "mdr" has been translated to "lol" and letter repetitions were also kept (e.g. "ouiii" has been translated to "yesss"). For our experiments, we have divided the Cr#pbank into a test set and a blind test set containing 777 comments each.

We also consider in our experiments, the MTNT corpus (Michel and Neubig, 2018), a dataset made of French sentences that were collected on Reddit and translated into English by professional translators. We used their designated test set and added a blind test set of 599 sentences we sampled from the MTNT validation set. The Cr#pbank and MTNT corpora both differ in the domain they consider, their

collection date, and in the way sentences were collected to ensure they are noisy enough. We will see in Section 4 that the Cr#pbank contains much more variations and noise than the MTNT corpus.

Table 3 presents examples of UGC sentences and their translation found in these two corpora. As shown by these examples, UGC sentences contain many orthographic and grammatical errors and differ from canonical language both in their content (i.e. the topic they address and/or the vocabulary they are using) and their structure. Several statistics of these two corpora are reported in Table 1. As expected, our two UGC test sets have a substantially higher token to type ratio than the canonical test corpora, indicating a higher lexical diversity.

3.2 Machine Translation Systems

We experiment with three MT models: a traditional phrase-based approach and two neural models.

3.2.1 Phrase-based Machine Translation

We use the Moses (Koehn et al., 2007) toolkit as our phrase-based model, using the default features and parameters.

The language model is a 5-gram language model with Knesser-Ney smoothing on the target side of the parallel data. We decided to consider only the parallel data (and not any monolingual data) so that the PBSMT and NMT systems use exactly the same data.

3.2.2 seq2seq model

The first neural model we consider is a seq2seq bi-LSTM architecture with global attention decoding. The seq2seq model was trained using the XNMT toolkit (Neubig et al., 2018).[5] It consists in a 2-layered Bi-LSTM layers encoder and 2-layered Bi-LSTM decoder. It considers, as input, word embeddings of 512 components and each LSTM units has 1 024 components. A dropout probability of 0.3 was introduced (Srivastava et al., 2014). The model was trained using the ADAM optimizer (Kingma and Ba, 2015) with vanilla parameters ($\alpha = 0.02$, $\beta = 0.998$). Other more specific settings include keeping unchanged the learning rate (LR) for the first two epochs, a LR decay method based on the improvement of the performance on

---

[4]Popular French websites devoted respectively to video-games and health.

[5]We decided to use XNMT, instead of OpenNMT in our experiments in order to compare our results to the ones of Michel and Neubig (2018).

Corpus	#sentences	#tokens	ASL	TTR
train set				
WMT	2.2M	64.2M	29.7	0.20
Small	9.2M	57.7M	6.73	0.18
Large	34M	1.19B	6.86	0.25
test set				
OpenSubTest	11,000	66,148	6.01	0.23
WMT	3,003	68,155	22.70	0.23

Corpus	#sentences	#tokens	ASL	TTR
UGC test set				
Cr#pbank	777	13,680	17.60	0.32
MTNT	1,022	20,169	19.70	0.34
UGC blind test set				
Cr#pbank	777	12,808	16.48	0.37
MTNT	599	8,176	13.62	0.38

Table 1: Statistics on the French side of the corpora used in our experiments. *TTR stands for Type-to-Token Ratio, ASL for average sentence length.*

UGC Corpus		Example
MTNT	FR (src)	Je sais mais au final c'est moi que le client va supplier pour son offre et comme **Jsui** un gars cool, **jfai** au mieux.
	EN(ref)	I don't know but in the end I am the one who will have to deal with the customer begging for his offer and because **I'm** a cool guy, **I do** whatever I can to help him.
Cr#pbank	FR (src)	si vous me comprenez **vivé** la **mm** chose ou *[vous]* **avez passé le cap** je **pren tou** ce qui peu m'aider.
	EN (ref)	if you understand me **leave** the **same** thing or **have gotten over it** I **take everything** that can help me.

Table 3: Excerpts of the UGC corpora considered. Common UGC idiosyncrasies are highlighted: non-canonical contractions, spelling errors, missing elements, colloquialism, etc. See (Foster, 2010; Seddah et al., 2012; Eisenstein, 2013) for more complete linguistic descriptions.

the development set and a 0.1 label smoothing (Pereyra et al., 2017).

3.2.3 Transformer architecture

We consider a vanilla Transformer model (Vaswani et al., 2017) using the implementation proposed in the OpenNMT framework (Klein et al., 2018). It consists of 6 layers with word embeddings of 512 components, a feed-forward layers made of 2 048 units and 8 self-attention heads. It was trained using the ADAM optimizer with OpenNMT default parameters.

3.3 Data processing

3.3.1 Preprocessing

All of our datasets were tokenized with byte-pair encoding (BPE) (Sennrich et al., 2016) using sentencepiece (Kudo and Richardson, 2018). We use a BPE vocabulary size of 16K. As a point of comparison we also train a system on Large OpenSubs with 32K BPE operations. As usual, the training corpora were cleaned so each sentence has, at least, 1 token and, at most, 70 tokens.

We did not perform any other pre-processing. In particular, the original case of the sentences was left unchanged in order to help disambiguate subword BPE units (see example in Figure 1) especially for Named Entities that are vastly present in our two UGC corpora.

3.3.2 Post-processing : handling OOVs

Given the high number of OOVs in UGC, special care must be taken in choosing the strategy to handle them. The BPE pre-processing aims at encoding rare and unknown words as sequence of subword units reducing the number of tokens for which the model has no information. But, because of the many named-entities, contractions and unusual character repetitions, this strategy is not effective for UGC as it leads the input sentence to contain many unknown BPE tokens (that are all mapped to the special symbol <UNK> before translating).

The most common strategy for handling OOVs in machine translation systems is simply copying the unknown tokens from the source sentence to the translation hypothesis. This is done in the Moses toolkit (using the alignments produced during translation) and in OpenNMT (that uses the soft-alignments to copy the source token with the highest attention weight at every decoding step when necessary). At the time we conducted the MT experiments, the XNMT toolkit (Neubig et al., 2018) has no straightforward possibilities of replacing unknown tokens present in the test set.[6] For our seq2seq NMT predictions, we performed such replacement through aligning the translation hypothesis with the source sentences (both already tokenized with BPE) with fastalign (Dyer et al., 2013) and copying the source words aligned with the <UNK> token.

4 Measuring noise levels as corpus divergence

Several metrics have been proposed to quantify the domain drift between two corpora. In particular, the perplexity of a language model the KL-divergence between the character-level 3-gram distribution of the train and test sets were two useful measurements capable of estimating the noise-level of UGC corpora as shown respectively by Martínez Alonso et al. (2016) and Seddah et al. (2012).

We also propose a new metric to estimate the noise level tailored to the BPE tokenization. The *BPE stability*, BPEstab, is an indicator of how many BPE-compounded words tend to form throughout a test corpus. Formally BPEstab is defined as:

$$\frac{1}{N} \cdot \sum_{v \in \mathcal{V}} \text{freq}(v) \cdot \frac{\text{n\_unique\_neighbors}(v)}{\text{n\_neighbors}(v)} \qquad (1)$$

where N is the number of tokens in the corpus, $\mathcal{V}$ the BPE vocabulary, freq(v) the frequency of the token v and n_unique_neighbors(v) the number of unique tokens that surrounds the token v. Neighbors are counted only within the original word limits. Low average BPE stability refers to a more variable BPE neighborhood, and thus, higher average vocabulary complexity.

Table 4 reports the noise-level of our test sets introduced in Section 3.1 with respect to our largest training set, Large OpenSubtitles. These measures all show how divergeent are our UGC corpora from our largest training set. As shown by its OOVs ratio and its KL-divergence score, our Cr#pbank corpus is much more noisier than the MTNT corpus, making it a more difficult target in our translation scenario.

5 Experimental Results

5.1 MT Performance

Table 5 reports the BLEU scores[7] achieved by the three systems we consider on the different combinations of train/test sets. These results show that, while NMT systems achieve the best scores on in-domain settings, their performance drops when the test set departs from the training data. On the contrary, the phrase-based system performs far better in out-domain setting than in-domain settings. It even appears that the quality of the translation of phrase-based system increases with the noise-level (as measured by the metrics introduced in §4): when trained on OpenSubtitles, its score for the Cr#pbank is surprisingly better than for in-domain data. This is not the case for neural models. In the next section we present a detailed error analysis to explain this observation.

Interestingly enough, we also notice that a MT system trained on the OpenSub corpora performed much better on UGC test sets than the system trained on the WMT collection. To further investigate whether this observation results from a badly chosen number of BPE operations, we have also trained using the Large OpenSubtitles corpus tokenized with a 32K operation BPE. We have selected these numbers of BPE operations (16K and 32K), beacause they are often used as maintream values, but this BPE parameter has been shown to have a significant impact on the MT system performance (Salesky et al., 2018; Ding et al., 2019). Thus, the number of merging BPE operations should be carefully optimized in order to garantee the best performance. However, this matter is out of the scope of our work.

Comparing both Large OpenSubtitles with BPE tokenization 16K and 32K, BLEU scores reveal that PBSMT has considerably lower performance as the vocabulary size doubles. Regarding the seq2seq NMT and, specially, PBSMT, we can notice these systems underperform for such vocabulary size, whereas the Transformer architecture shows slightly better performances. However, the Transformer still does not outperforms our best PBSMT benchmark on Cr#pbank. It is worth noting that performances of the in-domain test OpenSubsTest are kept almost invariable for PBSMT both and NMT models.As expected, these performance gaps between PBSMT and NMT models are

---

[6]Note that the models described in (Michel and Neubig, 2018) do not handle unknown words, its reported translation performance (Table 8 in the Appendix) would be thus underestimated if compared to our own results on the MTNT (Table 5).

[7]All BLEU scores evaluation are computed with SacreBLEU (Post, 2018).

↓ Metric / Test set →	Cr#pbank[†]	MTNT[†]	Newstest	OpenSubsTest
3-gram KL-Div	1.563	0.471	0.406	0.0060
%OOV	12.63	6.78	3.81	0.76
BPEstab	0.018	0.024	0.049	0.13
PPL	599.48	318.24	288.83	62.06

Table 4: Domain-related measure on the source side (FR), between Test sets and `Large OpenSubtitles` training set. Dags indicate UGC corpora.

	PBSMT				seq2seq				Transformer			
	Crap	MTNT	News	Open	Crap	MTNT	News	Open	Crap	MTNT	News	Open
WMT	20.5	21.2	22.5†	13.3	17.1	24.0	**29.1†**	16.4	15.4	21.2	27.4†	16.3
Small	28.9	27.3	20.4	26.1†	26.1	28.5	24.5	28.2†	27.5	28.3	26.7	31.4†
Large	**30.0**	**28.6**	22.3	27.4†	21.8	22.8	17.3	28.5†	26.9	28.3	26.6	31.5†
Large 32K	22.7	22.1	16.1	27.4†	25.3	27.2	21.9	28.4†	27.8	28.5	27.1	**31.9†**

Table 5: BLEU score results for our three models for the different train-test combinations. All the MT predictions have been treated to replace UNK tokens according to Section 3.3.2. The best result for each test set is marked in bold, best result for each system (row-wise) in blue color and score for in-domain test sets with a dag. 'Crap', 'MTNT', 'News' and 'Open' stand, respectively, for the `Cr#pbank`, `MTNT`, `newstest'14` and `OpenSubtitlesTest` test sets.

substantial to out-of-domain test corpora, whereas scores on the in-domain test sets remain almost invariable regardless the chosen BPE vocabulary size.

5.2 Error Analysis

The goal of this section is to analyze both quantitatively and qualitatively the output of NMT systems to explain their poor performance in translating UGC. Several works have already identified two main limits of NMT systems: translation dropping and excessive token generation, also known as over-generation (Roturier and Bensadoun, 2011; Kaljahi et al., 2015; Kaljahi and Samad, 2015; Michel and Neubig, 2018). We will analyze in detail how these two problems impact our models in the following subsections.

It is also interesting to notice how performances lowered on the `LargeOpenSubtitles` system tokenized with 16K BPE operations for the `seq2seq` system. Specifically the `newstest'14` translation results, for which we noticed a drop of 7.2 BLEU points with respect to the `SmallOpenSubtitles` configuration, despite having roughly 4 times more training data. This is due to a faulty behaviour of the `fastalign` method, directly caused by a considerable presence of UNK on the seq2seq output. Concisely, there were 829 UNK tokens on the newtest'14 prediction for the `Small` model and 3,717 of such tokens in the output of the Large setup. As soon as we double the number of operations on the further to train the `Large 32K` system, performances on all the out-of domain testsets substantially increase, having 862 UNK tokens on the `newstest'14`. This points to the fact that keeping the same size of BPE vocabulary while increasing the size of the trainig data several times causes to have too many UNK subword tokens on cross-domain corpora due to a small vocabulary given the size and the lexical variability of the training corpus. This is also suggested by the fact that the `LargeOpenSubtitles 16K` system results for the in-domain test set are the only ones with no performance loss. On the othe hand, it is important to note that the PBSMT and `Transformer` architecture did not showed a performance decrease for the Large model either.

Additionally, the PBSMT results for the `Large 32K` system are considerably lower than for any of the other 2 `OpenSubtitles` configurations. This shows that the PBSMT performs worse when we have 32K vocabulary size keeping the same data size, when compared to the `Large` system results. We hypothesize that this is caused by a loss of generalization capability due to the fact that phrase-tables are less factorized when having bigger vocabularies of whole words, rather than relatively few sub-word vocabulary elements.

5.2.1 Translation Dropping

By manually inspecting the systems outputs, we found that NMT models tend to produce shorter outputs than the translation hypotheses of our phrase-based system, often avoiding to translate the noisiest parts of the source sentence, such as in the example described in Figure 1. Sato et al. (2016) reports a similar observation.

Analyzing the attention matrices shows that this issue is often triggered by very unusual token sequences (e.g. letter repetitions that are quite frequent in UGC corpora), or when the BPE tokenization results in a subword token that can generate a translation that has a high probability according to a corpus of canonical texts. For instance, in Figure 1, a rare BPE token, part of the Named Entity "teen wolf" gets confused with the very common french token "te" *(you)*. As a consequence, the seq2seq model suddenly stops translating because the hypothesis "I want to look at you" is a very common English sentence with a much lower perplexity than the (correct) UGC translation. Similar pattern can be observed with the Transformer architecture in case of rare token sequences on the source side, such as in the third example of Table 9, causing the translation to stop abruptly.

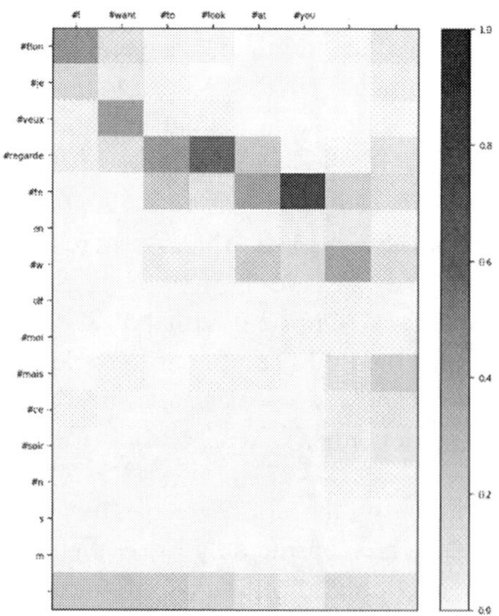

Figure 1: Attention matrix for the source sentence 'Bon je veux regardé teen wolf moi mais ce soir nsm*' predicted by a seq2seq model. *Ok, I do want to watch Teen Wolf tonight motherf..r*

Our phrase-based model does not suffer from this problem as there is no entry in the phrase table that matches the sequence of BPE tokens of the source sentence. This illustrates how hard alignment tables can be more efficient than soft-alignment produced by attention mechanisms for highly noisy cases, in particular when the BPE tokenization generates ambiguous tokens, which confuses the NMT model.

To quantify the translation dropping phenomenon, we show, in Figure 2, the distribution of the ratio between the reference (ground truth) translation sentence length and the one produced by PBSMT and NMT for Cr#pbank. This figure shows that both the NMT and Transformers models have a consistent tendency of producing shorter sentences than expected, while PBSMT does not. This is a strong evidence that NMT systems produce overall shorter translations, as has been noticed by several other authors. Moreover, there are a substantial percentage of the NMT predictions that are 60% shorter than the references, which demonstrates the presence of translations being dropped or shortened.

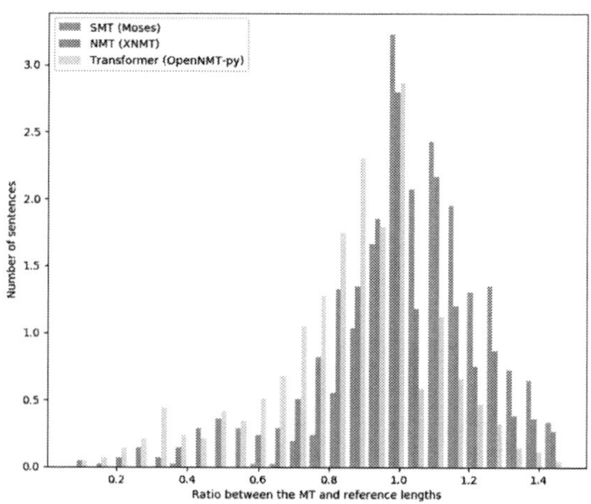

Figure 2: Distribution of Cr#pbank translations length ratio w.r.t ground truth translations.

5.2.2 Over-translation

A second well-known issue with NMT is that the model sometimes repeatedly outputs tokens lacking any coherence, thus adding considerable artificial noise to the output (Tu et al., 2016).

When manually inspecting the output, we noticed that this phenomenon occurred in UGC sentences that contain a rare, and often repetitive, sequence of tokens, such as those present in sentences like "ne spooooooooilez pas teen

wolf non non non et non je dis non"
(don't spoooool Teen wolf no and no I say no) in which the speaker emotion is expressed by repetitions of words or letters. The attention matrix obtained when translating such sentences with a `seq2seq` model often shows that the attention mechanism gets stalled due to the repetition of some BPE token (cf. the attention matrix in Figure 3 that corresponds to the example above). More generally, we noticed many cases in which the attention weights start focusing more and more on the end-of-sentence token until the translation is terminated while ignoring the source sentence tokens thereafter.

The transformer model exhibits similar problems (for instance it translates the previous example to "No no no no no no no no no no no no no no no no no no"). The PBSMT system does not suffer for this problem and arguably produces the best translation: "don't spooooooozt Teen Wolf, no, no, no, no, I say no".

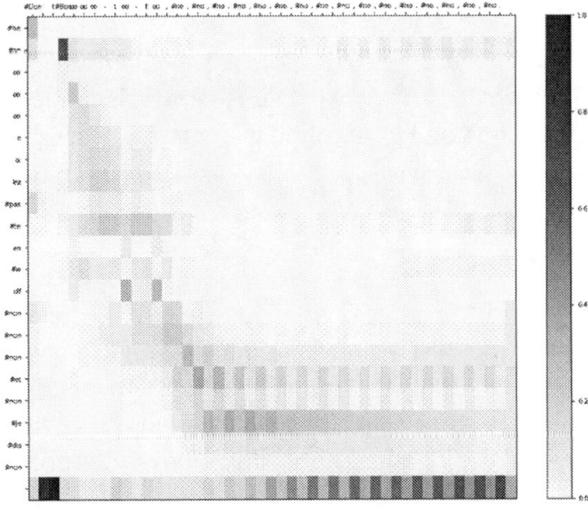

Figure 3: Attention matrix of a `seq2seq` model that exhibits the excessive token repetition problem. The sharp symbol (#) indicates spaces between words before the BPE tokenization.

To quantify the amount of noise artificially added by each of our models, we report, in Table 6 the Target-Source Noise Ratio (TSNR), recently introduced by Anastasopoulos (2019). A TSNR value higher than 1 indicates that the MT system adds more noise on top of the source-side noise, i.e. the rare and noisy tokens present in the source create even more noise on the output. This metric assumes that we have access to a corrected version of each source sentence. So in order to quan-

tify this noise, we manually corrected 200 source sentences of the `Cr#pbank` corpus. In Table 6, we can observe that PBSMT has a better TSNR score, thus adding less artifacts (including dropped translations) to the output. We notice that the gap between PBSMT and NMT architectures (about 0.3) is much larger when training on `WMT` than when training in our `OpenSubtitles` (about 0.1).

	PBSMT	seq2seq	Transformer
WMT	4.62	5.00	4.92
Small	4.11	4.27	4.19
Large	3.99	4.27	4.09

Table 6: Noise added by the MT system estimated with the TSNR metric for the `Cr#pbank` corpus, the lower the better.

5.2.3 Qualitative analysis

In Table 9, in the Appendix for space reasons, we present some more MT outputs to qualitatively compare the PBSMT and NMT models. These predictions were produced using `Large OpenSubtitles`, trained with 16K fixed size vocabulary. From Example 9.1, we can see both NMT models exhibiting better grammatical coherence on the output. Specifically, the Transformer displays the most well-formatted and fluid translation. From Example 9.2, the `seq2seq` model produces several potential translations to unknown expressions (*"Vous m'avez tellement soulé"*) and translates *"soulé"* → *"soiled"*. Note that *"flappy"* is also often translated as *"happy"* throughout the `Cr#pbank` translations. The Transformer model produces arguably the worst results for this example because of this unknown expression (*"You've got me so flappy"*). Example 9.3 shows one symptomatic example of the transformer producing a shorter translation than the source and a common tendency to the `seq2seq` and `Transformer` models to basically *"crash"* when problematic cases are added (bad casing, rare word, incorrect syntax..). Finally, on Example 9.4, we can notice that neither of the NMT systems can correctly translate the upper-cased source token *"CE SOIR"* → *"TONIGHT"*, whereas PBSMT achieves to do so. It is interesting to note that the `Transformer` model generated a non-existent word (*"SOIRY"*) in its attempt to translate the OOV.

6 Discussion

The results presented in the previous two sections confirm the conclusions of Anastasopoulos (2019) that found a correlation between NMT performance and the level of noise in the source sentence. Note that, for computational reasons we have considered a single NMT architecture in all our experiments. However, Sennrich and Zhang (2019) have recently shown that hyper-parameters such as batch size, size of BPE vocabulary, model depth, etc., can have a large impact on translation performance especially in low-resource scenario, a conclusion that should be confirmed in cross-domain setting such as the one considered in this work.

As shown by the differential of performance in favor of the smaller training sets when used with the neural models, our results suggest that the specificities of UGC raise new challenges for NMT systems that cannot simply be solved by feeding ours models more data. Nevertheless, Koehn and Knowles (2017) highlighted 6 challenges faced by Neural Machine Translation, one of them being the lack of data for resource poor-domain. This issue is strongly emphasized when it comes to UGC which does not constitute a domain on its own and which is subjected to a degree of variability only seen in the processing historical document over a large period of times (Bollmann, 2019) or in emerging dialects which can greatly varies over geographic or socio-demographic factors (transliterated Arabic dialects for example). This is why the availability of new UGC data sets is crucial and as such the release of the Cr#pbank is a welcome, small, stone in the edifice that will help evaluating machine translation architectures in near-real conditions such as blind testing.

In order to avoid common leaderboard pitfalls in such settings, we did not use the Cr#pbank's blind test set for any of our experiments, neither did we for the MTNT validation test. Nevertheless, evaluating models on unseen data is necessary, the more being the better. Therefore, in the absence of a MTNT blind test, we used a sample of its validation set, approximately matching the same average sentence length than its reference test set. In Table 7 are presented results of our best systems, based on their performance on our UGC test sets. They confirm the tendency exposed earlier: our PBSMT system is more robust to noise than our transformer-based NMT

with respectively +4.4 and +11.4 BLEU points for the MTNT and Cr#pbank blind tests. For completeness, we run the seq2seq system of Michel and Neubig (2018), trained on their own data set (Europarl-v7, news-commentary-v10), without any domain-adaptation, on our blind tests. Results are on the same range than the same seq2seq model we trained on our edited data set (WMT). It would be interesting to see how their domain-adaptation technique, fine-tuning on the target domain data, which brought their system's performance to BLEU 30.29 on the MTNT test set, would fare on unseen data. As UGC domain is a constantly moving, almost protean, target, adding more data seems unsustainable on the long run. Exploring unsupervised adaptive normalization could provide a solid alternative.

System	Blind Test Sets	
	MTNT	Cr#pbank
Large 16K - PBSMT	**29.3**	**30.5**
Large 32K - Transformer	24.9	19.1
N&G18	19.3	13.3
N&G18 + our UNK	21.9	15.4

Table 7: BLEU score results comparison on the Cr#pbank and MTNT blind test sets. N&G18 stands for (Michel and Neubig, 2018)'s baseline system

7 Conclusions

This work evaluates the capacity of both phrase-based and NMT models to translate UGC. Our experiments show that phrase-base systems are more robust to noise than NMT systems and we provided several explanations about this *relatively* surprising fact, among which the discrepancy between BPE tokens as interpreted by the translation model at decoding time and the addition of lexical noise factors are among the most striking. We have also shown, by producing a new data set with more variability, that using more training data was not necessarily the solution for coping with UGC idiosyncrasies. The aim of this work is of course not to discourage the NMT system deployment for UGC, but to better understand what in PBSMT methods contribute to noise robustness.

In our future work, we plan to see whether theses conclusions still hold for other languages and even noisier corpora. We also plan to see whether it is possible to bypass the limitations of NMT systems we have identified by pre-processing and normalizing the input sentences.

References

Antonios Anastasopoulos. 2019. An analysis of source-side grammatical errors in NMT. In *Proceedings of the 2019 ACL Workshop BlackboxNLP: Analyzing and Interpreting Neural Networks for NLP*, pages 213–223, Florence, Italy. Association for Computational Linguistics.

Dzmitry Bahdanau, Kyunghyun Cho, and Yoshua Bengio. 2015. Neural machine translation by jointly learning to align and translate. In *Proceedings of the 3rd International Conference on Learning Representations, ICLR 2015, San Diego, CA, USA, May 7-9, 2015, Conference Track Proceedings*.

Yonatan Belinkov and Yonatan Bisk. 2018. Synthetic and natural noise both break neural machine translation. In *Proceedings of the 6th International Conference on Learning Representations, ICLR 2018, Vancouver, BC, Canada, April 30 - May 3, 2018, Conference Track Proceedings*.

Yonatan Belinkov, Nadir Durrani, Fahim Dalvi, Hassan Sajjad, and James R. Glass. 2017. What do neural machine translation models learn about morphology? In *Proceedings of the 55th Annual Meeting of the Association for Computational Linguistics, ACL 2017, Vancouver, Canada, July 30 - August 4, Volume 1: Long Papers*, pages 861–872.

Luisa Bentivogli, Arianna Bisazza, Mauro Cettolo, and Marcello Federico. 2016. Neural versus phrase-based machine translation quality: a case study. In *Proceedings of the 2016 Conference on Empirical Methods in Natural Language Processing, EMNLP 2016, Austin, Texas, USA, November 1-4, 2016*, pages 257–267.

Ondrej Bojar, Rajen Chatterjee, Christian Federmann, Yvette Graham, Barry Haddow, Matthias Huck, Antonio Jimeno-Yepes, Philipp Koehn, Varvara Logacheva, Christof Monz, Matteo Negri, Aurélie Névéol, Mariana L. Neves, Martin Popel, Matt Post, Raphael Rubino, Carolina Scarton, Lucia Specia, Marco Turchi, Karin M. Verspoor, and Marcos Zampieri. 2016. Findings of the 2016 conference on machine translation. In *Proceedings of the First Conference on Machine Translation, WMT 2016, colocated with ACL 2016, August 11-12, Berlin, Germany*, pages 131–198.

Marcel Bollmann. 2019. A large-scale comparison of historical text normalization systems. In *Proceedings of the 2019 Conference of the North American Chapter of the Association for Computational Linguistics: Human Language Technologies, Volume 1 (Long and Short Papers)*, pages 3885–3898, Minneapolis, Minnesota. Association for Computational Linguistics.

Sheila Castilho, Joss Moorkens, Federico Gaspari, Rico Sennrich, Vilelmini Sosoni, Yota Georgakopoulou, Pintu Lohar, Andy Way, Antonio Valerio, Antonio Valerio Miceli Barone, and Maria Gialama. 2017. A comparative quality evaluation of pbsmt and nmt using professional translators. In *Proceedings of MT Summit XVI, vol.1: Research Track, Nagoya, Japan, September 18-22, 2017*.

Kyunghyun Cho, Bart van Merrienboer, Dzmitry Bahdanau, and Yoshua Bengio. 2014. On the properties of neural machine translation: Encoder-decoder approaches. In *Proceedings of SSST@EMNLP 2014, Eighth Workshop on Syntax, Semantics and Structure in Statistical Translation, Doha, Qatar, 25 October 2014*, pages 103–111.

Shuoyang Ding, Adithya Renduchintala, and Kevin Duh. 2019. A call for prudent choice of subword merge operations. *CoRR*, abs/1905.10453.

Meghan Dowling, Teresa Lynn, Alberto Poncelas, and Andy Way. 2018. SMT versus NMT: preliminary comparisons for irish. In *Proceedings of the Workshop on Technologies for MT of Low Resource Languages, LoResMT@AMTA 2018, Boston, MA, USA, March 21, 2018*, pages 12–20.

Nadir Durrani, Fahim Dalvi, Hassan Sajjad, Yonatan Belinkov, and Preslav Nakov. 2019. One size does not fit all: Comparing NMT representations of different granularities. In *Proceedings of the 2019 Conference of the North American Chapter of the Association for Computational Linguistics: Human Language Technologies, NAACL-HLT 2019, Minneapolis, MN, USA, June 2-7, 2019, Volume 1 (Long and Short Papers)*, pages 1504–1516.

Chris Dyer, Victor Chahuneau, and Noah A. Smith. 2013. A simple, fast, and effective reparameterization of IBM model 2. In *Proceedings of the Human Language Technologies: Conference of the North American Chapter of the Association of Computational Linguistics, June 9-14, 2013, Westin Peachtree Plaza Hotel, Atlanta, Georgia, USA*, pages 644–648.

Jacob Eisenstein. 2013. What to do about bad language on the internet. In *Proceedings of the 2013 conference of the North American Chapter of the association for computational linguistics: Human language technologies*, pages 359–369.

Jennifer Foster. 2010. "cba to check the spelling": Investigating parser performance on discussion forum posts. In *Human Language Technologies: The 2010 Annual Conference of the North American Chapter of the Association for Computational Linguistics*, pages 381–384, Los Angeles, California. Association for Computational Linguistics.

Sébastien Jean, KyungHyun Cho, Roland Memisevic, and Yoshua Bengio. 2015. On using very large target vocabulary for neural machine translation. In *Proceedings of the 53rd Annual Meeting of the Association for Computational Linguistics and the 7th International Joint Conference on Natural Language Processing of the Asian Federation of Natural Language Processing, ACL 2015, July 26-31, 2015, Beijing, China, Volume 1: Long Papers*, pages 1–10.

Nal Kalchbrenner and Phil Blunsom. 2013. Recurrent continuous translation models. In *Proceedings of the 2013 Conference on Empirical Methods in Natural Language Processing, EMNLP 2013, 18-21 October 2013, Grand Hyatt Seattle, Seattle, Washington, USA, A meeting of SIGDAT, a Special Interest Group of the ACL*, pages 1700–1709.

Rasoul Kaljahi, Jennifer Foster, Johann Roturier, Corentin Ribeyre, Teresa Lynn, and Joseph Le Roux. 2015. Foreebank: Syntactic analysis of customer support forums. In *Proceedings of the 2015 Conference on Empirical Methods in Natural Language Processing*, pages 1341–1347.

Zadeh Kaljahi and Rasoul Samad. 2015. *The role of syntax and semantics in machine translation and quality estimation of machine-translated user-generated content*. Ph.D. thesis, Dublin City University.

Diederik P. Kingma and Jimmy Ba. 2015. Adam: A method for stochastic optimization. In *Proceedings of the 3rd International Conference on Learning Representations, ICLR 2015, San Diego, CA, USA, May 7-9, 2015, Conference Track Proceedings*.

Guillaume Klein, Yoon Kim, Yuntian Deng, Vincent Nguyen, Jean Senellart, and Alexander M. Rush. 2018. Opennmt: Neural machine translation toolkit. In *Proceedings of the 13th Conference of the Association for Machine Translation in the Americas, AMTA 2018, Boston, MA, USA, March 17-21, 2018 - Volume 1: Research Papers*, pages 177–184.

Philipp Koehn, Hieu Hoang, Alexandra Birch, Chris Callison-Burch, Marcello Federico, Nicola Bertoldi, Brooke Cowan, Wade Shen, Christine Moran, Richard Zens, Chris Dyer, Ondrej Bojar, Alexandra Constantin, and Evan Herbst. 2007. Moses: Open source toolkit for statistical machine translation. In *ACL 2007, Proceedings of the 45th Annual Meeting of the Association for Computational Linguistics, June 23-30, 2007, Prague, Czech Republic*.

Philipp Koehn and Rebecca Knowles. 2017. Six challenges for neural machine translation. In *Proceedings of the First Workshop on Neural Machine Translation, NMT@ACL 2017, Vancouver, Canada, August 4, 2017*, pages 28–39.

Taku Kudo and John Richardson. 2018. Sentencepiece: A simple and language independent subword tokenizer and detokenizer for neural text processing. In *Proceedings of the 2018 Conference on Empirical Methods in Natural Language Processing, EMNLP 2018: System Demonstrations, Brussels, Belgium, October 31 - November 4, 2018*, pages 66–71.

An Nguyen Le, Ander Martinez, Akifumi Yoshimoto, and Yuji Matsumoto. 2017. Improving sequence to sequence neural machine translation by utilizing syntactic dependency information. In *Proceedings of the Eighth International Joint Conference on Natural Language Processing, IJCNLP 2017, Taipei, Taiwan, November 27 - December 1, 2017 - Volume 1: Long Papers*, pages 21–29.

Pierre Lison, Jörg Tiedemann, and Milen Kouylekov. 2018. Opensubtitles2018: Statistical rescoring of sentence alignments in large, noisy parallel corpora. In *Proceedings of the Eleventh International Conference on Language Resources and Evaluation, LREC 2018, Miyazaki, Japan, May 7-12, 2018*.

Thang Luong, Hieu Pham, and Christopher D. Manning. 2015. Effective approaches to attention-based neural machine translation. In *Proceedings of the 2015 Conference on Empirical Methods in Natural Language Processing, EMNLP 2015, Lisbon, Portugal, September 17-21, 2015*, pages 1412–1421.

Héctor Martínez Alonso, Djamé Seddah, and Benoît Sagot. 2016. From noisy questions to Minecraft texts: Annotation challenges in extreme syntax scenario. In *Proceedings of the 2nd Workshop on Noisy User-generated Text (WNUT)*, pages 13–23, Osaka, Japan. The COLING 2016 Organizing Committee.

Haitao Mi, Baskaran Sankaran, Zhiguo Wang, and Abe Ittycheriah. 2016. Coverage embedding models for neural machine translation. In *Proceedings of the 2016 Conference on Empirical Methods in Natural Language Processing, EMNLP 2016, Austin, Texas, USA, November 1-4, 2016*, pages 955–960.

Paul Michel and Graham Neubig. 2018. MTNT: A testbed for machine translation of noisy text. In *Proceedings of the 2018 Conference on Empirical Methods in Natural Language Processing, Brussels, Belgium, October 31 - November 4, 2018*, pages 543–553.

Matteo Negri, Marco Turchi, Marcello Federico, Nicola Bertoldi, and M. Amin Farajian. 2017. Neural vs. phrase-based machine translation in a multi-domain scenario. In *Proceedings of the 15th Conference of the European Chapter of the Association for Computational Linguistics, EACL 2017, Valencia, Spain, April 3-7, 2017, Volume 2: Short Papers*, pages 280–284.

Graham Neubig, Matthias Sperber, Xinyi Wang, Matthieu Felix, Austin Matthews, Sarguna Padmanabhan, Ye Qi, Devendra Singh Sachan, Philip Arthur, Pierre Godard, John Hewitt, Rachid Riad, and Liming Wang. 2018. XNMT: the extensible neural machine translation toolkit. In *Proceedings of the 13th Conference of the Association for Machine Translation in the Americas, AMTA 2018, Boston, MA, USA, March 17-21, 2018 - Volume 1: Research Papers*, pages 185–192.

Gabriel Pereyra, George Tucker, Jan Chorowski, Lukasz Kaiser, and Geoffrey E. Hinton. 2017. Regularizing neural networks by penalizing confident output distributions. In *5th International Conference on Learning Representations, ICLR 2017, Toulon,*

France, April 24-26, 2017, Workshop Track Proceedings.

Matt Post. 2018. A call for clarity in reporting BLEU scores. In *Proceedings of the Third Conference on Machine Translation: Research Papers, WMT 2018, Belgium, Brussels, October 31 - November 1, 2018*, pages 186–191.

Johann Roturier and Anthony Bensadoun. 2011. Evaluation of mt systems to translate user generated content. *Proceedings of Machine Translation Summit XIII, Xiamen, China*, pages 244–251.

Elizabeth Salesky, Andrew Runge, Alex Coda, Jan Niehues, and Graham Neubig. 2018. Optimizing segmentation granularity for neural machine translation. *CoRR*, abs/1810.08641.

Takayuki Sato, Jun Harashima, and Mamoru Komachi. 2016. Japanese-english machine translation of recipe texts. In *Proceedings of the 3rd Workshop on Asian Translation, WAT@COLING 2016, Osaka, Japan, December 2016*, pages 58–67.

Djamé Seddah, Benoît Sagot, Marie Candito, Virginie Mouilleron, and Vanessa Combet. 2012. The french social media bank: a treebank of noisy user generated content. In *COLING 2012, 24th International Conference on Computational Linguistics, Proceedings of the Conference: Technical Papers, 8-15 December 2012, Mumbai, India*, pages 2441–2458.

Rico Sennrich, Barry Haddow, and Alexandra Birch. 2016. Neural machine translation of rare words with subword units. In *Proceedings of the 54th Annual Meeting of the Association for Computational Linguistics, ACL 2016, August 7-12, 2016, Berlin, Germany, Volume 1: Long Papers*.

Rico Sennrich and Biao Zhang. 2019. Revisiting low-resource neural machine translation: A case study. In *Proceedings of the 57th Conference of the Association for Computational Linguistics, ACL 2019, Florence, Italy, July 28- August 2, 2019, Volume 1: Long Papers*, pages 211–221.

Nitish Srivastava, Geoffrey E. Hinton, Alex Krizhevsky, Ilya Sutskever, and Ruslan Salakhutdinov. 2014. Dropout: a simple way to prevent neural networks from overfitting. *J. Mach. Learn. Res.*, 15(1):1929–1958.

Ilya Sutskever, Oriol Vinyals, and Quoc V. Le. 2014a. Sequence to sequence learning with neural networks. In *Advances in Neural Information Processing Systems 27: Annual Conference on Neural Information Processing Systems 2014, December 8-13 2014, Montreal, Quebec, Canada*, pages 3104–3112.

Ilya Sutskever, Oriol Vinyals, and Quoc V. Le. 2014b. Sequence to sequence learning with neural networks. In *Advances in Neural Information Processing Systems 27: Annual Conference on Neural Information Processing Systems 2014, December 8-13 2014, Montreal, Quebec, Canada*, pages 3104–3112.

Zhaopeng Tu, Zhengdong Lu, Yang Liu, Xiaohua Liu, and Hang Li. 2016. Modeling coverage for neural machine translation. In *Proceedings of the 54th Annual Meeting of the Association for Computational Linguistics (Volume 1: Long Papers)*, pages 76–85, Berlin, Germany. Association for Computational Linguistics.

Ashish Vaswani, Noam Shazeer, Niki Parmar, Jakob Uszkoreit, Llion Jones, Aidan N Gomez, Ł ukasz Kaiser, and Illia Polosukhin. 2017. Attention is all you need. In I. Guyon, U. V. Luxburg, S. Bengio, H. Wallach, R. Fergus, S. Vishwanathan, and R. Garnett, editors, *Advances in Neural Information Processing Systems 30*, pages 5998–6008. Curran Associates, Inc.

Yonghui Wu, Mike Schuster, Zhifeng Chen, Quoc V. Le, Mohammad Norouzi, Wolfgang Macherey, Maxim Krikun, Yuan Cao, Qin Gao, Klaus Macherey, Jeff Klingner, Apurva Shah, Melvin Johnson, Xiaobing Liu, Lukasz Kaiser, Stephan Gouws, Yoshikiyo Kato, Taku Kudo, Hideto Kazawa, Keith Stevens, George Kurian, Nishant Patil, Wei Wang, Cliff Young, Jason Smith, Jason Riesa, Alex Rudnick, Oriol Vinyals, Greg Corrado, Macduff Hughes, and Jeffrey Dean. 2016. Google's neural machine translation system: Bridging the gap between human and machine translation. *CoRR*, abs/1609.08144.

Appendix

↓ System / Test set →	Newstest'14	Discusstest'15	MTNT[†]
out-of-domain set-up			
WMT-seq2seq N&G18	28.93	30.76	23.27
WMT-seq2seq (Ours)	28.70	30.00	23.00
domain adaptation set-up			
WMT-seq2seq N&G18+fine tuning	-	-	30.29

Table 8: BLEU score results comparison between our seq2seq system and thoses reported by Michel and Neubig (2018). None of the system outputs have been treated to replace UNK tokens. Dags indicate UGC corpora. N&G18 stands for (Michel and Neubig, 2018)'s system.

①	src	**Nen sans rire, j'ai bu hier soir** mais ca faisait deux semaines.
	ref	Yeah no kidding, I drank last night but it had been two weeks.
	PBSMT	**No, no, I've been drinking last night**, but it's been two weeks.
	seq2seq	**No laughing, I drank last night**, but it's been two weeks.
	Transformer	**No kidding, I drank last night**, but it's been two weeks.
②	src	**Vous m'avez tellement soulé avec votre** flappy bird j'sais pas quoi. Mais je vais le télécharger.
	ref	You annoyed me so much with your flappy bird whatever. But I'm going to download it.
	PBMST	**You're so drunk with your flappy bird** I don't know. But I'm going to download.
	seq2seq	**You have soiled me happy bird** I don't know what, but I'm going to download it.
	Transformer	**You've got me so flappy** I don't know what, but I'm gonna download it.
③	src	**Vos gueul ac vos** Zlatan
	ref	**Shut the fck up with your** Zlatan.
	PBMST	**Your scream in your** Zlatan
	seq2seq	**Your shrouds with your** Zlatan
	Transformer	Zlatan!
④	src	**CE SOIR Y A L'ÉPISODE DE** #TeenWolf OMFGGGG
	ref	**TONIGHT THERE'S THE** #TeenWolf **EPISODE** OMFGGGGG
	PBMST	**Tonight's It At The EPISODE OF** #Teen Wolf OMFGGGG
	seq2seq	Teenwolf OMFGGGGGGGGGG
	Transformer	**THIS SOIRY HAS THE** #TeenWOL OMFGGGGGGGGGG

Table 9: Examples from our noisy UGC corpus.

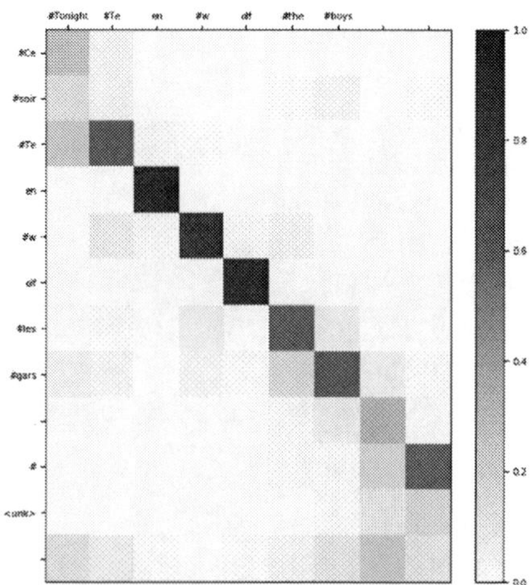

Figure 4: Attention matrix for the source sentence 'Ce soir Teen Wolf les gars.*' showing a proper translation thanks to correct casing of the named-entity BPE parts. *Tonight Teen Wolf guys.*

Bootstrapping UD treebanks for Delexicalized Parsing

Prasanth Kolachina
University of Gothenburg
`prasanth.kolachina@gu.se`

Aarne Ranta
University of Gothenburg
`aarne@chalmers.se`

Abstract

Standard approaches to treebanking traditionally employ a waterfall model (Sommerville, 2010), where annotation guidelines guide the annotation process and insights from the annotation process in turn lead to subsequent changes in the annotation guidelines. This process remains a very expensive step in creating linguistic resources for a target language, necessitates both linguistic expertise and manual effort to develop the annotations and is subject to inconsistencies in the annotation due to human errors.

In this paper, we propose an alternative approach to treebanking—one that requires writing grammars. This approach is motivated specifically in the context of Universal Dependencies, an effort to develop uniform and cross-lingually consistent treebanks across multiple languages. We show here that a bootstrapping approach to treebanking via interlingual grammars is plausible and useful in a process where grammar engineering and treebanking are jointly pursued when creating resources for the target language. We demonstrate the usefulness of synthetic treebanks in the task of delexicalized parsing, a task of interest when working with languages with no linguistic resources and corpora. Experiments with three languages reveal that simple models for treebank generation are *cheaper* than human annotated treebanks, especially in the lower ends of the learning curves for delexicalized parsing, which is relevant in particular in the context of low-resource languages.

1 Introduction

Treebanking remains a vital step in the process of creating linguistic resources for a language – a practice that was established in the last 2-3 decades (Marcus et al., 1994). The process of treebanking involves training human annotators in order to obtain high-quality annotations. This is a human-intensive and costly process where multiple iterations are performed to refine the quality of the linguistic resource. Grammar engineering is a complementary approach to creating linguistic resources: one that requires a different kind of expertise. These two approaches have remained orthogonal for obvious reasons: treebanks are primarily necessary to induce abstractions in NLU (Natural Language Understanding) models from data, while grammars are themselves abstractions arising from linguistic knowledge. Abstractions induced from data have proven themselves to be useful for robust NLU tasks, while grammars are better at precision tasks involving NLG (Natural Language Generation).

Given the resources required for treebanking, synthetic treebanks have been proposed and used as substitute in cross-lingual parsing for languages where treebanks do not exist. Such treebanks are created using parallel corpora where parse trees in one language are bootstrapped into a target language using alignment information through annotation projection (McDonald et al., 2011; Tiedemann, 2014) or using machine translation systems to bootstrap existing treebanks in one or more source language(s) to the target language (Tiedemann and Agic, 2016; Tyers et al., 2018). More recently, synthetic treebanks are generated for both real and artificial languages using multilingual treebanks by learning feasible parameter combinations (Wang and Eisner, 2016) – Wang and Eisner (2018) show that such treebanks can be useful to select the most similar language to train a parsing model for an unknown language.

At the same time, grammar-based treebanking approaches have been shown to work in monolingual setups—to derive rich linguistic representations defined by explicit grammars (Oepen et al., 2004). These approaches are carried out by parsing raw corpora with a target grammar and using an additional human disambiguation phase. Alternatively, existing treebanks are matched against the target grammar further reducing the human effort in disambiguation: these approaches face a challenge of under-specification in the source treebanks (Angelov, 2011). In the current paper, we propose a hybrid of these two methods: we use abstract syntax grammars as core linguistic abstraction to generate synthetic treebanks for a grammar that can be translated to target representations with high precision.

The question of annotation costs and ways to minimize the dependence on such annotated corpora has been a recurring theme in the field for the last two decades (Ngai and Yarowsky, 2000; Garrette and Baldridge, 2013). This question has also been extensively addressed in the context of dependency treebanks. We revisit this question in context of Universal Dependencies and recent work on the interplay between interlingua grammars and multilingual dependency trees in this scheme (Kolachina and Ranta, 2016; Ranta and Kolachina, 2017; Ranta et al., 2017). The use of interlingua grammars to bootstrap dependency treebanks guarantees two types of consistencies: multilingual treebank consistency and intra-treebank consistency. We study the efficacy of these dependency treebanks using learning curves of a transition-based parser in a *delexicalized parsing* setup. The delexicalized parsing setup allows for generation of parallel UD treebanks in multiple languages with minimal prerequisites on language-specific knowledge.

Another rationale behind the the current work in the context of cross-lingual parsing is while synthetic treebanks offer a "cheap" alternative, the signal for the target language is limited by the quality of the MT system. On the other hand, interlingua grammars provide a high-quality signal about the target language. High quality using interlingual grammars refers to accurate generation of word-order and morphology – although lexical selection in translation is still a problem. There have not been previous attempts in cross-lingual

parsing to our knowledge studying the effect of these.

This paper is structured as follows: Section 2 gives the relevant background on interlingua grammars and the algorithm used to generate UD trees given treebank derived from an interlingua grammar. Section 3 describes our algorithm to bootstrap treebanks for a given interlingua grammar and parallel UD treebanks from them along with an intrinsic evaluation of these bootstrapped UD treebanks. Section 4 shows the parsing setup we use and Section 5 details the results of the parsing experiments.

2 Grammatical Framework

Grammatical Framework (GF) is a multilingual grammar formalism using abstract syntax trees (ASTs) as primary descriptions (Ranta, 2011). Originating in compilers, AST is a tectogrammatical tree representation that can be shared between languages. A GF grammar consists of two parts – an abstract syntax shared between languages and concrete syntax that is defined for each language. The abstract syntax defines a set of categories and a set of functions, as shown in Figure 1. The functions defined in the abstract syntax specify the result of putting subparts of two categories together and the concrete syntax specifies how the subparts are combined i.e. word-order preferences and agreement constraints specific to the language.

A comprehensive implementation of a multilingual grammar in GF is the **Resource Grammar Library**, GF-RGL (Ranta, 2009), which currently has concrete syntaxes for over 40 languages, ranging from Indo-European through Finno-Ugric and Semitic to East Asian languages. [1] This implementation contains a full implementation of the morphology of the language, and a set of 284 syntactic constructors that correspond to the core syntax of the language. Also included is a small lexicon of 500 lexical concepts from a set of 19 categories, of which 10 correspond to different subcategorization frames of verbs, 2 classes of nouns and adjectives. These grammars are *reversible*-i.e. they can be used for parsing and simultaneous multilingual generation into multiple languages. The concrete syntaxes for all the languages define the rules for these syntactic constructors and

---

[1]The current status of GF-RGL can be seen in
`http://www.grammaticalframework.org/lib/doc/synopsis.html` which also gives access to the source code.

abstract syntax   dependency configuration

```
PredVP   : NP   -> VP   -> Cl    nsubj   head
ComplV2  : V2   -> NP   -> VP    head    dobj
AdvVP    : VP   -> Adv  -> VP    head    advmod
DetCN    : Det  -> CN   -> NP    det     head
ModCN    : AP   -> CN   -> CN    amod    head
UseN     : N          -> CN     head
UsePron  : Pron -> NP           head
PositA   : A          -> AP     Head

cat A                           ADJ
cat Adv                         ADV
cat Det                         DET
cat N                           NOUN
cat Pron                        PRON
cat V2                          VERB
```

Figure 1: Abstract syntax of a GF grammar and its specification for UD scheme. Also shown is an example AST for the sentence *the black cat sees us today*. Any function with a definition written as $f : C_1 \rightarrow C_2 \rightarrow ...C_n \rightarrow C$; can be rewritten as a context-free rule $f.\ C ::= C_1 C_2 ...C_n$.

the lexical concepts. The expressivity of these grammars is equivalent to a PMCFG (Seki et al., 1991), which makes parsing complexity of this formalism polynomial in sentence length. Polynomial parsing with high exponents can still be too slow for many tasks, and is also brittle if the grammars are designed to not over-generate. But generation using GF grammars has been shown to be both precise and fast, which suggests the idea of combining data-driven parsing with grammar-driven generation. We refer the interested reader to Ljunglöf (2004) for discussion on expressivity of this formalism and Angelov (2011); Angelov and Ljunglöf (2014) for discussion on probabilistic parsing using GF grammars.

2.1 gf2ud

Kolachina and Ranta (2016) propose an algorithm to translate ASTs to dependency trees, that takes a specification of the abstract syntax of the GF grammar (referred to as *configurations*, see Figure 1) which describes the mapping between the grammar and a target dependency scheme, in this case Universal Dependencies. These configurations can be interpreted as a synchronous grammar over the abstract syntax as source and dependency scheme as target.

The first step in this transducer is a recursive annotation that marks for each function in the AST, one of the arguments as head and specifies labels for the other arguments, as specified by the configuration. The algorithm to extract the resulting dependency tree from the *annotated AST* is simple.

- for each leaf X (which corresponds to a lexical item) in the AST
  - trace the path up towards the root until you encounter a label L
  - from the node immediately above L, follow the **spine** (the unlabeled branches) down to another leaf Y
  - Y is the head of X with label L

At the end of these two steps, the resulting data-structure is an *abstract dependency tree* (ADT shown in Figure 2). It should be noted that the order of nodes shown in the ADT does not reflect the surface order that is specific to a language. The ADT combined with the concrete syntax of a language and concrete configurations (when necessary) results in the corresponding full UD tree. The concrete configurations are necessary to provide appropriate labels to syncategorematic words like auxiliary verbs and negation particles. Additionally, the category configuration on the abstract

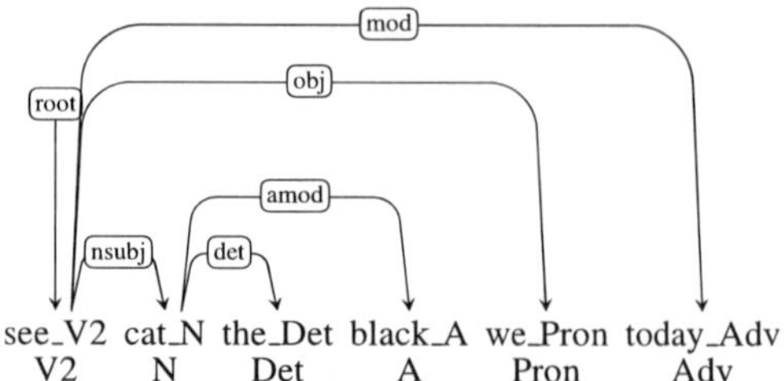

Figure 2: ADT for the sentence *the black cat sees us today*. The nodes in the ADT correspond to lexical functions defined in the grammar. Also shown is the UD part-of-speech tag sequence. Note that the order of nodes does not reflect the surface order in any particular language.

syntax can be augmented with a language-specific category configurations to generate the morphological features in the dependency tree with a desired tag set.

Kolachina and Ranta (2016) show that their method can be used to generate partially labeled UD trees for 30 languages when the corresponding concrete syntax is available. They also show that using configurations defined on abstract syntax alone and depending on the availability of the concrete syntax, a large fraction (around 75–85% of edges) of the dependency treebanks can be generated automatically. This is done with small treebanks of ASTs – a UD treebank of 104 ASTs and a GF treebank of 400 ASTs. Their results show that parallel UD treebanks can be bootstrapped using ASTs and interlingua grammars, the usefulness of such treebanks however is not addressed in that work. Full UD treebanks can be generated when concrete configurations (those addressing syncategorematic words) are additionally available for the language.

3 Bootstrapping AST and UD treebanks

The abstract syntax component of a GF grammar is an algebraic datatype definition, which can also be seen as a context-free grammar (CFG). The disambiguation model defined in GF uses a context-free probability distribution defined on the abstract syntax. The advantage of defining the distribution on the abstract syntax is that it allows for transfer of distribution to languages for which GF treebanks do not exist. The context-free distribution decomposes the probability estimate of a tree as the product of probabilities of the sub-trees and the probability of the function applied to these sub-

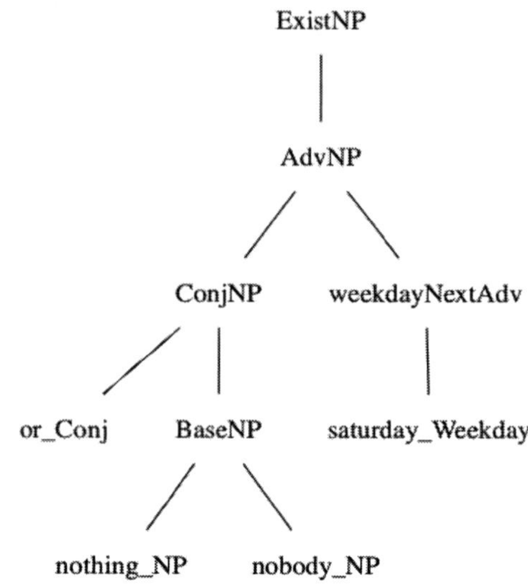

(a) An AST of an existential clause bootstrapped using our model.

there   is   nothing   or   nobody   next   Saturday
det   finns   inget   eller   ingen   nästa   lördag

(b) Linearization of the AST in English and Swedish

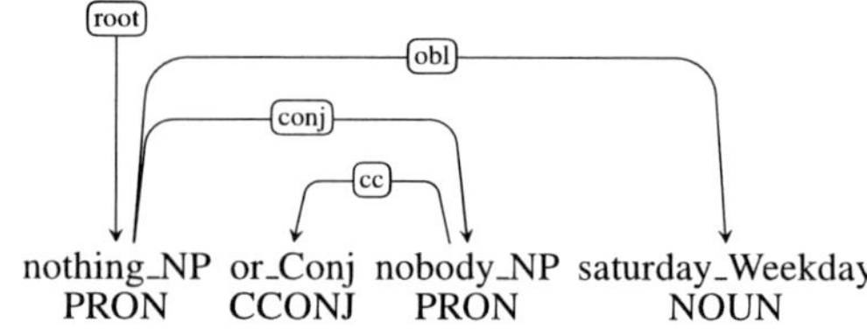

(c) ADT corresponding to the above example that has to be delexicalized.

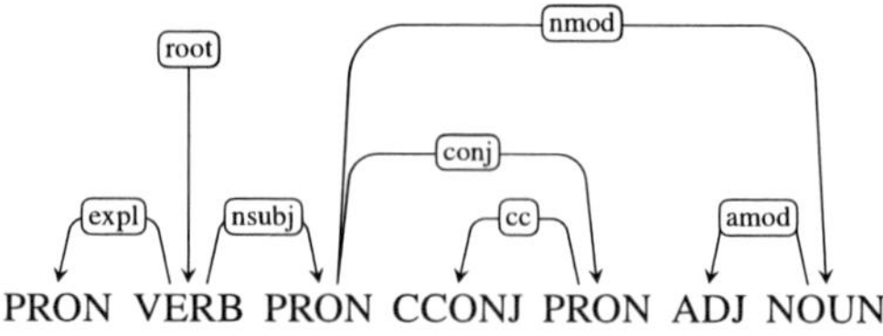

(d) The delexicalized UD tree in both English and Swedish shares the same part-of-speech tag sequence and dependency labels

Figure 3: Example of a bootstrapped AST and UD tree and the intermediate ADT.

trees. The probabilistic abstract syntax grammar can therefore be defined in terms analogous to a probabilistic CFG (PCFG). The probability distribution over the set of categories in the grammar is also included in the distribution corresponding to the abstract syntax.

We use this formulation as a starting point and generate ASTs for a given grammar. The ASTs bootstrapped using the probability model defined above are correct in terms of the grammar but do not follow the selectional preferences that encode semantic preferences verbs have for their arguments typically found in language. For this reason, we refer to the bootstrapped treebanks as "synthetic" data.

Additionally, while the algorithm used to bootstrap ASTs does not change depending on whether the grammar includes a lexicon or not, it is significantly faster depending the size of the grammar. Stacking `gf2ud` defined using abstract configurations on top of these bootstrapped ASTs results in a treebank of ADTs. Alternatively, the concrete syntax of a language can straightforwardly be used to *linearize* a corpus of the target language. The concrete syntax and the concrete configurations when available are used to generate fully labelled UD treebanks for a target language. Figure 3 shows an example of a synthetic AST and delexicalized UD tree bootstrapped using the RGL.

The bootstrapping algorithm uses a parameter corresponding to the maximum depth of the trees d to be generated. The generative story is as follows:

- Pick a category C using the distribution over categories defined in the probability model.
- Select a function F with the definition $C_1 \rightarrow C_2 \rightarrow ... \rightarrow C_n \rightarrow C$ according to the conditional distribution $P(F|C)$.
- Recursively apply the same step to build subtrees of maximum depth $d - 1$, t_{C_1}, t_{C_2} ... t_{C_n} of categories C_1, C_2 ... C_n respectively.
- Return $(F\ t_{C_1}\ t_{C_2}\ ..\ t_{C_n})$.

3.1 Differences against UDv2

The design of the RGL and corresponding configurations do not contain all of the structures defined in the UD annotation scheme. The missing structures fall into two major categories: labels that depend on the lexical realization in a specific language, and structures that correspond to specific linguistic constructions that are not part of the core RGL syntax. Examples of the first

Language	H(P_{UD})	H(P_{GF})	Cross-entropy
Afrikaans	39.59	58.34	63.12
Arabic	40.00	42.13	51.38
Basque	44.19	51.19	54.21
Bulgarian	32.09	53.76	61.23
Catalan	44.49	49.37	57.39
Chinese	39.25	42.10	59.76
Danish	44.85	55.28	63.39
Dutch	48.99	49.67	61.27
English	50.52	45.31	58.17
Estonian	39.45	43.82	49.35
Finnish	47.86	41.52	54.39
French	43.41	49.43	53.47
German	41.35	49.35	51.29
Greek	29.48	41.13	49.17
Hindi	32.99	43.18	54.27
Italian	38.55	51.37	59.64
Japanese	27.34	40.18	47.25
Latin	42.07	43.47	49.89
Latvian	49.75	49.91	59.26
Norwegian (bokmal)	40.29	45.97	53.17
Norwegian (nynorsk)	37.29	44.56	56.32
Persian	33.07	47.29	47.16
Polish	23.85	41.27	49.83
Portuguese	40.84	48.73	53.60
Romanian	47.31	52.31	57.12
Russian	39.14	47.92	52.84
Spanish	46.36	52.17	57.73
Swedish	35.36	47.41	51.39
Urdu	33.70	42.14	58.73
Icelandic	N/A	51.26	N/A
Thai	N/A	41.23	N/A

Table 1: Entropy values of probability distributions P(label—(head-pos)) for different languages estimated from real (P_{UD}) and bootstrapped (P_{GF}) treebanks. If a language has more than one treebank in the UD distribution, we select one treebank as the primary treebank and use that to estimate the distribution and in the parsing experiments. Languages for which a UD treebank does not exist but is included in GF-RGL are listed towards the bottom of the table.

type include multi-word expressions and proper nouns (labeled using `fixed` and `flat` label). In the second class, are ellipsis and paratactic constructions in addition to labels that are used in robust analysis of web text (`orphan`, `goeswith` and `reparandum`). Examples that cover these labels can be generated by re-writing the grammar: however, we found very few instances of these in the treebanks. Finally, another variation in the bootstrapped treebanks is in the case of label subtypes that are optionally defined in a language-specific manner. While the configurations allow for accurate generation of certain labels (e.g. `obl:agent` in the case of passive agents), recovering similar information in other instances is not possible without a significant redesign of the RGL (e.g. `obl:tmod` for temporal modifiers). We address this issue by restricting `gf2ud` to generate only the core labels in UD and ignore subtype labels uniformly across languages.

Table 1 shows the entropies of the conditional probability distribution defined as probability of a UD label given the part-of-speech tag of the head.

The distributions are estimated on both the synthetic UD treebank and a human annotated UD treebank [2] Also shown in the table are the cross-entropy values between the distribution estimated from the synthetic and the original treebanks.

4 UD Parsing

The bootstrapped UD treebanks are used to train delexicalized parsing models. We choose to work with the delexicalized UD treebanks for two reasons: first, the context-free assumption in the probabilistic model defined on the abstract syntax makes the tree generation decomposable, but selectional preferences are not encoded in the generative model used for bootstrapping the ASTs. Secondly, generating a full UD treebank assumes the availability of an interlingua lexicon – which reduces the portability of this approach to new languages.[3] For both these reasons, we restrict ourselves to strictly delexicalized UD treebanks in our parsing experiments.

We are interested in the following three use-cases depending on the size of the training data (N) available for inducing parsing models.

- When $N \leq 1K$ sentences[4] are available for a language. There are around 20 treebanks in the current UD distribution that match this criterion and almost all these treebanks have been manually annotated from scratch. This corresponds to the scenario of under-resourced languages, where either the monolingual corpus for treebank or annotators for treebanking are scarce. This scenario strongly corresponds to our proposed idea of simultaneous grammar engineering and tree-banking.

- When $1K \leq N \leq 5K$ sentences[5] are available for a language. There are around 18 treebanks in the current UD distribution that match this criterion. While one can argue that these languages are not really under-resourced, this setup matches the typical case of training domain-specific parsers either for a particular domain like bio-medical or legal texts.

- The case where treebanks are larger than either of the two previous scenarios $N \geq 5K$. This setup is interesting to test the limit of how useful are bootstrapped ASTs and UD treebanks to train parsing models.

For each of these use-cases, we train parsing models using data from both human annotated UD treebanks and synthetic treebanks for different sizes of training data. The resulting parsing models are evaluated using labelled attachment scores, obtained by parsing the test set of the UD treebank for the language in question. We experiment with an off-the-shelf transition-based dependency parser that gives good results in the dependency parsing task (Straka and Straková, 2017). In the ideal case the experiments need to be carried out using multiple parsers from both the transition-based and graph-based paradigms. We leave that for future work.

5 Experiments

We ran experiments with 3 languages – English, Swedish and Finnish in this paper. In addition to the availability of a concrete syntax for the language, our approach also requires concrete configurations for the languages (Kolachina and Ranta, 2016) in order to bootstrap full UD trees. Table 2 shows statistics about the concrete configurations for the RGL grammar for the languages. The probability distribution defined on the RGL was estimated using the GF-Penn treebank (Marcus et al., 1994; Angelov, 2011) of English. This raises another question – how well does the distribution defined on the abstract syntax of the RGL estimated from monolingual data transfer across other languages. The bootstrapping algorithm was restricted to generate 20K ASTs of depth less than 10.[6]

We use UDPipe (Straka and Straková, 2017) to train parsing models, using comparable settings to the baseline systems provided in the CoNLL18 shared task (Zeman and Hajič, 2018). Gold tokenization and part-of-speech tags are used in both training and testing the parser. This was done to control for differences in tagging performance across the synthetic and original UD treebanks. The models are trained using the primary treebanks from Universal Dependencies v2.3 distribution.[7] We plot the learning curves for parsing

---

[2] The UD treebanks are taken from the v2.3 distribution.

[3] There is ongoing work on developing interlingual lexica from linked data like WordNet (Virk et al., 2014; Angelov and Lobanov, 2016).

[4] This approximately corresponds to 20K tokens.

[5] This approximately corresponds to 20K – 100K tokens.

[6] Trees of depth less than 4 were filtered out in the process.

[7] The notion of primary treebank for a language has been

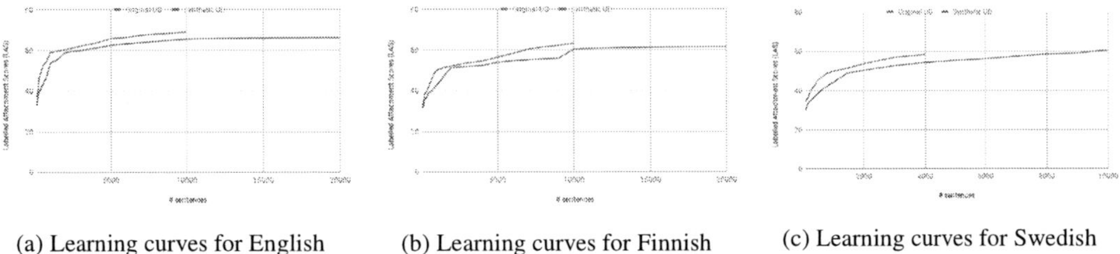

(a) Learning curves for English   (b) Learning curves for Finnish   (c) Learning curves for Swedish

Figure 4: Learning curves for parsing models of trained on original UD and synthetic UD treebanks.

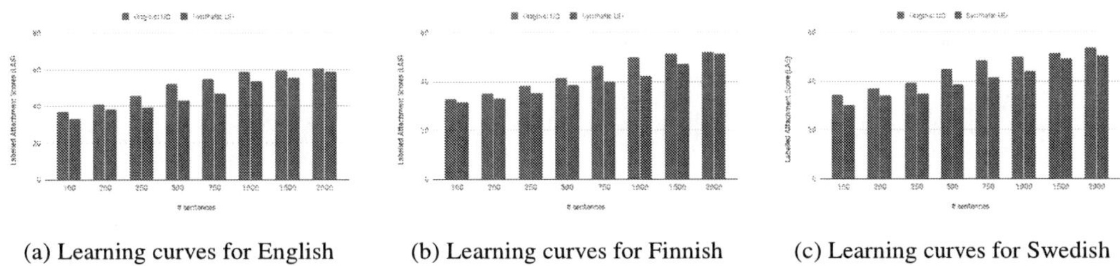

(a) Learning curves for English   (b) Learning curves for Finnish   (c) Learning curves for Swedish

Figure 5: Learning curves shown using bar plots for parsing models trained on less than 1000 sentences from original UD and 2000 sentences from synthetic UD treebanks.

Language	Abstract	Concrete	Morph-features
English	143	21	57
Swedish	143	25	59
Finnish	143	31	57

Table 2: Estimate of the effort required in `gf2ud`. The abstract configurations are the same for all languages, while the concrete functions and morph-features are defined for each language. The first column corresponds to configurations for syntactic constructors in the RGL, and second column corresponds to constructors that use syncategorematic words in the linearization.

models in Figure 4 trained on both the original and synthetic treebank data for each use case outlined in Section 4. The learning curves were plotted using the LAS accuracies obtained on the test set for the three languages using models trained on both the original and the synthetic treebanks. It is seen from the learning curves that models trained on the synthetic treebanks do not outperform the models trained using original UD treebanks.

However, the full learning curves shown in Figure 4 do not tell the complete story. Figure 5 shows the learning curves (visualized using bar plots) for English, Finnish and Swedish in the setup where less than 1K sentences from UD tree-

banks are used. It is clear from the plots for all the three languages that the synthetic treebanks are sub-optimal when directly compared against real treebanks of the **same size**. However, what is interesting is that parsing models in this range (i.e. $N \leq 1K$) with synthetic treebanks quickly reach comparable accuracies to using real treebank data, with an approximate effective data coefficient of 2.0. In other words comparable accuracies can be obtained using roughly twice the amount of synthetic data, generated for free by the abstract syntax grammar.

It is interesting to note that the learning curves using the synthetic data for the English parsing models become comparably flat in our setup with less than 5K sentences (shown in Figure 6a). Despite the lower improvements with increasing treebank sizes, there is still a consistent improvement in parsing accuracies with the best accuracy of 65.4 LAS using 10K synthetic samples (shown in Figure 6b). This pattern is consistent across Swedish and Finnish, which allows us to draw the conclusion that while the effective data coefficient is smaller, the synthetic treebanks are still useful to improve parsing accuracies.

6   Related Work

The current trend in dependency parsing is directed towards using synthetic treebanks in an attempt to cover unknown languages for which

made obsolete in UD v2.3 distribution - with all treebanks being assigned a code. So, we use the term primary in this paper to refer to EWT for English, TDT for Finnish and Talbanken for Swedish.

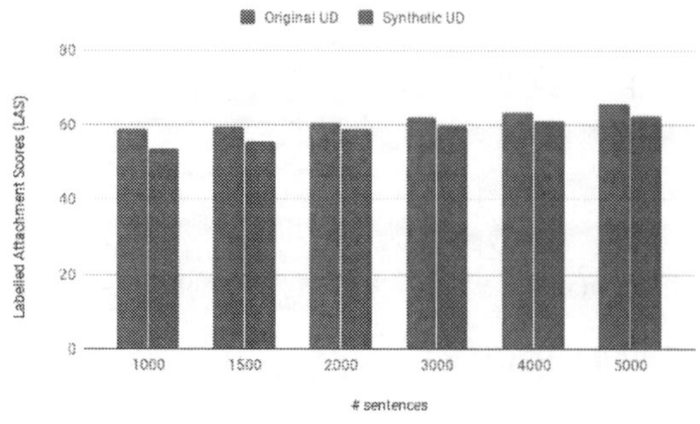 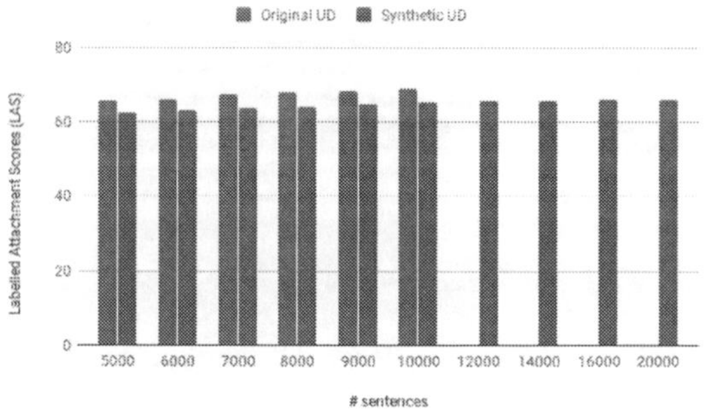

(a) Learning curves for English with N between 1K and 5K samples

(b) Learning curves for English with N between 5K and 10K samples

Figure 6: Learning curves shown using bar plots for parsing models of English

resources are minimal or do not exist altogether. Such treebanks rely on various auxiliary resources: parallel corpora (Tiedemann, 2014), multilingual word-embeddings (Xiao and Guo, 2014), MT system for the target language (Tiedemann and Agic, 2016; Tyers et al., 2018) or more minimally, tagged corpora in the target language (Wang and Eisner, 2018).

Tiedemann and Agic (2016) propose a method to generate synthetic treebanks for new languages using machine translation systems to transfer cross-linguistic information from resource-rich language to under-resourced languages. This work builds on top of many previous approaches to cross-lingual parsing using parallel corpora and multilingual word-embeddings. The synthetic treebanks generated in the current work are are different in two ways:

- we assume multilingual abstraction and the concrete syntaxes are available, namely the GF-RGL to generate language-independent samples in the form of ASTs.
- we also assume that a distribution of the target language is not available and what is available is a distribution on the abstract syntax that generalizes to other languages.

Hence, the resulting treebank is licensed by a grammar, and high-precision cross-linguistic information is specified, but the distribution over the resulting treebank is different from the distribution obtained using the real treebanks. An alternative to the method of bootstrapping UD treebanks is to use `ud2gf` (Ranta and Kolachina, 2017) as a way to translate existing UD treebanks to GF treebanks, that are licensed by a grammar.

The current work also relates to more recent work in data-augmentation for dependency parsing (Sahin and Steedman, 2018) and more generally in NLP (Sennrich et al., 2016). The augmentation methods are designed to address data scarcity by exploiting monolingual corpora or generating synthetic samples in multilingual applications. However, the underlying abstractions used to generate the synthetic data are induced from auxiliary corpora.

Jonson (2006) show that synthetic corpora generated using a GF grammar can be used to build language models for speech recognition. Experiments in their work show that synthetic in-domain examples generated using the grammar when combined with large out-of-domain data result in significant reduction of word error rate of the speech recognizer. This work falls in line with similar approaches to combine corpus driven approaches with rule-based systems (Bangalore and Johnston, 2004), as a way to combine the statistical information available from corpora with good coverage resulting from rule-based abstractions especially when working with restricted domains. In this paper, we restrict ourselves to utilizing synthetic treebanks for parsing, and leave the discussion on ways to combine synthetic treebanks with real treebanks as future work. This choice is primarily motivated by our interest in grammar-based development of dependency treebanks as opposed to the traditional way of treebanking – by training human annotators.

7 Conclusions

In the current paper, we propose an alternative approach to cross-lingual treebanking — one that recommends grammar engineering. Multilingual abstractions that facilitate bootstrapping of cross-lingual treebanks have been previously explored in the setup of low precision high recall methods. These methods presume the availability of different resources in order to induce the cross-linguistic signal – parallel or multilingual corpora, word embeddings etc. Our approach explores the opposite direction – multilingual grammars of high precision are used to bootstrap parallel treebanks. While these multilingual grammars are not easy to develop, the question of how useful such grammars are is one that has been largely unexplored in the context of cross-lingual syntactic parsing.

We use a context-free probability model to generate ASTs that are used to bootstrap parallel UD treebanks in 3 languages. Experiments in delexicalized parsing show that these treebanks are useful in two scenarios – when data in the target language is minimal ($<$1K sentences) and small ($<$5K sentences). In the future, we intend to look at ways to generate synthetic treebanks from existing UD treebanks of languages using `ud2gf` (Ranta and Kolachina, 2017), that aims to address the lack of syntactic distributions in our synthetic treebanks. We also did not pursue the obvious direction of combining the real and synthetic treebanks in the current work: we leave this for future work. Another direction that is of interest is to augment existing treebanks with syntactic variations to quantify the need for regular syntactic variants in parser development, such as converting declaratives to questions, varying tense and polarity, adding and removing modifiers, and so on. String-based augmentation (as opposed to precise grammar-based generation) in this direction has already shown promising results (Sahin and Steedman, 2018).

Acknowledgements

We want to thank Joakim Nivre, Richard Johansson, Filip Ginter, Lilja Øvrelid and Marco Kuhlmann for the discussion and the anonymous reviewers for helpful comments on this work. The project has been funded by the REMU project (Reliable Multilingual Digital Communication, Swedish Research Council 2012-5746).

References

Krasimir Angelov. 2011. *The Mechanics of the Grammatical Framework*. Ph.D. thesis, Chalmers University of Technology.

Krasimir Angelov and Peter Ljunglöf. 2014. Fast Statistical Parsing with Parallel Multiple Context-Free Grammars. In *Proceedings of the 14th Conference of the European Chapter of the Association for Computational Linguistics*, pages 368–376, Gothenburg, Sweden. Association for Computational Linguistics.

Krasimir Angelov and Gleb Lobanov. 2016. Predicting Translation Equivalents in Linked WordNets. In *Proceedings of the Sixth Workshop on Hybrid Approaches to Translation (HyTra6)*, pages 26–32, Osaka, Japan. The COLING 2016 Organizing Committee.

Srinivas Bangalore and Michael Johnston. 2004. Balancing data-driven and rule-based approaches in the context of a Multimodal Conversational System. In *HLT-NAACL 2004: Main Proceedings*, pages 33–40, Boston, Massachusetts, USA. Association for Computational Linguistics.

Dan Garrette and Jason Baldridge. 2013. Learning a Part-of-Speech Tagger from Two Hours of Annotation. In *Proceedings of the 2013 Conference of the North American Chapter of the Association for Computational Linguistics: Human Language Technologies*, pages 138–147, Atlanta, Georgia. Association for Computational Linguistics.

Rebecca Jonson. 2006. Generating Statistical Language Models from Interpretation Grammars in Dialogue Systems. In *11th Conference of the European Chapter of the Association for Computational Linguistics*.

Prasanth Kolachina and Aarne Ranta. 2016. From Abstract Syntax to Universal Dependencies. *Linguistic Issues in Language Technology*, 13(3).

Peter Ljunglöf. 2004. *The Expressivity and Complexity of Grammatical Framework*. Ph.D. thesis, Department of Computing Science, Chalmers University of Technology and University of Gothenburg.

Mitchell Marcus, Grace Kim, Mary Ann Marcinkiewicz, Robert MacIntyr, Ann Bies, Mark Ferguson, Karen Katz, and Britta Schasberger. 1994. The Penn Treebank: Annotating Predicate Argument Structure. In *HUMAN LANGUAGE TECHNOLOGY: Proceedings of a Workshop held at Plainsboro, New Jersey, March 8-11, 1994*, pages 114–119.

Ryan McDonald, Slav Petrov, and Keith Hall. 2011. Multi-Source Transfer of Delexicalized Dependency Parsers. In *Proceedings of the 2011 Conference on Empirical Methods in Natural Language Processing*, pages 62–72, Edinburgh, Scotland, UK. Association for Computational Linguistics.

Grace Ngai and David Yarowsky. 2000. Rule Writing or Annotation: Cost-efficient Resource Usage for Base Noun Phrase Chunking. In *Proceedings of the 38th Annual Meeting of the Association for Computational Linguistics*, pages 117–125, Hong Kong. Association for Computational Linguistics.

Stephan Oepen, Dan Flickinger, Kristina Toutanova, and Christopher D. Manning. 2004. LinGO Redwoods: A Rich and Dynamic Treebank for HPSG. *Research on Language and Computation*, 2(4):575–596.

Aarne Ranta. 2009. The GF Resource Grammar Library. *Linguistic Issues in Language Technology*, 2(2).

Aarne Ranta. 2011. *Grammatical Framework: Programming with Multilingual Grammars*. CSLI Publications, Stanford.

Aarne Ranta and Prasanth Kolachina. 2017. From Universal Dependencies to Abstract Syntax. In *Proceedings of the NoDaLiDa 2017 Workshop on Universal Dependencies (UDW 2017)*, pages 107–116, Gothenburg, Sweden. Association for Computational Linguistics.

Aarne Ranta, Prasanth Kolachina, and Thomas Hallgren. 2017. Cross-Lingual Syntax: Relating Grammatical Framework with Universal Dependencies. In *Proceedings of the 21st Nordic Conference on Computational Linguistics*, pages 322–325, Gothenburg, Sweden. Association for Computational Linguistics.

Gozde Gul Sahin and Mark Steedman. 2018. Data Augmentation via Dependency Tree Morphing for Low-Resource Languages. In *Proceedings of the 2018 Conference on Empirical Methods in Natural Language Processing*, pages 5004–5009, Brussels, Belgium. Association for Computational Linguistics.

Hiroyuki Seki, Takashi Matsumura, Mamoru Fujii, and Tadao Kasami. 1991. On multiple context-free grammars. *Theoretical Computer Science*, 88(2):191–229.

Rico Sennrich, Barry Haddow, and Alexandra Birch. 2016. Improving Neural Machine Translation Models with Monolingual Data. In *Proceedings of the 54th Annual Meeting of the Association for Computational Linguistics (Volume 1: Long Papers)*, pages 86–96, Berlin, Germany. Association for Computational Linguistics.

Ian Sommerville. 2010. *Software Engineering*, 9th edition. Addison-Wesley Publishing Company, USA.

Milan Straka and Jana Straková. 2017. Tokenizing, POS Tagging, Lemmatizing and Parsing UD 2.0 with UDPipe. In *Proceedings of the CoNLL 2017 Shared Task: Multilingual Parsing from Raw Text to Universal Dependencies*, pages 88–99, Vancouver, Canada. Association for Computational Linguistics.

Jörg Tiedemann. 2014. Rediscovering Annotation Projection for Cross-Lingual Parser Induction. In *Proceedings of COLING 2014, the 25th International Conference on Computational Linguistics: Technical Papers*, pages 1854–1864, Dublin, Ireland. Dublin City University and Association for Computational Linguistics.

Jörg Tiedemann and Zeljko Agic. 2016. Synthetic Treebanking for Cross-Lingual Dependency Parsing. *The Journal of Artificial Intelligence Research (JAIR)*, 55:209–248.

Francis Tyers, Mariya Sheyanova, Aleksandra Martynova, Pavel Stepachev, and Konstantin Vinogorodskiy. 2018. Multi-source synthetic treebank creation for improved cross-lingual dependency parsing. In *Proceedings of the Second Workshop on Universal Dependencies (UDW 2018)*, pages 144–150, Brussels, Belgium. Association for Computational Linguistics.

Shafqat Mumtaz Virk, K.V.S Prasad, Aarne Ranta, and Krasimir Angelov. 2014. Developing an interlingual translation lexicon using WordNets and Grammatical Framework. In *Proceedings of the Fifth Workshop on South and Southeast Asian Natural Language Processing*, pages 55–64, Dublin, Ireland. Association for Computational Linguistics and Dublin City University.

Dingquan Wang and Jason Eisner. 2016. The Galactic Dependencies Treebanks: Getting More Data by Synthesizing New Languages. *Transactions of the Association for Computational Linguistics*, 4:491–505.

Dingquan Wang and Jason Eisner. 2018. Synthetic Data Made to Order: The Case of Parsing. In *Proceedings of the 2018 Conference on Empirical Methods in Natural Language Processing*, pages 1325–1337, Brussels, Belgium. Association for Computational Linguistics.

Min Xiao and Yuhong Guo. 2014. Distributed Word Representation Learning for Cross-Lingual Dependency Parsing. In *Proceedings of the Eighteenth Conference on Computational Natural Language Learning*, pages 119–129, Ann Arbor, Michigan. Association for Computational Linguistics.

Daniel Zeman and Jan Hajič. 2018. Proceedings of the CoNLL 2018 Shared Task: Multilingual Parsing from Raw Text to Universal Dependencies. Brussels, Belgium. Association for Computational Linguistics.

Lexical Resources for Low-Resource PoS Tagging in Neural Times

Barbara Plank
Department of Computer Science
ITU, IT University of Copenhagen
Denmark
bplank@itu.dk

Sigrid Klerke
Department of Computer Science
ITU, IT University of Copenhagen
Denmark
sikl@itu.dk

Abstract

More and more evidence is appearing that integrating symbolic lexical knowledge into neural models aids learning. This contrasts the widely-held belief that neural networks largely learn their own feature representations. For example, recent work has shown benefits of integrating lexicons to aid cross-lingual part-of-speech (PoS). However, little is known on how complementary such additional information is, and to what extent improvements depend on the coverage and quality of these external resources. This paper seeks to fill this gap by providing a thorough analysis on the contributions of lexical resources for cross-lingual PoS tagging in neural times.

1 Introduction

In natural language processing, the deep learning revolution has shifted the focus from conventional hand-crafted symbolic representations to dense inputs, which are adequate representations learned automatically from corpora. However, particularly when working with low-resource languages, small amounts of symbolic lexical resources such as user-generated lexicons are often available even when gold-standard corpora are not. Recent work has shown benefits of combining conventional lexical information into neural cross-lingual part-of-speech (PoS) tagging (Plank and Agić, 2018). However, little is known on how complementary such additional information is, and to what extent improvements depend on the coverage and quality of these external resources.

The contribution of this paper is in the analysis of the contributions of models' components (tagger transfer through annotation projection vs. the contribution of encoding lexical and morphosyntactic resources). We seek to understand under which conditions a low-resource neural tagger

benefits from external lexical knowledge. In particular:

a) we evaluate the neural tagger across a total of 20+ languages, proposing a novel baseline which uses retrofitting;

b) we investigate the reliance on dictionary size and properties;

c) we analyze model-internal representations via a probing task to investigate to what extent model-internal representations capture morphosyntactic information.

Our experiments confirm the synergetic effect between a neural tagger and symbolic linguistic knowledge. Moreover, our analysis shows that the composition of the dictionary plays a more important role than its coverage.

2 Methodology

Our base tagger is a bidirectional long short-term memory network (bi-LSTM) (Graves and Schmidhuber, 2005; Hochreiter and Schmidhuber, 1997; Plank et al., 2016) with a rich word encoding model which consists of a character-based bi-LSTM representation $\vec{cw}$ paired with pre-trained word embeddings $\vec{w}$. Sub-word and especially character-level modeling is currently pervasive in top-performing neural sequence taggers, owing to its capacity to effectively capture morphological features that are useful in labeling out-of-vocabulary (OOV) items. Sub-word information is often coupled with standard word embeddings to mitigate OOV issues. Specifically, i) word embeddings are typically built from massive unlabeled datasets and thus OOVs are less likely to be encountered at test time, while ii) character embeddings offer further linguistically plausible fallback for the remaining OOVs through modeling intra-word relations. Through these approaches, multilingual PoS tagging has seen tangible gains from neural methods in the recent years.

2.1 Lexical resources

We use linguistic resources that are user-generated and available for many languages. The first is WIKTIONARY, a word type dictionary that maps words to one of the 12 Universal PoS tags (Li et al., 2012; Petrov et al., 2012). The second resource is UNIMORPH, a morphological dictionary that provides inflectional paradigms for 350 languages (Kirov et al., 2016). For Wiktionary, we use the freely available dictionaries from Li et al. (2012). UniMorph covers between 8-38 morphological properties (for English and Finnish, respectively).[1] The sizes of the dictionaries vary considerably, from a few thousand entries (e.g., for Hindi and Bulgarian) to 2M entries (Finnish Uni-Morph). We study the impact of smaller dictionary sizes in Section 4.1.

The tagger we analyze in this paper is an extension of the base tagger, called *distant supervision from disparate sources* (DSDS) tagger (Plank and Agić, 2018). It is trained on projected data and further differs from the base tagger by the integration of lexicon information. In particular, given a lexicon src, DSDS uses $\vec{e}_{src}$ to embed the lexicon into an l-dimensional space, where $\vec{e}_{src}$ is the concatenation of all embedded m properties of length l (empirically set, see Section 2.2), and a zero vector for words not in the lexicon. A property here is a possible PoS tag (for Wiktionary) or a morphological feature (for Unimorph). To integrate the type-level supervision, the lexicon embeddings vector is created and concatenated to the word and character-level representations for every token: $\vec{w} \circ \vec{cw} \circ \vec{e}$.

We compare DSDS to alternative ways of using lexical information. The first approach uses lexical information directly during decoding (Täckström et al., 2013). The second approach is more implicit and uses the lexicon to induce better word embeddings for tagger initialization. In particular, we use the dictionary for retrofitting off-the-shelf embeddings (Faruqui et al., 2015) to initialize the tagger with those. The latter is a novel approach which, to the best of our knowledge, has not yet been evaluated in the neural tagging literature. The idea is to bring the off-the-shelf embeddings closer to the PoS tagging task by retrofitting the embeddings with syntactic clusters derived from the lexicon.

We take a deeper look at the quality of the lex-

icons by comparing tag sets to the gold treebank data, inspired by Li et al. (2012). In particular, let T be the dictionary derived from the gold treebank (development data), and W be the user-generated dictionary, i.e., the respective Wiktionary (as we are looking at PoS tags). For each word type, we compare the tag sets in T and W and distinguish six cases:

1. NONE: The word type is in the training data but not in the lexicon (out-of-lexicon).

2. EQUAL: $W = T$

3. DISJOINT: $W \cap T = \emptyset$

4. OVERLAP: $W \cap T \neq \emptyset$

5. SUBSET: $W \subset T$

6. SUPERSET: $W \supset T$

In an ideal setup, the dictionaries contain no disjoint tag sets, and larger amounts of equal tag sets or superset of the treebank data. This is particularly desirable for approaches that take lexical information as type-level supervision.

2.2 Experimental setup

In this section we describe the baselines, the data and the tagger hyperparameters.

Data We use the 12 Universal PoS tags (Petrov et al., 2012). The set of languages is motivated by accessibility to embeddings and dictionaries. We here focus on 21 dev sets of the Universal Dependencies 2.1 (Nivre and et al., 2017), test set results are reported by Plank and Agić (2018) showing that DSDS provides a viable alternative.

Annotation projection To build the taggers for new languages, we resort to annotation projection following Plank and Agić (2018). In particular, they employ the approach by Agić et al. (2016), where labels are projected from multiple sources to multiple targets and then decoded through weighted majority voting with word alignment probabilities and source PoS tagger confidences. The wide-coverage Watchtower corpus (WTC) by Agić et al. (2016) is used, where 5k instances are selected via data selection by alignment coverage following Plank and Agić (2018).

Baselines We compare to the following alternatives: type-constraint Wiktionary supervision (Li et al., 2012) and retrofitting initialization.

---

[1] More details: `http://unimorph.org/`

| | Dev sets (UD2.1) | | | |
Language	5k	TC_W	Retro	DsDs
Bulgarian (bg)	89.8	89.9	87.1	**91.0**
Croatian (hr)	84.7	85.2	83.0	**85.9**
Czech (cs)	**87.5**	**87.5**	84.9	87.4
Danish (da)	89.8	89.3	88.2	**90.1**
Dutch (nl)	88.6	89.2	86.6	**89.6**
English (en)	86.4	**87.6**	82.5	87.3
Finnish (fi)	81.7	81.4	79.2	**83.1**
French (fr)	**91.5**	90.0	89.8	91.3
German (de)	85.8	87.1	84.7	**87.5**
Greek (el)	80.9	**86.1**	79.3	79.2
Hebrew (he)	75.8	75.9	71.7	**76.8**
Hindi (hi)	63.8	63.9	63.0	**66.2**
Hungarian (hu)	**77.5**	**77.5**	75.5	76.2
Italian (it)	92.2	91.8	90.0	**93.7**
Norwegian (no)	91.0	91.1	88.8	**91.4**
Persian (fa)	43.6	43.8	**44.1**	43.6
Polish (pl)	84.9	84.9	83.3	**85.4**
Portuguese	92.4	92.2	88.6	**93.1**
Romanian (ro)	84.2	84.2	80.2	**86.0**
Spanish (es)	90.7	88.9	88.9	**91.7**
Swedish (sv)	89.4	89.2	87.0	**89.8**
Avg(21)	83.4	83.6	81.3	**84.1**
Germanic (6)	88.5	88.9	86.3	**89.3**
Romance (5)	90.8	90.1	88.4	**91.4**
Slavic (4)	86.7	86.8	84.6	**87.4**
Indo-Iranian (2)	53.7	53.8	53.5	**54.9**
Uralic (2)	79.6	79.4	79.2	**79.6**

Table 1: Replication of results on the dev sets. 5k: model trained on only projected data; TC_W: type constraints; Retro: retrofitted initialization.

Hyperparameters We use the same setup as Plank and Agić (2018), i.e., 10 epochs, word dropout rate (p=.25) and l=40-dimensional lexicon embeddings for DsDs, except for down-scaling the hidden dimensionality of the character representations from 100 to 32 dimensions. This ensures that our probing tasks always get the same input dimensionality: 64 (2x32) dimensions for $\vec{cw}$, which is the same dimension as the off-the-shelf word embeddings. Language-specific hyperparameters could lead to optimized models for each language. However, we use identical settings for each language which worked well and is less expensive, following Bohnet et al. (2018). For all experiments, we average over 3 randomly seeded runs, and provide mean accuracy.

We use the off-the-shelf Polyglot word embeddings (Al-Rfou et al., 2013). Word embedding initialization provides a consistent and considerable boost in this cross-lingual setup, up to 10% absolute improvements across 21 languages when only 500 projected training instances are available (Plank and Agić, 2018). Note that we em-

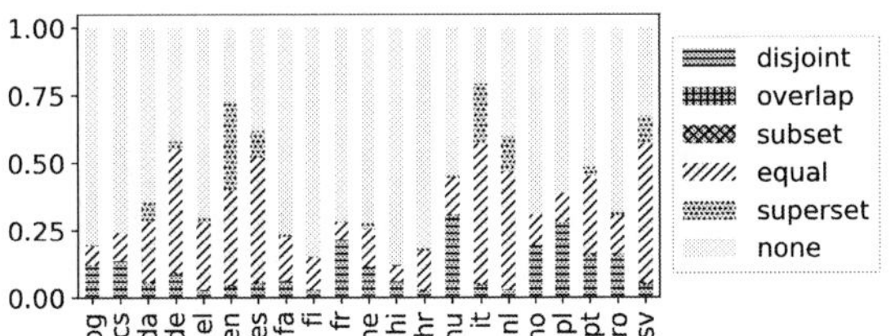

Figure 1: Analysis of Wiktionary vs gold (dev set) tag sets. 'None': percentage of word types not covered in the lexicon. 'Disjoint': the gold data and Wiktionary do not agree on the tag sets. See Section 2.1 for details on other categories.

pirically find it to be best to *not* update the word embeddings in this noisy training setup, as that results in better performance, see Section 4.4.

3 Results

Table 1 presents our replication results, i.e., tagging accuracy for the 21 individual languages, with means over all languages and language families (for which at least two languages are available). There are several take-aways.

Inclusion of lexical information Combining the best of two worlds results in the overall best tagging accuracy, confirming Plank and Agić (2018): Embedding lexical information into a neural tagger improves tagging accuracy from 83.4 to 84.1 (means over 21 languages). On 15 out of 21 languages, DsDs is the best performing model. On two languages, type constraints work the best (English and Greek). Retrofitting performs best only on one language (Persian); this is the language with the overall lowest performance. On three languages, Czech, French and Hungarian, the baseline remains the best model, none of the lexicon-enriching approaches works. We proceed to inspect these results in more detail.

Analysis Overall, type-constraints improve the baseline but only slightly (83.4 vs 83.6). Intuitively, this more direct use of lexical information requires the resource to be high coverage and a close fit to the evaluation data, to not introduce too many pruning errors during decoding due to contradictory tag sets. To analyze this, we look at the tag set agreement in Figure 1. For languages for which the level of *disjoint* tag set information is low, such as Greek, English, Croatian, Finnish and Dutch, type constraints are expected to help. This is in fact the case, but there are exceptions,

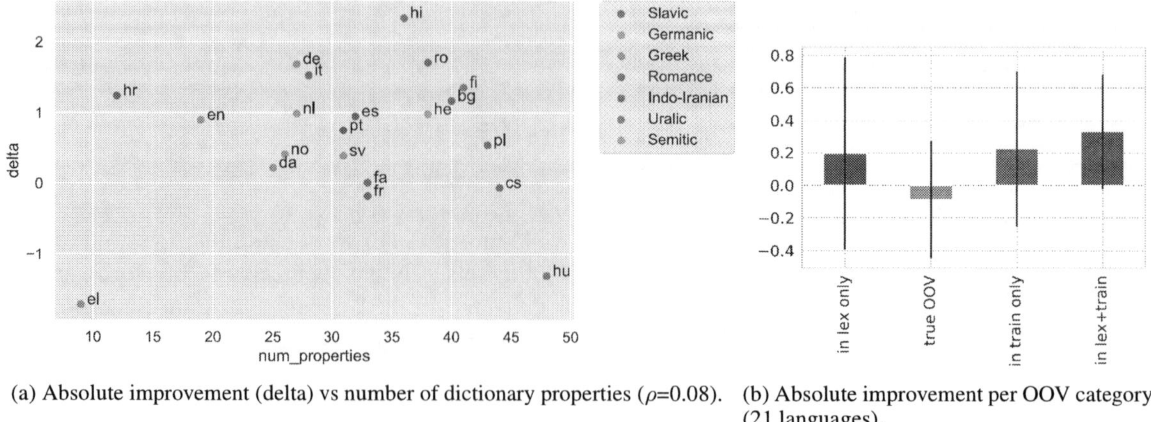

(a) Absolute improvement (delta) vs number of dictionary properties (ρ=0.08).

(b) Absolute improvement per OOV category (21 languages).

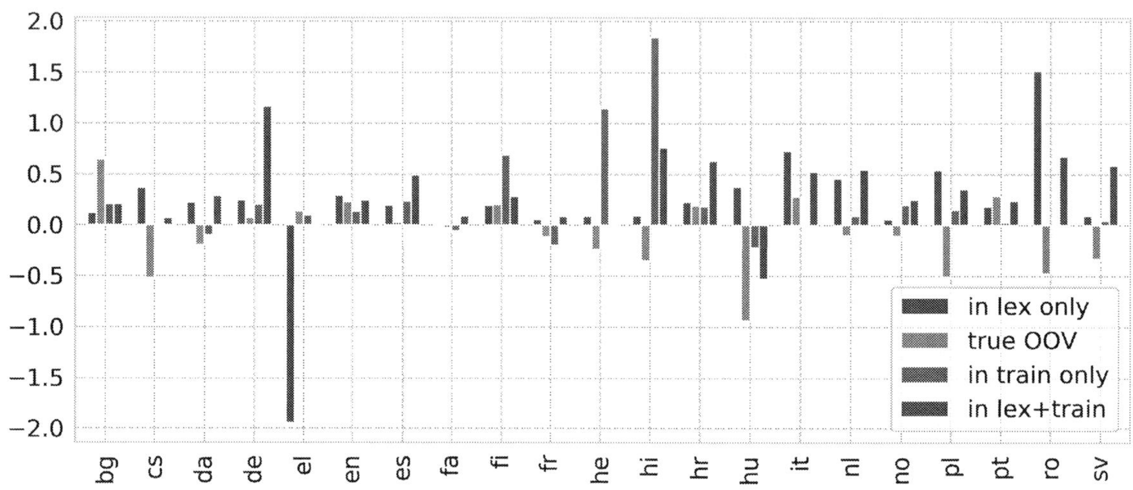

(c) Per language analysis: absolute improvements of DsDs over the baseline for words in the lexicon, in the training data, in both or in neither (true OOVs).

Figure 2: Analysis of OOVs and dictionary properties.

such as Finnish. Coverage of the lexicon is also important, and for this morphologically rich language, the coverage is amongst the lowest (c.f. large amount of the 'none' category in Figure 1).

The more implicit use of lexical information in DsDs helps on languages with relatively high dictionary coverage and low tag set disagreement, such as Danish, Dutch and Italian. Compared to type constraints, embedding the lexicon also helps on languages with low dictionary coverage, such as Bulgarian, Hindi, Croatian and Finnish, which is very encouraging and in sharp contrast to type constraints. The only outlier remains Greek.

Figure 2 (a) plots the absolute improvement in tagging accuracy over the baseline versus the number of properties in the dictionaries. Slavic and Germanic languages cluster nicely, with some outliers (Croatian). However, there is only a weak positive correlation (ρ=0.08). More properties do not necessarily improve performance, and lead to sparsity. The inclusion of the lexicons results in higher coverage, which might be part of the explanation for the improvement of DsDs. The question remains whether the tagger learns to rely only on this additional signal, or it generalizes beyond it. Therefore, we first turn to inspecting out-of-vocabulary (OOV) items. OOV items are the key challenge in part-of-speech tagging, i.e., to correctly tag tokens unseen in the training data.

In Figure 2 (b) and (c), we analyze accuracy improvements on different groups of tokens: The *in lex+train* tokens that were seen both in the lexicon and the training data, the *in train only* tokens seen in the training data but not present in the lexicon, the *in lex only* tokens that were present in the lexicon but not seen in the training data and the *true OOV* tokens that were neither seen in training nor present in the lexicon. Figure 2 (b) shows means over the 21 languages, Figure 2 (c) provides details per language. The first take-away is that in many cases the tagger does learn to use information beyond the coverage of the lexicon. The embedded knowledge helps the tagger to improve on tokens which are in train only (and are thus not in the lexicon, green bars). For true OOVs (orange bars), this is the case for some languages as well Figure 2 (c), i.e., improvements on true OOVs can be observed for Bulgarian, German, Greek, English, Finish, Croatian, Italian and Portuguese. Over all 21 languages there is a slight drop on true OOVs: -0.08, but this is a mean over all languages, for which results vary, making it important to look beyond the aggregate level. Over all languages except for Hungarian, the tagger, unsurprisingly, improves over tokens which are both in the lexicon and in the training data (see further discussion in Section 4).

4 Discussion

Here we dig deeper into the effect of including lexical information by a) examining learning curves with increasing dictionary sizes, b) relating tag set properties to performance, and finally c) having a closer look at model internal representations, by comparing them to the representations of the base model that does not include lexical information. We hypothesize that when learning from dictionary-level supervision, information is propagated through the representation layers so as to generalize beyond simply relying on the respective external resources.

4.1 Learning curves

The lexicons we use so far are of different sizes (shown in Table 1 of Plank and Agić (2018)), spanning from 1,000 entries to considerable dictionaries of several hundred thousands entries. In a low-resource setup, large dictionaries might not be available. It is thus interesting to examine how tagging accuracy is affected by dictionary size. We examine two cases: randomly sampling dictionary entries and sampling by word frequency, over increasing dictionary sizes: 50, 100, 200, 400, 800, 1600 word types. The latter is motivated by the fact that an informed dictionary creation (under limited resources) might be more beneficial. We estimate word frequency by using the UD training data sets (which are otherwise not used).

Figure 3 (a) provides means over the 21 languages (with confidence intervals of ± 1 standard deviation based on three runs). We note that sampling by frequency is overall more beneficial than random sampling. The biggest effect of sampling by frequency is observed for the Romance language family, see Figure 3 (b). It is noteworthy that more dictionary data is not always necessarily beneficial. Sometimes a small but high-frequency dictionary approximates the entire dictionary well. This is for instance the case for Danish, where sampling by frequency approximates the entire dictionary well ('all' achieves 90.1, while using 100 most frequent entries is close: 89.93). Frequency sampling also helps clearly for Italian, but here having the entire dictionary results in the overall highest performance.

For some languages, the inclusion of lexical information does not help, not even at smaller dictionary sizes. This is the case for Hungarian, French and Czech. For Hungarian using the entire dictionary drops performance below the baseline. For Czech, this is less pronounced, as the performance stays around baseline. Relating these negative ef-

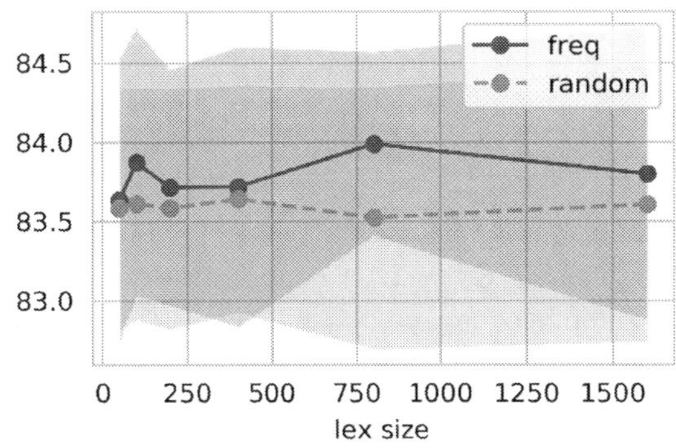

(a) Average effect over 21 languages of high-freq and random dictionaries

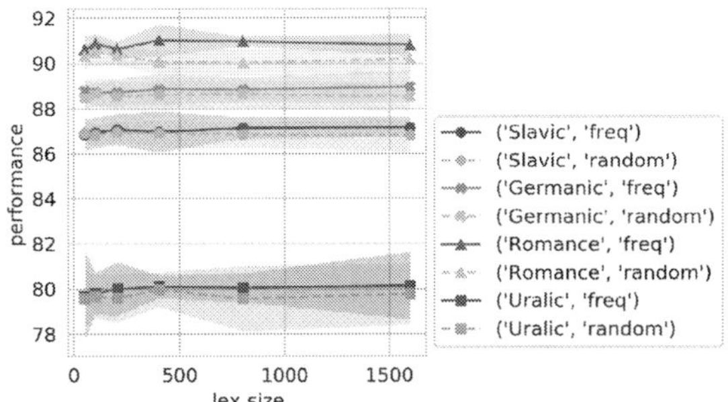

(b) Effect for subset of language families of high-freq and random dictionaries

Figure 3: Learning curves over increased dictionary sizes.

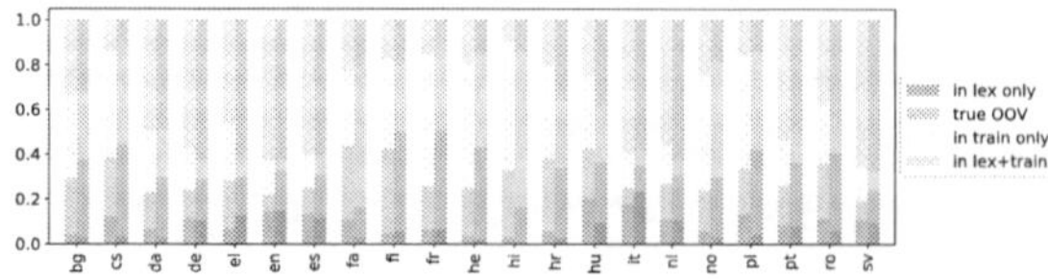

Figure 4: Proportion of tokens unseen in the training data, in the lexicon or in both (true OOV's). Lighter bars are proportion of correctly labeled portion, dark bars are proportion of errors.

fects to the results from the tag set agreement analysis (Figure 1), we note that Hungarian is the language with the largest *disjoint* tag set. Albeit the coverage for Hungarian is good (around .5), including too much contradictory tag information has a clear deteriorating effect. Consequently, neither sampling strategy works. Czech, which has less coverage, sees a negative effect as well: half of the dictionary entries have disjoint tag sets. Italian is the language with the highest dictionary coverage *and* the highest proportion of equal tag sets, thereby providing a large positive benefit.

We conclude that when dictionaries are not available, creating them by targeting high-frequency items is a pragmatic and valuable strategy. A small dictionary, which does not contain too contradictory tag sets, can be beneficial.

4.2 Analysis of correct/incorrect predictions

In the following we analyze correctly and incorrectly labeled tokens. Because we are analyzing differences between languages as well as between errors and successes we abstract away from the underlying sample size variation by comparing proportions.

The analysis inspects the differences in proportions on four subsections of the development set, as introduced above: the *in lex+train* tokens, the *in train only* tokens, the *in lex only* tokens and the *true OOVs*. The proportion of these four data subsets in the correctly and the incorrectly labeled tokens are shown side by side in Figure 4 in lighter and darker shades, respectively. If the OOV-status of a word was unrelated to performance, the lighter and darker bars would be of identical size. This is not the case and we can observe that the true OOVs make up a significantly larger share of the errors than of successes (two-tailed paired Student's t-test: $p = 0.007$). Similarly, seen across all languages the shift in the size of the proportion of

true OOVs is made up by more correct labeling of a larger proportion of *in train only* (two-tailed paired Student's t-test: $p = 0.014$) and *in lex only* (two-tailed paired Student's t-test: $p = 0.020$), whereas the proportion of *in lex+train* does not significantly differ between the correctly and incorrectly labeled parts (two-tailed paired Student's t-test: $p = 0.200$).[2]

4.3 Probing word encodings

Probing tasks, or diagnostic classifiers, are separate classifiers which use representations extracted from any facet of a trained neural model as input for solving a separate task. Following the intuition of Adi et al. (2017), if the target can be predicted, then the information must be encoded in the representation. However, the contrary does not necessarily hold: if the model fails it does not necessarily follow that the information is not encoded, as opposed to not being encoded in a useful way for a probing task classifier.

As the internal representations stored in neural models are not immediately interpretable, probing tasks serve as a way of querying neural representations for interpretable information. The probing task objective and training data is designed to model the query of interest. The representation layer we query in this work is the word-level output from the character embedding sub-model. This part of the word-level representation starts out uninformative and thus without prior prediction power on the classifier objectives.

The pre-trained word embeddings stay fixed in our model (see Section 4.4). However, the character-based word encodings get updated: This holds true both for the BASE system and the DsDs tagger. As a target for assessing the flow of information in the neural tagger, we thus focus on the character-based word encodings.

The word-level is relevant as it is the granularity at which the tagger is evaluated. The word embeddings may already have encoded PoS-relevant information and the lexicon embeddings explicitly encodes PoS-type-level information. By contrast, the character-based word encodings are initialized to be uninformative and any encoding of PoS-related information is necessarily a result of the neural training feedback signal.

For these reasons we query the character-based word representations of the tagger in order to com-

---

[2]Significance based on an α-level of 0.05

pare variation between the base tagger and the DsDs lexicon-enriched architecture.

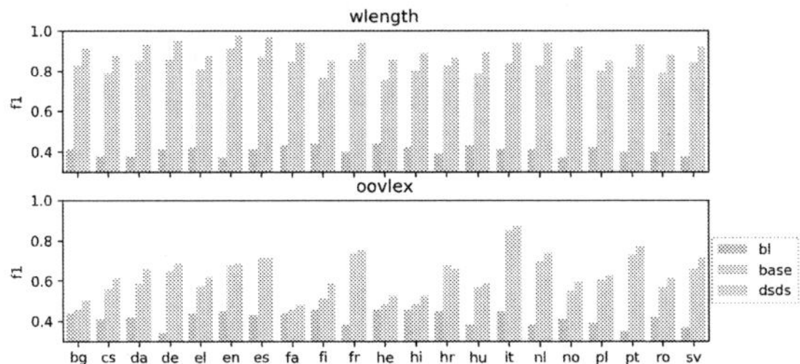

Figure 5: Macro F1 scores for stand-alone classifiers on the probing tasks of predicting which words are long and which are in the lexicon, respectively. The baseline (bl) is a simple majority baseline. The base- and DsDs-informed classifiers were trained on character-based word representations from the neural taggers with and without access to lexical information, respectively.

We employ two binary probing tasks: predicting which words are long, i.e., contain more than 7 characters[3], and predicting which words are in the lexicon. The word length task is included as a task which can be learned independently of whether lexicon information is available to the neural model. Storing length-related information might help the model distinguish suffix patterns of relevance to PoS-tagging.

Following Shi et al. (2016) and Gulordava et al (2018), we use a logistic regression classifier setup and a constant input dimensionality of 64 across tasks (Conneau et al., 2018). The classifiers are trained using 10-fold cross-validation for each of three trained runs of each neural model and averaged. We include a majority baseline and report macro F1-scores, as we are dealing with imbalanced classes. The training vocabulary of both probing tasks is restricted to the neural tagger training vocabulary, that is, all word types in the projected training data, as these are the representations which have been subject to updates during training of the neural model. Using the projected data has the advantage that the vocabulary is similar across languages as the data comes from the same domain (Watchtower).

The results on the word length probing task shown on the top half of Figure 5 confirm that information relevant to distinguishing word length is being encoded in the neural representation, as expected. It is intriguing that the lexicon-informed DsDs representation encodes this information even at higher degree.

On the task of classifying which words are in the lexicon, all neural representations beat the majority baseline, but we also see that this task is harder, given the higher variance across languages. With Spanish (es) and Croatian (hr) as the only exceptions, the DsDs-based representations are generally encoding more of the information relevant to distinguishing which words are in the lexicon, confirming our intuitions that the internal representations were altered. Note, however, that even the base-tagger is able to solve this task above chance level. This is potentially an artifact of how lexicons grow where it would be likely for several inflections of the same word to be added collectively to the lexicon at once, and since the character representations can be expected to produce more similar representations of words derived from the same lemma the classifier will be able to generalize and perform above chance level without the base-model representations having ever been exposed to the lexical resource.

4.4 Updating in light of noisy data?

When training a tagger with noisy training data and pre-trained embeddings, the question arises whether it is more beneficial to freeze the word embeddings or update them. We hypothesize that freezing embeddings is more beneficial in noisy training cases, as it helps to stabilize the signal from the pre-trained word embeddings while avoiding updates from the noisy training data. To test this hypothesis, we train the base tagger on high-quality gold training data (effectively, the UD training data sets), with and without freezing the word embeddings layer. We find that updating the word embedding layer is in fact beneficial in the high-quality training data regime: on average +0.4% absolute improvement is obtained (mean over 21 languages). This is in sharp contrast to the noisy training data regime, in which the baseline accuracy drops by as much as 1.2% accuracy. Therefore, we train the tagger with pre-trained embeddings on projected WTC data and freeze the word embeddings lookup layer during training.

---

[3]Considering words of 7 characters or more to be long is based on the threshold that was experimentally tuned in the design of the readability metric LIX (Björnsson, 1983). This threshold aligns well with the visual perceptual span within which proficient readers from grade four and up can be expected to automatically decode a word in a single fixation (Sperlich et al., 2015)

5   Related work

In recent years, natural language processing has witnessed a move towards deep learning approaches, in which automatic representation learning has become the de facto standard methodology (Collobert et al., 2011; Manning, 2015).

One of the first works that combines neural representations with semantic symbolic lexicons is the work on *retrofitting* (Faruqui et al., 2015). The main idea is to use the relations defined in semantic lexicons to refine word embedding representations, such that words linked in the lexical resource are encouraged to be closer to each other in the distributional space.

The majority of recent work on neural sequence prediction follows the commonly perceived wisdom that hand-crafted features are obsolete for deep learning methods. They rely on end-to-end training without resorting to additional linguistic resources. Our study contributes to the increasing literature to show the utility of linguistic resources for deep learning models by providing a deep analysis of a recently proposed model (Plank and Agić, 2018). Most prior work in this direction can be found on machine translation (Sennrich and Haddow, 2016; Chen et al., 2017; Li et al., 2017; Passban et al., 2018), work on named entity recognition (Wu et al., 2018) and PoS tagging (Sagot and Martínez Alonso, 2017) who use lexicons, but as n-hot features and without examining the cross-lingual aspect.

Somewhat complementary to evaluating the utility of linguistic resources empirically is the increasing body of work that uses linguistic insights to try to understand what properties neural-based representations capture (Kádár et al., 2017; Adi et al., 2017; Belinkov et al., 2017; Conneau et al., 2018; Hupkes et al., 2018). Shi et al. (2016) and Adi et al. (2017) introduced the idea of probing tasks (or 'diagnostic classifiers'), see Belinkov and Glass for a recent survey (Belinkov and Glass, 2019). Adi et al. (2017) evaluate several kinds of sentence encoders and propose a range of probing tasks around isolated aspects of sentence structure at the surface level (sentence length, word content and word order). This work has been greatly expanded by including both syntactic and semantic probing tasks, careful sampling of probing task training data, and extending the framework to make it encoder agnostic (Conneau et al., 2018). A general observation here is that task-specific knowledge is needed in order to design relevant diagnostic tasks, which is not always straightforward. For example, Gulordava (2018) investigate whether RNNs trained using a language model objective capture hierarchical syntactic information. They create nonsensical construction so that the RNN cannot rely on lexical or semantic clues, showing that RNNs still capture syntactic properties in sentence embeddings across the four tested languages while obfuscating lexical information. There is also more theoretical work on investigating the capabilities of recurrent neural networks, e.g., Weiss et al. (2018) show that specific types of RNNs (LSTMs) are able to use counting mechanisms to recognize specific formal languages.

Finally, linguistic resources can also serve as proxy for evaluation. As recently shown (Agić et al., 2017), type-level information from dictionaries approximates PoS tagging accuracy in the absence of gold data for cross-lingual tagger evaluation. Their use of high-frequency word types inspired parts of our analysis.

6   Conclusions

We analyze DsDs, a recently-proposed low-resource tagger that symbiotically leverages neural representations and symbolic linguistic knowledge by integrating them in a soft manner. We replicated the results of Plank and Agić (2018), showing that the more implicit use of embedding user-generated dictionaries turns out to be more beneficial than approaches that rely more explicitly on symbolic knowledge, such a type constraints or retrofitting. By analyzing the reliance of DsDs on the linguistic knowledge, we found that the composition of the lexicon is more important than its size. Moreover, the tagger benefits from small dictionaries, as long as they do not contain tag set information contradictory to the evaluation data. Our quantitative analysis also sheds light on the internal representations, showing that they get more sensitive to the task. Finally, we found that freezing pre-trained word embeddings complement the learning signal well in this noisy data regime.

Acknowledgements

We kindly acknowledge the support of NVIDIA Corporation for the donation of the GPUs and Amazon for an Amazon Research Award.

References

Yossi Adi, Einat Kermany, Yonatan Belinkov, Ofer Lavi, and Yoav Goldberg. 2017. Fine-grained analysis of sentence embeddings using auxiliary prediction tasks. In *ICLR*.

Željko Agić, Anders Johannsen, Barbara Plank, Héctor Alonso Martínez, Natalie Schluter, and Anders Søgaard. 2016. Multilingual projection for parsing truly low-resource languages. *Transactions of the Association for Computational Linguistics*, 4:301–312.

Željko Agić, Barbara Plank, and Anders Søgaard. 2017. Cross-lingual tagger evaluation without test data. In *Proceedings of the 15th Conference of the European Chapter of the Association for Computational Linguistics: Volume 2, Short Papers*. Association for Computational Linguistics.

Rami Al-Rfou, Bryan Perozzi, and Steven Skiena. 2013. Polyglot: Distributed word representations for multilingual nlp. *arXiv preprint arXiv:1307.1662*.

Yonatan Belinkov, Nadir Durrani, Fahim Dalvi, Hassan Sajjad, and James Glass. 2017. What do neural machine translation models learn about morphology? In *Proceedings of the 55th Annual Meeting of the Association for Computational Linguistics (Volume 1: Long Papers)*, pages 861–872. Association for Computational Linguistics.

Yonatan Belinkov and James Glass. 2019. Analysis methods in neural language processing: A survey. *Transactions of the Association for Computational Linguistics*, 7.

C. H. Björnsson. 1983. Readability of newspapers in 11 languages. *Reading Research Quarterly*, 18(4):480–497.

Bernd Bohnet, Ryan McDonald, Goncalo Simoes, Daniel Andor, Emily Pitler, and Joshua Maynez. 2018. Morphosyntactic tagging with a meta-bilstm model over context sensitive token encodings. *arXiv preprint arXiv:1805.08237*.

Huadong Chen, Shujian Huang, David Chiang, and Jiajun Chen. 2017. Improved neural machine translation with a syntax-aware encoder and decoder. In *Proceedings of the 55th Annual Meeting of the Association for Computational Linguistics (Volume 1: Long Papers)*, pages 1936–1945. Association for Computational Linguistics.

Ronan Collobert, Jason Weston, Léon Bottou, Michael Karlen, Koray Kavukcuoglu, and Pavel Kuksa. 2011. Natural language processing (almost) from scratch. *Journal of Machine Learning Research*, 12(Aug):2493–2537.

Alexis Conneau, Germán Kruszewski, Guillaume Lample, Loïc Barrault, and Marco Baroni. 2018. What you can cram into a single .. vector: Probing sentence embeddings for linguistic properties. In *Proceedings of the 56th Annual Meeting of the Association for Computational Linguistics (Volume 1: Long Papers)*, pages 2126–2136. Association for Computational Linguistics.

Manaal Faruqui, Jesse Dodge, Sujay Kumar Jauhar, Chris Dyer, Eduard Hovy, and Noah A. Smith. 2015. Retrofitting word vectors to semantic lexicons. In *Proceedings of the 2015 Conference of the North American Chapter of the Association for Computational Linguistics: Human Language Technologies*, pages 1606–1615. Association for Computational Linguistics.

Alex Graves and Jürgen Schmidhuber. 2005. Framewise phoneme classification with bidirectional lstm and other neural network architectures. *Neural Networks*, 18(5):602–610.

Kristina Gulordava, Piotr Bojanowski, Edouard Grave, Tal Linzen, and Marco Baroni. 2018. Colorless green recurrent networks dream hierarchically. In *Proceedings of the 2018 Conference of the North American Chapter of the Association for Computational Linguistics: Human Language Technologies, Volume 1 (Long Papers)*, pages 1195–1205. Association for Computational Linguistics.

Sepp Hochreiter and Jürgen Schmidhuber. 1997. Long short-term memory. *Neural computation*, 9(8):1735–1780.

Dieuwke Hupkes, Sara Veldhoen, and Willem Zuidema. 2018. Visualisation and'diagnostic classifiers' reveal how recurrent and recursive neural networks process hierarchical structure. *Journal of Artificial Intelligence Research*, 61:907–926.

Ákos Kádár, Grzegorz Chrupała, and Afra Alishahi. 2017. Representation of linguistic form and function in recurrent neural networks. *Computational Linguistics*, 43(4):761–780.

Christo Kirov, John Sylak-Glassman, Roger Que, and David Yarowsky. 2016. Very-large scale parsing and normalization of wiktionary morphological paradigms. In *Proceedings of the Tenth International Conference on Language Resources and Evaluation (LREC 2016)*. European Language Resources Association (ELRA).

Junhui Li, Deyi Xiong, Zhaopeng Tu, Muhua Zhu, Min Zhang, and Guodong Zhou. 2017. Modeling source syntax for neural machine translation. In *Proceedings of the 55th Annual Meeting of the Association for Computational Linguistics (Volume 1: Long Papers)*, pages 688–697, Vancouver, Canada. Association for Computational Linguistics.

Shen Li, João Graça, and Ben Taskar. 2012. Wiki-ly supervised part-of-speech tagging. In *Proceedings of the 2012 Joint Conference on Empirical Methods in Natural Language Processing and Computational*

Natural Language Learning, pages 1389–1398, Jeju Island, Korea. Association for Computational Linguistics.

Christopher D Manning. 2015. Computational linguistics and deep learning. *Computational Linguistics*, 41(4):701–707.

Joakim Nivre and et al. 2017. Universal dependencies 2.1.

Peyman Passban, Qun Liu, and Andy Way. 2018. Improving character-based decoding using target-side morphological information for neural machine translation. In *Proceedings of the 2018 Conference of the North American Chapter of the Association for Computational Linguistics: Human Language Technologies, Volume 1 (Long Papers)*, pages 58–68. Association for Computational Linguistics.

Slav Petrov, Dipanjan Das, and Ryan McDonald. 2012. A universal part-of-speech tagset. In *Proceedings of the Eight International Conference on Language Resources and Evaluation (LREC'12)*, Istanbul, Turkey. European Language Resources Association (ELRA).

Barbara Plank and Željko Agić. 2018. Distant supervision from disparate sources for low-resource part-of-speech tagging. In *Proceedings of the 2018 Conference on Empirical Methods in Natural Language Processing*, pages 614–620. Association for Computational Linguistics.

Barbara Plank, Anders Søgaard, and Yoav Goldberg. 2016. Multilingual part-of-speech tagging with bidirectional long short-term memory models and auxiliary loss. In *Proceedings of the 54th Annual Meeting of the Association for Computational Linguistics (Volume 2: Short Papers)*, pages 412–418. Association for Computational Linguistics.

Benoît Sagot and Héctor Martínez Alonso. 2017. Improving neural tagging with lexical information. In *Proceedings of the 15th International Conference on Parsing Technologies*, pages 25–31, Pisa, Italy. Association for Computational Linguistics.

Rico Sennrich and Barry Haddow. 2016. Linguistic input features improve neural machine translation. In *Proceedings of the First Conference on Machine Translation*, pages 83–91, Berlin, Germany. Association for Computational Linguistics.

Xing Shi, Inkit Padhi, and Kevin Knight. 2016. Does string-based neural mt learn source syntax? In *Proceedings of the 2016 Conference on Empirical Methods in Natural Language Processing*, pages 1526–1534. Association for Computational Linguistics.

Anja Sperlich, Daniel J. Schad, and Jochen Laubrock. 2015. When preview information starts to matter: Development of the perceptual span in german beginning readers. *Journal of Cognitive Psychology*, 27(5):511–530.

Oscar Täckström, Dipanjan Das, Slav Petrov, Ryan McDonald, and Joakim Nivre. 2013. Token and type constraints for cross-lingual part-of-speech tagging. *Transactions of the Association for Computational Linguistics*, 1:1–12.

Gail Weiss, Yoav Goldberg, and Eran Yahav. 2018. On the practical computational power of finite precision rnns for language recognition. In *Proceedings of the 56th Annual Meeting of the Association for Computational Linguistics (Volume 2: Short Papers)*, pages 740–745. Association for Computational Linguistics.

Minghao Wu, Fei Liu, and Trevor Cohn. 2018. Evaluating the utility of hand-crafted features in sequence labelling. In *Proceedings of the 2018 Conference on Empirical Methods in Natural Language Processing*, pages 2850–2856. Association for Computational Linguistics.

Gender Bias in Pretrained Swedish Embeddings

Magnus Sahlgren
RISE
Sweden
`magnus.sahlgren@ri.se`

Fredrik Olsson
RISE
Sweden
`fredrik.olsson@ri.se`

Abstract

This paper investigates the presence of gender bias in pretrained Swedish embeddings. We focus on a scenario where names are matched with occupations, and we demonstrate how a number of standard pretrained embeddings handle this task. Our experiments show some significant differences between the pretrained embeddings, with word-based methods showing the most bias and contextualized language models showing the least. We also demonstrate that a previously proposed debiasing method does not affect the performance of the various embeddings in this scenario.

1 Introduction

The motivation for this study is the currently widespread practice of using pretrained embeddings as building blocks for NLP-related tasks. More specifically, we are concerned about such usage by actors in the public sector, for instance government agencies and public organizations. It is obvious how the presence of (gender or racial) bias would be potentially serious in applications where embeddings are used as input to decision support systems in the public sector.

As an example, in Sweden limited companies must be approved and registered by the Swedish Companies Registration Office. One important (and internationally unique) step in this registration procedure is the approval of the company name, which is decided by case handlers at the Registration Office. Their decision is based on several factors, one of which is the appropriateness of the company name in relation to the company description. Now, imagine the hypothetical use case in which the case handlers use a decision support system that employs pretrained embeddings to quantify the similarity between a suggested company name and its company description. Table 1 exemplifies what the results might look like. In this fictive example, the company description states that the company will do business with cars, and the name suggestions are composed of a person name in genitive and the word "cars" (i.e. "Fredrik's cars"). We use pretrained Swedish ELMo embeddings (Che et al., 2018) to compute the distance between the name suggestion and the company description.

The results demonstrate that male person names ("Magnus" and "Fredrik") are closer to "cars" in the ELMo similarity space than female person names ("Maria" and "Anna"). If such results are used as input to a decision support system for deciding on the appropriateness of a company name suggestion in relation to a company description, we might introduce gender bias into the decision process. We subscribe to the view that such bias would be unfair and problematic.

The point of this paper is therefore to investigate gender bias when using existing and readily available pretrained embeddings for tasks relating to names and occupations. We include both word-based embeddings produced using

Name suggestion	Company description	Distance
Magnus bilar	Bolaget ska bedriva verksamhet med bilar	0.028
Fredriks bilar	Bolaget ska bedriva verksamhet med bilar	0.038
Marias bilar	Bolaget ska bedriva verksamhet med bilar	0.044
Annas bilar	Bolaget ska bedriva verksamhet med bilar	0.075

Table 1: Examples of gender bias with respect to occupations using pretrained ELMo embeddings.

`word2vec` and `fastText`, as well as character-based (and WordPiece-based) contextualized embeddings produced using `ELMo` and the multilingual `BERT`. The next section covers related work. We then discuss the various embeddings in Section 3, before we then turn to some experimental evidence of bias in the embeddings, and we also show that the previously proposed debiasing method is unable to handle gender bias in our scenario.

2   Related work

Research regarding bias and stereotypes expressed in text and subsequently incorporated in learned language models is currently a vivid field. Caliskan et al. (2017) show that learned embeddings exhibit every linguistic bias documented in the field of psychology (such as that flowers are more pleasant than insects, musical instruments are preferred to weapons, and personal names are used to infer race). Garg et al. (2018) show that temporal changes of the embeddings can be used to quantify gender and ethnic stereotypes over time, and Zhao et al. (2017) suggest that biases might in fact be amplified by embedding models.

Several researchers have also investigated ways to counter stereotypes and biases in learned language models. While the seminal work by Bolukbasi et al. (2016a, 2016b) concerns the identification and mitigation of gender bias in *pretrained* word embeddings, Zhao et al. (2018) provide insights into the possibilities of *learning* embeddings that are gender neutral. Bordia and Bowman (2019) outline a way of training a recurrent neural network for word-based language modelling such that the model is gender neutral. Park et al. (2018) discuss different ways of mitigating gender bias, in the context of abusive language detection, ranging from debiasing a model by using the hard debiased word embeddings produced by Bolukbasi et al. (2016b), to manipulating the data prior to training a model by swapping masculine and feminine mentions, and employing transfer learning from a model learned from less biased text.

Gonen and Goldberg (2019) contest the approaches to debiasing word embeddings presented by Bolukbasi et al. (2016b) and Zhao et al. (2018), arguing that while the bias is reduced when measured according to its definition, i.e., dampening the impact of the general gender direction in the vector space, "the actual effect is mostly hiding the bias, not removing it". Further, Gonen and Gold-berg (2019) claim that a lot of the supposedly removed bias can be recovered due to the geometry of the vector representation of the gender neutralized words.

Our contribution consists of an investigation of the presence of gender bias in pretrained embeddings for Swedish. We are less interested in bias as a theoretical construct, and more interested in the effects of gender bias in actual applications where pretrained embeddings are employed. Our experiments are therefore tightly tied to a real-world use case where gender bias would have potentially serious ramifications. We also provide further evidence of the inability of the debiasing method proposed by Bolukbasi et al. (2016b) to handle the type of bias we are concerned with.

3   Embeddings

We include four different standard embeddings in these experiments: `word2vec`, `fastText`, `ELMo` and `BERT`. There are several pre-trained models available in various web repositories. We select one representative instance per model, summarized in Table 2 (next page).

These models represent different types of embeddings. `word2vec` (Mikolov et al., 2013) builds embeddings by training a shallow neural network to predict a set of context words based on a target word (this is the so-called *skipgram* architecture; if we instead predict the target word based on the context words the model is called *continuous bag of words*). The network learns two sets of vectors, one for the target terms (the embedding vectors), and one for context terms. The objective of the network is to learn vectors such that their dot product correspond to the log likelihood of observing word pairs in the training data. `fastText` (Bojanowski et al., 2017) uses the same neural network architecture, but incorporates character information by using character n-grams instead of whole words in the prediction step.

It should be noted that most applications of the above-mentioned vectors use only the embeddings for the target terms. In fact, many repositories with pretrained vectors do not even contain the context embeddings. When the downstream task focuses on *associative* relations (which is the case in the present scenario with names and occupations), it would be beneficial to be able to use *both* target and context vectors, since using only one of these will result in more *paradigmatic* similarities.

Model	Source Code Repository	Training data
`word2vec`	`vectors.nlpl.eu`	CoNLL17 data
`fastText`	`github.com/facebookresearch/fastText`	Wikipedia
`ELMo`	`github.com/HIT-SCIR/ELMoForManyLangs`	CoNLL18 data
`BERT`	`github.com/google-research/bert`	Wikipedia

Table 2: The pre-trained embeddings and models included in these experiments were downloaded in April 2019 from the following URLs. **word2vec**: `vectors.nlpl.eu/repository/11/69.zip`, **fastText**: `dl.fbaipublicfiles.com/fasttext/vectors-crawl/cc.sv.300.bin.gz`, **ELMo**: `vectors.nlpl.eu/repository/11/173.zip`, **BERT**: `storage.googleapis.com/bert_models/2018_11_23/multi_cased_L-12_H-768_A-12.zip`

`ELMo` (Peters et al., 2018) is a deep character-based neural network that learns embeddings by predicting the next token given an input sequence. The network architecture includes both convolutional and (bidirectional) LSTM layers, and produces an embedding that that is sensitive to the particular context of the input sequence. `ELMo` is thus different from `word2vec` and `fastText` in the sense that it produces *contextualized* embeddings, which has proven to be highly beneficial when using the embeddings as representation in downstream NLP tasks such as classification, entity recognition, and question answering.

`BERT` (Devlin et al., 2018) is similar to `ELMo` in the sense that it uses a deep neural network architecture and produces contextualized embeddings. However, it differs in the type of network used. `BERT` uses a (bidirectional) Transformer network that relies exclusively on attention, and the model is trained using a masked language model task, similar to a cloze test. Contrary to `ELMo`, `BERT` is not character-based, but relies on WordPiece tokenization of the input data. This has some potentially problematic effects when tokenizing proper names. As an example, the Swedish male name "Henrik" gets tokenized as ["hen", "##rik"], with "rik" probably deriving from the Swedish word "rik" (eng. "rich"). It would have been desirable to *not* use WordPiece tokenization for proper names.

In the following experiments, pre-trained `ELMo` and `BERT` are used to produce contextualized embeddings both for individual words (such as names or places) and for texts (such as company descriptions). Pre-trained `word2vec` and `fastText` are used to look up individual words, and for texts we follow standard practice and average the vectors of the component words. Since proper names in Swedish use uppercase for the initial letter, we retain the casing information for all models that can handle such vocabulary, which in our case are all models except `word2vec`.

4 Data

In order to investigate whether our concerns about gender bias in pretrained Swedish embeddings are valid, we collect lists of the 100 most common Swedish female and male first names from Statistics Sweden (`www.scb.se`). We also collect lists of the most typical female and male occupations from the same source, as shown in Tables 3 and 4 (next page). These are the most common occupations for women and men as compiled by Statistics Sweden, together with the percentage of women and men in each occupation.

Since our interest in this paper is bias, we do not include occupations that have less than (or close to) 50% occurrence of women or men (such cases are marked by $*$ in the tables). This leaves us with 18 typically female occupations, and 15 typically male occupations. Some of the remaining occupations are very similar to each other, and we therefore collapse them to one occupation (marked by numbers in the tables), resulting in 14 distinct female occupations and 14 distinct male occupations. For each of these *gendered occupations*, we also list a number of synonyms, collected from `wikipedia.se` and `framtid.se`. Morphological variants of each term are included.

5 Experiment 1: names and occupations

As a first experiment, we compute the similarity between the names and the occupations using the different embeddings. We do this by computing the similarity between each name and each occupation. Table 5 shows the percentage of female and male names that are on average more similar to a female vs. male occupation. Numbers in parentheses are based on only *the most similar* oc-

Occupation (Swedish)	Occupation (English)	% women
[1]Undersköterska	Assistant nurse	92
Barnskötare	Nanny	89
Grundskollärare	Primary school teacher	75
Förskollärare	Preschool teacher	96
[2]Butikssäljare, fackhandel	Shop sales	61
[3]Vårdbiträde	Care assistant	81
Kontorsassistent och sekreterare	Secretary	79
Städare	Cleaner	75
Personlig assistent	Personal assistant	74
[2]Butikssäljare, dagligvaror	Retail sales	67
[3]Vårdare, boendestödjare	Housing assistant	73
Restaurang- och köksbiträde	Restaurant assistant	65
Planerare och utredare	Planner	63
Grundutbildad sjuksköterska	Nurse	90
[4]Ekonomiassistent	Accountant assistant	88
[1]Undersköterska, vård- och specialavdelning	Nursing staff	91
* Företagssäljare	Company sales	27
* Kock och kallskänka	Chef	52
[4]Redovisningsekonomer	Accountant	79
Socialsekreterare	Social worker	86

Table 3: The 20 most common occupations for Swedish women in 2016 according to Statistics Sweden (www.scb.se).

Occupation (Swedish)	Occupation (English)	% men
Företagssäljare	Company sales	73
Lager- och terminalpersonal	Warehouse staff	79
Mjukvaru- och systemutvecklare	Software developer	80
Lastbilsförare	Truck driver	94
Träarbetare, snickare	Carpenter	99
Maskinställare och maskinoperatörer	Machine operator	86
* Butikssäljare, fackhandel	Shop sales	39
Fastighetsskötare	Janitor	86
Motorfordonsmekaniker och fordonsreparatör	Vehicle mechanic	97
Installations- och serviceelektriker	Electrician	98
* Butikssäljare, dagligvaror	Retail sales	33
* Grundskollärare	Primary school teacher	25
Underhållsmekaniker och maskinreparatör	Maintenance mechanic	95
* Planerare och utredare	Planner	37
* Restaurang- och köksbiträde	Restaurant assistant	35
[1]Ingenjör och tekniker inom elektroteknik	Electrical technician	87
[1]Civilingenjörsyrke inom elektroteknik	Electrical engineer	84
Verkställande direktör	CEO	84
Buss- och spårvagnsförare	Bus driver	86
VVS-montör	Plumber	99

Table 4: The 20 most common occupations for Swedish men in 2016 according to Statistics Sweden (www.scb.se).

Model	**Male names** Male occupations	**Male names** Female occupations	**Female names** Male occupations	**Female names** Female occupations
`word2vec`	91 (86)	9 (14)	99 (98)	1 (2)
`fastText`	4 (10)	96 (90)	100 (100)	0 (0)
`ELMo`	96 (63)	4 (37)	49 (87)	51 (13)
`BERT`	37 (54)	63 (46)	76 (55)	24 (45)

Table 5: Percentage of female and male names that are on average more similar to a female vs. male occupation. The similarities are calculated based on the original embeddings, before the application of the debiasing step described in Section 6. Numbers in parentheses only count the single most similar occupation for each name.

cupation for each name. As an example, imagine we only have two female and male occupations, and that the name "Anna" has the similarities 0.47 and 0.78 to the female occupations, and the similarities 0.12 and 0.79 to the male occupations. In this example, "Anna" would be closer to the female occupations when counting the average similarities (0.625 vs. 0.455), but closer to the male occupations when only considering the most similar examples (0.79 vs. 0.78).

There are several ways in which an embedding could show bias in this setting. The arguably most detrimental effect would be if the embedding grouped male names with male occupations and female names with female occupations. Somewhat less severe, but still problematic, would be if the embedding grouped all names with female or male occupations. A completely unbiased model would not show any difference between the female and male names with respect to female and male occupations.

The numbers in Table 5 demonstrate some interesting differences between the different embeddings. `word2vec` shows a clear tendency to group both male and female names with male occupations. `fastText`, on the other hand, shows a bias for female occupations for male names, and for male occupations for female names. This is a very interesting difference, given that the only algorithmic difference between these models is the inclusion of character n-grams in the latter model.

The results for `ELMo` and `BERT` show some interesting differences too. `ELMo` groups the male names with the male occupations, but is less biased for the female names. When counting only the single most similar occupation, `ELMo` shows a similar tendency as `word2vec` and groups both male and female names with male occupations. `BERT`, on the other hand, seems slightly more balanced, with a tendency similar to `fastText` when counting the average similarities. When only counting the single most similar occupation, `BERT` is almost perfectly balanced between female and male occupations.

6 Debiasing embeddings

We apply the debiasing methodology in (Bolukbasi et al., 2016b) to the pretrained embedddings. Debiasing a given vector space involves finding the general direction in it that signifies gender using a set of predefined *definitional pairs*, and then removing the direction from all vectors except those corresponding to words that are naturally *gender specific*.

The definitional pairs are word pairs expressing among themselves a natural distinction between the genders, e.g., *he – she*, and *mother – father*. In our setting, there are 10 such pairs. The gender specific words are words that also carry a natural gender dimension that should not be corrected during the debiasing phase of the vector space. We use the same methodology for growing a seed set of gender specific words into a larger set as described in (Bolukbasi et al., 2016b), and end up with 486 manually curated gender specific words, including e.g., *farfar* (paternal grandfather), *tvillingsystrar* (twin sisters), and *matriark* (matriarch).

The definitional pairs are used to find a *gender direction* in the embedding space, which is done by taking the difference vector of each of the definitional pairs (i.e. $w_1 - w_2$), and then factorizing the mean-centered difference vectors using PCA, retaining only the first principal component, which will act as the gender direction. The vector space is then *hard debiased*[1] in the sense that the gen-

---

[1] The alternative is *soft debiasing*, in which one tries to strike a balance between keeping the pairwise distances

Model	Male names Male occupations	Male names Female occupations	Female names Male occupations	Female names Female occupations
`word2vec`	88 (89)	12 (11)	95 (93)	5 (7)
`fastText`	0 (10)	100 (90)	100 (99)	0 (1)
`ELMo`	99 (87)	1 (13)	26 (71)	74 (29)
`BERT`	0 (50)	100 (50)	97 (52)	3 (48)

Table 6: Percentage of female and male names that are on average more similar to a female vs. male occupation. The similarities are calculated based on the debiased version of each model. Numbers in parentheses only count the single most similar occupation for each name.

der direction b is removed from the embeddings of all non-gender specific words w using orthogonal projection: $w' = w - b \times \frac{w \cdot b}{b \cdot b}$.

The approach described by (Bolukbasi et al., 2016b) includes an *equalize* step to make all gender neutral words equidistant to each of the members of a given *equality* set of word pairs. The equality set is application specific, and since the current investigation of Swedish language embeddings does not naturally lend itself to include an equality set, the debiasing of the embeddings does not involve equalization in our case.

We apply the method described above to all pre-trained embeddings in Table 3, as well as to the token vectors generated by `ELMo` and `BERT`. Although it is not clear whether the proposed debiasing method is applicable to embeddings produced by contextualized language models, we argue that it is reasonable to treat the contextualized models as black boxes, and rely only on their output, given the proposed use case.

7 Experiment 2: names and occupations (revisited)

We repeat the experiment described in Section 5, but using the debiased embeddings. Table 6 summarizes the results. It is clear that the debiasing method does not have any impact on the results in these experiments. The tendencies for the word-based embeddings `word2vec` and `fastText` are more or less identical before and after debiasing. The most striking differences between Table 5 and Table 6 are the results for `ELMo` and `BERT`, which become less balanced after applying the debiasing method. `ELMo` actually shows a clearer gender distinction *after* debiasing, with male names being more similar to male occupations, and female names being more similar to fe-

male occupations. `BERT` also becomes less balanced *after* debiasing, grouping male names with female occupations, and female names with male occupations, when considering the average similarities. When counting only the most similar occupation per name, `BERT` is still well balanced after debiasing.

8 Experiment 3: company names and company descriptions

The experiments in the previous sections are admittedly somewhat simplistic considering the scenario discussed in the Introduction: quantifying the similarity between a company name and a company description. In particular the contextualized language models are not primarily designed for generating token embeddings, and it is neither clear what kind of quality we can expect from such un-contextualized token embeddings, nor whether they are susceptible to the debiasing operation discussed in Section 6. In order to provide a more realistic scenario, we also include experiments where we compute the similarity between a set of actual company descriptions and a set of fictive company names generated from the lists of male and female names by adding the term "Aktiebolag" (in English limited company) after each name.[2]

The company descriptions are provided by the Swedish Companies Registration Office, and contain approximately 10 company descriptions for each of the sectors *construction work*, *vehicles and transportation*, *information technologies*, *health and health care*, *education*, and *economy*. Based on Tables 3 and 4, we consider the descriptions from the first three sectors to be representative of typically male occupations, and the descriptions from the latter three sectors to be representative

---

among all vectors and decreasing the influence of the gender specific direction.

[2]It is not uncommon for names of limited companies (in Sweden) to feature a person name and the term "Aktiebolag".

Model	Male names Male occupations	Male names Female occupations	Female names Male occupations	Female names Female occupations
`word2vec`	29 (29)	71 (71)	30 (30)	70 (70)
`fastText`	60 (61)	40 (39)	60 (61)	40 (39)
`ELMo`	52 (53)	48 (47)	53 (54)	47 (46)
`BERT`	42 (40)	58 (60)	41 (41)	59 (59)

Table 7: Percentage of female and male names that are on average more similar to a female vs. male occupation. The similarities are calculated based on the original embeddings, using the names and occupations in context. Numbers in parentheses only count the single most similar occupation for each name.

of typically female occupations.

We generate vectors for each of the descriptions and for each fictive company name (i.e. a male or female name, followed by "Aktiebolag"). For the word-based models (`word2vec` and `fastText`), we take the average of the embeddings of the words in the descriptions and the name. For the contextualized language models (`ELMo` and `BERT`), we generate vectors for each description and each fictive name. In the case of `ELMo` we take the average over the three LSTM layers, and for `BERT` we use the output embedding for the [CLS] token for each of the input sequences.

The results are summarized in Table 7. It is clear that these results are significantly more balanced than the results using tokens only. Even so, there are still some interesting differences between the embeddings. Contrary to the results in Tables 5 and 6, `word2vec` now shows a bias for female occupations, and `fastText` now shows a bias for male occupations. `ELMo` and `BERT` seem more balanced, with `ELMo` showing almost perfectly balanced results, and `BERT` showing a slight bias for female occupations.

Even though the biases apparently are different when considering tokens in comparison with considering texts, there *are* still biases in all models in both cases. The only exception in our experiments is `ELMo`, when used for texts instead of tokens. We hypothesize that the results for `BERT` are negatively affected by artefacts of the WordPiece tokenization, as discussed in Section 3.

9 The effect of debiasing on embeddings

So far, we have shown that all Swedish pretrained embeddings included in this study exhibit some degree of gender bias when applied to a real-world scenario. We now turn to investigate the effect the hard debiasing operation has on the embedding spaces, using the intrinsic evaluation methodology of Bolukbasi et al. (2016b). In this setting, a number of analogy pairs are extracted for the original and debiased embeddings, and human evaluators are used to asses the number of appropriate and stereotypical pairs in the respective representations. Bolukbasi et al. (2016b) used 10 crowdworkers to classify the analogy pairs as being appropriate or stereotypical. Their results indicated that 19% of the top 150 analogies generated using the original embedding model were deemed gender stereotypical, while the corresponding figure for the hard debiased model was 6%.

We carry out a similar, but smaller, evaluation exercise using the analogy pairs generated by the original Swedish `word2vec` and `fastText` models, as well as their debiased counterparts.[3] We use *hon − han* (*she − he*) as seed pair, and score all word pairs in the embeddings with respect to the similarity of the word pair's difference vector to that of the the seed pair. The top 150 pairs are manually categorized as either *appropriate*, *gender stereotypical*, or *uncertain* by the authors.

The results of the annotation are shown in Table 8 (next page). Due to the limited extent of the evaluation, we can only use these results for painting the big picture. First of all, there is a relatively small overlap between the analogy pairs in the top 150 of the original models, and the top lists of the debiased models: for `word2vec`, only 42 of the analogy pairs in the original list are also in the list produced by the debiased model. The corresponding number for `fastText` is 31. This means that the debiasing operation changes

---

[3]It would have been preferable to also include `ELMo` and `BERT` in this experiment, but generating vectors for large vocabularies using these models takes a prohibitively long time, and it is neither clear whether the resulting token embeddings make sense, not whether the debiasing operation is applicable to the resulting embeddings.

Analogies quality	Original word2vec	Debiased word2vec	Original fastText	Debiased fastText
Appropriate	97	52	135	36
Stereotypical	3	13	5	4
Uncertain	18	36	0	45

Table 8: The number of appropriate, stereotypical, and uncertain analogies in the top 150 pairs for the original and debiased embeddings. The numbers are the analogy pairs for which the annotators agree on the category.

the embedding space to a large extent. Second, there is a considerable amount of annotator uncertainty involved, either regarding the plausibility of a given analogy pair, or regarding its appropriateness. This is manifested by an increase of the number of uncertain analogy pairs that the annotators agree on between the original and debiased models (both for `word2vec` and `fastText`). However, the most interesting findings have to do with the number of stereotypical analogy pairs. The number of stereotypical analogy pairs output by the Swedish models is small compared to the numbers reported by Bolukbasi et al. (2016b). Further, the number of stereotypical pairs is *larger* in the debiased `word2vec` model than in the original model (we anticipated that it should be lower). It thus seems as if the debiasing operation makes the `word2vec` embedding space *more* biased. For `fastText`, the number of such pairs are slightly fewer in the debiased model compared to its original counterpart.

10 Discussion

This paper has shown that pretrained Swedish embeddings *do* exhibit gender bias to varying extent, and that the debiasing operation suggested by Bolukbasi et al. (2016a) does not have the desired effect, neither in the task of matching person names with occupations, nor in the case of the gender stereotypes being present among the top ranked analogy pairs generated by the models. Our experiments also indicate that word-based embeddings are more susceptible to bias than contextualized language models, and that there is an unexpectedly large difference in the biases shown by `word2vec` and `fastText`, something we believe requires further study.

Although contextualized language models appear to be more balanced with respect to gender bias in our experiments, there *is* still bias in these models; in particular if they are used to generate

token embeddings, but also when they are used to generate representations for texts – `ELMo`, which produces almost perfect scores in Table 7, may still show bias in individual examples, such as those in Table 1. We acknowledge the possibility that it may not be appropriate to use contextualized language models to generate embeddings for individual tokens, but we also believe such usages to occur in real-world applications, and we therefore consider it relevant to include such examples in these experiments.

The debiasing operation proposed by Bolukbasi et al. (2016a) does nothing to rectify the situation in our setting. On the contrary, the debiased models still show significant gender bias, and in the case of `ELMo` and `BERT`, the bias actually becomes more prevalent *after* debiasing. (However, we are aware that the debiasing operation may neither be intended nor suitable for such representations.) Furthermore, our (admittedly small) analogy evaluation shows that debiasing actually introduces *more* stereotypical word pairs in the `word2vec` model.

Why then does not debiasing the Swedish word-based embeddings produce results similar to those of Bolukbasi et al. (2016a)? One of the big differences between the Swedish pretrained `word2vec` model and the one used by Bolukbasi et al. is the size of the vocabulary. The Swedish model contains 3M+ word types, while Bolukbasi et al. constrained their experiments to include only lower-cased words shorter than 20 characters, omitting digits and words containing punctuation, from the top 50,000 most frequent words in the model. By doing so, Bolukbasi et al. effectively removed many person names from the model. A large portion of the word pairs in our analogy lists produced by the original model consist of person names (e.g., *Anna – Jakob*), which we consider to be *appropriate*, and their presence on the top 150 list contribute to the comparatively low number of *stereotypical* pairs. The debiasing operation of the word-based models remove many of the persons name pairs from the top list, giving way for potentially stereotypical pairs. Thus, the increase of stereotypical pairs on the top list of analogy pairs generated by a debiased model is more likely to be due to the debiasing operation effectively removing many of the names from the top list, than the model being more biased in the first place.

Since our experiments have focused on pretrained embeddings readily available on the Internet, which have been trained on different types and different sizes of data, we cannot speculate about the extent to which a particular learning algorithm amplifies or distorts bias. We believe this is an interesting direction for further research, and we aim to replicate this study using a variety of embeddings trained on the same data.

References

Piotr Bojanowski, Edouard Grave, Armand Joulin, and Tomas Mikolov. 2017. Enriching word vectors with subword information. *Transactions of the Association for Computational Linguistics*, 5.

Tolga Bolukbasi, Kai-Wei Chang, James Y. Zou, Venkatesh Saligrama, and Adam Kalai. 2016a. Man is to computer programmer as woman is to homemaker? debiasing word embeddings. *arXiv preprint arXiv:1607.06520*.

Tolga Bolukbasi, Kai-Wei Chang, James Y Zou, Venkatesh Saligrama, and Adam T Kalai. 2016b. Man is to computer programmer as woman is to homemaker? debiasing word embeddings. In *Advances in neural information processing systems*, pages 4349–4357.

Shikha Bordia and Samuel R. Bowman. 2019. Identifying and reducing gender bias in word-level language models. In *NAACL Student Research Workshop*.

Aylin Caliskan, Joanna J Bryson, and Arvind Narayanan. 2017. Semantics derived automatically from language corpora contain human-like biases. *Science*, 356(6334):183–186.

Wanxiang Che, Yijia Liu, Yuxuan Wang, Bo Zheng, and Ting Liu. 2018. Towards better UD parsing: Deep contextualized word embeddings, ensemble, and treebank concatenation. In *Proceedings of the CoNLL 2018 Shared Task: Multilingual Parsing from Raw Text to Universal Dependencies*, pages 55–64, Brussels, Belgium. Association for Computational Linguistics.

Jacob Devlin, Ming-Wei Chang, Kenton Lee, and Kristina Toutanova. 2018. Bert: Pre-training of deep bidirectional transformers for language understanding. *arXiv preprint arXiv:1810.04805*.

Nikhil Garg, Londa Schiebinger, Dan Jurafsky, and James Zou. 2018. Word embeddings quantify 100 years of gender and ethnic stereotypes. *Proceedings of the National Academy of Sciences*, 115(16):E3635–E3644.

Hila Gonen and Yoav Goldberg. 2019. Lipstick on a pig: Debiasing methods cover up systematic gender biases in word embeddings but do not remove them. In *Proceedings of the Annual Conference of the North American Chapter of the Association for Computational Linguistics (NAACL)*.

Tomas Mikolov, Ilya Sutskever, Kai Chen, Greg Corrado, and Jeffrey Dean. 2013. Distributed representations of words and phrases and their compositionality. In *Proceedings of the 26th International Conference on Neural Information Processing Systems - Volume 2*, NIPS'13, pages 3111–3119, USA. Curran Associates Inc.

Ji Ho Park, Jamin Shin, and Pascale Fung. 2018. Reducing gender bias in abusive language detection. In *Proceedings of the 2018 Conference on Empirical Methods in Natural Language Processing*, pages 2799–2804.

Matthew Peters, Mark Neumann, Mohit Iyyer, Matt Gardner, Christopher Clark, Kenton Lee, and Luke Zettlemoyer. 2018. Deep contextualized word representations. In *Proceedings of the 2018 Conference of the North American Chapter of the Association for Computational Linguistics: Human Language Technologies, Volume 1 (Long Papers)*, pages 2227–2237.

Jieyu Zhao, Tianlu Wang, Mark Yatskar, Vicente Ordonez, and Kai-Wei Chang. 2017. Men also like shopping: Reducing gender bias amplification using corpus-level constraints. In *Proceedings of the 2017 Conference on Empirical Methods in Natural Language Processing*.

Jieyu Zhao, Yichao Zhou, Zeyu Li, Wei Wang, and Kai-Wei Chang. 2018. Learning gender-neutral word embeddings. In *Proceedings of the 2018 Conference on Empirical Methods in Natural Language Processing*, pages 4847–4853, Brussels, Belgium. Association for Computational Linguistics.

A larger-scale evaluation resource of terms and their shift direction for diachronic lexical semantics

Astrid van Aggelen♠ **Antske Fokkens**◇ **Laura Hollink**♠ **Jacco van Ossenbruggen** ♠◇
♠ Centrum Wiskunde Informatica, Amsterdam, Netherlands
◇ Vrije Universiteit Amsterdam, Netherlands
`a.e.van.aggelen@cwi.nl`, `antske.fokkens@vu.nl`

Abstract

Determining how words have changed their meaning is an important topic in Natural Language Processing. However, evaluations of methods to characterise such change have been limited to small, handcrafted resources. We introduce an English evaluation set which is larger, more varied, and more realistic than seen to date, with terms derived from a historical thesaurus. Moreover, the dataset is unique in that it represents change as a shift from the term of interest to a WordNet synset. Using the synset lemmas, we can use this set to evaluate (standard) methods that detect change between word pairs, as well as (adapted) methods that detect the change between a term and a sense overall. We show that performance on the new data set is much lower than earlier reported findings, setting a new standard.

1 Introduction

Determining how words have changed their meaning is an important topic in Natural Language Processing (Tang, 2018; Kutuzov et al., 2018; Tahmasebi et al., 2018). Using large diachronic corpora, computational linguistics has provided methods that can detect or qualitatively explain semantic change automatically. In particular, several approaches have been introduced that use distributional semantic models representing different time periods in diachronic corpora (Gulordava and Baroni, 2011; Mitra et al., 2014; Kulkarni et al., 2015, e.g.).

Researchers have illustrated through compelling examples that these methods can detect semantic shift, like *cell* obtaining the meaning of 'phone' and *gay* shifting from 'cheerful' to 'homosexual' (Mitra et al., 2014, e.g.) and have reported high accuracy on small evaluation sets of selected examples. Hamilton et al. (2016) even report 100% accuracy in detecting known change on 28 word pairs. As a result, these approaches have been enthusiastically adopted (Wohlgenannt et al., 2019; Orlikowski et al., 2018; Kutuzov et al., 2016; Martinez-Ortiz et al., 2016, e.g.). However, it has been called into question how reliable these methods really are (Hellrich and Hahn, 2016a; Dubossarsky et al., 2017).

These developments show that there is both a wide interest in using distributional semantic models to assess semantic change and an urgent need for better insight into the possibilities and limitations of these methods. It is therefore unsurprising that three recent survey papers on the topic all list the lack of proper evaluation and, in particular, the absence of large-scale evaluation sets, as a key challenge for this line of research (Tang, 2018; Kutuzov et al., 2018; Tahmasebi et al., 2018).

In this paper, we automatically derive HiT, the largest English evaluation set to date, from a historical thesaurus. HiT consists of terms linked to WordNet (Fellbaum, 2012) entries that represent senses they gained or lost. We introduce *sense shift assessment* as a task, enabled by this dataset, that identifies whether a sense of a term of interest was coming in our out of use, based on its changed relationship with all lemmas of the sense. This is a variation of a task introduced by Hamilton et al. (2016) that assesses the relationship of the terms of interest with individual other terms. The sense shift assessment instead uncovers the conceptual change that explains multiple observed trends between word pairs. Cross-checking and summarising individual observations also means drawing more informed conclusions. Furthermore, the use of WordNet sense representations allows for the dataset entries to be automatically derived rather than manually (expert) collected, hence limiting the effect of bias. We use HiT to answer two main research questions. First, how well can current methods detect sense shift on a larger and more varied evaluation set? Second, how, by taking a full synset as a representation of meaning, does the task of detecting sense shift compare to studying word pairs in isolation? The main contributions of this paper are as follows. First, the new evaluation set, consisting of 756 target words and 3624 word pairs. Second, we show that current methods perform quite poorly on this more challenging set, thus confirming that this set introduces a new benchmark. We also identify lexical factors that contribute to these differences.

2 Related Work

This section provides an overview of previous work on detecting lexical semantic change through distributional semantic models.

Distributional models of meaning are motivated by the hypothesis that words with similar meanings will occur in similar contexts (Harris, 1954; Firth, 1957). Tahmasebi et al. (2011) and Mitra et al. (2014) induce clusters of terms that temporally co-occur in particular syntactic patterns, and (qualitatively or quantitatively) trace their development. Their approach forms a bridge from previous document-based approaches (Blei and Lafferty, 2006; Wang and McCallum, 2006, e.g.) to the window-based models that are currently widely used.

Gulordava and Baroni (2011) and Jatowt and Duh (2014) were among the first to use trends in similarity between distributional representations. The former detect change within single terms by tracing their self-similarity. The latter, like we do, interpret the change of a term by contrasting it with other terms. In recent work, the most common type of distributional models used to assess semantic shift are known as prediction models (Kim et al., 2014; Kulkarni et al., 2015; Hamilton et al., 2016, e.g). In this paper, we use embeddings that gave the best results in Hamilton et al. (2016) and are created through the skip-gram method included in word2vec (Mikolov et al., 2013).

Until recently, semantic shifts were determined by comparing the distributional nearest neighbours of a term in one time period to its neighbours in another (see e.g. Tahmasebi et al. (2011)). However, such an inspection is difficult to carry out at scale, is not suited for disappearing senses - distant neighbours are hard to assess - and is prone to bias, especially when the aim is to confirm hypoth-

esized trends. Hamilton et al. (2016) use a predetermined list of terms to which the target term got more and less related over time. This variation alleviates the problem of bias and introduces 'more distant neighbours' into the analysis, but with just 28 term pairs it is still very small-scale.

Basile and McGillivray (2018) are, to our knowledge, the first to exploit a large historical dictionary as an evaluation source. The aim of their work is to detect changed terms and their change point, based on dips in the self-similarities, with the Oxford English Dictionary as the gold standard. To verify whether the observed change point corresponds to a new dictionary sense, the time-specific nearest neighbours of the term are contrasted with the dictionary definition. This work could have provided the evaluation set for the task addressed in this paper. However, as far as we know, the authors have not enriched the data with said nearest neighbours nor made them available. Hence, the current work is still the first to provide a large-scale evaluation set based on a dictionary.

3 A large-scale sense shift assessment set

This section describes a new evaluation set that links terms of interest (target terms) to rich synset representations of their old and new senses. This means that in an experimental setting (such as that in Section 5), the target term can be contrasted to a predetermined, varied set of terms. We also adapt two existing evaluation sets, HistWords (Hamilton et al., 2016) and the Word Sense Change Testset[1] (Tahmasebi and Risse, 2017), into datasets of the same format.

3.1 Deriving a sense shift assessment set

The new dataset, which we call **HiT**, is derived from **The Historical Thesaurus of the University of Glasgow** (Kay et al., 2019). This thesaurus lists (nearly all) English terms organised in a conceptual hierarchy of senses. It also documents the time period in which a term was attested and assumed to be active in the given sense. For instance, one entry says that the verb *bray* was used in the sense of 'Grind/pound' (in turn a subconcept of 'Create/make/bring about') for the period 1382 till 1850. The thesaurus does not indicate how any listed sense of a word relates to previous, concurrent or future ones. Hence, it is unclear whether

---

[1]`http://doi.org/10.5281/zenodo.495572`

the term underwent a process of semantic narrowing or broadening, or whether it lost or gained a sense altogether. The change that is considered here is a broad notion of rising or declining senses.

For HiT we use all terms in senses that came up between 1900 and 1959 and all terms in senses that disappeared - which were less numerous - between 1850 and 1959. To enrich the thesaurus terms, we identify their WordNet synsets and check if each of these expresses the intended meaning. This check is based on the overlap between the thesaurus definition and the synset terms. If any term from the synset (excluding the target term itself) overlaps with any of the terms from the thesaurus definition (in the example above, the terms are {*create, make, bring about, grind, pound*}), we assume that the synset in question provides the intended sense. The verb *bray* appears in WordNet under two polylexical synsets: {*bray, hee-haw*}, and {*bray, grind, mash, crunch, comminute*}. Due to the overlapping term *grind*, the thesaurus entry is matched with the latter, meaning 'reduce to small pieces or particles by pounding or abrading', but not with the former ('laugh loudly and harshly').

Newly emerging senses from the thesaurus provide gold standard instances that are supposed to attract the vector of the target term. Disappearing senses, on the other hand - such as 'grind' for *bray* after 1850 - are gold standard instances from which the target term should move away. Table 1 shows how the *bray* example translates to a HiT entry of a vanishing sense with the WordNet synonyms used as reference terms.

Only entries with at least one identified WordNet synset are included. This results in a dataset of 756 target terms exhibiting 979 sense shifts.

target term	POS	sense (WN synset) ⌊ reference term	shift	onset
bray	v.	grind.v.05 ⌊ grind, mash, crunch, comminute	-1	1850

Table 1: Example excerpt from an entry of HiT. Shift label -1 means a move away from the given meaning.

Validation To establish the accuracy of the WordNet matching method, two raters independently annotated a subset of 191 entries. The agreement between the raters (i.e. the proportion of agreement above chance level) is assessed using Cohen κ for two raters (Cohen, 1960). Also, we assessed how well the raters' judgement corresponded to the output of the automated WordNet

matching, i.e., the supposed gold standard.

Rater 1 verified whether the algorithm had selected the correct synset or not. To counteract an effect of bias from the gold standard, rater 2 did not work with the gold standard, rather indicating for any given WordNet synset whether it represented the given definition. These findings were then translated to a judgement of the algorithm output in line with rater 1. The annotators agreed on the evaluation by 97.9 per cent; by Cohen's chance-normalised norm ($\kappa = 0.789$, $z = 11$, $p < 0.001$), this is generally thought of as 'substantial' agreement. Except for 10 (rater 1) and 9 (rater 2) instances out of 191, the raters' judgements corresponded to that of the algorithm, an error rate of approximately 5 per cent. We consider this high enough to take the outcome of the synset linking method as the gold standard.

3.2 Transforming existing datasets

The thesaurus-derived dataset, HiT, qualitatively differs from existing evaluation sets in its automated construction and in its representation of senses by a synset rather than selected terms. In order to compare this set to previously used datasets, we adapt two standard evaluation sets semi-automatically to link the target words they contain to synsets representing the given old or new senses.

HistWords (Hamilton et al., 2016) (HW) contains 28 word pairs that saw their similarity increase or decrease over time, based on 9 target terms. HistWords states the onset of the change - no end date - and the gold standard shift direction. For instance, since 1800, *awful* has moved towards *mess* and *disgusting* and away from *impressive*.

The Word Sense Change Testset (WSCT) (Tahmasebi and Risse, 2017) lists terms that acquired a new sense and unchanged control words. It gives the type of change the term underwent (no change, new, broader, or narrower sense), a short explanation of the change and the onset date of the change. For instance, *memory* acquires a new related sense 'digital memory' in 1960 whilst keeping its existing sense 'human memory'.

From HW to HW+ and from WSCT to WSCT+. Every entry from WSCT and HW is treated as a separate change event, with an onset date and a description; some target terms have more than one change event. For each such event, the affected sense(s) are selected out of all candidate senses, i.e. all WordNet synsets that correspond to the target lemma (in the correct part of speech). This synset selection process happened manually, by comparing the lexical information in WordNet against the change description in the source data. More details about the annotation process are given below. The outcomes determine the change type listed for the combination of target term and synset in the enriched datasets **WSCT+** and **HW+**. The target term is thought to move towards any synset (and towards all terms of the synset) that captures an increasingly common sense, and away from any synset that expresses an increasingly uncommon sense. For any synset that does not capture any described change, its relation to the target term is described as unchanged or unknown. See Table 2 for an example.

Annotation process and validation. The selection was carried out by the first author; this was then evaluated by two co-authors for HW+ and one co-author for WSCT+. In the case of three raters, we used Fleiss' extension of Cohen's method (Fleiss, 1971). The raters judged the shift direction of the target term with respect to all candidate concepts (synsets): towards (+1), away from (-1) one another, or no change (0). The evaluation set of word-sense combinations was larger than the final dataset (Table 3), as it included synsets with just the target term. The raters were given the following data: the change description and the time of change, given in HW or WSCT; the (given or inferred) part of speech; the candidate WordNet concept that connects the two terms; and corresponding WordNet data such as the definition and the set of terms in the synset. For WSCT+ (N=129 target-sense pairs), the two raters agreed by 88.4 per cent, which, chance-normalised (Cohen's $\kappa = 0.63$, $z = 7.26$, $p < 0.01$) is thought to be 'substantial'. The raters then agreed on the final set of gold standard labels. On HW+ (N=70 target-sense pairs), the three raters agreed almost perfectly (Fleiss' $\kappa = 0.83$, $z = 16$, $p < 0.01$), and the ratings by the first author were taken as the gold standard.

Resulting datasets The evaluation sets all provide two types of pairings: target terms paired with reference terms and target terms with synsets. The gold standard for the individual word pairs - target word and synonym - corresponds to the gold standard for the whole synset. After the inter-rater evaluation, synsets with just one term (the target

target term	POS	sense (WN synset)	t	shift
		⌊ reference term		
memory	n.	memory.n.03	1960	0
		⌊ retention, retentiveness, retentivity		
memory	n.	memory.n.04	1960	1
		⌊ computer memory, storage, computer storage, store, memory board		

Table 2: Excerpts from two entries of WSCT+. Shift label 0 means we have no evidence the word changed with respect to the given sense. Label 1 means a shift towards the indicated meaning (and its associated terms).

term) were omitted, as the experiment requires reference terms. Table 3 provides an overview of the resulting evaluation sets next to HistWords as a baseline. HiT does not show any overlap with the other datasets except for a single target term lemma (verb *call*) in common with HW+, however with the described change in a different meaning.

dataset	HW	HW+	WSCT+	HiT
dataset type	existing	adapted	adapted	new
target words (TWs)	9	9	23	756
TW+term	28	117	213	3624
converging	18	41	56	1173
diverging	10	24	0	2451
unchanged/-known	0	52	157	0
TW+sense	n.a.	42	93	979
converging	n.a.	10	23	282
diverging	n.a.	10	0	697
unchanged/-known	n.a.	22	70	0

Table 3: Contents of the evaluation sets, which come in two variants: target terms paired with other terms and paired with WordNet senses (synsets). This allows the datasets to be used for the two types of evaluation used here.

4 Experiment

Two tasks are addressed in the experiment. Word shift assessment (**WordShiftAssess**) (Hamilton et al., 2016) is summarised as follows: given a target term, a reference term, and a time period, did the two terms become closer in meaning (gold standard label 1) or did their meanings move apart (label -1)? Sense shift assessment (**SenseShiftAssess**) goes as follows: given a target term, a WordNet synset, and a time period, did the target term in the given period move towards or away from the given sense? To be comparable to previous findings, we evaluate the datasets on both tasks. This section outlines the methods and the experimental setup.

4.1 Change assessment for word-word pairs

Our method of determining shift direction was proposed by Hamilton et al. (2016). It depends on the availability of distributional representations for the target term and reference terms, corresponding to the synset lemmas, at regular intervals between the start and the end of the period of interest. The successive cosine similarities of the embeddings of the target and reference term are (Spearman) correlated with the time index (e.g. 1800, 1810, .., 1990). If the correlation is positive, the target term is taken to have moved towards the reference term; if it is negative, away from it. Given the binary classification setting, the statistical significance of the correlation factor has no clear interpretation. However, we include it to comply with earlier reported findings and for readers to judge the potential of the method for a three-way classification with a null category.

4.2 Change assessment for word-sense pairs

To address SenseShiftAssess, we suggest two broad approaches. The first starts from the method outlined in Section 4.1. That is, for any target-sense pair, we start from the given target word paired with all lemmas of the synset, and the trend of the cosine similarities (Spearman ρ and p) for each of these word pairs. Then, we either take the most-observed sign of ρ as the outcome (**majority vote**), or we promote one word pair to exemplify the sense shift as a whole. Assuming that an observed strong trend is likely to be correct, **argmax(corr)** takes the sign of the highest absolute ρ value of all word pairs in the synset as the synset assessment. **argmin(p(corr))** does the same for the observation the correlation coefficient of which has the lowest p value.

The second approach we suggest, **average vec.**, operates on a lower level, as it aggregates the distributional representations of the synset lemmas into an average vector, for every time slice separately. The target term and the averaged representation are then treated like a word pair (Section 4.1).

4.3 Experimental setup

We apply word shift assessment on HW, HW+, WSCT+, and HiT. The reference terms of HW+, WSCT+ and HiT come from WordNet; those in HW are readily taken from the source. Figure 1 illustrates how the term *awful* from HW+ compares with its individual WordNet synonyms over time.

Sense shift assessment is applied to WSCT+, HW+ and HiT, i.e. all sets that could be enriched with sense information. To continue with the example in Figure 1, sense shift assessment translates the word-based observations into a single as-

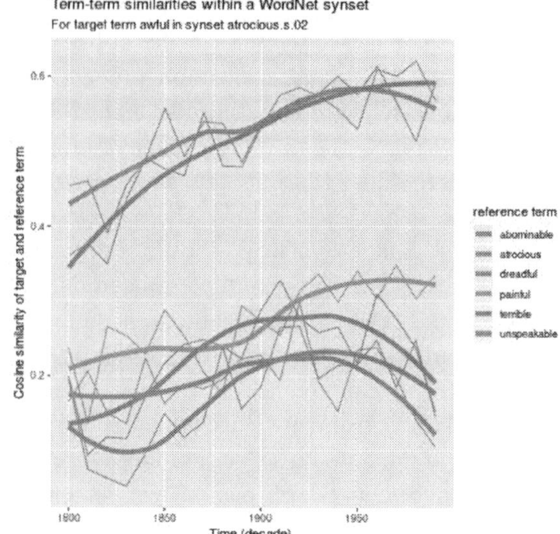

Figure 1: WordShiftAssess with WordNet-based reference terms: target term *awful* is individually contrasted with all terms from synset `atrocious.s.02`: *abominable, atrocious dreadful, painful*, etc. The fitted lines illustrate the observed trend in cosine similarities, such as the growing similarity between *awful* and *terrible*.

sessment of the changed relation of *awful* with respect to the whole synset.

Distributional vectors. We use word embeddings provided by Hamilton et al. (2016) of size 300, trained through skip-gram with negative sampling (SGNS) for every decade separately on three corpora: the Corpus of Historical American English (Davies, 2015) (COHA), the complete English Google N-Gram corpus (Michel et al., 2011), and the English Fiction corpus, a subset of the Google N-Gram corpus. The embeddings are not (part of speech) disambiguated, and can stand for several lemmas at once. We employ the embeddings for every decade from the attested onset of change up to and including the last available embedding, trained on the 1990s subcorpus.

Handling of missing and infrequent data. Some terms appear infrequently in some slices of the corpus. The code that accompanies Hamilton et al. (2016) deals with these cases by padding the cosine time series with a zero for the dimension (i.e. time slice) in which either or both of the terms was insufficiently frequent (under 500 times, except for COHA). However, this biases the outcome, since zero is the smallest cosine similarity value. Given that low word frequencies are more common in the corpora of the first few decades, this setting makes it more likely to find

cosine time series								ρ
t_1	...	t_{10}	t_{11}	t_{12}	t_{13}	t_{14}	t_{15}	
0	...	**0**	0.25	0.29	0.29	0.20	0.18	**0.77**
NA	...	**NA**	0.25	0.29	0.29	0.20	0.18	**-0.7**

Table 4: Similarity values based on infrequent data must not be padded with zero as this biases the correlation value towards a positive value. In the word pair *delimit-define*, padding the values for decades t_1 (in fact, 1850) through to t_{11} (1940) with zeros would lead to a conclusion opposite to the ground truth stating that these terms move away from each other; hence these observations are treated as missing data (NA) instead.

a rising trend in cosine similarities. As this is an unwanted effect, we treated cosine values based on low-frequency numbers as missing values. Table 4 illustrates the difference between the caveat explained here and the approach taken. A further count filter ensures that all results (correlations) are based on at least five cosine values.

5 Results

Table 5 shows the proportion of word pair observations (**WordShiftAssess**) displaying the expected trend in cosine similarities for every dataset and training corpus. The significance reported is the proportion of *correct* findings (i.e. with an upper limit of 100%) with a Spearman ρ significant on the 0.05 level. Whether the correlation coefficient is significant depends on its magnitude as well as the number of cosine values considered. The latter in turn depends on the change onset - the longer the time series, the more observations - minus observations that were based on too little data and were left out (see Section 4.3). N expresses how many of the word pair entries from the datasets (Table 3) which displayed a real shift (unchanged words were not used) resulted in a cosine time series of at least five observations (see Section 4.3). This depends in part on the corpus, some of which have much greater coverage than other ones, particularly the complete English corpus, eng-all. For instance, the results for HiT for eng-all are based on 1461 word pairs as opposed to a mere 746 for COHA and 772 for English fiction, out of a dataset total of 3624 shifted terms. Moreover, eng-all resulted in more statistically significant correct outcomes than COHA and eng-fic. We therefore focus on the results based on eng-all in particular.

HiT appears more challenging than WSCT+ and HW+. On eng-all, just under 60 per cent of all entries were correctly assessed, as opposed to around 70 per cent for WSCT+ and 80 per cent

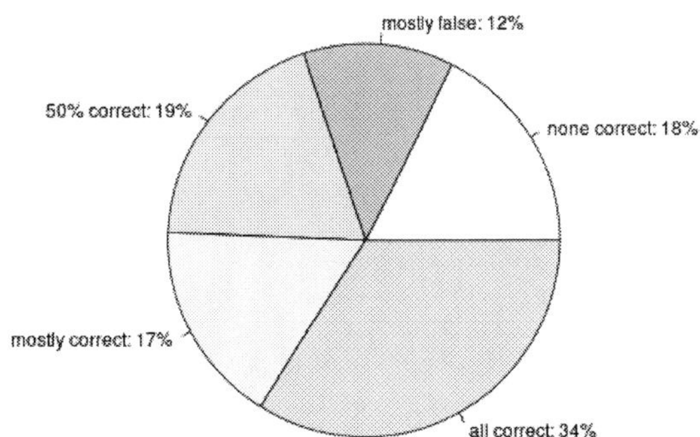

Figure 2: Proportions of correct word pairs (i.e. displaying the expected similarity trend) within synsets for HiT (on eng-all). In just over half of the cases, the synset contained more correct than incorrect observations (bottom half of the pie chart).

for HW+. The significance levels show a similar pattern, hence even the word pairs that showed the predicted trend did so less clearly for HiT than for the other datasets. The outcomes on COHA and eng-fic confirm the pattern for eng-all: HiT figures consistently lag behind WSCT+ and even further behind HW+. While eng-all and eng-fic give similar levels of accuracy, on COHA, the outcomes for HiT are below chance level.

HiT differs from WSCT+ and HW+ in that the target terms were not selected for the task at hand. Unsurprisingly, the automatically selected dictionary terms offer a more challenging evaluation set than the purposely selected terms in HW+ and WSCT+. The difference observed between HW and HW+ reveals a similar trend concerning hand-picked reference terms compared to (semi)-automatically selected ones: the performance on HW+ is about 20 per cent lower than for HW. In sum, the selection of term pairs has great impact.

Table 6 shows the proportion of target-sense entries that were correctly assessed (**SenseShiftAssess**), based on several possible aggregations of word pair level findings. Looking, firstly, at the different methods, argmin(p(corr)) performed best. Hence, the word pair within a synset that shows the most statistically robust change is the best indicator of the conceptual change of the target term. For HiT this resulted in 61.3% correct on eng-all and up to 64.0 % on eng-fic. The added performance over argmax(corr), whilst marginal (e.g. for HiT, 61.1 % on eng-all and 61.9% on eng-fic), suggests that balancing the correlation factor with the number of observations leads to better judgements than looking at the

WordShiftAssess	eng-all				coha				eng-fic			
	HiT	wsct+	HW+	HW	HiT	wsct+	HW+	HW	HiT	wsct+	HW+	HW
correct (%)	**58.0**	**69.2**	**79.5**	**100.0**	**45.6**	54.5	63.6	85.7	**59.5**	62.5	66.7	88.2
sig (%)	38.4	66.7	60.0	88.9	29.1	33.3	19.0	66.7	24.0	40.0	30.0	46.7
N	1461	13	44	27	746	11	33	21	772	8	30	17

Table 5: Results of determining the shift direction of a target word with respect to a reference word (WordShiftAssess).

SenseShiftAssess												
corpus	**eng-all**				**coha**				**eng-fic**			
dataset	HiT	wsct+	HW+	HW	HiT	wsct+	HW+	HW	HiT	wsct+	HW+	HW
average vec.	**57.8**	**100.0**	**88.9**	-	44.1	50.0	57.1	-	**58.9**	100.0	66.7	-
argmax(corr)	**61.1**	100.0	84.6	-	46.4	80.0	53.8	-	61.9	100.0	66.7	-
majority vote	**50.7**	100.0	76.9	-	**36.0**	80.0	53.8	-	**49.7**	75.0	66.7	-
argmin(p(corr))	**61.3**	100.0	84.6	-	46.8	80.0	53.8	-	**64.0**	75.0	66.7	-
N average vec.	374	2	9	-	204	2	7	-	214	1	6	
N other methods	450	5	13	-	278	5	13	-	286	4	12	-

Table 6: Results of determining the shift direction of a target word with respect to a reference word (SenseShiftAssess).

magnitude of the correlation alone. Averaging the vectors of all reference terms (average vec.) was less reliable an aggregation overall than promoting one word pair to represent the synset. However, it still did better than the majority vote, which required more than half of the word pairs in a synset to display the expected shift pattern. For HiT, this did not surpass chance level on any of the corpora. Hence, within a synset, false observations can be as numerous as or outweigh true ones, and heuristics are needed to find the signal in the noise.

SenseShiftAssess was expected to suffer less from noisy results that occur on the word level (WordShiftAssess). However, the improvement observed over the word pair results was marginal. For instance, for HiT on eng-all, the synset-level approach was correct in 61 per cent of cases at best, as opposed to 58 per cent on the word pair level. HW+ and WSCT+ did benefit more from the synset aggregation, but the small sample size makes it hard to draw conclusions from this. Figure 2 shows how much we can rely on the terms within a synset to display the anticipated change in relation to the target term (for HiT and eng-all). The vast majority of synsets - all except 18 per cent - contain at least one word pair that displays the true shift. This means that SenseShiftAssess on HiT is feasible, at least in theory, and the maximum accuracy attainable on eng-all is 82 per cent. A third of all synsets (34%) have all word pairs displaying the predicted shift; hence the lower limit is 34 per cent. There were more synsets with mostly correct than mostly false examples, and more synsets with just correct (33 per cent) than just false (17 per cent) ones. Based on the slightly higher odds of picking a correct than an incorrect example, our selection methods are perhaps not informed by the most determining factors. To know how we can find the signal in noisy word pair patterns, we must first understand what causes noise. This question is addressed next.

6 Follow-up analysis

We examine several lexical and corpus factors that may play a role in the outcomes. For every term in a word pair, we look at its polysemy, its frequency in the training corpus, and its typicality as a representation of the underlying concept. Table 7 breaks down the WordShiftEval results by the combined lexical properties of target and reference term. For every entry type we distinguish (e.g. a low-polysemous target term paired with a high-polysemous reference term), we examine the proportion of the result set it accounts for, and the observed tendency for such word pairs to display the expected shift pattern. Due to its fewer outcomes, WSCT+ was left out of this analysis.

When a term is ambiguous, i.e. when it tends to occur in various semantic and syntactic contexts, its distributional representation might be less suitable to reflect any single one of these. Polysemy is difficult to define (Ravin and Leacock, 2000). Here, we define the **polysemy** of a term by its total number of synsets divided by the number of different parts of speech it can occur in. We tested different thresholds for considering a term polysemous, from two to six synsets per part of speech, which all revealed similar results. The results we report are based on a minimum of three, four and

| | | | entry type (N.B.: 'low' can mean more or less challenging, depending on the property) | | | | | | | |
| | | | low-low | | low-high | | high-low | | high-high | |
property	threshold	corpus	accuracy	proportion	accuracy	proportion	accuracy	proportion	accuracy	proportion
polysemy	3*	HiT	**63.8**	17.8	**60.9**	18.2	**62.8**	18.4	**52.7**	45.6
	3*	HW	100	37	100	29.6	100	18.5	100	**14.8**
	3*	HW+	70.6	38.6	71.4	31.8	100	20.5	100	**9.1**
polysemy	4*	HiT	**66.4**	**32.2**	**58.1**	21.1	**59.6**	17.5	**47.9**	**29.3**
	4*	HW	100	51.9	100	25.9	100	11.1	100	11.1
	4*	HW+	82.1	63.6	60	22.7	100	9.1	100	4.5
polysemy	5*	HiT	**64.8**	**45.3**	**58.7**	19.7	**53**	14.9	**45.9**	**20.1**
	5*	HW	100	70.4	100	14.8	100	14.8	-	0
	5*	HW+	81.8	75	40	11.4	100	11.4	100	2.3
frequency	100k	HiT	65.7	**33.9**	**61.4**	17.2	58.6	17.1	47.6	**31.8**
	100k	HW	100	**18.5**	100	11.1	100	22.2	100	**48.1**
	100k	HW+	80	34.1	66.7	13.6	81.2	36.4	85.7	15.9
frequency	10k	HiT	**65.1**	**7.5**	**74.5**	14.8	63.5	12.9	**52.4**	64.8
	10k	HW	-	**0**	-	0	100	11.1	100	88.9
	10k	HW+	-	**0**	-	0	76.9	29.5	80.6	70.5
frequency	5k	HiT	52.5	**2.7**	**74.3**	9.9	68.8	9.7	54.8	77.8
	5k	HW	-	**0**	-	0	100	7.4	100	92.6
	5k	HW	-	**0**	-	0	66.7	13.6	81.6	86.4
centrality	1*	HiT	**56.4**	75.8	**62.4**	10.2	**66.9**	9.7	**56.5**	4.2
	1*	HW	-	-	-	-	-	-	-	-
	1*	HW+	76	56.8	75	27.3	100	15.9	-	0
	2*	HiT	**54.5**	**54.3**	60.2	18.4	63.5	16.5	**63.9**	10.8
	2*	HW	-	-	-	-	-	-	-	-
	2*	HW+	66.7	**34.1**	81.8	25	100	9.1	85.7	31.8

*high polysemy means the term has min. [THRESHOLD] total synsets / total parts of speech
*high centrality means the term has the intended concept as synset number [THRESHOLD] at most

Table 7: WordShiftEval results broken down by the frequency, centrality, and polysemy of the terms that make up the entries.

five senses per part of speech. Depending on the threshold T, the most-observed type of word pair amongst the HiT results is that of two polysemous terms (45.6 % of the result set, $T = 3$), two relatively unpolysemous terms (45.3%, $T = 5$), or equal proportions of the two ($T = 4$).

The proportion of correctly classified term pairs is unequally distributed across polysemy classes, in particular for HiT. Word pairs with two non-polysemous (i.e. relatively unambiguous) terms are consistently more likely to see their shift direction assessed correctly (64-66% correct, depending on the polysemy threshold) than word pairs with two polysemous terms (46-53% correct), which have an almost equal chance of getting correctly or incorrectly classified. Entries with a single polysemous term consistently fall somewhere between these two trends. Compared to HiT, HW and HW+ have notably smaller proportions of polysemous term pairs, with as little as 9.1% polysemous pairs (under $T = 3$) for HW and 14.8% for HW+, as opposed to 45.6% for HiT.

A low corpus **frequency** was expected to negatively impact the results. With a small number of occurrences used to collect (train) the vector representations, these risk being less stable and reliable. We take the frequencies underlying the 1990s eng-all vector corpus as a proxy for the overall frequencies of the terms and use several frequency cut-offs (5k, 10k and 100k). HiT clearly displays more lower-frequent terms than HW and HW+. For instance, under a cutoff value of 100k, HiT has about the same proportion of low-frequent (33.9%) and high-frequent pairs (31.8%), while HW has clearly more high-frequent (48.1%) than low-frequent pairs (18.5%). Also, HiT is the only set that contains entries made up of terms with frequencies under 5k and 10k.

Looking at the results on HiT when both terms were very sparse (under 5k) the assessment is just ad random (52.5%), but with a higher threshold of 10k the sparse pairs were more likely to be correctly classified (65.1%). At the same time, high-frequent term pairs with target and reference term both over 10k instances showed to be difficult to classify (52.4%). Taken together, these findings suggest that while higher-frequency terms are not always more suitable, a minimum number of instances is indispensable for reliable results.

By **centrality** we mean how good a contemporary example of the intended concept a term is. To this end we look at the synset that connects target and reference term. If the (target or reference) term has this sense listed among its top senses in WordNet, we assume it is exemplary. For the target term this is also an assessment of whether the change took place in (what is now) its primary, second, or in a more distant sense. For instance, we assess the target term *shrewd* in its currently most prevalent sense 'marked by practical hardheaded intelligence' (synset `astute.s.01`). While the reference term *astute* is central to this concept, *sharp* is not, as it is only the sixth sense listed for this term. Hence *shrewd-astute* might be a better example of the shift than *shrewd-sharp*. HW was excluded from the analysis, as the terms in it are not related through WordNet synsets.

We consider two cut-off points: one that examines just the first sense and a less strict one that includes the second listed sense. For the former, the (rare) word pairs in HiT that were made up of two strong terms (4.2%) surprisingly had the same proportion correct (56.5%) as the much larger group of word pairs (75.8%) with two weak terms (56.4% correct). This might be an artefact due the small sample size, as the groups with a single strong term did show higher accuracies (62.4% and 66.9%) than those with none. Under the looser definition of centrality, the accuracy of the shift assessment on HiT increases with the centrality of the terms involved, from 54.5% on weak pairs up to 63.9% on strong pairs. HW+ displays the same trend. However, with a much higher proportion of weak term pairs and a lower proportion of strong pairs than HW+, the HiT results are more at risk of centrality effects.

7   Conclusion

This work offers the largest and most realistic dataset for assessing sense change to date, HiT, which provides 3624 English word pairs and 979 word-synset pairs. HiT is made available along with this publication (click here or look for Sense-ShiftEval on GitHub) and can be automatically extended with more entries. Our experiments have given a number of insights. Firstly, they show how brittle the state-of-the-art method really is. When applied to HiT rather than to small sets of handcrafted examples, the state-of-the-art performance drops dramatically. The error analysis shows in what way existing evaluation data are privileged, if not to say biased: they contain fewer polysemous terms, fewer terms that are less exemplary for the intended concept, and fewer terms modelled on a low number of examples in the corpus. All of these are factors inherent to natural language, which a robust model of sense change will need to handle. The analysis showed that these factors indeed hindered our ability to assess shift direction. For this reason, the two corpus-independent factors, polysemy and centrality, will be incorporated as features in the dataset, to be able to select more or less challenging entries and to assess the effect of these factors on the outcomes.

Complementary to the findings above, several studies have demonstrated that noise is inherent to distributional approaches and stems from factors both computational - e.g. cross-temporal vector alignment (Dubossarsky et al., 2017) - and fundamental, by the mere variance found in natural text corpora (Hellrich and Hahn, 2016). Experimental validation was not the focus of this paper, but we would encourage follow-up work with more rigid experimental checks, including control conditions and non-aligned (e.g. see Dubossarsky et al. (2019)) or count-based vectors.

Given the presence of noise, it is crucial to cross-check findings. HiT is unique in that it caters for this with multiple synonymous entries per target term. We have presented a number of ways to derive holistic, sense-level insights. Some aggregations were more promising than others. The term pair with the largest and most significant cosine trend often displayed the predicted trend. However, averaging the vector representations of all synonyms did not sufficiently cancel out noise.

A logical next step would be to exploit lexical factors for sense-level evaluations, i.e., to select the most representative term pair of a synset based on its centrality to the concept and its (lack of) ambiguity. A preliminary experiment on HiT showed that selection by centrality outperforms some other evaluation techniques. This will be the topic of follow-up work.

Acknowledgements

This work was supported in part by VRE4EIC under the Horizon 2020 research and innovation program, grant agreement No 676247, and by the Netherlands Organization of Scientific Research (Nederlandse Organisatie voor Wetenschappelijk Onderzoek, NWO) as part of VENI grant 275-89-029 awarded to Antske Fokkens. We thank Pia Sommerauer, Aysenur Bilgin, and the anonymous reviewers for their invaluable feedback.

References

Pierpaolo Basile and Barbara McGillivray. 2018. Exploiting the web for semantic change detection. In *International Conference on Discovery Science*, pages 194–208. Springer.

David M Blei and John D Lafferty. 2006. Dynamic topic models. In *Proceedings of the 23rd international conference on Machine learning*, pages 113–120. ACM.

Jacob Cohen. 1960. A coefficient of agreement for nominal scales. *Educational and psychological measurement*, 20(1):37–46.

Mark Davies. 2015. Corpus of Historical American English (COHA).

Haim Dubossarsky, Simon Hengchen, Nina Tahmasebi, and Dominik Schlechtweg. 2019. Time-out: Temporal referencing for robust modeling of lexical semantic change. *arXiv preprint arXiv:1906.01688*.

Haim Dubossarsky, Daphna Weinshall, and Eitan Grossman. 2017. Outta control: Laws of semantic change and inherent biases in word representation models. In *Proceedings of the 2017 conference on empirical methods in natural language processing*, pages 1136–1145.

Christiane Fellbaum. 2012. Wordnet. *The Encyclopedia of Applied Linguistics*.

John Rupert Firth. 1957. A synopsis of linguistic theory, 1930-1955. *Studies in linguistic analysis*.

Joseph L Fleiss. 1971. Measuring nominal scale agreement among many raters. *Psychological bulletin*, 76(5):378.

Kristina Gulordava and Marco Baroni. 2011. A distributional similarity approach to the detection of semantic change in the Google Books Ngram corpus. In *Proceedings of the GEMS 2011 Workshop on Geometrical Models of Natural Language Semantics*, pages 67–71. Association for Computational Linguistics.

William L Hamilton, Jure Leskovec, and Dan Jurafsky. 2016. Diachronic word embeddings reveal statistical laws of semantic change. In *Proceedings of the 54th Annual Meeting of the Association for Computational Linguistics (Volume 1: Long Papers)*, pages 1489–1501.

Zellig S Harris. 1954. Distributional structure. *Word*, 10(2-3):146–162.

Johannes Hellrich and Udo Hahn. 2016. Bad companyneighborhoods in neural embedding spaces considered harmful. In *Proceedings of COLING 2016, the 26th International Conference on Computational Linguistics: Technical Papers*, pages 2785–2796.

Johannes Hellrich and Udo Hahn. 2016a. Bad companyneighborhoods in neural embedding spaces considered harmful. In *COLING (16)*, page 27852796.

Adam Jatowt and Kevin Duh. 2014. A framework for analyzing semantic change of words across time. In *Proceedings of the 14th ACM/IEEE-CS Joint Conference on Digital Libraries*, pages 229–238. IEEE Press.

Christian Kay, Jane Roberts, Michael Samuels, Iren Wotherspoon, and Marc Alexander. 2019. The historical thesaurus of english.

Yoon Kim, Yi-I Chiu, Kentaro Hanaki, Darshan Hegde, and Slav Petrov. 2014. Temporal analysis of language through neural language models. *ACL 2014*, page 61.

Vivek Kulkarni, Rami Al-Rfou, Bryan Perozzi, and Steven Skiena. 2015. Statistically significant detection of linguistic change. In *Proceedings of the 24th International Conference on World Wide Web*, pages 625–635. ACM.

Andrey Kutuzov, Lilja Øvrelid, Terrence Szymanski, and Erik Velldal. 2018. Diachronic word embeddings and semantic shifts: a survey. *arXiv preprint arXiv:1806.03537*.

Andrey Borisovich Kutuzov, Elizaveta Kuzmenko, and Anna Marakasova. 2016. Exploration of registerdependent lexical semantics using word embeddings. In *Proceedings of the Workshop on Language Technology Resources and Tools for Digital Humanities (LT4DH)*, pages 26–34.

Carlos Martinez-Ortiz, Tom Kenter, Melvin Wevers, Pim Huijnen, Jaap Verheul, and Joris Van Eijnatten. 2016. Design and implementation of shico: Visualising shifting concepts over time. In *HistoInformatics 2016*, volume 1632, pages 11–19.

Jean-Baptiste Michel, Yuan Kui Shen, Aviva Presser Aiden, Adrian Veres, Matthew K Gray, Joseph P Pickett, Dale Hoiberg, Dan Clancy, Peter Norvig, Jon Orwant, et al. 2011. Quantitative analysis of culture using millions of digitized books. *science*, 331(6014):176–182.

Tomas Mikolov, Kai Chen, Greg Corrado, and Jeffrey Dean. 2013. Efficient estimation of word representations in vector space. *arXiv preprint arXiv:1301.3781*.

Sunny Mitra, Ritwik Mitra, Martin Riedl, Chris Biemann, Animesh Mukherjee, and Pawan Goyal. 2014. Thats sick dude!: Automatic identification of word sense change across different timescales. In *Proceedings of the 52nd Annual Meeting of the Association for Computational Linguistics (Volume 1: Long Papers)*, pages 1020–1029.

Matthias Orlikowski, Matthias Hartung, and Philipp Cimiano. 2018. Learning diachronic analogies to analyze concept change. In *Proceedings of the Second Joint SIGHUM Workshop on Computational Linguistics for Cultural Heritage, Social Sciences, Humanities and Literature*, pages 1–11.

Yael Ravin and Claudia Leacock. 2000. Polysemy: an overview. *Polysemy: Theoretical and computational approaches*, pages 1–29.

Nina Tahmasebi, Lars Borin, and Adam Jatowt. 2018. Survey of computational approaches to diachronic conceptual change. *arXiv preprint arXiv:1811.06278*.

Nina Tahmasebi and Thomas Risse. 2017. Word sense change testset. This work has been funded in parts by the project "Towards a knowledge-based culturomics" supported by a framework grant from the Swedish Research Council (2012–2016; dnr 2012-5738). This work is also in parts funded by the European Research Council under Alexandria (ERC 339233) and the European Community's H2020 Program under SoBigData (RIA 654024).

Nina Tahmasebi, Thomas Risse, and Stefan Dietze. 2011. Towards automatic language evolution tracking, a study on word sense tracking. In *Joint Workshop on Knowledge Evolution and Ontology Dynamics*.

Xuri Tang. 2018. A state-of-the-art of semantic change computation. *Natural Language Engineering*, 24(5):649–676.

Xuerui Wang and Andrew McCallum. 2006. Topics over time: a non-markov continuous-time model of topical trends. In *Proceedings of the 12th ACM SIGKDD international conference on Knowledge discovery and data mining*, pages 424–433. ACM.

Gerhard Wohlgenannt, Ariadna Barinova, Dmitry Ilvovsky, and Ekaterina Chernyak. 2019. Creation and evaluation of datasets for distributional semantics tasks in the digital humanities domain. *arXiv preprint arXiv:1903.02671*.

Some steps towards the generation of diachronic WordNets

Yuri Bizzoni
Saarland University
Saarbrücken, Germany
`yuri.bizzoni@uni-saarland.de`

Marius Mosbach
Saarland University
Saarbrücken, Germany
`mmosbach@lsv.uni-saarland.de`

Dietrich Klakow
Saarland University
Saarbrücken, Germany
`dietrich.klakow@lsv.uni-saarland.de`

Stefania Degaetano-Ortlieb
Saarland University
Saarbrücken, Germany
`s.degaetano@mx.uni-saarland.de`

Abstract

We apply hyperbolic embeddings to trace the dynamics of change of conceptual-semantic relationships in a large diachronic scientific corpus (200 years). Our focus is on emerging scientific fields and the increasingly specialized terminology establishing around them. Reproducing high-quality hierarchical structures such as WordNet on a diachronic scale is a very difficult task. Hyperbolic embeddings can map partial graphs into low dimensional, continuous hierarchical spaces, making more explicit the latent structure of the input. We show that starting from simple lists of word pairs (rather than a list of entities with directional links) it is possible to build diachronic hierarchical semantic spaces which allow us to model a process towards specialization for selected scientific fields.

1 Introduction

Knowledge of how conceptual structures change over time and how the hierarchical relations among their components evolve is key to the comprehension of language evolution. Recently, the distributional modelling of relationships between concepts has allowed the community to move a bit further in understanding the true mechanisms of semantic organization (Baroni and Lenci, 2010; Kochmar and Briscoe, 2014; Marelli and Baroni, 2015), as well as in better mapping language change in terms of shifts in continuous semantic values (Hamilton et al., 2016; Hellrich and Hahn, 2017; Stewart and Eisenstein, 2017). In the past decades, extensive work has also gone into creating databases of hierarchical conceptual-semantic relationships, the most famous of these ontologies probably being WordNet (Miller, 1995). These

hand-made resources are tools of high quality and precision, but they are difficult to reproduce on a diachronic scale (Bizzoni et al., 2014), due to word form changes (De Melo, 2014) and shifts in meaning (Depuydt, 2016), which always make it hard to determine "when", over a period of time, a new lexical hierarchy is in place (Kafe, 2017).

A recent attempt to integrate hierarchical structures, typical of lexical ontologies, and the commutative nature of semantic spaces are hyperbolic embeddings (Nickel and Kiela, 2017). Hyperbolic embeddings have shown to be able to learn hierarchically structured, continuous, and low-dimensional semantic spaces from ordered lists of words: it is easy to see how such technology can be of interest for the construction of diachronic dynamic ontologies. In contrast to hand-made resources, they can be built quickly from historical corpora, while retaining a hierarchical structure absent in traditional semantic spaces. In their work Nickel and Kiela (2017) have extensively evaluated hyperbolic embeddings on various tasks (taxonomies, link prediction in networks, lexical entailment), evaluating in particular the ability of these embeddings to infer hierarchical relationships without supervision.

This paper is a first attempt in the direction of using hyperbolic semantic spaces to generate *diachronic lexical ontologies*. While count-based and neural word embeddings have often been applied to historical data sets (Jatowt and Duh, 2014; Kutuzov et al., 2018), and the temporal dimension has even solicited innovative kinds of distributional spaces (Dubossarsky et al., 2015; Bamler and Mandt, 2017), this is to the best of our knowledge the first attempt to model a diachronic corpus through hierarchical, non-euclidean semantic spaces. The literature on hyperbolic embeddings has until now mainly focused on reproducing lexical and social networks from contemporary data (Chamberlain et al., 2017; Nickel and Kiela,

2018).

We demonstrate that these kinds of word embeddings, while far from perfect, can capture relevant changes in large scale lexico-semantic relations. These relations are on the "vertical" axis, defining a super-subordinate structure latent in the data. But we also show that meaningful relations between words are preserved on the "horizontal" axis (similarity of meaning, common semantic belonging) as typically captured by distributional spaces and topic models.

While distributional semantic spaces can be built from unconstrained texts, the main conceptual limitation of hyperbolic embeddings probably lies in the fact the user always needs to pre-compose (and so pre-interpret) their input in the form of a list of entities linked by a set of parent–children relations; we thus show a simple system to collect *undirected* relations between entities that require less pre-interpretation of the texts at hand and a broader lexical coverage, giving more value to the information provided by the spaces.

Our main contributions are thus two. First, we apply hyperbolic embeddings to a diachronic setting, for which hand-crafted hierarchical resources are extremely difficult to create. Second, we introduce a system to design training inputs that do not rely on directional lists of related word pairs as in previous works. This is particularly advantageous as the system does not need a pre-interpretation nor a pre-formulation of the data in terms of explicit hierarchy and it allows a wider terminological coverage than the previous systems.

2 Methodology

2.1 Data

As our data set, we use the Royal Society Corpus (RSC; version 4.0; Kermes et al. (2016))[1], containing around 10.000 journal articles of the Transactions and Proceedings of the Royal Society in London (approx. 32 million tokens). The time span covered is from 1665 to 1869 and the corpus is split up into five main periods (*1650*: 1665-1699, *1700*: 1700-1749, *1750*: 1750-1799, *1800*: 1800-1849, *1850*: 1850-1869).

As meta-data annotation, the RSC provides e.g. title, author, year, and journal of publication. Crucial for our investigation is the annotation of sci-

entific disciplines (18 in total), which has been approximated by topic modeling (Blei et al., 2003) using Mallet (Fankhauser et al., 2016). Each document is annotated with primary topic and secondary topic, each with confidence scores. We select two groups: (1) the primary topics Chemistry and Physiology, which are subdivided in two sub-groups (Chemistry I and II and Physiology I and II) and thus might indicate more pronounced specialization tendencies, (2) Botany and Galaxy, both forming only one topic each, and thus possibly reflecting less pronounced specialization tendencies. Table 1 presents a detailed corpus statistics on tokens, lemmas and sentences across decades.

decade	tokens	lemmas	sentences
1660-69	455,259	369,718	10,860
1670-79	831,190	687,285	17,957
1680-89	573,018	466,795	13,230
1690-99	723,389	581,821	17,886
1700-09	780,721	615,770	23,338
1710-19	489,857	383,186	17,510
1720-29	538,145	427,016	12,499
1730-39	599,977	473,164	16,444
1740-49	1,006,093	804,523	26,673
1750-59	1,179,112	919,169	34,162
1760-69	972,672	734,938	27,506
1770-79	1,501,388	1,146,489	41,412
1780-89	1,354,124	1,052,006	37,082
1790-99	1,335,484	1,043,913	36,727
1800-09	1,615,564	1,298,978	45,666
1810-19	1,446,900	1,136,581	42,998
1820-29	1,408,473	1,064,613	43,701
1830-39	2,613,486	2,035,107	81,500
1840-49	2,028,140	1,565,654	70,745
1850-59	4,610,380	3,585,299	146,085
1860-69	5,889,353	4,474,432	202,488
total	31,952,725	24,866,457	966,469

Table 1: Corpus statistics of the RSC per decade.

2.2 Approach

Our approach encompasses (1) extraction of relations from data to serve as training data (edge extraction), (2) modeling hyperbolic embeddings on the obtained data, and (3) testing on selected benchmarks.

Edge extraction. In order to select relevant entities, we used the word clusters of a topic model trained on the whole RSC corpus (Fankhauser et al., 2016; Fischer et al., 2018), which generated circa 50 meaningful clusters, mainly belonging to disciplines (such as Paleontology, Electromagnetism) or objects of interest (such as Solar System or Terrestrial Magnetism).

---

[1] We obtained the RSC from the CLARIN-D repository at http://hdl.handle.net/21.11119/0000-0001-7E8B-6.

topic label	words in topic
Chemistry	acid baro-selenite acid.-when hydroguretted salifiable diethacetone subphosphate meta-furfurol chlorionic causticity acidt acld pyromeconate chloric acids pyroxylic diethyl acid* acid. iodic
Galaxy	stars star to1 nebulosity milky-way facula rethe constellations nebulae lyrce nebula nebule presidencies pole-star st nebulhe sun-spots stars* nebulosities magnet.-

Table 2: The first 20 words from the Chemistry and the galactic Astronomy topic clusters.

For this study, we selected the topics of Chemistry, Physiology, Botany, and galactic Astronomy. Chemistry and Physiology during the time span covered by our corpus undergo a significant inner systematization, which is mirrored by the fact that they are both represented in to two distinct and cohesive topics in our topic model. Botany and galactic Astronomy also underwent major changes during the covered years, but, despite important systematization efforts, kept a more multi-centered conceptual architecture: as a consequence, they represent less cohesive clusters, with more noise and internal diversity. Since the meaningful clusters drawn from topic modeling were relatively small, we populated them through cosine similarity in euclidean semantic spaces built on the same corpus, so as to attain lists of circa 500 elements, of the kind shown in Table 2. Notwithstanding the predictable amount of noise present in these lists, they keep a relative topical cohesion[2].

Based on this selection of words, for each of the five 50-years periods of the RSC, we extract a list of bigrams, i.e. pairs of words of entities of interest.

While usually the training input to model hyperbolic word embeddings is based on directional lists of related word pairs (e.g. the *Hearst patterns* extracted via rule-based text queries (Roller et al., 2018; Le et al., 2019)), we decided to opt for a more "agnostic" method to create input lists for our model.

We consider two words as related if they occur in the same sentence, and we do *not* express any

hierarchical value or direction between the words constituting the input lists: the input can be viewed as an undirected graph[3].

On simple cases, this way of extracting undirected edges appears to work well. As an example, in Figure 1 we show the output space of the Wikipedia article on Maslow's Hierarchy of Needs (a very hierarchical topic). In this case, the keywords were selected manually and the text was simple in its exposition of the theory. According to the hierarchy exposed in the article, human needs are as follows: physiological needs (food, water, shelter, sleep), safety (health, financial, well-being), social needs (family, intimacy, friendships), self-esteem, self-actualization (parenting), transcendence. In the hyper-space resulting from this text, the word *needs* occupies the root of the hierarchy: it is the closest point to the origin of the axes and has, consequently, the smallest norm. The six categories of needs described in the input page directly follow as hyponyms: *physiological, safety, social, self-esteem, self-actualization, transcendence*. The specific kinds of needs mainly cluster as hyponyms of such categories: for example *water, food, sleep, shelter* are all very close in the space, higher in norm, and located as direct hyponyms of *physiological* (they are closer to *physiological* than to the other categories).

The case we are going to deal with in this paper is much more complex: the lists of terms were selected automatically and the corpus is diachronic, technical in nature, and occasionally noisy.

On our corpus, we obtain through our system of edge extraction lists of variable length, between 500 and 5000 pairs depending on the topic and period. While this approach makes the input noisier and the model potentially more prone to errors, the system requires way less starting assumptions on the nature of the data, guarantees a larger coverage than the previous methods, and re-introduces the principle of unstructured distributional profiling so effective in euclidean semantic spaces.

Poincare hierarchical embeddings. For training hyperbolic semantic spaces, we rely on gensim's implementation of Poincare word embeddings. Here, we apply the Poincare hyperspace semantic model recently described by Nickel and Kiela (2017) on each 50-year period of the RSC corpus. We train each model for 20 epochs, di-

---

[2]Stop words like adverbs, pronouns, determiners and prepositions are also rare in the lists.

[3]Basically, each word pair is twice in the list: (1) word A related to word B, and (2) word B related to word A.

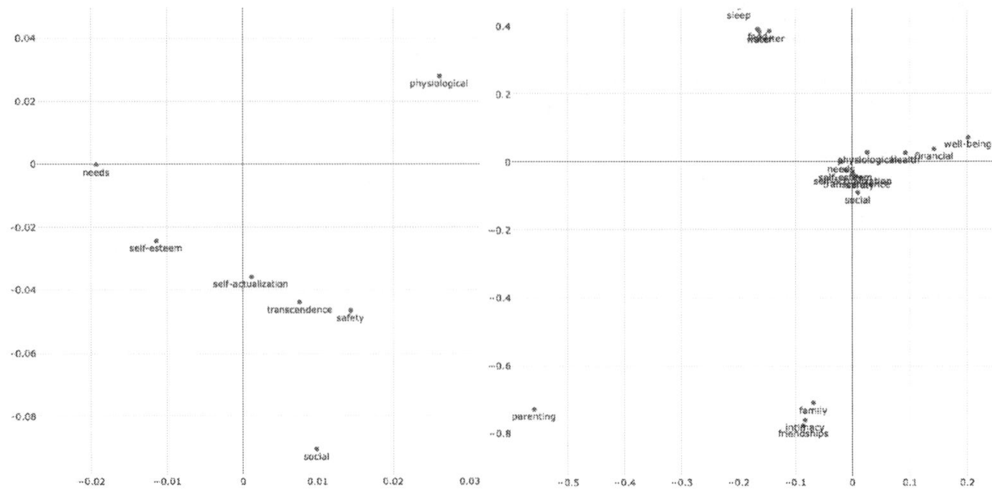

Figure 1: The center of the disk (left) and the whole space (right) as extracted from a Wikipedia article on the Hierarchy of Needs. The main needs cluster around the root of the hierarchy, while their hyponyms cluster to the periphery, but tendentially closer to their hypernymic category than to the others. Note that the space organizes words along the hypernym-hyponym hierarchical line, and ignores other kinds of hierarchy: *physiological*, albeit being treated as more "basic" in the input text, is not closer to *needs* than *transcendence*.

rectly setting a bi-dimensional output. Since our Poincare models generate 2d spaces, we can visualize them without losing any information.

Benchmarks. Since a gold standard to verify the qualities and pitfalls of diachronic hyperbolic semantic spaces is lacking, and it is of not obvious generation, we use two different benchmarks to perform partial tests of the results. The first benchmark is the correlation between the number of WordNet senses and words' norm in the spaces. The other benchmark is the same topic modeling described above: we use it to test whether the words that happen to be in the same topic also cluster together in our spaces.

3 Analysis and results

Having a look at the semantic spaces resulting from the four topics we selected, we can already see that Chemistry and Physiology develop a particularly centralized structure, with few elements in the center and a large crown of peripheral terminology, while Botany and galactic Astronomy return less clear symptoms of their inner ordering.

Figure 2, for example, illustrates hyperbolic embeddings of the Chemistry field for each 50-year period (1650s-1850s). The closer to the center, the more abstract (and potentially ambiguous) the meaning of the words should be, while the

more distant from the center, the more we should find specialized terminology. In an ideal semantic hyper-space, the center should represent the real root of the ontology, and its edges should represent the most distant leaves.

In some disciplines (mainly Chemistry and Physiology), we observe the emergence of a clearly centralized and hierarchical evolution, while in others (Biology and Astronomy) we see the development a more multi-central, complicated sort of conceptual organization.

Comparing the evolution of Chemistry with galactic Astronomy (see Figure 3), we can see that the development towards hierarchization does apply to both, but is more pronounced in the Chemistry space.

Figure 4, for clarity, shows only selected labels on the spaces of the 1650s and the 1850s: some words pertaining to the empirical framework, such as *inquires* and *investigations*, and technical terms at various degrees of specificity (still mostly absent in the 1650s space). We see how simple forms of conceptual hierarchization appear in the latter space: for example *compound* moves to the center of the disk, close to a cluster including terms like *substance* and *matter* (and others not included for clarity, such as *solution*), all being more abstract in meaning. *Actions* becomes a hypernym of *investigations* and *inquiries*. Instead, the more spe-

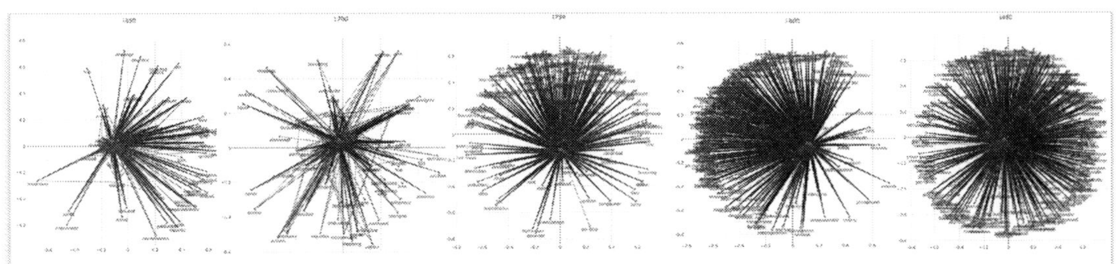

Figure 2: Evolution of the space with original edges for Chemistry.

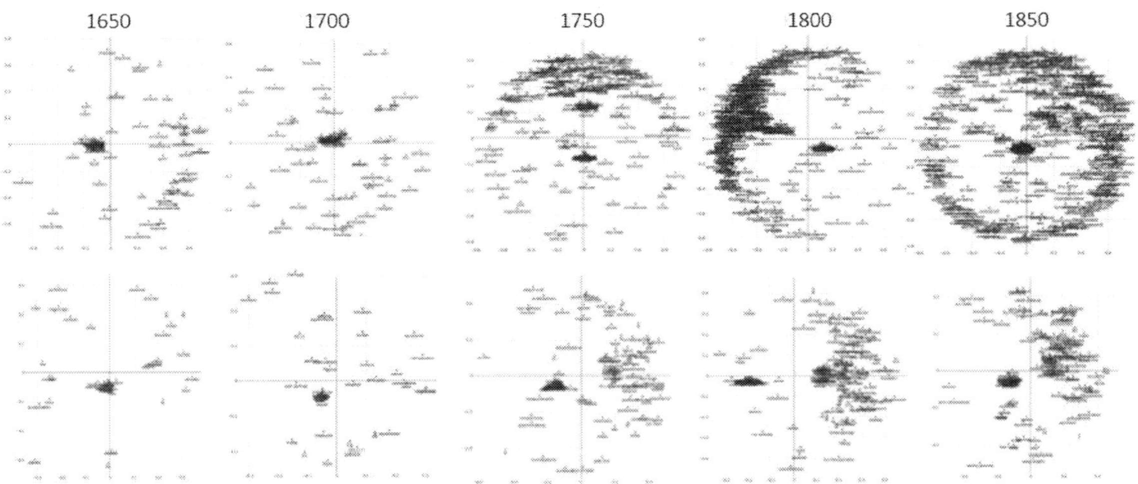

Figure 3: Evolution of the spaces for Chemistry (top row) and galactic Astronomy (bottom row). The high level of hierarchization in Chemistry appears evident. Galactic Astronomy maintains a more chaotic outlook despite the increase of terminology; still, a cluster of terms can be seen growing in the center of the space, while the periphery of the spaces becomes more dense.

cialized terms tend to be located at the edge of the disk, such as *ammoniac* vs. *ammonium-salt*, *anhydride* vs. *carboneous* vs. *gas-carbon*, or *oxide* vs. *protoxide*. See also Table 3 for some examples of developing hierarchization.

This tendency to cluster more clearly abstract/generic and specialized terms is visible in all four disciplines, and is mirrored in the evolution of the structure of the spaces. Measuring the variations in the overall norm of all words, and in the average norm of the 30 elements with the highest and lowest norm of the space for each of the four fields taken into consideration (see Table 4), we record in all cases a tendency to an increasing hierarchization, with small clusters of words moving towards the center and larger numbers of words clustering further away at the periphery of the hyper-disk (see Figure 5 for the highly centralized space of Physiology in the last period of our corpus). Even in Galaxy, the least cohesive of the topics, we notice a steady growth of the average norm (from 3.2 to 20.9), indicating an extension of the periphery. Comparing the results with a "control group" (see again Table 4) formed by sentimental terms (*happiness*, *misery*), which are present throughout the corpus but are neither the topic of the papers nor undergo systematic conceptualizations, there is no hierarchization tendency. Moreover, on average the norm of the 30 most peripheral words steadily increases through time. The tendency of words to increasingly populate more peripheral areas of the disk can be seen as an indication of the increased formation of specialized meanings within particular scientific fields (see Figure 6 for an example).

In Table 4, we show a compendium of these observations for each topic, while in Figure 7 we show the average norm of all words in the space for each discipline through time. It can be seen that the control group does not show most of the trends pictured by the other topics – centralization of a group of words, average increase of the norm,

Epoch	cluster	plant	flowers
1650	clusters, triple, larger	juice, stem, plants	bud, roots, tree
1700	dark-grey, situation, clusters	species, seed, juice	leaves, tree, trees
1750	clusters, nebula, nebulae	flowers, fruit, piece	fruit, branches, plant
1800	nebulosity, clusters, nebulae	leaf-stalk, leaves, roots	shurbs, stem, horse-chestnut
1850	clusters, stellar, nebulae	flowered, seeded, soil	petals, stamina, pistilla

Table 3: Nearest descendants for *cluster*, *plant* and *flowers* in diachronic Poincare spaces for galactic Astronomy (in the first case) and Botany (second and third case). It is possible to observe the emergence of *stellar* as a kind of cluster; of the division between flowered and seeded plants (an antithesis that became meaningful towards the XIX century); and of specific elements of a flower's anatomy, such as the stamen, which were particularly relevant in the studies on flowers' sexuality (mid XIX century).

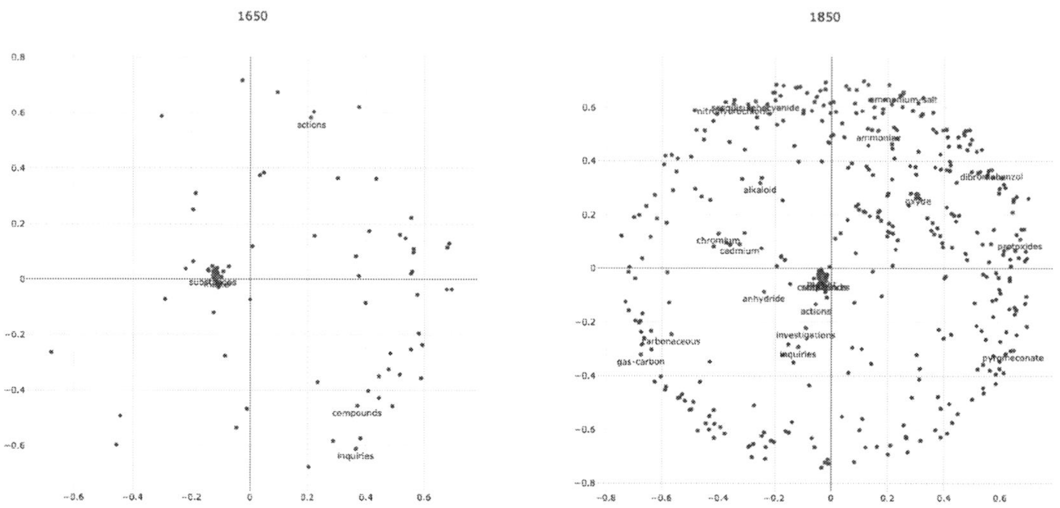

Figure 4: Selected nodes (in violet) from 1850s Chemistry, as compared to the 1650s. In *Compounds* joins *Substances* and *Matter* to the top of the hierarchy, while *Actions* becomes a hypernym of *Inquires* and *Investigations*. Raw chemical hierarchies can be seen forming at the edges of the hyperdisc.

extension of the peripheries – while a slight trend towards the increase of the norm of the most peripheral words can also be observed in this group.

WordNet comparison. Due to the practical and theoretical difficulties of using contemporary WordNet as a benchmark to validate historical ontologies (should we expect an ideal algorithm to return us a close WordNet similarity on historical data?), we do not use WordNet to directly compare the structure of the spaces (as Nickel and Kiela (2017) do for contemporary data sets), but to correlate the number of WordNet senses a word has with respect to its norm in each period. We notice that in all the considered disciplines, the correlation between the number of senses a word has and its vector's norm is not null, and tends to increase over time (see e.g. Table 5 for Physiol-

ogy). The words at the center of the hyper-disk tend more and more to overlap with highly polysemous words in contemporary English, while the words that cluster at the edges of the disk correlate more and more with highly specialized words in contemporary English (words with one or two senses at most). Table 5 shows the top 30 words with the lowest norm (most abstract in meaning) and the highest norm (most specialized) for Physiology through time. Both groups show a tendency towards fewer senses over time, indicating increased semantic specialization and decreasing polysemy. Also, in all epochs the first group displays on average more senses than the second group. Table 6 presents Pearson correlation between WordNet senses and words' norms per period across topics, showing an increasing correla-

Epoch	Physiology			Chemistry			Botany			Galaxy			Control		
	H	L	%>.3	H	L	%>.3	H	L	%>.3	H	L	%>.3	H	L	%>.3
1650	0.06	0.53	**45.2**	0.09	0.57	**43.7**	0.10	0.21	**4.3**	0.06	0.20	**3.2**	0.13	0.02	**0.0**
1700	0.11	0.47	**32.4**	0.04	0.44	**33.3**	0.09	0.18	**6.2**	0.02	0.30	**5.3**	0.07	0.01	**0.0**
1750	0.08	0.64	**57.6**	0.09	0.65	**61.2**	0.11	0.43	**3.7**	0.05	0.30	**5.2**	0.10	0.06	**0.0**
1800	0.06	0.68	**67.9**	0.12	0.70	**71.2**	0.10	0.36	**18.0**	0.05	0.35	**15.1**	0.13	0.08	**0.1**
1850	0.06	0.62	**64.1**	0.05	0.69	**69.3**	0.10	0.40	**24.7**	0.04	0.47	**20.9**	0.13	0.07	**0.0**

Table 4: Average norm for the 30 elements with the highest (H) and lowest (L) norm and percentage of elements with norm higher than .3 for each period and discipline.

Epoch	WordNet senses	
	abstract	specialized
1650	11.2	3.4
1700	6.6	4.2
1750	10.9	2.2
1800	5.2	1.03
1850	5.2	0.6

Table 5: Average number of WordNet senses for the 30 terms with the lowest norm (column 2) and for the 30 terms with the highest norm (column 3) in the space of Physiology.

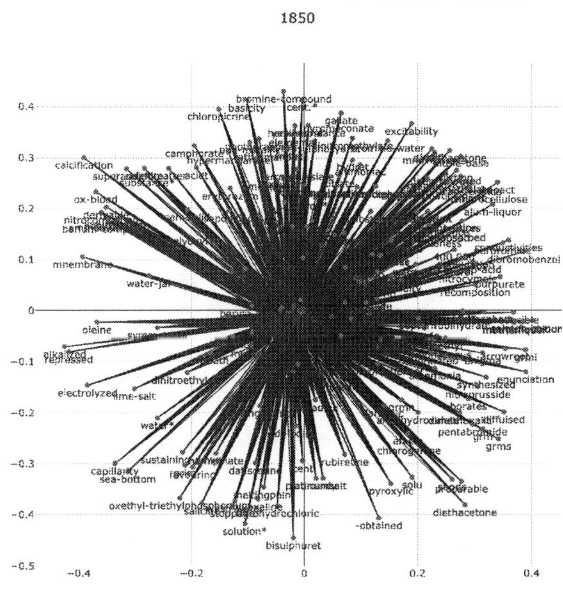

Figure 5: Physiology space (with original edges) for the last period. The centralized hierarchical structure is clearly visible.

tion.

Topic clustering. All four the selected topics show a tendency to increase their words' average norm and the distance between the center and the edge of the disk. The two topics that show stronger symptoms of conceptual hierarchization, Chemistry and Physiology, were also distinguished in two lexical sub-topics by our original topic model. The emergence of these sub-topics was mainly due to the changes in word usage caused by relevant scientific discoveries (like for example the systematization of elements in Chemistry) that created vocabularies and conceptual systems that had scarce interactions with one another. In Table 7, we show that the average cosine similarity between the words belonging to the one sub-topic tends to stay higher than their average similarity to the words belonging to the other sub-topic: the topical distance between the two groups is not lost in the hierarchization.

4 Discussion

We have built diachronic semantic hyperspaces for four scientific topics over a large historical English corpus stretching from 1665 to 1869. We have shown that the resulting spaces present the characters of a growing hierarchization of concepts, both in terms of inner structure and in terms of light comparison with contemporary semantic resources (growing Pearson correlation between norm and WordNet senses). We have shown that while the same trends are visible in all four disciplines, Chemistry and Physiology present more accentuated symptoms of hierarchization, while the group of control had even few or no signs of hierarchization.

Specialization in scientific language. This work is part of a larger project aimed to trace the linguistic development of scientific language toward an optimal code for scientific communication (Degaetano-Ortlieb and Teich, 2018, 2019). One mayor assumption is the diachronic development towards specialization – as a scientific field develops, it will become increasingly specialized and expert-oriented.

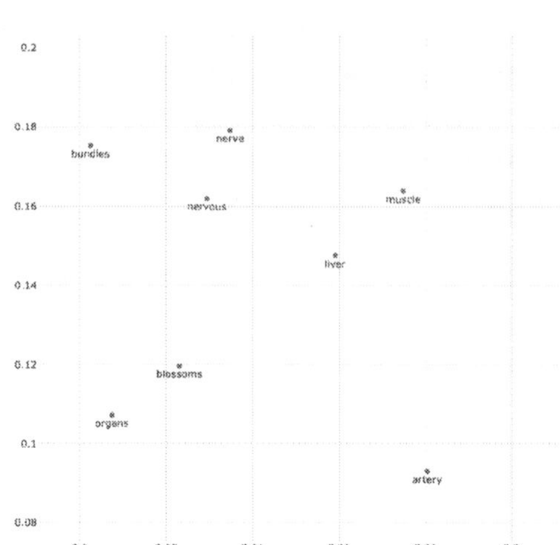
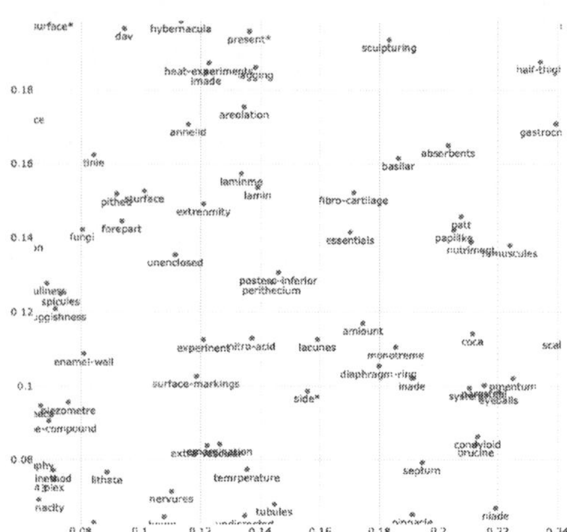

Figure 6: Population of the same area of the hyper-disk for Physiology in the first and last epoch. More specialized and technical terms tend to populate the same level in the "hierarchy".

Epoch	Physiology I and II	Chemistry I and II	Galaxy	Botany	Control
1650	-0.37	-0.42	-0.50	-0.09	-0.06
1700	-0.20	-0.44	-0.35	-0.05	0.67
1750	-0.40	-0.45	-0.43	-0.24	-0.34
1800	-0.42	-0.46	-0.16	-0.22	-0.17
1850	-0.41	-0.46	-0.37	-0.32	-0.16

Table 6: Pearson correlation between WordNet senses and word's norm per period per topic.

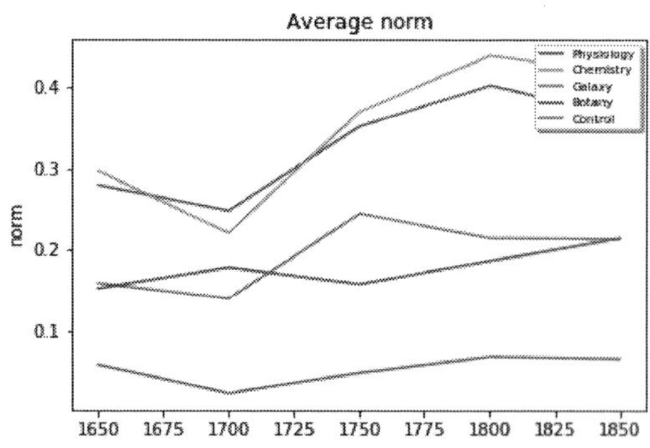

Epoch	P in	P out	C in	C out
1650	.58	.59	.54	.55
1700	.60	.60	.56	.56
1750	.53	.53	.50	.49
1800	.51	.50	.48	.47
1850	.50	.47	.47	.44

Table 7: Topic detectability. Average cosine similarity for elements pertaining to the same sub-topic (in) and elements pertaining to different sub-topics (out) in Physiology (P) and Chemistry (C) through time.

Figure 7: For all four disciplines the average words' norm increases through time. This is due to the expansion of the hyperspace periphery: words become more specialized, hierarchies become deeper. The control group (sentiment terms) does not show this tendency.

Thus, as a field specializes, it develops more technical and differentiated vocabulary (Halliday, 1988; Teich et al., 2016). For the disciplines investigated here increased specialization over time appears clearly in our hyperspaces showing a tendency towards the use of more peripheral words and deeper hierarchies.

Considerations on validity of our baselines. Finding valid, meaningful baselines to evaluate hierarchies based on a diachronic corpus is not a trivial task. Comparing them to the topic model's results on the same corpus was possibly the most sensible one, but we should not expect too much on that side: Hyperbolic embeddings are not specifically designed to tell topics apart, and if words pertaining to slightly different topics (such as two kinds of chemistry) happen to be on the same level of conceptual abstraction, it is fair to expect them quite near in the hyper-disk geography.

At the same time, comparing our results to WordNet makes sense only partially: the conceptual structures of WordNet are 150 years more recent than the ones discussed in the most recent of our spaces, and it is wrong to assume a priori that their distribution in a historical hierarchy should be similar. So we relied on internal analysis and qualitative considerations, but baselines for these kinds of tasks would be highly needed to better test diachronic ontologies.

Considerations on our extraction system. To collect our data, we used a very simple and non-committal approach that feeds the models with less information than usually provided in the literature.

However, choosing the words with some care and working on large numbers, our models do not seem completely at a loss in front of the noise of the input data. With differences due to the noise of the word lists and the development of the fields, a tendency for specialized terms to cluster as hyponyms of more abstract and polysemous words could be observed in all four disciplines. In future work, we intend to accurately test this procedure by means of contemporary data sets.

Dynamic diachronic WordNets. Hand crafted, historical ontologies of concepts are extremely expensive in terms of person/hour, not considering the amount of expertise and skills required to build a hierarchy of concepts based on the knowledge and beliefs of a different time. We speculate that these sorts of technologies can be a step towards an easier, and more dynamic way of building corpus-induced ontologies, offering for example raw material to be polished by human experts.

References

Robert Bamler and Stephan Mandt. 2017. Dynamic word embeddings. In *Proceedings of the 34th International Conference on Machine Learning-Volume 70*, pages 380–389. JMLR. org.

Marco Baroni and Alessandro Lenci. 2010. Distributional memory: A general framework for corpus-based semantics. *American Journal of Computational Linguistics*, 36(4):673–721.

Yuri Bizzoni, Federico Boschetti, Harry Diakoff, Riccardo Del Gratta, Monica Monachini, and Gregory R Crane. 2014. The making of ancient greek wordnet. In *LREC*, volume 2014, pages 1140–1147.

David M. Blei, Andrew W. Ng, and Michael I. Jordan. 2003. Latent Dirichlet Allocation. *Journal of Machine Learning Research*, 3:993–1022.

Benjamin Paul Chamberlain, James Clough, and Marc Peter Deisenroth. 2017. Neural embeddings of graphs in hyperbolic space. *arXiv preprint arXiv:1705.10359*.

Gerard De Melo. 2014. Etymological wordnet: Tracing the history of words. In *Proceedings of LREC 2014*, pages 1148–1154.

Stefania Degaetano-Ortlieb and Elke Teich. 2018. Using relative entropy for detection and analysis of periods of diachronic linguistic change. In *Proceedings of the 2nd Joint SIGHUM Workshop on Computational Linguistics for Cultural Heritage, Social Sciences, Humanities and Literature at COLING2018*, pages 22–33, Santa Fe, NM, USA.

Stefania Degaetano-Ortlieb and Elke Teich. 2019. Toward an optimal code for communication: The case of scientific English. *Corpus Linguistics and Linguistic Theory*, 0(0):1–33. Ahead of print.

Katrien Depuydt. 2016. Diachronic semantic lexicon of dutch (diachroon semantisch lexicon van de nederlandse taal; diamant). In *DH*, pages 777–778.

Haim Dubossarsky, Yulia Tsvetkov, Chris Dyer, and Eitan Grossman. 2015. A bottom up approach to category mapping and meaning change. In *NetWordS*, pages 66–70.

Peter Fankhauser, Jörg Knappen, and Elke Teich. 2016. Topical diversification over time in the royal society corpus. Digital Humanities 2016, Krakow 1116 July 2016, Krakow. Jagiellonian University; Pedagogical University.

Stefan Fischer, Jorg Knappen, and Elke Teich. 2018. Using topic modelling to explore authors' research fields in a corpus of historical scientific english. In *Proceedings of DH 2018*.

M.A.K. Halliday. 1988. On the Language of Physical Science. In Mohsen Ghadessy, editor, *Registers of Written English: Situational Factors and Linguistic Features*, pages 162–177. Pinter, London.

William L Hamilton, Jure Leskovec, and Dan Jurafsky. 2016. Cultural shift or linguistic drift? comparing two computational measures of semantic change. In *Proceedings of the Conference on Empirical Methods in Natural Language Processing. Conference on Empirical Methods in Natural Language Processing*, volume 2016, page 2116. NIH Public Access.

Johannes Hellrich and Udo Hahn. 2017. Exploring diachronic lexical semantics with JeSemE. In *Proceedings of ACL 2017, System Demonstrations*, pages 31–36, Vancouver, Canada. Association for Computational Linguistics.

Adam Jatowt and Kevin Duh. 2014. A framework for analyzing semantic change of words across time. In *Proceedings of the 14th ACM/IEEE-CS Joint Conference on Digital Libraries*, pages 229–238. IEEE Press.

Eric Kafe. 2017. How stable are wordnet synsets? In *LDK Workshops*, pages 113–124.

Hannah Kermes, Stefania Degaetano-Ortlieb, Ashraf Khamis, Jörg Knappen, and Elke Teich. 2016. The Royal Society Corpus: From Uncharted Data to Corpus. In *Proceedings of the 10th LREC*, Portorož, Slovenia. ELRA.

Ekaterina Kochmar and Ted Briscoe. 2014. Detecting learner errors in the choice of content words using compositional distributional semantics. In *Proceedings of COLING 2014, the 25th International Conference on Computational Linguistics: Technical Papers*, pages 1740–1751.

Andrey Kutuzov, Lilja Øvrelid, Terrence Szymanski, and Erik Velldal. 2018. Diachronic word embeddings and semantic shifts: a survey. *arXiv preprint arXiv:1806.03537*.

Matt Le, Stephen Roller, Laetitia Papaxanthos, Douwe Kiela, and Maximilian Nickel. 2019. Inferring concept hierarchies from text corpora via hyperbolic embeddings. *arXiv preprint arXiv:1902.00913*.

Marco Marelli and Marco Baroni. 2015. Affixation in semantic space: Modeling morpheme meanings with compositional distributional semantics. *Psychological review*, 122(3):485.

George A. Miller. 1995. Wordnet: A lexical database for english. *Commun. ACM*, 38(11):39–41.

Maximilian Nickel and Douwe Kiela. 2018. Learning continuous hierarchies in the lorentz model of hyperbolic geometry. *arXiv preprint arXiv:1806.03417*.

Maximillian Nickel and Douwe Kiela. 2017. Poincaré embeddings for learning hierarchical representations. In *Advances in neural information processing systems*, pages 6338–6347.

Stephen Roller, Douwe Kiela, and Maximilian Nickel. 2018. Hearst patterns revisited: Automatic hypernym detection from large text corpora. *arXiv preprint arXiv:1806.03191*.

Ian Stewart and Jacob Eisenstein. 2017. Making" fetch" happen: The influence of social and linguistic context on nonstandard word growth and decline. *arXiv preprint arXiv:1709.00345*.

Elke Teich, Stefania Degaetano-Ortlieb, Peter Fankhauser, Hannah Kermes, and Ekaterina Lapshinova-Koltunski. 2016. The Linguistic Construal of Disciplinarity: A Data Mining Approach Using Register Features. *Journal of the Association for Information Science and Technology (JASIST)*, 67(7):1668–1678.

An evaluation of Czech word embeddings

Karolína Hořeňovská

Charles University, Faculty of Mathematics and Physics

Institute of Formal and Applied Linguistics

`horenovska@ufal.mff.cuni.cz`

Abstract

We present an evaluation of Czech low-dimensional distributed word representations, also known as word embeddings. We describe five different approaches to training the models and three different corpora used in training. We evaluate the resulting models on five different datasets, report the results and provide their further analysis.

1 Introduction

Distributed word representations, often referred to as word embeddings, have received a lot of attention in recent years, and they have been used to improve results in many NLP tasks. The term itself refers to representing words as low-dimensional real-valued vectors (usually with dimensionality of 50-1000), and is opposed to explicit sparse representations, i.e. representing words as high-dimensional vectors of 0s and 1s (usually with dimensionality in the tens of thousands).

Many different models have been proposed (see section 2). By their nature, these models are language-independent (given the language can be tokenized) but usually the reported results are measured using only English. This is encouraged not only by English being the standard scientific language, but also by the availability of English text corpora and, even more importantly, English datasets to evaluate the models on.

We have decided to perform an intrinsic evaluation of embedding models on Czech. We have identified several successful models to evaluate, collected existing datasets to evaluate them on and designed two more datasets to extend the evaluation. We should note that we do not perform downstream-task evaluation, even though it might not correlate well with the intrinsic evaluation (Tsvetkov et al., 2015). We also use the models

with their default parameters and only try changing the corpus they are trained on.

The rest of the paper is organized as follows: first, we describe related work (section 2). We continue with a description of selected models (section 3), corpora used in training (section 4) and the datasets (section 5). Finally, we present the results (section 6).

2 Related work

Related work could be clustered into three groups of papers.

First, we should mention papers performing evaluation of Czech word embeddings. Such evaluation exists for Word2Vec and GloVe using analogy corpus (Svoboda and Brychcín, 2016), however we are not aware of any more recent evaluation (which would cover also more recent models). Still, some papers evaluate some word embeddings in the context of a new dataset, as is the case of Czech similarity-relatedness dataset (Konopik et al., 2017).

Second, there are intrinsic evaluations of embeddings. These are usually part of new model proposals but there are exceptions. A notable one is a comparison by Baroni et al (2014), and also the work by Levy and Goldbert (2014), though this paper proposes another objective to solving analogies. Tsvetkov (2015) should also be mentioned for showing that intrinsic evaluation of embeddings need not correlate with performance on downstream tasks, and Nayak et al (2016) proposed a suite to test word embeddings.

Finally, there are model proposals. The most famous one is probably Word2Vec (Mikolov et al., 2013a), which has later been extended to fastText (Bojanowski et al., 2017). Despite being so well known, Word2Vec is neither the older (cf. e.g. the work by Schütze (1993)) nor the only one. Another famous models include GloVe (Pennington et al., 2014), LexVec (Salle et al., 2016b), ELMo

(Peters et al., 2018) or a recent model BERT (Devlin et al., 2018).

In addition to models themselves, there are proposals on altering the trained model so that it better fits a purpose, e.g. by transforming the vector space to get vectors of synonyms closer to each other and increase the distance between antonym vectors (Faruqui et al., 2014; Mrkšić et al., 2016).

3 Selected models

In this section, we outline each of the selected models. We also report which implementation we use in our experiments.

Following some literature, we characterize each model as either *predictive* (trained by learning to predict a word) or *counting* (trained using co-occurences counts).

Unfortunately, it has not been feasible to train some model-corpus combinations.[1] We were not able to train fastText on Czech National Corpus using forms and LexVec on Czech National Corpus using either forms or lemmata. We have also not trained BERT on our own, instead, we only use a pre-trained model.

3.1 Word2Vec

Word2Vec (Mikolov et al., 2013a,b) is probably the most famous neural embedding model. The same name actually refers to two different architectures – called continuous bag of words (CBOW) and skip-gram (SG).

Both architectures are basically feed-forward networks. CBOW's inputs are words (tokens) within another word's context and its golden output is the surrounded word. Often, context window of size 5 is used, i.e. five words preceding and five words following the predicted word form the inputs. There's one projection layeyr between input and output layers. For skip-gram, it is the other way round, i.e. one word forms the input and words surrounding it are predicted. In both architectures, all words share the projection layer, which reduces the number of parameters to train, and thus the training time.

When using Word2Vec without specifying architecture, skip-gram is usually the default as it performs better in most evaluation. However, since Svoboda and Brychcín (2016) found out CBOW performed better in their experiments on Czech, we experiment with both architectures.

We use Word2Vec implementation provided in the gensim library (Řehůřek and Sojka, 2010).

An important concept introduced in the second paper (Mikolov et al., 2013b) is negative sampling: when training a word vector, other words are randomly sampled from the corpus and the model is penalized for high similarity of their vectors.

3.2 FastText

FastText (Bojanowski et al., 2017) is an extension of Word2Vec skip-gram which incorporates subword information in resulting vectors. Words are prefixed and suffixed with boundary symbols and vectors are then trained not only for all words but also for all n-grams appearing in any of the words. Boundary symbols are important to distinguish short words from n-grams appearing inside words. Using n-gram embeddings, even vectors for out-of-vocabulary words (i.e. words not present in training corpus) can be generated.

Please note that even though Bojanowski et al. (2017) describe the model as using skip-gram, it can integrate with CBOW architecture. We have tried using both architectures.

We use the implementation provided in gensim library (Řehůřek and Sojka, 2010).

3.3 GloVe

GloVe (Pennington et al., 2014) is a counting model which utilizes co-occurence matrix, i.e. numbers of times a word occurs within the context of another word. The basic idea is that if some words are related to the same concept, the probability of appearing in their context is much higher for these words than for any other word. This ratios need to be captured by the resulting model. The formulae to capture these similarities/ratios are further weighted so that rarely seen co-occurences contribute little to the resulting vectors (through loss function) and there's a limit to which frequent co-occurencies might contribute.

We use the original implementation provided by authors.[2]

3.4 LexVec

LexVec (Salle et al., 2016b,a; Salle and Villavicencio, 2018) is, like GloVe, a counting model. It again utilizes co-occurence matrix and weights the

---

[1]We hope to overcome this limitation in our future works.

[2]https://github.com/stanfordnlp/GloVe

errors so that more frequent co-occurences contribute more. It however also employs the negative sampling (originally introduced as an extension to skip-gram Word2Vec (Mikolov et al., 2013b)) to force scattering vectors of unrelated words.

Since the first paper, LexVec has been extended with positional context (i.e. it is not important only whether word a appeared in the context of word b but also whether it was to the left or to the right and how many words there were in between), the ability to use external memory for storing the co-occurences (which allows to train on a huge corpus), and finally with subword information (which allows deriving vectors even for out-of-vocabulary words).

We use the original implementation provided by authors.[3]

3.5 BERT

BERT (Devlin et al., 2018), which stands for bidirectional encoder representations from transformer, is a neural predictive model. It is trained on sentences rather than on words themselves (actually, its inputs are sentence pairs) but it does produce word embeddings. It's training can be viewed as a two-step process, the model is first pre-trained using specific tasks and then fine-tuned using downstream tasks.

The two tasks used to pretrain the model are next sentence prediction (i.e. deciding whether the second sentence really followed the first one in original text or if it was picked at random) and something the authors call masked language model, which is very close to a cloze test (Taylor, 1953). The idea is that some amount of randomly chosen words is masked (i.e. replaced with a special token), and the model has to correctly predict them.

We do not train the model, we use the distributed multilingual model [4] and our department wrapper around it.

Because of its different nature, we evaluate this model only on similarity datasets (those described in subsections 5.2 and 5.3).

4 Corpora

In this section, we briefly describe the corpora we use to train the models on.

Apart from using different models and corpora to train on, we have also experimented with two more settings: token form (i.e. training either on forms as they appear in the corpora, or on lemmata) and keeping/substituting numbers. The second idea is rather a concept, though concretized in numbers – some words have similar function but come in many different forms (and remain distinct when lemmatized) so their token counts are low and they do not take big part in the training. However, their similar function suggests that they could still be useful in defining contexts/concepts. We therefore tried also substituting all numbers (i.e. tokens tagged as C= by MorphoDiTa tool) with a meta-word.

For lemmatization of both corpora and datasets, we have used the MorphoDiTa tool (Straková et al., 2014).

4.1 Czech Wikipedia dump

As is common in natural language processing, we use Wikipedia dump as a training corpus. This corpus consists of short documents (hundreds to thousands words), the style is encyclopedic but not really expert. No shuffling has to happen, all co-occurences are kept as they are. Unfortunately, Czech Wikipedia is rather small when compared to the English version, thus we expect it to produce worse results.

We have used the dump from 1st May 2019. We have processed the dump with wikiextractor[5] and tokenized it using MorphoDiTa (Straková et al., 2014) tool.

4.2 CzEng

CzEng (Bojar et al., 2016) is a parallel Czech-English corpus. The texts in it are of varied domains, including news, fiction, laws, movie subtitles and tweets. It is shuffled at block level, i.e. only a few consecutive sentences are kept together each time. Each sentence is associated with its domain but it is not possible to reconstruct the original documents.

We have used version 1.7 and only extracted the Czech part of CzEng, keeping the tokenization and lemmatization provided in CzEng. We have reordered the sentences so that all sentences which share the domain are grouped together.

---

[3]https://github.com/alexandres/lexvec
[4]https://github.com/google-research/bert

[5]http://attardi.github.io/wikiextractor/

4.3 Czech National Corpus

Czech National Corpus (Křen et al., 2016) is a large corpus of written Czech. Version SYN v4, which we have used, contains texts of varying types, however news are by far the most common. (This version is not considered representative because of the prevailing news, but it is much larger than representative CNC subcorpora.) The corpus is again shuffled at block level, sentences are linked with the exact document they come from but their order cannot be reconstructed.

5 Datasets

We describe the existing (as well as no-longer-existing) datasets suitable for the evaluation of Czech word embeddings.

5.1 RG-65 Czech (unavailable)

RG-65 Czech (Krčmář et al., 2011) is (or perhaps used to be) a Czech version of the famous Rubenstein-Goodenough set (Rubenstein and Goodenough, 1965), a set on word relatedness.

In the original set, the data are triplets: two words and a mean relatedness score as annotated by human annotators, there are 65 word pairs.

The authors decided to translate the word pairs, using a reference on the original meanings. Pair relatedness was annotated by 24 human annotators of varying age, gender and education. During the translation and annotation process, a total of 10 pairs was omitted since one of the words could not be easily translated (or it would be translated to exactly the same word as the other).

Unfortunately, this dataset seems not to be available any more. The URL provided in the paper does not work, neither does the first author's email. We have tried contacting another author of the paper but they did not have the data.

We therefore do not evaluate on this dataset, however we think it should be listed when discussing all relevant datasets.

5.2 WordSim353-CZ

WordSim353-CZ (Cinková, 2016) is a Czech version of WordSim (Finkelstein et al., 2002), which is another dataset on word relatedness. The data are again triplets, word pair and a score (though technically the Czech dataset contains other information for each pair).

The author decided to create a dataset as similar as possible to the original, which especially means she encouraged the annotators to annotate relatedness, even though the name refers to similarity.

During the process of creating the dataset, four candidate translations were suggested for each of the original pairs, and 25 annotators annotated all reasonable pairs. The authors then selected the pairs so that the correlation between Czech and English rankings is maximal.

A version with all annotated pairs is available but we stick to the selected subset in our experiments.

5.3 Czech similarity and relatedness

The dataset for Czech similarity and relatedness (Konopik et al., 2017) not only enables another evaluation of word similarity, it also addresses the problem of scoring words which are closely related but not really similar (those may be e.g. antonyms or pairs like beach and sand). This dataset contains 953 words.

The authors decided to build the dataset from several different resources. They translated random pairs from several English datasets, RG-65 (Rubenstein and Goodenough, 1965), WordSim (Finkelstein et al., 2002), MTurk (Radinsky et al., 2011), Rare words (Luong et al., 2013) and MEN (Bruni et al., 2014). They also mined translational data using Moses (Koehn et al., 2007) and CzEng (Bojar et al., 2016), language part of Czech general study tests SCIO, and they invented a few pairs on their own.

Word pairs were annotated by 5 annotators and each of them annotated both similarity and relatedness, the annotators achieved Spearman correlation of 0.81.

The dataset itself does not contain only the word pairs and their scores but also examples of their usage, examples of ambiguities (sentences containing the same word with different meaning) and examples of the two words co-occuring; all examples were taken from the Czech National Corpus.

5.4 Czech analogy corpus

Czech analogy corpus was presented as a part of embedding-related experiments by Svoboda and Brychcín (2016), and it mimics the Google analogy test set.[6]

---

[6]http://download.tensorflow.org/data/questions-words.txt

It contains 11 relationship categories. Of those, 4 are purely semantic (capital cities and three groups of antonym relations, further divided based on part-of-speech), 3 are purely syntactic (noun plural, verb past tense, adjective gradation), 3 are rather syntactic (gender variation of job names and of nationalities, grammatic number variation of pronouns, including pairs like I and we) and 1 is rather semantic (family relations, i.e. he-cousin to she-cousin as father to mother). While family relations is in fact gender variation of family roles, feminime variants usually cannot be derived from masculine ones.

There is also a phrase version which contains some additional categories but we use the version containing single words only.

5.5 Extended semantic analogies

We have developed four additional analogy categories and word pairs representing those categories. These categories are: old or even archaic words and more modern words with the same / close enough meaning, e.g. *biograf* and *kino* 'cinema'; diminutives, e.g. *máma* 'mum' and *maminka* 'mummy'; more foreign-sounding (often expert) words and their more Czech-sounding variants, e.g. *akceptovat* and *přijmout* '(to) accept'; and synonyms.

While we understand and acknowledge the ambiguity of listed relations, we believe some ambiguity accompanies also antonyms and family relations, and we are curious about the model performance.

5.6 Synonym retrieval

We propose evaluating word embeddings also on synonym retrieval. Using our department thesaurus, we have randomly selected 500 words known to have at least 5 synonyms. (No two tested words are synonyms of each other.)

For each tested word, we find 10 words having the most similar vectors and we evaluate the top-1, top-3 and top-5 precision. We do it both with respect to the answer really given and with respect to an oracle which would move true synonyms to top positions whenever they would appear within the 10 candidates.

Please note that even though Leeuwenberg et al (2016) have shown that relative cosine similarity is a better approach to synonym extraction, it does not make a great difference in our case because we do not need to set a similarity threshold between synonyms and non-synonyms.

6 Results

We evaluated all trained models on all available datasets, with the exception of BERT embeddings which were only evaluated on WordSim353-CZ and Czech similarity and relatedness dataset. Please keep in mind that we were not able to train fastText on Czech National Corpus using forms and LexVec on Czech National Corpus using either forms or lemmata.

When evaluating analogies, we have tried using both 3CosAdd suggested by Mikolov et al (2013b) and 3CosMul suggested by Levy and Goldbert (2014) as similarity objective. To evaluate similarity, we use cosine similarity in all tasks.

Since the number of trained and evaluated models is high, we do not report results for each of the models. Instead, we do the following:

- Divide the tasks into five groups: syntactic analogies, semantic analogies, extended analogies, similarity/relatedness assignment and synonym retrieval. For each group, we identify all models which achieve the best result on any task within this group, and for all such models, we report results on all tasks within this group. We also report the performace of BERT embeddings on the similarity/relatedness group.

- Report a basic approximation of parameter volatility, given by differences in performance when only the parameter in question is changed.

- Discuss the patterns we have noticed during our examination of all results.

Table 1 shows the results on syntactic analogies. Please note that the dominance of models trained on forms is expected since models trained on lemmata are not able to solve purely syntactic tasks (plural, past tense, pronouns, gradation). The nonzero accuracy of lemmatized models on plural is only possible due to a dataset lemmatization error.

The achieved accuracies are pleasing, with a notable exception of pronoun analogies. We suspect this could be because the pronoun analogies in fact mix several aspects, i.e. there are pairs like *já* 'I' - *my* 'we' but also *mého* 'my (sg., i.e. my thing)' - *mých* 'my (pl., i.e. my things)', instead of *mého*

	fastText Wiki forms 3CosMul	Word2Vec CNC forms 3CosAdd	Word2Vec CNC forms 3CosMul	LexVec CzEng forms 3CosMul	fastText CNC lemmata 3CosMul
Plural	**71.85**	64.11	64.04	68.17	2.70
Jobs	83.92	**87.54**	85.35	80.72	75.00
Past tense	**89.02**	66.58	67.84	87.79	0.00
Pronouns	7.54	9.79	**10.98**	10.45	0.00
Gradation	60.00	62.50	60.00	**70.00**	0.00
Nations	43.18	25.19	28.03	40.15	**67.52**

Table 1: Results on syntactic analogies; numbers were always kept in place; both Word2Vec and fastText were trained using CBOW architecture

	LexVec CzEng lemmata meta 3CosAdd	Word2Vec Wiki lemmata meta 3CosAdd	LexVec Wiki forms numbers 3CosAdd	Word2Vec CNC lemmata meta 3CosAdd	LexVec CzEng lemmata numbers 3CosMul
Anto-nouns	**23.33**	13.44	17.28	14.72	18.56
Anto-adj	20.96	**31.71**	3.54	23.17	20.15
Anto-verbs	6.79	5.27	**13.66**	7.68	6.70
City/state	5.35	41.62	3.03	**54.72**	5.08
Family	45.99	41.98	8.03	43.83	**48.61**

Table 2: Results on semantic analogies;

	CNC numbers 3CosMul	CNC meta 3CosAdd	CNC meta 3CosMul	CzEng numbers 3CosMul
Archaic	**18.92**	15.92	17.72	7.56
Diminutives	25.97	**27.66**	**27.66**	13.97
Expert	23.09	19.63	**23.48**	14.19
Synonyms	20.27	19.79	19.79	**26.71**
Total	22.80	21.32	**23.17**	14.83

Table 3: Results on extended analogies; all models were trained using Word2Vec with CBOW architecture, corpus was always lemmatized

'my' - *našeho* 'our'. The possessive pronouns are also given in genitive/accusative (same forms are used for both cases) while the personal pronouns are given in nominative.

Results on semantic analogies are reported in table 2, and results on extended analogies are given in table 3.

Consistently with Svoboda and Brychcín (2016), we have found that CBOW outperforms skip-gram on Czech, which is not consistent with the results observed on English (Mikolov et al., 2013b). We hypothesize this could be due to relatively free word order and strong inflection and conjugation found in Czech. For example, while the two sentences *Profesor pochválil studenta* and *Studenta pochválil profesor* 'A professor praised a student', have a different meaning with respect to topic-focus articulation, they can be both utilized in Czech to communicate roughly the same thing. In English, changing the word order would also require transforming the verb. Therefore, a single Czech word could be less predictive than a single English word, making skip-gram less effective.

The best result is not always achieved using the largest corpus available. Out of 15 analogy classes, 4 are best solved when training on

Wikipedia dump. The difference is very subtle for noun plural, rather subtle for past tense and verb antonyms (with LexVec trained on CzEng being the second in all cases) but high for adjective antonyms (the best non-wiki model achieves accuracy of 25.67). While we are not able to truly explain, we suspect several factors could be responsible: Wikipedia dump is probably more consistent in style than both other corpora (which are compilations of various sources); many pages originated as English Wikipedia translation and thus are likely to follow English stylistics, making the language more similar to English; its encyclopaedic nature could make the language more regular in general. Perhaps these properties could outweight the corpus size.

However, CNC in general gives good results on extended analogies. We suppose its size does make an advantage, though indirectly, by making the appearance of queried words in the corpus more likely and their contexts more recognizable (some words are unusual in Czech, especially words from archaic and expert analogies).

We notice that while syntactic analogies are better solved by models trained on forms (with the exception of gendered nationality analogies), most semantic analogies are better solved by models trained on lemmata. We suppose this is due to large numbers of word forms for each lemma (a prototypic Czech noun has 14 forms, adjectives and verbs have even more), further strengthened by lemmata having some basic sense disambiguation annotation.

The exception to lemmata performing better are verbal antonyms. The best lemma-based model achieves accuracy of 10.18, which is notably lower than the best result. We are not sure about the cause. However, verbs have lots of forms (which all get lemmatized to the same string) and many verbal forms contain auxiliary words, often also verbal. The combination of that could make distinguisting contexts more difficult.

Table 4 gives the results on similarity tasks. To evaluate BERT on Czech similarity and relatedness dataset, we extracted all example sentences (which are given to demonstrate the use of the word with the desired meaning) and inferred the embeddings of all words in them. We then used the embeddings of the queried words to evaluate the model.[7]

We were quite surprised to see the relatively low results of BERT, compared to other models. We suspect the elimination of accented characters could hurt BERT performance since accents may differentiate meaning in Czech and the removal of accented characters might produce the same string (as turning both *malý* 'small (masculine)' and *malá* 'small (feminime)' into *mal*; *můra* 'moth' and *míra* 'measure, rate' to *mra*) or even to valid Czech words (as turning *zeď* 'wall' into *ze* 'from'). However, this should be rather rare, except for systematic occurences as with the masculine and feminime adjectives.

We find it more likely that BERT performance is hurt by inferring embeddings of rather artificial sentences. For WordSim, the sentences had only the queried words. For the similarity and relatedness dataset, these were true sentences, but without further context.

The results on synonym retrieval are reported in table 5. We again see that CBOW architecture outperforms skip-gram, which might be because of relatively free word order in Czech. The effect could be even stronger in context of synonym retrieval, as the distinction e.g. between subject and object could also be the distinction between (near-)synonym and (near-)antonym verb.

The corpus size might be a more important factor than model selection for synonym retrieval. Even though moving from forms to lemmata helps both in general and specifically with this task, models trained on unlemmatized CNC often outperformed models trained on lemmatized CzEng. However, Word2Vec/CBOW trained on smaller lemmatized corpus still outperformed other models trained on CNC. Unfortunately, we cannot be sure about the performance of LexVec on CNC but its performance on CzEng is 30%-70% of word2vec/CBOW performance with the remaining parameters matching.

We have also noticed that while oracle precision is good, the synonyms often do not come first. The exact precisions differ but for all models, the real precision is one third to one half of oracle precision.

In all our experiments, GloVe did not perform

---

[7]Technically, we first associated the word with a unique

identifier, added the identifier and the inferred embedding to a special model using gensim, and finally evaluated this special model against the translation of the dataset into the identifiers. The identifiers are needed since embeddings are contextualized, i.e. different for the same word in different contexts, but gensim only supports mapping one word to one embedding.

	fastText CNC meta	LexVec CzEng numbers	BERT
SimRel/Similarity	**72.45**	65.39	46.90
SimRel/Relatedness	**66.51**	62.14	38.63
WordSim353-CZ	69.17	**70.41**	13.88

Table 4: Results (Spearman correlation coefficient) on similarity tasks; All models were trained on lemmatized corpus; fastText was trained using CBOW architecture

	numbers	meta-numbers
Top-1 oracle	**78.10**	74.79
Top-3 oracle	47.80	**49.45**
Top-5 oracle	32.07	**32.48**
Top-1 precision	**35.12**	33.88
Top-3 precision	**26.86**	26.45
Top-5 precision	21.65	**22.15**

Table 5: Results on synonym retrieval; Models were trained using Word2Vec/CBOW on lemmatized CNC

well. The rank of best performing GloVe model was usually around 30, therefore being worse than about a quarter of all other models. It is however possible that GloVe would benefit from tweaking the parameters more carefully. Altering a parameter often has the opposite effect on GloVe than on other modesl, which also encourages this assumption. Still, it should be noted that this result again is consistent with the findings of Svoboda and Brychcín (2016), who discovered GloVe performed worse than Word2Vec on Czech.

Despite all the research into incorporating subword information into embeddings (which is, among other, motivated by morphologically rich languages), models trained on lemmata perform better that their counterparts trained on forms. Tasks which require form distinguishing are a natural exception to this. We suspect this gap is partially caused by some forms being quite different from its lemma (and therefore hardly connectable on form/subword level), by lots of forms being only seemingly similar (sharing a long substring but meaning a different thing), and also by some forms appearing in specific contexts only (making the model learn a relation more specific than it should be).

However, we believe performing a strictly syntactic evaluation of embeddings which would focus on deriving correctly inflected/conjugated

forms would be an interesting experiment to evaluate to benefits of subword information in morphologically rich languages.

As has been already mentioned, CBOW outperforms skip-gram on Czech. The difference is bigger on syntactic analogies; CBOW advantage is less clear in fastText models than Word2Vec models and on similarity tasks (in which CBOW only outperforms skip-gram if trained on lemmata).

Word2Vec with CBOW architecture generally performs well, though there are tasks (especially similarity assignment) on which LexVec gives notably better results.

Number substitution with meta-words alters the results only slightly. Though sometimes the best result is achieved by a model trained on text with those meta-words, the substitution hurts more often than it helps.

Similarly, the difference in analogy performance between different similarity objectives is rather subtle, though it is notable that semantic analogies are generally best solved with 3CosAdd objective while syntactic analogies are generally best solved with 3CosMul. However, this pattern is not repeated in extended analogies which are mostly semantic but best solved with 3CosMul (though the results on extended analogies are low which might further reduce the effect of similarity objective).

In general, training on CzEng instead of CNC results in worse results, suggesting CNC is more appropriate for training word embeddings. The difference of size is likely to play a role, but without further investigations we cannot eliminate the possibility that the fact that CzEng is comprised of more different text types also worsens (or possibly improves) the results.

The comparison of training with CzEng and Wikipedia dump is less one-sided. In most cases, moving from CzEng to Wikipedia dump has a negative impact, however it does improve the re-

Parameter	Mean	Deviation	Maximum
model	9.61	12.62	87.54
corpus	7.22	9.38	55.61
form/lemma	13.87	19.85	89.02
form/lemma*	5.89	6.36	30.30
numbers	1.13	1.70	15.00
similarity objective	1.58	2.34	18.54

Table 6: Approximation of parameter volatility given by the distribution of performance differences (percent points) when altering the parameter with all remaining parameters fixed; Minimum difference is always 0; similarity objective is only taken into account on analogy tasks; * line refers to values when skipping noun plural, past tense, pronouns and gradation which are by nature unsolvable by lemmata-based models

sults on several task/model combinations (especially syntactic analogies). We also noticed that on similarity assignment, LexVec performs better than most models when both are trained on CzEng but worse when trained on Wikipedia dump (the comparison for CNC is not available). The effects of moving from CNC to Wikipedia dump are similar to effects of moving from CNC to CzEng (i.e. usually negative).

7 Conclusion

We have presented an intrinsic evaluation of Czech word embeddings. We have evaluated several models trained on three different corpora, using different strategies during the training process. We have evaluated the resulting embeddings on a variaty of tasks – analogy, similarity, synonym retrieval.

The most important of our findings, regarding model selection, are that GloVe model using the default parameter settings does not seem to work well on Czech, that CBOW architecture of Word2Vec/fastText generally outperforms the Skip-gram architecture (unlike on English) and that LexVec performs fairly well in our experiments. It is worth noting that model selection affected the results more than corpus selection.

While bigger corpus might be expected to give better results, our results regarding corpus size are mixed. In most cases, the best performing model is trained on CNC, the largest corpus we have used, and if the best result is achieved using CzEng, the model is usually LexVec (which we were not able to train on CNC). However, the best result in several tasks is achieved using Wikipedia dump. We hypothesize the encyclopaedic nature of Wikipedia and the similarity of its language to English (following from many pages being translated or based on their English counterparts) could be important factors.

We have also found that models trained on lemmatized corpus usually perform better. Given that lemmatization tools are available for Czech, we would therefore recommend lemmatizing the text even when training on models which employ subword information. We hypothesize the differences of forms as well as some basic sense disambiguation might play a role.

We have several future goals which have emerged from the described work. Obviously, overcoming the limitations and being able to train all models on any corpus is one of them. We expect to try reformumalting the analogy task so that there can be more than one correct answer (which is clearly useless for tasks like currect capitals but might be interesting for tasks like antonyms or diminutives). We would also like to create more syntactic tasks to further evaluate the benefits of subword information, train the models on corpora subsets to better evaluate the effect of using bigger corpus, and carefully evaluate analogies and synonym retrieval using contextualized embeddings.

Acknowledgement

This work has been supported by the grant No. 1704218 of the Grant Agency of Charles University and the grant No. 19-19191S of the Grant Agency of Czech Republic. It has been using language resources and tools stored and distributed by the LINDAT/CLARIN project of the Ministry of Education, Youth and Sports of the Czech Republic (project LM2015071). The research was also partially supported by SVV project number 260 453.

References

Marco Baroni, Georgiana Dinu, and Germán Kruszewski. 2014. Don't count, predict! a systematic comparison of context-counting vs. context-predicting semantic vectors. In *Proceedings of the 52nd Annual Meeting of the Association for Computational Linguistics (Volume 1: Long Papers)*, volume 1, pages 238–247.

Piotr Bojanowski, Edouard Grave, Armand Joulin, and Tomas Mikolov. 2017. Enriching word vectors with subword information. *Transactions of the Association for Computational Linguistics*, 5:135–146.

Ondřej Bojar, Ondřej Dušek, Tom Kocmi, Jindřich Libovický, Michal Novák, Martin Popel, Roman Sudarikov, and Dušan Variš. 2016. CzEng 1.6: Enlarged Czech-English Parallel Corpus with Processing Tools Dockered. In *Text, Speech, and Dialogue: 19th International Conference, TSD 2016*, number 9924 in Lecture Notes in Computer Science, pages 231–238, Cham / Heidelberg / New York / Dordrecht / London. Masaryk University, Springer International Publishing.

Elia Bruni, Nam-Khanh Tran, and Marco Baroni. 2014. Multimodal distributional semantics. *Journal of Artificial Intelligence Research*, 49:1–47.

Silvie Cinková. 2016. Wordsim353 for czech. In *International Conference on Text, Speech, and Dialogue*, pages 190–197. Springer.

Jacob Devlin, Ming-Wei Chang, Kenton Lee, and Kristina Toutanova. 2018. Bert: Pre-training of deep bidirectional transformers for language understanding. *arXiv preprint arXiv:1810.04805*.

Manaal Faruqui, Jesse Dodge, Sujay K Jauhar, Chris Dyer, Eduard Hovy, and Noah A Smith. 2014. Retrofitting word vectors to semantic lexicons. *arXiv preprint arXiv:1411.4166*.

Lev Finkelstein, Evgeniy Gabrilovich, Yossi Matias, Ehud Rivlin, Zach Solan, Gadi Wolfman, and Eytan Ruppin. 2002. Placing search in context: The concept revisited. *ACM Transactions on information systems*, 20(1):116–131.

Philipp Koehn, Hieu Hoang, Alexandra Birch, Chris Callison-Burch, Marcello Federico, Nicola Bertoldi, Brooke Cowan, Wade Shen, Christine Moran, Richard Zens, et al. 2007. Moses: Open source toolkit for statistical machine translation. In *Proceedings of the 45th annual meeting of the association for computational linguistics companion volume proceedings of the demo and poster sessions*, pages 177–180.

Miloslav Konopik, Ondřej Pražák, and David Steinberger. 2017. Czech dataset for semantic similarity and relatedness. In *Proceedings of the International Conference Recent Advances in Natural Language Processing, RANLP 2017*, pages 401–406.

Lubomír Krčmář, Miloslav Konopík, and Karel Jezek. 2011. Exploration of semantic spaces obtained from Czech corpora. In *DATESO*, pages 97–107.

Michal Křen, Václav Cvrček, Tomáš Čapka, Anna Čermáková, Milena Hnátková, Lucie Chlumská, Tomáš Jelínek, Dominika Kováříková, Vladimír Petkevič, Pavel Procházka, Hana Skoumalová, Michal Škrabal, Petr Truneček, Pavel Vondřička, and Adrian Zasina. 2016. SYN v4: large corpus of written czech. LINDAT/CLARIN digital library at the Institute of Formal and Applied Linguistics (ÚFAL), Faculty of Mathematics and Physics, Charles University.

Artuur Leeuwenberg, Mihaela Vela, Jon Dehdari, and Josef van Genabith. 2016. A minimally supervised approach for synonym extraction with word embeddings. *The Prague Bulletin of Mathematical Linguistics*, 105(1):111–142.

Omer Levy and Yoav Goldberg. 2014. Linguistic regularities in sparse and explicit word representations. In *Proceedings of the eighteenth conference on computational natural language learning*, pages 171–180.

Thang Luong, Richard Socher, and Christopher Manning. 2013. Better word representations with recursive neural networks for morphology. In *Proceedings of the Seventeenth Conference on Computational Natural Language Learning*, pages 104–113.

Tomas Mikolov, Kai Chen, Greg Corrado, and Jeffrey Dean. 2013a. Efficient estimation of word representations in vector space. *arXiv preprint arXiv:1301.3781*.

Tomas Mikolov, Ilya Sutskever, Kai Chen, Greg S Corrado, and Jeff Dean. 2013b. Distributed representations of words and phrases and their compositionality. In *Advances in neural information processing systems*, pages 3111–3119.

Nikola Mrkšić, Diarmuid O Séaghdha, Blaise Thomson, Milica Gašić, Lina Rojas-Barahona, Pei-Hao Su, David Vandyke, Tsung-Hsien Wen, and Steve Young. 2016. Counter-fitting word vectors to linguistic constraints. *arXiv preprint arXiv:1603.00892*.

Neha Nayak, Gabor Angeli, and Christopher D Manning. 2016. Evaluating word embeddings using a representative suite of practical tasks. In *Proceedings of the 1st Workshop on Evaluating Vector-Space Representations for NLP*, pages 19–23.

Jeffrey Pennington, Richard Socher, and Christopher Manning. 2014. Glove: Global vectors for word representation. In *Proceedings of the 2014 conference on empirical methods in natural language processing (EMNLP)*, pages 1532–1543.

Matthew E Peters, Mark Neumann, Mohit Iyyer, Matt Gardner, Christopher Clark, Kenton Lee, and Luke

Zettlemoyer. 2018. Deep contextualized word representations. *arXiv preprint arXiv:1802.05365*.

Kira Radinsky, Eugene Agichtein, Evgeniy Gabrilovich, and Shaul Markovitch. 2011. A word at a time: computing word relatedness using temporal semantic analysis. In *Proceedings of the 20th international conference on World wide web*, pages 337–346. ACM.

Radim Řehůřek and Petr Sojka. 2010. Software Framework for Topic Modelling with Large Corpora. In *Proceedings of the LREC 2010 Workshop on New Challenges for NLP Frameworks*, pages 45–50, Valletta, Malta. ELRA. `http://is.muni.cz/publication/884893/en`.

Herbert Rubenstein and John B Goodenough. 1965. Contextual correlates of synonymy. *Communications of the ACM*, 8(10):627–633.

Alexandre Salle, Marco Idiart, and Aline Villavicencio. 2016a. Enhancing the lexvec distributed word representation model using positional contexts and external memory. *arXiv preprint arXiv:1606.01283*.

Alexandre Salle and Aline Villavicencio. 2018. Incorporating subword information into matrix factorization word embeddings. In *Proceedings of the Second Workshop on Subword/Character LEvel Models*, pages 66–71.

Alexandre Salle, Aline Villavicencio, and Marco Idiart. 2016b. Matrix factorization using window sampling and negative sampling for improved word representations. In *Proceedings of the 54th Annual Meeting of the Association for Computational Linguistics (Volume 2: Short Papers)*, volume 2, pages 419–424.

Hinrich Schütze. 1993. Word space. In *Advances in neural information processing systems*, pages 895–902.

Jana Straková, Milan Straka, and Jan Hajič. 2014. Open-Source Tools for Morphology, Lemmatization, POS Tagging and Named Entity Recognition. In *Proceedings of 52nd Annual Meeting of the Association for Computational Linguistics: System Demonstrations*, pages 13–18, Baltimore, Maryland. Association for Computational Linguistics.

Lukáš Svoboda and Tomáš Brychcín. 2016. New word analogy corpus for exploring embeddings of Czech words. In *International Conference on Intelligent Text Processing and Computational Linguistics*, pages 103–114. Springer.

Wilson L Taylor. 1953. "Cloze procedure": A new tool for measuring readability. *Journalism Bulletin*, 30(4):415–433.

Yulia Tsvetkov, Manaal Faruqui, Wang Ling, Guillaume Lample, and Chris Dyer. 2015. Evaluation of word vector representations by subspace alignment. In *Proceedings of the 2015 Conference on Empirical Methods in Natural Language Processing*, pages 2049–2054.

Language Modeling with Syntactic and Semantic Representation for Sentence Acceptability Predictions

Adam Ek   **Jean-Phillipe Bernardy**   **Shalom Lappin**

Centre for Linguistic Theory and Studies in Probability
Department of Philosophy, Linguistics and Theory of Science
University of Gothenburg
{adam.ek, jean-philippe.bernardy, shalom.lappin}@gu.se

Abstract

In this paper, we investigate the effect of enhancing lexical embeddings in LSTM language models (LM) with syntactic and semantic representations. We evaluate the language models using perplexity, and we evaluate the performance of the models on the task of predicting human sentence acceptability judgments. We train LSTM language models on sentences automatically annotated with universal syntactic dependency roles (Nivre et al., 2016), dependency tree depth features, and universal semantic tags (Abzianidze et al., 2017) to predict sentence acceptability judgments. Our experiments indicate that syntactic depth and tags lower the perplexity compared to a plain LSTM language model, while semantic tags increase the perplexity. Our experiments also show that neither syntactic nor semantic tags improve the performance of LSTM language models on the task of predicting sentence acceptability judgments.

1 Introduction

Lau et al. (2014) show that human acceptability judgments are graded rather than binary. It is not entirely obvious what determines sentence acceptability for speakers and listeners. However, syntactic structure and semantic content are clearly central to acceptability judgments. In fact, as Lau et al. (2015, 2017) show, it is possible to use a language model, augmented with a scoring function, to predict acceptability. Standard RNN language models perform fairly well on the sentence acceptability prediction task.

By experimenting with different sorts of enrichments of the training data, one can explore their effect on both the perplexity and the predictive accuracy of the LM. For example, Bernardy et al. (2018) report that including contextual information in training and testing improves the performance of an LSTM LM on the acceptability task, when contextual information is contributed by preceding and following sentences in a document.

Here we report several experiments on the possible contribution of symbolic representations of semantic and syntactic features to the accuracy of LSTM LMs in predicting human sentence acceptability judgments. [1]

For semantic tags, we use the Universal Semantic Tagging scheme, which provides language independent and fine-grained semantic categories for individual words (Abzianidze et al., 2017). We take our syntactic roles from the Universal Dependency Grammar scheme (Nivre et al., 2016). This allows us to assign to each word in a sentence a semantic and a syntactic role, respectively.

Our working hypothesis is that for a language model the syntactic and semantic annotations will highlight semantic and syntactic patterns observed in the data. Therefore sentences that exhibit these patterns should be more acceptable than sentences which diverge from them. One would expect that if we get lower perplexity for one of the tagging scheme LMs, then its performance would improve on the acceptability prediction task. Clearly, better performance on this task indicates that tagging supplies useful information for predicting acceptability.

2 Experimental Setup

First, we train a set of language models, some of them on tag annotated corpora, and some on plain text. While we are interested in the effect of the tags on model perplexity, our main concern is to measure the influence of the tags on an LSTM

---

[1]Our training and test sets, and the code for generating our LSTM LM models are available at https://github.com/GU-CLASP/predicting-acceptability.

LM's predictive power in the sentence acceptability task.

We implement four variants of LSTM language models. The first model is a plain LSTM that predicts the next word based on the previous sequence of words. The second, third and fourth models predict the next word w_i conditioned on the previous sequence of words and tags, for which we write $P_M(w_i)$. For a model M that uses syntactic or semantic information:

$$P_M(w_i) = P(w_i|(w_{i-1}, t_{i-1}), ..., (w_{i-n}, t_{i-n})) \tag{1}$$

We stress that the current tag (t_i) is not given when the model predicts the current word (w_i).

Using the main hyperparameters from a previous similar experiment (Bernardy et al., 2018), all language models use a unidirectional LSTM of size 600. We apply a drop-out of 0.4 after the LSTM layer. The models are trained on a vocabulary of 100,000 words. We randomly initialise word embeddings of size 300 dimensions, and tag embeddings of size 30 dimensions. Each model is trained for 10 epochs.

Following the literature on acceptability (Lau et al., 2015, 2017; Bernardy et al., 2018), we predict a judgment by applying a variant of the scoring function SLOR (Pauls and Klein, 2012) to a model's predictions.

2.1 SLOR

To estimate sentence acceptability, we use a length-normalized *syntactic log-odds ratio* (hereafter simply referred to as SLOR). We use SLOR rather than any other measurements since it was shown to have the best results in a previous study (Lau et al., 2015). It is calculated by taking the logarithm of the ratio to the probability of the sentence s predicted by a model M (P_M) with the probability predicted by the unigram model (P_U), divided by the length of the sequence $|s|$.

$$SLOR_M(s) = \frac{\log(P_M(s)) - \log(P_U(s))}{|s|} \tag{2}$$

where $P_M(s) = \prod_{i=1}^{|s|} P_M(w_i)$, and $P_U(s) = \prod_{i=1}^{|s|}(P_U(w_i))$. This formula discounts the effect of both word frequency and sentence length on the acceptability score that it assigns to the sentence. SLOR has been found to be a robustly effective scoring function for the acceptability prediction task (Lau et al., 2015).

2.2 Model evaluation

We evaluate the model by calculating the Weighted Pearson correlation coefficient between the SLOR score assigned by the model and the judgments assigned by the annotators.

Even though we show only the mean judgment in Figure 3, each data point comes also with a variance (there is heteroscedasticity). Thus we have chosen to weight the data points with the inverse of the variance when computing the Pearson correlation, as is standard when computing least square regression on heteroscedastic data.

We report the weighted correlation point wise between all models, and between each model and the human judgments. Additionally, we perform three experiments where we shuffle the syntactic and semantic representations in the test sentences. This is done to determine if the tags provide useful information for the task.

2.3 Language Model Training Data

For training the LMs we selected the English part of the CoNLL 2017 dataset (Nivre et al., 2017). The input sentences were taken from a subset of this corpus. We used only 1/10 of the total CoNNL 2017 Wikipedia corpus, randomly selected. We took out all sentences whose dependency root is not a verb, thus eliminating titles and other non-sentences. We also removed all sentences longer than 30 words. After filtering, the training data contained 87M tokens and 5.3M sentences.

3 Semantic Tags

We train a LSTM model for predicting semantic tags. We use this model to tag both the training set extracted from the CoNLL 2017 corpus, and the crowdsource annotated test set (described in Section 6).

The Universal semantic tagging scheme provides fine-grained semantic tags for tokens. It includes 80 different semantic labels. The semantic tags are similar to Part-of-Speech (POS) tags, but they are intended to generalise and to semantically disambiguate POS tags. For many purposes, POS tags do not provide enough information for semantic processing, and this is where semantic tags come into play. A significant element of POS disambiguation consists in assigning proper nouns to semantic classes (named entities). In this way, the scheme also provides a form of named entity recognition. The scheme is designed to be language independent. Annotations currently exist for English, German, Dutch and Italian, but we only use the English labels in our model.

The corpus of semantically tagged sentences that we use comes from the Parallel Meaning Bank (PMB) (Abzianidze et al., 2017). It contains 1.4M tagged tokens divided into 68,177 sentences[2]. The dataset is extracted from a variety of sources: Tatoeba, News Commentary, Recognizing Textual Entailment (RTE), Sherlock Holmes stories, and the Bible. The sentences are split into gold and silver annotations, where the gold has been manually annotated, and the silver has been annotated by a parser with manual corrections. The silver annotations are mostly correct, but may contain some errors.

Example (1) below is a semantically tagged sentence, taken from the PMB corpus. It includes two pronouns 'he' and 'his'. Both of these instanti-

(1)   He   took   his   book   .
        PRO   EPS   HAS   CON   NIL

ate the same POS, but their semantic classes are distinct. The first is a simple third person pronoun, while the second is a possessive pronoun. Semantic tags are able to handle this distinction, by assigning PRO (pronoun) to the third person pronoun, and HAS (possessive) to the possessive pronoun.

3.1 Semantic Tagging Model

To assign semantic tags to the CoNNL 2017 training corpus and our training set we use a bidirectional LSTM of size 256, with a standard configuration. The model is trained with a batch size of 512 sentences. The word embeddings are of size 256 and are randomly initialized. The model is implemented with keras (Chollet et al., 2015). We stress that this model is separate from the language models used to predict sentence acceptability.

The semantic tagging model is trained for a maximum of 1024 epochs, with early stopping if the validation loss does not improve after 32 epochs. For each epoch, we feed the model 64 batches of 512 randomly selected sentences. The model observes 32,768 sentences (e.g. roughly half of the corpus) per epoch. To select the best model we left out 1024 gold annotated sentences,

[2]Available for download at https://pmb.let.rug. nl/releases/sem-0.1.0.zip

randomly selected, and we used them for validation.

Performance   The model was validated on 1.5% of the sentences with gold annotations. The remaining data were used for training. This split was chosen because the primary goal of this model is a downstream task, namely tagging data for language modeling. We wish to maximise the number of sentences in the training data.

The model finished after 33 epochs, with a final validation loss of 0.317 and a validation accuracy of 91.1%. The performance of our model is similar to that of (Bjerva et al., 2016).

4 Syntactic Tags

To introduce syntactic information into our model in an explicit way, we provide it with Universal Dependency Grammar (UD) roles. The UD annotation scheme seeks to develop a unified syntactic annotation system that is language independent (Nivre et al., 2016). UD implements syntactic annotation through labelled directed graphs, where each edge represents a *dependency relation*. In total, UD contains 40 different dependency relations (or tags). For example, the sentence *'There is no known cure'* (taken from the CoNLL2017 Wikipedia corpus) is annotated as the dependency graph shown in Figure 1.

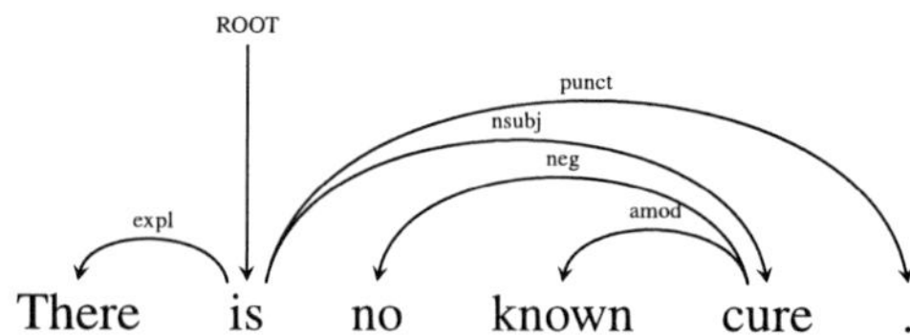

Figure 1: Dependency Graph

The model gives the label of the dependency originating from each word, which we call the *syntactic role* of the word. This label is provided as an additional feature for each word *in the input* to our language model. The model does not attempt to predict these roles. For the above sentence, the information given to our syntactic tag trained models would be:

    There   is   no   known   cure
     expl   root   neg   amod   nsubj

We use the Stanford Dependency Parser (Chen and Manning, 2014) to generate syntactic tags for the training and test sets.

5 Syntactic Depth

In addition to using syntactic and semantic tags, we also experiment with syntactic depth. To assign a depth to word n, we compute the number of common ancestors in the tree between word n and word $n + 1$. The last word is arbitrarily assigned depth 0. This method was proposed by Gómez-Rodríguez and Vilares (2018) for constituent trees, but the method works just as well for dependency trees. An example tree is shown below:

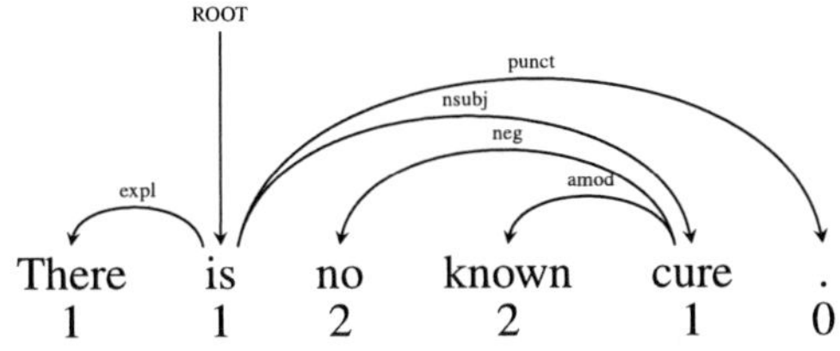

Figure 2: Linearized dependency graph

6 Test Set

The test set for evaluating our LMs comes from the work of Lau et al. (2015, 2017). 600 sentences were extracted from the BNC corpus (BNC Consortium, 2007) and filtered for length ($8 < |s| < 25$). After this filtering 500 sentences remained and were put through a round-trip machine translation process, from English to Norwegian, Spanish, Chinese or Japanese, and then back to English. In total, the test set contains 2500 sentences: 500 original sentences, and 500 from each language used for round-trip translation (i.e. Norwegian, Spanish, Chinese and Japanese). The purpose of using round-trip MT is to introduce a wide variety of infelicities into some of the sentence in our test set. This insures variation in acceptability judgements across the examples of the set.

We used Amazon Mechanical Turk (AMT) crowdsourcing to obtain acceptability judgments. The annotators were asked to rate the sentences based on their naturalness (as opposed to the theoretically committed notion of *well-formedness*) on a scale of 1 to 4. On average, each sentence had 14 annotators after filtering (for a more detailed description see (Lau et al., 2017)).

The results are shown in Table 1. The original sentences, and the sentences that were round-trip translated through Norwegian and Spanish have a higher mean rating than the sentences translated through Japanese and Chinese. The standard deviation is slightly higher for all the sentences which underwent round-trip translation, which is to be expected.

Table 1: Mean judgments and standard deviation for the test set.

SENTENCES	MEAN	ST-DEV
en	3.51	0.46
en–no–en	3.13	0.70
en–es–en	3.12	0.69
en–zh–en	2.42	0.72
en–ja–en	2.14	0.74

7 Results

Below we denote the plain LSTM LM by LSTM, the LM with syntactic tags as +SYN, the LM with semantic tags as +SEM, and the LM with syntactic tree depth as +DEPTH. We denote the models with shuffled tags by using the star (*) as a modifier.

7.1 Language Model Perplexity

We report in Table 3 the training loss for the plain-LSTM language model, and for the LSTM language models enhanced with syntactic and semantic tags. At the end of the training, the language model conditioned on syntactic tags shows the lowest loss. By definition loss is the logarithm of the perplexity. The semantic tag LM exhibits the highest degree of loss. It seems that the syntactic tags reduce LM perplexity, while the semantic tags increase it.

7.2 Acceptability Predictions

The matrix in Table 2 gives the results for the sentence acceptability prediction task. Each entry r_j^i indicates the weighted Pearson correlation r between $SLOR_i$ and $SLOR_j$. Scatter plots showing the correlation between human and model predictions are given in Figure 3

The plain LSTM performs close to the level that Bernardy et al. (2018) report for the same type of LM, trained and tested on English Wikipedia data. This indicates the robustness of this model for the sentence acceptability prediction task, given that, unlike the LSTM of Bernardy et al. (2018), it is trained on Wikipedia text, but tested on a BNC test set. Therefore, it sustains a relatively high level of performance on an out of domain test set.

Table 2: Weighted Pearson correlation between prediction from different models on the SMOG1 dataset. * indicates that the tags have been shuffled.

	HUMAN	LSTM	+SYN	+SYN*	+SEM	+SEM*	+DEPTH	+DEPTH*
HUMAN	1.00							
LSTM	**0.58**	1.00						
+SYN	0.55	0.96	1.00					
+SYN*	0.39	0.76	0.75	1.00				
+SEM	0.54	0.81	0.78	0.61	1.00			
+SEM*	0.52	0.81	0.78	0.63	0.96	1.00		
+DEPTH	0.56	0.97	0.97	0.74	0.79	0.79	1.00	
+DEPTH*	0.46	0.87	0.85	0.73	0.72	0.72	0.86	1.00

Table 3: Training loss and accuracy for the language modeling task.

MODEL	LOSS	ACCURACY
LSTM	5.04	0.24
+SYN	**4.79**	0.26
+SEM	5.23	0.21
+DEPTH	4.88	0.27

We also tested a model that combined depth markers and syntactic tags, which is, in effect, a full implicit labelled dependency tree model. Interestingly, its Pearson correlation of 0.54 was lower than the ones achieved by the syntactic tag and depth LSTM LMs individually.

None of the enhanced language models increases correlation with human judgments compared to the plain LSTM. Neither does the additional information significantly reduce correlation.

Shuffling the tags causes a drop of 0.16 in correlation for syntactic tags, and a drop of 0.1 for tree depth. Shuffling the semantic tags also lowers the correlation, but only by a small amount (-0.02).

8 Discussion

8.1 Semantic Tags

As can be observed in Table 3, the semantic tags show the highest loss during training. This indicates that semantic tags increase the perplexity of the model, and do not help to predict the next word in a sentence. Despite this, +SEM correlates fairly well with human judgments ($r = 0.54$).

The results obtained with shuffled semantic tags (+Sem*) are revealing. They yield a correlation factor nearly as high as the non-shuffled tags ($r = 0.53$). This suggests that the semantic tags *do not provide any useful information* for the prediction

task. This hypothesis is further confirmed by the high correlation between the non-shuffled and the shuffled semantic tag LMs ($r = 0.96$).

The question of why semantic tags do not reduce perplexity, or why randomly assigned semantic tags are almost as good as non-shuffled tags at predicting acceptability requires further study. One possibility is that the tagging model does not perform as well on the ConLL 2017 Wikipedia subset, or the BNC test set, as it does on the PMB corpus. It may be the case that since the domains are somewhat different, the model is not able to accurately predict tags for our training and test sets. Similarly, we do not know the accuracy of the Stanford Dependency Parser on the BNC test set.

8.2 Syntactic Tags

Providing syntactic tags improves the language model, but not the correlation of its predictions with mean human acceptability judgments. However, shuffling the syntactic tags does lower the correlation substantially. This indicates that syntactic tags significantly influence the predictions of the language model.

8.3 Tree Depth

The depth marker enriched LSTM performs best of all the feature enhanced models. Shuffling the markers significantly degrades accuracy, and the non-shuffled depth model achieves a reduction in perplexity. However, it still performs below the simple LSTM on the acceptability prediction task

It may be the case that the plain LSTM already acquires a significant amount of latent syntactic information, and adding explicit syntactic role labeling does not augment this information in a way that is accessible to LSTM learning. This con-

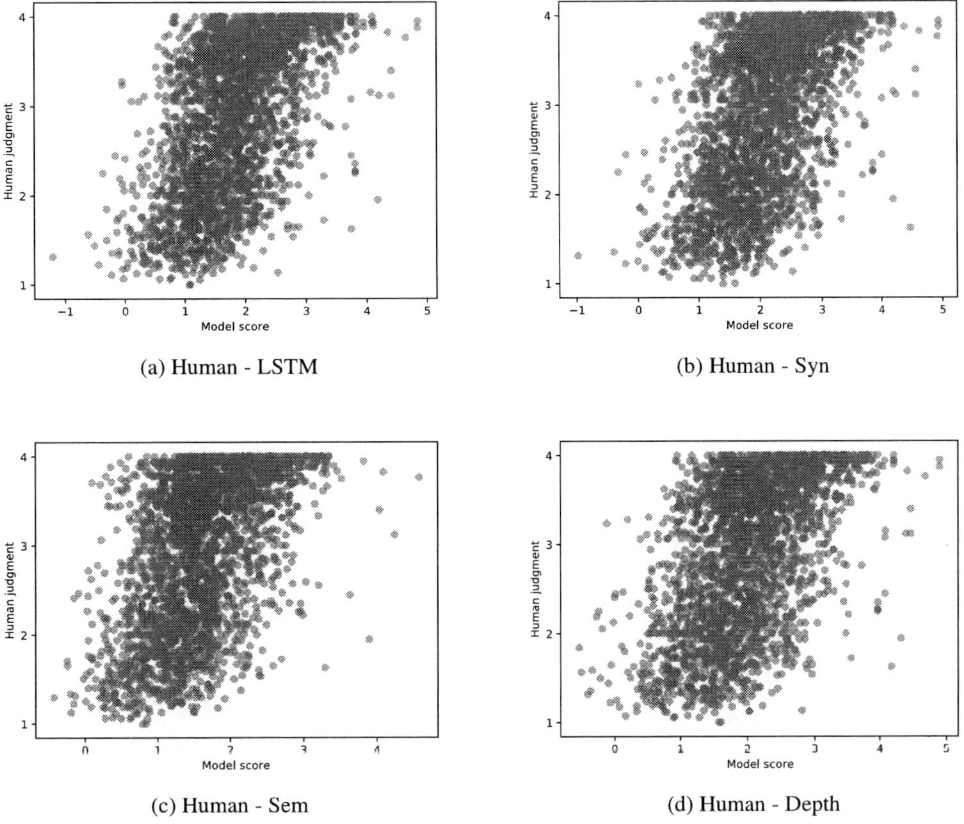

(a) Human - LSTM   (b) Human - Syn

(c) Human - Sem   (d) Human - Depth

Figure 3: Scatter plots showing the weighted Pearson correlation between human acceptability judgments (y-axis) and model predictions (x-axis).

clusion is supported by the work of Bernardy and Lappin (2017) on syntactic agreement. They observe that replacing a significant portion of the lexicon of an LSTM with POS tags degrades its capacity to predict agreement.

In general, our results do not show that syntactic and semantic information plays no role in the performance of any LM for the acceptability prediction task. It seems clear that the simple LSTM model learns both semantic and syntactic relations among words and phrases, but represents these in a distributed way through the encoding of lexical embeddings in vectors. In fact, there is a body of work which shows that such LSTMs recognise complex long-distance syntactic relations (Linzen et al., 2016; Bernardy and Lappin, 2017; Gulordava et al., 2018; Lakretz et al., 2019).

8.4 Error analysis

We analyse the models in two ways. First, we explore how they score sentences in the test set as categorised by the round-trip translation language that the sentences went through. Second, we look at two example sentences for which no model did particularly well.

8.4.1 Model performance on test sentences

To analyse the scores assigned by the model in comparison to the human judgments we first need to normalise the scores. We do this by dividing the score assigned to each sentence by the maximum score assigned. Thus, the relative score of a sentence indicates how close it is to the highest acceptability judgment.

The mean relative score of the human judgments and model scores are presented in Table 4. We observe that the models generally appear to assign a lower relative score than humans. But all models also appear to follow the general trend of human judgments and assign a lower score to the Chinese and Japanese round-trip translated sentences compared to the Spanish, Norwegian and original sentences. However, looking at the numbers the difference in magnitude for Chinese and

Japanese sentences is rather large. The Chinese and Japanese sentences have a lower relative score of 0.27 and 0.35 respectively. But for models, this difference is only ≈ 0.07 and ≈ 0.12 respectively. This indicates that while the models are able to see some acceptability differences between the subclasses of test sentences, the models do not penalize these sentences as much as humans.

Table 4: Comparison of the average relative score assigned by the models and humans for the different sentences in the test set.

MODEL	EN	NO	ES	ZH	JA
Human	0.88	0.78	0.78	0.61	0.53
LSTM	0.41	0.40	0.40	0.34	0.29
+SYN	0.46	0.44	0.45	0.39	0.35
+SEM	0.39	0.36	0.37	0.30	0.28
+DEPTH	0.45	0.43	0.44	0.38	0.34

We also note that the models consistently assign much lower relative scores than the human annotators do to most of the sentences. This, biases their scores in favour of the Chinese and Japanese target sentences, since these are typically 'worse' than their original English sources, or the Norwegian and Spanish targets, according to the human judges (see Table 1).

We also compare the worst scoring sentences between the models. This was done by splitting the predictions into two sets: (a) model scores above the average[3] and (b) model scores below the average. We sort these sets by their difference to the humans and select the top 20 sentences for each model. Table 5 shows the intersection of sentence sets for the different models.

Table 5: Shared erroneous sentences between the models.

MODEL	LSTM	+SYN	+SEM	+DEPTH
LSTM	40			
+SYN	30	40		
+SEM	19	15	40	
+DEPTH	30	28	17	40

We observe that the syntactic tag and depth models share many sentences with each other, and with the plain LSTM, but not as many with the

---

[3]We compare scores by dividing each score by it's maximum value, as described previously.

semantic model. This shows that the difficult sentences for the semantic model are different than those for the syntactic and plain models.

8.4.2 Model and human performance

We use the relative scores from the previous section to select sentences for examination. We look at two types of cases, one in which the model predicts a higher score than the human judgments, and the other where the model predicts a lower score than human judgments. For both cases we select a sentence at random.

We begin by considering an example to which the model assigns a higher score than humans do. The sentence went through Chinese:

(1) '1.5% Hispanic or Latino of any race population.'

The sentence lacks a verb, and the modifier-noun construction 'race population' is lexically strange. It is interesting to note that our syntactic models (+SYN and +DEPTH) both assign a high score to this sentence, while the semantic and plain LM assign a lower score (which is closer to the human judgment). We would think that the model using syntactic tags would pick up on the missing verb, and so penalize the sentence. The scores for the sentence (1) are shown in Table 6:

Table 6: Human judgments and model scores for sentence (1).

MODEL	RELATIVE	ABSOLUTE
HUMAN	0.40	1.62
LSTM	0.77	3.74
+SYN	0.90	4.47
+SEM	0.71	3.29
+DEPTH	0.85	4.17

For (1), the LM enhanced with semantic tags gave the sentence the lowest score. The syntactic and depth model gave the sentence a high score (0.90 and 0.85 respectively). This indicates that while still assigning the sentence a relatively high score, the semantic and plain LM rate the sentence closer to humans than the syntactical LM.

In the second case, (2), the sentence is one of the original English sentences:

(2) 'ACS makes a special "FAT" heavy duty BMX freewheel in 14T and 16T with 3/16 "teeth compatible only with 3/16" chains.'

The human annotators gave it an appropriately high score, but the models did not, as indicated in table Table 7.

Table 7: Human judgments and model scores for sentence (2).

MODEL	RELATIVE	ABSOLUTE
HUMAN	0.80	3.23
LSTM	-0.007	-0.03
+SYN	0.002	0.01
+SEM	0.26	1.20
+DEPTH	0.02	-0.01

Again, we can see that the LM enhanced with semantic tags performed the best (i.e. assigned the sentence the highest score). The sentence has a few features which might make it difficult for the standard LM and syntactically enhanced language models. The sentence contains a high number of quotations, acronyms (e.g. ACS) and specialized terms (e.g. 3/16). The dependency tags do not treat these words in any special way. Because the words arc rarc thcy arc not likcly candidatcs. The semantic tags will treat these words in a different manner, since it contains tags for named entities and quantities.

8.5 Pre-Trained Language Models

Recently several large pre-trained language models using transformation architecture, like BERT (Devlin et al., 2018), or bidirectional LSTM with attention, such as ELMo (Peters et al., 2018), have achieved state of the art results across a variety of NLP tasks. We opted not to experiment with any of these pre-trained language models for our task. The LSTM architecture of our LMs is far simpler, which facilitates testing the contribution of explicit feature representation to correlation in the acceptability prediction task, and perplexity for the language modeling task.

9 Related Work

There has been a considerable amount of work showing that encoding tree representations in deep neural networks, particularly LSTMs, improves their performance on semantic relatedness tasks. So, for example, Tai et al. (2015) show that Tree-LSTMs outperform simple LSTMs on SemEval 2014 Task 1, and sentiment classification. Similarly, Gupta and Zhang (2018) argue that by adding progressive attention to a Tree-LSTM it is possible to improve its performance on several semantic relatedness tasks.

Williams et al. (2018) describe a number of experiments with latent tree learning RNNs. These models learn tree structures implicitly, rather than through training on a parse annotated corpus. They construct their own parses. Williams et al. (2018) state that they outperform Tree-LSTM and other DNN models on semantic relatedness applications, and the Stanford Natural Language Inference task. Interestingly, the parse trees that they construct are not consistent across sentences, and they do not resemble the structures posited in formal syntactic or semantic theories. This result is consistent with our finding that LSTMs learn syntactic and semantic patterns in a way that is quite distinct from the classifications posited in classical grammatical and semantic systems of representation.

Finally, Warstadt and Bowman (2019) discuss the performance of several pre-trained transformer models on classifying sentences in their Corpus of Linguistic Acceptability (CoLA) as acceptable or not. These models exhibit levels of accuracy that vary widely relative to the types of syntactic and morphological patterns that appear in CoLA.

It is important to recognise that CoLA is a very different sort of test set from the one that we use in our experiments. It is drawn from linguists' examples intended to illustrate particular sorts of syntactic construction. It is annotated for binary classification according to linguists' judgments. By contrast, our BNC test set consists of naturally occurring text, where a wide range of infelicities are introduced into many of the sentences through round trip machine translation. It is annotated through AMT crowd sourcing with gradient acceptability judgments. Given these significant differences in design and annotation between the two test sets, applying our models to CoLA would have taken us beyond the scope of the sentence acceptability task, as specified in (Lau et al., 2015, 2017; Bernardy et al., 2018),

Moreover, our experiments are not focused on identifying the best performing model as such. Instead, we are interested in ascertaining whether enriching the training and test data with explicit syntactic and semantic classifier representations contributes to LSTM learning for the sentence acceptability prediction task.

10 Conclusions

We present experiments that explore the effect of enhancing language models with syntactic and semantic tags, and dependency tree depth markers, for the task of predicting human sentence acceptability judgments. The experiments show that neither syntactic nor semantic tags, nor tree depth indicators improve the correlation between an LSTM LM and human judgments. Our experiments also show that syntactic tags provide information that is useful for language modeling, while semantic tags do not. However, further experiments are needed to verify our results for semantic tags. The model that we used for tagging, rather than the information in the tags themselves, may be responsible for the observed result.

Surprisingly our initial hypothesis that lower training perplexity produces better acceptability prediction has been overturned. We have not observed any correlation between the perplexity of an LM and its accuracy in acceptability prediction. The SLOR scoring function may mask an underlying connection between preplexity and prediction accuracty.

Our tentative conclusion from these experiments is that simple LSTMs already learn syntactic and semantic properties of sentences through lexical embeddings only, which they represent in a distributional manner. Introducing explicit semantic and syntactic role classifiers does not improve their capacity to predict the acceptability of sentences, although such information may be useful in boosting the performance of deep neural networks on other tasks.

In future work, we plan to test other sources of information for the language models. One possibility is to use constituency, rather than dependency tree depth. We also plan to experiment with different combinations of tags for the language models, such as models that use both semantic and syntactic roles.

11 Acknowledgments

The research reported in this paper was supported by grant 2014-39 from the Swedish Research Council, which funds the Centre for Linguistic Theory and Studies in Probability (CLASP) in the Department of Philosophy, Linguistics, and Theory of Science at the University of Gothenburg. We are grateful to Stephen Clark for helpful advice on encoding syntactic trees in lexical embedding vectors for LSTMs. We would also like to thank our colleagues at CLASP for helpful discussion of some of the ideas presented here.

References

Lasha Abzianidze, Johannes Bjerva, Kilian Evang, Hessel Haagsma, Rik Van Noord, Pierre Ludmann, Duc-Duy Nguyen, and Johan Bos. 2017. The parallel meaning bank: Towards a multilingual corpus of translations annotated with compositional meaning representations. *arXiv preprint arXiv:1702.03964.*

Jean-Philippe Bernardy and Shalom Lappin. 2017. Using deep neural networks to learn syntactic agreement. *Linguistic Issues In Language Technology*, 15(2):15.

Jean-Philippe Bernardy, Shalom Lappin, and Jay Han Lau. 2018. The influence of context on sentence acceptability judgements. In *Proceedings of the 56th Annual Meeting of the Association for Computational Linguistics (Volume 2: Short Papers)*, pages 456–461.

Johannes Bjerva, Barbara Plank, and Johan Bos. 2016. Semantic tagging with deep residual networks. *arXiv preprint arXiv:1609.07053.*

BNC Consortium. 2007. The british national corpus, version 3 (bnc xml edition). 2007. *Distributed by Oxford University Computing Services on behalf of the BNC Consortium.*

Danqi Chen and Christopher Manning. 2014. A fast and accurate dependency parser using neural networks. In *Proceedings of the 2014 conference on empirical methods in natural language processing (EMNLP)*, pages 740–750.

François Chollet et al. 2015. Keras. `https:// keras.io`.

Jacob Devlin, Ming-Wei Chang, Kenton Lee, and Kristina Toutanova. 2018. Bert: Pre-training of deep bidirectional transformers for language understanding. *arXiv preprint arXiv:1810.04805.*

Carlos Gómez-Rodríguez and David Vilares. 2018. Constituent Parsing as Sequence Labeling. *arXiv:1810.08994 [cs].* ArXiv: 1810.08994.

Kristina Gulordava, Piotr Bojanowski, Edouard Grave, Tal Linzen, and Marco Baroni. 2018. Colorless green recurrent networks dream hierarchically. In *Proceedings of the 2018 Conference of the North American Chapter of the Association for Computational Linguistics: Human Language Technologies, Volume 1 (Long Papers)*, pages 1195–1205, New Orleans, Louisiana. Association for Computational Linguistics.

Amulya Gupta and Zhu Zhang. 2018. To attend or not to attend: A case study on syntactic structures for semantic relatedness. In *Proceedings of the 56th Annual Meeting of the Association for Computational Linguistics (Volume 1: Long Papers)*, pages 2116–2125, Melbourne, Australia. Association for Computational Linguistics.

Yair Lakretz, German Kruszewski, Theo Desbordes, Dieuwke Hupkes, Stanislas Dehaene, and Marco Baroni. 2019. The emergence of number and syntax units in lstm language models. *arXiv preprint arXiv:1903.07435*.

Jey Han Lau, Alexander Clark, and Shalom Lappin. 2014. Measuring gradience in speakers grammaticality judgements. In *Proceedings of the Annual Meeting of the Cognitive Science Society*, 36.

Jey Han Lau, Alexander Clark, and Shalom Lappin. 2015. Unsupervised Prediction of Acceptability Judgements. In *Proceedings of the 53rd Annual Meeting of the Association for Computational Linguistics and the 7th International Joint Conference on Natural Language Processing (Volume 1: Long Papers)*, pages 1618–1628, Beijing, China. Association for Computational Linguistics.

Jey Han Lau, Alexander Clark, and Shalom Lappin. 2017. Grammaticality, Acceptability, and Probability: A Probabilistic View of Linguistic Knowledge. *Cognitive Science*, 41(5):1202–1241.

Tal Linzen, Emmanuel Dupoux, and Yoav Goldberg. 2016. Assessing the ability of LSTMs to learn syntax-sensitive dependencies. *Transactions of the Association for Computational Linguistics*, 4:521–535.

Joakim Nivre, Željko Agić, Lars Ahrenberg, and et al. 2017. Universal dependencies 2.0. LINDAT/CLARIN digital library at the Institute of Formal and Applied Linguistics (ÚFAL), Faculty of Mathematics and Physics, Charles University.

Joakim Nivre, Marie-Catherine De Marneffe, Filip Ginter, Yoav Goldberg, Jan Hajic, Christopher D Manning, Ryan T McDonald, Slav Petrov, Sampo Pyysalo, Natalia Silveira, et al. 2016. Universal dependencies v1: A multilingual treebank collection. In *LREC*.

Adam Pauls and Dan Klein. 2012. Large-scale syntactic language modeling with treelets. In *Proceedings of the 50th Annual Meeting of the Association for Computational Linguistics: Long Papers-Volume 1*, pages 959–968. Association for Computational Linguistics.

Matthew E. Peters, Mark Neumann, Mohit Iyyer, Matt Gardner, Christopher Clark, Kenton Lee, and Luke Zettlemoyer. 2018. Deep contextualized word representations. In *Proc. of NAACL*.

Kai Sheng Tai, Richard Socher, and Christopher D. Manning. 2015. Improved semantic representations from tree-structured long short-term memory networks. In *Proceedings of the 53rd Annual Meeting of the Association for Computational Linguistics and the 7th International Joint Conference on Natural Language Processing (Volume 1: Long Papers)*, pages 1556–1566, Beijing, China. Association for Computational Linguistics.

Alex Warstadt and Samuel R. Bowman. 2019. Grammatical analysis of pretrained sentence encoders with acceptability judgments. *CoRR*, abs/1901.03438.

Adina Williams, Andrew Drozdov, and Samuel R Bowman. 2018. Do latent tree learning models identify meaningful structure in sentences? *Transactions of the Association of Computational Linguistics*, 6:253–267.

Comparing linear and neural models for competitive MWE identification

Hazem Al Saied
ATILF, Université de Lorraine
France
halsaied@atilf.fr

Marie Candito
LLF, Université Paris Diderot
France
marie.candito@gmail.com

Mathieu Constant
ATILF, Université de Lorraine
France
mathieu.constant@univ-lorraine.fr

Abstract

In this paper, we compare the use of linear versus neural classifiers in a greedy transition system for MWE identification. Both our linear and neural models achieve a new state-of-the-art on the PARSEME 1.1 shared task data sets, comprising 20 languages. Surprisingly, our best model is a simple feed-forward network with one hidden layer, although more sophisticated (recurrent) architectures were tested.

The feedback from this study is that tuning a SVM is rather straightforward, whereas tuning our neural system revealed more challenging. Given the number of languages and the variety of linguistic phenomena to handle for the MWE identification task, we have designed an accurate tuning procedure, and we show that hyperparameters are better selected by using a majority-vote within random search configurations rather than a simple best configuration selection.

Although the performance is rather good (better than both the best shared task system and the average of the best per-language results), further work is needed to improve the generalization power, especially on unseen MWEs.

1   Introduction

Multi-word expressions (MWE) are composed of several words (more precisely of elements that are words in some contexts) that exhibit irregularities at the morphological, syntactic and/or semantic level. For instance, *"prendre la porte"* is a French verbal expression with semantic and morphological idiosyncrasy because (1) its idiomatic meaning (*"to leave the room"*) differs from its literal meaning (*"to take the door"*) and (2) the idiomatic reading would be lost if *"la porte"* were used in the plural. Identifying MWE is known to be challenging (Constant et al., 2017), due to the highly lexical nature of the MWE status, the various degrees of the MWE irregularities and the various linguistic levels in which these show. In this paper we focus on the task of identifying *verbal* MWEs, which have been the focus of two recent shared tasks, accompanied by data sets for 20 languages: PARSEME shared task ST.0 (Savary et al., 2017) and ST.1 (Ramisch et al., 2018). Verbal MWEs are rather rare (one every 4 sentences overall in ST1.1 data sets) but being predicates, they are crucial to downstream semantic tasks. They are unfortunately even more difficult to identify than other categories of MWEs: they are more likely to be discontinuous sequences and to exhibit morphological and structural variation, if only the verb generally shows full inflectional variation, allows adverbial modification and in some cases syntactic reordering such as relativization.

Our starting point to address the MWE identification task is to reuse the system of Al Saied et al. (2018), an enhanced version of the winning system of ST.0, a transition system using a linear (SVM) model. Our objective has been to incorporate neural methods, which are overwhelming in current NLP systems. Neural networks have brought substantial performance improvements on a large variety of NLP tasks including transition-based parsing (e.g. Kiperwasser and Goldberg (2016) or Andor et al. (2016)), in particular thanks to the use of distributed representations of atomic labels, their ability to capture contextual information. Moreover, neural methods supposedly learn combinations from simple feature templates, as an alternative to hand-crafted task-specific feature engineering.

Yet, using neural methods for our task is challenging, the sizes of the available corpus are relatively modest (no ST.1 language has more than 5000 instances of training MWEs), albeit neural models generally have more parameters to learn than linear models. Indeed, the best systems at the shared tasks ST.0 and ST.1 (Al Saied et al., 2017; Waszczuk, 2018) (in closed track) are not neural and surpassed some neural approaches.

In this paper, we carefully describe and compare the development and tuning of linear versus neural classifiers, to use in the transition system for MWE identification proposed in Al Saied et al. (2018), which itself built on the joint syntactic / MWE analyzer of Constant and Nivre (2016). We set ourselves the constraints (i) of building systems that are robust across languages, hence using the same hyperparameter configuration for all languages and (ii) of using lemma and POS information but not syntactic parses provided in the PARSEME data sets, so that the resulting systems require limited preprocessing. We report a systematic work on designing and tuning linear and neural transition classifiers, including the use of resampling, vocabulary generalization and several strategies for the selection of the best hyperparameter configuration. We address both the open and closed tracks of the PARSEME ST.1, i.e with and without external resources (which in our case amount to pre-trained word embeddings).

The contributions of our work are:

- a new state-of-the art for the MWE identification task on the PARSEME ST1.1 data sets. Our neural model obtains about a four-point error reduction on an artificial score mixing the best results for each language, and 4.5 points compared to the best participating system (even though we do not use syntactic parses);

- a report on which hyperparameters proved crucial to obtain good performance for the neural models, knowing that a basic feed-forward network without class balancing showed high instability and achieves very poorly (average F-score between 15% and 30%);

- an alternative strategy for tuning the hyperparameters, based on trends in random search

(Bergstra and Bengio, 2012);

- a fine-grained analysis of the results for various partitions of the MWE, shedding light on the necessity to address unknown MWE (not seen in train);

- a negative result concerning the basic semi-supervised strategy of using pre-trained word embeddings.

We discuss the related work in Section 2, data sets in Section 3 and the transition system in Section 4. Linear and neural models are described in Sections 5 and 6, and the tuning methodology in Section 7. We present experiments and discuss results in Sections 8 and 9, and conclude in Section 10.

2   Related work

Supervised MWE identification has made significant progress in the last years thanks to the availability of new annotated resources (Schneider et al., 2016; Savary et al., 2017; Ramisch et al., 2018). **Sequence tagging methods** have been largely used for MWE identification. In particular, first studies experimented IOB or IOB-like annotated corpora to train conditional random fields (CRF) models (Blunsom and Baldwin, 2006; Constant and Sigogne, 2011; Vincze et al., 2011) or other linear models (Schneider et al., 2014).

Recently, Gharbieh et al. (2017) experimented on the DiMSUM data set various IOB-based MWE taggers relying on different deep learning models, namely multilayer perceptron, recurrent neural networks and convolutional networks. They showed that convolutional networks achieve better results. On the other hand, Taslimipoor and Rohanian (2018) used pre-trained non-modifiable word embeddings, POS tags and other technical features to feed two convolutional layers with window sizes 2 and 3 in order to detect n-grams. The concatenation of the two layers is then passed to a Bi-LSTM layer.
Legrand and Collobert (2016) used a phrase representation concatenating word embeddings in a fixed-size window, combined with a linear layer in order to detect contiguous MWEs. They reach state-of-the-art results on the French Treebank (Abeillé et al., 2003; Seddah et al., 2013). Rohanian et al. (2019) integrate an attention-based

L	S	T	MWE	L	S	T	MWE
RO	43	782	4.7	DE	7	130	2.8
PT	22	473	4.4	LT	5	090	0.3
BG	18	399	5.4	HU	5	120	6.2
FR	17	421	4.6	EL	4	123	1.4
TR	17	335	6.1	EN	4	053	0.3
IT	14	342	3.3	FA	3	045	2.5
PL	13	220	4.1	ES	3	097	1.7
HE	12	238	1.2	HR	2	054	1.5
SL	10	202	2.4	HI	1	018	0.5
EU	08	117	2.8				

Table 1: The number of **Sentences**, **Tokens** and **MWEs** in train sets of ST.1 **Languages**. Dev and test sets have all a close number of MWEs (between 500 and 800). Languages are represented by their ISO 639-1 code and all table numbers are scaled and rounded (1/1000).

neural model with a graph convolutional neural network to produce an efficient model that outperforms the state-of-the-art on certain languages of the PARSEME Shared Task 1.1.

The work of Waszczuk (2018) extends a sequential CRF to tree structures, provided that MWEs form connected syntactic components and that dependency parse trees are given as input. Dependency trees are used to generate a hypergraph of possible traversals and a binary classifier labels nodes as MWEs or not using local context information. A multi-class logistic regression is then used to determine the globally optimal traversal. This method has showed very competitive scores on the data sets of the PARSEME ST1.1, by ranking first overall on the closed track.

By contrast, some authors have used **Transition systems**, introducing a greedy structured method that decomposes the MWE prediction problem into a sequence of local transition predictions. Constant and Nivre (2016) proposed a two-stack transition system to jointly perform MWE identification and syntactic parsing. Al Saied et al. (2017) experimented a partial implementation of this system for identifying and categorizing verbal MWEs. This system eliminates the syntactic aspects of Constant and Nivre (2016)'s system and learn a SVM model using linguistic and technical features to classify transitions. Relying on Al Saied et al. (2017), Stodden et al. (2018) replaced the linear model with a convolutional module that transforms the sparse feature vectors into continuous ones and connect them to a dense layer.

Name	Cond.	Action
SHIFT	$\beta \neq \emptyset$	$(\sigma, i \lvert \beta, \gamma) \Rightarrow (\sigma \lvert i, \beta, \gamma)$
REDUCE	$\sigma \neq \emptyset$	$(\sigma \lvert i, \beta, \gamma) \Rightarrow (\sigma, \beta, \gamma)$
MERGE	$\lvert \sigma \rvert > 1$	$(\sigma \lvert i, j, \beta, \gamma) \Rightarrow (\sigma \lvert (i, j), \beta, \gamma)$
MARK	$\sigma \neq \emptyset$	$(\sigma \lvert i, \beta, \gamma) \Rightarrow (\sigma \lvert i, \beta, \gamma \cup (i))$

Figure 1: Set of transitions, each with its precondition.

3 Data sets

For our investigation, we focus on the data sets of the PARSEME Shared Task on *verbal* MWE identification edition 1.1 (Ramisch et al., 2018), thereafter ST.1. Table 1 provides statistics on this data set, which includes 20 languages[1] covering a wide range of families and corpus sizes. All languages come with train and test sets, and all but EN, HI and LT have a development set. They contain tokenized sentences in which MWEs are annotated. Each token comes with its word and lemma forms and its part of speech (POS) tag. ST.1 also has extra linguistic annotations such as morphological features and syntactic dependency trees, but we do not use them for the purpose of the paper. One MWE instance is either a set of several potentially non-continuous tokens, or a single token compounding multiple words (namely a multiword token, hereafter MWT).[2] Data sets also contain rare MWEs embedded in another one, and overlapping MWEs.

4 System description

Transition system A transition system incrementally builds the expected output structure by sequentially applying a *transition* to a *configuration* that encodes the state of the system, outputting a new configuration. It has been used in particular to build a syntactic tree for a given input sentence (Nivre, 2004), and to build both the syntactic tree and the MWE list (Constant and Nivre, 2016). We use such a system here to build the list of MWEs only. We reuse the transition system of Al Saied et al. (2018), simplified in that we do not predict the MWE types.

In this system, a configuration is a triplet $c = (\sigma, \beta, \gamma)$, where β is a buffer of (remaining) tokens, σ is a stack of "elements", which are either single tokens or binary trees of tokens, and γ is the list of elements that have been

---

[1] We used all languages but Arabic due to licence issues.

[2] MWTs are extremely marginal for all ST.1 languages except German (30%) and Hungarian(75%)

Trans		Configuration $= (\sigma, \beta, \gamma)$
$F_i(s)$	$\Rightarrow$	[ ], [Take, .., account], [ ]
SHIFT	$\Rightarrow$	[Take], [the, .., account], [ ]
SHIFT	$\Rightarrow$	[Take, the], [fact, .., account], [ ]
REDUCE	$\Rightarrow$	[Take], [fact, .., account], [ ]
SHIFT	$\Rightarrow$	[Take, fact], [that, .., account], [ ]
...		
SHIFT	$\Rightarrow$	[Take, give], [up, into, account], [ ]
SHIFT	$\Rightarrow$	[Take, give, up], [into, account], [ ]
MERGE	$\Rightarrow$	[Take, (give, up)], [into, account], [ ]
MARK	$\Rightarrow$	[Take, (give, up)], [into, account] , [(give, up)]
REDUCE	$\Rightarrow$	[Take], [into, account], [(give, up)]
SHIFT	$\Rightarrow$	[Take, into], [account], [(give, up)]
MERGE	$\Rightarrow$	[(Take, into)], [account], [(give, up)]
SHIFT	$\Rightarrow$	[(Take, into), account], [ ], [(give, up)]
MERGE	$\Rightarrow$	[((Take, into), account)], [ ], [(give, up)]
MARK	$\Rightarrow$	[((Take, into), account)], [ ], (give, up), ((Take, into), account)]
REDUCE	$\Rightarrow$	[ ], [ ], [(give, up), ((Take, into), account)]

Figure 2: Application of the oracle transition sequence for the sentence *Take the fact that I didn't give up into account*, containing two verbal MWEs: *Take into account* and *give up*.

Tuning	BoR	TB	Feature template
Prelim	+	+	Unigrams S_0, S_1, B_0
Prelim	+	+	Bigrams $S_0 S_1, S_0 B_0, S_0 B_1, S_1 B_0$
Prelim	+	+	Lemma ngrams and POS ngrams
Prelim	+	+	S_0 in MWT dictionary
Prelim	-	-	Resampling
Rdm Sch	-	-	word forms ngrams
Rdm Sch	+	-	Unigram B_1
Rdm Sch	+	-	Bigram $S_0 B_2$
Rdm Sch	+	-	Trigram $S_1 S_0 B_0$
Rdm Sch	+	+	Distance between S_0 and S_1
Rdm Sch	+	+	Distance between S_0 and B_0
Rdm Sch	+	-	MWE component dictionary
Rdm Sch	-	-	Stack length
Rdm Sch	+	+	Transition history (length 1)
Rdm Sch	-	+	Transition history (length 2)
Rdm Sch	+	-	Transition history (length 3)
$\mathbf{F}_G$	62.5	60	

Table 2: Linear model feature hyperparameters. First column: **prelim** if the hyperparameter was fixed once and for all given preliminary tests vs. **Rdm Sch** for tuning via random search (see Section 7). Best of random **BoR** column: whether the template is activated (+) or not (-) in the best performing hyperparameter set of the random search. Trend-based **TB**: same but for the trend-based hyperparameter set (cf. section 7). The last line provides the corresponding global F-scores on dev sets of the three pilot languages (BG, PT and TR).

identified as MWEs so far[3]. To build the list of MWEs for a given input sentence $w_1, w_2, ...w_n$, the system starts by the initial configuration $(\sigma = [\,], \beta = [w_1, ..., w_n], \gamma = [\,])$, and applies a sequence of transitions until a terminal configuration is reached, namely here when both the buffer and stack are empty. The transition set, and their precondition is described in Figure 1. Note the MERGE transition creates complex stack elements, by merging the top 2 elements of the stack[4].

The identification of a MWE made of m components $t_1, ..., t_m$ necessitates $m - 1$ MERGEs, and one final MARK. The REDUCE transition allows to manage discontinuities in MWEs. Note that MARK identifies S_0 as MWE, but does not remove it from the stack, hence enabling to identify some cases of embedded MWEs (we refer to Al Saied et al. (2018) for the precise expressive power). At prediction time, we use a greedy algorithm in which the highest-scoring applicable transition according to a classifier is applied to the current configuration.

Learning algorithm and oracle To learn this transition classifier, we use the static deterministic oracle of Al Saied et al. (2018). For any input sentence and list of gold MWEs, the oracle defines a unique sequence of transitions, providing example pairs (config / next transition to apply). Transitions have a priority order (MARK > MERGE > REDUCE > SHIFT), and the oracle greedily applies the highest-priority transition that is compatible with the gold analysis. MERGE is gold-compatible whenever S_0 and S_1 are part of the same gold MWE.[5] For REDUCE to be gold-compatible, S_0 must not be strictly included in a gold MWE. Moreover, either S_0 is not a gold MWE, or it is already marked as MWE.

Figure 2 shows the application of the oracle transition sequence for a sentence with two MWEs.[6]

5 Linear model

In order to compare linear and neural models for MWE identification, we reused the best

---

[3]In all the following, we use $\sigma|i$ to denote a stack with top element i and remainder σ, and $i|\beta$ for a buffer with first token i followed by the elements in β. S_i and B_i denote the ith element of the stack and buffer respectively, starting at 0.

[4]Hence S_i elements are either single tokens or binary trees of tokens. In the latter case, their linguistic attributes (lemma, POS, word form) are obtained by simple concatenation over their components.

[5]Note that this order will lead to left-branching binary trees for elements in the stack.

[6]The system is implemented in Python 2.7, using Keras and Scikit-learn libraries. The code is available at `https://github.com/hazemalsaied/MWE.Identification/releases/tag/v.1` under MIT licence.

performing linear model of Al Saied et al. (2018), namely a SVM, in a one versus rest scheme with linear kernel and squared hinge loss.

We used the feature templates of Al Saied et al. (2018) minus the syntactic features, since we focus on MWE identification independently of syntactic parsing. Table 2 displays the list of feature templates. We detail the "S_0 in MWT dictionary" and "MWE component dictionary" templates, the other features names being rather transparent: "S_0 in MWT dictionary" feature fires when S_0 lemma is a MWT at least once in train, and binary features fire when either S_0, S_1, B_0, B_1 or B_2 belong to at least one train multi-token MWE.

We ran some preliminary experiments which led us to set some hyperparameters once and for all (first four lines of Table 2). In particular, we ended up not using resampling to balance the class distribution, because it proved quite detrimental for the linear model, contrary to the neural models. We then performed tuning for all the other features (cf. section 7).

6 MLP model

Though we investigated various neural architectures[7], the "baseline" multi-layer perceptron (hereafter MLP) proved to be the best in the end. It is a plain feed-forward network, with an embedding layer concatenating the embeddings for the POS of S_0, S_1, B_0 and B_1 and for either their word form or lemma (hyperparameter), fully connected to a dense layer with ReLU activation, in turn connected to the output layer with softmax activation.

Table 3 provides the exhaustive list of MLP hyperparameters, along with their possible values and their optimal values for the most performing

---

[7]We tried in particular (1) a MLP with several hidden layers; (2) a MLP fed with a bidirectional recurrent layer to represent the sequence of elements $S_0 S_1 B_0$; (3) We also built a model inspired by Kiperwasser and Goldberg (2016) in which the recurrent (LSTM) embeddings of certain focus elements (S_0, S_1, B_0 and B_1) are dynamically concatenated and fed into a MLP, with back-propagation for a whole sentence instead of for each transition. The recurrent representations of the focus elements are supposed to encode the relevant contextual information of these elements in the sentence. These models suffered from either a non-competitive performance or a very unstable loss (36.7 for the bidirectional MLP and 8.4 for kiperwasser on test data sets of ST1.1).

configurations. Lines 1 to 9 correspond to embedding and initialization hyperparameters: Lines (**1, 2**) concern which elements to include as additional input (Use B_2, Use B_{-1})[8], (**3**) which form for input tokens (Lemmatization), (**4, 5**) which size for token and POS tag embeddings (Token and POS dimensions), (**6**) whether the embeddings are initialized randomly or pre-trained (pre-trained), (**7**) whether the embeddings are Trainable or not, and (**8**) how to generate embedding vectors for stack elements: as the average of tree token embeddings or as their sum (Averaging).

Vocabulary For the neural model, when S_i or B_i are missing, a special dummy word is used instead. Moreover, we investigated an aggressive reduction of the known vocabulary. We compared 2 strategies to define it: in *exhaustive vocabulary* mode, hapaxes are replaced at training time by a UNK symbol, with probability 0.5. In *compact vocabulary* mode, any token (or complex element) whose lemma is never a component of a MWE in the training set is replaced by UNK. Note that in both modes, the used vocabulary contains the concatenated symbols in case of complex S_i elements.

Resampling Given that tokens are mostly not part of a VMWE, the transitions for their identification are very rare, leading to a very skewed class distribution.[9] Resampling techniques aiming at balancing class distribution are known to be efficient in such a case (Chawla, 2009). Moreover, preliminary experiments without resampling showed unstable loss and rather low performance. We thus used in subsequent experiments a hybrid resampling method composed of (**1**) under sampling, that removes training sentences non containing any MWE, and (**2**) random oversampling, that forces a uniform distribution of the classes by randomly duplicating minority class instances (all but SHIFT) (Chawla, 2009). Preliminary experiments showed that without these strategies, the systems suffered from very unstable loss and low performance, which led us to systematically use these two strategies in the subsequent experiments.

---

[8] B_{-1} is the last reduced element (its right-most token if it is a complex stack element).

[9]For all ST.1 languages, the transitions in training sets are approximately distributed as follows: 49% for SHIFT, 47% for REDUCE, 3% for MERGE and 1% for MARK.

Type	Hyperparameter	Range or set	BoR_c	BoR_o	TB
Embedding and initialisation	Use B_2	{True, False}	True	True	True
	Use B_{-1}	{True, False}	True	False	True
	Lemmatization	{True, False}	True	True	True
	Token dimension	[100, 600]	157	300	300
	POS dimension	[15, 150]	147	132	35
	Pre-trained	{True, False}	False	True	True | False
	Trainable	{True, False}	True	True	True
	Averaging	{True, False}	False	True	True
	Vocabulary	{Compact, Exhaustive}	True	False	True
Dense	Unit number	[25, 600]	85	56	75
	Dropout	{.1, .2,... .6}	0.3	0.1	0.4
Sampling	Focused / Frequency threshold	{True, False} / {5, 10,... 30}	False / -	False / -	False / -
	Over loss / Loss coefficient	{True, False} / [1, 40]	False / 1	False / 1	False / 1
Train	Learning rate	[.01, .2]	0.017	0.095	0.03
	Batch size	{16, 32, 48, 64, 128}	128	16	48
$\mathbf{F}_G$ on all languages (on dev sets if available or 20% of train)			61.2	57.8	63.5 | 64.3

Table 3: MLP hyperparameters and their possible values ("range or set" column). Best-of-random closed (**BoR**$_c$) and Best-of-random open (**BoR**$_o$) columns: hyperparameter values in best configurations according to random search on the three pilot languages, in closed and open tracks. Last column: Trend-based (**TB**) configuration (see text in section 7). Last line: global F-scores for these configurations, calculated using the average precision and recall for all ST.1 languages. The models are fit on truncated training sets of the three pilot languages (BG, PT and TR) (cf. section 7).

Tuning explored two supplementary resampling techniques: "focused" oversampling which aims at mimicking a minimum number of occurrences for all MWEs. When set, training instances with MERGE and MARK transitions are duplicated for each training MWE below a frequency threshold. "Over loss" hyperparameter penalizes the model when it fails to predict MERGE and MARK, by multiplying the loss by a coefficient (see Table 3).

7 Tuning methodology

The tuning phase served us to choose a hyperparameter configuration for the linear model and the neural model, in closed and open track. In our case, we experimented open track for the neural model only, by using pre-trained embeddings instead of random initialization. We thus consider three cases: closed track linear, closed track MLP and open track MLP.

For each of these three cases, in order to enforce the robustness across languages of the selected hyperparameters, we aimed at selecting the same hyperparameter configuration for all the languages.

Yet, to reduce the tuning time, we have chosen to work on three pilot languages, from three different language families. But because the various training sets have various sizes, we tried to neutralize this variation by using training sets of average size. This led us to choose three languages (Bulgarian, Portuguese and Turkish) among ST.1 languages having training sets bigger than average and to tune the hyperparameters using training sets truncated to that average size ($270k$ tokens) and evaluating on dev sets.

Multilingual metric: the official metric for the PARSEME shared task is the macro average of the F-scores over all languages (hereafter F_{AVG}). Yet we noted that although macro-averaging precision and recall is appropriate because the number of dev and test MWEs is almost the same for all languages, averaging the F-scores of all languages sometimes substantially differs (e.g. by 2 points) from taking the F-score of the macro-averaged precision and the macro-averaged recall (hereafter F_G). We thus use F_{AVG} for comparability with the shared task results, but also report the F_G score, and use the latter during tuning.

Random search: To tune the hyperparameters on the three pilot languages, we used random search, which proved to be more efficient than grid search when using the same computational budget, because it allows to search larger ranges of values (Bergstra and Bengio, 2012). We thus run about 1000 trials for SVM, closed track MLP and open track MLP. For the SVM, random search used a uniform distribution for the hyperparameters, which are all boolean. For the MLP, the random hyperparameter values are generated from either a set of discrete values using a uniform distribution or from a range of continuous values using logarithmic distribution. For the MLP, each resulting random hyperparameter configuration was run on each pilot language twice, using always the same two seeds 0 and 1[10]. We then averaged the precision and recall on the dev sets, for the three languages and the two seeds (i.e. use the global F-score F_G).

Selecting hyperparameter configurations: Random hyperparameter search for the three pilot languages led us to use two strategies to select the hyperparameter sets. The first one is simply to select the best performing hyperparameter sets (shown in column **BoR** in Table 2 for the linear model, and in the **BoR**$_c$ and **BoR**$_o$ columns in Table 3). Yet, we noted that some hyperparameters varied a lot among the top performing systems. We thus investigated to build a "**trend-based**" configuration, by selecting each hyperparameter value according to the observed trend among the top k best configurations (with k=500/250 for MLP/SVM)[11]. This results in two sets for the linear model (best-of-random and trend-based, in closed mode) and four configurations for the MLP: best-of-random or trend-based, in closed or open mode.

We then trained these six configurations on the full-size training sets for all ST.1.1 languages, using two seeds (0 and 1), and retaining the best seed for each language. For the MLP case, the global F-scores on dev sets are provided in the last row of Table 3. Interestingly, the trend-based configuration largely beats the best-of-random configurations, both in closed and open tracks[12]. This shows that choosing hyperparameter values independently of each other is compensated by choosing more robust values, by using the top k best performing systems instead of one.

Note that for the linear case, the trend-based configuration does not surpass the best performing random search configuration (the last line of

---

[10]Preliminary experiments showed a relative stability when changing seeds, hence we used only two seeds in the end. Changing seeds was useless for the linear model which is more stable.

[11]We chose the values using an approximate majority vote, using a graphical visualization of the hyperparameter values in the top k best performing systems.

[12]Moreover, the best-of-random open configuration showed instability when switching from the three pilot languages to all languages, leading to a null score for Hindi (hence the rather low global F-score of 57.8).

Language	Closed track			Open track	
	SVM	MLP$_c$	ST.1	MLP$_o$	ST.1
BG	63.3	**66.8**	62.5	**67.7**	65.6
HR	55.4	**59.3**	55.3	**59.0**	47.8
LT	38.0	**45.7**	32.2	**45.3**	22.9
PL	69.4	**71.8**	67.0	**72.2**	63.6
SL	53.5	62.7	**64.3**	**61.2**	52.3
DE	49.5	**51.5**	45.3	**49.9**	45.5
EN	28.4	31.4	**32.9**	31.9	**33.3**
ES	39.2	**40.0**	34.0	**39.7**	38.4
FR	**61.1**	59.0	56.2	58.8	**60.9**
IT	**55.7**	55.0	49.2	**56.5**	45.4
PT	**68.9**	67.8	62.1	**70.4**	68.2
RO	80.9	83.5	**85.3**	82.0	**87.2**
HI	66.8	64.9	**73.0**	64.9	**72.7**
FA	75.4	70.6	**77.8**	70.6	**78.4**
EL	57.8	**62.2**	49.8	**61.4**	58.0
EU	80.7	**82.1**	75.8	**80.2**	77.0
HE	43.3	**45.2**	23.3	**47.3**	38.9
HU	91.7	**92.4**	90.3	**92.6**	85.8
TR	47.5	**52.1**	45.2	47.9	**58.7**
F_{AVG}	59.3	**61.3**	56.9	**61.0**	57.9
F_G	60.8	**62.6**	57.8	**62.3**	58.7
F_G best sys			54.0		58.1

Table 4: MWE-based F-scores for ST.1 languages on test sets using our tuned **SVM** and **MLP** models, fit on train and dev sets when available. **ST.1** stands for the most performing scores of the shared task for each language in closed and open tracks. All ST.1 systems fit training and development sets except the system that produced the best score of BG on closed track. Languages are grouped according to their linguistic families (Slavic, Germanic, Romance, Indo-Iranian and other).) F_{AVG} is the official metric (average F-scores). F_G is the global F-score (see Section 7). In the F_{AVG} and F_G lines, the best ST.1 per-language scores are used, whereas the last line concerns the F_G score of the best ST.1 systems (Waszczuk, 2018; Taslimipoor and Rohanian, 2018).

Table 2). This asymmetry could mean that the number of random trials is sufficient for the linear case, but not for the neural models, and that a trend-based strategy is advantageous within a limited computational budget.

8 Experiments and results

Table 4 provides identification scores on test sets, for our tuned SVM and MLP models for each ST.1 language, along with the best score of ST.1 for each language, in open and closed tracks. It also displays overall scores using both the official ST.1 metrics (F_{AVG}) and the more precise F_G score introduced in section 7. This F_G score for the ST.1 results is computed in two modes: in line F_G, the ST.1 columns correspond to artificially averaging the best result of each language (in closed / open tracks), whereas "F_G best sys" is the score of the best system of ST.1. The differences between SVM and MLP$_c$ results are significant[13]

---

[13]We used a MWE-based McNemar test.

for all languages except EU, HU, LT and PL.

For both F_{AVG} and F_G metrics, results show that MLP models significantly outperforms all other systems both in the closed and open tracks. In the closed track, MLP surpasses SVM by 1.8 points, the best ST.1 systems per language by 4.8 points, and the best ST.1 system (Waszczuk, 2018) by 8.6 points. In the open track, MLP beats the best ST.1 system (Taslimipoor and Rohanian, 2018) by 4.2 points, and the best ST.1 systems per language by 3.6 points[14].

In the closed track, MLP ranks first for 11 languages, while the SVM model and the best ST.1 systems per language reach the first position respectively for three and five languages. In open track, MLP achieves the highest scores for 13 languages while ST.1 systems beat it for six languages. These results tend to validate the robustness of our approach across languages. Regarding language families, MLP reports remarkable gains for Slavic languages and languages from the *other* family, but achieve lower performance on Indo-Iranian languages when compared with best ST.1 results. For Romance languages, our models surpass the ST.1 best results (except for RO), and the SVM model is globally better than the MLP.

Comparing the results of the open and the closed track, we can observe that the use of pre-trained word embeddings has no significant impact on the MLP results. This might mean that static embeddings are not well-suited for representing tokens both when used literally and within MWE. This tendency would deserve more investigation using other word embedding types, in particular contextualized ones (Devlin et al., 2018).

9   Discussion

Performance analysis   In order to better understand the strengths and weaknesses of the various systems, we provide in Table 5 an in-depth performance analysis of our models, on dev sets, broken-down by various classifications of MWEs,

namely (1) whether a dev MWE was seen in train (and if so, more than 5 times or not) or unseen; (2) whether the MWE is continuous or has gaps; and (3) according to the MWE length. The table provides the proportions of each subclass within the gold dev set and within the predictions of each model (% columns), in addition to the average precision and recall over all languages, and the global F_G score, for each model. Overall, neural models (in closed and open tracks) tends to get better recall than the SVM model (56 and 57, versus 49) but lower precision (70 versus 86), which is coherent with the use of embeddings.

Generalization power   Without surprise, the global F-score on seen MWEs is high for all our systems (> 80), and it is still above 75 for MWEs with frequency ≤ 5. Yet this masks that the neural models have comparable precision and recall on seen MWEs, whereas the SVM has better precision than recall. Now when turning to the unseen category, we can observe that all systems get very low performance.

In comparison with MLP models, the most important advantage of SVM is its (little) ability to generalize ($F_G = 12$ on unseen MWEs), whereas the MLPs have none at all. Note that frequency ≤ 5 is sufficient for the MLP models to surpass the linear model. For comparison, the average F-scores on test sets of the PARSEME ST.1 for unseen MWEs range from 0 to almost 20. This very low generalization of our MLP models is understandable since tuning led us to favor the compact vocabulary mode, which agressively reduces the known vocabulary to seen MWE components. Yet our best result on unseen MWEs with a MLP with exhaustive vocabulary mode only achieves $F_G = 4$ on unseen MWEs.

It appears that for all models, more than 90% of the unindentified MWEs (the silence) are either unseen or with frequency ≤ 5, which clearly shows that the frequency of a MWE in train set is the crucial trait for identification. Further analysis is needed to study the performance according to the literal versus MWE ambiguity rate.

Continuous/discontinuous   MWEs   MLP models show better performances for discontinuous MWEs than SVM, whereas they reach

---

[14]It is worth noting that the model of Rohanian et al. (2019), published while writing this paper, outperforms our scores for the languages they use for evaluating their model (EN:41.9, DE:59.3, FR:71.0, FA:80.0) on the ST.1 test sets. However, this model exploits syntactic information (See Section 2).

Type	%	SVM				MLP_o				MLP_c			
		%	F_G	P	R	%	F_G	P	R	%	F_G	P	R
All	-	-	63	86	49	-	62	70	56	-	63	70	57
Seen	63	93	80	89	72	99	81	83	80	98	82	82	82
- Freq > 5	26	37	80	84	77	37	82	81	82	36	81	81	82
- Freq <= 5	38	56	75	86	67	62	77	79	76	61	78	79	77
Unseen	37	7	12	44	7	1	0	7	0	2	2	10	1
Contin.	67	77	69	88	57	75	69	84	59	74	70	83	60
Discont.	33	23	45	78	31	25	50	77	37	26	50	75	37
Length 1 (MWT)	6	7	84	93	77	7	82	89	77	7	84	91	78
Length 2	78	84	64	86	51	85	65	82	54	85	66	81	56
Length 3	13	8	40	66	29	7	40	69	28	7	40	66	29

Table 5: Performance of our tuned models, on all languages, with models fit on train and evaluated on dev sets if available, otherwise fit on 80% of train and evaluated on the rest (with seed 0 for MLP models). First line: performance on all languages. Subsequent lines: break-down according to various MWE classifications (first column). Second column: proportion of the subclass in gold dev set. For each model (SVM, $MLP_{o(open)}$ and $MLP_{c(losed)}$), we report for each subclass: the proportion of the subclass in the system prediction, the global F-score (F_G), Precision (P) and Recall (R).

comparable scores for continuous MWEs. In particular, they display a 5-point gain in F-score, due to a 6-point gain in recall on discontinuous MWEs.

MWE length The three systems display comparable scores regarding MWE length. Results validate the intuition that the shorter the MWE, the easier it is to identify.

10 Conclusion

We described and compared the development of linear versus neural classifiers to use in a transition system for MWE identification (Al Saied et al., 2018). Surprisingly, our best neural architecture is a simple feed-forward network with one hidden layer, although more sophisticated architectures were tested. We achieve a new state-of-the art on the PARSEME 1.1 shared task data sets, comprising 20 languages.

Our neural and linear models surpass both the best shared task system (Waszczuk, 2018) and the artificial average of the best per-language results. Given the number of languages and the variety of linguistic phenomena to handle, we designed a precise tuning methodology.

Our feedback is that the development of the linear (SVM) system was pretty straightforward, with low variance between the configurations. For the neural models on the contrary, preliminary runs led to low and unstable performance. Class balancing proved crucial, and our proposal to select hyperparameter values using majority vote on the top k best performing systems in random search also proved beneficial.

Although our systems are competitive, their generalization power reveals disappointing: performance on unseen MWEs is very low for the linear model (F-score=12) and almost zero for the neural models (whereas the shared task results range from 0 to 20 for unseen MWEs). Basic semi-supervised experiments, consisting in using pre-trained word embeddings, did not bring any improvement. Static embeddings might not be suitable representations of MWE components, as their behavior differs when used literally or within a MWE. This definitely calls for future work that can incorporate information on semantic irregularity.

Acknowledgement

This work was partially funded by the French National Research Agency (PARSEME-FR ANR-14-CERA-0001).

References

Anne Abeillé, Lionel Clément, and François Toussenel. 2003. Building a treebank for French. In Anne Abeillé, editor, *Treebanks*. Kluwer, Dordrecht.

Hazem Al Saied, Marie Candito, and Matthieu Constant. 2017. The ATILF-LLF system for parseme shared task: a transition-based verbal multiword expression tagger. In *Proceedings of the 13th Workshop on Multiword Expressions (MWE 2017)*, pages 127–132, Valencia, Spain. Association for Computational Linguistics.

Hazem Al Saied, Marie Candito, and Matthieu Constant. 2018. A transition-based verbal multiword expression analyzer. In *Multiword expressions at length and in depth: Extended papers from the MWE 2017 workshop*, volume 2, page 209. Language Science Press.

Daniel Andor, Chris Alberti, David Weiss, Aliaksei Severyn, Alessandro Presta, Kuzman Ganchev, Slav Petrov, and Michael Collins. 2016. Globally normalized transition-based neural networks. *arXiv preprint arXiv:1603.06042*.

James Bergstra and Yoshua Bengio. 2012. Random search for hyper-parameter optimization. *Journal of Machine Learning Research*, 13(Feb):281–305.

Phil Blunsom and Timothy Baldwin. 2006. Multilingual deep lexical acquisition for hpsgs via supertagging. In *Proceedings of the 2006 Conference on Empirical Methods in Natural Language Processing*, pages 164–171, Sydney, Australia. Association for Computational Linguistics.

Nitesh V Chawla. 2009. Data mining for imbalanced datasets: An overview. In *Data mining and knowledge discovery handbook*, pages 875–886. Springer.

Mathieu Constant, Gülşen Eryiğit, Johanna Monti, Lonneke Van Der Plas, Carlos Ramisch, Michael Rosner, and Amalia Todirascu. 2017. Multiword expression processing: A survey. *Computational Linguistics*, 43(4):837–892.

Matthieu Constant and Joakim Nivre. 2016. A transition-based system for joint lexical and syntactic analysis. In *Proceedings of the 54th Annual Meeting of the Association for Computational Linguistics (Volume 1: Long Papers)*, pages 161–171, Berlin, Germany. Association for Computational Linguistics.

Matthieu Constant and Anthony Sigogne. 2011. Mwu-aware part-of-speech tagging with a crf model and lexical resources. In *Proceedings of the Workshop on Multiword Expressions: from Parsing and Generation to the Real World*, pages 49–56. Association for Computational Linguistics.

Jacob Devlin, Ming-Wei Chang, Kenton Lee, and Kristina Toutanova. 2018. BERT: pre-training of deep bidirectional transformers for language understanding. *CoRR*, abs/1810.04805.

Waseem Gharbieh, Virendrakumar Bhavsar, and Paul Cook. 2017. Deep learning models for multiword expression identification. In *Proceedings of the 6th Joint Conference on Lexical and Computational Semantics (*SEM 2017)*, pages 54–64, Vancouver, Canada. Association for Computational Linguistics.

Eliyahu Kiperwasser and Yoav Goldberg. 2016. Simple and accurate dependency parsing using bidirectional lstm feature representations. *arXiv preprint arXiv:1603.04351*.

Joël Legrand and Ronan Collobert. 2016. Phrase representations for multiword expressions. In *Proceedings of the 12th Workshop on Multiword Expressions*, pages 67–71, Berlin, Germany. Association for Computational Linguistics.

Joakim Nivre. 2004. Incrementality in deterministic dependency parsing. In *Proceedings of the ACL Workshop Incremental Parsing: Bringing Engineering and Cognition Together*, pages 50–57, Barcelona, Spain. Association for Computational Linguistics.

Carlos Ramisch, Silvio Cordeiro, Agata Savary, Veronika Vincze, Verginica Mititelu, Archna Bhatia, Maja Buljan, Marie Candito, Polona Gantar, Voula Giouli, et al. 2018. Edition 1.1 of the parseme shared task on automatic identification of verbal multiword expressions. In *the Joint Workshop on Linguistic Annotation, Multiword Expressions and Constructions (LAW-MWE-CxG-2018)*, pages 222–240.

Omid Rohanian, Shiva Taslimipoor, Samaneh Kouchaki, Le An Ha, and Ruslan Mitkov. 2019. Bridging the gap: Attending to discontinuity in identification of multiword expressions. *arXiv preprint arXiv:1902.10667*.

Agata Savary, Carlos Ramisch, Silvio Cordeiro, Federico Sangati, Veronika Vincze, Behrang Qasem-iZadeh, Marie Candito, Fabienne Cap, Voula Giouli, and Ivelina Stoyanova. 2017. The parseme shared task on automatic identification of verbal multiword expressions.

Nathan Schneider, Emily Danchik, Chris Dyer, and Noah A. Smith. 2014. Discriminative lexical semantic segmentation with gaps: running the MWE gamut. *TACL*, 2:193–206.

Nathan Schneider, Dirk Hovy, Anders Johannsen, and Marine Carpuat. 2016. Semeval-2016 task 10: Detecting minimal semantic units and their meanings (dimsum). In *Proceedings of the 10th International Workshop on Semantic Evaluation (SemEval-2016)*, pages 546–559.

Djamé Seddah, Reut Tsarfaty, Sandra Kübler, Marie Candito, Jinho D. Choi, Richárd Farkas, Jennifer Foster, Iakes Goenaga, Koldo Gojenola Galletebeitia, Yoav Goldberg, Spence Green, Nizar Habash, Marco Kuhlmann, Wolfgang Maier, Joakim

Nivre, Adam Przepiórkowski, Ryan Roth, Wolfgang
Seeker, Yannick Versley, Veronika Vincze, Marcin
Woliński, Alina Wróblewska, and Eric Villemonte
de la Clergerie. 2013. Overview of the SPMRL 2013
shared task: A cross-framework evaluation of parsing morphologically rich languages. In *Proceedings of the Fourth Workshop on Statistical Parsing of
Morphologically-Rich Languages*, pages 146–182,
Seattle, Washington, USA. Association for Computational Linguistics.

Regina Stodden, Behrang QasemiZadeh, and Laura
Kallmeyer. 2018. Trapacc and trapaccs at parseme
shared task 2018: Neural transition tagging of verbal multiword expressions. In *Proceedings of the
Joint Workshop on Linguistic Annotation, Multiword Expressions and Constructions (LAW-MWE-
CxG-2018)*, pages 268–274.

Shiva Taslimipoor and Omid Rohanian. 2018. Shoma
at parseme shared task on automatic identification of vmwes: Neural multiword expression tagging with high generalisation. *arXiv preprint
arXiv:1809.03056*.

Veronica Vincze, István Nagy, and Gábor Berend.
2011. Multiword expressions and named entities in
the Wiki50 corpus. In *Proc. of RANLP 2011*, pages
289–295, Hissar.

Jakub Waszczuk. 2018. Traversal at parseme shared
task 2018: Identification of verbal multiword
expressions using a discriminative tree-structured
model. In *Proceedings of the Joint Workshop on
Linguistic Annotation, Multiword Expressions and
Constructions (LAW-MWE-CxG-2018)*, pages 275–
282.

Syntax-based identification of light-verb constructions

Silvio Ricardo Cordeiro
LLF, Université Paris Diderot
Paris, France
silvioricardoc@gmail.com

Marie Candito
LLF, Université Paris Diderot
Paris, France
marie.candito@linguist.univ-paris-diderot.fr

Abstract

This paper analyzes results on light-verb construction identification, distinguishing between known cases that could be directly learned from training data from unknown cases that require an extra level of semantic processing. We propose a simple baseline that beats the best results of the PARSEME 1.1 shared task (Savary et al., 2018) for the known cases, and couple it with another simple baseline to handle the unknown cases. We additionally present two other classifiers based on a richer set of features, with results surpassing these best results by 7 percentage points.

1 Introduction

Light-verb constructions (LVCs), such as the expression *pay visit*, are a linguistic phenomenon coupling a verb and a stative or eventive noun, in which the verb itself is only needed for morphosyntactic purposes, its syntactic dependents being semantically related to the noun. For instance in the sentence *John paid me a visit*, the subject and object of *paid* play the roles of the visitor and the visited. The verb's semantics is either bleached or redundant with that of the noun (as in *commit crime*) (Savary et al., 2018). This mismatch between syntax and semantics has to be taken care of for semantically-oriented tasks to recover the full predicate-argument structure of the noun, since at least one of its semantic arguments of the noun is generally attached to the verb in plain syntactic treebanks.[1] Moreover, the fact

that the verb choice is conventionalized and semantically bleached makes LVC identification an important requirement in semantic tasks such as machine translation (Cap et al., 2015).

Because of their syntactico-semantic characteristics, LVCs are generally considered difficult to circumscribe and annotate consistently (Bonial and Palmer, 2016). Yet recently, the PARSEME 2018 shared-task has brought forth a collection of corpora containing verbal multiword expression (VMWE) annotations across 19 languages (Ramisch et al., 2018), including LVCs. The reported inter-annotator agreement is variable across languages, but the macro-averaged chance-corrected kappa is overall 0.69, which is generally considered to denote a good agreement. In the annotated corpora, the category of LVCs[2] accounted for a third of all expressions (Savary et al., 2018). The annotation was performed in a separate layer, largely independent from the underlying syntactic framework, and relied on semantic properties of the verb (bleached or redundant in the given context) and both semantic and syntactic properties of the noun: it should be stative or eventive and take at least one semantic argument, and it should be possible to have all the syntactic arguments of the verb realized within a NP headed by the noun (for instance out of *John paid me a visit*, one can create the NP *John's visit to me*).

A total of 13 systems participated in the PARSEME shared-task, predicting VMWEs occurrence in the test corpora. Results for each system varied across different systems and target languages, in which expressions that had been seen in the test corpus were predicted with variable accuracy. However, expressions that had never been seen in the test corpus were hardly ever predicted by most systems (the best F-score on unseen-

---

[1] For instance, Nivre and Vincze (2015) report that for the majority of the 18 UD languages at that time, in a structure like *X takes a photo of Y* in English, X is attached to the verb, but the Y argument is attached to the noun. In some annotation schemes, the Y would be attached to the verb too. Note though that some treebanks do annotate the LVC status (e.g. in Hungarian). Additional semantic annotation of LVC can be found e.g. in propbank (Bonial and Palmer, 2016).

[2] Unless otherwise stated, this paper refers to the 1.1 edition of the PARSEME shared task, and to the category LVC.full (as opposed to LVC.cause).

in-train expressions in the closed track is below 20%).

In this paper, we investigate the task of LVC identification in running text. The main contributions of this paper are: (1) we propose handling the task of LVC identification differently depending on whether it was seen in the training corpus; (2) we present a simple baseline that surpasses all systems for seen LVCs; (3) we propose and evaluate different techniques for the prediction of unseen LVCs, which we then compare to the state of the art.

The remainder of this paper is structured as follows: Section 2 presents the related work; Section 3 describes the methodology that will be employed; Section 4 describes the results; and finally, Section 5 presents our conclusions.

2 Related Work

LVC identification may follow one of two strategies: (a) LVC candidates are initially proposed based on lexicosyntactic patterns, and are then classified as LVC or non-LVC based on other criteria; (b) a variant of the BIO scheme (Ramshaw and Marcus, 1999) is employed so as to directly classify each token as belonging or not to an LVC. The former method allows the use of features that encompass the LVC as a whole, while the latter can be more easily implemented in the framework of some machine learning algorithms.

Most works in the literature concerning LVC identification focus on annotations in a particular language, often with a language-specific understanding of LVCs. Vincze et al. (2013) adapt a dependency parser so as to identify Hungarian LVC candidates as a byproduct of parsing, which they then evaluate on the Szeged Dependency Treebank with LVC annotations. Nagy T. et al. (2013) extract English LVC candidates involving a verb and a dependent noun with a specific dependency label. A J48 and an SVM classifier are then considered, using lexical and morphosyntactic features from the corpus, as well as semantic features from WordNet. The latter was found to contribute to better results when compared to earlier works that relied purely on morphosyntactic and statistical features (Tu and Roth, 2011). Chen et al. (2015) detect English LVCs in the BNC and OntoNotes corpora, using the PropBank layer to select LVC candidates composed of an eventive noun linked one of 6 known light verbs. The candidates are then filtered based on semantic features, including WordNet synsets and hypernym relations.

More recently, the PARSEME shared-task saw 13 system submissions that tried to predict LVCs along with other VMWEs for annotated corpora in 19 languages (Ramisch et al., 2018). Overall, the best F_1 scores across all languages in the open track were obtained by the SHOMA system, which employed a pipeline of CNNs, a Bi-LSTM, and and optional CRF layer (Taslimipoor and Rohanian, 2018). MWE prediction followed a variant of the BIO scheme that allowed multiple tags per token, with input features including a set of pre-trained embeddings (leading the system to compete in the open track category), POS tags, and a set of word-shape features.

In the closed track, the TRAVERSAL system obtained the best overall results for MWEs in general as well as for LVCs. It uses a syntax-based approach, in which each node in the syntax tree was classified as part of an MWE or not (Waszczuk, 2018). The classifier resembles a second-order CRF, but rather than considering the previous 2 tokens at each point, it considers the parent and left-sibling. Features included the lemma, POS tag and dependency relation.

Rather than predicting each token as being part of an LVC or not, the varIDE system use a Naive Bayes classifier to tag LVC candidates (Pasquer et al., 2018). These were extracted based on all possible token combinations whole multi-set of lemmas corresponded to an LVC that had been seen in the training corpus (no attempts were made at predicting unseen LVCs). Classifier features included POS tags and morphological information.

Graph convolutional neural networks have also been used in the identification of VMWE candidates for subsequent classification (Rohanian et al., 2019). In this work, the network is combined with an attention mechanism so as to improve the accuracy of long-range predictions, and a Bi-LSTM layer is used to classify these predictions and produce the final output. The system uses contextualized embeddings (ELMo) and outperforms the state of the art for the four languages for which results are reported.

3 Methods and materials

Our LVC identification technique consists of two main stages: (1) extraction of LVC candidates based on syntactic patterns; and (2) classification of candidates based on a set of lexical, morphological, syntactic and semantic features, concerning both the candidate as a whole and its components.

3.1 Extraction of candidates

The first step of LVC identification in a target corpus is to identify candidates. While LVCs are commonly thought of as a combination of a verb and noun acting as its direct object, other configurations can be attested in the PARSEME corpora. This may be due to morphosyntactic variations (e.g. passive voice), the presence of more complex noun phrases (instead of a single noun), non-standard analyses (e.g. verbs that are tagged as adjectives) or other language-specific idiosyncrasies. A robust candidate extraction method should handle this variation, and we do so by using the morphosyntactic patterns of the LVCs in the training corpora, using the provided UD parses.

So we start by extracting language-specific morphosyntactic patterns from the training LVCs. More specifically, for each LVC annotated in a training corpus, we retain a representation involving the POS tag and the syntactic relation between components (henceforth referred to as a "pattern"). If the LVC does not form a connected tree (e.g. *to give a series of lectures*), the pattern will additionally include the minimum number of nodes that makes the tree connected (if two nodes are only connected by the root node, we discard the occurrence instead). In the example above, the extracted pattern would be: $\text{VERB}_1 \xrightarrow{\text{obj}} (\text{NOUN}_2) \xrightarrow{\text{nmod}} \text{NOUN}_3$ (the components of the LVC being those not within brackets).

The number of extracted patterns ranges from 14 (Slovene) to 185 (Farsi), with an average of 90 patterns per language. We then sort the patterns based on how many occurrences of LVCs led to each pattern. As expected, the patterns follow a Zipfian distribution. For example, for the French training data, the most common pattern is $\text{VERB}_1 \xrightarrow{\text{obj}} \text{NOUN}_2$ with 977 occurrences; the second is $\text{NOUN}_1 \xrightarrow{\text{acl}} \text{VERB}_2$ with 150 occurrences (as in for instance *a picture taken yesterday*); the third is $\text{VERB}_1 \xrightarrow{\text{nsubj:pass}} \text{NOUN}_2$ with 58 occurrences (as in *this picture was taken yesterday*); and so on[3].

The most common patterns are then used to identify LVC candidates in the train, development and test data, using the Grew tool (Bonfante et al., 2018). Obviously, using unlexicalized patterns results in getting a vast majority of candidates that are not LVCs, and this is even more true for rare patterns. We experimented with two pattern selecting stagies: topN, in which we take the N most common patterns (we considered values of $N \in \{1, 5, 10, 20, 50\}$); and atleastNoccurs, in which we take all patterns that originated from at least N occurrences in the training corpus (we considered $N \in \{2, 5, 10, 50\}$). Moreover, for each pattern p containing $\xrightarrow{\text{label}} \text{NOUN}_i$, we add a pattern p' replacing this subpattern by $\xrightarrow{\text{label}} (\text{NOUN}_j) \xrightarrow{\text{conj}} \text{NOUN}_i$[4].

Using the selected patterns, we identify LVC candidates in the development and test corpora, but also in the training corpora, so as to obtain positive and negative LVC candidates to train a binary classifier. For each identified candidate, we produce a set of features which may be related either to the whole LVC, or to its components.[5]

3.2 Features

The PARSEME 1.1 data contains test/development and training data for 19 languages. The training data contained an average of 1171 LVCs per language (σ=948, ranging from 78 for English to 2952 for Turkish). Most corpora contain morphosyntactic information (in most cases obtained by an external parser, and in most cases representing data using the POS and dependency tagsets recommended by UD).

For a given candidate c, we first extract the verb component v and predicative noun component n. This is in general trivial, but in order to cover all cases, v is taken to be the leftmost token that has POS tag VERB, or the leftmost AUX, or the leftmost ADJ, or the leftmost token in c, while n is the leftmost NOUN, leftmost PROPN, or leftmost token that is not v. In all the features, we use the lemmas of v and n. We then extract the following features:

- F_1: One-hot representing the pattern used to predict the candidate (see Section 3.1).

- F_2: Fraction of true LVCs among all candi-

---

[3]Note that the majority of LVCs has two components only, but some do contain additional components, such as prepositions when they are required to connect the verb and the noun.

[4]This alternative pattern would cover the expression *make adjustment* in *make an effort and an adjustment*, for which two occurrences of LVCs would be annotated according to the PARSEME guidelines.

[5]For the training data, we take the union of gold LVCs and LVC candidates identified through syntactic patterns, since the patterns do not cover all gold LVCs.

	BG	DE	EL	ES	EU	FA	FR	HE	HR	HU	IT	PL	PT	RO	SL	TR	μAvg
%seen	60	26	50	48	86	61	68	45	29	75	71	66	74	90	57	44	62
Coverage (seen)	98	100	100	95	94	91	99	82	93	86	90	97	95	96	100	98	95
Coverage (unseen)	73	84	91	98	98	90	91	78	96	86	72	90	93	33	92	95	90

Table 1: Fraction of LVC annotations that were *seen* in train, and LVC candidate coverage (highest recall achievable, if all candidates are predicted as LVC) — evaluated on the development sets.

dates in train that have the same pattern and lexical items (lemma-wise comparison) as c (-1 if unseen in train).

- F_3: POS tag of v and n.

- F_4: Dependency relation between v and n (NONE if not directly connected).

- F_5: One-hot for the number of components of c (with the rationale that LVCs of length higher than 2 may display more non-standard behavior due to the additionally lexicalized words).

- F_6: One-hot for the number of gaps (extraneous words that do not belong to the LVC), between the leftmost and rightmost components of c, in the underlying sentence.

- F_C: Binary contextual features from the underlying UD parses. Features are defined for every observed $\langle$key, value$\rangle$ pair in the morphological CoNLLU column (e.g. $\langle$Tense, Past$\rangle$), as well as every observed $\langle$column, value$\rangle$ pair for the UD columns FORM, LEMMA, XPOS, UPOS and DEPREL (e.g. $\langle$FORM, took$\rangle$, $\langle$LEMMA, picture$\rangle$, $\langle$POS, NOUN$\rangle$). These features are binary in value, and indicate whether the $\langle$key, value$\rangle$ pair is present for c. A feature is considered present if it appears in at least one of the direct dependents of n or v. We consider only the top t features with the highest mutual information and whose underlying pairs appear in at least ℓ LVCs.

While it is clear that LVC identification would greatly benefit from fine-grained semantic clues such as noun predicativeness, such information is not readily available for most languages under study. We consider instead on a set of unsupervised features that can be constructed for all languages based on distributional semantic models. In particular, we consider the *fasttext* (Bojanowski et al., 2017) set of pretrained word embeddings (which is also used by the SHOMA system) as a basis for semantic features.

- F_E: Word embeddings for the lemma of the verb and noun (300 dimensions each).

- F_k^1: k-nearest neighbors of the underlying noun n. Considered neighbors are all nouns that are paired up with the underlying verb v in at least one LVC candidate in the training set, whether true LVC or not. We select the top k neighbors whose embedding has highest cosine against n's embedding. Each neighbor is either *seen-in-LVC* (it is part of at least one true LVC) or an *unseen-in-LVC* (it is part of false positives only). The final value of the feature is the sum of the scores of the k neighbors, where a seen-in-LVC neighbor has score $+1$ and an unseen-in-LVC neighbor has score -1.

- F_k^c: Same as F_k^1, but each neighbor's score that is being summed up is additionally weighted by the underlying cosine.

3.3 LVC classifiers

We present below two LVC candidate binary classifiers based on the features above: SVM and FFN. We compare them against two simple baselines: Majority, which only predicts LVCs seen in train, and kNN, which we use either for all LVCs or for those unseen in train, in combination with Majority for the seen LVCs. Note we consider a predicted or gold LVC to be seen in train when the training corpus contains at least one gold LVC with same lemmas, in whatever order and with whatever syntactic pattern.

- Majority baseline: Predict a candidate as LVC if and only if it has been annotated more often than not in the training corpus (i.e. the value of feature F_2 is greater than 0.5).

- kNN baseline: Predict a candidate as LVC if and only if the value of feature F_k^c is positive,

Configuration	BG	DE	EL	ES	EU	FA	FR	HE	HR	HU	IT	PL	PT	RO	SL	TR	μAvg
Maj (seen)	72	84	76	89	81	83	93	68	91	91	87	92	86	90	70	38	81
kNN (seen)	62	84	76	89	79	81	92	66	91	91	83	89	82	37	60	46	78
FFN (seen)	74	78	82	94	87	87	94	67	92	92	86	90	88	87	68	71	**85**
SVM (seen)	70	74	84	86	86	89	93	64	91	91	84	89	90	72	76	57	84
kNN (unseen)	08	08	24	22	32	30	30	04	13	13	11	20	32	00	04	24	22
FFN (unseen)	15	18	27	29	22	55	31	05	21	33	12	22	25	00	08	27	28
SVM (unseen)	15	15	33	20	42	63	37	02	24	46	10	31	45	00	10	34	**34**

Table 2: F_1 scores on Majority and kNN baselines (F_k^c with $k = 2$) , along with the best configuration for the SVM and FFN classifiers — on the development sets.

meaning that within the k nominal neighbors of the noun n of the candidate, the total cosine of seen-in-LVC surpasses that of the unseen-in-LVC neighbors.

- SVM: Support vector machine with RBF kernel. Positive and negative examples are balanced through compensating class weights. We use a 3-fold grid-search to select for the best combination of classifier hyperparameters for each language; we consider the values $C \in \{1, 10, 20, 50, 100\}$ and $\gamma \in \{0.5, 0.1, 0.05, 0.01\}$.

- FFN: Feed-forward network with a 100-neuron hidden layer, using tanh as an activation function and 50% dropout. The network uses an SGD optimizer[6] and negative log-likelihood loss. Positive training examples are duplicated as much as needed so as to be balanced against negative examples. The final list of examples is shuffled, and fed into the classifier in batches of size $B \in \{1, 2, 4, 8, 16\}$. Training is performed for a number e of epochs, such that epoch $e + 1$ would have had higher loss on the validation set (10% of train). One-hot features are implemented as a layer of trainable embeddings instead (300 dimensions for lemmas; 5 dimensions for dependency relations, for F_5 and F_6).

3.4 Evaluation

We explore hyperparameters on the 16 languages that contained a development set, and evaluate the final systems on the test set for all 19 languages (using both training and development set for training). Evaluation of LVC predictions for each language uses the MWE-based F_1 score from of the PARSEME shared task (Ramisch et al., 2018). We modified its evaluation script so as to output scores

for seen and unseen LVCs: it first labels a LVC (whether gold or predicted) as "seen" if there exists at least one gold LVC occurrence with the same set of lemmas in the training set, and unseen otherwise. The two labels are then evaluated separately.

We also present a micro-average score (μAvg), in which the F_1 scores of all languages are averaged with a weight that is proportional to the number of LVCs in that languages test (or development) set.[7] On test sets, we compare our results with SHOMA and TRAVERSAL, the two highest-scoring systems in the shared-task.[8]

4 Results

Table 1 presents the fraction of LVCs in the development set that can also be seen in the training set. In the lower end, German dev LVCs were only seen in train 26% of the time, mostly due to the small training set in this language. In the higher end, 90% of Romanian LVCs had a counterpart in the training set, suggesting that a simple baseline focusing on seen LVCs should already yield good results for this language.

The last two rows in Table 1 present the coverage (i.e. recall) in the initial step of LVC candidate extraction, for the strategy atleastNoccurs with $N = 2$. This strategy was found to yield the best results in both SVM and FFN settings during early experiments. It can be seen that, despite variation across languages, mainly due to training corpus size differences, the micro-averaged coverage is 95% for dev LVCs seen in train, and slightly

---

[6]Basic tuning of the learning rate led us to use 0.01.

[7]We chose to use micro-average, since the test sets across languages don't have the same number of sentences, for reasons that are independent of the linguistic properties of each.

[8]We used the predicted test sets of all participating systems (made available by the shared task organizers at `https://gitlab.com/parseme/sharedtask-data/tree/master/1.1/system-results`), filtering them to consider LVCs only. The best systems in open and closed tracks (SHOMA and TRAVERSAL) are the same when considering all verbal MWEs or LVCs only.

Configuration	BG	DE	EL	EN	ES	EU	FA	FR	HE	HI	HR	HU	IT	LT	PL	PT	RO	SL	TR	μAvg
Maj (seen)	74	67	85	64	60	87	84	85	70	90	87	94	82	48	87	89	81	75	53	80
kNN (seen)	71	67	78	64	61	83	84	87	64	89	89	92	80	47	88	87	38	62	58	78
SVM (seen)	75	67	80	65	60	86	87	89	66	94	80	94	83	38	89	91	67	79	77	81
FFN (seen)	82	69	79	67	64	87	86	89	69	92	85	94	82	48	88	93	74	69	87	**83**
SHOMA (seen)	64	00	79	00	39	88	88	66	73	88	43	78	66	49	69	87	93	52	79	76
TRAV (seen)	62	53	66	34	44	82	81	70	58	81	64	87	64	45	76	78	83	63	66	72
kNN (unseen)	14	09	23	23	17	16	21	34	05	44	18	24	13	08	19	28	00	05	36	22
SVM (unseen)	17	24	34	19	07	17	57	29	07	61	17	36	06	07	39	39	67	13	43	**31**
FFN (unseen)	20	18	18	33	20	19	45	25	06	64	16	29	12	15	33	31	00	07	34	29
SHOMA (unseen)	21	00	36	03	13	35	62	37	19	53	19	14	04	08	22	35	29	00	50	**31**
TRAV (unseen)	08	00	18	14	10	11	41	31	05	42	21	23	00	01	20	24	00	00	23	20
Maj + kNN	53	26	62	31	36	81	64	62	30	68	45	77	63	28	60	74	69	34	44	57
kNN	56	26	59	32	37	77	65	64	29	67	46	76	62	28	61	72	28	31	49	57
SVM	61	40	66	26	35	79	77	65	41	77	44	81	70	28	71	78	67	63	61	**63**
FFN	53	26	43	40	36	74	74	51	21	78	42	75	44	30	60	68	57	26	56	56
SHOMA	50	00	60	02	22	79	78	51	43	72	24	59	46	29	51	70	86	28	64	56
TRAVERSAL	44	15	47	18	26	70	65	52	30	62	32	68	51	23	52	62	73	38	44	50

Table 3: F_1 scores (split for seen LVCs, unseen LVCs and overall) for the Majority and kNN baselines, the best configuration of our SVM and FFN classifiers, and the highest-scoring systems in the shared-task (SHOMA and TRAV(ERSAL)) — evaluated on the test sets.

lower (90%) for unseen ones.

We tuned the hyperparameters on the development sets. For every system, the same configuration is used for all languages. The best kNN configuration is F_k^c with k=2; the best SVM and FFN configurations are both $F_{1..6}$, F_C (t=30, ℓ=30), F_E.

Table 2 presents the scores obtained by these best configurations on the development sets. Across seen LVCs, both the Majority and kNN baselines have considerably high scores (F_1=81 and 78 respectively, but the highest results are obtained by FFN and SVM (F_1=85 and 84). For the unseen LVCs, results are quite lower, and there is a bigger gap between the kNN baseline (F_1=0.22) and the best system on unseen, namely the SVM (F_1=0.34).

Table 3 presents system results for the same configurations when evaluated against the test sets. On seen LVCs here again, the Majority baseline is slightly higher than the kNN baseline. However, both baselines beat the best systems from the shared-task (that we recomputed for LVCs only). Results for SVM (F_1=81) are comparable to the Majority baseline (F_1=81) while FFN obtains the highest score (F_1=83).

When we consider LVCs that were not seen in training data, results are much lower. The kNN baseline obtains an F_1=0.22, while SHOMA obtains F_1=0.31, as does our SVM, while results for FFN are slightly weaker. When predictions for both seen and unseen LVCs are taken together, FFN and SHOMA have comparable scores (F_1=56), while the baselines (either Major-

ity+kNN or kNN alone) is slightly higher. The best system overall is the SVM (F_1=63).

5 Conclusion

In this paper, we considered the task of identifying LVCs in running text. We propose to use data-driven language-specific syntactic patterns for the extraction of LVC candidates out of syntactic parses, followed by a binary classification of the candidates into LVC or not.

We proposed a strong baseline combining different methods for LVC candidates depending on whether they were seen in the training set or not ("seen" meaning a LVC with same lemmas is annotated at least once in the training set). The baseline for seen cases tags a candidate as LVC if the training occurrences with same lemmas are more often tagged as LVC than not. The baseline for unseen cases uses the similarity of the predicative noun with the nouns of the training candidates, in a distributional semantic model. We also proposed supervised classifiers (a SVM and a feed-forward neural network) trained using internal and contextual morphosyntactic and semantic features, and working independently of the seen/unseen status.

Overall the SVM system is our best one, surpassing the best shared task system on LVCs (SHOMA, (Taslimipoor and Rohanian, 2018)) by 7 percentage points. When evaluating performance separately on seen and unseen LVCs, the feed-forward network performs a little better on seen LVCs, but less well on unseen ones. It also appears that our results for seen LVCs surpass the best shared-task results even in the case of the baseline, in spite of a much simpler technique of supervised learning. For unseen LVCs, results are globally quite lower. The best performance is F_1=31%, achieved both by the SHOMA system and our SVM. Our kNN-inspired baseline achieves F_1=22% only, a performance that would rank second for unseen LVCs in the shared task.

Given the quality of predictions for seen LVCs, future works should focus on improving prediction for the unseen expressions. Such task could be achieved through an evaluation of different types of neural network. Other semantically-motivated language-independent features should also be considered, so as to estimate the candidate noun's abstractness and predicativeness, as well as the level of semantic bleaching in the use of the verb. Finally, future works should investigate using a model for contextualized word embeddings such as BERT (Devlin et al., 2018)), despite the difficulty of covering the 19 languages of the PARSEME datasets.

Acknowledgements

We would like to thank Bruno Guillaume for advice in using Grew. This work was partially funded by the French National Research Agency (PARSEME-FR ANR-14-CERA-0001).

References

Piotr Bojanowski, Edouard Grave, Armand Joulin, and Tomas Mikolov. 2017. Enriching word vectors with subword information. *Transactions of the Association for Computational Linguistics*, 5:135–146.

Guillaume Bonfante, Bruno Guillaume, and Guy Perrier. 2018. *Application of Graph Rewriting to Natural Language Processing*. Wiley Online Library.

Claire Bonial and Martha Palmer. 2016. Comprehensive and consistent propbank light verb annotation. In *LREC*.

Fabienne Cap, Manju Nirmal, Marion Weller, and Sabine Schulte im Walde. 2015. How to account for idiomatic German support verb constructions in statistical machine translation. In *Proceedings of the 11th Workshop on Multiword Expressions*, pages 19–28, Denver, Colorado. Association for Computational Linguistics.

Wei-Te Chen, Claire Bonial, and Martha Palmer. 2015. English light verb construction identification using lexical knowledge. In *Proceedings of the Twenty-Ninth AAAI Conference on Artificial Intelligence*, AAAI'15, pages 2375–2381. AAAI Press.

Jacob Devlin, Ming-Wei Chang, Kenton Lee, and Kristina Toutanova. 2018. BERT: pre-training of deep bidirectional transformers for language understanding. *CoRR*, abs/1810.04805.

István Nagy T., Veronika Vincze, and Richárd Farkas. 2013. Full-coverage identification of English light verb constructions. In *Proceedings of the Sixth International Joint Conference on Natural Language Processing*, pages 329–337, Nagoya, Japan. Asian Federation of Natural Language Processing.

Joakim Nivre and Veronika Vincze. 2015. Light verb constructions in universal dependencies. In *Poster at the 5th PARSEME meeting, Iasi, Romania*.

Caroline Pasquer, Carlos Ramisch, Agata Savary, and Jean-Yves Antoine. 2018. VarIDE at PARSEME shared task 2018: Are variants really as alike as two peas in a pod? In *Proceedings of the Joint Workshop on Linguistic Annotation, Multiword Expressions and Constructions (LAW-MWE-CxG-2018)*, Santa Fe, New Mexico, USA. Association for Computational Linguistics.

Carlos Ramisch, Silvio Ricardo Cordeiro, Agata Savary, Veronika Vincze, Verginica Barbu Mititelu, Archna Bhatia, Maja Buljan, Marie Candito, Polona Gantar, Voula Giouli, Tunga Güngör, Abdelati Hawwari, Uxoa Iñurrieta, Jolanta Kovalevskaitė, Simon Krek, Timm Lichte, Chaya Liebeskind, Johanna Monti, Carla Parra Escartín, Behrang Qasemi-Zadeh, Renata Ramisch, Nathan Schneider, Ivelina Stoyanova, Ashwini Vaidya, and Abigail Walsh. 2018. Edition 1.1 of the PARSEME shared task on automatic identification of verbal multiword expressions. In *Proceedings of the Joint Workshop on Linguistic Annotation, Multiword Expressions and Constructions (LAW-MWE-CxG-2018)*, pages 222–240, Santa Fe, New Mexico, USA. Association for Computational Linguistics.

Lance A Ramshaw and Mitchell P Marcus. 1999. Text chunking using transformation-based learning. In *Natural language processing using very large corpora*, pages 157–176. Springer.

Omid Rohanian, Shiva Taslimipoor, Samaneh Kouchaki, Le An Ha, and Ruslan Mitkov. 2019. Bridging the gap: Attending to discontinuity in identification of multiword expressions. In *Proceedings of the 2019 Conference of the North American Chapter of the Association for Computational Linguistics: Human Language Technologies, Volume 1 (Long and Short Papers)*, pages 2692–2698, Minneapolis, Minnesota. Association for Computational Linguistics.

Agata Savary, Marie Candito, Verginica Barbu Mititelu, Eduard Bejček, Fabienne Cap, Slavomír

Čéplö, Silvio Ricardo Cordeiro, Gülşen Cebiroğlu Eryiğit, Voula Giouli, Maarten Van Gompel, Yaakov HaCohen-Kerner, Jolanta Kovalevskaitė, Simon Krek, Chaya Liebeskind, Johanna Monti, Carla Parra Escartín, Lonneke Der, Behrang Qasemi Zadeh, Carlos Ramisch, and Veronika Vincze. 2018. *PARSEME multilingual corpus of verbal multiword expressions*. Berlin: Language Science Press.

Shiva Taslimipoor and Omid Rohanian. 2018. SHOMA at PARSEME Shared Task on automatic identification of VMWEs: Neural multiword expression tagging with high generalisation. *arXiv preprint arXiv:1809.03056.*

Yuancheng Tu and Dan Roth. 2011. Learning English light verb constructions: contextual or statistical. In *Proceedings of the Workshop on Multiword Expressions: from Parsing and Generation to the Real World*, pages 31–39. Association for Computational Linguistics.

Veronika Vincze, János Zsibrita, and István Nagy T. 2013. Dependency parsing for identifying Hungarian light verb constructions. In *Proceedings of the Sixth International Joint Conference on Natural Language Processing*, pages 207–215, Nagoya, Japan. Asian Federation of Natural Language Processing.

Jakub Waszczuk. 2018. TRAVERSAL at PARSEME Shared Task 2018: Identification of verbal multiword expressions using a discriminative tree-structured model. In *Joint Workshop on Linguistic Annotation, Multiword Expressions and Constructions (LAW-MWE-CxG-2018)*.

Comparing the Performance of Feature Representations for the Categorization of the Easy-to-Read Variety vs Standard Language

Marina Santini
RISE Research Institutes of Sweden
(Division ICT - RISE SICS East)
Stockholm, Sweden
marina.santini@ri.se

Benjamin Danielsson
Linköping University
(IDA)
Linköping, Sweden
benda425@student.liu.se

Arne Jönsson
RISE Research Institutes of Sweden
& Linköping University (IDA)
Linköping, Sweden
arne.jonsson@liu.se

Abstract

We explore the effectiveness of four feature representations – bag-of-words, word embeddings, principal components and autoencoders – for the binary categorization of the easy-to-read variety vs standard language. "Standard language" refers to the ordinary language variety used by a population as a whole or by a community, while the "easy-to-read" variety is a simpler (or a simplified) version of the standard language. We test the efficiency of these feature representations on three corpora, which differ in size, class balance, unit of analysis, language and topic. We rely on supervised and unsupervised machine learning algorithms. Results show that bag-of-words is a robust and straightforward feature representation for this task and performs well in many experimental settings. Its performance is equivalent or equal to the performance achieved with principal components and autoencorders, whose preprocessing is however more time-consuming. Word embeddings are less accurate than the other feature representations for this classification task.

1 Introduction

Broadly speaking, a language variety is any specific form of language variation, such as standard language, dialects, registers or jargons. In this paper, we focus on two language varieties, namely the standard language variety and the easy-to-read variety. In this context, "standard language" refers to the official and ordinary language variety used by a population as a whole, or to a variety that is normally employed within a community. For example, "Standard English" is the form of the English language widely accepted as the usual correct form, while within the medical community it is the specialized medical jargon that is considered to be standard language. In contrast, the easy-to-read variety is a simpler version of a standard language. The need of an easy-to-read variety stems from the difficulties that certain groups of people experience with standard language, such as people with dyslexia and other learning disabilities, the elderly, children, non-native speakers and so on. In order to meet the needs of a simpler language that makes information easy to read and understand for all, European Standards have been established[1], and an important initiative like Wikipedia has created a special edition called Simple English Wikipedia[2]. These are not isolated phenomena. For instance, in Sweden public authorities (sv: *myndigheter*) provide an easy-to-read version (a.k.a. simple Swedish or sv: lättläst) of their written documentation.

Both in the case of the Simple English Wikipedia and in the case of Swedish public authorities, the simplified documents are manually written. Since the manual production of simplified texts is time-consuming, the task called Text Simplification (TS) is very active in Natural Language Processing (NLP) in the attempt to streamline this type of text production. TS is a fast-growing research area that can bring about practical benefits, e.g. the automatic generation of simplified texts. There is, however, a TS subtask that is still underexplored: the categorization of the easy-to-read variety vs standard language. The findings presented in this paper contribute to start filling this gap. The automatic separation of standard texts from easy-to-read texts could be particularly useful for other TS subtasks, such as the bootstrapping of monolingual corpora from the web or the

---

[1] https://easy-to-read.eu/wp-content/uploads/2014/12/EN_Information_for_all.pdf

[2] https://simple.wikipedia.org/wiki/Main_Page

extraction of simplified terminology. Other areas that could benefit from it include information retrieval (e.g. for the retrieval of easy-to-read or patient-friendly medical information) and deep learning-based dialogue systems (e.g. customized chatbots for expert users or naive users).

The research question we would like to answer is: *which is the most suitable feature representation for this categorization task?* In order to answer this question, we compare four different feature representations that can potentially make sense of the lexical makeup that differentiates easy-to-read from standard language, namely bag-of-words (BoWs), word embeddings, principal components and autoencoders. It goes without saying that these four feature representations are just a few of the many possible feature representations for this kind of task. We start our long-term exploration with these four feature representations because they are straightforward and easy to extract automatically from any corpora. We test the efficiency of the four feature representations with three types of machine learning algorithms: traditional supervised machine learning, deep learning and clustering[3]. The experiments are based on three corpora belonging to different domains. From these corpora, we extracted three datasets of different sizes, different class balance, different units of analysis (sentence vs document), different languages (Swedish and English).

The ultimate goal of the experiments presented in this paper is to propose a first empirical baseline for the categorization of the easy-to-read variety vs standard language.

2   Previous Work

As mentioned above, the automatic separation of standard language from the easy-to-read variety is underinvestigated, but it could be useful for several TS subtasks, such as the bootstrapping (Baroni and Bernardini, 2004) of monolingual parallel corpora (Caseli et al., 2009), of monolingual comparable corpora (Barzilay and Elhadad, 2003) or the exploitation of regular corpora (Glavaš and Štajner, 2015). Extensive work exists in TS (Saggion, 2017). The most advanced work focuses on the implementation of neural text simplification systems that are able to simultaneously perform lexical simplification and content reduction

(Nisioi et al., 2017).

In this paper, however, we do not focus on the creation of TS systems, but rather on the sheer downstream categorization task of separating standard language from the easy-to-read variety. To our knowledge, limited research exists in this area, which mostly focuses on the discrimination between the specialized language used by domain experts and the language used by non-experts (a.k.a. laypeople or the lay). This type of distinction is required in some domains (e.g. medical and legal domains), where the specialized jargon hinders the understanding of "ordinary" people, i.e. people without specialized education, who struggle to get a grip on professional sublanguages. In the experiments reported in Santini et al. (2019), it is shown that it is possible to successfully discriminate between medical web texts written for experts and for laypeople in Swedish. Results are encouraging and we use one of their datasets in the experiments presented here.

Other corpora are available that can be used for the automatic categorization of the easy-to-read variety vs standard language. For instance, the Simple English Wikipedia corpus[4] (Kauchak, 2013), and the DigInclude corpus[5] in Swedish (Rennes and Jönsson, 2016). However, neither Simple English Wikipedia nor DigInclude have ever been used for this text categorization task. We use them in this context for the first time.

3   Corpora and Datasets

In our experiments, we use three corpora, two in Swedish and one in English. More precisely, we rely on 1) a subset of the eCare corpus (Santini et al., 2019) in Swedish; 2) a subset of the DigInclude corpus (Rennes and Jönsson, 2016) in Swedish and 3) a subset of the Simple English Wikipedia corpus (Kauchak, 2013) in English.

The eCare corpus is a domain-specific web corpus. The domain of interest is the medical field of chronic diseases. From the current version of the corpus we re-use a labelled subset. The eCare subset contains 462 webpages without boilerplates. The webpages have been labelled as 'lay' or 'specialized' by a lay native speaker. Lay sublanguage is an *easy-to-read* version of the *standard language* (the medical jargon) used by healthcare pro-

---

[3]The umbrella term 'categorization' is used to cover these three machine learning approaches.

[4]http://www.cs.pomona.edu/~dkauchak/simplification/

[5]https://www.ida.liu.se/~arnjo82/diginclude/corpus.shtml

fessionals. The 462 webpages of the eCare dataset (amounting to 424,278 words) have been labelled in the following way: 388 specialized webpages (66%) and 154 lay webpages (33%). The dataset is unbalanced. The unit of analysis that we use in these experiments is the *document*.

The DigInclude corpus is a collection of easy-to-read sentences aligned to standard language sentences. The corpus has been crawled from a number of Swedish authorities' websites. The DigInclude datasets contains 17,502 sentences, 3,827 simple sentences (22%) and 13,675 standard sentences (78%), amounting to 233,094 words. The dataset is heavily unbalanced. The unit of analysis is the *sentence*.

The Simple English Wikipedia (SEW) corpus was generated by aligning Simple English Wikipedia and standard English Wikipedia. Two different versions of the corpus exist (V1 and V2). V2 has been packaged in sentences and in documents. We used the subset of V2 divided into sentences. The SEW dataset contains 325,245 sentences, 159,713 easy-to-read sentences (49.1%) and 165,532 standard sentences (50.9%), amounting to 7,191,133 words. The dataset is fairly balanced. The unit of analysis is the *sentence*.

4   Features Representations and Filters

At the landing page of Simple English Wikipedia, it is stated: "We use Simple English words and grammar here." Essentially, this statement implies that the use of basic vocabulary and simple grammar makes a text easier to read. In these experiments we focus on the effectiveness of feature representations based on **lexical items** and leave the exploration of grammar-based tags for the future.

In this section, we describe the four feature representations, as well as the filters that have been applied to create them. These filters and the methods described in Section 5 are included in the Weka Data Mining workbench (Witten et al., 2016)[6]. All the experiments performed with the Weka workbench can be replicated in any other workbench, or programmatically in any programming language. We use Weka here for the sake of fast reproducibility, since Weka is easy to use also for those who are not familiar with the practicalities of machine learning. Additionally, it is open source, flexible and well-documented.

In the experiments below several filters have been stacked together via the *Multifilter* metafilter, which gives the opportunity to apply several filtering schemes sequentially to the same dataset.

BoWs.   BoWs is a representation of text that describes the occurrence of single words within a document. It involves two things: a vocabulary of known words and a weighing scheme to measure the presence of known words. It is called a "bag" of words, because any information about the order or structure of words in the document is discarded. The model is only concerned with whether known words occur in the document, not where in the document, or with which other words they co-occur. The *advantage* of BoWs is simplicity. BoWs models are simple to understand and implement and offer a lot of flexibility for customization. Preprocessing can include different levels of refinement, from stopword removal to stemming or lemmatization, and a wide range of weighing schemes. Usually, lexical items in the form of BoWs represent the topic(s) of a text and are normally used for topical text classification. Several related topics make up a domain, i.e. a subject field like Fashion or Medicine. Here we use BoWs for a different purpose, which is to detect the different level of **lexical sophistication** that exists between the easy-to-read variety and standard language. Intuitively, easy-to-read texts have a much plainer and poorer vocabulary than texts written in standard language. The *rationale* of using BoWs in this context is then to capture the lexical diversification that characterizes easy-to-read and standard language texts.

Starting from datasets in string format, we applied *StringToWordVector*, which is an unsupervised filter that converts string attributes into a set of attributes representing frequencies of word occurrence. For all the corpora, we selected the TF and IDF weighing schemes, normalization to lowercase and normalization to the length of the documents. Lemmatization, stemming and stopword removal were not applied. The number of words that were kept varies according to the size of corpus. The complete settings of this and all the other filters described below are fully documented in the companion website.

Word embeddings.   Word embeddings are one of the most popular representations of document vocabulary to date, since they have proved to be

---

[6]Open source software freely available at `https://www.cs.waikato.ac.nz/ml/weka/`

effective in many tasks (e.g. sentiment analysis, text classification, etc.). The *advantage* of word embeddings lies in their capability to capture the context of a word in a document, as well as semantic and syntactic similarity. The basic idea behind word embeddings is to "embed" a word vector space into another. The big intuition is that this mapping could bring to light something new about the data that was unknown before. More specifically, word embeddings learn both the meanings of the words and the relationships between words because they capture the implicit relations between words by determining how often a word appears with other words in the training text. The *rationale* of using word embeddings in this context is to account for both semantic and syntactic representations, traits that can be beneficial for the categorization of language varieties.

Word embeddings can be native or pretrained. Here we use the pretrained Polyglot Embeddings (Al-Rfou et al., 2013) for Swedish (polyglot-sv) and for English (polyglot-en).

Principal Components. Principal Component Analysis (PCA) involves the orthogonal transformation of possibly correlated variables into a set of values of linearly uncorrelated variables called principal components. This transformation is defined in such a way that the first principal component explains the largest possible variance, and each succeeding component in turn explains the highest variance possible under the constraint that it is orthogonal to the preceding components. The *advantage* of PCA is to reduce the number of redundant features, which might be common but disturbing when using a BoWs approach, thus possibly improving text classification results. The *rationale* of using PCA components in this context is to ascertain whether feature reduction is beneficial for the categorization of language varieties.

To perform PCA and the transformation of the data, we wrapped *PrincipalComponents* filter on the top of the *StringToWordVector* filter, via the Multifilter metafilter. The *PrincipalComponents* filter is an unsupervised filter that chooses enough principal components (a.k.a eigenvectors) to account for 95% of the variance in the original data.

Autoencoders. Similar to PCA, the basic idea behind autoencoders is dimensionality reduction. However, autoencoders are much more flexible than PCA since they can represent both linear and non-linear transformation, while PCA can only perform linear transformation. Additionally, autoencoders can be layered to form deep learning networks. They can also be more efficient in terms of model parameters since a single autoencoder can learn several layers rather than learning one huge transformation as with PCA. The *advantage* of using autoencoders in this context is to transform inputs into outputs with the minimum possible error (Hinton and Salakhutdinov, 2006). The *rationale* of their use here is to determine whether they provide a representation with enriched properties that is neater than other reduced representations.

In these experiments, autoencoders are generated using the *MLPAutoencoder* filter stacked on the top of the *StringToWordVector* filter, via the Multifilter metafilter. This *MLPAutoencoder* filter gives the possibility of creating contractive autoencoders, which are much more efficient than standard autoencoders (Rifai et al., 2011).

5 Methods, Baselines and Evaluation

In this section, we describe the categorization schemes, the baselines and the evaluation metrics used for comparison.

Methods. We use three different learning methods, namely an implementation of SVM, an implementation of multilayer perceptron (MLP) and an implementation of K-Means for clustering. The rationale behind these choices is to compare the behaviour of the four feature representations described above with learning schemes that have a different inductive biases, and to assess the difference (if any) between the performance achieved with labelled data (supervised algorithms) and unlabelled data (clustering). We calculate a random baseline with the ZeroR classifier. All the categorization schemes are described below.

ZeroR: baseline classifier. The ZeroR is based on the Zero Rule algorithm and predicts the class value that has the most observations in the training dataset. It is more reliable than a completely random baseline.

SVM: traditional supervised machine learning. SVM is a classic and powerful supervised machine learning algorithm that performs extremely well in text classification tasks with numerous features. Weka's SVM implementation is called SMO and includes John Platt's sequential minimal optimization algorithm (Platt, 1998) for training a support vector classifier (Joachims, 1998).

Since two corpora are highly unbalanced, we also combined SMO with filters that can correct class unbalance. More specifically, we relied on *ClassBalancer*, which reweights the instances in the data so that each class has the same total weight; *Resample*, which produces a random subsample of a dataset using either sampling with replacement or without replacement; *SMOTE*, which resamples a dataset by applying the Synthetic Minority Oversampling TEchnique (SMOTE); and *SpreadSubsample*, which produces a random subsample of a dataset. All the models built with SMO are based on Weka's standard parameters.

Multilayer Perceptron: Deep Learning. Weka provides several implementations of MLP. We relied on the WekaDeeplearning4j package that is described in Lang et al. (2019). The main classifier in this package is named Dl4jMlpClassifier and is a wrapper for the DeepLearning4j library[7] to train a multilayer perceptron. While features like BoWs, principal components and autoencoders can be fed to any classifiers within the Weka workbench (if they are wrapped in filters), word embeddings can be handled only by the Dl4jMlpClassifier (this explains *N/A* in Table 2). We used the standard configuration of the Dl4jMlpClassifier (which includes only one output layer) for BoWs, principal components and autoencoders. Conversely, the configuration used with word embeddings was cutomized in the following way: word embeddings were passed through four layers (two convulational layers, a GlobalPoolingLayer and a OutputLayer); the number of epochs was set to 100; the instance iterator was set on CnnTextEmbeddingInstanceIterator; we used the polyglot embeddings for Swedish and English, as mentioned above.

K-Means: Clustering. We compare the performance of the supervised classification with clustering (fully unsupervised categorization). We use the traditional K-Means algorithm (Arthur and Vassilvitskii, 2007) that in Weka is called SimpleKMeans. Since we know the number of classes in advance (i.e. two classes), we evaluate the quality of the clusters against existing classes using the option *Classes to cluster evaluation*, which first ignores the class attribute and generates the clus-

ters, then during the test phase assigns classes to the clusters, based on the majority value of the class attribute within each cluster.

Evaluation metrics. We compare the performances on the Weighted Averaged F-Measure (*AvgF*), which is the sum of all the classes' F-measures, each weighted according to the number of instances with that particular class label.

In order to reliably assess the performance based on AvgF, we also use *k-statistic* and the *ROC area value*. K-statistic indicates the agreement of prediction with true class; when the value is 0 the agreement is random. The quality of a classifier can also be assessed with the help of the ROC area value which indicates the area under the ROC curve (AUC). It is used to measure how well a classifier performs. The ROC area value lies between about 0.500 to 1, where 0.500 (and below) denotes a bad classifier and 1 denotes an excellent classifier.

ZeroR Baselines. Table 1 shows a breakdown of the baselines returned by the ZeroR classifier on the three corpora. These baselines imply that the k-statistic is 0 and the ROC area value is below or equal to 0.500.

6 Results and Discussion

The main results are summarized in Table 2 and Table 3. As shown in in Table 2, by and large both SMO and the Dl4jMlpClassifier have equivalent or identical performance on all datasets in combination with BoWs and principal components (we observe however that the Dl4jMlpClassifier is definitely slower than SMO). Word embeddings have a slightly lower performance than BoWs and principal components on the eCare and SEW subsets. Autoencoders perform well (0.82) in combination with SMO on the eCare subset, less so (0.77) when running with the Dl4jMlpClassifier. The performance of clustering with BoWs on eCare gives an encouraging 0.59 (6 points above the ZeroR baseline of 0.53), while the performance with principal components and autoencoders is below the ZeroR baselines. In short, BoWs, which is the simplest and the most straightforward feature representation in this set of experiments, has a performance that is equivalent or identical to other more complex feature representations.

But what do the classifiers learn when they are fed with BoWs? The classifiers learn the

---

[7]https://deeplearning.cms.waikato.ac.nz/

Table 1: ZeroR baselines, breakdown

	Class	k	Acc(%)	Err(%)	P	R	F	ROC
eCare Subset (462 webpages)	lay (154 webpages)	0.00	66.66	33.33	0.00	0.00	0.00	0.490
	specialized (308 webpages)				0.66	1.00	0.80	0.490
	AvgF						**0.53**	
DigInclude Subset (17,502 sentences)	simplified (3,827 sentences)	0.00	78.13	21.86	0.00	0.00	0.00	0.500
	specialized (13,675 sentences)				0.78	1.00	0.87	0.500
	AvgF						**0.68**	
SEW Subset (325,235 sentences)	simplified (159,708 sentences)	0.00	50.89	49.10	0.00	0.00	0.00	0.500
	specialized (165,527 sentences)				0.50	1.00	0.67	0.500
	AvgF						**0.34**	

Table 2: Summary table (AvgF): easy-to-read variety vs standard language

Dataset	Features	SMO	DI4jMlp	K-Means
eCare Subset	BoW Features	0.80	0.80	0.59
	Word Embeddings	N/A	0.75	N/A
	Principal Components	0.80	0.81	0.44
	Autoencoders	0.82	0.77	0.50
DigInclude Subset	BoW	0.72	0.72	0.29
	Word Embeddings	N/A	0.72	N/A
	Principal Components	0.73	0.72	0.19
	Autoencoders	0.68	0.68	0.33
SEW Subset	BoW	0.58	0.56	0.43
	Word Embeddings	N/A	0.55	N/A
	Principal Components	0.55	0.56	0.49
	Autoencoders	0.52	0.51	0.49

Table 3: Summary table (AvgF): unbalanced datasets (BoWs + class balancing filters applied to SMO)

Dataset	NoFilter	ClassBalancer	Resample	SpreadSample	SMOTE
eCare Subset	0.80	0.81	0.81	0.80	0.81
DigInclude Subset	0.72	0.68	0.66	0.73	0.74

words that have been automatically selected by the StringToWordVector filter. Interestingly, since we did not apply stopword removal, the lexical items selected by the filter are mostly function words and common lexical items. An example is shown in Table 4.

Table 4: 5 top frequent words and 5 bottom frequent words in one of the SEW models

Word	Freq
the	237021
of	159924
in	149698
and	135958
a	135867
...	...
...	...
usually	1517
international	1503
municipatlity	1449
show	1415
island	1277

At first glance, it might appear counter-intuitive that BoWs, which are very simple features that do not take syntax and word order into account, can perform well in this kind of task. However, we surmize that this is the effect of the presence of stopwords. As stopwords have not been removed (see settings reported earlier), the classifiers do not learn 'topics' – since content words are pushed down in the rank of the frequency list – but rather the distribution of function words, that are instead top-ranked and represent "structural" lexical items that capture the syntax rather than the meaning of texts. Essentially, function words can be seen as a kind of subliminal syntactic features. What is more, in the corpora some words are domain-specific and difficult, while others are easy and common. Apparently, this *difficult vs easy* variation in the vocabulary helps the classification task. The full list of the words extracted by the StringToWordVectorFilter (utilized alone or as the basis of other filters) is available on the companion website.

The snap verdict of this set of experiments is that BoWs are a valuable feature representation for this kind of task. Their added value is that they need little preprocessing and no additional conversion schemes, as it is required by principal components and autoencoders. BoWs seem to be a robust feature representation that accounts for both syntactic information and lexical sophistication.

As for word embeddings, it seems that their full potential remains unleashed in this context. Theoretically, word embeddings would be an ideal feature representation for this task because they combine syntax and semantics and they could capture simplification devices both at lexical and morpho-syntactic level. However, this does not fully happen here. As a matter of fact, it has already been noticed elsewhere that word embeddings might have an unstable behaviour (Wendlandt et al., 2018) that needs to be further investigated.

Table 5: SMO, breakdown

SMO: eCare Subset							
BOW	k	Acc(%)	Err(%)	P	R	F	ROC
lay	0.56	80.92	19.04	0.72	0.68	0.70	0.779
specialized				0.84	0.87	0.85	0.779
AvgF						**0.80**	
PCA	k	Acc(%)	Err(%)	P	R	F	ROC
lay	0.58	80.30	19.69	0.71	0.68	0.70	0.774
specialized				0.84	0.86	0.85	0.774
AvgF						**0.80**	
Autoenc	k	Acc(%)	Err(%)	P	R	F	ROC
lay	0.60	82.16	17.83	0.72	0.75	0.73	0.804
specialized				0.87	0.85	0.86	0.804
AvgF						**0.82**	

(a) eCare

SMO: DigInclude Subset							
BOW	k	Acc(%)	Err(%)	P	R	F	ROC
simplified	0.13	79.04	20.95	0.61	0.11	0.18	0.546
standard				0.79	0.98	0.88	0.546
AvgF						**0.72**	
PCA	k	Acc(%)	Err(%)	P	R	F	ROC
simplified	0.14	78.80	21.19	0.56	0.14	0.22	0.555
standard				0.80	0.97	0.77	0.555
AvgF						**0.73**	
Autoenc	k	Acc(%)	Err(%)	P	R	F	ROC
simplified	0.00	78.49	21.50	0.00	0.00	0.00	0.500
standard				0.78	1.00	0.87	0.500
AvgF						**0.68**	

(b) DigInclude

SMO: SEW Subset							
BOW	k	Acc(%)	Err(%)	P	R	F	ROC
simplified	0.23	61.81	38.18	0.61	0.61	0.61	0.618
standard				0.62	0.62	0.62	0.618
AvgF						**0.61**	
PCA	k	Acc(%)	Err(%)	P	R	F	ROC
simplified	0.13	57.08	42.91	0.57	0.45	0.51	0.569
standard				0.56	0.67	0.61	0.569
AvgF						**0.56**	
Autoenc	k	Acc(%)	Err(%)	P	R	F	ROC
simplified	0.04	52.67	47.32	0.52	0.42	0.46	0.525
standard				0.53	0.62	0.57	0.525
AvgF						**0.52**	

(c) SEW

the unit of analysis, since the classifiers are not biased towards the majority class and k-statistic and ROC area values are quite robust (mostly above 0.500 and above 0.800 respectively). Additonally, the dataset is small, and this might also facilitate the learning. Clustering with BoWs is well above the ZeroR baseline, while with the other feature representations the performance is below the baseline thresholds.

Table 6: DI4jMlpClassifier, breakdown

DI4jMlpClassifier: eCare Subset							
BOW	k	Acc(%)	Err(%)	P	R	F	ROC
lay	0.57	80.08	19.91	0.67	0.78	0.72	0.890
specialized				0.88	0.80	0.84	0.890
AvgF						**0.80**	
Embed	k	Acc(%)	Err(%)	P	R	F	ROC
lay	0.45	75.79	24.20	0.63	0.65	0.64	0.807
specialized				0.82	0.81	0.81	0.807
AvgF						**0.75**	
PCA	k	Acc(%)	Err(%)	P	R	F	ROC
lay	0.58	80.73	19.26	0.68	0.79	0.73	0.900
specialized				0.88	0.81	0.84	0.900
AvgF						**0.81**	
Autoenc	k	Acc(%)	Err(%)	P	R	F	ROC
lay	0.52	77.07	22.92	0.61	0.84	0.71	0.872
specialized				0.90	0.73	0.81	0.872
AvgF						**0.77**	

(a) eCare

DI4jMlpClassifier: DigInclude Subset							
BOW	k	Acc(%)	Err(%)	P	R	F	ROC
simplified	0.18	72.86	27.13	0.37	0.35	0.36	0.667
standard				0.82	0.83	0.82	0.667
AvgF						**0.72**	
Embed	k	Acc(%)	Err(%)	P	R	F	ROC
simplified	0.10	77.24	22.75	0.41	0.13	0.20	0.587
standard				0.80	0.94	0.86	0.587
AvgF						**0.72**	
PCA	k	Acc(%)	Err(%)	P	R	F	ROC
simplified	0.16	72.94	27.05	0.36	0.31	0.33	0.650
standard				0.81	0.84	0.83	0.650
AvgF						**0.72**	
Autoenc	k	Acc(%)	Err(%)	P	R	F	ROC
simplified	0.00	78.49	21.50	0.00	0.00	0.00	0.500
standard				0.78	1.00	0.87	0.500
AvgF						**0.68**	

(b) DigInclude

DI4jMlpClassifier: SEW Subset							
BOW	k	Acc(%)	Err(%)	P	R	F	ROC
simplified	0.13	56.50	43.49	0.55	0.57	0.56	0.594
standard				0.57	0.55	0.56	0.594
AvgF						**0.56**	
Embed	k	Acc(%)	Err(%)	P	R	F	ROC
simplified	0.10	55.26	44.73	0.54	0.53	0.53	0.586
standard				0.55	0.57	0.56	0.586
AvgF						**0.55**	
PCA	k	Acc(%)	Err(%)	P	R	F	ROC
simplified	0.10	55.21	44.78	0.54	0.55	0.55	0.577
standard				0.56	0.54	0.55	0.577
AvgF						**0.55**	
Autoenc	k	Acc(%)	Err(%)	P	R	F	ROC
simplified	0.04	52.14	47.85	0.51	0.60	0.55	0.535
standard				0.53	0.44	0.48	0.535
AvgF						**0.51**	

(c) SEW

We observe that the classification results are promising on the eCare subset (see breakdown in Tables 5a, 6a and 7a). Arguably, a factor has contributed to achieve this performance: the unit of analysis. Certainly, classification at document level is easier because the classifier has more text to learn from. Surprisingly, the unbalance of the eCare dataset seems to be somehow mitigated by

The DigInclude subset (see breakdown in Tables 5b, 6b, and 7b) is quite problematic from a classification standpoint. It is highly unbalanced and the unit of analysis is the sentence. The classification models built with BoWs, word embeddings and principal components in combination with SMO and the DI4jMlpClassifier are very close to random (see the value of k-statistic and the ROC area value). Although the AvgF values in the summary table (Table 2) seem to be decent for a binary classification problem, they are actually misleading, because the classifiers perform poorly on the minority class, as revealed by the low value of k-statistic and the ROC area value shown in the breakdown tables (Tables 5b and 6b). Classification with autoencoders is perfectly random (k-statistic 0.00 and ROC area value 0.500). Clustering results are very poor with all feature representations. Arguably, with this dataset the learning is hindered by two factors: the high class unbalance and the very short text that makes up a sentence. While in the case of the eCare subset, unbalance is compensated by the longer text of webpages, with DigInclude the sentence does not allow any generalizable learning. Given these results, a different approach must be taken for datasets like DigInclude. Solutions to address these problems include changing the unit of analysis from sentences to documents (if possible) and/or applying a different classification approach e.g. a cost-sensitive classifier of the kind used to predict rare events, e.g. Ali et al. (2015) or Krawczyk (2016). Algorithms used for fraud detection (Sundarkumar and Ravi, 2015) could also be useful.

The SEW corpus (see Tables 5c, 6c and 7c) is balanced and the unit of analysis is the sentence. The performance is promising because it is well above the ZeroR baseline (0.32). The best performance is with the combination of SMO and BoWs that reaches an AvgF of 0.58 with only a limited number of features. Word embeddings perform slightly worse than BoWs (but the running time is much longer). Clustering is definitely encouraging and much above the baseline level with all features representations.

Since the eCare and DigInclude datasets are both unbalanced, we applied class balance correctors. Table 8 shows the breakdown of SMO on the eCare subset in combination with four balancing filters. The performance with filters is similar to the performance without filters. This is true also if we look at the performance (P, R, AvgF) of the minority class (the lay class). K-statistic is stable (greater than 0.50) as are the ROC area values (greater than 0.700). Essentially, this means that this dataset, although unbalanced, does not need a class balancing filter. As pointed out earlier, we

suppose that it is the unit of analysis used for the classification (the webpage) that has a positive effect on the results since the classifier learns more from an extended text (i.e. several sentences about a coherent topic) than from a single sentence.

Conversely, on the DigInclude subset (see full breakdown in Table 9), two filters (ClassBalancer and Resample) out of four filters produce lower AvgF values than the performance with no filters. A bit paradoxically, this might be good news if we are interested in the performance on the minority class (i.e. the simplified class). When we look at the performance breakdown, we notice a big gap between P and R on the minority class. Without filters, the P of the simplified class is decent (0.61), while the R is very low (0.11). When applying a ClassBalancer and Resample, the P of the minority class jumps down to about 0.30, but R soars up to above 0.60. Thus, although the AvgF values with these two filters are lower than the SMO without any filter, the performance on the individual classes is more balanced. The best performance

Table 7: K-means, breakdown

K-means: eCare					
BOW	Acc(%)	Err(%)	P	R	F
lay	60.82	39.18	0.48	0.75	0.56
specialized			0.81	0.53	0.64
AvgF					**0.59**
PCA	Acc(%)	Err(%)	P	R	F
lay	51.95	48.05	0.32	0.50	0.39
specialized			0.65	0.47	0.54
AvgF					**0.44**
Autoenc	Acc(%)	Err(%)	P	R	F
lay	54.55	45.45	0.37	0.57	0.45
specialized			0.71	0.53	0.61
AvgF					**0.50**

(a) eCare

Simple K-means: DigInclude					
BOW	Acc(%)	Err(%)	P	R	F
simplified	75.78	24.22	0.21	0.93	0.35
standard			0.73	0.04	0.08
AvgF					**0.29**
PCA	Acc(%)	Err(%)	P	R	F
simplified	78.09	21.91	0.21	0	0
standard			0.78	0.99	0.87
AvgF					**0.19**
Autoenc	Acc(%)	Err(%)	P	R	F
simplified	54.54	45.46	0.22	0.62	0.33
standard			0.79	0.40	0.53
AvgF					**0.37**

(b) DigInclude

K-means: SEW					
BOW	Acc(%)	Err(%)	P	R	F
simplified	50.27	49.73	0.46	0.17	0.25
standard			0.50	0.80	0.62
AvgF					**0.43**
PCA	Acc(%)	Err(%)	P	R	F
simplified	50.37	49.63	0.48	0.49	0.48
standard			0.50	0.50	0.50
AvgF					**0.49**
Autoenc	Acc(%)	Err(%)	P	R	F
simplified	50.46	49.55	0.48	0.54	0.51
standard			0.50	0.45	0.47
AvgF					**0.49**

(c) SEW

is, in our view, with SMOTE, which achieves an AvgF of 0.74 with a k-statistic of 0.24 and a ROC area value of 0.624. The P and R of the minority class are balanced (0.41 in both cases). This is indeed an encouraging result for this dataset. It is to be acknowledged however that all the classifiers based on the DigInclude subset shown in Table 9 are rather weak, since both k-statistic and ROC area values are rather modest.

Table 8: eCare - Class balancing filters, breakdown

eCare: SMO NoFilter							
BOW	k	Acc(%)	Err(%)	P	R	F	ROC
lay	0.56	80.90	19.04	0.72	0.68	0.70	0.797
specialized				0.84	0.87	0.85	0.779
AvgF						**0.80**	

eCare: SMO ClassBalancer							
BOW	k	Acc(%)	Err(%)	P	R	F	ROC
lay	0.57	81.16	18.83	0.72	0.69	0.71	0.782
specialized				0.85	0.87	0.86	0.782
AvgF						**0.81**	

eCare: SMO Resample							
BOW	k	Acc(%)	Err(%)	P	R	F	ROC
lay	0.58	81.81	18.18	0.74	0.70	0.72	0.789
specialized				0.85	0.87	0.86	0.789
AvgF						**0.81**	

eCare: SMO Spreadsubsample							
BOW	k	Acc(%)	Err(%)	P	R	F	ROC
lay	0.56	80.95	19.04	0.72	0.68	0.70	0.779
specialized				0.84	0.87	0.85	0.779
AvgF						**0.808**	

eCare: SMO SMOTE							
BOW	k	Acc(%)	Err(%)	P	R	F	ROC
lay	0.57	81.16	18.83	0.73	0.68	0.70	0.781
specialized				0.84	0.87	0.86	0.781
AvgF						**0.81**	

7 Conclusion and Future Work

In this paper, we explored the effectiveness of four feature representations – BoWs, word embeddings, principal components and autoencoders – for the binary categorization of the easy-to-read variety vs standard language. The automatic separation of these two varieties would be helpful in tasks where it is important to identify a simpler version of the standard language. We tested the effectiveness of these four representations on three datasets, which differ in size, class balance, unit of analysis, language and topic. Results show that BoWs is a robust and straightforward feature representation that performs well in this context. Its performance is equivalent or equal to the performance of principal components and autoencorders, but these two representations need additional data conversion steps that do not pay off in terms of performance. Word embeddings are less accurate than the other feature representations for this classification task, although theoretically they should be able to achieve better results. As mentioned in the Introduction, several other feature representations could be profitably tried out for this task. We started off with the simplest ones, all based on individual lexical items. We propose the findings presented in this paper as empirical baselines for future work.

We will continue to explore categorization schemes in a number of additional experimental settings. First, we will try to pin down why word embeddings are less robust than other feature representations in this context. Then, we will explore the performance of other feature representations suitable for the task, e.g. lexical and morphological n-grams as well as features based on syntactic complexity. We will also explore other classification paradigms, e.g. BERT (Devlin et al., 2018), and extend our investigation on the impact of the unit of analysis (e.g. by using the DigInclude and SEW versions that contain documents rather than sentences). Last but not least, we will try out approaches specifically designed to address the problem of unbalanced datasets.

Table 9: DigInclude - Class balancing filters, breakdown

DigInclude: SMO NoFilter							
BOW	k	Acc(%)	Err(%)	P	R	F	ROC
simplified	0.13	79.04	20.95	0.61	0.11	0.18	0.546
standard				0.79	0.98	0.88	0.546
AvgF						**0.72**	

DigInclude: SMO ClassBalancer							
BOW	k	Acc(%)	Err(%)	P	R	F	ROC
simplified	0.22	65.24	34.57	0.34	0.62	0.44	0.645
standard				0.86	0.66	0.74	0.645
AvgF						**0.68**	

eCare: SMO Resample							
BOW	k	Acc(%)	Err(%)	P	R	F	ROC
simplified	0.19	63.92	36.07	0.32	0.61	0.42	0.629
standard				0.85	0.64	0.73	0.629
AvgF						**0.66**	

eCare: SMO Spreadsubsample							
BOW	k	Acc(%)	Err(%)	P	R	F	ROC
simplified	0.18	75.39	24.60	0.40	0.28	0.33	0.584
standard				0.81	0.88	0.84	0.584
AvgF						**0.73**	

eCare: SMO SMOTE							
BOW	k	Acc(%)	Err(%)	P	R	F	ROC
simplified	0.24	74.30	25.69	0.41	0.41	0.41	0.624
standard				0.83	0.83	0.83	0.624
AvgF						**0.74**	

Companion Website & Acknowledgements

Companion website: http://www.santini.se/nodalida2019

This research was supported by E-care@home, a "SIDUS – Strong Distributed Research Environment" project, funded by the Swedish Knowledge Foundation [kk-stiftelsen, Diarienr: 20140217]. Project website: http://ecareathome.se/

References

Rami Al-Rfou, Bryan Perozzi, and Steven Skiena. 2013. Polyglot: Distributed word representations for multilingual nlp. In *Proceedings of the Seventeenth Conference on Computational Natural Language Learning*, pages 183–192, Sofia, Bulgaria. Association for Computational Linguistics.

Aida Ali, Siti Mariyam Shamsuddin, and Anca L Ralescu. 2015. Classification with class imbalance problem: a review. *Int. J. Advance Soft Compu. Appl*, 7(3):176–204.

David Arthur and Sergei Vassilvitskii. 2007. k-means++: The advantages of careful seeding. In *Proceedings of the eighteenth annual ACM-SIAM symposium on Discrete algorithms*, pages 1027–1035.

Marco Baroni and Silvia Bernardini. 2004. Bootcat: Bootstrapping corpora and terms from the web. In *LREC*.

Regina Barzilay and Noemie Elhadad. 2003. Sentence alignment for monolingual comparable corpora. In *Proceedings of the 2003 conference on Empirical methods in natural language processing*, pages 25–32. Association for Computational Linguistics.

Helena M Caseli, Tiago F Pereira, Lucia Specia, Thiago AS Pardo, Caroline Gasperin, and Sandra Maria Aluísio. 2009. Building a brazilian portuguese parallel corpus of original and simplified texts. *Advances in Computational Linguistics, Research in Computer Science*, 41:59–70.

Jacob Devlin, Ming-Wei Chang, Kenton Lee, and Kristina Toutanova. 2018. Bert: Pre-training of deep bidirectional transformers for language understanding. *arXiv preprint arXiv:1810.04805*.

Goran Glavaš and Sanja Štajner. 2015. Simplifying lexical simplification: Do we need simplified corpora? In *Proceedings of the 53rd Annual Meeting of the Association for Computational Linguistics and the 7th International Joint Conference on Natural Language Processing (Volume 2: Short Papers)*, volume 2, pages 63–68.

Geoffrey E Hinton and Ruslan R Salakhutdinov. 2006. Reducing the dimensionality of data with neural networks. *Science*, 313(5786):504–507.

Thorsten Joachims. 1998. Text categorization with support vector machines: Learning with many relevant features. In *European conference on machine learning*, pages 137–142. Springer.

David Kauchak. 2013. Improving text simplification language modeling using unsimplified text data. In *Proceedings of the 51st annual meeting of the association for computational linguistics (volume 1: Long papers)*, volume 1, pages 1537–1546.

Bartosz Krawczyk. 2016. Learning from imbalanced data: open challenges and future directions. *Progress in Artificial Intelligence*, 5(4):221–232.

Steven Lang, Felipe Bravo-Marquez, Christopher Beckham, Mark Hall, and Eibe Frank. 2019. Wekadeeplearning4j: A deep learning package for weka based on deeplearning4j. *Knowledge-Based Systems*.

Sergiu Nisioi, Sanja Štajner, Simone Paolo Ponzetto, and Liviu P Dinu. 2017. Exploring neural text simplification models. In *Proceedings of the 55th Annual Meeting of the Association for Computational Linguistics (Volume 2: Short Papers)*, pages 85–91.

John C Platt. 1998. Sequential minimal optimization: a fast algorithm for training support vector machines. *MSRTR: Microsoft Research*, 3(1):88–95.

Evelina Rennes and Arne Jönsson. 2016. Towards a corpus of easy to read authority web texts. In *Proceedings of the Sixth Swedish Language Technology Conference (SLTC2016), Umeå, Sweden*.

Salah Rifai, Pascal Vincent, Xavier Muller, Xavier Glorot, and Yoshua Bengio. 2011. Contractive auto-encoders: Explicit invariance during feature extraction. In *Proceedings of the 28th International Conference on International Conference on Machine Learning*, pages 833–840. Omnipress.

Horacio Saggion. 2017. Automatic text simplification. *Synthesis Lectures on Human Language Technologies*, 10(1):1–137.

Marina Santini, Arne Jönsson, Wiktor Strandqvist, Gustav Cederblad, Mikael Nyström, Marjan Alirezaie, Leili Lind, Eva Blomqvist, Maria Lindén, and Annica Kristoffersson. 2019. Designing an extensible domain-specific web corpus for "layfication": A case study in ecare at home. In *Cyber-Physical Systems for Social Applications*, pages 98–155. IGI Global.

G Ganesh Sundarkumar and Vadlamani Ravi. 2015. A novel hybrid undersampling method for mining unbalanced datasets in banking and insurance. *Engineering Applications of Artificial Intelligence*, 37:368–377.

Laura Wendlandt, Jonathan K Kummerfeld, and Rada Mihalcea. 2018. Factors influencing the surprising instability of word embeddings. *arXiv preprint arXiv:1804.09692*.

Ian H Witten, Eibe Frank, Mark A Hall, and Christopher J Pal. 2016. *Data Mining: Practical machine learning tools and techniques*. Morgan Kaufmann.

Unsupervised Inference of Object Affordance from Text Corpora

Michele Persiani
Department of Computing Science
Umeå University
Umeå, Sweden
michelep@cs.umu.se

Thomas Hellström
Department of Computing Science
Umeå University
Umeå, Sweden
thomash@cs.umu.se

Abstract

Affordances denote actions that can be performed in the presence of different objects, or possibility of action in an environment. In robotic systems, affordances and actions may suffer from poor semantic generalization capabilities due to the high amount of required hand-crafted specifications. To alleviate this issue, we propose a method to mine for object-action pairs in free text corpora, successively training and evaluating different prediction models of affordance based on word embeddings.

Affordance; Natural Language Processing; Robotics; Intention Recognition; Conditional Variational Autoencoder;

1   Introduction

The term "affordance" was introduced by the American psychologist Gibson (Greeno, 1994) to describe what an animal can do in a given environment. It has since then been extensively utilized, interpreted, and re-defined (see (Çakmak Mehmet R. Doğar et al., 2007) for an overview) in fields such as robotics (Zech et al., 2017), human-computer-interaction (Schneider and Valacich, 2011) or human-robot-interaction (HRI) (E. Horton et al., 2012). Several interpretations for affordance exist in the literature, we use the term in a loose way to denote actions that can be performed with objects. As a simplified first approach we assume a one-to-many mapping G: *Objects* → *Affordances*. The object "door" may, for example, be used to perform the actions "open", "close", and "lock".

This paper presents how G may be learned from free-text corpora. The results show how it is possible to learn a generative model G that, given an object name, generates affordances according to a probability distribution that matches the used training data. Qualitatively results also indicate that the model manages to generalize, both to previously unseen objects and actions.

The paper is organized as follows. In Section II and III we give a brief literature review on affordances from different fields. The developed method is described in Section IV, and results from the evaluation are presented in Section V. The paper is finalized by conclusions in Section VI.

2   Affordances

When learned, the mapping G can be used in several ways in artificial systems, for example, by visually identifying objects in the environment or in the verbal dialogue with the user, suitable actions can be inferred by applying G to the observed objects. The objects and actions can then be used for shared planning or intent recognition (Bonchek-Dokow and Kaminka, 2014), thus allowing closer cooperations with the user.

For example, the mapping G may be used in a robot to decide how it should act within a given context that affords certain actions. In HRI, a service robot may for example suggest its user to read a book after it being visually detected or mentioned. Affordances may also be useful for object disambiguation. When a robot is told to "pick it up!", the robot only has to consider objects that are "pickable" in the current scene (E. Horton et al., 2012). Alternatively, affordances may be used to infer the human's intention, which may guide the robot's behavior (Bonchek-Dokow and Kaminka, 2014). If a user expresses will of talking to his children, a robot may infer that the user want to call them, and suggest making a phone call. Inference of affordances may also be used to design robots that are understandable by humans, since mutually perceived affordances may contribute to explaining a robot's behavior (Hellström and Bensch, 2018), and thereby increase interaction quality (Bensch et al., 2017).

Classical planning require knowledge about the actions that are possible in a certain situation, i.e. its afforded actions. For simple scenarios, it could suffice to enumerate all objects in the current scene, to later score their affordances and finally select the most promising to activate.

Affordances can be organized in a hierarchy, thus exposing relations or subsumptions between actions (Antanas et al., 2017; Zech et al., 2017). Assuming that a door affords the action *open*, it is clear that in order to be opened, several actions must be performed in a precise sequence (e.g. turn the handle, push the handle). Objects that offer the same grouped sequence of actions could then be represented as similar in a latent space.

Antanas et al. (Antanas et al., 2017) relate affordances to the symbol grounding problem. In the attempt of grounding the object *door*, we could say it is an object affording *open, close,* etc.: it is grounded over those actions. Further stress is also put on describing affordances as relations between objects and qualities of objects. A pear can be cut with a knife because it's soft, while a hard surface could instead be just scraped. The blade of the knife affords cut only if used in conjunction with soft enough objects. This relational hypothesis is supported by neuroscience studies showing how motor cortices are activated faster if a tool is presented together with another contextual object, rather than alone (Borghi et al., 2012).

Depending on the desired level of abstraction, affordances can be represented on different levels (Zech et al., 2017). We broadly distinct two categories, namely symbolic and sub-symbolic. In symbolic form, affordances are expressed through symbols, and every symbol enjoys certain relations with other symbols. This usually gives rise to the possibility of having a knowledge-base, containing entities such as *affords(knife, cut, pear)*, and organizing them in a graph. Sub-symbolic encodings (such as through neural networks) are instead useful to obtain percepts (Persiani et al., 2018). By clustering the perceptual/procedural space, we obtain entities (the centroids) that may or may not be utilizable as symbols, depending on the nature of the input space and subsequent calculations.

Inference of affordances from images (Zech et al., 2017) is an example of sub-symbolic approach. This is related to object recognition/segmentation, and corresponds to associating afforded actions to different visual regions of the object. Recognized affordance regions can be used for object categorization (Dag et al., 2010). For example, in a kitchen environment objects having two graspable regions could be identified as pans or containers. This is especially useful for robotic manipulation tasks (Yamanobe et al., 2017): a planner for a gripper must have knowledge about the geometric shape of the parts that can actually be grasped.

Ruggeri and Di Caro (Ruggeri and Caro, 2013) propose methodologies on how to build ontologies of affordances, also linking them to mental models and language. If we think at the phrase "The squirrel climbs the tree", we can create a mental image for it, imaging how it reaches the top. If an elephant climbs the tree instead, surely some semantic mismatch will soon arise. The mental model doesn't fit because the tree doesn't afford climbing to the elephant. The opposite might instead apply for scenarios like *"Lifting a trunk"*.

3   Related work

Unsupervised extraction of object-action pairs from free text corpora has been a relevant point in recent Natural Language Processing (NLP) research. Differently from the other methods, corpora can be mined by different techniques with the goal of finding in an unsupervised manner relationships between objects, properties of objects and actions. Chao et al. (Chao et al., 2015) show how in NLP objects and actions can be connected through the introduction of a latent space. They argue that building such a space is equivalent to obtaining a co-occurrence table, referred to as the "affordance matrix". In their approach every object-action word pair is scored through a similarity measure in the latent space, and only the pairs over a certain threshold are retained as signaling the presence of affordance. The affordance matrix, together with other automatically extracted properties and relations (altogether referred to as commonsense knowledge), such as expected location for objects, can be then used to build PKS (Planning with Knowledge and Sensing (Petrick and Bacchus, 2002)) planners (Petrick and Bacchus, 2002; Kaiser et al., 2014).

In (Chen et al., 2019), the authors map semantic frames to robot action frames using semantic role labeling, showing how a language model can yield the likelihood of possible arguments. Their proposed *Language-Model-based Commonsense Reasoning* (LMCR) will give as more probable an instruction such as *"Pour the water in the glass."* rather than *"Pour the water in the plate."*. The LMCR is trained over semantic frames by using mined knowledge about semantic roles and can be used to rank robot action frames by testing the different combinations of the available objects. When searching for an object where to pour water, the LMCR is used to rank the available objects.

4   Method

We trained a generative model for the one-to-many mapping $G : Objects \rightarrow Affordances$ using pairs of the type *<object, action>*. These pairs were generated by *semantic role labeling* of sentences from a selected corpus. Objects and actions were represented by *wordvectors* throughout the process, as is illustrated in Fig. 1. The model allows to rank the different affordances for a given object name, as names of actions that can per performed on it. By employing a neural network model rather than a tabular model we investigate whether wordvectors encoding allows for the generalization the in mapping object-action.

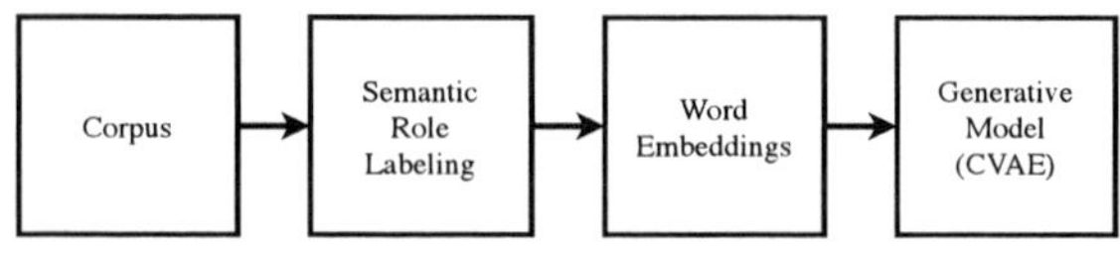

Figure 1: Steps taken to obtain the generative model.

4.1   Corpus

As data source we used the *Yahoo! Answers Manner Questions* (YAMC) dataset[1] containing 142,627 ques-

---

[1] Obtained at *https://webscope.sandbox.yahoo.com/catalog.php?datatype=l*. Accessed May 16, 2019.

tions and corresponding answers. The corpus is a distillation of all questions gathered from the platform *Yahoo! Answers* during the year 2007. It is a small subset of all questions, selected for their linguistic properties such as good quality measured in terms of vocabulary and length.

This specific corpus was selected due to the nature of its content. Our hypothesis is that being a collection of QA regarding daily living, the actions and objects being mentioned are more closely related to affordance than the ones in other corpora such as Wikipedia.

4.2 Semantic Role Labeling

In NLP, semantic roles denote the semantic functions that words have in a given phrase (Carreras and Márquez, 2004). For example, in the phrase "John looks in the mirror", the words "looks in" (denoted V) refer to the action being performed. "John" identifies the agent carrying out the action (denoted $A0$), and "the mirror" is the object (denoted $A1$) being target of the action.

Semantic role labeling (Gildea and Jurafsky, 2002) is the task of assigning semantic roles to words or groups of words in a sentence. A variety of tools exist for this task, with different conventions for the associated roles. As an example, for (Sutherland et al., 2015), the SE-MAFOR parser (Das et al., 2010) was used to infer human intention in verbal commands to a robot. In the current paper we used the parser in SENNA (Collobert et al., 2011), which is a software tool distributed with a non-commercial license.

After parsing the corpus using SENNA, phrases with semantic roles $A1$ and V of size one were selected. Each action V was lemmatized into the basic infinitive form since we were not interested in discriminating temporal or other variants of the verbs.

Finally, all pairs $(A1,V)$ that appeared at least seven times were used to create data samples *<object, action>*. This number was found to filter out spurious pairs. A fictional example illustrating possible generated sample pairs *<object, action>* is shown in Table 4.2.

Phrase	<object, action>
Add flour.	<flour, add>
Crack the egg.	<egg, crack>
Set the mixer on two steps.	<mixer, set>
Whip using the mixer.	<mixer, use>
Open the oven.	<oven, open>
Enjoy the cake.	<cake, enjoy>

Table 4.2 Examples of object-action pairs generated from phrases in a recipe.

Objects and actions are further filtered based on a *concreteness* value (Kaiser et al., 2014), that correspond to how close they are to being physical entities rather than abstract ones. To do so, for every sense of every object we navigate the WordNet entity hierarchy

and retain that sense only if it is a child node of *physical entity*. Only objects with a ratio of physical senses above a certain threshold are kept. We apply the same procedure to actions but regarding them as physical if they are child of *move, change, create, make.*

4.3 Dataset

The words in each generated pair *<object, action>* were converted to wordvectors to provide numeric data to be used in the subsequent experiments. All data was divided into a training set comprising of 734,002 pairs, and a test set comprising 314,572 pairs. Special care was taken to include different objects in training and test data sets. This would allow us to test in a more aggressive way the generalization capabilities of the trained models. The data contained $N_O = 33,655$ distinct object names and $N_A = 11,923$ distinct action names.

4.4 Word Embeddings

Word embeddings (Collobert et al., 2011) model every word x as a dense vector W_x. Words that co-occur often in the corpus have similar associated vectors, and enjoy linear or non-linear properties reflecting semantic or syntactic relationships such as analogies(Drozd et al., 2016). $W_{king} - W_{man} \approx W_{queen} - W_{woman}$ (semantic analogy), or $W_{lift} - W_{lifted} \approx W_{drop} - W_{dropped}$ (syntactic analogy). Similarity of words is often measured though cosine distance of the vectors. For a review on analogy tests see (Finley et al., 2017).

GloVe (Pennington et al., 2014) and Word2Vec (Mikolov et al., 2013) are common approaches to create word embeddings. We trained Word2Vec over YAMC to get embeddings for words that were most specific for our dataset. The selected dimensionality for the wordvectors was 100.

4.5 Generative Model

We compare three different models in how good they are in predicting $P(A|O)$ provided the evidence in the data. A *Conditional Variational Autoencoder* (CVAE) (Doersch, 2016) trained on off-the-shelf GloVe embeddings with dimensionality 200, a CVAE trained on word2vec embeddings fitted on the YAMC dataset, a *K-NN* model.

4.5.1 Conditional Variational Autoencoder

A CVAE is a trainable generative model that learns a conditional probability distribution $P(A|O)$ while keeping a stochastic latent code in its hidden layers. They can be divided into two coupled layers: an encoder and a decoder. The encoder transforms the input distribution into a certain latent distribution $Q_\phi(z|A, O)$, while the decoder reconstructs the original vectors from its latent representation z together with the conditioning input o, with output distribution equal to $P_\varphi(A'|z, o)$.

The encoder's latent layer is regularized to be close to certain parametric prior $Q_\vartheta(z|O)$. The lower-bound loss function for the CVAE is:

$$L_{CVAE} = \mathbb{E}[\log P_\varphi(A'|z,o)] - \lambda D_{KL}(Q_\phi(z|A,O)||q_\vartheta(z|O)) \quad (1)$$

The first term accounts for how good the autoencoder reconstructs the input given its latent representation. The second term regularizes the hidden latent space to be close to a certain posterior distribution. The factor λ balances how regularization is applied during learning. Starting from zero it is linearly grown up to one as the learning epochs advance. This technique addresses the *vanishing latent variable problem* and is referred to as KL annealing (Bowman et al., 2016).

φ, ϕ, ϑ denotes the three disjoint sets of parameters of the components that are simultaneously involved in learning. More specifically, they represent set of weights for the three neural network composing the CVAE. The CVAE was trained using the training set generated as described above, and was implemented using the Keras (Chollet et al., 2015) library for Python.

In order to search for a most direct relationship between objects and actions in wordvectors space, we keep the autoencoder with one hidden layer in both encoder and decoder. Nevertheless, nonlinearity of the output function of the hidden units proved necessary to yield a high accuracy. We set the dropout value for the hidden layers of the autoencoder to 0 (no features are dropped during the training phase), as this setting proved better performance in all of the experiments.

4.5.2 Nearest Neighbor

For a given input object o, the Nearest Neighbors model predicts $P(A|o)$ as $P(A|o')$, where o' is the closest object in training data. o' is found by cosine similarity of the wordvectors o and o'. $P(a'|o')$ is computed as $N(a',o')/N(o')$, where $N(.)$ is the counting of occurrences in training data.

Input	Output
door	open, pull, put, loosen, grab, clean, leave, get, slide, shut
egg	hatch, poach, implant, lay, crack, peel, spin, whip, float, cook
wine	pour, add, mix, dry, rinse, melt, soak, get, use, drink
book	read, get, write, purchase, find, use, sell, print, buy, try
cat	declaw, deter, bathe, bath, spay, pet, scare, feed, attack
money	loan, inherit, double, owe, withdraw, save, waste, cost, earn, donate
knife	scrape, cut, brush, chop, use, roll, pull, remove, slide, rub
body	trick, adapt, tone, adjust, recover, starve, cleanse, respond, flush, exercise

Table 4.5.2 Examples of actions generated by the CVAE. For every input object the 10 most probable outputs are sorted from high to low probability.

5 Evaluation

By sampling the model, we obtain names of possible actions A. As described above, the sampling follows the estimated conditional probabilities $P(A|O)$. Hence, actions with high probability are generated more frequently than actions with low probability. Since the CVAE outputs actions in numeric wordvector format, these actions are "rounded" to the closest action word appearing in the dictionary. This is equivalent to a *K-NN* classification with $K = 1$. A few examples of the most probable generated actions for CVAE are shown in Table 4.5.2.

Evaluation of generative models is in general seen as a difficult task (Theis et al., 2015; Hendrycks and Basart, 2017; Kumar et al., 2018), and one suggestion is that they should be evaluated directly with respect to the intended usage (Theis et al., 2015). In that spirit we evaluated how often our models produced affordances that were correct in the sense that they exactly matched test data with unseen objects. For a model $P_k(A|O)$ we define an accuracy measure as follows:

Algorithm 1 Accuracy computation of a model $P_k(A|O)$

1: **procedure** ACCURACY($P_k(A|O), l, m$,test_set)
2:      $s \leftarrow$ size(test_set)
3:      $x \leftarrow 0$
4:      **for** $(o_i, a_i) \in$ test_set **do**
5:          $A_o \leftarrow P_k(A|o_i)$ ▷ Output of the k-th model, sampled m times, with $m >> 1$
6:          SORT(A_o) ▷ The list of actions is sorted in descending order
7:          $sel_{il} \leftarrow$ FIRST(A_o, l) ▷ The most frequent actions up to l are kept
8:          **if** $a_i \in sel_{il}$ **then**
9:              $x \leftarrow x + 1$ ▷ x is increased when a_i is contained in sel_{il}
10:          **end if**
11:      **end for**
12:      $accuracy_k \leftarrow \frac{x}{s}$
13: **end procedure**

This measure tests how good a model replicates test data, and is meant to be a quantitative evaluation. Two different CVAEs are evaluated, the first with data encoded with GloVe-200 embeddings, the second with word2vec embeddings obtained over YAMC. We evaluated CVAE, K-NN and a baseline model by the described procedure. As baseline model we used a prior $P(A|O) = P(A)$, that is the probability distribution of actions over all objects. For every action a, $P(a) = N_a/N_{tot}$, where N_a is the number of times a appeared in the dataset. Accuracy computed on the test set for the different models are presented in Figure 2.

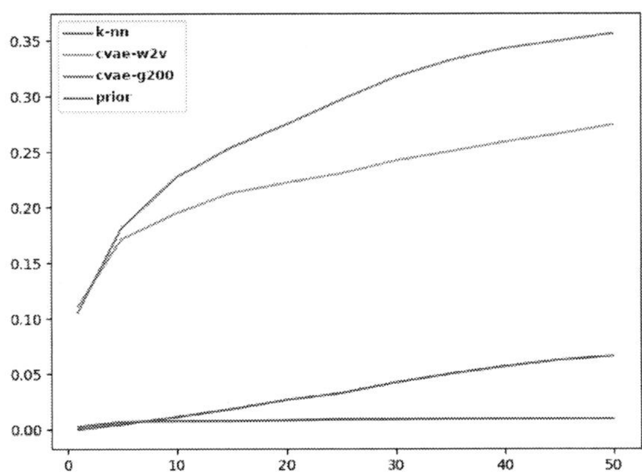

Figure 2: Computed accuracy for the different models. The X axis shows different percentages of retained output actions, starting from the most probable ones (parameter L). The Y axis shows the obtained accuracy.

The K-NN model fails to generalize the task: jumping to the closest object and outputting the empirical probability for it yield performances just above zero, also lower to the baseline.

We explain the K-NN performance as being this low due to the fact that similarity of objects (using cosine distance) does not encode similarity of associated actions. Supporting this hypothesis there is also the necessity of having nonlinear layers in the autoencoder in order to achieve high accuracy values. From this consideration we conclude that in word embedding space the mapping object-action is non-linear using the off-the-shelf embedding features.

The two CVAEs performance is higher, reaching a score of 0.35 with the off-the-shelf wordvectors. Additionally, we observed that training word2vec embeddings over the corpus lead to overfitting: performance computed over the test set comprising unseen objects is lower than the performance obtained with general purpose wordvectors.

6 Conclusions

With the goal of mining knowledge about affordance from corpora, we presented an unsupervised method that extracts object-action pairs from text using Semantic Role Labeling. The extracted pairs were used to train different models predicting $P(A|O)$: two Conditional Variational Autoencoders and one K-NN model. The presented results show that, on unseen objects, a CVAE trained on off-the-shelf wordvectors performs significantly better than the other tested models. Furthermore, we show how the K-NN model fails to generalize on our specific benchmark task, having performance even lower than the baseline model.

Knowledge about affordance, even in simple forms such as a object-action mapping, is relevant for applications such as inference of intent or robot planning. In robotics, planning requires a high amount of specifica-

tions inserted in the domain description, usually resulting in most of the decision rules being hand-crafted. With this paper, we present an algorithm allowing the leverage of knowledge about affordance present in corpora, thus allowing for a method of generating of at least a part the domain automatically.

Future work related to this research will be about improving the method by which the object-action pairs are mined, followed by reasearch on how this knowledge can be transformed to be used for robotic planning and intent recognition problems.

Acknowledgement

This work has received funding from the European Union's Horizon 2020 research and innovation program under the Marie Skłodowska-Curie grant agreement No 721619 for the SOCRATES project.

References

Laura Antanas, Ozan Arkan Can, Jesse Davis, Luc De Raedt, Amy Loutfi, A. Persson, Alessandro Saffiotti, Emre Ünal, Deniz Yuret, and Pedro Zuidberg dos Martires. 2017. Relational symbol grounding through affordance learning : An overview of the reground project. In *International Workshop on Grounding Language Understanding (GLU). Stockholm, Sweden: Satellite of INTERSPEECH.*

Suna Bensch, Alexander Jevtić, and Thomas Hellström. 2017. On interaction quality in human-robot interaction. In *International Conference on Agents and Artificial Intelligence (ICAART)*, pages 182–189.

Elisheva Bonchek-Dokow and Gal A Kaminka. 2014. Towards computational models of intention detection and intention prediction. *Cognitive Systems Research*, 28:44–79.

Anna M Borghi, Andrea Flumini, Nikhilesh Natraj, and Lewis A Wheaton. 2012. One hand, two objects: Emergence of affordance in contexts. *Brain and cognition*, 80(1):64–73.

Samuel R. Bowman, Luke Vilnis, Oriol Vinyals, Andrew M. Dai, Rafal Józefowicz, and Samy Bengio. 2016. Generating sentences from a continuous space. In *Proceedings of the 20th SIGNLL Conference on Computational Natural Language Learning, CoNLL 2016, Berlin, Germany, August 11-12, 2016*, pages 10–21.

Xavier Carreras and Lluìs Márquez. 2004. Introduction to the conll-2004 shared task: Semantic role labeling.

Yu-Wei Chao, Zhan Wang, Rada Mihalcea, and Jia Deng. 2015. Mining semantic affordances of visual object categories. In *CVPR*, pages 4259–4267. IEEE Computer Society.

Haonan Chen, Hao Tan, Alan Kuntz, Mohit Bansal, and Ron Alterovitz. 2019. Enabling robots to understand incomplete natural language instructions using commonsense reasoning. *CoRR*.

François Chollet et al. 2015. https://keras.io Keras.

Ronan Collobert, Jason Weston, Léon Bottou, Michael Karlen, Koray Kavukcuoglu, and Pavel Kuksa. 2011. Natural language processing (almost) from scratch. *J. Mach. Learn. Res.*, 12:2493–2537.

Nilgun Dag, Ilkay Atil, Sinan Kalkan, and Erol Sahin. 2010. Learning affordances for categorizing objects and their properties. In *2010 20th International Conference on Pattern Recognition*, pages 3089–3092. IEEE.

Dipanjan Das, Nathan Schneider, Desai Chen, and Noah A. Smith. 2010. Probabilistic frame-semantic parsing. In *Human Language Technologies: The 2010 Annual Conference of the North American Chapter of the Association for Computational Linguistics*, HLT '10, pages 948–956, Stroudsburg, PA, USA. Association for Computational Linguistics.

Carl Doersch. 2016. Tutorial on variational autoencoders.

Aleksandr Drozd, Anna Gladkova, and Satoshi Matsuoka. 2016. Word embeddings, analogies, and machine learning: Beyond king-man+ woman= queen. In *Proceedings of COLING 2016, the 26th International Conference on Computational Linguistics: Technical Papers*, pages 3519–3530.

Thomas E. Horton, Arpan Chakraborty, and Robert St. Amant. 2012. Affordances for robots: A brief survey. In *Avant. Pismo Awangardy Filozoficzno-Naukowej, 2*, volume 3, pages 70–84.

Gregory Finley, Stephanie Farmer, and Serguei Pakhomov. 2017. What analogies reveal about word vectors and their compositionality. In *Proceedings of the 6th Joint Conference on Lexical and Computational Semantics (*SEM 2017)*, pages 1–11. Association for Computational Linguistics.

Daniel Gildea and Daniel Jurafsky. 2002. Automatic labeling of semantic roles. *Comput. Linguist.*, 28(3):245–288.

James G Greeno. 1994. Gibson's affordances. *Psychological Review*, 101(2):336–342.

Thomas Hellström and Suna Bensch. 2018. Understandable robots - what, why, and how. *Paladyn, Journal of Behavioral Robotics*, 9(1).

Dan Hendrycks and Steven Basart. 2017. A quantitative measure of generative adversarial network distributions.

Peter Kaiser, Mike Lewis, Ronald PA Petrick, Tamim Asfour, and Mark Steedman. 2014. Extracting common sense knowledge from text for robot planning. In *2014 IEEE International Conference on Robotics and Automation (ICRA)*, pages 3749–3756. IEEE.

Ashutosh Kumar, Arijit Biswas, and Subhajit Sanyal. 2018. ecommercegan : A generative adversarial network for e-commerce. *arXiv preprint arXiv:1801.03244*.

Maya Çakmak Mehmet R. Doğar, Emre Uur, and Erol Şahin. 2007. Affordances as a framework for robot control. In *Proceedings of the 7th international conference on epigenetic robotics, epirob07*.

Tomas Mikolov, Kai Chen, Gregory S. Corrado, and James A. Dean. 2013. Efficient estimation of word representations in vector space. *CoRR*.

Jeffrey Pennington, Richard Socher, and Christopher D. Manning. 2014. Glove: Global vectors for word representation. In *In EMNLP*.

Michele Persiani, Alessio Mauro Franchi, and Giuseppina Gini. 2018. A working memory model improves cognitive control in agents and robots. *Cognitive Systems Research*, 51:1–13.

Ronald PA Petrick and Fahiem Bacchus. 2002. A knowledge-based approach to planning with incomplete information and sensing. In *AIPS*, volume 2, pages 212–222.

Alice Ruggeri and Luigi Di Caro. 2013. How affordances can rule the (computational) world. In *AIC@AI*IA*.

C. Schneider and J. Valacich. 2011. *Enhancing the Motivational Affordance of Human–Computer Interfaces in a Cross-Cultural Setting*, pages 271–278. Physica-Verlag HD, Heidelberg.

Alexander Sutherland, Suna Bensch, and Thomas Hellström. 2015. Inferring robot actions from verbal commands using shallow semantic parsing. In *Proceedings of the 17th International Conference on Artificial Intelligence ICAI'15*, pages 28–34.

Lucas Theis, Aäron van den Oord, and Matthias Bethge. 2015. A note on the evaluation of generative models. *CoRR*.

Natsuki Yamanobe, Weiwei Wan, Ixchel G Ramirez-Alpizar, Damien Petit, Tokuo Tsuji, Shuichi Akizuki, Manabu Hashimoto, Kazuyuki Nagata, and Kensuke Harada. 2017. A brief review of affordance in robotic manipulation research. *Advanced Robotics*, 31(19-20):1086–1101.

Philipp Zech, Simon Haller, Safoura Rezapour Lakani, Barry Ridge, Emre Ugur, and Justus Piater. 2017. Computational models of affordance in robotics: a taxonomy and systematic classification. *Adaptive Behavior*, 25(5):235–271.

Annotating evaluative sentences for sentiment analysis: a dataset for Norwegian

Petter Mæhlum, Jeremy Barnes, Lilja Øvrelid, and Erik Velldal
University of Oslo
Department of Informatics
`{pettemae, jeremycb, liljao, erikve}@ifi.uio.no`

Abstract

This paper documents the creation of a large-scale dataset of evaluative sentences – i.e. both subjective and objective sentences that are found to be sentiment-bearing – based on mixed-domain professional reviews from various news-sources. We present both the annotation scheme and first results for classification experiments. The effort represents a step toward creating a Norwegian dataset for fine-grained sentiment analysis.

1 Introduction

Sentiment analysis is often approached by first locating the relevant, sentiment-bearing sentences. Traditionally, one has distinguished between subjective and objective sentences, where only the former were linked to sentiment (Wilson, 2008). Objective sentences typically present facts about the world, whereas subjective sentences express personal feelings, views, or beliefs. More recently, however, it has become widely recognized in the literature that subjectivity should not be equated with opinion (Liu, 2015): On the one hand, there are many subjective sentences that do not express sentiment, e.g., *I think that he went home*, and on the other hand there are many objective sentences that do, e.g., *The earphone broke in two days*, to quote some examples from Liu (2015). Additionally, sentences often contain several polarities in a single sentence, which complicates the labeling of a full sentence as positive or negative.

This paper documents both the annotation effort and first experimental results for sentence-level evaluative labels added to a subset of the data in the Norwegian Review Corpus (NoReC) (Velldal et al., 2018), a corpus of full-text reviews from a range of different domains, collected from several of the major Norwegian news sources.

The annotated subset, dubbed NoReC$_{eval}$, covers roughly 8000 sentences across 300 reviews and 10 different thematic categories (literature, products, restaurants, etc.).

Sentences are labeled to indicate whether they are *evaluative*, i.e. where they are intended by the author (or some other opinion holder) to serve as an evaluation or judgment. They are not, however, annotated with respect to positive/negative polarity. The reason for this is that polarity is often mixed at the sentence-level. Hence, we defer annotating polarity to a later round of phrase-level annotation. Although most of the sentences labeled as evaluative will be subjective and personal, they can also include objective sentences. Moreover, our annotation scheme singles out a particular category of evaluative sentences called *fact-implied non-personal*, following the terminology of Liu (2015). Evaluative sentences are also further sub-categorized as to whether they are considered *on-topic* with respect to the object being reviewed, and whether they express the *first-person* view of the author.

The annotation scheme is described in further detail in Sections 3 and 4. We start, however, by briefly outlining relevant previous work and background in Section 2. In Section 5 we describe more practical aspects of the annotation procedure and go on to analyze inter-annotator agreement in Section 6, before Section 7 summarizes the resulting dataset. In Section 8, we analyze the corpus experimentally and present a series of preliminary classification experiments using a wide range of state-of-the-art sentiment models including CNNs, BiLSTMs and self-attention networks, before we in Section 9 conclude and outline some remaining avenues for future work. The dataset and the annotation guidelines are made available, along with code for replicating the experiments.[1]

---

[1] `https://github.com/ltgoslo/norec_eval`

2 Background and related work

In this section we briefly review some of the previous annotation efforts (for English) that are most relevant for our work.

Toprak et al. (2010) present a sentiment-annotated corpus of consumer reviews. In a first pass, sentences are annotated with respect to relevancy to the overall topic and whether they express an evaluation. In a second pass, sentences that were marked as relevant and evaluative are further annotated with respect to whether they are *opinionated* (i.e. express a subjective opinion) or *polar-facts* (i.e. factual information that implies evaluation). In addition to evaluations, they also identify sources (opinion holders), targets (the entity or aspect that the sentiment is directed towards), modifiers, positive/negative polarity and strength, and anaphoric expressions.

Also working with review data, Scheible and Schütze (2013) present a simplified annotation scheme which appears similar in spirit to the first pass of annotation described by Toprak et al. (2010). Scheible and Schütze (2013) annotate sentences with respect to what they call *sentiment relevance*, indicating whether they are informative for determining the sentiment of a document. Sentiment relevant sentences can be either subjective or objective, but must be on topic and convey some evaluation of the object under review.

Van de Kauter et al. (2015) present a fine-grained scheme for annotation of polar expressions at the sub-sentential level. They distinguish between two types of sentiment; *explicit* sentiment on the one hand, corresponding to private states, and *implicit* sentiment on the other, corresponding to factual information that implies a positive/negative evaluation (van de Kauter et al., 2015). The latter category corresponds to what is refered to as *polar-facts* by Toprak et al. (2010) or *objective polar utterances* by Wilson (2008). The annotations of van de Kauter et al. (2015) also identify sources, targets, and modifiers. Acknowledging that the distinction between implicit/explicit sentiment is not always clear cut, polar expressions are labeled with a graded numerical value indicating a continuum ranging from objective to subjective.

Liu (2015) proposes various sub-categorizations of what he calls *opinionated* expressions along several dimensions. Among the most relevant for our work is the distinction

between *subjective* and *fact-implied opinions*. The subjective expressions are further sub-categorized as either *emotional* or *rational*, and the fact-implied can be either *personal* or *non-personal* (Liu, 2015). In the order they are listed above, these sub-categorizations can perhaps be seen to correspond to four bins of the subjective–objective continuum defined by van de Kauter et al. (2015). Liu (2015) also differentiates between first-person and non-first-person opinions, where non-first-person indicates that the opinion is held by someone other than the author of the sentence.

In the next section we describe the choice of label categories used in our sentence-level annotation of NoReC reviews.

3 Annotation scheme

Our annotation approach corresponds to some degree to that of Scheible and Schütze (2013) or the first step described by Toprak et al. (2010) – see discussion above – in that we assign labels only at the sentence-level and without marking polarity (as this might be mixed at the sentence-level), and include both subjective and objective sentences. However, our approach is slightly more fine-grained in that we also explicitly annotate evaluative sentences with respect to being on-topic or not, and with respect to expressing a first-person opinion of the author or not. Finally, we also single out one particular sub-class of evaluative sentences, namely those that in the terminology of Liu (2015) are fact-implied non-personal. These sentences might require special treatment, where proper identification might be more dependent on taking the overall domain and discourse context into account (Liu, 2015). In this section we provide more details and examples for the various label types in our annotation scheme.

Evaluative Following Toprak et al. (2010), we use the term *evaluative* to refer to any sentence that expresses or implies a positive or negative evaluation, regardless of its subjectivity. An example of an evaluative sentence can be found in (1) below which contains the positive evaluation signaled by the adjective *lekkert* 'tastefully'.

(1) *Det hele var også lekkert presentert.*
    The whole was also tastefully presented.
    'Everything was tastefully presented.'

Our EVAL label roughly comprises the three opinion categories described by Liu (2015) as emotional, rational and fact-implied personal. Sentences including emotional responses (arousal) are very often evaluative and involve emotion terms like e.g. *elske* 'love', *like* 'like' or *hate* 'hate'. Sentences that lack the arousal we find in emotional sentences may also be evaluative, for instance by indicating worth and utilitarian value, e.g. *nyttig* 'useful' or *verdt (penger, tid)* 'worth (money, time)'.

Evaluative fact-implied non-personal There are actually two types of evaluative sentences in our scheme: simply *evaluative* (labeled EVAL) as in (1) above, or the special case of *evaluative fact-implied non-personal* (FACT-NP).

A sentence is labeled as FACT-NP when it is a fact or a descriptive sentence but evaluation is implied, and the sentence does not involve any personal experiences or judgments. (In contrast, objective sentences expressing personal experiences – so-called *fact-implied personal* in the terminology of Liu (2015) – are not seen as objective to the same degree, and are labeled as EVAL.) FACT-NP-labeled sentences are usually understood to be evaluative because we interpret them based on common (societal, cultural) background knowledge, and they are often highly context dependent. The example in (2) illustrates a FACT-NP-labeled sentence which simply states factual information, however, within the context of a car review, it clearly expresses a positive evaluation.

(2) *178   hestekrefter.*
     178   horsepowers.
     '178 horsepower.'

Note that the definition of FACT-NP departs from what at first might appear like similar categories reported in the literature, like factual *implicit* sentiment (van de Kauter et al., 2015), *polar-facts* (Toprak et al., 2010) or *objective polar utterances* (Wilson, 2008), in that it does not include so-called *personal* fact-implied evaluations (Liu, 2015). This latter class is in our scheme subsumed by EVAL. The reason for this is that we found them to have a more explicit and personal nature, separating them from the purely objective FACT-NP sentences described above.

Non-evaluative Sentences that do not fall into either of these two categories (EVAL and FACT-NP) are labeled non-evaluative (NONE). An example of this category can be found in (3),

which is taken from a restaurant review. Even though this sentence clearly describes a personal experience, it is still a factual statement that does not express any sort of evaluation.

(3) *Jeg   har   aldri   spist   den   oransje*
     I   have   never   eaten   the   orange
     varianten   av   sorten,   sa   Fredag.
     variant   of   kind.the,   said   Fredag.
     'I have never tasted the orange kind, said Fredag'

On-topic or not Sentences that are identified as evaluative, in either the EVAL or FACT-NP sense, are furthermore labeled with respect to two other properties: (*i*) whether the author is the one expressing the evaluation, and (*ii*) whether the evaluation is on topic or not.

Sentences that are not-on-topic are labeled ¬OT. For an example, see (4), where the review is about a music album, but the sentence expresses an evaluation about the author upon whose book the album is based, and does not reflect the reviewer's evaluation of the album itself.

(4) *Jeg   liker   Aune   Sand.*
     I   like   Aune   Sand
     'I like Aune Sand [name of author].'

The class of sentiment-bearing sentences that are not considered relevant or on-topic are typically not marked in other annotation efforts, e.g. by Toprak et al. (2010) or Scheible and Schütze (2013). However, from a modeling perspective, we expect it will be difficult in practice to correctly identify evaluative sentences that are on-topic while leaving out those that are not, at least without going beyond the standard sentence-level models typically applied in the field today and move towards more discourse-oriented modeling. By explicitly labeling the not-on-topic cases we are able to quantify this effect, both with respect to human annotations and system predictions.

First person or not Sentences where the author is not the holder of the evaluation, are labeled ¬FP ('not-first-person'). An example is provided in (5) where the holder of the opinion is not the author of the review, but rather the subject noun phrase *ekte astronauter* 'real astronauts'.

(5) *Ekte   astronauter   har   også   sett*
     real   astronauts   have   also   seen
     filmen   og   skryter   hemningsløst   av
     movie.the   and   boast   unrestrainedly   of
     dens   autentisitet
     its   authenticity

'Real astronauts have also seen the movie and boast highly of its authenticity'

Mixed class sentences   A sentence may include several types of evaluative expressions. In these cases, we label a sentence as EVAL if it contains both EVAL and FACT-NP, as in example (6) below.

(6)   *Dette gir   et   gjennomsnitt   på   27,3*
       this   gives   an   average   on   27,3
       MB/sek   som   er   meget   bra.
       MB/sec   which   is   very   good
       'This gives us an average of 27,3 MB / sec, which is very good.'

Similarly, we refrain from labeling ¬OT and ¬FP if a sentence contains any sentiment expression that is first-person or on topic respectively.

4   Annotation challenges / special cases

Below, we provide some more details about particular annotation decisions related to various special cases, including some challenges.

Modality   In our annotation guidelines, the treatment of modals depends on the specific modal verb in use. In particular, we found that some modals like *burde* 'should' are frequently used to indicate evaluation, as in the example (7) below.

(7)   *Hun burde   hatt   med   seg   en*
       She   should   had   with   herself   an
       opplevelse   i   tillegg.
       experience   in   addition.
       'On top of this she should have brought with her an experience.'

Conditionals   Conditional sentences also require special attention. In particular, so-called irrealis sentences, i.e., sentences that indicate hypothetical situations, have been excluded in some previous sentence-level annotation efforts (Toprak et al., 2010), but we wish to include them as long as they clearly indicate evaluation. A seemingly common use of irrealis is to indicate negative evaluation by expressing a future condition, indicating that the current situation is less optimal, as in (8) below.

(8)   *Bare Elvebredden   får   nok   arbeidskraft*
       Only   Elvebredden   gets   enough   work-power
       [...]   gleder   Robinson   &   Fredag
       [...]   look-forward   Robinson   &   Fredag
       seg   til   å   komme   tilbake
       themselves   to   INF   come   back
       'If only Elvebredden had more waiters, Robinson & Fredag would gladly return'

Questions   Questions often have a similar role in expressing evaluations as the conditionals discussed above. Often a sentence may question some aspect of the object in question, also indicating a negative evaluation of the current state of the object, as in (9) below, labeled EVAL.

(9)   *Et "mimrespill"   skal   vel   stimulere*
       A   memory-game   should   well   stimulate
       mer   enn   korttidsminnet?
       more   than   shortterm.memory.the?
       'Shouldn't a "memory game" stimulate more than the short term memory?'

Cross-sentential evaluation   An evaluative expression may sometimes span across several sentences. Since our annotation is performed at the sentence-level, annotations may not span across sentences. We decided to label adjacent sentences that were strongly related identically. In examples (10) and (11) below, for instance, the first sentence contains a general comment about the action scenes penned by a given book author, but this is tied to the topic of the review (the author's new book *Gjenferd* 'Ghost') only in the sentence following it. In our annotation, these two sentences were both annotated as EVAL.

(10)   *Min   største   innvending   er   at*
        my   biggest   objection   is   that
        actionscenene   til   Nesbø   har   en
        action.scenes.the   of   Nesbø   has   a
        tendens   til   å   få   noe
        tendency   to   INF   get   something
        tegneserieaktig   overdrevent   over   seg.
        cartoon.like   exaggerated   over   themselves
        'My biggest objection is that Nesbø's action scenes have a tendency to give an exaggerated cartoon-like expression.'

(11)   *Det   gjelder   også   i   "Gjenferd".*
        That   applies   also   in   "Gjenferd"
        'That also applies in "Gjenferd" [book title].'

Other examples of evaluative expressions spanning sentences are lists of reasons following or preceding a more clearly evaluative expression, and sentences where the target and polar expression are split, as in a question–answer structure.

External objective evaluation   Another challenging type of sentence encountered during annotation are sentences where the author refers to prizes or evaluations by people other than the author, as in (12) below. These expressions are marked as ¬FP, but evaluation-wise they can be seen from two angles: Is the author using the phrase to express an explicit positive evaluation, in which case it would be marked as EVAL, or is the author reporting a fact, in which case it is marked as FACT-NP. The same problem applies to words like *populær* 'popular' or *folkekjær* 'loved by the people', although these words tend towards EVAL, while nominations like in (12) tend towards FACT-NP.

(12) *[...] er både Ejiofor og Fassbender*
[...] are both Ejiofor and Fassbender
Oscar-nominert.
Oscar-nominated .
'[...]] both Ejiofor and Fassbender have been Oscar-nominated.'

In this case, the evaluation has been performed by a different group of people at an earlier stage and the evaluation is also not of the object being reviewed, and is therefore marked as ¬OT, ¬FP and FACT-NP.

Higher-level topic evaluation   At times the annotators also found sentences where the evaluation is at a higher ontological level than the object being reviewed, as in sentence (13), where the review is about a specific edition of a series of games called *Buzz*, but the evaluation is about the series as a whole.

(13) *Da   tror   jeg Buzz   kan fenge   i*
Then think I   Buzz can captivate in
mange   år   til   [...].
many   years   more [...]
'Then I think Buzz [game] can captivate for many more years'

In these cases, it was decided that as long as the object being reviewed is a close subclass of the target of the evaluation, it is reasonable to assume that the author wrote this sentence in order to say something about the overall quality of the actual object under review, and thus the sentence above is labeled EVAL.

5   Annotation procedure

Annotation was performed using the WebAnno tool (Eckart de Castilho et al., 2016), and annotators were able to see the whole review in order to judge sentences in context. There were five annotators in total (students with background in linguistics and language technology) and all sentences were doubly-annotated. In cases of disagreement, another of the annotators would consider the sentence a second time and resolve the

conflict. Problematic sentences would be discussed at a meeting with all annotators present.

The annotation guidelines were fine-tuned in three rounds using two sets of texts. The first set contained 10 texts, representing each of the thematic categories in NoReC, in order to provide the annotators with as much variation as possible. These texts were annotated by two of the annotators, and the results were discussed, forming the basis of the guidelines. The same annotators then annotated a second set of 8 texts, trying to strictly adhere to the guidelines. After a second fine-tuning, the remaining annotators would annotate the first set, and the guidelines were again fine-tuned in accordance with the new disagreements. These texts are not included when calculating the agreement scores reported below.

6   Inter-annotator agreement

Inter-annotator agreement scores for the main three categories EVAL, FACT-NP, and NONE are presented in Table 1, calculated as F_1-scores between pairs of annotators on the complete set of sentences. We find that agreement among the annotators is high for the EVAL sentences and for the overall score. Agreement is much lower for the FACT-NP label, however, likely reflecting the fact that these sentences have no clear sentiment expression, with interpretation more heavily depending on context and domain-specific knowledge.

We also computed annotator agreement for the attribute categories ¬OT and ¬FP, restricted to the subset of sentences labeled EVAL,[2] yielding F_1 of 0.59 and 0.56, respectively. In other words, we see that the agreement is somewhat lower for these subcategories compared to the top-level label EVAL. Possible reasons for this might be that although problems with these attributes seem to be resolved quickly in annotator meetings, they might pose difficulties to the individual annotator, as sometimes these attributes can be context dependent to an extent that makes them difficult to infer from the review text by itself.

Kenyon-Dean et al. (2018) problematizes a practice often seen in relation to sentiment annotation, namely that complicated cases – e.g. sentences were there is annotator disagreement – are discarded from the final dataset. This makes the

---

[2]For the FACT-NP subset there were too few instances of these attributes (prior to adjudication) for agreement to be meaningfully quantified; 1 for ¬OT and 0 for ¬FP.

EVAL	FACT−NP	NONE	all
0.84	0.22	0.87	0.82

Table 1: F_1 inter-annotator agreement for each top-level label.

data non-representative of real text and will artificially inflate classification results on the annotations. In our dataset, we not only include the problematic cases, but also explicitly flag sentences for which there was disagreement among annotators (while also indicating the resolved label). This can be of potential use for both error analysis and model training, as we will also see in Section 8.3. Finally, note that we also found interesting differences in agreement across review domains and this too is something we return to when discussing experimental results in Section 8.3.

7 Corpus statistics

Table 2 presents the distribution of the annotated classes (EVAL, FACT−NP and NONE), as well as the attributes ¬OT and ¬FP in terms of absolute number and proportion of sentences across the different review domains (screen, music, literature, etc.). The resulting corpus contains a total of 298 documents and 7961 total sentences.

In general, we may note that there is a large proportion of evaluative sentences in the corpus, a fact which is unsurprising given the review genre. EVAL sentences are in a slight majority in the corpus (just above 50%) followed by NONE which accounts for 46% of the sentences, while the FACT−NP label makes up a little less than 4% of the sentences.

We observe that the evaluative sentences (EVAL or FACT−NP) are not evenly distributed across the different thematic categories. The category with the highest percentage of evaluative sentences – restaurants – tend to be written in a personal style, with vivid descriptions of food and ambience. In contrast, stage reviews tend to be written in a non-personal style, largely avoiding strong evaluations. Unsurprisingly, the product category has a higher number of FACT−NP sentences, as they contain several objective but evaluative product descriptions. The low proportion of EVAL sentences found in the literature category is somewhat sur-

prising, as one would not normally consider literature reviews as especially impersonal. However, music reviews in this corpus tend to be written in a personal, informal style, which is reflected in the high rate of EVAL sentences.

The corpus contains a total of 396 ¬OT sentences and 109 ¬FP sentences. Most of the evaluative sentences are thus on topic, and most evaluations belong to the author. The percentages of the attributes ¬OT and ¬FP are quite evenly distributed among the different domains, with the exception of one apparent outlier: the 31.33% of ¬FP sentences in the sports domain. This is probably due to the interview-like style in one of the reviews, reporting the evaluations of several different people. Reviews about video games seem to have a slightly higher percentage of ¬OT sentences. This could be due to a large number of comparisons with earlier games and different gaming consoles in these texts.

8 Experiments

In this section we apply a range of different architectures to provide first baseline results for predicting the various labels in the new corpus. Data splits for training, validation and testing are inherited from NoReC.

8.1 Models

We provide a brief description of the various classifiers below. Additionally, we provide a majority baseline which always predicts the EVAL class as a lower bound. Note that all classifiers except the bag-of-words model take as input 100 dimensional fastText skipgram embeddings (Bojanowski et al., 2016), trained on the NoWaC corpus (Guevara, 2010), which contains over 680 Million tokens in Bokmål Norwegian. The pre-trained word embeddings were re-used from the NLPL vector repository[3] (Fares et al., 2017).

BOW learns to classify the sentences with a linear separation estimated based on log likelihood optimization with an L2 prior using a bag-of-words representation.

AVE (Barnes et al., 2017) uses the same L2 logistic regression classifier as BOW, but instead using as input the average of the word vectors from a sentence.

CNN (Kim, 2014) is a single-layer convolutional neural network with one convolutional layer

---

[3] http://vectors.nlpl.eu/repository/

Domain	Docs	Sents	EVAL		FACT−NP		NONE		¬OT		¬FP	
			#	%	#	%	#	%	#	%	#	%
Screen	110	2895	1359	46.94	50	1.73	1486	51.33	160	11.36	20	1.42
Music	101	1743	1055	60.53	48	2.75	640	36.72	100	9.07	23	2.09
Literature	35	930	327	35.16	31	3.33	572	61.51	50	13.97	18	5.03
Products	22	1156	619	53.55	127	10.99	410	35.47	36	4.83	10	1.34
Games	13	520	278	53.46	23	4.42	219	42.12	37	12.29	6	1.99
Restaurants	6	268	167	62.31	10	3.73	91	33.96	4	2.26	6	3.39
Stage	8	264	100	37.88	6	2.27	158	59.85	7	6.60	0	0.0
Sports	2	149	78	52.35	5	3.36	66	44.3	2	2.41	26	31.33
Misc	1	36	20	55.56	0	0.0	16	44.44	0	0.0	0	0.0
Total	298	7961	4003	50.28	300	3.77	3658	45.95	396	9.20	109	2.53

Table 2: Distribution of documents, sentences and labels across the thematic categories of reviews. Note that the percentages for ¬OT and ¬FP are relative to evaluative (EVAL or FACT−NP) sentences.

on top of pre-trained embeddings. The embedding layer in convoluted with filters of size 2, 3, and 4 with 50 filters for each size and then 2-max pooled. This representation is then passed to a fully connected layer with *ReLU* activations and finally to a softmax layer. Dropout is used after the max pooling layer and *ReLU* layer for regularization.

BiLSTM is a one-layer bidirectional Long Short-Term Network (Graves et al., 2005) with word embeddings as input. The contextualized representation of each sentence is the concatenation of the final hidden states from the left-to-right and right-to-left LSTM. This representation is then passed to a softmax layer for classification. Dropout is used before the LSTM layers and softmax layers for regularization.

SAN is a one-layer self-attention network (Vaswani et al., 2017) with relative position representations (Shaw et al., 2018) and a single set of attention heads, which was previously shown to perform well for sentiment analysis (Ambartsoumian and Popowich, 2018). The network uses a variant of the attention mechanism (Bahdanau et al., 2014) which creates contextualized representations of the original input sequence, such that the contextualized representations encode both information about the original input, as well as how it relates to all other positions.

8.2 Experimental Setup

We apply the models to five experimental setups. The main task is to classify each sentence as *evaluative* (EVAL), *fact-implied non-personal* (FACT−NP), or *non-evaluative* (NONE). In order to provide a view of how difficult it is to model the secondary properties mentioned in Section 3,

Model	EVAL	FACT−NP	NONE	Overall
majority	66.2	0.0	0.0	49.5
Bow	69.6	0.0	64.4	65.8
Ave	75.4	0.0	70.4	71.6
Cnn	**76.3** (0.7)	0.0 (0.0)	72.2 (0.7)	73.1 (0.3)
BiLSTM	76.1 (0.1)	6.0 (4.8)	72.1 (0.1)	72.7 (0.1)
San	76.2 (0.1)	**7.1** (3.1)	**72.3** (0.3)	**73.7** (0.1)

Table 3: Per class F_1 score and overall micro F_1 of baseline models on the main classification task. For the neural models mean micro F_1 and standard deviation across five runs are shown.

two additional binary classification tasks are performed; determining if the sentence is on topic (OT) and if the opinion expressed is from a first-person perspective (FP). Only the best performing model from the main experiment above is applied for these subtask, and the model is trained and tested separately on the two subsets of sentences annotated as EVAL and FACT−NP, leading to four binary classification experiments in total.

For all models, we choose the optimal hyper-parameters by performing a random search on the development data. Given that neural models are sensitive to random initialization parameters, we run each neural experiment five times with different random seeds and report means for both per-class and micro F_1 in addition to their standard deviation.

8.3 Results

Table 3 shows the results for all models on the main three-way classification task. All classifiers perform better than the majority baseline (at 49.5

F_1 overall). Of the two logistic regression classifiers, the AVE model based on averaged embeddings as input performs much better than the standard discrete bag-of-words variant (65.8 vs. 71.6 overall). While the AVE model proves to be a strong baseline, the three neural models have the strongest performance. The CNN achieves the best results on the EVAL class (76.3) and improves 1.8 ppt over AVE on NONE. While overall results are quite even, the strongest model is SAN – the self-attention network – which achieves an overall F_1 of 73.7. This model also proves more stable in the sense of having slightly lower variance across the multiple runs, at least compared to the CNN.

The easiest class to predict is EVAL, followed closely by NONE. The most striking result is that is appears very difficult for all models to identify the FACT-NP class. This is largely due to the few examples available for FACT-NP, as well as the fact that FACT-NP sentences do not contain clear lexical features that separate them from EVAL and NONE. This confirms the intuitions presented in Section 3. Only BILSTM and SAN manage to make positive predictions for FACT-NP, but the scores are still very low (with 7.1 F_1 being the best) and we see that the variance across runs is high. An analysis of the strongest model (SAN) shows that the model tends to confuse FACT-NP nearly equally with EVAL (15 errors) and NONE (20 errors), while only correctly predicting this category 6 times, suggesting this category is difficult for the models to capture.

Performance per domain   Table 4 breaks down the F_1 score of the SAN model across the different review domains. We observe that there are fairly large differences in performance, and furthermore that these can not simply be explained just by differences in the number of training examples for each domain (cf. the class distributions in Table 2). We see that sentences from the literature reviews appear difficult to classify, despite being relatively well represented in terms of training examples, while the opposite effect can be seen for the games category. The lowest performance is seen for the product reviews, which is unsurprising given that – despite having a high number of examples – it is arguably the most heterogeneous category in the dataset, in addition to having a relatively high proportion of the difficult FACT-NP sentences.

Domain	F_1
Screen	77.5 (2.2)
Music	76.1 (1.3)
Literature	66.0 (1.3)
Products	65.0 (0.8)
Games	77.6 (2.2)
Restaurants	69.6 (1.5)
Stage	70.0 (2.2)

Table 4: Per domain micro F_1 score of the SAN model. Note that the test set does not contain sentences from the Sports or Misc domains.

Human agreement vs model performance   We also computed the inter-annotator agreement scores per domain, again as pairwise micro F_1, and found that while the agreement tends to vary less than model performance, the two scores yield a similar relative ranking of domains in terms of difficulty. For example, the two domains with the highest prediction scores, Games and Screen (with F_1 of 77.6 and 77.5, respectively), also have the highest inter-annotator agreement (82.6 and 83.8). The two domains with lowest prediction F_1, Products and Restaurants (65.0 and 69.6, respectively), also have the lowest agreement (77.54 and 78.5).

As described in Section 3, while annotator disagreements have been resolved, we have chosen to mark them in the final dataset. An error analysis of the classifier predictions show there is a strong correlation between inter-annotator agreement and errors that the classification models make (using a χ^2 test, p $\ll$ 0.01). This suggests that these examples are inherently more difficult, and lead to disagreement for both human and machine learning classifiers.

On-topic and first-person   Table 5 shows the results of applying the SAN architecture to the four binary tasks. The sentences which are on-topic (OT) and first-person (FP) are the easiest to classify (F_1 ranging from 92.8 to 99.4), while the not-on-topic ($\neg$OT) and not-first-person ($\neg$FP) are very difficult (0.0 – 11.3 F_1). None of the models are able to correctly predict the $\neg$FP class. In order to distinguish this class, some kind of co-reference resolution likely needs to be included in the model, as simple lexical information cannot distinguish them from FP. Note, however, that the prediction scores for $\neg$FP need to be taken with a

Model	Subset	OT	¬OT	Avg.	FP	¬FP	Avg.
SAN	EVAL	93.5 (0.1)	11.3 (4.3)	88.5 (1.0)	99.4 (0.0)	0.0 (0.0)	98.9 (0.0)
	FACT-NP	97.2 8 (0.0)	0.0 (0.0)	94.6 (0.0)	92.8 (0.0)	0.0 (0.0)	86.5 (0.0)

Table 5: Per-class and micro F_1 for the self-attention network trained to predict whether an example is on topic (OT) or not (¬OT) or whether the opinion is expressed by the first person (FP) or not (¬FP). The models are trained and tested on the subset of sentences annotated as evaluative (EVAL) and fact-implied (FACT-NP).

grain of salt as there are too few instances in the test data to give reliable estimates; 5 in each of the EVAL and FACT-NP subsets. The same is true of the ¬OT predictions for FACT-NP (8 test instances). We see that the network is able to predict to some degree (11.3) the ¬OT class for EVAL, but the absolute score is still low, which also reflects the inter-annotator scores. Once information about aspect or target expressions is added to the data in future annotation efforts, we hope that this might be leveraged to more accurately predict 'on-topicness'.

9 Summary and outlook

This paper has described an annotation effort focusing on evaluative sentences in a subset of the mixed-domain Norwegian Review Corpus, dubbed NoReC$_{eval}$. Both subjective and objective sentences can be labeled as evaluative in our annotation scheme. One particular category of objective sentences, conveying so-called *fact-implied non-personal* sentiment, is given a distinct label, as this category might need special treatment when modeling. Evaluative sentences are also assigned labels that indicate whether they are on topic and express a first-person point of view.

The paper also reports experimental results for predicting the annotations, testing a suite of different linear and neural architectures. While the neural models reach a micro F_1 of nearly 74 on the three-way task, none of them are able to successfully predict the underrepresented minority-class FACT-NP, misclassifying it nearly equally as often with EVAL as with NONE. Additional experiments show that it is difficult to classify sentences as not-on-topic (¬OT) and not-first-person (¬FP), indicating that important of this in future research on sentiment analysis. Moreover, our error analysis also showed that the cases where annotators disagree (flagged in the data) are also difficult for the classifiers to predict correctly.

Note that, in our annotation scheme, we only annotate sentences as sentiment-bearing (i.e. evaluative), not with positive/negative polarity values, as labeling polarity on the sentence-level only makes sense for sentences that do not contain mixed sentiment. Although such datasets are not uncommon, we argue that this is a rather idealized classification task not in line with the goal of the current effort. In immediate follow-up work, however, we will perform fine-grained sentiment annotation where we label in-sentence sentiment expressions and their polarity, in addition to sources (holders) and targets (aspect expressions). In later iterations we plan to also analyze additional information that can be compositionally relevant to polarity like negation, intensifiers, verbal valence shifters, etc. The dataset and the annotation guidelines are made available, along with code for replicating the experiments.[4]

Acknowledgements

This work has been carried out as part of the SANT project (Sentiment Analysis for Norwegian Text), funded by the Research Council of Norway (grant number 270908). We also want to express our gratitude to the annotators, who in addition to the first author includes Anders Næss Evensen, Carina Thanh-Tam Truong, Tita Enstad, and Trulz Enstad. Finally, we thank the anonymous reviewers for their valuable feedback.

References

Artaches Ambartsoumian and Fred Popowich. 2018. Self-attention: A better building block for sentiment analysis neural network classifiers. In *Proceedings of the 9th Workshop on Computational Approaches to Subjectivity, Sentiment and Social Media Analysis*, pages 130–139, Brussels, Belgium.

---

[4]https://github.com/ltgoslo/norec_eval

Dzmitry Bahdanau, Kyunghyun Cho, and Yoshua Bengio. 2014. Neural machine translation by jointly learning to align and translate. *arXiv e-prints*, abs/1409.0473.

Jeremy Barnes, Roman Klinger, and Sabine Schulte im Walde. 2017. Assessing State-of-the-Art Sentiment Models on State-of-the-Art Sentiment Datasets. In *Proceedings of the 8th Workshop on Computational Approaches to Subjectivity, Sentiment and Social Media Analysis*, pages 2–12, Copenhagen, Denmark.

Piotr Bojanowski, Edouard Grave, Armand Joulin, and Tomas Mikolov. 2016. Enriching word vectors with subword information. *arXiv preprint arXiv:1607.04606*.

Richard Eckart de Castilho, Éva Mújdricza-Maydt, Seid Muhie Yimam, Silvana Hartmann, Iryna Gurevych, Anette Frank, and Chris Biemann. 2016. A Web-based Tool for the Integrated Annotation of Semantic and Syntactic Structures. In *Proceedings of the Workshop on Language Technology Resources and Tools for Digital Humanities, LT4DH@COLING*, pages 76–84, Osaka, Japan.

Murhaf Fares, Andrey Kutuzov, Stephan Oepen, and Erik Velldal. 2017. Word vectors, reuse, and replicability: Towards a community repository of large-text resources. In *Proceedings of the 21st Nordic Conference of Computational Linguistics*, pages 271–276, Gothenburg, Sweden.

Alex Graves, Santiago Fernández, and Jürgen Schmidhuber. 2005. Bidirectional LSTM Networks for Improved Phoneme Classification and Recognition. In *Artificial Neural Networks: Biological Inspirations - ICANN 2005, LNCS 3697*, pages 799–804. Springer-Verlag Berlin Heidelberg.

Emiliano Raul Guevara. 2010. NoWaC: a large web-based corpus for Norwegian. In *Proceedings of the NAACL HLT 2010 Sixth Web as Corpus Workshop*, pages 1–7, NAACL-HLT, Los Angeles.

Marjam van de Kauter, Bart Desmet, and Véronique Hoste. 2015. The good, the bad and the implicit: a comprehensive approach to annotating explicit and implicit sentiment. *Language Resources and Evaluation*, 49:685–720.

Kian Kenyon-Dean, Eisha Ahmed, Scott Fujimoto, Jeremy Georges-Filteau, Christopher Glasz, Barleen Kaur, Auguste Lalande, Shruti Bhanderi, Robert Belfer, Nirmal Kanagasabai, Roman Sarrazingendron, Rohit Verma, and Derek Ruths. 2018. Sentiment analysis: It's complicated! In *Proceedings of the 2018 Conference of the North American Chapter of the Association for Computational Linguistics and Human Language Technologies*, pages 1886–1895, New Orleans, Louisiana.

Yoon Kim. 2014. Convolutional Neural Networks for Sentence Classification. In *Proceedings of the 2014 Conference on Empirical Methods in Natural Language Processing*, pages 1746–1751, Doha, Qatar.

Bing Liu. 2015. *Sentiment analysis: Mining Opinions, Sentiments, and Emotions*. Cambridge University Press, Cambridge, United Kingdom.

Christian Scheible and Hinrich Schütze. 2013. Sentiment relevance. In *Proceedings of the 51st Annual Meeting of the Association for Computational Linguistics*, pages 954–963, Sofia, Bulgaria.

Peter Shaw, Jakob Uszkoreit, and Ashish Vaswani. 2018. Self-attention with relative position representations. In *Proceedings of the 2018 Conference of the North American Chapter of the Association for Computational Linguistics: Human Language Technologies, Volume 2 (Short Papers)*, pages 464–468, New Orleans, Louisiana.

Cigdem Toprak, Niklas Jakob, and Iryna Gurevych. 2010. Sentence and expression level annotation of opinions in user-generated discourse. In *Proceedings of the 48th Annual Meeting of the Association for Computational Linguistics*, pages 130–139, Uppsala, Sweden.

Ashish Vaswani, Noam Shazeer, Niki Parmar, Jakob Uszkoreit, Llion Jones, Aidan N Gomez, Ł ukasz Kaiser, and Illia Polosukhin. 2017. Attention is all you need. In I. Guyon, U. V. Luxburg, S. Bengio, H. Wallach, R. Fergus, S. Vishwanathan, and R. Garnett, editors, *Advances in Neural Information Processing Systems 30*, pages 5998–6008. Curran Associates, Inc.

Erik Velldal, Lilja Øvrelid, Cathrine Stadsnes Eivind Alexander Bergem, Samia Touileb, and Fredrik Jørgensen. 2018. NoReC: The Norwegian Review Corpus. In *Proceedings of the 11th edition of the Language Resources and Evaluation Conference*, pages 4186–4191, Miyazaki, Japan.

Theresa Wilson. 2008. Annotating subjective content in meetings. In *Proceedings of the 6th edition of the Language Resources and Evaluation Conference*, pages 2738–2745, Marrakech, Morocco.

An Unsupervised Query Rewriting Approach Using N-gram Co-occurrence Statistics to Find Similar Phrases in Large Text Corpora

Hans Moen[1], Laura-Maria Peltonen[2], Henry Suhonen[2,3], Hanna-Maria Matinolli[2], Riitta Mieronkoski[2], Kirsi Telen[2], Kirsi Terho[2,3], Tapio Salakoski[1] and Sanna Salanterä[2,3]

[1]Turku NLP Group, Department of Future Technologies, University of Turku, Finland
[2]Department of Nursing Science, University of Turku, Finland
[3]Turku University Hospital, Finland
{hanmoe,lmemur,hajsuh,hmkmat,
ritemi,kikrte,kmterh,sala,sansala}@utu.fi

Abstract

We present our work towards developing a system that should find, in a large text corpus, contiguous phrases expressing similar meaning as a query phrase of arbitrary length. Depending on the use case, this task can be seen as a form of (phrase-level) query rewriting. The suggested approach works in a generative manner, is unsupervised and uses a combination of a semantic word n-gram model, a statistical language model and a document search engine. A central component is a distributional semantic model containing word n-grams vectors (or embeddings) which models semantic similarities between n-grams of different order. As data we use a large corpus of PubMed abstracts. The presented experiment is based on manual evaluation of extracted phrases for arbitrary queries provided by a group of evaluators. The results indicate that the proposed approach is promising and that the use of distributional semantic models trained with uni-, bi- and trigrams seems to work better than a more traditional unigram model.

1 Introduction

When searching to see if some information is found in a text corpus, it may be difficult to formulate search queries that precisely match all relevant formulations expressing the same information. This becomes particularly difficult when the information is expressed using multiple words, as a phrase, due to the expressibility and complexity of natural language. Single words may have several synonyms, or near synonyms, which refer to the same or similar underlying concept (e.g. "school" vs "gymnasium"). When it comes to multi-word phrases and expressions, possible variations in word use, word count and word order complicate things further (e.g. "consume food" vs "food and eating" or "DM II" vs "type 2 diabetes mellitus").

An important task for a search engine is to try to bridge the gap between user queries and how associated phrases of similar meaning (semantics) are written in the targeted text. In this paper we present our work towards enabling phrase-level query rewriting in an unsupervised manner. Here we explore a relatively simple generative approach, implemented as a prototype (search) system. The task of the system is, given a query phrase as input, generate and suggest as output contiguous candidate phrases from the targeted corpus that each express similar meaning as the query. These phrases, input and output, may be of any length (word count), and not necessarily known as such before the system is presented with the query. Ideally, all unique phrases with similar meaning as the query should be identified. For example, the query might be: "organizational characteristics of older people care". This exact query phrase may or may not occur in the target corpus. Regardless, a phrase candidate of related meaning that we want our system to identify in the targeted corpus could then be: "community care of elderly". In this example, the main challenges that we are faced with are: 1) how can we identify these four words as a relevant phrase, and 2) decide that its meaning is similar to that of the query. Depending on the use case, the task can be seen as a form of query rewriting/substitution, paraphrasing or a restricted type of query expansion. Relevant use cases include information retrieval, information extraction, question–answering and text summarization. We also aim to use this functionality to support manual annotation. For that purpose the system will be tasked with finding phrases that have similar meaning as exemplar phrases and queries provided by the user, and/or as previously annotated text spans. An unsupervised approach like we are aiming for would be particularly valuable for corpora and in domains that lack relevant labeled training data, e.g. in the form of search history logs, needed for supervised paraphrasing and query rewriting approaches.

The presented system relies on a combination of primarily three components: A distributional semantic model of word n-gram vectors (or embeddings), containing unigrams, bigrams and trigrams; A statistical language model; And a document search engine. Briefly explained, the way the system works is by first generating a set of plausible phrase (rewrite) candidates for a given query. This is done by first composing vector representation(s) of the query, and then searching for and retrieving n-grams that are close by in the semantic vector space. These n-grams are then concatenated to form the phrase candidates. In this process, the statistical language model helps to quickly discard phrases that are likely nonsensical. Next the phrases are ranked according to their similarity to the query, and finally the search engine checks which phrase candidates actually exist in the targeted corpus, and where.

Similar to Zhao et al. (2017) and Gupta et al. (2019) we explore the inclusion of word n-grams of different sizes in the same semantic space/model. One motivation for this is that they both found this to produce improved unigram representations compared to only training with unigram co-occurrence statistics. Another motivation is that we want to use the model to not only retrieve unigrams that are semantically close to each other, but also bigrams and trigrams.

2   Related Work

Unsupervised methods for capturing and modeling word-level semantics as vectors, or embeddings, have been popular since the introduction of Latent Semantic Analysis (LSA) (Deerwester et al., 1990) around the beginning of the 1990s. Such word vector representations, where the underlying training heuristic is typically based on the distributional hypothesis (Harris, 1954), usually with some form of dimension reduction, have shown to capture word similarity (synonymy and relatedness) and analogy (see e.g. Agirre et al. (2009); Mikolov et al. (2013)). Methods and toolkits like Word2Vec (Mikolov et al., 2013) and GloVe (Pen-

nington et al., 2014) are nowadays commonly used to (pre-)train word embeddings for further use in various NLP tasks, including supervised text classification with neural networks. However, recent methods such as ELMo (Peters et al., 2017) and BERT (Devlin et al., 2018) use deep neural networks to represent context sensitive word embeddings, which achieves state-of-the-art performance when used in supervised text classification and similar.

Further, there are several relatively recent works focusing on using and/or representing n-gram information as semantic vectors (see e.g. Bojanowski et al. (2016); Zhao et al. (2017); Poliak et al. (2017); Gupta et al. (2019)), possibly to further represent clauses, sentences and/or documents (see e.g. Le and Mikolov (2014); Pagliardini et al. (2018)) in semantic vector spaces.

A relatively straight forward approach to identify and represent common phrases as vectors in a semantic space is to first use some type of collocation detection. Here the aim is to identify sequences of words that co-occur more often than what is expected by chance in a large corpus. One can then train a semantic model where identified phrases are treated as individual tokens, on the same level as words, like it is done in Mikolov et al. (2013).

In the works mentioned so far, the focus is on distributional semantics for representing and calculating semantic similarity and relatedness between predefined lexical units and/or of predefined length (words/n-grams, collocations, clauses, sentences, etc.). Dinu and Baroni (2014) and Turney (2014) take things a step further and approach the more complex and challenging task of using semantic models to enable phrase generation. Their aim is similar to ours: given an input query (phrase) consisting of k words, generate as output t phrases consisting of l words that each expresses its meaning. Their approaches rely on applying a set of separately trained vector composition and decomposition functions able to compose a single vector from a vector pair, or decompose a vector back into estimates of its constituent vectors, possibly in the semantic space of another domain or language.

Dinu and Baroni (2014) also apply vector composition and decomposition in a recursive manner for longer phrases ($t \leq 3$). Their focus is on mapping between unigrams, bigrams and trigrams. As output their system produce one vector per word which represent the (to be) generated phrase. Here the evaluation primarily assumes that $t = 1$, i.e. the nearest neighbouring word in the semantic model, belonging to the expected word class, is extracted per vector to form the output phrase. However, no solution is presented for when $t > 1$ other than independent ranked lists of semantically similar words to each vector.

Turney (2014) explores an approach targeting retrieval of multiple phrases for a single query (i.e. $t > 1$), evaluated on unigram to bigram and bigram to unigram extraction. Here he applies a supervised ranking algorithm to rank the generated output candidates. For each input query, the evaluation checks whether or not the correct/expected output (phrase) is among the list of top hundred candidates.

It is unclear how well these two latter approaches potentially scale beyond bigrams or trigrams. Further, they assume that the length of the input/output phrases is known in advance. However, the task that we are aiming for is to develop a system that can take any query phrase of arbitrary (sub-sentence) length as input. As output it should suggest phrases that it identifies in a large document corpus which express the same or similar information/meaning. Here the idea is that we only apply upper and lower thresholds when it comes to the length of the output phrase suggestions. In addition, we do not want to be concerned with knowledge about word classes in the input and output phrases. We are not aware of previous work presenting a solution to this task.

In the next section, Section 3, we describe how our system works. In Section 4 we present a preliminary evaluation followed by discussion and plans for future work directions.

3 Methods

3.1 Semantic Model Training

In order to train a semantic n-gram model of unigrams, bigrams and trigrams, we initially explored two approaches. First using the Word2Vecf (Levy and Goldberg, 2014) variation of the original Word2Vec toolkit, where one can freely customize the word-to-context training instances as individual rows in the training file – each row containing one source word and one target context to predict. We opted for a skip-gram representation of the training corpus, meaning, for each row in the customized training file, we put the source n-gram and one of its neighboring n-grams as target context. The size of the sliding window is decided by how many neighboring (context) n-grams we include for each source n-gram. Overlap between the source n-gram and target n-grams is allowed.

However, we found that Word2Vecf only allows training using negative sampling. As an alternative approach we simply used the original Word2Vec toolkit, with the skip-gram architecture, hierarchical softmax optimization and a window size of one, to train on the same word-to-context organized training file intended for Word2Vecf. This means that it sees and trains on only two n-grams (cf. word–context pair) at a time. Based on preliminary testing we found this latter approach to produce semantic models that seemed to best capture n-gram semantics for our use case.

The text used for training the semantic model is first stemmed using the Snowball stemmer. This is done to normalize inflected word forms, reduce the number of unique n-grams and consequently the size of the model, as well as creating more training examples for the remaining n-grams. Mapping back to full-form words and phrases is later done using a document search engine, as explained below.

3.2 Phrase-Level Query Rewriting System

Our system works in a generative way when trying to find phrases from a target corpus that are semantically similar to a query phrase. We describe this as a five-step process/pipeline.

Step 1: As a first step we generate a set of query vectors for each of the different n-gram orders in the model – uni, bi and tri. We simply generate these vectors by normalizing and summing the associated n-gram vectors from the semantic model. In addition, if a word (or all words in a n-grams when n > 1) is found in a stopword list[1], we give these vectors half weight. As an example: given the query "this is a query", we generate three query vectors, $\overrightarrow{q_{1\text{-}g}}$, $\overrightarrow{q_{2\text{-}g}}$ and $\overrightarrow{q_{3\text{-}g}}$ as follows:

$$\overrightarrow{q_{1\text{-}g}} = sum(\frac{1}{2}\overrightarrow{\text{this}}, \frac{1}{2}\overrightarrow{\text{is}}, \frac{1}{2}\overrightarrow{\text{a}}, \overrightarrow{\text{query}}) \quad (1)$$

$$\overrightarrow{q_{2\text{-}g}} = sum(\frac{1}{2}\overrightarrow{\text{this\_is}}, \frac{1}{2}\overrightarrow{\text{is\_a}}, \overrightarrow{\text{a\_query}}) \quad (2)$$

$$\overrightarrow{q_{3\text{-}g}} = sum(\frac{1}{2}\overrightarrow{\text{this\_is\_a}}, \overrightarrow{\text{is\_a\_query}}) \quad (3)$$

---

[1] We use the NLTK (Bird et al., 2009) stopword list for English.

If, let's say, the query only contains one word, we can not generate query bigram or trigram vectors. Also, not all n-grams might be found in the semantic model. To compensate for this possibility, we keep track of the *coverage percentage* of each composed vector. This is later used when calculating similarity between the query and the generated phrase candidates (see step 4).

Step 2: Having composed the query vectors, the second step focuses on using the semantic model to extract the most similar n-grams. For each query vector, $\overrightarrow{q_{1\text{-}g}}$, $\overrightarrow{q_{2\text{-}g}}$ and $\overrightarrow{q_{3\text{-}g}}$, we extract semantically similar unigrams, bigrams and trigrams that are near in the semantic space. As a distance measure we apply the commonly used cosine similarity measure (cos). We use a cut-off threshold and a max count as parameters to limit the number of retrieved n-grams and further the number of generated phrase candidates in step 3.

Step 3: The third step focuses on generating candidate phrases from the extracted n-grams. This is primarily done by simply exploring all possible permutations of the extracted n-grams. Here we apply the statistical language model, trained using the KenLM toolkit (Heafield, 2011), to efficiently and iteratively check if nonsensical candidate phrases are being generated. For n-grams where n > 1 we also combine with overlapping words – one overlapping word for bigrams and one or two overlapping words for trigrams. As an example, from the bigrams: "a_good" and "good_cake", we can construct the phrase "a good cake" since "good" is overlapping.

The generation of a phrase will end if no additional n-grams can be added, or if the length reaches a maximum word count threshold relative to the length of the query[2]. If, at this point, a phrase has a length that is below a minimum length threshold[3], it will be discarded. Finally, we also conduct some simple rule-based trimming of candidates by mainly removing stopwords if they occur as the rightmost word(s).

Step 4: After having generated a set of candidate phrases, we now rank these by their similarity to the query. For each phrase candidate we compose phrase vectors ($\overrightarrow{p_{n\text{-}g}}$) in the same way as we did for the query. That said, we observed that the trigram coverage of the semantic model is relatively

low compared to unigrams and bigrams. This is a result of us using a minimum n-gram occurrence count threshold of 20 when training the semantic model. Thus, for the presented experiment, we decided to exclude trigrams in the similarity scoring function.

As already mentioned, not all n-grams may be found in the semantic model. Thus, we also incorporate what we refer to as coverage information for each $\overrightarrow{q_{n\text{-}g}} - \overrightarrow{p_{n\text{-}g}}$ pair. The underlying intuition is to let query vectors and phrase candidate vectors with low model coverage have a lower influence on the overall similarity score. For example, if phrase p is "this is a phrase", which consist of three bigrams, but the semantic model is missing the bigram "a_phrase", the coverage of $\overrightarrow{p_{2\text{-}g}}$, i.e. $cov(\overrightarrow{p_{2\text{-}g}})$, becomes $2/3 = 0.66$. The coverage of a $\overrightarrow{q_{n\text{-}g}} - \overrightarrow{p_{n\text{-}g}}$ pair is simply the product of their coverage, i.e. $cov(\overrightarrow{q_{n\text{-}g}}) \times cov(\overrightarrow{p_{n\text{-}g}})$.

The overall similarity function $sim(q, p)$ for a query q and a phrase candidate p is as follows:

$$sim(q, p) = \frac{1}{cov_{sum}} \sum_{n=1}^{2} \sum_{m=1}^{2} \left(cos(\overrightarrow{q_{n\text{-}g}}, \overrightarrow{p_{m\text{-}g}}) \right.$$
$$\left. \times cov(\overrightarrow{q_{n\text{-}g}}) \times cov(\overrightarrow{p_{m\text{-}g}}) \right) \tag{4}$$

Where cos is cosine similarity, $cov(\overrightarrow{q_{n\text{-}g}})$ and $cov(\overrightarrow{p_{m\text{-}g}})$ refer to their coverage in the semantic model, and cov_{sum} is:

$$cov_{sum} = \sum_{n=1}^{2} \sum_{m=1}^{2} \left(cov(\overrightarrow{q_{n\text{-}g}}) \times cov(\overrightarrow{p_{m\text{-}g}}) \right) \tag{5}$$

Finally, all candidate phrases generated from a query are ranked in descending order.

Step 5: In the final step we filter out the candidate phrases that are not found in the targeted text corpus. To do this we have made the corpus searchable by indexing it with the Apache Solr search platform[4]. Since the candidate phrases are at this point stemmed, we use a text field analyzer that allows matching of stemmed words and phrases with inflected versions found in the original text corpus. In this step we also gain information about how many times each phrase occur in the corpus, and where. By starting with the most similar candidate phrase, the search engine is used to filter out non-matching phrases until the

---

desired number of existing phrases are found, or until there are no more candidates left.

In addition, the system checks to see if an exact match of the query exist in the corpus. If this is the case, it removes any phrase candidate that are either a subphrase of the query or contains the entire query as a subphrase. This is a rather strict restriction, but for evaluation purposes it ensures that the system does not simply find and suggest entries of the original query phrase (with some additional words), or subphrases of it.

4 Experiment

Evaluating the performance of such a system is challenging due to the complexity of the task and the size of the text corpus. We are not aware of evaluation data containing gold standards for this task. Also, the complexity of the task makes it difficult to apply suitable baseline methods to compare against.

We decided to conduct a relatively small experiment, relying on manual evaluation, with the aim of getting an insight into strengths and weaknesses of the system. As text corpus we use a collection of PubMed abstracts consisting of approximately 3.6B tokens. Since our approach is unsupervised, we use this same data set for both training and testing. Six people (aka evaluators) with background as researchers and practitioners in the field of medicine were asked to provide 10 phrases of arbitrarily length, relevant to their research interests. The requirements were that the phrases should be intended for PubMed, more or less grammatically correct, and preferably consist of two or more words. This resulted in 69[5] phrases of different topics, length and complexity, with an average word count of 4.07. These serve as *query phrases*, or simply *queries*, for the remainder of this experiment.

Next, we use three different versions of the system, Ngram, Unigram and Ngram$_{restr}$ (described below) to separately generate and suggest 20 candidate phrases for each query. The evaluators were then given the task of assessing/rating if these phrases expressed the same information, similar information, topical relatedness or were unrelated to the query. Each evaluator assessed the suggestions for the query phrases they provided themselves[6]. The five-class scale used for rating

Class	Description
1	Same information as the query.
2	Same information as the query and has additional information.
3	Similar information as the query but is missing some information.
4	Different information than the query but concerns the same topic.
5	Not related to the query.

Table 1: Classes used by the evaluators when rating phrases suggested by the system.

the phrase suggestions can be seen in Table 1. In total, 1380 phrases were assessed for each system (69×20).

System - Ngram: Here the system is employed as it is described in Section 3.2. We prepared the training data for the semantic n-gram model with a window size equivalent to 3. Minimum occurrence count for inclusion was 20^7. A dimensionality of 200 was used and otherwise default hyper parameters.

System - Unigram: Here we use a more traditional semantic model containing only unigrams. We trained the model using Word2Vec with skip-gram architecture, a dimensionality of 200, window size of 3, minimum inclusion threshold of 20, and otherwise default hyper parameters. This model was used to both extract relevant words and to calculate similarity between phrases and the query. Comparing this to the Ngram variant should provide some insight into the effect of training/using semantic models with word n-grams.

System - Ngram$_{restr}$: Here we add an additional restriction to the default setup (Ngram) by removing any generated phrase candidates containing one or more bigrams found in the query (based on their stemmed versions). The intention is to see if the system is still able to find phrases of related information to a query, despite not allowed to use any word pairs found in it.

In all system versions we use a statistical language model (KenLM (Heafield, 2011)) trained on the mentioned text corpus with an order of 3. We set the phrase inclusion likelihood threshold to

---

[5]One person submitted 19 phrases.

[6]No overlapping evaluation were conducted, so no inter-rater agreement information is available.

[7]Unique unigrams = 0.8M, bigrams = 6.5M, trigrams = 15.7M.

Class	System		
	Ngram	**Unigram**	**Ngram**$_{restr}$
1	13.99%	9.78%	8.48%
2	17.61%	12.54%	16.30%
3	24.13%	23.04%	16.23%
4	22.61%	25.14%	24.06%
5	21.67%	29.49%	34.93%
1+2	31.59%	22.32%	24.78%
1+2+3+4	78.33%	70.51%	65.07%

Table 2: Manual evaluation results.

−11.2. We strived to select parameters that made the system variants produce, on average, approximately the same number of phrase candidates (step 2 and 3). The number of phrase candidates generated in step 3 varied significantly depending on the query and system, from some thousands to some tens of thousands.

5   Results, Discussion and Future Work

Table 2 shows how the evaluators rated the (rewrite) phrases extracted by the various system setups. With the Ngram variant, when allowed to suggest 20 phrases, 31.59% of these contain the same information as the query phrases – possibly with some additional information (rated class 1+2). 78.33% of the suggested phrases concerns the same topic as the query phrases, i.e. rated class 1+2+3+4. The latter indicate the percentage of phrases that could be relevant to the user when it comes to query-based searching. Overall the results show that the system is indeed capable of generating, finding and suggesting (from the PubMed abstracts corpus) phrases that expresses similar meaning as the query. Table 3 shows examples of a few queries, rewrite suggestions by the system and their ratings by the evaluators.

Using a semantic model trained on word n-grams of different orders simultaneously (Ngram) achieves better results than using a unigram model (Unigram). This supports the findings in Zhao et al. (2017) and Gupta et al. (2019).

Naturally, the restricted Ngram$_{restr}$ variant achieves lower scores than Ngram. However, the performance differences are not that great when looking at the percentage of phrases rated as class 2. This suggests that the system finds phrases containing some additional information and/or phrases with words and expressions describing other degrees of specificity. Further, de-spite not allowed to suggest phrases containing bigrams found in the associated queries, it still achieves a higher 1+2 score than Unigram.

For some expressions used in the queries, there might not exist any good alternatives. Or, these might not exist in the PubMed abstracts corpus. For example, given the query "hand hygiene in hospitals". Since Ngram$_{restr}$ is not allowed to suggest phrases containing the expression "hand hygiene", or even "hygiene in", it has instead found and suggested some phrases containing somewhat related concepts such as "hand-washing" and "hand disinfection". However, for other queries the system had an arguably easier time. For example, for the query "digestive tract surgery" it suggests phrases like "gastrointestinal (GI) tract operations" (rated as class 1) and "gastrointestinal tract reconstruction" (rated as class 2). In other cases, the same meaning of a phrase is more or less retained when simply changing the word order (e.g. "nurses' information needs" vs "information nurses need").

We observed that step 5 typically took less time to complete for Ngram compared to Unigram. This could indicate that Ngram – using the n-gram model – is better at producing phrases that are likely to exist in the corpus. Another factor here is the effect of using the n-gram model in the ranking step (step 4), which retains some word order information from the queries.

A weakness of the conducted experiment is that we do not have a true gold standard reflecting if there actually exist any phrases in the corpus of similar meaning to the queries, or how many there potentially are. Still, the results show that the proposed system is indeed able to generate and suggest phrases whose information expresses the same or similar meaning as the provided queries, also when there are no exact matches of the query in the corpus. A planned next step is to look into other evaluation options. One option is to create a gold standard for a set of predefined queries using a smaller corpus. However, it can be difficult to manually identify and decide which phrases are relevant to a given query. Another option is to use the system to search for concepts and entities that has a finite set of known textual variants – e.g. use one variant as query and see if it can find the others. Alternatively, an extrinsic evaluation approach would be to have people use the system in an interactive way for tasks related to phrase-level

Query phrase	Rewrite suggestions by the system	Rating
infection prevention and control in hospital	• prevent and control hospital infections	1
	• control and prevent nosocomial infection	2
	• infection control and preventative care	4
information system impact	• information system influence	1
	• impact of healthcare information systems	2
	• health information system : effects	2
attitude and hand hygiene	• knowledge and attitude towards hand hygiene	2
	• Hand Hygiene : Knowledge and Attitudes	2
	• handwashing practices and attitudes	3
assessment of functional capacity of older people	• the functional assessment of elderly people	1
	• functional capacity of the elderly	3
	• the functional status of elderly individuals	4
facial muscle electromyography	• electromyography of facial muscles	1
	• electromyography (EMG) of masticatory muscles	2
	• facial muscle recording	3
treatment of post-operative nausea and vomiting	• postoperative nausea and vomiting (PONV) treatment	1
	• control of postoperative nausea and vomiting (PONV)	1
	• treatment of emesis , nausea and vomiting	4
fundamental care	• fundamental nursing care	2
	• palliative care is fundamental	2
	• holistic care , spiritual care	4
pain after cardiac surgery	• postoperative pain after heart surgery	1
	• postoperative pain management after cardiac surgery	2
	• discomfort after cardiac surgery	4

Table 3: Examples of a few queries, rewrite suggestions by the system and their ratings by the evaluators.

searching and matching, and then collect qualitative and/or quantitative feedback regarding impact on task effectiveness.

So far, not much focus has been placed on system optimization. For example, no multithreading was used in the phrase generation steps. The average time it took for the system to generate and find 20 phrases in the PubMed abstracts corpus for a query was about 30 seconds. This varied quite a bit depending on the number of n-grams extracted in step 2, the semantic model used and the length of the query. One bottleneck seems to be step 5 which is dependent on the size and status of the document index. However, it is worth noting that we have observed this to take only a few seconds for smaller corpora. For use in search scenarios where response time is critical, offline generation for common queries is an option. Further, this could for example serve to produce training data for supervised approaches.

As future work, system optimization will aim towards having the system generate as few non-relevant phrase candidates as possible while avoiding leaving out relevant ones. This includes making the search in the vector space (semantic model) to be as precise as possible (query vector composition) with a wide enough search for semantically similar n-grams (cos similarity cutoff threshold). Also, the similarity measure used to rank the phrase candidates relative to the query ($sim(q, p)$) is important for the performance of the system. As future work we also plan to look into the possibility of incorporating ways to automatically exclude non-relevant phrase candidates, e.g. by using a similarity cut-off threshold. Other text similarity measures and approaches could be tried, such as some of those shown to perform well in the SemEval STS shared tasks (Cer et al., 2017). In our relatively straight forward vector composition approach, each word/n-gram are weighted equally (except for stopwords). Improvements may be gained by incorporating some sort of statistical word weighting, like TF-IDF (Salton and Buckley, 1988). Other vector composition approaches could also be considered. Further, we also plan to explore other approaches to generating semantic text representations, such as Sent2Vec (Pagliardini et al., 2018). Also approaches like ELMo (Peters et al., 2017) and BERT (Devlin et al., 2018) could be applicable for this purpose. Additionally, one could also explore the use of cross-lingual semantic models for tasks related to translation.

Some times the system had a hard time finding phrases reflecting all the information in some of the more lengthy and complex queries – possibly referring to multiple topics. For example, "means to reduce the duration of surgical operations" and "a systematic approach to infection control". For some of the queries one can assume that no contiguous (sub-sentence) phrases exist among the PubMed abstracts that expresses the same meaning. However, something that is missing from our current pipeline is some kind of query segmentation step. We are now treating each query as a single expression. As future work, especially in the context of query-based free-text searching, we aim to incorporate some sort of query segmentation which may split the query into smaller parts dependent on its complexity and the number of topics it refers to. Here we also want to explore the possibility of having wildcards in the query.

Overall we find these initial results to be promising. Further exploration and evaluation of the presented approach and system is needed. This includes looking into potential improvements and extensions, such as those mentioned above.

6 Conclusion

In this paper we have described a prototype system intended for the task of finding, in a large text corpus, contiguous phrases with similar meaning as a query of arbitrary length. For each of the 69 queries provided by a group of evaluators, we tested the system at finding 20 phrases expressing similar information. As corpus a large collection of PubMed abstracts were used. The results indicate that using a semantic model trained on word n-grams of different orders (1–3) simultaneously is beneficial compared to using a more traditional word unigram model. Further, when restricting the system from suggesting phrases containing bi-grams from the corresponding queries, the results indicate that the system is still able to find and suggest relevant phrases.

Acknowledgments

This research was supported by the Academy of Finland (315376). We would like to thank Suwisa Kaewphan for helping out with the preprocessing of the PubMed abstracts data set.

References

Eneko Agirre, Enrique Alfonseca, Keith Hall, Jana Kravalova, Marius Paşca, and Aitor Soroa. 2009. A study on similarity and relatedness using distributional and wordnet-based approaches. In *Proceedings of Human Language Technologies: NAACL 2009*, pages 19–27. Association for Computational Linguistics.

Steven Bird, Edward Loper, and Ewan Klein. 2009. *Natural Language Processing with Python*. OReilly Media Inc., Sebastopol, California, USA.

Piotr Bojanowski, Edouard Grave, Armand Joulin, and Tomas Mikolov. 2016. Enriching word vectors with subword information. *CoRR*, abs/1607.04606.

Daniel Cer, Mona Diab, Eneko Agirre, Inigo Lopez-Gazpio, and Lucia Specia. 2017. SemEval-2017 task 1: Semantic textual similarity multilingual and crosslingual focused evaluation. In *Proceedings of the 11th International Workshop on Semantic Evaluation (SemEval-2017)*, Vancouver, Canada. Association for Computational Linguistics.

Scott Deerwester, Susan T. Dumais, George W. Furnas, Thomas K. Landauer, and Richard A. Harshman. 1990. Indexing by latent semantic analysis. *Journal of the American Society for Information Science*, 41(6):391–407.

Jacob Devlin, Ming-Wei Chang, Kenton Lee, and Kristina Toutanova. 2018. Bert: Pre-training of deep bidirectional transformers for language understanding. *arXiv preprint arXiv:1810.04805*.

Georgiana Dinu and Marco Baroni. 2014. How to make words with vectors: Phrase generation in distributional semantics. In *Proceedings of the 52nd Annual Meeting of the Association for Computational Linguistics (Volume 1: Long Papers)*, volume 1, pages 624–633.

Prakhar Gupta, Matteo Pagliardini, and Martin Jaggi. 2019. Better word embeddings by disentangling contextual n-gram information. *arXiv preprint arXiv:1904.05033*.

Zellig S. Harris. 1954. Distributional structure. *Word*, 10:146–162.

Kenneth Heafield. 2011. KenLM: Faster and smaller language model queries. In *Proceedings of the Sixth Workshop on Statistical Machine Translation*, WMT '11, pages 187–197, Stroudsburg, PA, USA. Association for Computational Linguistics.

Quoc Le and Tomas Mikolov. 2014. Distributed representations of sentences and documents. In *International conference on machine learning*, pages 1188–1196.

Omer Levy and Yoav Goldberg. 2014. Dependency-based word embeddings. In *Proceedings of the 52nd Annual Meeting of the Association for Computational Linguistics (Volume 2: Short Papers)*, volume 2, pages 302–308.

Tomas Mikolov, Ilya Sutskever, Kai Chen, Greg S. Corrado, and Jeff Dean. 2013. Distributed representations of words and phrases and their compositionality. In *Advances in Neural Information Processing Systems 26*, pages 3111–3119.

Matteo Pagliardini, Prakhar Gupta, and Martin Jaggi. 2018. Unsupervised Learning of Sentence Embeddings using Compositional n-Gram Features. In *NAACL 2018 - Conference of the North American Chapter of the Association for Computational Linguistics*, pages 528–540. Association for Computational Linguistics.

Jeffrey Pennington, Richard Socher, and Christopher Manning. 2014. Glove: Global vectors for word representation. In *Proceedings of the 2014 conference on empirical methods in natural language processing (EMNLP)*, pages 1532–1543.

Matthew Peters, Waleed Ammar, Chandra Bhagavatula, and Russell Power. 2017. Semi-supervised sequence tagging with bidirectional language models. In *Proceedings of the 55th Annual Meeting of the Association for Computational Linguistics (Volume 1: Long Papers)*, pages 1756–1765.

Adam Poliak, Pushpendre Rastogi, M Patrick Martin, and Benjamin Van Durme. 2017. Efficient, compositional, order-sensitive n-gram embeddings. In *Proceedings of the 15th Conference of the European Chapter of the Association for Computational Linguistics: Volume 2, Short Papers*, pages 503–508.

Gerard Salton and Christopher Buckley. 1988. Term-weighting approaches in automatic text retrieval. *IPM*, 24(5):513–523.

Peter D Turney. 2014. Semantic composition and decomposition: From recognition to generation. *arXiv preprint arXiv:1405.7908*.

Zhe Zhao, Tao Liu, Shen Li, Bofang Li, and Xiaoyong Du. 2017. Ngram2vec: Learning improved word representations from ngram co-occurrence statistics. In *Proceedings of the 2017 Conference on Empirical Methods in Natural Language Processing*, pages 244–253.

Compiling and Filtering ParIce: An English-Icelandic Parallel Corpus

Starkaður Barkarson
The Árni Magnússon Institute
for Icelandic Studies
`starkadur.barkarson@`
`arnastofnun.is`

Steinþór Steingrímsson
The Árni Magnússon Institute
for Icelandic Studies
`steinthor.steingrimsson@`
`arnastofnun.is`

Abstract

We present ParIce, a new English-Icelandic parallel corpus. This is the first parallel corpus built for the purposes of language technology development and research for Icelandic, although some Icelandic texts can be found in various other multilingual parallel corpora. We map which Icelandic texts are available for these purposes, collect and filter aligned data, align other bilingual texts we acquired and describe the alignment and filtering processes. After filtering, our corpus includes 39 million Icelandic words in 3.5 million segment pairs. We estimate that our filtering process reduced the number of faulty segments in the corpus by more than 60% while only reducing the number of good alignments by approximately 9%.

1 Introduction

In recent years machine translation (MT) systems have achieved near human-level performance in a few languages. They rely heavily on large amounts of parallel sentences. This can pose problems for inflected languages like Icelandic, where a substantial amount of data is necessary to cover common word forms of frequent words. For training statistical (SMT) and neural (NMT) machine translation systems, parallel data quality is important and may weaken performance if inadequate, especially for NMT (see e.g. Khayrallah and Koehn (2018)). A vital part of compiling good parallel corpora is thus to assess how accurate the alignments are.

In addition to MT, parallel corpora have been employed for many tasks, including the creation of dictionaries and ontologies, multilingual and cross-lingual document classification and various annotation projection across languages. See e.g. Steinberger et al. (2012) for a discussion on the many aspects of parallel corpora usage.

This paper introduces ParIce, the first parallel corpus focusing only on the English-Icelandic language pair. There have been few available multilingual parallel corpora including Icelandic texts and those that exist vary in quality. Our primary aim was to build a corpus large enough and of good enough quality for training useful MT systems, while we also want it to be useful for other purposes, such as those listed above. The project plan for a language technology program for Icelandic, set to start in fall 2019, notes that for a quality MT system, a parallel corpus of 25-35 million sentence pairs is preferable, although 2 million may be sufficient for initial experiments with state-of-the-art methods (Nikulásdóttir et al., 2017). This first version of ParIce includes 3.5 million sentence pairs. That is quite far from the ambitious aim set forward in the project plan, but is hopefully sufficient to get meaningful results when used to train MT systems.

We started by mapping what parallel data was available and assessed its quality. We then collected unaligned bilingual texts and aligned and filtered them. In the filtering process we want to remove as many bad segment pairs as possible, while maximizing the number of good sentence pairs we hold on to. There is considerable literature on filtering parallel texts. Taghipour et al. (2011) point out that a lack of properly labeled training data makes it hard to use discriminative methods. They utilize unsupervised methods for outlier detection. To reduce reliance on labeled examples, Cui et al. (2013) conduct a PageRank-style random walk algorithm to iteratively compute the importance score of each sentence pair. The higher the score, the better the quality. Xu and Koehn (2017) tackle the problem of insufficient labeled data by creating synthetic noisy data to train a classifier that identifies known good sentence pairs from a noisy corpus.

In this paper we describe our semi-supervised method of using an NMT system trained on part of the corpus, and a bootstrapped dictionary to iteratively assess and score the sentence pairs. We then show how using the score to filter out low quality data results in a better quality corpus.

2 Available texts

The data mapping was twofold. First we looked for available parallel corpora with Icelandic and English texts. Then we looked for texts available to us in both languages that we could align and had permission to publish with open licenses.

2.1 Aligned data

We collected over 1.9 million English-Icelandic sentence pairs from other parallel corpora (see Table 1), mostly from the Opus project[1] but also from the Tilde MODEL corpus[2], ELRC[3] and a multilingual parallel bible corpus[4].

Opus (Tiedemann, 2012) has a variety of different parallel corpora in multiple languages. In the EN-IS language pair there are film and tv subtitles collected from OpenSubtitles[5], texts from localization files for KDE4, Ubuntu and Gnome and a collection of translated sentences from Tatoeba[6], an online collection of sentences and their translations, created by volunteers.

ELRC (European Language Resource Coordination) offers among others a parallel corpus that was derived from Icelandic and English texts from the Statistics Iceland (SI) website[7].

From the Tilde MODEL corpus (Rozis and Skadins, 2017) we include the EN-IS language pair from a corpus of texts from the European Medicines Agency document portal.

A parallel corpus of the bible in 100 languages (Christodoulopoulos and Steedman, 2015) is available online. This includes the Icelandic

Corpus	Sentence pairs	Bad alignments (%)
The Bible[4]	31,085	0.5
EMA[8]	420,297	3.3
Gnome[9]	5,431	n/a
KDE4[9]	87,575	45.0
OpenSubtitles[9]	1,368,170	8.3
Statistics Iceland[10]	2,360	8.0
Tatoeba[9]	8,139	0.0
Ubuntu[9]	2,127	2.5
TOTAL	**1,923,060**	

Table 1: Pair count and ratio of bad alignments in the parallel corpora available.

translation from 1981 and the King James version of the English bible.

An examination of random sentences from these corpora revealed that the sentence pairs were sometimes faulty. This could be due to misalignment, mistranslation or other causes. Thus, in cases where we could obtain the raw data that the corpora were compiled from, we realigned them using our methods. For the EMA corpus we only had the raw data in pdf-files and decided against harvesting the texts from these files for realignment. The raw data for the SI corpus was not available on the ELRC-website, and we did not scrape the SI website for this project. The Tatoeba data is collected in such a way that there is no reason to align it again, and inspection of the data from GNOME indicated that the alignments were of insufficient quality and that mending them would prove hard so we decided to exclude them from our corpus.

2.2 Unaligned data

Regulations, directives and other documents translated for the members of the European Economic Area (EEA) were obtained from the EFTA-website[11], where they are available in both pdf and html format.

The Icelandic Sagas have been translated into numerous languages. Some of these translations are out of copyright and available in English on Project Gutenberg[12]. The Icelandic texts were obtained from the SAGA corpus (Rögnvaldsson and Helgadóttir, 2011). We also selected four books from Project Gutenberg, which were available in

---

[1] http://opus.nlpl.eu
[2] https://tilde-model.s3-eu-west-1.amazonaws.com/Tilde_MODEL_Corpus.html
[3] Available at the ELRC-SHARE repository
[4] http://christos-c.com/bible/
[5] http://www.opensubtitles.org
[6] http://tatoeba.org
[7] https://www.statice.is
[8] Part of the Tilde MODEL corpus
[9] Part of the OPUS corpus
[10] Created by ELRC

[11] https://www.efta.int
[12] https://www.gutenberg.org

translation on Rafbókavefurinn[13], a website with a collection of books in Icelandic in the public domain. The purpose of this was to experiment with aligning literary translations.

3 Compiling ParIce

We employed a two-step process to pair the sentences. First the texts were aligned with LF Aligner, except in cases where no alignment was necessary (see Section 3.1.2). Then the alignment was assessed and filtered.

3.1 Alignment

We used LF Aligner[14], which relies on Hunalign (Varga et al., 2005) for automatic sentence pairing. It aligns sentences in two languages by using a dictionary and information on sentence length.

3.1.1 Dictionary

We created a makeshift dictionary of over 12 thousand lemmas (D1) by scraping the Icelandic Wiktionary. In the case of nouns, pronouns and adjectives all possible inflections are listed on Wiktionary and were included in D1,

We ran LF Aligner, using D1, in the first pass of the alignment process. Afterwards the data was sent through the filtering process described in Section 3.2. We then used bitextor-builddics (Esplà-Gomis, 2009), to create another dictionary (D2). Builddics takes as an input source language segments in one file and target language segments in another. It then compares corresponding lines and builds a bilingual dictionary. Finally, D2 was expanded by getting all possible word forms of every Icelandic word in the dictionary from the Database of Modern Icelandic Inflection (DMII) (Bjarnadóttir, 2005). For each Icelandic word in D2, all the possible lemmas were found in DMII and every word form was retrieved for each lemma. D2 contains approx. 31 thousand lemmas, not counting different word forms. We used this dictionary for a second run of alignment on all the corpora.

3.1.2 Texts not requiring alignment

Texts from localization files (KDE4 and Ubuntu) are aligned by design. Some lines also contain strings that are not proper words but placeholders. In order to have less noisy texts these were

[13]https://rafbokavefur.is
[14]http://sourceforge.net/projects/aligner

removed. The Tatoeba segments were also not re-aligned, as the segments are created by translation.

3.2 Assessment and filtering

Aside from the cases where there was no need for assessment due to the nature of the data (Tatoeba, Bible), or because the alignments had already been filtered (KDE4, Ubuntu), we start by assessing the quality of the alignment and filtering out all lines deemed bad. A rough inspection of the aligned texts reveals that bad alignments usually come in chunks. If an error occurs in one alignment it has a tendency to affect the alignment of one or more sentences that follow since LF Aligner can take several lines to find the right path again.

As part of the filtering process we translate the English text of each sentence pair into Icelandic and then compare the translations to the Icelandic sentence and score each pair depending on that comparison. Every chunk of sentence pairs that has unfavorable scoring is deleted, but the sentence pairs that are not deleted are used to expand the dictionary (D2). These steps of translating, scoring, filtering and expanding the dictionary are repeated several times.

Before describing the filtering pipeline in detail we describe the scoring process.

3.3 Scoring

All English segments were translated into Icelandic by employing these two methods:

i) All possible translations were obtained from dictionary D2 for every word in the English sentence, thus creating a multiset for each word.

ii) We used OpenNMT (Klein et al., 2017) to train an MT system, using a 1 million segment translation memory provided by the Translation Centre of the Ministry for Foreign Affairs, and parallel corpora obtained from Opus. The system was used to translate each English sentence into Icelandic.

Since Icelandic is an inflected language it was necessary to take into account every word form. As described in Section 3.1.1, the D2 dictionary included all possible word forms but for the translated sentence obtained with OpenNMT all word forms were obtained by using DMII and a multiset created for each word of the translated sentence.

The score for every sentence was calculated by finding the average of score1 and score2. Score1 is the ratio of words in the Icelandic sentence found in any of the multisets created by either the first or

	Before Filtering	Accepted Pairs	Accepted Pairs (%)	Bad Accepted Pairs (%)	Bad Deleted Pairs (%)
The Bible	32,964	32,964	100.0	0.0	n/a
Books	16,976	12,416	73.1	3.5	38.0
EEA	2,093,803	1,701,172	81.3	5.0	63.5
EMA	420,297	404,333	96.2	1.3	45.0
ESO	12,900	12,633	97.9	0.5	46.0
KDE4	137,724	49,912	36.2	9.0	n/a
OpenSubtitles	1,620,037	1,305,827	80.6	1.4	37.0
Sagas	43,113	17,597	40.8	11.0	55.5
Statistics Iceland	2,481	2,288	92.2	5.0	56.0
Tatoeba	8,263	8,263	100.0	0.0	n/a
Ubuntu	11,025	10,572	95.9	2.0	n/a
TOTAL	**4,399,582**	**3,557,977**	**80.9**		

Table 2: Pair count before and after filtering as well as ratio of accepted pairs and deleted pairs that were deemed bad during the assessment.

the second method of translation. Score2 was calculated by finding the ratio of multisets, created with dictionary D2, that contained a word form appearing in the Icelandic sentence, and the ratio of multisets, created with OpenNMT/DMII, that contained a word form appearing in the Icelandic sentence, and then selecting the higher ratio. Sentence pair (1) gets 1.0 as score1 since each word in the Icelandic sentence would be found in the multisets, and 0.38 as score2 since only three of eight multisets would contain a word appearing in the Icelandic sentence. The score would thus be 0.69.

(1)   a.   Hann gekk inn. *(e. He walked in)*
       b.   As he walked in he sang a song.

The score for each document is the average score for all sentence pairs.

3.3.1 Filtering

We set up a filtering pipeline, sending one subcorpus through it at a time. Steps 4-8 in the pipeline, detailed below, were repeated several times with the conditions for "good" sentence pairs strict at first but more lenient in later iterations. The conditions were controlled by thresholds and deletion rules described in step 7 below.

Our filtering pipeline is set up as follows:

1. Aligned sentences are cleaned of all out-of-vocabulary unicode symbols, as some symbols cause problems in parsing.

2. The aligned texts are divided into files, one for each document in the text. The process deletes faulty files, defining faulty to be ones that contain either unusually few and large aligned segments or a very low ratio of Icelandic letters (i.e. *ð, þ, ö*) in the Icelandic segments, indicating that they might have been obtained by inadequate OCR.

3. The English segments are automatically translated to Icelandic with the OpenNMT system, as described in Section 3.3.

4. The English segments are translated using dictionary D2, as described in Section 3.3.

5. Each sentence pair is scored.

6. Files receiving on average a score below a given threshold for their segment pairs are deleted. The assumption is that the English and Icelandic files being aligned are not compatible or only compatible in minor parts.

7. Sentences are deleted according to one of two rules: i) If a certain number of pairs in a row have a score under a given threshold, they are deleted. ii) If a certain number of pairs in a row have a score above a given threshold, they are not deleted but all other pairs are deleted. The second rule is more strict and is usually only used during the first iteration. For both rules, the number of pairs in a row and the threshold have different values selected for each iteration and subcorpus.

8. Two text files are created from the accepted sentence pairs: English in one file and Ice-

landic in the other, with sentences matching on line number. The files are used to create a new dictionary with bitextor-builddics which is appended to dictionary D2.

In OpenSubtitles there often exist many versions of both English and Icelandic subtitles for the same film. Therefore we sometimes chose between several files from the corpus. Working with the Sagas, we sometimes had two translations of the same Saga. The files receiving the highest score, after going through the pipe, were selected.

4 Resulting dataset

Before filtering the texts we had 4,399,582 sentence pairs in total, see Table 2. During the filtering process 841,605 pairs were deleted, 19.13%. The resulting dataset contains 3,557,977 pairs.

4.1 Quality assessment

We manually assessed the alignment quality of the new corpus as well as the pre-existing corpora by checking from 200 to 800 sentence pairs in each subcorpus, depending on its size. If the sentences were not in agreement, if a large chunk was erroneous or if a sentence in one language contained a segment not found in the other language the pair was classified as bad.

The quality of ParIce varies between subcorpora, from containing no bad alignments to 11.0%. Approximately 3.5% of the alignments in the corpus are bad, while the ratio was 8% in the pre-existing corpora. See Table 1 for quality estimates of the pre-existing corpora and Table 2 for quality estimates of ParIce.

5 Filter assessment

We checked a random sample of 100 to 400 of the deleted pairs in each subcorpus, depending on the number of deleted lines, and counted the amount of bad pairs. The results are shown in Table 2. When we compare this assessment to the assessment of the final version of ParIce, we can estimate the reduction of errors in the filtering process. If we exclude the alignments of KDE4 and Ubuntu, which were not sent through the main filtering pipeline, then 753,340 of 4,250,833 alignments, or 17.72%, were deleted during the filtering process. Of these 53.0% were bad, given that the ratio is the same as in our random samples, and the filtering process reduced the number of faulty

segments in the corpus by 77.0% while it only reduced the number of good ones by 9.5%.

6 Availability

ParIce can be downloaded from `http://www.malfong.is`. Available sentences have been PoS-tagged with a BiLSTM tagger (Steingrímsson et al., 2019), lemmatized with Nefnir (Ingólfsdóttir et al., 2019) and word aligned with GIZA++ (Och and Ney, 2003).

The corpus is also searchable on `http://malheildir.arnastofnun.is` in a search tool powered by Korp (Borin et al., 2012).

7 Conclusion and future work

From a fragmented collection of around 1.9 million sentence pairs of unknown quality, and other data, we have built the ParIce corpus of approx. 3.5 million sentence pairs, assessed to be of acceptable quality. This enables the Icelandic language technology community, and others, to experiment with building MT systems for the English-Icelandic language pair.

While increasing alignment quality, our method filters out many perfectly good sentence pairs. It is necessary both to improve the filtering and the alignment processes. For better alignments a better dictionary is crucial. In the absence of a better dictionary, multiple iterations of aligning and filtering, where the aligned data is used to grow the dictionary in every iteration, could be helpful.

For better filtering adding features to our scoring algorithm might be beneficial. Hangya and Fraser (2018) follow Lample et al. (2018) and train monolingual word embeddings for two languages and map them to a shared space without any bilingual signal. They use these bilingual word embeddings for parallel corpus filtering. This approach could prove useful for our purposes.

The web is our best prospect for growing the corpus. We have yet to see how much the ParaCrawl project will collect of Icelandic parallel data, but can expect filtering to be important for that dataset (see e.g. Koehn et al. (2018)).

It would be useful to try to estimate how good MT systems trained on this data can get, and whether our filtering and realigning methods are useful for that purposes. Training MT systems on data from different stages and evaluating BLEU scores should thus be added as part of our pipeline, when working on future versions of ParIce.

References

Kristín Bjarnadóttir. 2005. Modern icelandic inflections. In H. Holmboe, editor, *Nordisk Sprogteknologi 2005*. Museum Tusculanums Forlag, Copenhagen, Denmark.

Lars Borin, Markus Forsberg, and Johan Roxendal. 2012. Korp – the corpus infrastructure of språkbanken. In *Proceedings of LREC 2012. Istanbul: ELRA*, pages 474–478.

Christos Christodoulopoulos and Mark Steedman. 2015. A massively parallel corpus: the bible in 100 languages. *Language Resources and Evaluation*, 49(2):375–395.

Lei Cui, Dongdong Zhang, Shujie Liu, Mu Li, and Ming Zhou. 2013. Bilingual data cleaning for SMT using graph-based random walk. In *Proceedings of the 51st Annual Meeting of the Association for Computational Linguistics (Volume 2: Short Papers)*, pages 340–345, Sofia, Bulgaria. Association for Computational Linguistics.

Miquel Esplà-Gomis. 2009. Bitextor: a Free/Opensource Software to Harvest Translation Memories from Multilingual Websites. In *Proceedings of MT Summit XII*, Ottawa, Canada. Association for Machine Translation in the Americas.

Viktor Hangya and Alexander Fraser. 2018. An unsupervised system for parallel corpus filtering. In *Proceedings of the Third Conference on Machine Translation: Shared Task Papers*, pages 882–887, Belgium, Brussels. Association for Computational Linguistics.

Svanhvít Ingólfsdóttir, Hrafn Loftsson, Jón Daðason, and Kristín Bjarnadóttir. 2019. Nefnir: A high accuracy lemmatizer for Icelandic. In *Proceedings of the 22nd Nordic Conference of Computational Linguistics*, NODALIDA 2019, Turku, Finland.

Huda Khayrallah and Philipp Koehn. 2018. On the impact of various types of noise on neural machine translation. In *Proceedings of the 2nd Workshop on Neural Machine Translation and Generation*, pages 74–83, Melbourne, Australia. Association for Computational Linguistics.

Guillaume Klein, Yoon Kim, Yuntian Deng, Jean Senellart, and Alexander Rush. 2017. OpenNMT: Open-source toolkit for neural machine translation. In *Proceedings of ACL 2017, System Demonstrations*, pages 67–72, Vancouver, Canada. Association for Computational Linguistics.

Philipp Koehn, Huda Khayrallah, Kenneth Heafield, and Mikel L. Forcada. 2018. Findings of the WMT 2018 shared task on parallel corpus filtering. In *Proceedings of the Third Conference on Machine Translation: Shared Task Papers*, pages 726–739, Belgium, Brussels. Association for Computational Linguistics.

Guillaume Lample, Alexis Conneau, Marc'Aurelio Ranzato, Ludovic Denoyer, and Hervé Jégou. 2018. Word translation without parallel data. In *International Conference on Learning Representations*.

Anna Björk Nikulásdóttir, Jón Guðnason, and Steinþór Steingrímsson. 2017. *Language Technology for Icelandic 2018-2022: Project Plan*. Mennta og menningarmálaráðuneytið, Reykjavík, Iceland.

Franz Josef Och and Hermann Ney. 2003. A systematic comparison of various statistical alignment models. *Computational Linguistics*, 29(1):19–51.

Roberts Rozis and Raivis Skadins. 2017. Tilde MODEL - multilingual open data for EU languages. In *NODALIDA*, pages 263–265. Association for Computational Linguistics.

Eiríkur Rögnvaldsson and Sigrún Helgadóttir. 2011. Morphosyntactic tagging of Old Icelandic texts and its use in studying syntactic variation and change. In C. Sporleder, A. van den Bosch, and K. Zervanou, editors, *Language Technology for Cultural Heritage: Selected Papers from the LaTeCH Workshop Series*. Springer, Berlin.

Ralf Steinberger, Andreas Eisele, Szymon Klocek, Spyridon Pilos, and Patrick Schlüter. 2012. DGT-TM: A freely available translation memory in 22 languages. In *Proceedings of the Eighth International Conference on Language Resources and Evaluation (LREC-2012)*, pages 454–459, Istanbul, Turkey. European Language Resources Association (ELRA).

Steinþór Steingrímsson, Örvar Kárason, and Hrafn Loftsson. 2019. Augmenting a BiLSTM tagger with a morphological lexicon and a lexical category identification step. In *Proceedings of RANLP 2019*, Varna, Bulgaria.

Kaveh Taghipour, Shahram Khadivi, and Jia Xu. 2011. Parallel corpus refinement as an outlier detection algorithm. In *MT Summit XIII. Machine Translation Summit (MT-Summit-11), 13., September 19-23, Xiamen, China*. NA.

Jörg Tiedemann. 2012. Parallel data, tools and interfaces in opus. In *Proceedings of the 8th International Conference on Language Resources and Evaluation (LREC'2012)*.

Dániel Varga, László Németh, Péter Halácsy, András Kornai, and Viktor Nagy Viktor Trón. 2005. Parallel corpora for medium density languages. In *Proceedings of the RANLP 2005*, pages 590–596.

Hainan Xu and Philipp Koehn. 2017. Zipporah: a fast and scalable data cleaning system for noisy webcrawled parallel corpora. In *Proceedings of the 2017 Conference on Empirical Methods in Natural Language Processing*, pages 2945–2950, Copenhagen, Denmark. Association for Computational Linguistics.

DIM: The Database of Icelandic Morphology

Kristín Bjarnadóttir, Kristín Ingibjörg Hlynsdóttir, Steinþór Steingrímsson
The Árni Magnússon Institute for Icelandic Studies
University of Iceland
`kristinb@hi.is, kih4@hi.is, steinst@hi.is`

Abstract

The topic of this paper is The Database of Icelandic Morphology (DIM), a multipurpose linguistic resource, created for use in language technology, as a reference for the general public in Iceland, and for use in research on the Icelandic language. DIM contains inflectional paradigms and analysis of word formation, with a vocabulary of approx. 287,000 lemmas. DIM is based on The Database of Modern Icelandic Inflection, which has been in use since 2004. Whereas the older work was descriptive, the new version is partly prescriptive, making the data applicable in a greater range of projects than before.

1 Introduction

This paper describes The Database of Icelandic Morphology (DIM), containing the morphological analysis of approx. 287,000 Icelandic lemmas. The DIM is based on The Database of Modern Icelandic Inflection (DMII), a collection of inflectional paradigms first published in 2004, and originally conceived as a resource for language technology (LT) (Bjarnadóttir, 2012). The DMII has been restructured and extended to include information on word formation, and the analysis has been extended to include genre, style, domain, age, and various grammatical features. The original DMII was descriptive, but DIM is partly prescriptive, i.e., the "correctness" of both words and inflectional forms is marked in accordance with accepted rules of usage. This greatly improves the scope of applications using the data, from the purely analytical possibilities of the old DMII (used for e.g. search engines, PoS tagging, named entity recognition, etc.), to the productive possibilities of the DIM, such as correction and formulation of text. The additional analysis of morphological constituent structure also provides important

linkups between lexical items, as the morphology of Icelandic is extremely productive. The name DIM is here used inclusively for the new project, whereas DMII refers to the inflectional part only.[1]

DIM has five aspects:

- An LT data source for various uses (inclusive of the original format available from 2007)

- A new enhanced and enlarged website for the general public

- The prescriptive DMII Core which is a subset of the inflectional paradigms marked for correctness

- A morphological analysis (MorphIce) with binary constituent structure and lemmatization of constituents

- A data source for linguistic research utilizing the classifications in the database to the full.

The paper is structured as follows. Section 2 contains a short description of Icelandic morphology, to pinpoint the features of analysis needed for various LT uses, with a discussion of the difference of descriptive and prescriptive data. Section 3 describes the DIM database and discusses details of the classification system briefly. Section 4 describes the five main parts of DIM listed above, one by one, drawing out the benefits of the new classification system in each case, i.e., in the DIM

---

[1] The Icelandic name of the DMII is Beygingarlýsing íslensks nútímamáls, abbreviated BÍN. The abbreviation has become a household name in Iceland, with the noun BÍN assigned feminine gender, and the verb bína (with the object in the accusative) used of the search. As the name is so well known, it is not easy to rename the project, and thus BÍN is still used inclusively in Icelandic for the whole project, both DMII and DIM, i.e., BÍN-vefurinn (DMII Web, for inflection online), BÍN-máltæknigögn (DIM/DMII LT Data), BÍN-kjarninn (DMII Core), BÍN-orðföng (DIM Morphological Data, MorphIce)), and Rannsóknar-BÍN (DIM for Research).

Core, the DMII Web, MorphIce, the accessible LT data, and a website for linguists doing research on Icelandic. Section 5 gives details on availability and licensing, and Section 6 contains the conclusion.

2 DIM and the Morphology of Icelandic

Work on the DMII was started in 2002, at the Institute of Lexicography in Reykjavík (cf. Bjarnadóttir (2012) for a description of the project).[2] The database (and the analysis) was very limited in scope, due to considerations of finance and manpower. The result was a set of inflectional paradigms for Icelandic intended for LT use, and a website for the general public.[3] The downloadable LT data has been available in two formats, i.e., in a list of inflectional forms with grammatical tags, linked to a list of lemmas, and in a simple list of inflectional forms without any analysis. Up to date, the data has most popularly been downloaded as a CSV file, with the fields lemma; word class; domain; inflectional form; grammatical tag. The inflectional data for the genitive singular definite form of the masculine noun **köttur** "cat" is as follows, slightly simplified, with the grammatical tag in English:

köttur;416784;masc;kattarins;GEN.SG.+DEF;

This simple data has been used extensively in Icelandic LT projects to date, but these projects have shown the need for a more extensive analysis of Icelandic morphology, which is rich and full of variants and ambiguities, both in regard to inflection and word formation. The reasons are shortly addressed in the following subsections, insofar as they are reflected in the analysis used in DIM.

2.1 Inflection

The ratio of inflectional forms to paradigms in the original DMII is quite high, i.e., 5.8 million inflected forms to 270,000 paradigms, with up to 16 inflectional forms to a noun, 120 to an adjective, and 107 to a verb, excluding variants (Bjarnadóttir, 2012).[4] The inflectional categories for nouns are case (nom., acc., dat., gen.), number (sg., pl.), and definiteness (-/+);[5] for adjectives gender (masc., fem., neut.), case (4), number (2), definiteness (2), and degree (pos., comp., superl.); for finite verbs voice (active, mediopassive), mood (indicative, subjunctive), tense (present, past), number (sg., pl.) and person (1st, 2nd, 3rd).[6] For other word classes, some adverbs inflect for degree; personal pronouns inflect for person, case and number; other pronouns, the definite article and the numbers from one to four inflect for gender, case and number, etc. All these features are used in the tag set for the DMII, which is correspondingly large, cf. footnote 4.

The number of inflectional forms is, per se, not problematic, but the number of variant forms with the same grammatical tag within the same paradigm can be. A simple case in point is genitive forms taking different endings, as in the genitive singular of the masculine noun **lestur** "reading": **lestrar/lesturs**. These two genitive forms are equally acceptable, but restrictions on the usage of variants can, in other lexical items, be a question of context, style, and degree of acceptability. A case in point is the feminine noun **rödd** "voice" where the otherwise obsolete dative singular variant **röddu** is only used in contexts like **hárri röddu** "with a forceful voice" (i.e., "loudly, clearly"; this instrumental dative phrase construction is quite common). The result of the number of possible variants of inflectional endings (i.e., exponents of a grammatical category) is a rather large number of inflectional patterns or inflectional classes.[7]

The inflectional forms are highly ambiguous, and this can be demonstrated by the distribution of the inflectional endings. In the genitive plu-

---

[2]In 2006, The Institute of Lexicography merged with other institutions under the name The Árni Magnússon Institute for Icelandic Studies.

[3]It should be noted that the DMII is a set of hardcoded paradigms and not a rule-based inflectional system. The reasons for this are given in Bjarnadóttir (2012).

[4]The figures are from Bjarnadóttir (2012), but the number of inflectional forms of verbs quoted here is from the original DMII. The new DIM includes additional cliticized verb forms, and grammatical tags for impersonal constructions (i.e., verbs with oblique subjects), so the number of possible inflectional forms for a verb presently exceeds 300. That analysis is under review, and there are plans to review the PoS tag set for Icelandic which at present contains more than 670 possible morphosyntactic tags, of which 559 turn up in a corpus of 1.2 billion running words (Steingrímsson et al., 2018).

[5]Gender is a lexical category for nouns, not an inflectional one.

[6]The categories for non-finite verbs are not listed here.

[7]The paradigm of each word is run as a whole, i.e., all the inflectional variants are produced by one bundle of rules, instead of specifying that a word can belong to more than one inflectional class. There are at present (May 2019) 669 such inflectional classes in the DIM; the number fluctuates easily with new data.

ral, the universal ending for nouns is **-a**[8] (as in **anda**, gen.pl. for both the feminine noun **önd** "duck" and the masculine noun **andi** "spirit"), but the same ending is also one of the nom.sg. endings in feminine nouns, the acc./dat./gen.sg. ending in some masculine nouns, the acc.pl. ending in some masculine nouns, not to mention the function of the same ending in other word classes. The result is that inflectional forms are hugely ambiguous, with only 32% of the inflectional forms in the original DMII being unambiguous (Bjarnadóttir, 2012). Disambiguation is therefore an important task in Icelandic LT, and because of the idiosyncrasies of individual words in respect of variant inflectional forms this can only be achieved by referring to a lexicon.

2.2 Word Formation

In Icelandic, the morphological head of a word is the word-final base word or compound, depending on the binary structure of the word (cf. Bjarnadóttir (2017a) for a short reference). Compounds can be formed by joining any of the open word classes, but noun-noun compounds are by far the most common. The rules of compound formation are recursive, and there is no theoretical limit to the number of constituents in a compound, although compounds with more than six constituents are rare. An added complication is the fact that the first part of compounds (i.e., the modifier) can take a variety of combining forms. Nominal modifiers can appear as stems or inflected forms, most often in the genitive, singular or plural. The choice of forms is arbitrary, but not free, cf. examples in Table 1 where unacceptable compounds are marked by * (cf. also Bjarnadóttir (1995)).

Stem	Gen.sg.	Gen.pl.	Meaning
bóksala	*bókarsala	*bókasala	"book store"
*bókkápa	bókarkápa	bókakápa	"book cover"
*bókbúð	*bókarbúð	bókabúð	"book store"

Table 1: Examples of combining forms in Icelandic compounds.

The lemmatization of the modifiers is needed for disambiguation, as inflectional forms are highly ambiguous, as in the case of the genitive plural **anda** in **andagift** "spiritual gift" (i.e., "inspiration"), and **andapollur** "duck pond", where the lemma for **anda** in the first compound is the masculine noun **andi** "spirit, breath", but the feminine noun **önd** "duck" in the second compound.

The ambiguity of the combining forms is a reflection of the ambiguity of inflectional forms, and the most ambiguous of those in the DMII at present is **minni**, which shows up as 30 inflectional forms in four paradigms, i.e., in the neuter noun **minni** "memory" (5 inflectional forms: nom./acc./dat. sg., nom./acc.pl.); in the verb **minna** "remember" (4 inflectional forms, not counting impersonal ones: active voice, 1.p.sg. pres. indicative & subjunctive; 3.p.pl. pres. subjunctive); in the adjective **lítill** "small, little" (20 inflectional forms, i.e., comp., masc./fem. nom./acc./dat./gen.sg., and masc./fem./neut. nom./acc./dat./gen.pl.); and in the possessive pronoun **minn** "mine" (1 inflectional form, fem.dat.sg.). The ambiguity in combining forms is therefore linked to ambiguity elsewhere in the DIM.

2.3 Description vs. prescription

The DMII was originally created as a part of an effort to start work on LT at the start of the millennium, financed by the Icelandic Ministry for Education and Culture. The first version of the DMII was a set of XML files with 173,389 paradigms, made available on CDs for use in LT in 2004. The purpose was quite simple, the data was to be used in coping with the morphology in Icelandic texts, as well as in search engines and other tools requiring the information. The emphasis was being able to cope with Icelandic texts "as is", without regard to correct spelling, grammar, vocabulary, or style. In other words, the data was descriptive, as it had to function for analysis, but it was in no way suited for production. For that prescriptive data is needed, in order to conform with the established standards for good Icelandic.

Icelandic standards appear in the "Rules of spelling and punctuation" (*Ritreglur* (2016), *Reglur um greinamerkjasetningu* (2018)), published by the Ministry of Education and Culture, and in *Stafsetningarorðabókin* "The Dictionary of Spelling" (Sigtryggsson, 2016), published by the Árni Magnússon Institute for Icelandic Studies.[9] Various handbooks and grammar books, used in

---

[8]Except for a subset of feminine nouns and a (very) few neuter nouns where the generative plural ending is **-na**.

[9]These sources are available at the website of The Árni Magnússon Institute for Icelandic Studies, `https://arnastofnun.is` and at `https://malid.is`.

the school system, also function as prescriptive sources.

In order to make the transition from descriptive to prescriptive, the core vocabulary of the DMII has been checked against the standards mentioned above, adding extensive cross-referencing of less than optimal instances of usage to the standardized forms in the DMII. This applies both to spelling, inflectional forms, and to the vocabulary itself, as a part of good usage is considered to be in the choice of native words instead of loan words.

The mark-up of the prescriptive data, with the links from the less optimal forms to the prescribed ones, makes the data better suited for LT projects such as spell checkers, grammar checkers, and any kind of production of text, including teaching material such as grammatical exercises.

3 The structure of the DIM Database

The old DMII database has been restructured to achieve two main objectives. The first is to allow for more detailed information and classification (cf. Subsection 3.1), and the other to allow for configuring different aspects of the data for different use (cf. Section 4). Some parts of the new database have been designed from scratch and contain new types of data, such as the analysis of word formation which is linked to the other parts of DIM.

Examples of the detailed information added to the database are features of usage restrictions (syntactic, semantic, stylistic, etc.), different orthographic representations, and features of acceptability, as described in Subsection 3.1. In addition, a proposed part of the DIM, still only in the preliminary stages, is a repository of written word forms not found elsewhere in the DIM data, including obsolete forms, errors of all kinds, and abbreviations. These will be classified, dated, attributed to source, and be linked to the list of lemmas in the DIM proper. Extensive material of this type is ready for import into the database, both from lexicographic sources and from error analysis. This data allows for new analytic possibilities, both for language technology and linguistic research. It also extends the time frame of the data, by creating a place for older inflectional variants, as the DMII was originally confined to Modern Icelandic, cf. the name: The Database of Modern Icelandic Inflection. The inclusion of older data does not entail attempts at creating paradigms for Icelandic through the centuries; the data is too scarce for that. Experiments with using these peripheral word forms in LT have been made, cf. footnote 14 below.

3.1 Classification

DIM uses a new sorting and grading system for words and inflectional forms to differentiate between prescriptive and descriptive use, or to give researchers access to vocabulary containing relevant grammatical features. Following is a brief description of the main sorting categories, with a handful of examples in footnotes. The system is complex and a full exposition with examples is outside the scope here.

- **Grammatical features of words**: Used to mark words with certain features or restricted usage. Words can be marked for more than one feature. These include: Idiom bound, gender variation, older word form, restricted paradigm, loan word, spelling variants ... [10]

- **Value of inflectional forms**: Used for inflectional forms where two or more variants are presented, to indicate their status in respect of the other variant(s), with values like: equal, dominant, yielding, uncertain.[11]

- **Correctness Grade**: Used to mark a word's or variant's correctness according to prescriptive grammar rules and standardized spelling. Grades range from 0 to 5. Most words have a grade of 1, and this is the default value and stands for "Correct". Grades 2, 3 and 4 stand for "Used", "Not good" and "Very bad", depending on the level of "wrongness", 4 being the lowest grade. Grade 5 exists for words or inflectional forms that have somehow made it into the database but are so "wrong" that they

---

[10]Examples of "Grammatical features of words": Idiom bound: **almannavitorð** n.neut. "public knowledge", only used in the dative singular in the idiom *e-ð er á almanna-vitorði* "sth is public knowledge"; Gender variation: **engifer** n.masc. or n.neut. "ginger"; Older word form: **röddu** dat.sg. of **rödd** n.fem. "voice", cf. Subsection 2.1; Restricted paradigm: **munu** v. auxilary. The verb is finite only, active voice only, and there is no past tense in the indicative; Loan word: **engifer** n.masc. or n.neut. "ginger" (Loanwords, especially multisyllable ones, need marking as their inflection very often deviates from the inflection of the native vocabulary.); Spelling variants: **pósitívur/pósitívur** adj. "positive".

[11]Examples of "Values of inflectional forms": Equal: **dugir/dugar**, 3.p.sg.pres. active voice of **duga** v. "suffice"; Dominant: **rödd**, dat.sg. of **rödd** n.fem. "voice"; Yielding: **röddu**, dat.sg. (idiom bound) of **rödd** n.fem. "voice".

could not possibly be part of the language of an adult with a native speaker's competence in Icelandic, and so they are only visible in administrator mode. Words and inflectional variants classified by genre (cf. next paragraph) have the grade 0, standing for "Not applicable, depends on style or genre". This is because variants marked by genre are not incorrect, but they are not the most common correct form either.[12]

- **Genre**: Used to sort words and inflectional forms according to style or age. Values: Formal, informal, derogatory, obscene, rare, old-fashioned, obsolete, poetic language, regional. Genre is not a mandatory feature for words or variants.

- **Domain**: A semantic classification, used to classify named entities and domain specific vocabulary. These include several different kinds of names (e.g. Icelandic personal names, place names, etc.), and technical terms from different fields, etc. Most words are in the domain called Common language, which is the default value. All words belong to one domain only.[13] Domain specification only applies to words, not to inflectional forms.

- **Pronunciation**: Features of pronunciation are marked on words with possible discrepancies between pronunciation and spelling. Still a work in progress, this is meant for linguistic research, but it may be useful for speech synthesizers or speech analysis, etc.

- **Peripheral word forms:** Older word forms, spelling errors and other forms that do not fit within a paradigm are kept in a separate list and connected to a lemma in the database. This can be used to connect errors or old forms to the appropriate modern form.[14]

4 The Five Aspects of DIM

DIM has five aspects or conceptual units. All of them are part of one database; two of them are solely focused on inflection, i.e., the DMII Core (Subsection 4.1) and the DMII Website (Subsection 4.2), and one contains the word formations analysis, i.e., MorphIce (Subsection 4.3). The remaining two aspects contain different modes of access to the data, the LT Website for use in language technology (Subsection 4.4), and the Ling-Research for research on the language (Subsection 4.5).

4.1 The DMII Core

The DMII Core is designed to meet users' demands for data from the DMII in a prescriptive context, and it is created to be used for third party publication through an API, especially for language learners. The RESTful API is open for everyone to use. It allows users to send simple queries and receive full paradigms in JSON-format as a response. The data in the DMII Core only contains the core vocabulary of Icelandic, only standardized spelling, and only the most common or correct inflectional forms. This makes the data suited for creating teaching material and for other prescriptive uses. As the data in the DMII Core is simplified and the vocabulary limited, the omission of a word or variant does not imply that it is wrong. However, if a word or variant is found in the DMII Core, users should be able to trust that it is safe to use, i.e., correct, in all (or most) contexts.

The vocabulary of the DMII Core is based on the list of headwords in *The Modern Icelandic Dictionary* (Jónsdóttir and Úlfarsdóttir, 2016), and the 50,000 most frequent words (lemmas) in the *The Icelandic Gigaword Corpus* (Steingrímsson et al., 2018). The total number of paradigms in the DMII Core now stands at 56,867 (end of May 2019), as compared almost 287,000 in the whole of DIM.

The new classification system (cf. Subsection 3.1), is used to choose words and inflectional variants for the DMII Core. Only words and variants with a correctness grade of 1 (universally acceptable) are included in the DMII Core,

---

[12]Examples of "Correctness Grade": 1 (Correct, default value): **jafnvægi** n.neut. "balance". 2 (Used): **ballans** n.masc. "balance". The compound **jafnvægi** is considered better usage, it is also much more common.; 3 (Not good): **pósitífur** adj. "positive". According to *The Dictionary of Spelling* the correct form is **pósitívur**; 4 (Very bad): **líter** n.masc. "liter". The correct form is **lítri** n.masc. 0 (Grading is not applicable): **blóðgagl** "raven, vulture", poetic language (**blóð** "blood" and **gagl** "goose; bird").

[13]The result is that the common noun **hrafn** "raven" and the personal name **Hrafn** are shown in two different paradigms, although the inflection is identical.

[14]Cf. Daðason et al. (2014) for description of an LT tool for transposing older Icelandic texts to modern spelling, using data from a pilot project of this kind.

and the categories of genre included are "formal, informal, derogatory, obscene". (The excluded ones are "rare, old-fashioned, obsolete, poetic language, regional".) The only domain included in the DMII Core is common language (i.e., the default value), with a chosen selection of named entities, i.e., common Icelandic personal names, a few very common place names, and the most common names of institutions.

The paradigms in the DMII Core have been simplified as possible, without omitting equally valid variants, showing only the best forms, or the variants not limited by specific usage restrictions. The correctness grade is also used for inflectional forms, and only variants with correctness grade of 1 are included.

4.2 The DMII website

Individual paradigms have been accessible on the DMII website from 2004.[15] Extensively used by the Icelandic public as a reference on inflection, the website has been popular from the start, and the latest figures show that more than 200,000 users viewed over 1.7 million pages in the year starting June 1, 2018. (The total population of Iceland is approx. 360,000.) The figures are still rising, with 9% growth over the previous year. Originally, the data was set out to be purely descriptive, for use in analysing Icelandic text "as is", not just the "received" text adhering to the rather strict language norms officially advocated. To make the website more useful, notes on usage were placed with individual inflectional paradigms, pointing the way in the choice of variants, and containing information on restrictions on their use. These notes are in Icelandic only, and they were originally hand-crafted and not classified in any way. This makes the original website unsuited for any but speakers with native or near native knowledge of Icelandic, as the users themselves have to make the final choice between variants, with the help of the notes. In this context, the multitude and ambiguity of variant forms has to be stressed.

This mode of operation has not always been totally successful, as the descriptive nature of the data causes problems, even for native speakers of Icelandic. The expectation is that all word forms appearing on the site are "best usage", all spelling variants are "good", and all words shown on the website are acceptable, irrespective of genre, style,

etc. The tolerance for substandard usage appearing on the website is at times very low, as the users will let the editors know from time to time. The converse is also true, as some users expect all "acceptable" Icelandic words to be found in the DMII, in spite of clear statements to the contrary on the website, stating that the DMII is not exhaustive and not an authority on acceptable Icelandic vocabulary. The original duality of purpose in the DMII, i.e., the need for the maximum number of word forms found in texts for LT analysis vs. the needs of ordinary users for prescriptive data, has therefore caused some problems from the start.

The new version of the DMII website, to be opened in 2019, makes use of the work on classification in the DMII Core described in Subsection 3.1. Markings on variations in spelling and word formation, and any restrictions on use discovered in the work of adapting the standard, are carried over into the paradigms on the DMII website, in the form of better notes on usage, with extensive cross-references. To give one example of two words commonly causing confusion because of their spelling, the words **híði** "den" (as in "bear's den") and **hýði** "skin" (as in "banana skin") are pronounced in the same way. Each of these entries on the website gives both forms, explaining the semantic difference. In case of substandard spelling (as in writing **pósitífur** instead of **pósitívur** "positive"), a hyperlink to the appropriate spelling rule is provided, as published online at The Árni Magnússon Institute's portal for information on Icelandic usage.[16] The guidelines on the DMII website still warn the users that the DMII is **not** a spelling dictionary, but there are now referrals to the standard wherever possible.

4.3 MorphIce

The morphological analysis included in MorphIce gives full constituent structure, with lemmatized constituents. As compounding in Icelandic is extremely productive, this is of importance in LT tasks, as the data can be used to minimize the effect of out-of-vocabulary words. The data also serves for training of tools such as the compound splitter Kvistur (cf. Daðason and Bjarnadóttir (2014)), which has been used to estimate the probability of unknown compounds by the use of a preliminary version of the data in MorphIce. This data was originally analysed manually in the

---

[15] http://bin.arnastofnun.is

[16] https://malid.is

nineties (Bjarnadóttir, 2006) and will now be incorporated into the DIM. It is only with the creation of MorphIce that this data can be made freely available as a linguistic resource.

As stated in Subsection 2.2, compound formation in Icelandic is complex. The compound analysis in MorphIce assumes binary branching, and the rules are recursive, resulting in quite complex binary trees.

The data on each compound will give full details on each component, with links to the main index in the DIM, with DMII ids. All information on the inflection of each constituent word in the compound will therefore be accessible.[17] Bound constituents (affixes and combining forms) form a separate part of the data set, with information on the structures into which they fit. The format of the output is still under construction, but a sample of the analysis can be seen in the word **orðabókar-maður** "lexicographer" below, with the consituent parts **orð** "word", **bók** "book", and **maður** "man". The analysis is binary, with each item in the example showing the result of one process or word formation rule. These can be nested or not in the output, according to needs, but as stated above, the final format is still under construction. The numbers are the ids of the words in the DMII.

- orðabókarmaður:
  [[orðabókar]<gen.sg.orðabók.n.fem.404616>
  [maður]<n.masc.5763>]<n.masc.88516>

- orðabók:
  [[orða]<gen.pl.orð.n.neut.2635>
  [bók]<n.fem.11100>]<n.fem.404616>

A coding system for the binary trees is included in the data, with "0" for base words, "1" for a single join, "12" for a left-branching binary tree with three constituents, as in [[[orða][bókar]][maður]] above, etc. The granularity of the compound analysis can by adapted to the needs of each LT task, and the most detailed analysis will probably only be of interest to linguists.

The data in MorphIce will be linked to a dataset containing argument structure, presently found in

a pilot version on the website of The Árni Magnússon Institute for Icelandic Studies (Bjarnadóttir, 2017b). This data will be used to link multiword constructions, such as particle verbs and verbs with incorporated object, to their compound counterparts, as in **greina að** "separate" (i.e., "take apart", the compound verb **aðgreina** also exists), the past participle/adjective **aðgreindur**, the present participle **aðgreinandi**, and the noun **aðgreining**. Structures of this kind are very common in Icelandic, and finding and analysing multiword lexical entities and linking them to compounds helps in demarcating semantic units.

In the future, the plan is to make the binary trees themselves accessible online, but as yet the formulation of that project is only in the preliminary stages.

4.4 The LT Website

Datasets from DIM, for use in language technology, are available from a separate website. Until now, two versions of the data have been available for download on the old DMII website along with detailed descriptions of the datasets, in Icelandic and English. One version is the list of inflectional forms and lemmas, along with word class and grammatical tag, described in Section 2. The other is a simple list of word forms, without any classification or linkups. The new DIM-LT website still makes the DIM data available for download in those formats, but more configurations are available, constructed in cooperation with a select group of long-time users. The data available on the DIM-LT website is updated daily. For reproduction purposes, versioned datasets will be published periodically.

The dataset is published with an open license and is intended for use in the development of LT tools and methods, but it may also be suitable in other fields as well. The DIM-LT data is not intended for lookups. Users who build software that needs to do lookups in DIM at runtime will be encouraged to use the API, described in Sections 4.1 and 5, as that will allow them access at all times to the most recently updated data.

As well as providing access to downloadable data, the DIM-LT website has information on licensing, detailed information on all the grammatical features appearing in the inflectional paradigms, including lists of word classes, all inflectional categories and grammatical terms, and

---

[17]The inflection of Icelandic compounds is notoriously unpredictable, especially when there is a choice of variant forms, as in **útvegur** "fishing industry", gen.sg. **útvegs** (i.e., **út** "out" adv., **vegur** "road, way") vs. **akvegur** "road (for cars)", gen.sg. **akvegar** (aka "drive" verb, **vegur** "road"). In recursive compounding, such genitives do appear as modifiers. In such cases, the data should be sufficient for analysis, but perhaps not unerring in predictions for new compounds.

other relevant information, in Icelandic and English. The tag set in the downloadable data is in Icelandic, but English translations are accessible on the website.

4.5 DIM LingResearch

The DIM LingResearch is an adaptation of the editorial interface to the new database, to be made accessible for linguistic research. All features of the classification of words and inflectional forms will be accessible for the extraction of data. Some features have been specially included in the database with linguistic research in mind, such as categories of irregular pronunciation. To name an example, the vowel **a** is diphthongized when preceding **ng** (as in the word **bangsi** "teddy bear"), except in a few loanwords, such as **mangó** and **tangó**. This type of data is interesting for linguists working on morphophonemics, but it may also be useful for speech systems, etc. There are at present 16 pronunciation sets of this kind in the data, along with similar sets for various other features of word formation, etc.

5 Access and licencing

As described in previous sections, DIM is available in different configurations. The DMII Core is made available through an API through a permissive license that allows third parties to publish the data on the web. They are required not to modify the data and to give appropriate credit. All paradigms can be viewed individually on the new DMII website, as they have been on the old DMII website since 2004. Access is open to all and free of charge, but scraping the data or copying en masse is prohibited. For use in language technology or research on the language, the datasets are available for download with an open, permissive license, CC BY-SA. The same will apply to the MorphIce data. Finally, access to the DIM Ling-Research interface, intended for scholars, will be given upon request.

6 Conclusion

The data from the old DMII has been used extensively from 2004, when it was first made available. The initial dream was basically to create data for rather simple tools, like a decent search engine, etc. Very many of the projects using the data have far surpassed these expectations. Two of these projects are mentioned above, i.e., the com-

pound splitter Kvistur (cf. Subsection 4.3), and the spellchecker Skrambi, referred to in connection with the use of peripheral word forms (cf. Subsection 3.1, footnote 14).[18] Two very recent NLP-tools take advantage of DMII, the PoS Tagger ABLTagger (Steingrímsson et al., 2019) and the lemmatizer Nefnir, which is described in this current version of NoDaLiDa (Ingólfsdóttir et al., 2019). A list of additional projects is accessible on the DIM website.[19]

In fall 2019, the first projects will start in a national language technology programme, which will run for five years. The programme follows a plan set forward in 2017 (Nikulásdóttir et al., 2017), and aims to produce open systems for machine translation, spell and grammar checking, speech synthesis and speech recognition.

Extensive linguistic resources are needed for the new projects planned in the next five years. This is especially important for two reasons. First, the Icelandic language community is very small, and although Icelanders take pride in the production of a great deal of text (as evidenced in a blooming Icelandic literary scene, and the proliferation of Icelandic websites, etc.), the actual mass of text produced is nowhere close to the scale accessible in really large language communities. Even if all Icelandic texts from all times were accessible, very many word forms would probably only occur a few times, certainly not often enough to be useful in statistical analysis.[20] The other reason is the complexity of Icelandic morphology, both inflectional and morphological, with corresponding irregularities and ambiguities. It has therefore proved to be necessary to produce and store the morphological data, instead of writing a rule system for analysing the morphology on the go.

We see the work in the immediate future as ongoing excerption from the Gigaword Corpus (Steingrímsson et al., 2018), fine-tuning the analysis and classifications described in this paper, and ongoing cooperation with the users of the data, as they are the people who know what they need.

---

[18]Skrambi is available as an online spellchecker (`http:skrambi.bin.arnastofnun.is`), but it is also used in different versions for tasks such as correcting OCR texts, and to transpose older texts with unstandardized spelling from different periods to Modern Icelandic.

[19]`http:bin.arnastofnun.is`

[20]Some inflectional forms are not found at all, as is the case for the dative singular of the name of Odin's tree **Yggdrasill** which is not to be found in any of the Old Icelandic sources.

Acknowledgments

The restructuring of the DMII and the creation of DIM was made possible by a grant by the Icelandic Research Council in 2017. The authors wish to thank our co-workers in the project, without whom the project would not have taken shape: Samúel Þórisson, for the database, and Trausti Dagsson, for the creation of the new websites. Thanks are also due to our present and former colleagues at The Árni Magnússon Institute for Icelandic Studies and The University of Iceland who have been generous with their time, advice and assistance: Starkaður Barkarson, Jón Friðrik Daðason, Sigrún Helgadóttir, Halldóra Jónsdóttir, Jón Hilmar Jónsson, Ari Páll Kristinsson, Kristján Rúnarsson, Eiríkur Rögnvaldsson, Jóhannes B. Sigtryggsson, Einar Freyr Sigurðsson, Ásta Svavarsdóttir, Þórdís Úlfarsdóttir, Ágústa Þorbergsdóttir, Gunnar Thor Örnólfsson, and Katrín Axelsdóttir. Thanks are also due to the company Já.is for their generous support through the years.

References

Kristín Bjarnadóttir. 1995. Lexicalization and the Selection of Compounds for a Bilingual Icelandic Dictionary Base. *Nordiske studier i leksikografi*, (3):255–263.

Kristín Bjarnadóttir. 2006. *Afleiðsla og samsetning í generatífri málfræði og greining á íslenskum gögnum*. Orðabók Háskólans, Reykjavík, Iceland.

Kristín Bjarnadóttir. 2012. The Database of Modern Icelandic Inflection. In *LREC 2012 Proceedings: Proceedings of "Language Technology for Normalization of Less-Resourced Languages", SaLTMiL 8 – AfLaT*, pages 67–72.

Kristín Bjarnadóttir. 2017a. Phrasal compounds in Modern Icelandic with reference to Icelandic word formation in general. In Carola Trips and Jaklin Kornfilt, editors, *Further investigations into the nature of phrasal compounding*. Language Science Press, Berlin, Germany.

Kristín Bjarnadóttir. 2017b. https://notendur.hi.is/ kristinb/divs-2017.txt *ÍSLEX-venslamálfræði*. The Árni Magnússon Institute for Icelandic Studies, Reykjavík, Iceland.

Jón Friðrik Daðason and Kristín Bjarnadóttir. 2014. Utilizing constituent structure for compound analysis. In *Proceedings of LREC 2014. Reykjavik: ELRA*, pages 1637–1641.

Jón Friðrik Daðason, Kristín Bjarnadóttir, and Kristján Rúnarsson. 2014. The Journal Fjölnir for everyone: The post-processing of historical OCR texts. In *Proceedings of Language Resources and Technologies for Processing and Linking Historical Documents and Archives - Deploying Linked Open Data in Cultural Heritage. Reykjavik: ELRA*, pages 56–62.

Svanhvít Ingólfsdóttir, Hrafn Loftsson, Jón Daðason, and Kristín Bjarnadóttir. 2019. Nefnir: A high accuracy lemmatizer for Icelandic. In *Proceedings of the 22nd Nordic Conference of Computational Linguistics*, NODALIDA 2019, Turku, Finland.

Halldóra Jónsdóttir and Þórdís Úlfarsdóttir, editors. 2016. http://islenskordabok.arnastofnun.is *Íslensk nútímamálsorðabók*. The Árni Magnússon Institute for Icelandic Studies.

Anna Björk Nikulásdóttir, Jón Guðnason, and Steinþór Steingrímsson. 2017. https://notendur.hi.is/eirikur/mlt-en.pdf *Language Technology for Icelandic 2018-2022: Project Plan*. Mennta- og menningarmálaráðuneytið, Reykjavík, Iceland.

Jóhannes B. Sigtryggsson, editor. 2016. http://malid.is *Stafsetningarorðabókin*. The Árni Magnússon Institute for Icelandic Studies.

Steinþór Steingrímsson, Sigrún Helgadóttir, Eiríkur Rögnvaldsson, Starkaður Barkarson, and Jón Guðnason. 2018. Risamálheild: A Very Large Icelandic Text Corpus. In *Proceedings of the Eleventh International Conference on Language Resources and Evaluation*, LREC 2018, Miyazaki, Japan.

Steinþór Steingrímsson, Örvar Kárason, and Hrafn Loftsson. 2019. Augmenting a BiLSTM tagger with a morphological lexicon and a lexical category identification step. In *Proceedings of RANLP 2019*, Varna, Bulgaria.

Tools for supporting language learning for Sakha

Sardana Ivanova, Anisia Katinskaia, Roman Yangarber
University of Helsinki
`first.last@helsinki.fi`

Abstract

This paper presents an overview of linguistic resources available for the Sakha language, and presents new tools for supporting language learning for Sakha. The essential resources include a morphological analyzer, digital dictionaries, and corpora of Sakha texts. We extended an earlier version of the morphological analyzer/transducer, built on the Apertium finite-state platform. The analyzer currently has an adequate level of coverage, between 86% and 89% on two Sakha corpora. Based on these resources, we implement a language-learning environment for Sakha in the Revita computer-assisted language learning (CALL) platform. Revita is a freely available online language learning platform for learners beyond the beginner level. We describe the tools for Sakha currently integrated into the Revita platform. To our knowledge, at present this is the first large-scale project undertaken to support intermediate-advanced learners of a minority Siberian language.

1 Introduction

The Sakha language, also known by its exonym *Yakut*, is the language of an ethnic community, who mainly inhabit the Republic of Sakha in the Far East of Siberia, Russian Federation. According to the 2010 census, Sakha is the native language of 450,140 people, and is considered vulnerable due to its limited usage. Children do not use Sakha in all aspects of their life; they speak Sakha at home with family, but do not use it in school and socially.

Sakha belongs to the Northern group of the Siberian branch of the Turkic language family, and is agglutinative, as are all Turkic languages, (Ubryatova, 1982). It has complex, four-way vowel harmony, and a basic Subject-Object-Verb word order. The lexicon of Sakha consists of native Turkic

words, has many borrowings from the surrounding Mongolic and Tungusic languages, numerous loanwords from Russian, as well as words of unknown origin. Sakha makes extensive use of post-positions, which indicate syntactic relations and govern the grammatical case of nominals, (Forsyth, 1994).

In the digital sphere, Sakha can be considered a low-resource language. We report on our project to provide learning support for Sakha. Building on pre-existing digital resources, we aim to provide a learning platform for students (including adults) who are interested in strengthening their linguistic competency in Sakha.

The paper is structured as follows. Section 2 describes distinctive properties of the Sakha language and motivates the need for language-learning support by reviewing the social environment of the language. Section 3.1 presents an overview of previous work Sakha; Section 3.2 describes the Revita platform for language learning. Section 4 describes the instruments we integrate to support language learning for Sakha. In Section 5 we discuss initial results obtained with the tools. Sections 6 concludes with pointers for future work.

2 Sakha language

Sakha is the national language of the Sakha people, which, along with Russian, is one of the official languages of the Republic of Sakha (Yakutia), (Yartseva, 1990). The Sakha language differs significantly from other Turkic languages by the presence of a layer of vocabulary of unclear (possibly Paleo-Asiatic) origin, (Kharitonov, 1987). There are also a large number of words of Mongolic origin related to ancient borrowings, as well as late borrowings from the Russian language, (Tenishev, 1997).

2.1 Distinctive features

Vowels in Sakha follow complex vowel harmony rules. The features of the vowels within a word must agree in a strictly defined fashion. First, *palatal-*

velar harmony of vowels is observed in Sakha strictly sequentially and does not admit exceptions. If the first syllable contains a front vowel, then the vowels in all subsequent syllables in the word must be front. Otherwise, if the first syllable contains a back vowel, then the vowels in all subsequent syllables must be back. Second, *labial* vowel harmony requires that the sequence of vowels agree according to the degree of roundedness within adjacent syllables, (Sleptsov, 2018). For example:

- back+unrounded: "аҕа / аҕалардыын"
  [aɣa / aɣalardīn]
  "father/with fathers"
- back+rounded: "оҕо / оҕолордуун"
  [oɣo / oɣolordūn]
  "child / with children"
- front+unrounded: "эбэ / эбэлэрдиин"
  [ebe / ebelerdīn]
  "grandmother / with grandmothers"
- front+rounded: "бөрө / бөрөлөрдүүн"
  [börö / börölördǖn]
  "wolf / with wolves"

Thus, the vowels in the suffixes "-лар-" [lar], indicating the plural, and "-дыын" [dīn], indicating comitative case, undergo 4-way mutation according to vowel harmony.

In Sakha, the verb is the central part of speech, (Dyachkovsky et al., 2018). Some verbs can have multiple affixes (as in most Turkic languages), which can correspond to an entire clause or sentence in other languages, such as Russian. Sakha has no infinitive form for verbs, therefore a predicate that (in other languages) would include an infinitive is conveyed by various indirect means, for example:

- "суруйан бүтэрдэ": [surujan büterde]
  "he finished writing"
  (literally: *"he wrote, finished"*);
- "сатаан ыллыыр": [satān ıllīr]
  "he can sing"
  (literally: *"he knows how, sings"*);
- "бобуоххун син": [bobuoχχun sin]
  "you can forbid"
  (literally: *"you can, let's forbid"*).

Sakha is characterized by an exceptional variety of verbal tenses. In particular, according to (Korkina, 1970), 8 past forms are distinguished:

- proximal-past:
  "үлэлээтим" [üelētim]
  "I worked (recently)";

- remote-past:
  "үлэлээбитим" [ülelēbitim]
  "I worked (long ago)";
- past perfect:
  "үлэлээбиппин" [ülelēbippin]
  "In fact, I worked";
- episodic past:
  "үлэлээбиттээхпин" [ülelēbittēχpin]
  "I used to work on occasion";
- past imperfect:
  "үлэлиирим" [ülelīrim]
  "I worked in the past for some time";
- plusquamperfect:
  "үлэлээбит этим" [ülelēbit etim]
  "I had worked prior to that";
- episodic plusquamperfect:
  "үлэлээбиттээх этим" [ülelēbittēχ etim]
  "Long ago, I used to work".

The total number of tense forms exceeds 20.

One of the particularities of nouns is when *paired nouns* are marked with possessiveness, both components of the compound noun change *in parallel*, as the word is inflected:

- "баай-дуол" [bāj duol] *"wealth"*:
  "баайа-дуола" [bāja duola]
  (3rd person possessive, nominative case),
  "баайын-дуолун" [bājın duolun]
  (3rd person singular possessive, accusative)
- "сурук-бичик" [suruk bičik] *"writing"*:
  "сурукта-бичиктэ" [surukta bičikte]
  (partitive case),
  "суругу-бичиги" [surugu bičigi]
  (accusative case)

2.2 Socio-linguistic environment

According to (Vasilieva et al., 2013), since 1990, the percentage of ethnic Sakha has grown, reaching 45% of the total population in the Republic of Sakha. Ethnic Sakha together with other indigenous peoples of the North Siberia and the Far East comprise over 50% of the total population.

Vasilieva et al. (2013) has conducted surveys, which show a direct dependence of the level of linguistic proficiency on the *language of instruction* at school. A fluent level of proficiency is achieved by:

- respondents who had schooling in the Sakha language (34.5%)

- respondents who had studied in schools, where subjects were taught in Russian and partly in Sakha (27.4%).

Only 17.9% of respondents who had studied in Russian are fluent in Sakha. Respondents who speak Sakha poorly, or do not speak at all, graduated from Russian-speaking schools. Thus, as expected, linguistic skills and abilities in Sakha are poorer for those who had studied in Russian.

In work life, the Russian language is dominant for all age groups. In the two youngest age groups (16–25 and 26–35 years old), the use of Russian is growing, approaching 50%. This is due to the requirements of formal communication, terminological dependence, ethnically mixed composition of professional teams. On the other hand, after the completion of active professional life, the return to an increased usage of the original ethnic language is common, (Vasilieva et al., 2013).

In Yakutsk—the capital and the largest city of the Sakha Republic—one in three Sakha children lack the opportunity to study in their native language. This is a violation of the right to study in one's native language. The number of schools which offer teaching in Sakha in Yakutsk in 2002–2003 was 16, and dropped to 15 by 2003–2004. The number of schools where Sakha is studied as a subject decreased from 22 (in 2002–2003) to 16 (in 2003–2004). The number of Sakha language learners decreased from 6,377 to 2,902, (Vasilieva et al., 2013). According to the statistical report of the Ministry of Education of the Republic of Sakha in 2006–2007, the *cities* of the Republic had 147 schools with Russian language of instruction (61,055 children), 4 educational institutions with non-Russian languages of instruction (1014 children), 29 institutions with a mix of Russian and non-Russian languages of instruction (18,094 children). In 11 schools (serving 1,262 students) non-Russian languages are offered as optional subjects of study.

Vasilieva et al. (2013) indicate that this situation concerning the language of instruction of ethnic Sakha pupils has a direct correlation with other serious problems in terms of linguistic competency in Sakha and vitality of Sakha—acculturation and assimilation of urban youth, which will leads to linguistic conformism due to the lack of sufficient social opportunities for using the language.

3 Prior work

3.1 Sakha language resources

Despite the current advances in digitization, digital resources for the Sakha language are severely lacking. The creation of digital tools would strengthen the language in a number of ways, and several projects are being undertaken to support Sakha. We briefly mention some of them here.

The digital bilingual dictionary SakhaTyla.Ru[1] currently offers over 20,000 items from Sakha to Russian, over 35,000 items from Russian to Sakha, about 2,000 items from Sakha to English, and about 1,000 items from English to Sakha. In addition to translations, this dictionary also contains *examples of usage*, including idiomatic usage, for every item, which constitutes a base of lexical data, and can be highly useful for language learning and teaching. The base of examples from this dictionary is currently not utilized in our learning platform.

Leontiev (2015) has compiled a newspaper corpus of Sakha containing over 12 million tokens. The Sakha Wikipedia contains over 12,000 articles, which makes up a corpus of over 2 million tokens.[2]

A Sakha course on the educational platform Memrise offers a vocabulary of about 3100 words.[3]

Audio materials: Common Voice is a platform for crowdsourcing open-source audio datasets.[4] At present, it offers just under 2.5 hours validated voice recordings in Sakha. By comparison, English has almost 850 hours of audio content on the platform, and Russian has 50 hours.

In summary, few linguistic resources exists for Sakha.

3.2 Revita language learning platform

Revita is an e-learning platform, which uses methods from computer-assisted language learning (CALL) and intelligent tutoring systems (ITS).[5] The platform provides a language-independent foundation for language learning, which can be adapted to support new languages, by adding language-specific resources, without modifying the core system. The platform is used for language teaching and learning at several universities in Europe and Asia.

The goal of the system is to provide tools for language learning, (Katinskaia et al., 2018), and to support endangered languages, (Katinskaia and Yangarber, 2018; Yangarber, 2018). The system focuses on stimulating the student to actively produce language, rather than passively absorb exam-

---

[1]www.sakhatyla.ru

[2]sah.wikipedia.org

[3]www.memrise.com/course/153579/sakha-tylyn-leksikata-sakha-tyla-iakutskii/

[4]voice.mozilla.org/en/about

[5]revita.cs.helsinki.fi

ples of language use or grammatical rules. The system achieves this by helping students learn language from *stories*. The story can be any text, which the students can choose themselves. The platform takes an arbitrary text chosen by the user and uses it as practice material; it creates exercises for the student based on the text: the exercises are new every time the student practices with the text—to keep the practice sessions interesting and to reduce boredom. The computational engines in the platform analyze the text, and try to determine which concepts are best suited for the student to learn next.

The platform has been customized for several less-resourced Finno-Ugric languages: Erzya, Komi-Zyrian, Meadow Mari, North Saami, Udmurt; it has also been customized for Kazakh (also a Turkic language), and several others. Revita also offers a number of languages with larger resources: currently, the most developed are Finnish, Russian, and German, and initial support exists for Swedish, Spanish, Catalan, and French.

4   System for supporting Sakha

In this section we describe our work on adding the Sakha language to the Revita platform for language learning. The system is built on several lower-level linguistic tools and components.

4.1 Morphological analyzer

The morphological analyzer, part of the package called `apertium-sah`, was developed in the context of the Apertium platform, (Forcada et al., 2011). The analyzer is developed using the Helsinki Finite-State Toolkit (HFST), (Lindén et al., 2011). The lexicon and morphotactics are written in the `lexc` formalism, and the morphophonology is developed using the `twol` formalism, based on the Two-Level Morphology framework, (Koskenniemi, 1983). The transducers are compiled into a morphological analyzer and a generator. The transducer is two-directional: on one hand, it can map a surface form to all of its possible lexical forms; on the other hand, it can take a lexical form and generate all of its corresponding surface forms. That is, the transducer can be used both for analysis and for generation of surface forms.

For example, the surface form "атын" receives two analyses—lexical forms:

- ат [at] <n> <px3sg> <acc>
  Horse.Noun.Possessive-3sg.Accusative
  "his horse" (accusative)

- атын [atın] <adj>
  "other" Adjective (indeclinable)

We extended the initial, baseline version of the Apertium Sakha analyzer by adding lemmas to the lexicon based on their frequencies, which we computed from the Wikipedia corpus. Initially the analyzer had 4,303 stems. Table 1 gives the number of lexical items for each of the major parts of speech (POSs) in inital and extended analyzer versions.

Part of speech	Original	Improved
Noun	2,582	4,240
Proper noun	815	2,155
Adjective	464	1,362
Verb	278	1,038
Adverb	62	338
Numeral	58	89
Pronoun	15	17
Postposition	12	42
Conjunction	7	16
Determiner	10	16
Total:	4,303	9,313

Table 1: Number of stems per part of speech

The morphological tagset consists of 92 tags: 16 tags indicate parts of speech—noun, adjective, verb, postposition, etc.—and 76 tags indicate values for morphological subcategories, e.g., for case, number, person, possession, transitivity, tense, aspect, mood, etc. We consulted Ubryatova (1982) as the principal source of grammatical information.

4.2 Language learning platform

The platform offers the learner several exercise modes based on input stories: reading mode, practice mode, flashcards, crossword mode, etc.

In the *reading mode* learner can read a story, and request translations of unfamiliar words.

In the *practice mode* the system generates exercises based on the story, which user has uploaded to the system. The story undergoes several stages of analysis. At the lowest level the system uses the Sakha morphological analyzer, (Ivanova et al., (To appear). The story is presented in "snippets"—small pieces of text, about 50 tokens each, approximately one paragraph or 2–3 sentences in length. The system selects some of the tokens in the snippet to generate quizzes. Each quiz may be of several types: "cloze" (i.e., fill-in-the-blank quiz), multiple-choice, or a listening exercise (where the learner must type in the words s/he hears).

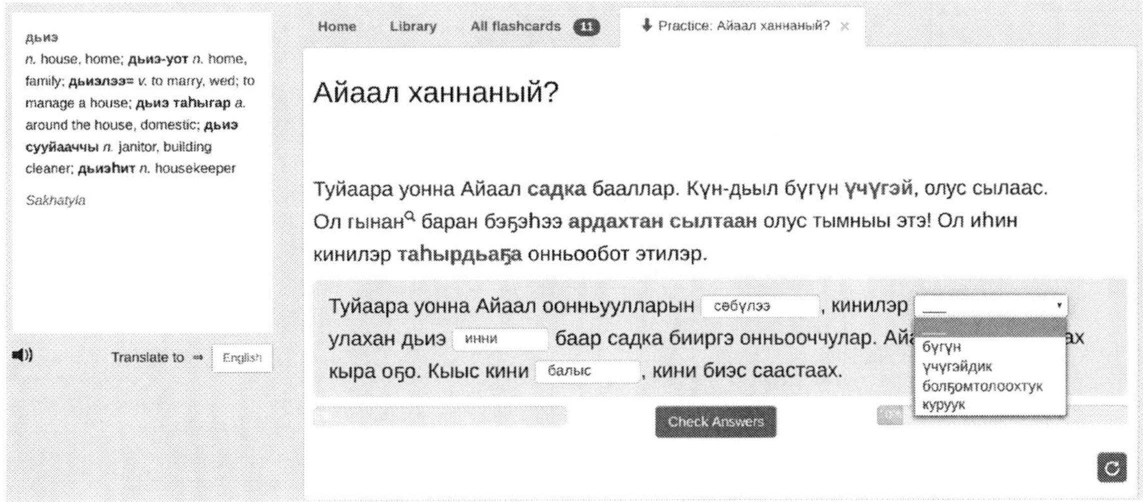

Figure 1: Practice mode

The system creates cloze quizzes from *inflected* parts of speech, i.e., nouns, verbs, etc. For example, the first sentence in the snippet in Figure 1 is

"Туйаара уонна Айаал оонньуулларын сөбүлүүллэр."

[tujāra uonna ajāl ōnnʲūlların söbülüller]

"Tuyaara and Ayaal like to play."

The current snippet of the story appears over a grey background, and contains cloze and multiple-choice exercises. The system created a cloze exercise, showing to the user only the base form (lemma) "сөбүлээ" [söbülē] (*"to like"*) of the surface form "сөбүлүүллэр" [söbülüller] (*"they like"*):

"Туйаара уонна Айаал оонньуулларын сөбүлээ ..."

[tujāra uonna ajāl ōnnʲūlların söbülē]

From the verb lemma the learner should guess which form of the hidden word fits the context best.

Multiple-choice quizzes are constructed also from non-inflected parts of speech (adverbs, postpositions, etc.) Tokens of similar part of speech are presented to the learner as "distractors"—incorrect answer options. Figure 1 shows a multiple-choice quiz for the token "куруук" [kurūk] (*"always"*) with other adverbs serving as distractors.

Listening exercises (optional) are generated from tokens in the story—the words are spoken by a speech synthesizer and the learner must enter the word that was pronounced. Currently, listening exercises are not available for Sakha; we plan to incorporate them into the system when text-to-speech (TTS) synthesis for Sakha becomes available.

The previous snippets—above the current snippet—show correctly answered questions—coloured in green—and incorrectly answered questions in blue.

The choice of candidates for exercises depends on the *user model*—based on the history of the user's previous answers. The system computes probabilities (weights) for potential candidates in the snippet. Exercises receive a lower probability if the student had mostly answered them correctly or mostly incorrectly in earlier sessions—since it means that they are too easy or too difficult for the learner at present.

In the *crossword mode*, a crossword is built based on the text. Exercises for the crossword are selected randomly, and according to the same principles as in practice mode.

The user can receive the translation of an unfamiliar word by clicking on it. The box on the left in Figure 1 shows a dictionary entry for a token clicked by the user—"дьиэ" [ʒie] (*"house"*). The learner can request a translation of an unfamiliar word in all practice modes. Translations are looked up in the SakhaTyla.Ru digital dictionary. The system records the words for which translations were requested into the user's own set of flashcards. In the flashcard mode the user can practice vocabulary, using timed repetition algorithms.

Stories for learning can be found on newspaper websites, such as edersaas.ru, kyym.ru, etc., or from the Sakha Wikisource.[6]

---

[6]https://sah.wikisource.org/

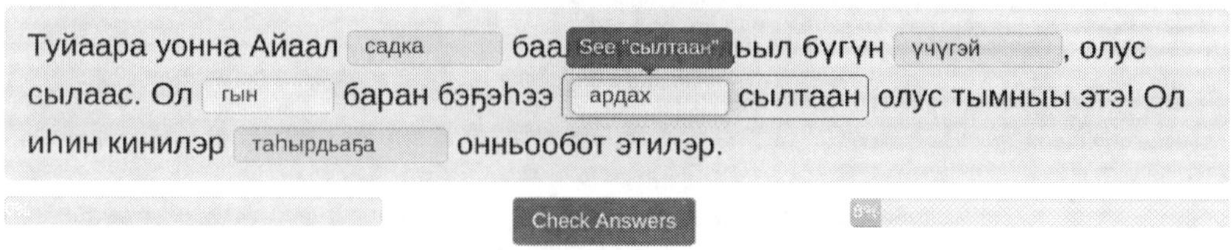

Figure 2: Example of a chunk

4.3 Chunking for exercises

Revita allows the language expert to customize the system for a new language by explicitly specifying rules for syntactic government and agreement. The system performs shallow parsing ("chunking") based on these rules, and uses the chunks when creating exercises, discussed in the previous section. Next we discuss how these rules can work for Sakha.

A government rule, R_g, may state:

(сылтаан, PostP) → [Ablative]

which means that the post-position lemma *сылтаан*, [sıltān], (meaning "because-of"), *governs the ablative* case of its preceding noun (or noun phrase).

A simple but quite general agreement rule, R_a, may state:

[{pos: Noun, case: \$X }
 + {pos: PostP, gov_case: \$X }   ]

Rule R_a consists of two elements/tokens, and describes case agreement. If a token with noun POS is followed by a token with postposition POS, they will form a unit (phrase) if the free variable \$X, indicating the value of the case feature of the noun and the case that the postposition governs, has the same value for both tokens.

Using these two rules, the systems will match all corresponding constructions in text. For example:

"... ардахтан сылтаан ... "

[ardaχtan sıltān]

Rain.Noun.ABL *because_of*.Post-position

"... *because of rain* ..."

The Revita language learning system uses these chunk rules to construct exercises. For example, the exercise based on the second sentence in Figure 2:

"Ол гын баран бэҕэһээ ардахт сылтаан олус тымныы этэ!"

[ol gın baran beɣehē ardaχ sıltān olus tımnī ete]

"But it was very cold yesterday because of the rain!"

Corpus	Tokens	% Coverage
Original analyzer:		
Wikipedia 2015	1,020,000	73.02
Kyym (newspaper)	1,040,000	71.36
Improved analyzer:		
Wikipedia 2019	2,195,565	89.28
Newspapers	16,436,999	86.41

Table 2: Coverage of the morphological analyzer

The boxes contain the *cloze* quizzes—exercises for the user. The system provides hints for each cloze. First, inside the box it shows the lemma of the word. Further, each phrase circled in red forms a chunk/unit—based on the government and agreement rules, such as R_g and R_a, above. Thus, the post-position "сылтаан" [sıltān] (*"because of"*), which governs the ablative case, links it to its preceding noun "ардах" [ardaχ] (*"rain"*) to hint to the user that the noun's surface form should be in the *ablative*.

5 Discussion

5.1 Analyzer coverage

Table 2 shows the coverage of the improved morphological analyzer, as compared to the original one. Coverage of the original analyzer was measured on the Wikipedia corpus (dump from 2015) and the "Kyym" Sakha newspaper.

The improved analyzer was tested on a Wikipedia dump from 2019, and the large newspaper corpus compiled by Leontiev (2015). Currently, the coverage on Wikipedia is about nine out of ten tokens, which is higher, as expected, since the analyzer was developed based on a frequency list from this corpus.

5.2 Learner engagement

We have presented the language learning platform to language experts and lecturers at the Department of the Sakha language, at the North-Eastern Federal University in Yakutsk, Russian Federation. The experts confirm that the language learning system can be a promising tool for enhancing instruction in Sakha. We also plan to introduce the learning system to Sakha learners in cooperation with *Yakutia.Team*, the organization for promoting Sakha language and culture.[7]

Releasing the system for use by language learners will yield mutual benefits for the learners as well as for the researchers. The learners receive a training platform which helps them improve their linguistic competency. From the interaction of the learners with the platform, the researchers receive valuable educational data, for modeling the process of learning Sakha, the patterns of mistakes that the learners make over time, and insights into how the learning system can be improved on the basis of the collected data.

5.3 Multiple admissibility

Multiple Admissibility (MA) in language learning occurs when more than one surface form of a given lemma fits syntactically and semantically within a given context. MA implies that multiple alternative answers are "correct" for the given context, not only the word that the author chose to use in the story. From the perspective of CALL and ITS (intelligent tutoring systems), MA forms a complex challenge, discussed in current research, (Katinskaia et al., 2019).

The Sakha language presents a particularly rich source of scenarios for multiple-admissible answers. Due to the agglutinative morphology of Sakha, the learner can add affixes to a word, which carry additional information or connotations to slightly alter the meaning of the word. We briefly discuss several such scenarios.

The category of *possessiveness*—possessive affixes on nominals—is one of the fundamental categories of Sakha grammar. Possessive forms are very common, and the scope of their usage is far wider than merely indicating possession in the strict sense; possessive affixes express a wide range of logical relations and connections between objects, which are often *not* related directly to the strict notion of possession, (Ubryatova, 1982). For example:

- "сылдьыбатах сир<u>им</u>"
  [sɪlʒɪbataχ sir<u>im</u>]
  "a place where <u>I</u> have not been"
  (literally: "<u>my</u> place, where ...")

---

[7]https://www.yakutia.team

- "билбэт киһит<u>э</u>"
  [bilbet kihi<u>te</u>]
  "man whom <u>s/he</u> doesn't know"
  (literally: "<u>her</u> man, whom ...").

We often find examples of using an impersonal form of a noun in place of a possessive form of a noun and vice versa, as in the following examples:

- Example of using an impersonal noun instead of a possessive noun:
  1a. Form which was used in a story:
      "⎡сааны⎤ ылан сүгэр"
      [sānɪ ɪlan süger]
      (*"he hung <u>a</u> gun on his shoulder"*)
  1b. The learner's input:
      "⎡саатын⎤ ылан сүгэр"
      [sātɪn ɪlan süger]
      (*"he hung <u>his</u> gun on his shoulder"*)

- Example of using a possessive form instead of an impersonal form:
  2a. Form which was used in a story:
      "мооннью̆ун уһатан ⎡уутун⎤ көрөр"
      [mōnnʲun uhatan ūtun körör]
      (*"craning his neck, he looks at (his) water"*)
  2b. The learner's input:
      "мооннью̆ун уһатан ⎡ууну⎤ көрөр"
      [mōnnʲun uhatan ūnu körör]
      (*"craning his neck, he looks at the water"*)

Secondly, Sakha has a highly developed system of verbal *aspects*. Aspect in Sakha can be expressed by various affixes or analytically. Aspect is one of the most commonly used grammatical categories in Sakha, which allows statements in the language to be expressive and precise, (Ubryatova, 1982). Eight forms are used to designate actions that have occurred prior to the present time.

As a result of this choice, it may be quite difficult to decide which form best fits the context, given only the base form of the word. For instance, it can be difficult to distinguish the "first past" perfect tense and recent past tense, because the results of both actions are connected with a present moment.

The verb form which was used in a story: first past perfect tense, indicative mood, third person, singular:

"Эһэм сиргэ сылдьан өрүү түргэн хаамыылаах, оттон бу сырыыга өссө чэпчэкитик үктэнэргэ дылы ⎡буолбут⎤."

[ehem sirge sılẕan örü türgen χāmīlāχ,
otton bu sırīga össö čepčekitik üktenerge
dılı | buolbut |]

*"Grandfather usually walks fast in the field, but
this time he also seems to step lighter"* (meaning,
the action is inferred from its result).

The learner's input was a verb form in the recent
past tense, indicative mood, third person, singular:

"Эһэм сиргэ сылдьан өрүү түргэн
хаамыылаах, оттон бу сырыыга өссө
чэпчэкитик үктэнэргэ дылы | буолла |."

[ehem sirge sılẕan örü türgen χāmīlāχ,
otton bu sırīga össö čepčekitik üktenerge
dılı | buolla |]

*"Grandfather usually walks fast in the field,
but this time he also steps lighter"* (meaning,
the action is observed by the speaker).

These and many other examples show that the
task of generating exercises automatically for Sakha
is far from trivial and requires much research due to
extensive multiple admissibility.

6 Conclusion and future work

This paper offers an overview of the resources available
for Sakha, and describes our work on creating
tools to support language learning for Sakha. Our
surveys of available resources demonstrate that they
are severely lacking.

We present the following tools and resources,
which we combine to create a system to support language
learning for Sakha:

- morphological analyzer, built on the Apertium
  platform,
- language learning system, built on the Revita
  platform,
- bilingual Sakha dictionaries,
- several Sakha corpora.

The morphological analyzer is an essential component
in any natural language processing (NLP)
system, without which little can be done to provide
computational tools for the language.

The functionality of the language learning system
is under development. For larger languages
many more linguistic resources and tools are available
than for Sakha. For example, currently, the
Sakha system has only noun–postposition government
rules. We plan to implement additional
shallow-parsing rules to provide intelligent error
feedback to the learners. For example, *verb–
complement government*:

"ангинанан ыалдьыбыт"
[anginanan ıalẕıbıt]
tonsillitis.Noun.INS *contract*.Verb.2SG.PAST
(*"s\he contracted tonsillitis"*).

The verb "ыарыы" [ıarıj] (*"to contract"*) governs
the *instrumental* case of the noun "ангина"
[angina] (*"tonsillitis"*).

Currently, the system employs chunking (shallow
parsing) to track instances of syntactic government.
The system can track more complex and longer-
range government with the help of deep parsing.
Once a parser for Sakha becomes available, it will
enable Revita to provide richer feedback to the
learner.

The Sakha analyzer needs further improvement
to reach higher coverage. The main work to be
done is extending the lexicon. While a good level of
coverage has been achieved with only 9,313 stems,
production-level morphological analyzers have at
least tens of thousands of stems—more typically,
hundreds of thousands. Once good coverage has
been achieved for the morphological analyzer, the
next step is to build models for morphological and
syntactic disambiguation.

As more advanced tools for Sakha become available,
they will be incorporated into Revita, to provide
richer functionality:

- Parsers, e.g., dependency parsers, such as
  based on the constraint-grammar formalism
  (commonly used in Apertium), or statistical or
  neural-network based parsers.
- Difficulty models—to predict the difficulty of
  a story for the user, and to assess the learner's
  level of competency—based on how well a
  learner handles easy vs. difficult stories.
- Disambiguation models—to disambiguate ambiguous
  tokens in text.
- Text-to-speech—to provide listening exercises
  based on text.
- Speech-to-text—to provide speaking exercises
  (not yet available).

Acknowledgements

This research was supported in part by the "Fin-
UgRevita" Project, Academy of Finland, Grant
267097, and EDUFI Fellowship TM-18-10846.

We are very grateful to Javad Nouri, Kim Salmi,
Max Koppatz, José María Hoya Quecedo, and Jue
Hou for their contributions.

References

Katja Bang. 2015. Language situation in the republic of Sakha (Yakutia). Master's thesis, University of Turku, School of Languages and Translation Studies.

Nikolay Dyachkovsky, Petr Sleptsov, K Fedorov, and M Cherosov. 2018. *Поговорим по-якутски. Самоучитель языка саха (Let's speak Sakha. Sakha language tutorial)*. Yakutsk: Bichik.

Mikel L Forcada, Mireia Ginestí-Rosell, Jacob Nordfalk, Jim O'Regan, Sergio Ortiz-Rojas, Juan Antonio Pérez-Ortiz, Felipe Sánchez-Martínez, Gema Ramírez-Sánchez, and Francis M Tyers. 2011. Apertium: a free, open-source platform for rule-based machine translation. *J. Machine Translation*, 25(2).

James Forsyth. 1994. *A history of the peoples of Siberia: Russia's North Asian colony 1581-1990*. Cambridge University Press.

Sardana Ivanova, Francis Tyers, and Jonathan Washington. (To appear). The Apertium implementation of finite-state morphological analysis for the Sakha language.

Anisia Katinskaia, Sardana Ivanova, and Roman Yangarber. 2019. Multiple admissibility: Judging grammaticality using unlabeled data in language learning. In *Proceedings of the 7th Workshop on Balto-Slavic Natural Language Processing*, pages 12–22.

Anisia Katinskaia, Javad Nouri, and Roman Yangarber. 2018. Revita: a language-learning platform at the intersection of ITS and CALL. In *Proceedings of LREC: 11th International Conference on Language Resources and Evaluation*, Miyazaki, Japan.

Anisia Katinskaia and Roman Yangarber. 2018. Digital cultural heritage and revitalization of endangered Finno-Ugric languages. In *Proceedings of the 3rd Conference on Digital Humanities in the Nordic Countries*, Helsinki, Finland.

Leonid Kharitonov. 1987. *Самоучитель якутского языка (Yakut language tutorial)*. Yakutsk Publishing.

Evdokia Korkina. 1970. *Наклонения глагола в якутском языке*. Moscow, Nauka.

Kimmo Koskenniemi. 1983. *Two-level morphology: A general computational model for word-form recognition and production*. Ph.D. thesis, Helsinki, Finland.

Nyurgun Leontiev. 2015. The newspaper corpus of the Yakut language. *TurkLang-2015*, page 233.

Krister Lindén, Erik Axelson, Sam Hardwick, Tommi A Pirinen, and Miikka Silfverberg. 2011. HFST—framework for compiling and applying morphologies. In *International Workshop on Systems and Frameworks for Computational Morphology*, pages 67–85. Springer.

Petr Sleptsov. 2018. *Саха тылын быһаарыылаах улахан тылдьыта: Большой толковый словарь якутского языка. (Large explanatory dictionary of the Yakut language: in 15 volumes)*. Novosibirsk, Nauka.

Edhem Tenishev. 1997. *Языки мира: Тюркские языки (Languages of the World: Turkic languages)*, volume 2. Moscow: Indrik.

Elizaveta Ubryatova. 1982. *Грамматика современного якутского литературного языка (Grammar of the modern Yakut literary language: Phonetics and morphology)*. Moscow, Nauka.

Rimma Vasilieva, M Degtyareva, N Ivanova, and L Semenova. 2013. *Современная этноязыковая ситуация в Республике Саха (Якутия): социопсихолингвистический аспект (Modern ethno-linguistic situation in the Republic of Sakha (Yakutia): sociopsycholinguistic aspect)*. Novosibirsk, Nauka.

Roman Yangarber. 2018. Support for endangered and low-resource languages via e-learning, translation and crowd-sourcing. In *FEL XXII: Proceedings of the 22nd Annual Conference of the Foundation for Endangered Languages*, pages 90–97. London: FEL & EL Publishing.

Viktoria Yartseva. 1990. *Лингвистический энциклопедический словарь (Linguistic encyclopedic dictionary)*. Moscow, Sovetskaya entsiklopediya.

Abstract

We show how to express the problem of finding an optimal morpheme segmentation from a set of labelled words as a 0/1 linear programming problem, and how to build on this to analyse a language's morphology. The approach works even when there is very little training data available.

1 Introduction

Many recent tools for morphological analysis use statistical approaches such as neural networks (Cotterell et al., 2018). These approaches can profitably use huge amounts of training data, which makes them ideal for high-resource languages. But if there is little training data available, statistical methods can struggle to learn an accurate model. And when they learn the wrong model, it is difficult to diagnose the error, because the model is a black box.

This paper presents a new approach to morphological analysis that produces human-understandable models and works even if only a few training words are given. The user gives a list of inflected words together with each word's morphosyntactic features and standard form (lemma):

standard	inflected	features
woman	women	Pl;Nom
baby	babies'	Pl;Gen
dog	dogs'	Pl;Gen
cat	cat's	Sg;Gen
lorry	lorries	Pl;Nom

Our tool then proposes, for each feature, the affixes and morphological rules which mark that feature. For the example above it suggests the following:

feature	context	morpheme
Gen	Sg	+'s*
Gen	Pl	+'*
Pl	Gen	+s*
Pl	Nom	+a+ $\rightarrow$ +e+
Pl		+y* $\rightarrow$ +ies*
Sg		+y*, +a+, ∅

Here, +'s* represents the *suffix* 's, and +a+ represents an *infix* a.[1] The table shows that both 's and an apostrophe can mark the genitive case; the second column means that the genitive was marked by 's only in singular nouns, and by an apostrophe only in plural nouns. An *s* suffix marks plural, and because of the tiny input data it was only seen in genitive nouns. Plural can be marked by an inner vowel change from *a* to *e* (indicated by the arrow), or by changing a final *y* to *ies*, in which case the singular form is marked by *a* or *y*.

The tool also segments the input words into morphemes consistent with the table of rules (the inferred stem is marked in bold):

standard	inflected
wom│a$_{\text{Sg}}$│**n**│$\varnothing_{\text{Nom}}$	**wom**│e$_{\text{Pl}}$│**n**│$\varnothing_{\text{Nom}}$
bab│y$_{\text{Sg}}$│$\varnothing_{\text{Nom}}$	**bab**│ies$_{\text{Pl}}$│'$_{\text{Gen}}$
dog│$\varnothing_{\text{Sg,Nom}}$	**dog**│s$_{\text{Pl}}$│'$_{\text{Gen}}$
cat│$\varnothing_{\text{Sg,Nom}}$	**cat**│'s$_{\text{Gen}}$│$\varnothing_{\text{Sg}}$
lorr│y$_{\text{Sg}}$│$\varnothing_{\text{Nom}}$	**lorr**│ies$_{\text{Pl}}$│$\varnothing_{\text{Nom}}$

Our key idea is a novel *morphological segmentation* algorithm used to produce the segmentation above (section 3). Once we have a segmentation, we use it to compute the rules on the left (section 4).

In this example, the rules inferred by our tool precisely capture the morphology of the input words, and the segmentation shows which rules are most common. We claim that, together, they can be used to perform high-quality morphological analysis. We validate this claim in section 5 by showing how to build on our tool to do reinflection.

2 Related Work

Morphological segmentation is a well-studied problem in NLP, with applications including machine translation (Green and DeNero, 2012), speech

---

[1]The tool also supports prefixes such as *un+, and circumfixes such as *ge+t* in the German *gerannt* (run; past participle). We explain the meaning of * and + in section 3.3.

recognition (Rajagopal Narasimhan et al., 2014) and information retrieval (Turunen and Kurimo, 2008); for a more detailed overview we refer the reader to Ruokolainen et al. (2016) or Hammarström and Borin (2011). Unsupervised learning (Harris, 1955; Creutz and Lagus, 2007; Goldsmith, 2001; Johnson, 2008; Poon et al., 2009) relies on unannotated text, and is perhaps the most popular approach, because of the large amount of unannotated text available for many languages, but it can suffer from low accuracy (Hammarström and Borin, 2011). One way to improve accuracy is to exploit semantic information (Sakakini et al., 2017; Vulić et al., 2017; Schone and Jurafsky, 2000; Soricut and Och, 2015). Another is minimally-supervised learning (Monson et al., 2007; Kohonen et al., 2010; Ruokolainen et al., 2013; Grönroos et al., 2014; Sirts and Goldwater, 2013; Ahlberg et al., 2014), which combines a large amount of unannotated text with a small amount of annotated text, and potentially provides high accuracy at a low cost.

Silfverberg and Hulden (2017) observe that in the Universal Dependencies project (Nivre et al., 2017), each word is annotated with its lemma and features, but not segmented. They study the problem of finding a segmentation for these words. Our segmentation algorithm solves the same problem, and can be used in their setting. We improve on their solution by using a constraint solver to achieve high accuracy even with limited data, and using a precise language for expressing affixes and rules, which allows us to use the resulting model to precisely analyse new words.

Luo et al. (2017) use Integer Linear Programming for unsupervised modelling of morphological families. They use ILP as a component of a larger training algorithm, so unlike our work they do not attempt to find a globally optimal solution. ILP has been used in other NLP applications outside of morphology (Berant et al., 2011; Roth and Yih, 2005; Clarke and Lapata, 2008).

3　Morphological segmentation

The input to our tool is a list of words, each annotated with its lemma and morphosyntactic features. From now on, we model the lemma as simply another feature; for example, the word "women" has the features Nom, Pl and woman.

The goal of this section is to divide each word into segments, and assign each feature of the word to one of those segments. A segment may consist of multiple discontinuous pieces, or be empty. In the segmentation on page 1, for example, the word *women* is segmented by assigning Pl the segment *e*, Nom the null segment, and *woman* the discontinuous segment *wom*n*. In general, the segment assigned to the lemma feature represents the stem of the word.

We say a segmentation is valid if for each word:

- Every letter is in exactly one segment.

- Each feature labels exactly one segment.

- Each segment is labelled with exactly one feature.[2]

There are many valid segmentations, some good, some bad. We consider a segmentation good if it is parsimonious: each morpheme should be marked by as few features as possible. Note that different forms of a word may be assigned different stems (e.g. *go* and *went*), but parsimony dictates that we share stems wherever reasonable. Perhaps surprisingly, finding the most parsimonious segmentation is an NP-hard problem, by reduction from set cover.

3.1　Segmentation as a constraint problem

We solve the segmentation problem using *zero-one linear programming* (0/1 LP). A 0/1 LP problem consists of a set of variables (e.g. $x, y, z, \ldots$) and a set of linear inequalities over those variables (e.g. $2x + 3y \geq z$ and $x \leq 2y + 3$). Given such a problem, a 0/1 LP solver finds an assignment of values to the variables that makes all the inequalities hold, and where all variables have the value 0 or 1. A 0/1 LP problem also specifies a linear term whose value should be minimised (e.g. $4x + y - z$), called the *objective function*. A 0/1 LP solver is guaranteed to find the solution that minimises the objective function, if a solution exists. The solver that we use is CPLEX (ILOG, 2009).

In this section we assume that we are given, in addition to the labelled words, a (possibly large) set of allowable segments for each feature, which we call *candidate morphemes*. How candidate morphemes are automatically generated is explained in section 3.2.

Our encoding uses the following variables. If m is a candidate morpheme of feature f, the variable

---

[2]This is an unrealistic assumption, but also fairly harmless: when a morpheme marks (e.g.) genitive plural, it will be assigned one of those features, but the inferred rules will show that it only occurs together with the other feature.

$S_{f,m}$ should be 1 if m is used to mark f, and 0 otherwise. If f is a feature with a candidate morpheme m that occurs in word w, and P is the set of positions in w occupied by m, then the variable $M_{w,P,f,m}$ should be 1 if this occurrence of m marks feature f, and 0 otherwise.

Example Suppose that we are given the problem of segmenting the Swedish word *hästarna* (the horses). For simplicity, suppose that we know that the stem of *hästarna* is *häst*, and that the possible affixes are *ar* and *na*. (For now, we ignore the fact that these should be suffixes; we deal with this in section 3.3.) This results in the following candidate morphemes:

feature	candidate morphemes
Pl	ar, na
Def	ar, na
häst	häst

The string *ar* appears at positions 5–6 in *hästarna*, and *na* appears at positions 7–8. Therefore, the encoding introduces the following variables: $S_{\text{Pl,ar}}$, $S_{\text{Pl,na}}$, $S_{\text{Def,ar}}$, $S_{\text{Def,na}}$, $S_{\text{häst,häst}}$, $M_{\text{häst,5–6,Pl,ar}}$, $M_{\text{häst,7–8,Pl,na}}$, $M_{\text{häst,7–8,Def,na}}$, $M_{\text{häst,1–4,häst,häst}}$.
We then generate the following constraints:

- *If a morpheme is used to mark a feature in a given word, it must be a genuine morpheme of that feature.* For each M-variable, if the M-variable is 1 then the corresponding S-variable must also be 1:

$$S_{f,m} \geq M_{w,P,f,m}$$

- *Each position of each word must be in exactly one segment.* For each position in each word, there must be exactly one M-variable that contains that position and whose value is 1. Thus for each position p of each word w we generate the following constraint:

$$\sum_{\substack{f \in \text{features of } w \\ m \in \text{candidate morphemes of } f \\ P \in \text{occurrences of } m \text{ in } w \text{ where } p \in P}} M_{w,P,f,m} = 1.$$

- *In each word, each feature must be mapped to exactly one morpheme.* For each feature f of each word w and feature f of w, exactly one M-variable must be 1:

$$\sum_{\substack{m \in \text{candidate morphemes of } f \\ P \in \text{occurrences of } m \text{ in } w}} M_{w,P,f,m} = 1.$$

Example For the above example, the first rule generates the following constraints, which force an S-variable to 1 when one of its M-variables is 1:

$$S_{\text{häst,häst}} \geq M_{\text{häst,1–4,häst,häst}}$$
$$S_{\text{Pl,ar}} \geq M_{\text{häst,5–6,Pl,ar}}$$
$$S_{\text{Pl,na}} \geq M_{\text{häst,7–8,Pl,na}}$$
$$S_{\text{Def,ar}} \geq M_{\text{häst,5–6,Def,ar}}$$
$$S_{\text{Def,na}} \geq M_{\text{häst,7–8,Def,na}}$$

The second rule generates the following constraints, since letters 1 to 4 can only be covered by *häst*, letters 5 to 6 by *ar* (either as Pl or Def), and letters 7 to 8 by *na*:

$$M_{\text{häst,1–4,häst,häst}} = 1$$
$$M_{\text{häst,5–6,Pl,ar}} + M_{\text{häst,5–6,Def,ar}} = 1$$
$$M_{\text{häst,7–8,Pl,na}} + M_{\text{häst,7–8,Def,na}} = 1$$

The third rule generates the following constraints, stating that *häst*, Pl and Def must be marked by exactly one morpheme each:

$$M_{\text{häst,5–6,Pl,ar}} + M_{\text{häst,7–8,Pl,na}} = 1$$
$$M_{\text{häst,5–6,Def,ar}} + M_{\text{häst,7–8,Def,na}} = 1$$
$$M_{\text{häst,1–4,häst,häst}} = 1$$

This set of constraints has two solutions:

1. One where Pl is assigned to *ar* and Def to *na*. In this solution, the following variables are 1 and the rest are 0: $S_{\text{häst,häst}}$, $S_{\text{Pl,ar}}$, $S_{\text{Def,na}}$, $M_{\text{häst,1–4,häst,häst}}$, $M_{\text{häst,5–6,Pl,ar}}$, $M_{\text{häst,7–8,Def,na}}$.

2. One where Def is assigned to *ar* and Pl to *na*.

In general, any valid segmentation of the input words is a solution to the constraint problem. To make the constraint solver find the best segmentation, we also supply an objective function to be minimised. In our case, we choose to minimise the total number of morpheme-feature pairs used. To achieve this, we supply the objective function

$$\sum_{\substack{f \in \text{features} \\ m \in \text{candidates of } f}} S_{f,m}.$$

Example Suppose that we add to our earlier example the word *hundars* (dogs'). Its stem is *hund* and its other features are Gen and Pl. We also add *s* to the candidate morphemes for Pl, Def and Gen.
The constraint solver finds the solution that minimises the value of the objective function, which

in this case means assigning *ar* to Pl, *s* to Gen and *na* to Def. The objective function's value is then 3 ($S_{\text{Pl,ar}} + S_{\text{Gen,s}} + S_{\text{Def,na}}$). This is the correct segmentation; the wrong segmentations are rejected because they have more feature-morpheme pairs and thus make the objective function larger.

3.2 Choosing the candidate morphemes: the naive approach

The constraint solver requires as input a set of candidate morphemes for each feature. Since the problem formulation requires that a morpheme or stem of a word in the dictionary must be a subsequence of that word, one option is to simply let the candidate morphemes of a feature f include all subsequences of all words that are annotated with feature f. This guarantees the optimal solution with respect to the given constraints. We have found two main problems with this approach.

1. While it works very well for small inputs (around 20 words), the constraint problem quickly becomes infeasible with larger sets of data, especially if many features are involved.

2. It does not consider the position of the morpheme in the word: the suffix *-s* is a plural marker in English, but the infix *-s-* is not.

We solve Problem 1 with an algorithm that guesses an approximate stem and then refines the guess. The algorithm is described in section 3.4.

To solve Problem 2, we now introduce morpheme patterns, which restrict the way in which morphemes can be applied: in this case, a morpheme that has been observed only as a suffix in the data should only occur to the right of the stem.

3.3 Morpheme patterns

If we do not distinguish prefixes, suffixes and infixes, we can not know whether the word seashells should be segmented as seashell|s or s|eashells or even sea|s|hells. *Morpheme patterns* allow us to make this distinction. A typical morpheme pattern is +s∗, which represents the suffix *s*.

Morpheme patterns act as jigsaw pieces that make sure each morpheme is placed in its appropriate position in relation to the stem. By using morpheme patterns, we restrict the way morphemes can be combined and obtain a more precise segmentation. The purpose of this section is to formalise what + and ∗ in patterns mean, and to extend the segmentation algorithm to respect the meaning of the patterns. Both stems and affixes are described using morpheme patterns, but their semantics are slightly different.

Stem Patterns For stems, a ∗ symbol marks a position where an affix can (but does not have to be) inserted. For example, m∗n∗ is the stem of *man*, where an *a* can be inserted in the infix position to make it singular, or an *e* to make it plural. In the suffix position, we can have the null morpheme, or add an affix such as *'s*. To accommodate word forms with multiple tokens, such as the German word *fängt an* (begins), with standard form *anfangen*, stems are represented by a set of patterns. The patterns of this set can be combined in any order, with or without a space. {f∗ng∗, an} is thus a stem of both word forms.

Affix Patterns Affix patterns include two special symbols, + and ∗. For an affix pattern to match a word, you must be able to obtain the word by replacing each + and ∗ with an appropriate string. For example, +s∗ matches *dogs'* by replacing + with *dog* and ∗ by an apostrophe. But there are two important restrictions:

- Each + must be replaced by a string that contains some part of the stem.

- Each ∗ must be replaced by a string that *does not* contain any part of the stem.

In effect, the + symbol determines where the stem must be placed in relation to the affix, while the ∗ symbol allows other affixes to be attached in its place. For example, the plural morpheme +s∗ in English must be placed after (but not necessarily directly after) a stem. Likewise, the genitive morpheme +'∗ must have the stem entirely on its left side. The two morphemes can be combined into +s'∗, and be placed after the stem *horse*∗, to produce the word *horses'*. The morpheme +ea+ must be placed where it has the stem on both sides, thus making it an infix. Together with the stem pattern br∗k∗, it produces the word *break*. Similarly, the morpheme +o+en∗ together with br∗k∗ produces the word *broken*. An affix pattern can in theory have any number of +-symbols.

Extra constraints In order to make the constraint solver follow the semantics of stem patterns and affix patterns, we must for each word add extra constraints for the stems and patterns that are incompatible. An affix and stem can both be chosen for a word only if the affix is in an appropriate position in relation to the stem. Thus, for all words w, and all pairs of M-variables $M_{w,P_1,f_1,m_1}, M_{w,P_2,f_2,m_2}$, we check if m_1 is a stem pattern, m_2 is an affix pattern and their positions P_1 and P_2 are incompatible. If so, we add a constraint that only one of them can be chosen:

$$M_{w,P_1,f_1,m_1} + M_{w,P_2,f_2,m_2} \leq 1$$

For example, supposing we have $+e+$ as a candidate morpheme for *plural*, $+s'$ as a candidate morpheme of *genitive*, and $bus*$ as a candidate stem of *buses'*, the constraint will not accept $bus|e|s'$ as a segmentation, since $+e+$ is required to be an infix of the stem.

3.4 The Algorithm

Considering all possible subsequences of all words yields an unmanageable number of variables for the constraint solver. We therefore need to identify the relevant subsequences, which is done in several steps.

1. As a first step, we approximate the stem as the longest common subsequence of the inflected word and the standard form:

standard	inflected	features
<u>wom</u>an	<u>wom</u>en	Pl;Nom
<u>bab</u>y	<u>bab</u>ies'	Pl;Gen
<u>dog</u>	<u>dog</u>s'	Pl;Gen
<u>lorry</u>	<u>lorry</u>	Sg;Nom

2. By removing the approximated stems, we simplify the problem to segmenting the non-stem part of each word. The resulting problem includes many duplicates, as well as having shorter strings to segment, making it feasible to naively consider every subsequence as a candidate for each feature listed with the word. The result is as follows.

$$
\begin{array}{lll}
\text{wom}\underline{\text{e}}\text{n} & \text{e} \rightarrow & \text{e} \mid \;\;\; \\
& & {}_{\text{Pl}} \;\;\; {}_{\text{Nom}} \\
\text{wom}\underline{\text{a}}\text{n} & \text{a} \rightarrow & \text{a} \mid \;\;\; \\
& & {}_{\text{Sg}} \;\;\; {}_{\text{Nom}} \\
\text{bab}\underline{\textbf{ies'}} & \text{ies'} \rightarrow & \text{ies} \mid \text{'} \\
& & {}_{\text{Pl}} \;\;\; {}_{\text{Gen}} \\
\text{bab}\underline{\text{y}} & \text{y} \rightarrow & \text{y} \mid \;\;\; \\
& & {}_{\text{Sg}} \;\;\; {}_{\text{Nom}} \\
\text{dog}\underline{\textbf{s'}} & \text{s'} \rightarrow & \text{s} \mid \text{'} \\
& & {}_{\text{Pl}} \;\;\; {}_{\text{Gen}} \\
\text{dog} & \rightarrow & \mid \;\;\; \\
& & {}_{\text{Sg}} \;\;\; {}_{\text{Nom}} \\
\text{lorry} & \rightarrow & \mid \;\;\; \\
& & {}_{\text{Sg}} \;\;\; {}_{\text{Nom}}
\end{array}
$$

We simplify the problem further, by automatically giving the null morpheme to features that are shared between the inflected form and the standard form. Since we do not allow any segment to be explained by multiple features, we can assume that the word difference is unrelated to the features that are shared between the two word forms. As an optimisation, when a word is annotated with a single non-shared feature, that feature is automatically paired with the entire non-stem part, and no subsequences are generated.

The approximated stem together with the segmentation of the remainder of the word makes a first approximation of a segmentation of the entire word. However, choosing the longest common subsequence as the stem does not always result in the best segmentation. In our example above, the *-y* is dropped in the stem of *baby*, but is included in the stem of *lorry*. A more consistent choice would be to drop it for *lorry* too, which we achieve in the next step.

3. Taking the morphemes chosen by the constraint solver in step 2, we generate additional stem candidates by removing from each word each possible choice of morpheme for the word's features. For example, in the segmentation to the left, we got $+y*$ as a morpheme of the *Sg* feature. Therefore, for any word with the *Sg* feature that ends in y, we generate a candidate stem where the *-y* suffix is dropped.

For *lorry*, we get the candidate stem *lorr** in addition to the approximated stem *lorry* from step 1. For *baby*, in addition to the suffix $+y$, we also consider the infix $+a+$ from *wom*n* in step 2 as a possibility for the singular morpheme. The candidate stems thus become *bab** and *b*by*.

4. Using the morphemes computed in step 1 and the stem candidates of step 3, we re-run the constraint solver and let it find the optimal choice of stems and morphemes. The chosen stems and morphemes are decoded from the 1-valued S-variables, while the segmentation can be decoded from the 1-valued M-variables.

4   Finding morphological rules

We have now discovered which morphemes mark each features. This section shows how to find inflections that change one morpheme to another, and morphemes that mark a combination of features.

4.1 Function features

In order to detect inflection rules that involve *replacing* one morpheme with another, such as the change of the suffix +*y*∗ into +*ie*∗ in English plural, we introduce the concept of *function features*. Without function features, we might find all of +*s*∗, +*es*∗ and +*ies*∗ as English plural morphemes. By adding function features, we can specify that +*s*∗ is generally used as the pluralisation morpheme, and when +*ies*∗ and +*es*∗ are used instead.

Function features are a special synthetic feature automatically added to some input words. They are added once we have segmented the input, and only for words where the standard and inflected form have the same stem. Let us take as an example the word *babies*, its standard form *baby*, and its stem *bab*∗. We first remove the stem from the standard form to get +*y*∗. Our idea is that, since +*y*∗ is a suffix, we will add the feature *From_Suffix_y* to the set of features of *babies*. We process the whole input this way, and then re-run the segmentation. Assuming there are several words in the input that share the same paradigm, the constraint solver will map +*s*∗ to *Plural* (because the pair (+*s*∗, *Plural*) is commonly occurring and shared by other words), and +*ie*∗ to the *From_Suffix_y* feature. This segmentation captures the fact that words ending in *y* often change to *ie* in plural. We can picture this process as: $\mathrm{bab(y \rightarrow ie)\,|_{Pl}\,s.}$

In the same way, the word-lemma pairs *men - man*, *wives - wife* and *mice - mouse* result in the stem changes +*a*+ → +*e*+, +*f*+ → +*v*+ and +*ous*+ → +*ic*+, after we synthesise the respective function features *From_Infix_a, From_Infix_f* and *From_Infix_ous*.

An inflection rule may also be specific to a part of the stem, such as the doubling of the letter *g* in *big - bigger*. To cover cases involving the last or first letter of the stem, we synthesise the feature *AddTo_Suffix_x*, where *x* is the last letter of the stem, and *AddTo_Prefix_x*, where *x* is the first letter of the stem. As an example, *bigger*, with the stem *big*∗, is given the additional feature *AddTo_Suffix_g*. The morpheme +*er*∗ is likely to be mapped to the comparative feature (due to its commonness in words in comparative form), while the remaining +*g*∗ is mapped to the *AddTo_Suffix_g* feature:

$$\mathrm{bi(g \rightarrow gg)\,|_{Comp}\,er}$$

We also capture the phenomenon where extra letters are inserted when adding an affix, such as the insertion of an extra *g* between the past tense marker *ge* and a stem beginning with the letter *e* in German. To do so, we identify the first and last letters of the stem and add them as synthesised features. In this case, this results in the extra feature *AddTo_Prefix_e*, the segmentation of *gegessen* (eaten) becomes $\mathrm{ge\,|_{Past}\,(e \rightarrow ge)ss\,|_{Past}\,en}$.

This algorithm is *not* language-specific: it works for any language where the concepts of prefix, infix, suffix, first and final letter affect inflection.

4.2 Morphemes with multiple features

Sometimes, a morpheme can be linked to more than one feature. For example, +*na*∗ in Swedish is a morpheme of definite form, but it occurs only in plural. To find such links we post-process the result returned by the constraint solver. For each morpheme m of each feature f, we collect all words whose segmentation uses morpheme m for feature f. The intersection of all features of all such word entries reveals what features always occur together with the combination of m and f.

5 Experimental Results

We evaluated our tool on four different problems: English nouns, Swedish nouns, Dutch verbs, and the SIGMORPHON 2018 shared task of morphological reinflection (Cotterell et al., 2018).

English nouns We tested our tool on 400 randomly selected English nouns from the GF resource grammar library (Ranta, 2009). The tool took 3.9s to run. Fig. 1 shows the morphemes chosen before and after the addition of function features.

From the test results, we randomly select 20 words to demonstrate their segmentations. The first segmentation, based on approximated stems (step 3 of the algorithm) is presented in Fig. 2.

Step 4 of the algorithm changes just one entry: the suffix *y* has been dropped from the stem of *sky*. None of the 20 word entries involves a function feature that was assigned to a non-null morpheme.

Combined morphemes Fig. 3 lists the morphemes with multiple features, as described in section 4.2. The list of combined features nicely shows many of the inflection rules appearing in the data.

Reducing the test data We repeat the experiment after reducing the test data to include only

First approximation of morphemes				
feature	**morphemes**			
Gen	*	+'s*	+'*	+e+'s*
	+v+'*			
Nom	*			
Pl	*	+s*	+ies*	+es* +e+
	+ren*	+v+s*	+ic+	
Sg	*	+y*	+a+	+f* +f+
	+oo+	+ous+		

Morphemes, including function features			
feature	**morphemes**		
Gen	*	+s'	+'s
Nom	*	+ous+	
Pl	*	+s*	
Sg	*	+a+	+oo+ +y*
	+f*	+f+	
Infix_a	*	+e+	
Infix_f	*	+v+	
Infix_oo	*	+ee+	+oo+
Infix_ous	*	+ic+	
Suffix_f	*	+ve*	+f*
Suffix_y	*	+ie*	+y*
AddToSuffix_d	*	+ren*	
AddToSuffix_h	*	+e*	

Figure 1: Chosen morphemes after each step

the 20 randomly selected words. After step 2, the segmentation based on 20 words is identical to the segmentation based on 400 words, with just one exception; the stem of *country* includes the suffix *y*. After step 3 and step 4, the segmentation is identical to the one based on 400 words.

Swedish nouns and Dutch verbs We also tested our method on a set of Swedish nouns and Dutch verbs. For Swedish nouns, our method works very well. The precision is 100% based on a set of 50 words, and 94% based on a set of 250 words. The erroneous results on the bigger data were because the algorithm noticed a vowel change in certain words and applied it universally, causing for example the stem of *grad* (degree) to wrongly become gr*d* instead of grad*, because of other words in which *a* becomes *ä* in the plural. For Dutch verbs, the precision was 80%, based on 50 words, and 74% based on 250 words. The errors made were similar to those on the Swedish test data.

Comparison with earlier work We compared our results on Swedish with those of Silfverberg and Hulden (2017), although they do not use the

	word	stem	morphemes
1	rivers'	river	+s'/Gen,Pl
2	breasts	breast	+s/Pl /Nom
3	river's	river	+'s/Gen /Sg
4	windows'	window	+s'/Gen,Pl
5	television's	television	+'s/Gen /Sg
6	country	countr+	+y/Sg /Nom
7	languages'	language	+s'/Gen,Pl
8	fire	fire	/Sg,Nom
9	number	number	/Sg,Nom
10	ceiling	ceiling	/Sg,Nom
11	question's	question	+'s/Gen /Sg
12	song	song	/Sg,Nom
13	airplane's	airplane	+'s/Gen /Sg
14	doors'	door	+s'/Gen,Pl
15	fires	fire	+s/Pl /Nom
16	water	water	/Sg,Nom
17	arts'	art	+s'/Gen,Pl
18	flowers'	flower	+s'/Gen,Pl
19	sky's	sky	+'s/Gen /Sg
20	ear	ear	/Sg,Nom

Figure 2: The segmentation of the 20 test words, based on the test data of 400 words

feature		**morpheme**	**combines with**
+a+	→	+e+	Pl
(*policeman → policemen and 1 other(s)*)			
+f+	→	+v+	Pl
(*wife → wives*)			
+oo+	→	+ee+	Pl,Gen
(*foot → feet's*)			
+ous+	→	+ic+	Pl,Nom
(*louse → lice*)			
Pl		+s'*	Gen
(*doctor → doctors' and 91 other(s)*)			
+d	→	+d*ren	Pl
(*child → children*)			
+h	→	+h*e	Pl
(*church → churches and 1 other(s)*)			
+f	→	+ve*	Pl,Gen
(*leaf → leaves'*)			
+y	→	+ie*	Pl
(*country → countries and 7 other(s)*)			

Figure 3: The combined features, where the feature of column 1 and morpheme of column 2 occur only in combination with the features of column 3

same dataset (in particular, ours only includes nouns). Our precision of 94% far exceeds their precision of 62%.[3] To find out why, we looked into what sort of errors both tools made. As mentioned above, our tool made one class of errors, inferring a vowel change where none was needed, but produced a plausible segmentation.

Their tool found many implausible segmentations; for example, *inkomst* (income) was sometimes segmented into i|nkomst, and *pension* into p|ension. Furthermore, it segmented words inconsistently: some occurrences of *inkomst* were (correctly) left as one segment. This means that the tool has not found the *simplest* explanation of the input data: its explanation requires more morphemes than necessary, such as *i*, *p* and *nkomst*. We avoid this problem since the constraint solver guarantees to find the globally minimal solution to the input constraints.

Secondly, their tool does not restrict where in a word a morpheme can occur. For example, the letter *a* can mark common nouns, such as *flicka* (girl). It only occurs as a suffix, but their tool uses it as a prefix to segment *arbetsinkomst* (income from work) into a|rbetsinkomst. By distinguishing different kinds of affixes, we avoid this problem.

Morphological Reinflection   We use an adapted version of our tool to solve the SIGMORPHON 2018 shared task of morphological (type level) reinflection (Cotterell et al., 2018). Given a lemma and set of morphological features, the task is to generate a target inflected form. For example, given the source form *release* and target features PTCP and PRS, the task is to predict the target form *releasing*.

Our approach requires a set of labelled training data, which we segment to obtain a list of affixes and their associated features. To predict the target inflected form of a word, we: 1) find the stem of the word, 2) find a word in the training data whose features match the target features, and 3) replace the stem of that word with that of the input word.

In more detail, in step 1, we check if the word contains any affixes that are associated with a feature belonging to the lemma. We remove any such affix from the word. There may be a choice of affixes for each feature so this results in a set of candidate stems. When considering a candidate stem, we also add the appropriate function features to the target feature list; for example, if the stem drops a suffix *suff* from the source form, we add

the feature *From_Suffix_suff*. In step 2, for each candidate stem, we collect the entries of the training data that match the target features (including the function features collected in step 1). Out of those, we pick the word whose stem best matches the source form. In step 3, we take this word, and replace its stem with the stem of the input word.

Language	Our system	Mean	Best
Arabic	25.6	14.77	45.2
	(2.95)	(6.63)	(1.77)
Galician	49.0	31.93	61.1
	(1.42)	(2.4)	(0.72)
Greek	27.9	15.76	32.3
	(3.02)	(4.89)	(1.83)
Karelian	32.0	47.93	94.0
	(1.4)	(1.53)	(0.1)
Russian	43.8	26.86	53.5
	(1.41)	(3.64)	(1.07)
Sanskrit	43.9	25.76	58.0
	(1.55)	(2.99)	(0.93)
Slovene	35.9	24.80	58.0
	(1.15)	(2.7)	(0.73)
Tatar	64.0	48.89	90.0
	(0.44)	(2.15)	(0.14)
Telugu	66.0	67.41	96.0
	(0.98)	(1.29)	(0.06)
West Frisian	43.0	32.52	56.0
	(1.86)	(1.85)	(1.01)

Figure 4: Results of reinflection. The first line gives the average accuracy and the second line the average Levenshtein distance from the right answer.

We evaluate our system on the *low* training data, the smallest of the three available sizes, which consists of 100 words for each of the 103 languages. The data includes a mixture of nouns, adjectives and verbs. 17 of the languages were excluded from the evaluation, because they involved a large number of features, resulting in a too long execution time. On the remaining 86 languages, our approach performs, with a few exceptions, in the better half, and often in the better third of the 27 submitted systems. For English, Czech, Greek, Livonian and Romanian, the accuracy is within 5% of the accuracy of the system with the highest score. Figure 4 shows the accuracy and Levenshtein distance of our system on a sample of languages, and the mean and best values of the systems that took part in the shared task. Our reinflection algorithm is very simple, but still competes with state-of-the-art sys-

---

[3]62% is the figure for *unlabelled* morphemes. The figures given in the paper for *labelled* morphemes are unfortunately erroneous.

tems, indicating that the underlying morphological analysis provided by our tool is of good quality.

6 Conclusion and Future Work

We have presented a method for morphological segmentation based on constraint solving. Our evaluation shows that it works well even given little training data, producing almost the same segmentation from 20 English words as it does from 400 words. It produces a morphological analysis precise enough that a simple reinflection algorithm built on it can compete with state-of-the-art systems. The reasons for this good precision are (a) the pattern semantics, which allows the solver to make precise distinctions between different kinds of morphemes, such as infix and suffix; (b) the use of function features to express replacement rules.

The paper also demonstrates that constraint solving is a useful alternative to machine learning for segmentation, particularly for low-resource languages where one must make the most of a small set of data. We hope that our paper spurs further research in this direction.There are many possible refinements to our technique and some of our ideas for future work are listed below.

More refined semantics for morphemes With a more refined semantics of morphemes, we can guide the constraint solver to pick a segmentation that follows the observed data in a more precise way. This can be done by restricting how a morpheme can be placed in relation to other morphemes. For example, the definite morpheme $+na*$ in Swedish always follows a plural morpheme ($+er*$, $+or*$ or $+ar*$), and never occurs directly after a stem. The morpheme semantics could be improved to allow these kind of restrictions, and the algorithm refined to automatically infer them from the data.

Improved function features Currently, we consider only the first and last letter of the stem for stem additions, as described in section 4. We are currently investigating generalising this idea by using the constraint solver to find the relevant segment of the stem. This would allow us to detect a wider range of morphological changes.

As an example, suppose we would like to find out which kinds of English words form their plural with $+es$. We could take all such words that occur in the input, and give the following segmentation problem to the constraint solver:

standard	features
bus	bus; Suffix_es
dress	dress; Suffix_es
box	box; Suffix_es
suffix	suffix; Suffix_es

The solution returned indicates which letter patterns are associated with the plural form $+es$:

$$\mathbf{bu}\big|\ {}^{\text{s}}_{\text{Suffix\_es}}$$
$$\mathbf{dres}\big|\ {}^{\text{s}}_{\text{Suffix\_es}}$$
$$\mathbf{bo}\big|\ {}^{\text{x}}_{\text{Suffix\_es}}$$
$$\mathbf{suffi}\big|\ {}^{\text{x}}_{\text{Suffix\_es}}$$

We could then introduce new features *AddTo_Suffix_s* and *AddTo_Suffix_x* to the original problem, whereupon the algorithm of Section 4 would find the correct function features. This method would be able to invent function features from an arbitrary substring of the given words.

Tweaking the objective function The objective function can be weighted to give higher or lower cost to stems or morphemes related to specific kinds of features. For example, by multiplying each term $S_{f,m}$ in the objective function by the length of m, we would recover the Minimum Description Length principle. It is left as future work to investigate how the choice of cost function affects the result in different settings.

Distinguishing between rules and exceptions Once a morpheme is used in a segmentation, the algorithm is sometimes too eager to use the same morpheme elsewhere. This means that adding more data sometimes leads to worse results, and errors in the input can cause unrelated words to be segmented wrongly. We plan to investigate using statistical methods to distinguish between morphological rules and exceptions; exceptions should not be applied everywhere, but rules should.

Scalability For most languages our tool works comfortably up to a thousand words or more, but for languages with many morphosyntactic features (such as Basque) it can struggle to deal with a hundred words. We would like to see if, by tackling features in smaller groups, it is possible to scale the approach to large inputs.

References

Malin Ahlberg, Markus Forsberg, and Mans Hulden. 2014. Semi-supervised learning of morphological paradigms and lexicons. In *Proceedings of the 14th*

Conference of the European Chapter of the Association for Computational Linguistics, Gothenburg, Sweden 26–30 April 2014*, pages 569–578.

Jonathan Berant, Ido Dagan, and Jacob Goldberger. 2011. Global learning of typed entailment rules. In *Proceedings of the 49th Annual Meeting of the Association for Computational Linguistics: Human Language Technologies*, pages 610–619, Portland, Oregon, USA. Association for Computational Linguistics.

James Clarke and Mirella Lapata. 2008. Global inference for sentence compression: An integer linear programming approach. *Journal of Artificial Intelligence Research*, 31:399–429.

Ryan Cotterell, Christo Kirov, John Sylak-Glassman, Géraldine Walther, Ekaterina Vylomova, Arya D McCarthy, Katharina Kann, Sebastian Mielke, Garrett Nicolai, Miikka Silfverberg, et al. 2018. The conll–sigmorphon 2018 shared task: Universal morphological reinflection. *arXiv preprint arXiv:1810.07125*.

Mathias Creutz and Krista Lagus. 2007. Unsupervised models for morpheme segmentation and morphology learning. *ACM Trans. Speech Lang. Process.*, 4(1):3:1–3:34.

John Goldsmith. 2001. Unsupervised learning of the morphology of a natural language. *Comput. Linguist.*, 27(2):153–198.

Spence Green and John DeNero. 2012. A class-based agreement model for generating accurately inflected translations. In *Proceedings of the 50th Annual Meeting of the Association for Computational Linguistics: Long Papers - Volume 1*, ACL '12, pages 146–155, Stroudsburg, PA, USA. Association for Computational Linguistics.

Stig-Arne Grönroos, Sami Virpioja, Peter Smit, and Mikko Kurimo. 2014. Morfessor flatcat: An hmm-based method for unsupervised and semi-supervised learning of morphology. In *Proceedings of COLING 2014, the 25th International Conference on Computational Linguistics: Technical Papers*, pages 1177–1185, Dublin, Ireland. Dublin City University and Association for Computational Linguistics.

Harald Hammarström and Lars Borin. 2011. Unsupervised learning of morphology. *Computational Linguistics*, 37(2):309–350.

Zellig S. Harris. 1955. From phoneme to morpheme. *Language*, 31(2):190–222.

IBM ILOG. 2009. *IBM ILOG CPLEX V12.1: User's manual for CPLEX*.

Mark Johnson. 2008. Using adaptor grammars to identify synergies in the unsupervised acquisition of linguistic structure. In *Proceedings of ACL-08: HLT*, pages 398–406, Columbus, Ohio. Association for Computational Linguistics.

Oskar Kohonen, Sami Virpioja, and Krista Lagus. 2010. Semi-supervised learning of concatenative morphology. In *Proceedings of the 11th Meeting of the ACL Special Interest Group on Computational Morphology and Phonology*, SIGMORPHON '10, pages 78–86, Stroudsburg, PA, USA. Association for Computational Linguistics.

Jiaming Luo, Karthik Narasimhan, and Regina Barzilay. 2017. Unsupervised learning of morphological forests. *Transactions of the Association for Computational Linguistics*, 5:353–364.

Christian Monson, Jaime Carbonell, Alon Lavie, and Lori Levin. 2007. Paramor: Minimally supervised induction of paradigm structure and morphological analysis. In *Proceedings of Ninth Meeting of the ACL Special Interest Group in Computational Morphology and Phonology*, pages 117–125, Prague, Czech Republic. Association for Computational Linguistics.

Joakim Nivre, Željko Agić, Lars Ahrenberg, Maria Jesus Aranzabe, Masayuki Asahara, and Aitziber et al. Atutxa. 2017. Universal dependencies 2.0. LINDAT/CLARIN digital library at the Institute of Formal and Applied Linguistics (ÚFAL), Faculty of Mathematics and Physics, Charles University.

Hoifung Poon, Colin Cherry, and Kristina Toutanova. 2009. Unsupervised morphological segmentation with log-linear models. In *Proceedings of Human Language Technologies: The 2009 Annual Conference of the North American Chapter of the Association for Computational Linguistics*, NAACL '09, pages 209–217, Stroudsburg, PA, USA. Association for Computational Linguistics.

Karthik Rajagopal Narasimhan, Damianos Karakos, Richard Schwartz, Stavros Tsakalidis, and Regina Barzilay. 2014. Morphological segmentation for keyword spotting.

Aarne Ranta. 2009. The gf resource grammar library.

Dan Roth and Wen-tau Yih. 2005. Integer linear programming inference for conditional random fields. In *Proceedings of the 22Nd International Conference on Machine Learning*, ICML '05, pages 736–743, New York, NY, USA. ACM.

Teemu Ruokolainen, Oskar Kohonen, Kairit Sirts, Stig-Arne Grönroos, Mikko Kurimo, and Sami Virpioja. 2016. A comparative study of minimally supervised morphological segmentation. *Comput. Linguist.*, 42(1):91–120.

Teemu Ruokolainen, Oskar Kohonen, Sami Virpioja, and Mikko Kurimo. 2013. Supervised morphological segmentation in a low-resource learning setting using conditional random fields. In *Proceedings of the Seventeenth Conference on Computational Natural Language Learning*, pages 29–37, Sofia, Bulgaria. Association for Computational Linguistics.

Tarek Sakakini, Suma Bhat, and Pramod Viswanath. 2017. Morse: Semantic-ally drive-n morpheme segment-er. In *Proceedings of the 55th Annual Meeting of the Association for Computational Linguistics (Volume 1: Long Papers)*, pages 552–561, Vancouver, Canada. Association for Computational Linguistics.

Patrick Schone and Daniel Jurafsky. 2000. Knowledge-free induction of morphology using latent semantic analysis. In *Fourth Conference on Computational Natural Language Learning and the Second Learning Language in Logic Workshop*.

Miikka Silfverberg and Mans Hulden. 2017. Automatic morpheme segmentation and labeling in universal dependencies resources. In *Proceedings of the NoDaLiDa Workshop on Universal Dependencies, UDW@NoDaLiDa 2017, Gothenburg, Sweden, May 22, 2017*, pages 140–145. Association for Computational Linguistics.

Kairit Sirts and Sharon Goldwater. 2013. Minimally-supervised morphological segmentation using adaptor grammars. *Transactions of the Association for Computational Linguistics*, 1:255–266.

Radu Soricut and Franz Och. 2015. Unsupervised morphology induction using word embeddings. In *Proceedings of the 2015 Conference of the North American Chapter of the Association for Computational Linguistics: Human Language Technologies*, pages 1627–1637, Denver, Colorado. Association for Computational Linguistics.

Ville T. Turunen and Mikko Kurimo. 2008. Speech retrieval from unsegmented finnish audio using statistical morpheme-like units for segmentation, recognition, and retrieval. *ACM Trans. Speech Lang. Process.*, 8(1):1:1–1:25.

Ivan Vulić, Nikola Mrkšić, Roi Reichart, Diarmuid Ó Séaghdha, Steve Young, and Anna Korhonen. 2017. Morph-fitting: Fine-tuning word vector spaces with simple language-specific rules. In *Proceedings of the 55th Annual Meeting of the Association for Computational Linguistics (Volume 1: Long Papers)*, pages 56–68, Vancouver, Canada. Association for Computational Linguistics.

Lexicon information in neural sentiment analysis:
a multi-task learning approach

Jeremy Barnes, Samia Touileb, Lilja Øvrelid, and Erik Velldal
University of Oslo
Department of Informatics
`{jeremycb,samiat,liljao,erikve}@ifi.uio.no`

Abstract

This paper explores the use of multi-task learning (MTL) for incorporating external knowledge in neural models. Specifically, we show how MTL can enable a BiLSTM sentiment classifier to incorporate information from sentiment lexicons. Our MTL set-up is shown to improve model performance (compared to a single-task set-up) on both English and Norwegian sentence-level sentiment datasets. The paper also introduces a new sentiment lexicon for Norwegian.

1 Introduction

Current state-of-the-art neural approaches to sentiment analysis tend not to incorporate available sources of external knowledge, such as polarity lexicons (Hu and Liu, 2004; Taboada et al., 2006; Mohammad and Turney, 2013), explicit negation annotated data (Morante and Daelemans, 2012; Konstantinova et al., 2012), or labels representing inter-annotator agreement (Plank et al., 2014). One reason for this is that neural models can already achieve good performance, even if they only use word embeddings given as input, as they are able to learn task-specific information (which words convey sentiment, how to resolve negation, how to resolve intensification) in a data-driven manner (Socher et al., 2013; Irsoy and Cardie, 2014). Another often overlooked reason is that it is not always entirely straightforward how we can efficiently incorporate this available external knowledge in the model.

Despite achieving strong results, neural models are known to be difficult to interpret, as well as highly dependent on the training data. Resources like sentiment lexicons, on the other hand, have the benefit of being completely transparent, as well as being easy to adapt or update. Additionally, lexicons are often less sensitive to domain and frequency effects and can provide high coverage and precision even for rare words. We hypothesize that these two views of sentiment are complimentary and that even competitive neural models can benefit from incorporating lexicon information.

In the current work, we demonstrate that multi-task learning (Caruana, 1993; Collobert et al., 2011) is a viable framework to incorporate lexicon information in a sentence-level sentiment classifier. Our proposed multi-task model shares the lower layers in a multi-layer neural network, while allowing the higher layers to adapt to either the main or auxiliary task. Specifically, the shared lower layers are a feed-forward network which uses a sentiment lexicon auxiliary task to learn to predict token-level sentiment. The higher layers use these learned representations as input for a BiLSTM sentiment model, which is trained on the main task of sentence-level classification. The intuition is that the representations learned from the auxiliary task give the model an advantage on the main task.

Compared to previous methods, our model has two advantages: 1) it requires *only a single sentiment lexicon*, and 2) the lexicon prediction model is *able to generalize to words that are not found in the lexicon*, increasing the overall performance. Experimental results are reported for both English and Norwegian, with the code[1] made available. While we rely on an existing sentiment lexicon for English, we introduce and make available a new lexicon for Norwegian.[2]

In the following, we first consider relevant related work (§ 2), and describe the sentiment lexicons (§ 3) and datasets (§ 4) that we use for our experiments. In § 5 we detail our proposed multi-task model, while § 6 presents the experimental results and error analysis. Finally, we summarize and point to future directions in § 7.

---

[1] `https://github.com/ltgoslo/mtl_lex`
[2] `https://github.com/ltgoslo/norsentlex`

2   Related work

In this section we briefly review previous relevant work related to (*i*) sentiment lexicons, (*ii*) lexicon-based approaches to sentiment analysis (SA), (*iii*) use of lexicon information in neural models, and finally (*iv*) multi-task learning in NLP.

Sentiment lexicons   Sentiment lexicons provide a valuable source of information about the prior affective orientation of words, oftentimes driven by theoretical approaches to emotion (Stone et al., 1962; Bradley et al., 1999). There are several freely available sentiment lexicons for English. One widely used lexicon is that of Hu and Liu (2004),[3] which was created using a bootstrapping approach from WordNet and a corpus of product reviews. This is the lexicon that forms the basis of the experiments in the current paper and we return to it in § 3.1. Other available lexicons include the MPQA subjectivity lexicon (Wilson et al., 2005) which contains words and expressions manually annotated as positive, negative, both, or neutral. SentiWordnet (Esuli and Sebastiani, 2006) contains each synset of the English WordNet annotated with scores representing the sentiment orientation as being positive, negative, or objective. The So-Cal (Taboada et al., 2011) English sentiment lexicon contains separate lexicons of verbs, nouns, adjectives, and adverbs. The words were manually labeled on a scale from extremely positive ($+5$) to extremely negative (-5), and all words labeled as neutral (0) were excluded from the lexicons.

While no high-quality sentiment lexicons for Norwegian are currently publicly available, there have been some previous attempts at generating lexicons for Norwegian. Hammer et al. (2014) used a set of 51 positive and 57 negative manually selected seed words to crawl three Norwegian thesauri in three iterations, to extract synonyms and antonyms at each iteration. These were thereafter used to build an undirected graph with words as nodes, and synonymy and antonymy relations as edges. A label propagation algorithm was applied to create a lexicon by identifying the strength and polarity of the non-seed words and calculating the weighted average of the connected nodes. They used the Norwegian full-form lexicon SCARRIE[4] to retrieve all forms of each word

in the lexicon. As a benchmark, they have also created two other lexicons: a machine translated version of the AFINN lexicon (Nielsen, 2011), and a manually corrected version of this translation. The generated lexicons were evaluated against reviews containing ratings (dice values) by summing the scores of each sentiment word present in a review, averaging these scores over the total number of words in the review, and assigning a final score based on threshold intervals. The authors also took into account the use of the sentiment shifter *ikke* (not) if it appeared two words before a word from the lexicons. Their results show that the translated lexicons outperformed, by mean absolute error with standard deviation, all of their automatically generated lexicons. Unfortunately, none of the lexicons are made available.

Bai et al. (2014) used a corpus of newspaper articles and discussion forums with a modified version of Pointwise Mutual Information (PMI) to compute the semantic orientation of candidate words against a list of seed words. They manually selected 7 positive and 7 negative words as seed words, and instead of using the entire corpus as candidate words they used a selection of the top 10,000 most frequent words in the corpus and a list of adjectives generated from their corpus using SCARRIE. Their results showed that the translated lexicons outperformed all of their generated lexicons, but unfortunately only the latter were made publicly available.

Lexicon-based approaches to SA   Early approaches to sentiment analysis classified documents based on the sum of *semantic orientation* scores of adjectives in a document. Often, researchers used existing lexicons (Stone et al., 1962), or extended these resources in a semi-supervised fashion, using WordNet (Hu and Liu, 2004; Kim and Hovy, 2004; Esuli and Sebastiani, 2006). Alternatively, an adjective's semantic orientation could be determined as the strength of association with positive words (*excellent*) or negative words (*poor*) as measured by Pointwise Mutual Information (Turney and Littman, 2003).

Researchers quickly discovered, however, that various linguistic phenomena, *e.g.* negation, intensifying adverbs, downtoners, *etc*, must be taken into account to correctly assign a sentiment score. Taboada et al. (2011) proposed an approach to determine the semantic orientation of documents which incorporates sentiment lexicons for adjec-

---

[3]Available at `https://www.cs.uic.edu/~liub/FBS/sentiment-analysis.html`

[4]`https://www.nb.no/sprakbanken/show?serial=sbr-9`

tives, nouns, verbs, and adverbs. Additionally, they included compositional rules for intensification, negation, and irrealis blocking. They showed that smaller, manually built lexicons outperform semi-supervised lexicon approaches and that their model is more robust to domain shifts than machine learning models.

Lexicons in neural approaches The general tendency in NLP when using neural approaches is to perform end-to-end learning without using external knowledge sources, relying instead solely on what can be inferred from (often pre-trained) word embeddings and the training corpus itself. This is also the case for neural sentiment modeling. However, there have been some attempts to include external knowledge like lexicon features into such models (Teng et al., 2016; Zou et al., 2018; Lei et al., 2018a; Bao et al., 2019a).

One notable example is the work of Shin et al. (2017) where several approaches are tested for how to incorporate lexicon information into a CNN for sentiment classification on the SemEval 2016 Task 4 dataset and the Stanford Sentiment Treebank (SST). Shin et al. (2017) create feature vectors that encode the positive or negative polarity values of words across a broad selection of different sentiment lexicons available for English. These word-level sentiment-score vectors are then combined with standard word embeddings in different ways in the CNN: through simple concatenation, using multiple channels, or performing separate convolutions. While all three approaches yield improvements for the SemEval data, performance deteriorates or remain unchanged for SST. The model used by Shin et al. (2017) requires information from six different lexicons, which is overly restrictive for most languages besides English, where one will typically not have the luxury of several publicly available sentiment lexicons.

Lei et al. (2018b) propose a different approach based on what they dub a 'Multi-sentiment-resource Enhanced Attention Network', where lexicon information is used for guiding an attention mechanism when learning sentiment-specific sentence representations. The approach shows promising results on both SST and the Movie Review data of Pang and Lee (2005), although the model also incorporates other types of lexicons, like negation cues and intensifiers.

In a similar spirit, Margatina et al. (2019) include features from a range of sentiment-related lexicons for guiding the self-attention mechanism in an LSTM. Bao et al. (2019b) generate features from several different lexicons that are added to an attention-based LSTM for aspect-based sentiment analysis.

In the current paper we will instead explore whether lexicon information can be incorporated into neural models using the framework of *multi-task learning*. This has two main advantages: 1) we require only a single sentiment lexicon, unlike much previous work, and 2) our model is able to generalize to sentiment words not seen in the lexicon as it only uses word embeddings as features. Below we review some relevant background on multi-task learning for NLP.

Multi-task learning Multi-task learning (MTL) (Caruana, 1993; Collobert et al., 2011), whereby a single machine learning model is simultaneously trained to perform two or more tasks, can allow a model to incorporate a useful inductive bias by restricting the search space of possible representations to those that are predictive for both tasks. MTL assumes that features that are useful for a certain task should also be predictive for similar tasks, and in this sense effectively acts as a regularizer, as it prevents the weights from adapting too much to a single task.

The simplest approach to MTL, *hard parameter sharing* (Caruana, 1993), assumes that all layers are shared between tasks except for the final predictive layer. This approach tends to improve performance when the auxiliary task is carefully chosen (Plank, 2016; Peng and Dredze, 2017; Martínez Alonso and Plank, 2017; Fares et al., 2018; Augenstein et al., 2018). What characteristics determine a useful auxiliary task, however, is still not completely clear (Bingel and Søgaard, 2017; Augenstein and Søgaard, 2017; Martínez Alonso and Plank, 2017; Bjerva, 2017).

Søgaard and Goldberg (2016) propose an improvement over hard parameter sharing that uses the lower layers of a multi-layer recurrent neural network to make predictions for low-level auxiliary tasks, while allowing higher layers to focus on the main task. In this work, we adopt a similar approach to incorporate sentiment lexicon information as an auxiliary task to improve sentence-level sentiment and evaluative-language classification.

3 Sentiment lexicons

We here describe the sentiment lexicons used in the experiments reported in § 5.

3.1 English sentiment lexicon

For English we use the sentiment lexicon compiled by Hu and Liu (2004), containing 4,783 negative words and 2,006 positive words. The sentiment lexicon was a bi-product of their task for predicting which reviews were positive and negative from a corpus of customer reviews of a range of products. Hu and Liu (2004) first PoS-tagged the review corpus to identify all the adjectives it contained, and then manually defined a list of 30 seed adjectives and their labels (positive or negative). The synsets and antonyms of the adjectives in the seed list were searched for in WordNet, and the positive and negative labels were automatically assigned based on the synonymy or antonymy relation of each word to the corresponding adjective from the seed list, iteratively growing the set of words in the lexicon. This has also enabled the inclusion of words that were not adjectives, which made the lexicon a mix of word classes and inflections.

3.2 Norwegian sentiment lexicon

We automatically translated (from English to Norwegian) the positive and negative words in the sentiment lexicon compiled by Hu and Liu (2004) described above. Thereafter, all the translations were manually inspected and corrected when necessary. If an English word had several senses that could be translated into different Norwegian words, these were manually added to the translations during the manual inspection. For example the English word *outstandingly* has been translated to the five following Norwegian words *bemerkelsesverdig*, *fortreffelig*, *fremstående*, *utmerket*, and *utsøkt*.

We have also decided to omit all multi-word expressions, and only keep single-word translations. For example the translations of the negative-labeled expressions *die-hard*, *layoff-happy*, *ultra-hardline*, *muscle-flexing*, *martyrdom-seeking*, *anti-israeli*; and positive-labeled expressions like *counter-attacks*, *well-positioned*, and *well-backlit* were not included.

Some other words were not translated because we either believed that they did not fit into the positive or negative categories, or because we

		Negative	Positive
Translated	All	3,917	1,601
	Adjectives	1,728	844
	Verbs	1,575	541
	Nouns	1,371	461
	Participle adjectives	146	97
Full-forms	All	14,839	6,103
	Adjectives	6,392	3,030
	Verbs	5,769	2,269
	Nouns	4,565	1,559
	Participle adjectives	938	368
Lemmas	All	4,939	2,004
	Adjectives	2,085	958
	Verb	942	371
	Noun	1,186	415
	Participle adjectives	934	366

Table 1: Overview of the Norwegian sentiment lexicon, showing counts for the manually inspected translations, the full-forms of the expanded version, and finally the lemmas found after expansion.

could not find an appropriate Norwegian translation. Examples of some of the originally negative-labeled words that fell into these categories are: *drones*, *vibration*, *miscellaneous*, *frost*, *funny*, *flirt*, *sober*, and *rhetorical*. Examples of positive-labeled words that were excluded are *work*, *hotcakes*, *rapport*, *dawn*, *illuminati*, *electrify*, *ftw*, and *instrumental*. We also removed all words that were present in both the positive and the negative lists. This process resulted in a Norwegian sentiment lexicon containing a collection of 3,917 negative and 1,601 positive words. Table 1 gives an overview of the word classes present in the translated Norwegian lexicon (*Translated*). Several words can overlap between word classes, for example 60 positive nouns and 123 negative nouns are also adjectives.

Similarly to the English lexicon, the resulting Norwegian lexicon contains a mix of word classes and inflected forms. In order to produce a more general version of the lexicon containing all possible word-forms (*Full-forms*), we have used the previously mentioned Norwegian full-form lexicon SCARRIE to expand the entries to include all inflected forms. This resulted in a lexicon of 14,839 negative words and 6,103 positive words. Table 1 gives a detailed overview of the content of the Norwegian lexicon, both with regards to the number of word-forms and lemmas, where participle adjectives are all words that can be both adjectives and participles.

Our preliminary experiments showed that using the Norwegian lexicon as directly translated yields similar results to using the expanded lexicon. In what follows we therefore only report results of using the translated and manually curated (but non-expanded) Norwegian lexicon. However, we make both versions of the lexicon publicly available.[5]

Additionally, we set aside 20 percent of each lexicon (1,357 words for English, 1,122 for Norwegian) as a development set to monitor the performance of the models on the auxiliary task.

4 Sentiment datasets

In the following we present the datasets used to train and evaluate our sentence-level classifiers.

4.1 English

The Stanford Sentiment Treebank (SST) (Socher et al., 2013) contains 11,855 sentences taken from English-language movie reviews. It was annotated for fine-grained sentiments (strong negative, negative, neutral, positive, strong positive) based on crowdsourcing. We perform experiments using the pre-defined train, development and test splits (of 8,455 / 1,101 / 2,210 sentences, respectively).

4.2 Norwegian

The Norwegian dataset used in this work forms part of the Norwegian Review Corpus NoReC (Velldal et al., 2018), consisting of full-text reviews from a range of different domains, such as restaurants, literature, and music, collected from several of the major Norwegian news sources. The particular subset used in the current work, dubbed NoReC$_{eval}$, comprises 7961 sentences across 298 documents that have been manually annotated according to whether or not each sentence contains an *evaluation*, as described by Mæhlum et al. (2019). Two types of evaluative sentence categories are distinguished (in addition to non-evaluative sentences): simple *evaluative* and a special case of *evaluative fact-implied non-personal*. The latter follows the terminology of Liu (2015), denoting factual, objective sentences which are used with an evaluative intent but without reference to personal experience. Example

(1) shows an evaluative sentence, labeled EVAL, which contains the positive evaluation signaled by the adjectives *sterk* 'strong/powerful' and *flott* 'great'.

(1) *Sterk   og   flott   film   om   hevntanker*
Strong and great movie about revenge
A powerful and great movie about revenge

Example (2) shows a fact-implied non-personal sentence, labeled FACT-NP, where a factual, objective statement is interpreted as expressing an evaluation given the context of a car review.

(2) *Firehjulsdriften kan kobles   inn og   ut*
Fourwheeldrive can switched in   and out
etter   behov.
after   need
The four wheel drive can be switched on and off as required

Unlike the English dataset discussed above, the annotation does not specify the polarity of the sentence. The rationale for this is that a sentence may contain more than one sentiment expression and have a mixed polarity, hence this type of annotation is better performed sub-sententially following an initial annotation of evaluative or sentiment-relevant sentences (Toprak et al., 2010; Scheible and Schütze, 2013).

We use the training, development and test splits as defined by Mæhlum et al. (2019), see the summary of corpus statistics in Table 2.

5 Multi-task learning of lexicon information in neural models

This section details our multi-task neural architecture for incorporating sentiment lexicon information into neural networks, as shown in Figure 1. Our multi-task model shares the lower layers (an embedding and fully connected layer), while allowing the higher layers to further adapt to the main and auxiliary tasks. Specifically, we use a sentiment prediction auxiliary task, where the goal is to correctly predict whether a single word is positive or negative, to improve the main task of sentence-level classification. Although the units of classification for the two tasks are different (word-level in the auxiliary task and sentence-level in the main), the auxiliary task can be assumed to be highly predictive for the main task, as sentiment bearing words are the main feature for identifying evaluative sentences and their polarity.

---

[5]https://github.com/ltgoslo/norsentlex

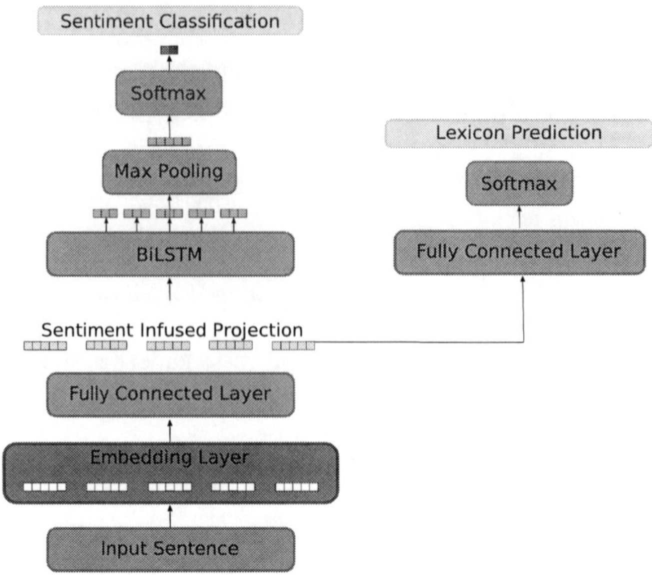

Figure 1: Our proposed multi-task model to incorporate lexicon information into a neural classifier.

	Train	Dev	Test
Documents	230	33	35
Sentences	5,915	1,151	895
Tokens	104,350	20,755	16,292

Table 2: Corpus counts for the Norwegian dataset.

Lexicon prediction model: We propose a lexicon prediction model, which given a word from a sentiment lexicon, predicts whether the word is positive or negative. We implement a multi-layer feed-forward network which uses word embeddings as input, ReLU non-linearities, and a softmax layer for classification. This model has previously shown promise for predicting abstractness (Köper and Schulte im Walde, 2017) and emotion ratings (Köper et al., 2017). We additionally use dropout (0.3) after the embedding layer for regularization.

Sentence-level prediction model: For sentiment classification, we use a bidirectional Long Short-Term Memory network to create contextualized representations of each token after being projected to the sentiment infused space. The final contextualized vectors at each time step are concatenated and then passed to a max pooling layer and finally to a softmax layer for classification. This single-task model trained without the lexicon

prediction task (STL) is also used as a baseline to measure the relative improvement.

Multi-task model: During training, the multi-task learning model (MTL) alternates between training one epoch on the main task and one epoch on the auxiliary task. Preliminary experiments showed that more complicated training strategies (alternating training between each batch or uniformly sampling batches from the two tasks) did not lead to improvements. For English we use 300 dimensional pre-trained embeddings from GoogleNews,[6] while for Norwegian we use 100 dimensional skip-gram fastText embeddings (Bojanowski et al., 2016) trained on the NoWaC corpus (Guevara, 2010). The pre-trained embeddings were re-used from the NLPL vector repository[7] (Fares et al., 2017). We train the model for 10 epochs using Adam (Kingma and Ba, 2014), performing early stopping determined by the improvement on the development set of the main task. Given that neural models are sensitive to the random initialization of their parameters, we perform five runs with different random seeds and show the mean and standard deviation as the final result for each model. We use the same five random seeds for all experiments to ensure a fair comparison between models.

---

[6]Available at https://code.google.com/archive/p/word2vec/.

[7]http://vectors.nlpl.eu/repository

Model	SST	NoReC$_{eval}$
LEXICON	14.7	37.2
BOW	37.4	45.0
BOW+LEXICON	38.9	45.8
LEX-EMB	34.7 (1.1)	48.9 (0.1)
STL	37.8 (3.1)	51.2 (2.6)
MTL	**42.4 (3.2)**	**52.8 (2.9)**

Table 3: Macro F_1 of models on the SST and NoReC$_{eval}$ sentence-level datasets. Neural models report mean and standard deviation of the scores over five runs.

Lexicon embedding Model: We also include an additional model (LEX-EMB), which uses the feed-forward network previously described to learn to predict word-level polarity and the same BiLSTM architectures for sentiment classification. Instead of jointly learning the two tasks, we first train the feed-forward model on the lexicon task and update the original embeddings. We then concatenate these learned sentiment embeddings to the original embeddings to create a sentiment informed representation of each word before passing them to the BiLSTM. All other parts of the models are the same as the STL model.

Baselines: We also include three non-neural baseline models: LEXICON, BOW, BOW+LEXICON. The LEXICON baseline uses the sentiment lexicon to create features for a Linear SVM. The inputs to the SVM were presented as sequences of labels representing the sentences of the datasets, such that each word present in the lexicons was labeled as either $+1$ or -1 for positive or negative words respectively, and the rest were labeled as 0. This was done to incorporate lexicon information, and predict classes based on the distribution of positive and negative words within sentences. The BOW baseline uses a bag-of-words representation of the data to train a Linear SVM. Finally, the BOW+LEXICON adds two additional features to the BOW model: the total number of tokens which are found in the positive and negative lists in the sentiment lexicons. We choose the optimal c value for each classifier on the development split.

6 Model results

Table 3 shows the Macro F_1 scores for all models on the SST and NoReC$_{eval}$ test sets. Note that previous work often uses accuracy as a metric on the SST dataset, but as we hypothesize that lexicon information may help the minority classes, we thought it important to give these equal weight. (A macro F_1 of 40.1 in our case corresponds to 46.7 accuracy). The BOW model performs quite well on SST, only 0.4 percentage points (ppt) worse than STL. On NoReC$_{eval}$, however, it performs much worse, which can be attributed to the the difficulty of determining if a sentence is non-evaluative or fact-implied using only unigram information, as these sentence types do not differ largely lexically.

BOW+LEXICON performs better than BOW on both datasets, although the difference is larger on SST (1.5 ppt vs. 0.8 ppt). This is likely due to sentiment lexicon features being more predictive for the sentiment task. Additionally, it outperforms the STL model by 1.1 ppt on SST, confirming that it is a strong baseline (Mohammad et al., 2013).

LEX-EMB is the weakest model on the SST dataset with 34.7 F_1 but performs better than the non-neural baselines on NoReC$_{eval}$ (48.9). STL performs better than LEXICON, BOW, and LEX-EMB on both tasks, as well as BOW+LEXICON on NoReC$_{eval}$. Finally, MTL is the best performing model on both tasks, with a difference of 3.5 ppt between MTL and the next best performing model on SST, and 1.6 ppt on NoReC$_{eval}$.

6.1 Error analysis

We perform an error analysis by comparing how the MTL model changes predictions when compared to the STL model. We create a confusion matrix of the predictions of each model on the SST and NoReC$_{eval}$ tasks over all five runs and show the relative differences in Figures 2 and 3. Positive numbers (dark purple) indicate that the MTL model made more predictions in this square, while negative numbers (white) indicate it made fewer predictions.

Counter-intuitively, the MTL model improves mainly on the neutral, strong positive, and strong negative classes, while performing relatively worse on the positive and negative classes. In general, the MTL makes fewer negative and positive predictions than the STL model. On the NoReC$_{eval}$ task, the MTL model leads to fewer ab-

Sentence	Gold	STL	MTL
Light, cute and forgettable.	neutral	negative	neutral
Despite some gulps the film is a fuzzy huggy.	positive	negative	positive
This is art paying homage to art.	positive	positive	neutral
Undercover Brother doesn't go far enough.	negative	negative	neutral

Table 4: Examples where MTL performs better and worse than STL. A red box indicates negative polarity (blue box indicates positive) according to the sentiment lexicon used to in the auxiliary training task.

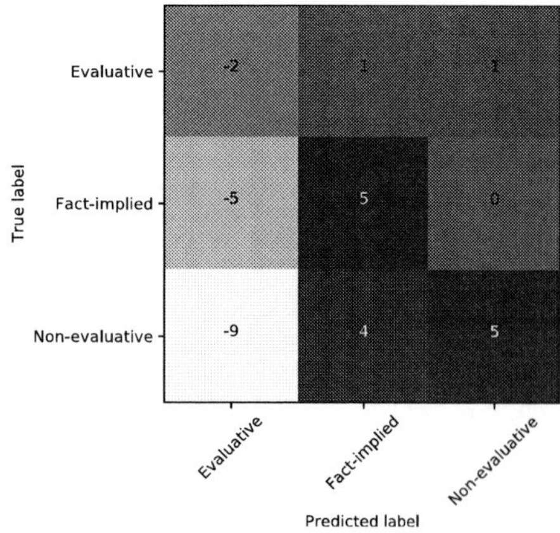

Figure 2: A relative confusion matrix on the SST task, where positive numbers (dark purple) indicate that the MTL model made more predictions than STL in the square and negative (white) indicate that it made fewer.

Figure 3: A relative confusion matrix on the NoReC$_{eval}$ task, where positive numbers (dark purple) indicate that the MTL model made more predictions than STL in the square and negative (white) indicate that it made fewer.

Model	English	Norwegian
LEX-EMB	**87.1 (0.2)**	**87.5 (0.2)**
MTL	86.7 (0.2)	72.4 (3.9)

Table 5: Mean accuracy and standard deviation of the MTL and LEX-EMB models over five runs on the Hu and Liu lexicon for English and the translated lexicon for Norwegian.

solute changes, but importantly reduces the number of non-evaluative sentences predicted as evaluative. Again, the MTL model has a tendency to reduce predictions for the majority class and increase them for the minority classes (fact-implied and non-evaluative). This seems to point to the regularizing effect of multi-task learning (Augenstein et al., 2018; Bingel and Søgaard, 2017). Table 4 additionally shows examples where MTL is better and worse than STL.

6.2 Lexicon prediction results

In this section, we evaluate the performance of the MTL and LEX-EMB models on the auxiliary lexicon prediction task. Table 5 shows that the LEX-EMB model outperform the MTL model on both English and Norwegian. For English the difference between models is small (0.4 ppt), while much larger for Norwegian (15.1 ppt). Rather than being attributed to differences in language, we hypothesize that the difference is due to task similarity. For English, the auxiliary task is much more predictive of the main task (sentence-level sentiment), while for Norwegian the main task of predicting evaluative, fact implied and non-evaluative does not depend as much on word-level sentiment. The MTL classifier in Norwegian therefore relies less on the auxiliary module.

Model	Lexicon	# tokens	SST
STL	–	–	37.8 (3.1)
MTL	SoCal	4,539	41.3 (3.1)
	SoCal Google	1,691	37.9 (0.3)
	NRC Emotion	4,460	41.5 (3.1)
	Hu and Liu	5,432	**42.4 (3.2)**

Table 6: Macro F_1 of models on the SST sentence-level datasets. We compare the MTL model on SST using different lexicons.

6.3 Other lexicons

In this section, we experiment with using different English lexicons as an auxiliary task for the MTL model. Specifically, we compare the following sentiment lexicons:

- SoCal: a sentiment lexicon compiled manually with words taken from several review domains (Taboada et al., 2011).

- SoCal Google: a semi-supervised lexicon created from a small set of seed words (Taboada et al., 2006) using a PMI-based technique and search engine queries (Turney and Littman, 2003).

- NRC Emotion: a crowd-sourced emotion lexicon which also contains polarity annotations (Mohammad and Turney, 2013).

- Hu and Liu: the sentiment lexicon described in § 2.

While the NRC Emotion lexicon already contains binary annotations, tokens in SoCal and SoCal Google are annotated on a scale from -5 to 5. We make these annotations binary by assigning positive polarity to tokens with a rating > 0 and negative for those < 0. Any neutral tokens are discarded. Table 6 shows that the MTL model is robust to different sources of sentiment information. The size of the dataset appears to be more important than the specific content, as all lexicons over 4,000 words achieve similar scores.

7 Conclusion

This paper proposes a method to incorporate external knowledge, in this case about word polarity in the form of sentiment lexicons, into a neural classifier through multi-task learning. We have performed experiments on sentence-level sentiment tasks for English and Norwegian, demonstrating that our multi-task model improves over a single-task approach in both languages. We provide a detailed analysis of the results, concluding that the multi-task objective tends to help the neutral and minority classes, indicating a regularizing effect.

We have also introduced a Norwegian sentiment lexicon, created by first machine-translating an English lexicon and manually curating the results. This lexicon, and its expansion to a full-form lexicon, are made freely available to the community. While our current model ignores subword information, *e.g. unimpressive*, and multiword expressions, *e.g. not my cup of tea*, including this information could further improve the results.

Although we have limited the scope of our auxiliary task to binary classification, using a regression task with sentiment and emotion labels may provide more fine-grained signal to the classifier. We also plan to experiment with a similar setup for targeted or aspect-level classification tasks.

Finally, it is important to note that the MTL approach outlined in this paper could also be applied to incorporate other types of external knowledge into neural classifiers for other types of tasks besides sentiment analysis.

Acknowledgements

This work has been carried out as part of the SANT project (Sentiment Analysis for Norwegian Text), funded by the Research Council of Norway (grant number 270908).

References

Isabelle Augenstein, Sebastian Ruder, and Anders Søgaard. 2018. Multi-task learning of pairwise sequence classification tasks over disparate label spaces. In *Proceedings of the 2018 Conference of the North American Chapter of the Association for Computational Linguistics: Human Language Technologies, Volume 1 (Long Papers)*, pages 1896–1906, New Orleans, Louisiana.

Isabelle Augenstein and Anders Søgaard. 2017. Multi-Task Learning of Keyphrase Boundary Classification. In *Proceedings of the 55th Annual Meeting of the Association for Computational Linguistics (Volume 2: Short Papers)*, pages 341–346, Vancouver, Canada.

Aleksander Bai, Hugo Hammer, Anis Yazidi, and Paal Engelstad. 2014. Constructing sentiment lexicons in Norwegian from a large text corpus. In *Proceedings of the 17th IEEE International Conference on Computational Science and Engineering*, pages 231–237, Chengdu, China.

Lingxian Bao, Patrik Lambert, and Toni Badia. 2019a. Attention and lexicon regularized LSTM for aspect-based sentiment analysis. In *Proceedings of the 57th Annual Meeting of the Association for Computational Linguistics: Student Research Workshop*, pages 253–259, Florence, Italy. Association for Computational Linguistics.

Lingxian Bao, Patrik Lambert, and Toni Badia. 2019b. Attention and lexicon regularized LSTM for aspect-based sentiment analysis. In *Proceedings of the 57th Annual Meeting of the Association for Computational Linguistics: Student Research Workshop*, pages 253–259, Florence, Italy.

Joachim Bingel and Anders Søgaard. 2017. Identifying beneficial task relations for multi-task learning in deep neural networks. In *Proceedings of the 15th Conference of the European Chapter of the Association for Computational Linguistics: Volume 2, Short Papers*, pages 164–169, Valencia, Spain.

Johannes Bjerva. 2017. Will my auxiliary tagging task help? Estimating Auxiliary Tasks Effectivity in Multi-Task Learning. In *Proceedings of the 21st Nordic Conference on Computational Linguistics*, pages 216–220, Gothenburg, Sweden.

Piotr Bojanowski, Edouard Grave, Armand Joulin, and Tomas Mikolov. 2016. Enriching word vectors with subword information. *arXiv preprint arXiv:1607.04606*.

Margaret M. Bradley, Peter J. Lang, Margaret M. Bradley, and Peter J. Lang. 1999. Affective norms for English Words (ANEW): Instruction manual and affective ratings.

Richard Caruana. 1993. Multitask learning: A knowledge-based source of inductive bias. In *Proceedings of the Tenth International Conference on Machine Learning*, pages 41–48. Morgan Kaufmann.

Ronan Collobert, Jason Weston, Léon Bottou, Michael Karlen, Koray Kavukcuoglu, and Pavel Kuksa. 2011. Natural language processing (almost) from scratch. *Journal of Machine Learning Research*, 12:2493–2537.

Andrea Esuli and Fabrizio Sebastiani. 2006. Sentiwordnet: A publicly available lexical resource for opinion mining. In *In Proceedings of the 5th Conference on Language Resources and Evaluation (LREC06)*, volume 6, pages 417–422, Genova, Italy.

Murhaf Fares, Andrey Kutuzov, Stephan Oepen, and Erik Velldal. 2017. Word vectors, reuse, and replicability: Towards a community repository of large-text resources. In *Proceedings of the 21st Nordic Conference of Computational Linguistics*, pages 271–276, Gothenburg, Sweden.

Murhaf Fares, Stephan Oepen, and Erik Velldal. 2018. Transfer and multi-task learning for nounnoun compound interpretation. In *Proceedings of the 2018 Conference on Empirical Methods in Natural Language Processing*, pages 1488–1498, Brussels, Belgium.

Emiliano Raul Guevara. 2010. NoWaC: a large web-based corpus for Norwegian. In *Proceedings of the NAACL HLT 2010 Sixth Web as Corpus Workshop*, pages 1–7, NAACL-HLT, Los Angeles.

Hugo Hammer, Aleksander Bai, Anis Yazidi, and Paal Engelstad. 2014. Building sentiment lexicons applying graph theory on information from three Norwegian thesauruses. In *Norsk Informatikkonferanse (NIK)*, Fredrikstad, Norway.

Minqing Hu and Bing Liu. 2004. Mining and summarizing customer reviews. In *Proceedings of the 10th ACM SIGKDD International Conference on Knowledge Discovery and Data Mining*, pages 168–177, Seattle, USA.

Ozan Irsoy and Claire Cardie. 2014. Deep Recursive Neural Networks for Compositionality in Language. In Z. Ghahramani, M. Welling, C. Cortes, N. D. Lawrence, and K. Q. Weinberger, editors, *Advances in Neural Information Processing Systems 27*, pages 2096–2104. Curran Associates, Inc.

Soo-Min Kim and Eduard Hovy. 2004. Determining the sentiment of opinions. In *Proceedings of the 20th International Conference on Computational Linguistics*, Geneva, Switzerland.

Diederik Kingma and Jimmy Ba. 2014. Adam: A method for stochastic optimization. *Proceedings of the 3rd International Conference on Learning Representations*.

Natalia Konstantinova, Sheila C.M. de Sousa, Noa P. Cruz, Manuel J. Maña, Maite Taboada, and Ruslan Mitkov. 2012. A review corpus annotated for negation, speculation and their scope. In *Proceedings of the Eighth International Conference on Language Resources and Evaluation*, pages 3190–3195, Istanbul, Turkey.

Maximilian Köper, Evgeny Kim, and Roman Klinger. 2017. IMS at EmoInt-2017: Emotion Intensity Prediction with Affective Norms, Automatically Extended Resources and Deep Learning. In *Proceedings of the 8th Workshop on Computational Approaches to Subjectivity, Sentiment and Social Media Analysis*, pages 50–57, Copenhagen, Denmark.

Maximilian Köper and Sabine Schulte im Walde. 2017. Improving verb metaphor detection by propagating abstractness to words, phrases and individual senses. In *Proceedings of the 1st Workshop on Sense, Concept and Entity Representations and their Applications*, pages 24–30, Valencia, Spain.

Zeyang Lei, Yujiu Yang, and Min Yang. 2018a. Sentiment lexicon enhanced attention-based lstm for sentiment classification. In *AAAI-2018-short paper*, page 81058106.

Zeyang Lei, Yujiu Yang, Min Yang, and Yi Liu. 2018b. A multi-sentiment-resource enhanced attention network for sentiment classification. In *Proceedings of the 56th Annual Meeting of the Association for Computational Linguistics*, pages 758–763, Melbourne, Australia.

Bing Liu. 2015. *Sentiment analysis: Mining Opinions, Sentiments, and Emotions*. Cambridge University Press, Cambridge, United Kingdom.

Petter Mæhlum, Jeremy Claude Barnes, Lilja Øvrelid, and Erik Velldal. 2019. Annotating evaluative sentences for sentiment analysis: a dataset for Norwegian. In *Proceedings of the 22nd Nordic Conference on Computational Linguistics (NoDaLiDa)*, Turku, Finland.

Katerina Margatina, Christos Baziotis, and Alexandros Potamianos. 2019. Attention-based conditioning methods for external knowledge integration. In *Proceedings of the 57th Annual Meeting of the Association for Computational Linguistics*, pages 3944–3951, Florence, Italy.

Héctor Martínez Alonso and Barbara Plank. 2017. When is multitask learning effective? Semantic sequence prediction under varying data conditions. In *Proceedings of the 15th Conference of the European Chapter of the Association for Computational Linguistics: Volume 1, Long Papers*, pages 44–53, Valencia, Spain.

Saif Mohammad, Svetlana Kiritchenko, and Xiaodan Zhu. 2013. NRC-canada: Building the state-of-the-art in sentiment analysis of tweets. In *Second Joint Conference on Lexical and Computational Semantics (*SEM), Volume 2: Proceedings of the Seventh International Workshop on Semantic Evaluation (SemEval 2013)*, pages 321–327, Atlanta, USA.

Saif M. Mohammad and Peter D. Turney. 2013. Crowdsourcing a Word-Emotion Association Lexicon. *Computational Intelligence*, 29(3):436–465.

Roser Morante and Walter Daelemans. 2012. ConanDoyle-neg: Annotation of negation cues and their scope in Conan Doyle stories. In *Proceedings of the Eight International Conference on Language Resources and Evaluation*, Istanbul, Turkey.

Finn Årup Nielsen. 2011. A new ANEW: Evaluation of a word list for sentiment analysis in microblogs. In *Proceedings of the ESWC2011 Workshop on Making Sense of Microposts: Big things come in small packages*, pages 93–98, Heraklion, Crete.

Bo Pang and Lillian Lee. 2005. Seeing stars: Exploiting class relationships for sentiment categorization with respect to rating scales. In *Proceedings of the 43rd Annual Meeting of the Association for Computational Linguistics*, pages 115–124, Ann Arbor, Michigan.

Nanyun Peng and Mark Dredze. 2017. Multi-task domain adaptation for sequence tagging. In *Proceedings of the 2nd Workshop on Representation Learning for NLP*, pages 91–100, Vancouver, Canada.

Barbara Plank. 2016. Keystroke dynamics as signal for shallow syntactic parsing. In *Proceedings of COLING 2016, the 26th International Conference on Computational Linguistics: Technical Papers*, pages 609–619, Osaka, Japan.

Barbara Plank, Dirk Hovy, and Anders Søgaard. 2014. Learning part-of-speech taggers with inter-annotator agreement loss. In *Proceedings of the 14th Conference of the European Chapter of the Association for Computational Linguistics*, pages 742–751, Gothenburg, Sweden.

Christian Scheible and Hinrich Schütze. 2013. Sentiment relevance. In *Proceedings of the 51st Annual Meeting of the Association for Computational Linguistics*, pages 954–963, Sofia, Bulgaria.

Bonggun Shin, Timothy Lee, and Jinho D. Choi. 2017. Lexicon integrated CNN models with attention for sentiment analysis. In *Proceedings of the 8th Workshop on Computational Approaches to Subjectivity, Sentiment and Social Media Analysis*, pages 149–158, Copenhagen, Denmark.

Richard Socher, Alex Perelygin, Jean Wu, Jason Chuang, Christopher D. Manning, Andrew Ng, and Christopher Potts. 2013. Recursive Deep Models for Semantic Compositionality Over a Sentiment Treebank. In *Proceedings of the 2013 Conference on Empirical Methods in Natural Language Processing*, pages 1631–1642, Seattle, Washington, USA.

Anders Søgaard and Yoav Goldberg. 2016. Deep multi-task learning with low level tasks supervised at lower layers. In *Proceedings of the 54th Annual Meeting of the Association for Computational Linguistics*, pages 231–235, Berlin, Germany.

Philip J. Stone, Robert F. Bales, J. Zvi Namenwirth, and Daniel M. Ogilvie. 1962. The general inquirer: A computer system for content analysis and retrieval based on the sentence as a unit of information. *Behavioral Science*, 7(4):484–498.

Maite Taboada, Caroline Anthony, and Kimberly Voll. 2006. Methods for Creating Semantic Orientation Dictionaries. In *Proceedings of the Fifth International Conference on Language Resources and Evaluation (LREC'06)*, Genoa, Italy. European Language Resources Association (ELRA).

Maite Taboada, Julian Brooke, Milan Tofiloski, Kimberly Voll, and Manfred Stede. 2011. Lexicon-based methods for sentiment analysis. *Computational linguistics*, 37(2):267–307.

Zhiyang Teng, Duy-Tin Vo, and Yue Zhang. 2016. Context-sensitive lexicon features for neural sentiment analysis. In *Proceedings of the 2016 Conference on Empirical Methods in Natural Language Processing*, pages 1629–1638, Austin, Texas. Association for Computational Linguistics.

Cigdem Toprak, Niklas Jakob, and Iryna Gurevych. 2010. Sentence and expression level annotation of opinions in user-generated discourse. In *Proceedings of the 48th Annual Meeting of the Association for Computational Linguistics*, pages 130–139, Uppsala, Sweden.

Peter Turney and Michael Littman. 2003. Measuring praise and criticism: Inference of semantic orientation from association. *ACM Transactions on Information Systems*, 21(4):315–346.

Erik Velldal, Lilja Øvrelid, Cathrine Stadsnes Eivind Alexander Bergem, Samia Touileb, and Fredrik Jrgensen. 2018. NoReC: The Norwegian Review Corpus. In *Proceedings of the 11th edition of the Language Resources and Evaluation Conference*, pages 4186–4191, Miyazaki, Japan.

Theresa Wilson, Janyce Wiebe, and Paul Hoffmann. 2005. Recognizing Contextual Polarity in Phrase-Level Sentiment Analysis. In *Proceedings of Human Language Technology Conference and Conference on Empirical Methods in Natural Language Processing*, pages 347–354, Vancouver, British Columbia, Canada.

Yicheng Zou, Tao Gui, Qi Zhang, and Xuanjing Huang. 2018. A lexicon-based supervised attention model for neural sentiment analysis. In *Proceedings of the 27th International Conference on Computational Linguistics*, pages 868–877, Santa Fe, New Mexico, USA. Association for Computational Linguistics.

Aspect-Based Sentiment Analysis Using BERT

Mickel Hoang
Chalmers University of Technology
Sweden
Hoangmicke@gmail.com

Oskar Alija Bihorac
Chalmers University of Technology
Sweden
Alija.bihorac@hotmail.com

Jacobo Rouces
Språkbanken, University of Gothenburg
Sweden
jacobo.rouces@gu.se

Abstract

Sentiment analysis has become very popular in both research and business due to the vast amount of opinionated text currently produced by Internet users. Standard sentiment analysis deals with classifying the overall sentiment of a text, but this doesn't include other important information such as towards which entity, topic or aspect within the text the sentiment is directed. Aspect-based sentiment analysis (ABSA) is a more complex task that consists in identifying both sentiments and aspects. This paper shows the potential of using the contextual word representations from the pre-trained language model BERT, together with a fine-tuning method with additional generated text, in order to solve out-of-domain ABSA and outperform previous state-of-the-art results on SemEval-2015 (task 12, subtask 2) and SemEval-2016 (task 5). To the best of our knowledge, no other existing work has been done on out-of-domain ABSA for aspect classification.

1   Introduction

Sentiment analysis, also known as opinion mining, is a field within natural language processing (NLP) that consists in automatically identifying the sentiment of a text, often in categories like negative, neutral and positive. It has become a very popular field in both research and industry due to the large and increasing amount of opinionated user-generated text in the Internet, for instance social media and product reviews. Knowing how users feel or think about a certain brand, product, idea or topic is a valuable source of information for companies, organizations and researchers, but it can be a challenging task. Natural language often contains ambiguity and figurative expressions that make the automated extraction of information in general very complex.

Traditional sentiment analysis focuses on classifying the overall sentiment expressed in a text without specifying what the sentiment is *about*. This may not be enough if the text is simultaneously referring to different topics or entities (also known as *aspects*), possibly expressing different sentiments towards different aspects. Identifying sentiments associated to specific aspects in a text is a more complex task known as aspect-based sentiment analysis (ABSA).

ABSA as a research topic gained special traction during SemEval-2014 (Pontiki et al., 2014) workshop, where it was first introduced as Task 4 and reappeared in the SemEval-2015 (Pontiki et al., 2015) and SemEval-2016 (Pontiki et al., 2016) workshops.

In parallel, within NLP, there have been numerous developments in the field of pre-trained language models, for example ELMo (Peters et al., 2018) and BERT (Devlin et al., 2019). These language models are pre-trained on large amounts of unannotated text, and their use has shown to allow better performance with a reduced requirement for labeled data and also much faster training. At SemEval-2016, there were no submissions that used such pre-trained language model as a base for the ABSA tasks. For this paper we will use BERT as the base model to improve ABSA models for the unconstrained evaluation, which permits using additional resources such as external training data, due to the pre-training of the base language model. More precisely, the contributions of this paper are as follows:

- It proposes the new ABSA task for out-of-domain classification at both sentence and text levels.

- To solve this task, a general classifier model is proposed, which uses the pre-trained language model BERT as the base for the contextual word representations. It makes use of the sentence pair classification model (Devlin et al., 2019) to find semantic similarities between a text and an aspect. This method outperforms all of the previous submissions, except for one in SemEval-2016.

- It proposes a combined model, which uses only one sentence pair classifier model from BERT to solve both aspect classification and sentiment classification simultaneously.

2 State-of-the-art

This chapter provides an overview of the techniques and models used throughout the rest of the paper, as well as existing state-of-the-art results.

Section 2.1 will cover the pre-trained model used in this paper, which has achieved state-of-the-art results in several NLP tasks, together with the architecture of the model and its key features. Thereafter, Section 2.2 will explain the ABSA task from SemEval-2016. Previous work with and without a pre-trained model will be briefly described in Section 2.3 and Section 2.4.

2.1 BERT

Pre-trained language models are providing a context to words, that have previously been learning the occurrence and representations of words from unannotated training data.

Bidirectional encoder representations from transformers (BERT) is a pre-trained language model that is designed to consider the context of a word from both left and right side simultaneously (Devlin et al., 2019). While the concept is simple, it improves results at several NLP tasks such as sentiment analysis and question and answering systems. BERT can extract more context features from a sequence compared to training left and right separately, as other models such as ELMo do (Peters et al., 2018).

The left and right pre-training of BERT is achieved using modified language model masks, called masked language model (MLM). The purpose of MLM is to mask a random word in a sentence with a small probability. When the model masks a word it replaces the word with a token [MASK]. The model later tries to predict the masked word by using the context from both left and right of the masked word with the help of transformers. In addition to left and right context extraction using MLM, BERT has an additional key objective which differs from previous works, namely next-sentence prediction.

Previous work

BERT is the first deeply bidirectional and unsupervised language representation model developed. There have been several other pre-trained language models before BERT that also use bidirectional unsupervised learning. One of them is ELMo (Peters et al., 2018), which also focuses on contextualized word representations. The word embeddings ELMo generates are produced by using a Recurrent Neural Network (RNN) named Long Short-Term Memory (LSTM) (Sak et al., 2014) to train left-to-right and right-to-left independently and later concatenate both word representations (Peters et al., 2018). BERT does not utilize LSTM to get the word context features, but instead uses transformers (Vaswani et al., 2017), which are attention-based mechanisms that are not based on recurrence.

Input Representaion

The text input for the the BERT model is first processed through a method called wordpiece tokenization (Wu et al., 2016). This produces set of tokens, where each represent a word. There are also two specialized tokens that get added to the set of tokens: classifier token [CLS], which is added to the beginning of the set; and separation token [SEP], which marks the end of a sentence. If BERT is used to compare two sets of sentences, these sentences will be separated with a [SEP] token. This set of tokens is later processed through three different embedding layers with the same dimensions that are later summed together and passed to the encoder layer: Token Embedding Layer, Segment Embedding Layer and Position Embedding Layer.

Transformers

Previous work in sequence modeling used the common framework sequence-to-sequence (seq2seq) (Sutskever et al., 2014), with techniques such as recurrent neural networks (RNNs) (Graves, 2013) and long short-term memory (LSTM) (Hochreiter and Schmidhuber, 1997).

The architecture of transformers is not based on RNNs but on attention mechanics (Vaswani et al., 2017), which decides what sequences are important in each computational step. The encoder does not only map the input to a higher dimensional space vector, but also uses the important keywords as additional input to the decoder. This in turn improves the decoder because it has additional information such which sequences are important and which keywords give context to the sentence.

Sentence Pair Classifier Task

Originally, BERT pre-trained the model to obtain word embeddings to make it easier to fine-tune the model for a specific task without having to make a major change in the model and parameters. Usually, only one additional output layer on top of the model was required to make the model more task-specific.

The Sentence Pair Classifier task deals with determining the semantic relations between two sentences. The model takes two texts as input, as described in Section 2.1, and outputs a label representing the type of relation between the sentences. This kind of task evaluates how good a model is on comprehensive understanding of natural language and the ability to do further inference on full sentences (Conneau et al., 2017). There is a benchmark that evaluates natural language understanding on models named general language understanding evaluation (GLUE) (Wang et al., 2018), which consists of several tasks such as multi-genre natural language inference (MNLI) (Williams et al., 2018), the semantic textual similarity benchmark (STS-B) (Cer et al., 2017) and Microsoft research paraphrase corpus (MRPC) (Dolan and Brockett, 2005).

Pre-training tasks

Supervised machine learning tasks are solved training a model from scratch with training data. NLP is a diversified field that contains many distinct tasks for which only small sets of human-labeled training data may be available. It has been proven that a large amount of training data increases the performance of deep learning models, for instance in the computer vision field with ImageNet (Deng et al., 2009). The same concept can be applied to deep language models. The development of a general purpose language model uses large amount of unannotated text, which is called pre-training, and the general purpose for the language model is to learn the contextual representation of words.

Language Models are key components in solving NLP problems and learn word occurrence and word prediction patterns based on unannotated text data. A language model learns the context by using techniques such as word embeddings which use vectors to represent the words in a vector space (Mikolov et al., 2013). With the large amount of training data, the language model learns that representations of words, depending on the context, allows similar words to have a similar representation.

Masked Language Model BERT uses a mask token [MASK] to pre-train deep bidirectional representations for the language model. But as opposed to conditional language models that train left-to-right or right-to-left to predict words, where the predicted word is positioned at the end or at the start of the text sequence, BERT masks a random word in the sequence. The other reason for using a mask token to pre-train is that the standard conditional language models are only able to explicitly train left-to-right or right-to-left because the words can indirectly "see itself" in a multi-layered context.

Next Sentence Prediction is used to understand the relationship between two text sentences. BERT has been pre-trained to predict whether or not there exists a relation between two sentences. Each of these sentences, sentence A and sentence B, has its own embedding dimensions.

Sentence A : [CLS] The man went to the store . [SEP]

Sentence B : He bought a gallon of milk . [SEP]

Label : IsNextSentence

During training, half of the time sentence B is the follow-up of sentence A in half and the IsNextSentence label is used. The other half of the time, a random sentence is chosen for sentence B and the IsNotNextSentence label is used.

2.2 Aspect-Based Sentiment Analysis

ABSA is a more complex task than traditional text-level sentiment analysis. It focuses on identifying the attributes or aspects of an entity mentioned in a text, together with the sentiment expressed towards each aspect.

ABSA was first introduced in SemEval-2014 (Pontiki et al., 2014), which provided a dataset with annotated reviews about restaurants and laptops. The ABSA task in SemEval-2014 did not contain full reviews until SemEval-2015 (Pontiki et al., 2015) and the dataset for SemEval-2016 did not change from 2015 except for additional test data.

The goal of the SemEval-2016 ABSA task is to identify opinions expressed towards specific aspect for a topic within customer reviews. Specifically, given a text review about a certain topic, from the dataset (e.g. laptop, restaurant), the objective for SemEval-2016, the goal is to address the following tasks:

Aspect category classification aims to identify the topic and aspect pair, which an opinion is expressed in the text. The topic and aspect should be chosen from an already defined set of topic types (e.g. LAPTOP, RESTAURANT, FOOD) and aspects (e.g. PRICE, QUALITY) per domain.

Opinion target expression (OTE) is the task of extracting the linguistic expression used in the text input that refers to the reviewed entity, for each entity-aspect pair. The OTE is defined with one starting and ending offsets in the sequence. If no entity is explicitly mentioned, the value returned is "NULL".

Sentiment polarity classification has the objective of predicting the sentiment polarity for each identified topic and aspect pair. The sentiment polarity is a value within the set {positive, negative, neutral, conflict}.

Subtask 1: Sentence Level. The input consists of one sentence, usually obtained from the fully text level text.

Subtask 2: Text Level. The input is a full review, where several aspects can be mentioned simultaneously and also different opinions on the same aspect can be given.

2.3 ABSA without BERT

The submissions that performed best at the SemEval-2016 ABSA challenges used mostly machine learning techniques such as support vector machines (SVM) (Joachims, 1998; Hsu et al., 2003) or conditional random field classifiers (Lafferty et al., 2001). Even though deep learning models have shown to perform well in sentiment analysis (Kim, 2014), the submissions employing deep learning techniques performed poorly that year.

The features used with the SVM were usually contextualized word representations extracted using GloVe (Pennington et al., 2014) or word lists, which were generated by extracting the nouns and adjectives from the datasets.

2.4 ABSA with BERT

BERT has shown to produce good results on NLP tasks (Wang et al., 2018) due to the large amounts of text it has been trained on. For tasks such as ABSA, performance has shown to improve with the help of an additional training on Review text, called Post-Training (Xu et al., 2019). To solve an ABSA task, the Post-Training paper constructed ABSA as a question answering problem, together with a machine reading comprehension technique for reviews called "review reading comprehension".

Solving ABSA as a sentence-pair classification task using BERT by constructing auxiliary sentence has been seen to improve the results, compared to the previous state-of-the-art models that used single-sentence classification (Sun et al., 2019).

3 Experiments

The models implemented in this paper are three: an aspect classification model, a sentiment polarity classification model, and a combined model for both aspect and sentiment classification. The aspect classification model, described in Section 3.4, uses sentence pair classification from BERT (Devlin et al., 2019). As it only predicts whether an aspect is related to a text or not, this model has the possibility to be used for out-of-scope aspects. The sentiment polarity classifier, described in Section 3.3, is a classification model that is trained to determine the sentiment labels (positive, negative, neutral, conflict) for a given aspect and text input. Finally, Section 3.5 explains the last model, which is a combination of both the sentiment and aspect classification models. It outputs a sentiment if the aspect is related, and otherwise it returns the unrelated label.

	Sentence Level			Text Level		
	Restaurant	Laptop	Both	Restaurant	Laptop	Both
Texts	2000	2500	4500	334	395	729
Unique Aspects	12	81	93	12	81	93
Aspects with Sentiment	2507	2908	5415	1435	2082	3517
Aspects without Sentiment	21493	199592	413085	2573	29913	64280
Total Aspects	24000	202500	418500	4008	31995	67797

Table 1: Distribution of data in each training dataset.

3.1 Pre-processing entity and aspect pairs for BERT

The format of the pairs in the SemEval-2016 dataset is originally structured in the form of "ENTITY#ASPECT". In order to fit better the BERT model when training and to be able have the pre-trained data in BERT to be applicable, we formatted it to have a sentence-like structure, so the pair "FOOD#STYLE_OPTIONS" gets parsed into "food, style options". This text is what we use as aspect.

3.2 Data generation

The dataset used in our experiments is reused from SemEval-2016 - Task 5 (Pontiki et al., 2016). Each sample in the dataset contains text that has been annotated with a list of aspects and sentiment polarity which consists of 'positive', 'neutral', 'negative' or 'conflict'. The annotations to be generated are those which have an aspect that are not related to the subject, for example, the text "The food tasted great!" and the aspect 'restaurant, ambience' do not have any relations.

As the dataset has a fixed amount of aspects (e.g. the Restaurant dataset has 12 different unique aspects), we can assume that each aspect that has not been annotated for a specific text is unrelated to said text. The aspects, which are not related to the text will be added to the list of aspects for the text with an 'unrelated' label instead of a sentiment label. Table 1 and Table 6 show the distribution of the original data and our generated data in the training and test dataset respectively.

Unbalanced data

The dataset from SemEval-2016 is originally very unbalanced, it becomes even more so when the unrelated data is generated, as seen in aspects without sentiment compared to aspects with sentiment in Table 1.

To compensate for the imbalance, we weight each label depending on how frequently they show up in the training set. The higher the frequency of a label, the lower the weight of the given label.

3.3 Sentiment Classifier

This is a model for predicting sentiment on a text, given a specific aspect. It is implemented using the architecture of the Sentence Pair classification model explained in Section 2.1, where the first input is the text to be evaluated, and the second input is the aspect that the text will be evaluated on. The output of this model will be one of the labels 'positive', 'negative', 'neutral' and 'conflict', where 'conflict' means that there are parts of the text where the aspect is judged positively and other parts where the aspect judged negatively.

3.4 Aspect Category Classifier

This is a model for aspect classification, with the structure of a Sentence Pair classifier described in Section 2.1, with the text and the aspect as input. This model is used to predict whether or not the aspect is related to the text or not, using labels 'related' and 'unrelated'. With the aspect as input, it is possible to handle out-of-domain aspects, i.e. outside the set of aspects the model was trained on.

3.5 Combined model

This model is structured as a multi-class classifier for predicting both the aspect and the sentiment using the structure of a Sentence Pair classification, described in Section 2.1. The model also takes the text and the aspect as input and returns a sentiment label if the aspect is related to the text, and the unrelated label otherwise.

The model can be used as an entire ABSA structure. It has the possibility to behave as either an aspect category model by mapping the polarity labels to 'related' or it can behave like a sentiment model by ignoring the value of the 'unrelated' label or it can behave as both at the same time.

4 Evaluation

The evaluation is based on the SemEval-2016 Task 5, more specifically the subtasks: aspect categorization in subtask 1 & 2, slot 1 and sentiment polarity in subtask 1 & 2, slot 3. The results for each model implemented are presented in the tables in Table 2a to Table 5c, with the previous state-of-the-art models as baseline.

The Aspect Category Classifier, the Sentiment Classifier, and the Combined Classifier, have all been trained on each dataset described in Table 1. This results in 18 models, where each of these models have been tested on every dataset described in Table 6. However, the text-level Hotel dataset was generated by concatenating all the sentence-level input to a full text and labelling the text with all the aspects corresponding to the sentences, because the Hotel dataset only consisted of the sentence level.

For the results in the tables of this section, we only show the best performing model for model type, in-domain, out-of-domain, text-level and sentence-level model. The dataset in which these models has been tested on can be found in the description of the tables.

4.1 Aspect Category Models

In this section, we evaluate how well the aspect categorization works with our models, which are described in Section 3.4 and Section 3.5. Each is trained in all the different domains and levels described in Table 1. As the performance of aspect category classifiers is only measured with F1-score in SemEval-2016, all the result tables in this section are ordered by F1 score in descending order.

In the tables within this section, the 'Model' column represents which model type it is. The combined model is defined as 'COM' and 'ASP' is the Aspect Category Classifier. The other two columns, Domain and Level, denote which domain and text type it was trained on.

For aspect classification, the text-level datasets in Table 3 produce better results than the sentence-level datasets in Table 2. In both of these tables, the aspect classifiers always outperform the combined classifiers. In out-of-scope evaluations, aspect classification performs better with classifiers that have been trained on datasets with more unique aspects.

Model	Domain	Level	F1	PRE	REC	ACC
ASP	REST	SENL	**79.9**	80.2	79.5	96.3
COM	REST	SENL	77.4	75.9	79.0	95.8
ASP	REST	TEXL	55.5	41.0	85.9	87.4
COM	LAPT	SENL	35.7	30.0	44.1	85.5
Baseline: BERT-PT			78.0	-	-	-
Baseline: NLANGP			73.0	-	-	-

(a) Results of Aspect models on dataset: Restaurant, Sentence-Level. BERT-PT (Xu et al., 2019) and NLANGP (Toh and Su, 2016) as baselines

Model	Domain	Level	F1	PRE	REC	ACC
ASP	BOTH	SENL	**51.7**	40.7	70.6	98.4
ASP	BOTH	TEXL	39.0	27.5	66.7	97.5
COM	BOTH	SENL	38.7	25.5	80.7	96.9
ASP	REST	SENL	5.7	3.0	67.3	73.5
Baseline: NLANGP			**51.9**	-	-	-

(b) Results of Aspect models on dataset: Laptop, Sentence Level. With NLANGP (Toh and Su, 2016) as baseline.

Model	Domain	Level	F1	PRE	REC	ACC
ASP	BOTH	SENL	**34.4**	23.3	65.9	89.1
COM	REST	SENL	34.1	22.9	67.5	88.7
ASP	LAPT	TEXL	33.8	28.2	42.1	92.8

(c) Performance of Aspect models on the dataset: Hotel, Sentence-Level.

Table 2: Best performance of aspect category classifiers in sentence-level datasets

Model	Domain	Level	F1	PRE	REC	ACC
ASP	REST	TEXL	**85.0**	84.2	85.9	88.7
COM	BOTH	TEXL	82.4	78.2	87.1	86.1
ASP	BOTH	SENL	78.8	81.9	76.0	84.7
COM	LAPT	TEXL	68.0	66.4	69.6	75.5
Baseline: GTI			84.0	-	-	-

(a) Results of Aspect models on dataset: Restaurant, Text-Level. Baseline: GTI (Álvarez-López et al., 2016).

Model	Domain	Level	F1	PRE	REC	ACC
ASP	BOTH	TEXL	**64.3**	60.9	68.1	92.3
COM	BOTH	TEXL	63.9	57.4	72.1	91.7
ASP	LAPT	SENL	61.0	58.7	64.6	91.6
COM	REST	SENL	21.6	12.3	87.4	37.0
Baseline: UWB			60.5	-	-	-

(b) Performance of Aspect models on the dataset: Laptop, Text-Level. UWB (Hercig et al., 2016) as baseline.

Model	Domain	Level	F1	PRE	REC	ACC
ASP	BOTH	TEXL	**60.8**	48.3	82.0	62.8
COM	LAPT	TEXL	59.4	53.7	66.4	68.0
COM	BOTH	SENL	58.8	45.2	84.0	58.5
ASP	REST	SENL	56.7	45.0	76.7	58.8

(c) Results of aspect category classifiers on the dataset: Hotel, Text-Level

Table 3: Best performance of aspect category classifiers in text-level datasets

4.2 Sentiment Models

In this section, we evaluate how well the sentiment classification performs with our models, which are described in Section 3.3 and Section 3.5. Each model trained on all the different domains and levels are described in Table 1. The F1 score measured on the tables in this section is a weighted average of the F1 on each label. As the performance of sentiment classifiers are only measured with accuracy in SemEval-2016, all the tables in this section is ordered by accuracy in descending order.

In the tables within this section, the 'Model' column represents which model type it is, 'COM' is the combined model, 'SEN' is the Sentiment Classifier. The other two columns, Domain and Level, is which domain and text type it was trained on.

For sentiment classification, in both Table 4 and Table 5, the combined classifiers always outperformed the sentiment classifiers. In out-of-scope scenarios, the classifiers which have been trained on sentence-level datasets outperform the classifiers which have been trained on the text-level datasets.

Model	Domain	Level	F1	PRE	REC	ACC
COM	BOTH	SENL	89.5	89.5	89.8	**89.8**
SEN	BOTH	SENL	89.2	89.6	89.5	89.5
COM	BOTH	TEXL	83.3	84.0	84.0	84.0
SEN	LAPT	SENL	81.6	84.0	81.2	81.2
Baseline: XRCE			-	-	-	88.1

(a) Performance of Sentiment models on the dataset: Restaurant, Sentence-Level. XRCE (Brun et al., 2016) as baseline.

Model	Domain	Level	F1	PRE	REC	ACC
COM	BOTH	SENL	83.2	83.6	82.8	**82.8**
SEN	LAPT	SENL	82.7	83.0	82.6	82.6
COM	REST	SENL	77.0	75.7	79.0	79.0
COM	BOTH	TEXL	76.2	76.1	76.7	76.7
Baseline: IIT-T			-	-	-	82.8

(b) Performance of Sentiment models on the dataset: Laptop, Sentence-Level. IIT-T (Kumar et al., 2016) as baseline.

Model	Domain	Level	F1	PRE	REC	ACC
COM	BOTH	SENL	90.0	91.0	89.5	**89.5**
SEN	BOTH	SENL	89.0	89.4	88.9	88.9
SEN	REST	SENL	87.0	86.9	87.3	87.3
COM	LAPT	SENL	86.2	86.0	87.0	87.0
COM	BOTH	TEXL	84.2	84.2	84.2	84.2
Baseline: lsislif			-	-	-	85.8

(c) Performance of Sentiment models on the dataset: Hotel, Sentence-Level. Lsislif (Hamdan et al., 2015) as baseline.

Table 4: Best performance of sentiment classifiers in sentence-level datasets

Model	Domain	Level	F1	PRE	REC	ACC
COM	BOTH	SENL	86.3	86.2	87.5	**87.5**
COM	BOTH	TEXL	84.7	84.1	86.6	86.6
SEN	REST	SENL	83.4	81.0	86.3	86.3
COM	LAPT	SENL	80.4	79.9	82.4	82.4
Baseline: UWB			-	-	-	81.9

(a) Results of aspect category classifiers on dataset: Restaurant, Text-Level. Baseline: GTI (Álvarez-López et al., 2016).

Model	Domain	Level	F1	PRE	REC	ACC
COM	BOTH	SENL	79.4	80.8	78.7	**78.7**
COM	REST	SENL	75.6	73.4	78.2	78.2
SEN	BOTH	SENL	77.1	76.7	77.8	77.8
COM	LAPT	TEXL	75.1	74.4	76.7	76.7
Baseline: ECNU			-	-	-	75.0

(b) Performance of Sentiment models on the dataset: Laptop, Text-Level. ECNU (Jiang et al., 2016) as baseline.

Model	Domain	Level	F1	PRE	REC	ACC
COM	BOTH	SENL	86.9	86.5	87.3	**87.3**
COM	REST	SENL	85.5	84.1	87.3	87.3
COM	BOTH	TEXL	85.4	84.9	86.4	86.4
SEN	BOTH	SENL	82.5	81.6	83.8	83.8
COM	LAPT	SENL	82.3	81.1	83.5	83.5

(c) Performance of Sentiment models on the dataset: Hotel, Text-Level

Table 5: Best performance of sentiment classifiers in text-level datasets

5 Discussion

Our proposed out-of-domain implementation performed well in the out-of-domain evaluation. In aspect category for hotels in Table 3c, which our aspect models have not been introduced to before, the model achieved a higher F1 score than the in-domain baseline for laptop F1 score in Table 3b. This shows the potential of using semantic similarities to find features for relations between aspect and a text input. However, to compare these models more in depth, a better measurement would be to look at both precision and recall, as the laptop domain has much more unique aspects, which in turn makes it more likely to predict more false positives which causes a lower precision.

For all the experiments and evaluation, we trained the models on each specific dataset and tried for the others. Our expectation was that the model would be able to improve the performance by using the combined dataset (restaurant & laptop) because it offers more features to use for the aspect classification task. This was not always the case, and we assume it has to

	Sentence Level			Text Level		
	Restaurant	Laptop	Hotel	Restaurant	Laptop	Hotel
Texts	676	782	226	90	80	30
Unique Aspects	12	81	28	12	81	28
Aspects with Sentiment	859	777	339	404	545	215
Aspects without Sentiment	7253	62565	5989	676	5935	625
Total Aspects	8112	63342	6328	1080	6480	840

Table 6: Data distribution in test datasets.

do with the difference between the amount of unique aspects in the domains. The aspect classifiers seem not to work well on the sentence-level test dataset. We suspect that the reason for this is that each sentence does not necessarily have enough information to validate whether an aspect is relevant for a text. A sentence-level text input example is "It wakes up super fast and is always ready to go", which is categorized as "LAPTOP#OPERATION_PERFORMANCE". In the out-of-domain and generalized model, this sentence does not provide the necessary information to make clear that the aspect is related to the sentence and instead can be applied to a lot of other aspects from other domains.

The combined model performs consistently better than the sentiment model in all domains. We believe that the reason for this is that the combined model is trained on a vast volume of "unrelated" data compared to the sentiment model, which allows it to learn to ignore redundant features when predicting the sentiment. However, the combined model performs worse than the aspect model in classifying relevant aspects. We conclude that the reason for this is that the combined model has to find what is relevant, which for this model is defined by the 4 sentiment polarity labels. This increases the complexity compared to the aspect model that was trained specifically on whether or not the aspect is relevant to the text.

A possible reason for why our model improves upon previous state-of-the-art models may be that it uses BERT for the word representation and can then employ the semantic similarities in the different word embeddings for the word, which captures the context, to find sentiments for an aspect in a text. Compared to the previous best models that generate one vector for each word, BERT uses positional word embeddings to generate different word embeddings for each word, depending on its position in the text. Another possible reason is the use of sentence-pair classification to compare the similarities of an aspect to a text instead of the previous best models that used single-sentence classification to determine what aspect is found in a text.

6   Conclusion

In this paper, we proposed an ABSA model that can predict the aspect related to a text for in-domain and out-of-domain. We achieve this by using the pre-trained language model BERT and fine-tuning it to a sentence pair classification model for the ABSA task. Moreover, we train the aspect classifier model with data that we generate, which consist of 'related' and 'unrelated' labels.

We further experimented with this approach for the sentiment classifier, by fine-tuning the model to find a relation between an aspect and a text and to make the model learn when the contextual representation showed a sentiment context. Furthermore, we proposed a combined model that can classify both aspect and sentiment using only one sentence pair classification model. Experimental results show that the combined model outperforms previous state-of-the-art results for aspect based sentiment classification.

References

Tamara Álvarez-López, Jonathan Juncal-Martínez, Milagros Fernández Gavilanes, Enrique Costa-Montenegro, and Francisco Javier González-Castaño. 2016. Gti at semeval-2016 task 5: Svm and crf for aspect detection and unsupervised aspect-based sentiment analysis. In *SemEval@NAACL-HLT*.

Caroline Brun, Julien Perez, and Claude Roux. 2016. XRCE at SemEval-2016 task 5: Feedbacked ensemble modeling on syntactico-semantic knowledge for aspect based sentiment analysis. In *Proceedings of the 10th International Workshop on Semantic Evaluation (SemEval-2016)*, pages 277–281, San Diego, California. Association for Computational Linguistics.

Daniel Cer, Mona Diab, Eneko Agirre, Iñigo Lopez-Gazpio, and Lucia Specia. 2017. SemEval-2017 task 1: Semantic textual similarity multilingual and crosslingual focused evaluation. In *Proceedings of the 11th International Workshop on Semantic Evaluation (SemEval-2017)*, pages 1–14, Vancouver, Canada. Association for Computational Linguistics.

Alexis Conneau, Douwe Kiela, Holger Schwenk, Loïc Barrault, and Antoine Bordes. 2017. Supervised learning of universal sentence representations from natural language inference data. In *Proceedings of the 2017 Conference on Empirical Methods in Natural Language Processing*, pages 670–680, Copenhagen, Denmark. Association for Computational Linguistics.

J. Deng, W. Dong, R. Socher, L. Li, Kai Li, and Li Fei-Fei. 2009. Imagenet: A large-scale hierarchical image database. In *2009 IEEE Conference on Computer Vision and Pattern Recognition*, pages 248–255.

Jacob Devlin, Ming-Wei Chang, Kenton Lee, and Kristina Toutanova. 2019. BERT: Pre-training of deep bidirectional transformers for language understanding. In *Proceedings of the 2019 Conference of the North American Chapter of the Association for Computational Linguistics: Human Language Technologies, Volume 1 (Long and Short Papers)*, pages 4171–4186, Minneapolis, Minnesota. Association for Computational Linguistics.

William B. Dolan and Chris Brockett. 2005. Automatically constructing a corpus of sentential paraphrases. In *Proceedings of the Third International Workshop on Paraphrasing (IWP2005)*.

Alex Graves. 2013. Generating sequences with recurrent neural networks. *CoRR*, abs/1308.0850.

Hussam Hamdan, Patrice Bellot, and Frederic Bechet. 2015. Lsislif: CRF and logistic regression for opinion target extraction and sentiment polarity analysis. In *Proceedings of the 9th International Workshop on Semantic Evaluation (SemEval 2015)*, pages 753–758, Denver, Colorado. Association for Computational Linguistics.

Tomáš Hercig, Tomáš Brychcín, Lukáš Svoboda, and Michal Konkol. 2016. UWB at SemEval-2016 task 5: Aspect based sentiment analysis. In *Proceedings of the 10th International Workshop on Semantic Evaluation (SemEval-2016)*, pages 342–349, San Diego, California. Association for Computational Linguistics.

Sepp Hochreiter and Jürgen Schmidhuber. 1997. Long short-term memory. *Neural Comput.*, 9(8):1735–1780.

Chih-Wei Hsu, Chih-Chung Chang, and Chih-Jen Lin. 2003. A practical guide to support vector classification. Technical report, Department of Computer Science, National Taiwan University.

Mengxiao Jiang, Zhihua Zhang, and Man Lan. 2016. ECNU at SemEval-2016 task 5: Extracting effective features from relevant fragments in sentence for aspect-based sentiment analysis in reviews. In *Proceedings of the 10th International Workshop on Semantic Evaluation (SemEval-2016)*, pages 361–366, San Diego, California. Association for Computational Linguistics.

Thorsten Joachims. 1998. Text categorization with support vector machines: Learning with many relevant features. In *Proceedings of the 10th European Conference on Machine Learning*, ECML'98, pages 137–142, Berlin, Heidelberg. Springer-Verlag.

Yoon Kim. 2014. Convolutional neural networks for sentence classification. In *Proceedings of the 2014 Conference on Empirical Methods in Natural Language Processing (EMNLP)*, pages 1746–1751, Doha, Qatar. Association for Computational Linguistics.

Ayush Kumar, Sarah Kohail, Amit Kumar, Asif Ekbal, and Chris Biemann. 2016. IIT-TUDA at SemEval-2016 task 5: Beyond sentiment lexicon: Combining domain dependency and distributional semantics features for aspect based sentiment analysis. In *Proceedings of the 10th International Workshop on Semantic Evaluation (SemEval-2016)*, pages 1129–1135, San Diego, California. Association for Computational Linguistics.

John D. Lafferty, Andrew McCallum, and Fernando C. N. Pereira. 2001. Conditional random fields: Probabilistic models for segmenting and labeling sequence data. In *Proceedings of the Eighteenth International Conference on Machine Learning*, ICML '01, pages 282–289, San Francisco, CA, USA. Morgan Kaufmann Publishers Inc.

Tomas Mikolov, Kai Chen, Greg Corrado, and Jeffrey Dean. 2013. Efficient estimation of word representations in vector space.

Jeffrey Pennington, Richard Socher, and Christopher Manning. 2014. Glove: Global vectors for word representation. In *Proceedings of the 2014 Conference on Empirical Methods in Natural Language Processing (EMNLP)*, pages 1532–1543, Doha, Qatar. Association for Computational Linguistics.

Matthew Peters, Mark Neumann, Mohit Iyyer, Matt Gardner, Christopher Clark, Kenton Lee, and Luke Zettlemoyer. 2018. Deep contextualized word representations. In *Proceedings of the 2018 Conference of the North American Chapter of the Association for Computational Linguistics: Human Language Technologies, Volume 1 (Long Papers)*, pages 2227–2237, New Orleans, Louisiana. Association for Computational Linguistics.

Maria Pontiki, Dimitrios Galanis, John Pavlopoulos, Harris Papageorgiou, Ion Androutsopoulos, and Suresh Manandhar. 2014. Semeval-2014 task 4: Aspect based sentiment analysis. *Proceedings of the*

8th international workshop on semantic evaluation (SemEval 2014), pages 27–35.

Maria Pontiki, Dimitris Galanis, Haris Papageorgiou, Ion Androutsopoulos, Suresh Manandhar, Mohammed AL-Smadi, Mahmoud Al-Ayyoub, Yanyan Zhao, Bing Qin, Orphée De Clercq, Veronique Hoste, Marianna Apidianaki, Xavier Tannier, Natalia Loukachevitch, Evgeniy Kotelnikov, Núria Bel, Salud Maria Jiménez-Zafra, and Gülşen Eryiğit. 2016. Semeval-2016 task 5 : aspect based sentiment analysis. In *Proceedings of the 10th International Workshop on Semantic Evaluation (SemEval-2016)*, pages 19–30. Association for Computational Linguistics.

Maria Pontiki, Dimitris Galanis, Haris Papageorgiou, Suresh Manandhar, and Ion Androutsopoulos. 2015. SemEval-2015 task 12: Aspect based sentiment analysis. In *Proceedings of the 9th International Workshop on Semantic Evaluation (SemEval 2015)*, pages 486–495, Denver, Colorado. Association for Computational Linguistics.

Hasim Sak, Andrew W. Senior, and Franoise Beaufays. 2014. Long short-term memory recurrent neural network architectures for large scale acoustic modeling. In *INTERSPEECH*, pages 338–342.

Chi Sun, Luyao Huang, and Xipeng Qiu. 2019. Utilizing BERT for aspect-based sentiment analysis via constructing auxiliary sentence. In *Proceedings of the 2019 Conference of the North American Chapter of the Association for Computational Linguistics: Human Language Technologies, Volume 1 (Long and Short Papers)*, pages 380–385, Minneapolis, Minnesota. Association for Computational Linguistics.

Ilya Sutskever, Oriol Vinyals, and Quoc V. Le. 2014. Sequence to sequence learning with neural networks. In *Proceedings of the 27th International Conference on Neural Information Processing Systems - Volume 2*, NIPS'14, pages 3104–3112, Cambridge, MA, USA. MIT Press.

Zhiqiang Toh and Jian Su. 2016. NLANGP at SemEval-2016 task 5: Improving aspect based sentiment analysis using neural network features. In *Proceedings of the 10th International Workshop on Semantic Evaluation (SemEval-2016)*, pages 282–288, San Diego, California. Association for Computational Linguistics.

Ashish Vaswani, Noam Shazeer, Niki Parmar, Jakob Uszkoreit, Llion Jones, Aidan N. Gomez, Lukasz Kaiser, and Illia Polosukhin. 2017. Attention is all you need.

Alex Wang, Amanpreet Singh, Julian Michael, Felix Hill, Omer Levy, and Samuel Bowman. 2018. GLUE: A multi-task benchmark and analysis platform for natural language understanding. In *Proceedings of the 2018 EMNLP Workshop BlackboxNLP: Analyzing and Interpreting Neural Networks for NLP*, pages 353–355, Brussels, Belgium. Association for Computational Linguistics.

Adina Williams, Nikita Nangia, and Samuel Bowman. 2018. A broad-coverage challenge corpus for sentence understanding through inference. In *Proceedings of the 2018 Conference of the North American Chapter of the Association for Computational Linguistics: Human Language Technologies, Volume 1 (Long Papers)*, pages 1112–1122, New Orleans, Louisiana. Association for Computational Linguistics.

Yonghui Wu, Mike Schuster, Zhifeng Chen, Quoc V. Le, Mohammad Norouzi, Wolfgang Macherey, Maxim Krikun, Yuan Cao, Qin Gao, Klaus Macherey, Jeff Klingner, Apurva Shah, Melvin Johnson, Xiaobing Liu, ukasz Kaiser, Stephan Gouws, Yoshikiyo Kato, Taku Kudo, Hideto Kazawa, Keith Stevens, George Kurian, Nishant Patil, Wei Wang, Cliff Young, Jason Smith, Jason Riesa, Alex Rudnick, Oriol Vinyals, Greg Corrado, Macduff Hughes, and Jeffrey Dean. 2016. Google's neural machine translation system: Bridging the gap between human and machine translation.

Hu Xu, Bing Liu, Lei Shu, and Philip S. Yu. 2019. Bert post-training for review reading comprehension and aspect-based sentiment analysis.

Political Stance Detection for Danish

Rasmus Lehmann
ITU Copenhagen
Denmark
`rasmus_lehmann@hotmail.com`

Leon Derczynski
ITU Copenhagen
Denmark
`ld@itu.dk`

Abstract

The task of stance detection consists of classifying the opinion expressed within a text towards some target. This paper presents a dataset of quotes from Danish politicians, labelled for stance, and also stance detection results in this context. Two deep learning-based models are designed, implemented and optimized for political stance detection. The simplest model design, applying no conditionality, and word embeddings averaged across quotes, yields the strongest results. Furthermore, it was found that inclusion of the quote's utterer and the party affiliation of the quoted politician, greatly improved performance of the strongest model.

Dansk abstrakt: I indeværende artikel præsenteres et annoteret datasæt over citater fra danske politikere, samt to Deep Learning-baserede modeller til brug ved identifikation af holdninger i de annoterede citater. Det konkluderes at den simpleste af de to modeller opnår de bedste resultater, samt at brug af information vedrørende citaternes kontekst forbedrer modellernes resultater.

1   Introduction

As a result of digitalization, the availability of information regarding the state of politics has never been greater, interviews, debates, party programs and articles all readily available online. This can be seen as a democratic benefit, contributing to the enlightenment of the population, giving individuals a basis on which to form their opinions and place their votes. However, the large amount of information available means the time required for keeping up to date on the state of politics becomes increasingly higher. A partial solution to this problem is to convert textual data into quantitative data, representing a large amount of text in a more compact fashion. This can be achieved using Natural Language Processing (NLP), the field concerned with the automatic parsing, analysis and understanding of text. Within this field is the task of stance detection, concerned with discerning the stance in a text towards some target. Building a model which can accurately solve the task of stance detection can help generate quantitative data regarding the state of Danish politics.

The objective of this work is two-fold; creating a dataset of quotes from politicians labelled for stance, allowing statistical analysis of opinions within parties and for each politician, and building a machine learning-based stance detection model, able to determine the stances within quotes in the generated dataset.

The task of collecting data for the dataset is defined as the extraction of quotes from news articles for all political parties within the Danish parliament. Here, considerations are made regarding the objectivity of the collected data, both taking into account the subjectivity of journalists, media outlets and the researcher.

The task of data labelling will be performed using the labels *for*, *against* and *neutral*. For this task, the subjectivity of the researcher is the primary concern, in regards to the objectivity and general applicability of the dataset.

The task of stance detection is defined as the automatic detection of a stance within a given quote towards some target, using the stance classes *for* and *against* the target, or as neither *for* nor *against* the target, which we call *neutral*. The goal of this work is to create a model which can perform this task, both to be used as a tool for political analysis and to expand the generated dataset by automatic labelling of quotes, as well as to be used as a benchmark for further research within the field of NLP in Danish.

2   Related Work

Stance detection has been addressed through a number of different model approaches, including probabilistic classifiers (Qazvinian et al., 2011), kernel-based classifiers (Mohammad et al., 2017; Enayet and El-Beltagy, 2017; Collins and Duffy, 2001) and ensemble learners (Zeng et al., 2016; Tutek et al., 2016). Recently, deep learning approaches have shown promise at this task. The two top performing teams of SemEval 2016 Task 6 both applied deep learning models (Zarrella and Marsh, 2016; Wei et al., 2016) as did those in RumourEval 2019 (Gorrell et al., 2019).

The task of stance detection has been applied widely within political analysis, both analyzing the stance of politicians towards a given topic (Lai et al., 2016; Skeppstedt et al., 2017), as is the task within this paper, and also to identify the stance of individuals towards some politician or policy (Aker et al., 2017; Augenstein et al., 2016; Mohammad et al., 2016; Johnson and Goldwasser, 2016; Iyyer et al., 2014). For several of these cases, the stance target has been mentioned explicitly in the data. This is not necessarily the case for the dataset generated for this paper, increasing the difficulty of the task significantly. Furthermore, all of these examples perform stance detection for English, whereas the dataset generated for this data is in Danish. This further increases the difficulty of the task, as fewer resources are available.

Enevoldsen and Hansen (2017) perform sentiment analysis in Danish using newspaper articles, using the AFINN dictionary over sentiment of Danish words (Årup Nielsen, 2011), performing ternary classification of articles using *for*, *against* and *neutral* labels. However, no research has been done within political stance detection in Danish (Kirkedal et al., 2019), and only very recently has any work been done for stance in Danish in the first place – just Lillie et al. (2019), published at the same time as this paper.

3   Data

We assembled a dataset of quotes from Danish politicians, extracted from articles from the Danish media outlet Ritzau. Considerations were made regarding the objectivity of the collected data, and seeing as Ritzau is owned by a conglomerate of media outlets from all areas of the political spectrum (Ritzau, 2019), it is assumed that articles from the media outlet will not contain bias

towards any given party. A data statement (Bender and Friedman, 2018) is in the appendix.

A shortlist of possible topics to include in the dataset was attained based on an opinion poll executed by Kvalvik (2017), seeking to identify the topics most important to the Danish population, when voting in the next election. Here, the five most important topics were identified as health policy, social policy, immigration policy, crime and justice policy and finally environment and climate policy. Immigration policy was chosen as the topic to be included in the dataset, due to alternative topics being defined too broadly to easily allow a clear definition of annotation guidelines.

3.1   Choice of Politicians

To accurately represent the full spectrum of Danish legislative politics, politicians from all political parties with seats in parliament are included in the dataset. From each party, ten politicians have been chosen for inclusion in the dataset. Politicians with seats in parliament have been prioritized over those without seats. For the parties with more than ten politicians in parliament, prioritization has been made as follows:

1. Ministers
2. Party heads
3. Speakers

    (a) Speakers within the five top topics of interest to the Danish population as presented by (Kvalvik, 2017)
    (b) Speakers not within the five top topics

4. Non-speaker Members of parliament

Considerations were made regarding the gender representativity within the dataset. The metrics just described yields the gender distribution presented in Table 1. It can be observed that the approach creates a skewed gender distribution of included politicians, but the skewness is judged to be within a reasonable margin, with 58% male and 42% female politicians.

3.2   Data Labelling

The choice of labelling convention is based on that applied by Mohammad et al. (2016) in organizing SemEval-2016 Task 6, which is concerned with the detection of stance within tweets, and the creation of a dataset for this task. Three classes are defined along which quotes are labelled, the first called *for*, declaring support of a given topic, the

Party	Males		Females	
	Count	%	Count	%
Alternativet	7	70	3	30
Dansk Folkeparti	5	50	5	50
Det Konservative Folkeparti	6	60	4	40
Enhedslisten	7	70	3	30
Liberal Alliance	6	60	4	40
Radikale Venstre	5	50	5	50
Socialdemokratiet	7	70	3	30
Socialistisk Folkeparti	3	30	7	70
Venstre	6	60	4	40
Total	**52**	**58**	**38**	**42**

Table 1: Gender distribution of dataset per party

second called *against*, declaring opposition to a given topic, and a third, called *neutral*, contains both quotes that are deemed to be neutral towards the topic, as well as quotes for which a specific stance can not be determined. During the initial labelling efforts, it was observed that not all gathered quotes could be categorized along the same axis, and it was therefore decided to divide the dataset into sub-topics.

3.2.1 Defining Sub-topics

A clear division of the dataset was found along whether the quote concerned immigration issues in the context of within the borders of Denmark, or in a more global context. The sub-topic National immigration policy (*national policy* for short) was defined as policy and topics that concern matters within Danish borders, such as the number of asylum seekers the country takes in, how these are housed, and what requirements should be set for them in regards to taking Danish education and employment. An example of a quote within this subtopic can be found below, which concerns the government's initiative to combat communities that they define as ghettos.

> *Det er godt, at der lægges op til højere straffe og en styrket politiindsats i ghettoer. Men regeringen skal passe på ikke at oversælge sit udspil. Det kan ikke løse alle problemer.*

> *It is good that harsher penalties and an increased police effort in ghettos is encouraged. But the government should be careful not to over-sell its proposal. It can not solve all problems.*
> Martin Henriksen, (Ritzau, 2018b)

Centralized immigration policy (*centralization* for short) is defined as policy and topics that concern immigration on a European or international level, for example distribution of asylum seekers among the member countries of EU, deterring immigrants at EU's boarders or the sending of im-

migrant from Denmark to refugee camps in other countries. An example of such a quote is:

> *Den danske regering bør i stedet sige til den italienske regering, at Danmark og Italien i fæl-lesskab kan transportere asylansøgerne tilbage til Afrika, så de kan blive sat af på kyste.*

> *The Danish government should instead tell the Italian government that Denmark and Italy can transport the asylum seekers back to Africa together, where they can be set ashore on the coast.*
> Martin Henriksen, (Ritzau, 2018f)

Some quotes fit both subtopics. In these cases, a duplicate quote is created, and one is labelled with each subtopic. An example of this is found below, where first half of the quote is concerning the free mobility of labour within EU, and immigration stemming from this, and the second half is concerned with the effect on immigration legislation changes on a Danish level.

> *Det er oplagt at se på, hvordan vi kan understøtte en højere grad af mobilitet i Europa, så danske virksomheder, der har brug for arbejdskraft, kan få den, uden det betyder den indvandring, som vil følge af at sætte beløbsgrænsen ned.*

> *It would be natural to look at, how we can support a higher level of mobility in Europe, so Danish companies that need laborers can get them, without it resulting in the immi-gration, which would result from lowering the threshold.*
> Mette Frederiksen, (Ritzau, 2018d)

3.2.2 Annotation Guidelines

The subtopic *national policy* is defined as tightening the policy within the borders of Denmark on the legislative fields of immigration, integration and asylum. Therefore, a quote would be classified as *for* this topic, if it exhibits one or more of the following traits.

- support for higher restrictions on immigrants or asylum seekers entering the country

- support for lowering public benefits to immigrants or asylum seekers

- a wish to get immigrants or asylum seekers to leave Denmark, after they have entered the country

- making demands specifically of immigrants or asylum seekers, for instance regarding taking language courses or job search

- seeking to make immigrants or asylum seekers change their culture or behaviour

- communicating explicitly or implicitly that immigration is a burden to Danish society

- wishing to implement changes in behaviour though negative incentives such as decreased public benefits

Quotes classified as *against* the *national policy* subtopic, on the other hand, will exhibit one or more of the following traits.

- support for lower restrictions on immigrants or asylum seekers entering the country

- support for higher public benefits to immigrants or asylum seekers

- immigrants or asylum seekers are free to stay, after having entered the country

- seeking to making fewer demands of, and give more freedom to, immigrants or asylum seekers

- not seeking to make immigrants or asylum seekers change their culture or behaviour

- communicating explicitly or implicitly that immigration is an asset to Danish society

- wishing to implement changes in behaviour though positive incentives such as increased public benefits

The subtopic *centralization* is defined as yielding decision power to EU, and/or solving more immigration issues on a European or international level, rather than on a national level, and *for* and *against* labels are thus more clearly defined for this subtopic. A *for* quote would support yielding power, an example of which is found below.

> *Europa har en fælles udfordring med flygtninge og migranter. Vi må have et fælles asylsystem.*

> *Europe has a mutual challenge with refugees and immigrants. We must have a common asylum system.*
> Rasmus Nordqvist, (Ritzau, 2018a)

On the other hand, an *against* quote would be opposed to yielding power, an example of which is found below.

> *Der er for mange spørgsmål, som står ubesvaret hen, og derfor mener vi, at man fra dansk side skal suspendere det samarbejde, indtil der er fuldstændig klarhed over, hvad regeringen har forpligtet sig til på Danmarks vegne.*

> *There are too many questions left unanswered, and therefore we believe that Denmark should suspend the collaborative efforts, until there is complete clarity regarding what the government has committed itself to on behalf of Denmark.*
> Martin Henriksen, (Ritzau, 2018g)

3.2.3 Resolving Grey Areas

Not all quotes contain explicit communication of a stance or even clear indicators, like the ones just described. To solve this issue, inspiration is taken from Mohammad et al. (2016), and the questions given to annotators. In line with Mohammad et al. (2016), when labelling quotes, stance is inferred from how the quotee refers to things and people aligned with or opposed to the topic. An example of this would be a politician indicating support towards a ban on the use of burkas, which falls within the subtopic of *national policy*. Seeing as the ban on burkas is a restriction of behaviour, the quote would be labelled as *for*, as the stance of the quote can be induced by proxy. Furthermore, when no clear stance is communicated, and no stance can be determined by proxy, the tone of the quote is analyzed, looking at the use of weighted words, for instance describing immigrants as resources, nuisances or in neutral terms.

4 Annotated Dataset

Looking at the quote count for the dataset as presented in Table 2, it is clear that the dataset is significantly skewed towards the *for* label, containing 57.2% of the quotes, with 23.4% labeled as *against* and 19.3% as neutral when observing the full dataset, and the skewness remains if looking at the two subsets in isolation. Such skewness has shown to be an issue for stance detection models in earlier research, an example of this being the SemEval-2017 competition Task 8, where the dataset contained a majority label with 66% of the data points in the train set and 74% of data points in the test set (Derczynski et al., 2017).

Another potential issue for the stance detection task is the size of the dataset, as a size of 898 instances might not be sufficient to learn the language patterns within the quotes.

4.1 Assessing Representativity in the Dataset

Out of the 90 politicians chosen to be included in the dataset, relevant quotes were only found in the

Party	Topic	F	A	N	Total
Alternativet	NP		7	2	9
	C	2			2
	Total	2	7	2	11
Dansk Folkeparti	NP	187	5	25	217
	C	5	18	7	30
	Total	192	23	32	247
Det Konservative Folkeparti	NP	18	1	5	24
	C	2			2
	Total	20	1	5	26
Enhedslisten	NP	3	26	5	34
	C		4	1	5
	Total	3	30	6	39
Liberal Alliance	NP	6	6	6	18
	C				0
	Total	6	6	6	18
Radikale Venstre	NP	7	68	18	93
	C	6		1	7
	Total	13	68	19	100
Socialdemokratiet	NP	92	20	42	154
	C	7	1	1	9
	Total	99	21	43	163
Socialistisk Folkeparti	NP	5	26	2	33
	C	2			2
	Total	7	26	2	35
Venstre	NP	144	14	54	212
	C	38	1	8	47
	Total	182	15	62	259
All parties	NP	462	173	159	**794**
	C	62	24	18	**104**
	Total	**524**	**197**	**177**	**898**

Table 2: Quote count overview for dataset, NP denoting *national policy*, C denoting *centralization*, F denoting For, A denoting Against and N denoting Neutral.

Ritzau database for 63 politicians. This might constitute an issue in terms of representativity, if a certain gender, party or political orientation is more likely to be quoted by news outlets.

Dividing parties based on their placement on the political axis, defining Alternativet, Enhedslisten, Radikale Venstre, Socialdemokratiet and Socialistisk Folkeparti as left-wing parties and Dansk Folkeparti, Det Konservative Folkeparti, Liberal Alliance and Venstre as right-wing parties, a skewness towards the right-wing parties within the dataset can be observed, as seen in Table 3. We observe an over-representation of right-wing parties with 61% of the quotes.

	Left-wing	Right-wing	Total
For	400	124	479
Neutral	105	72	177
Against	45	152	197
Total	**550**	**348**	**898**

Table 3: Quote count divided by political axis

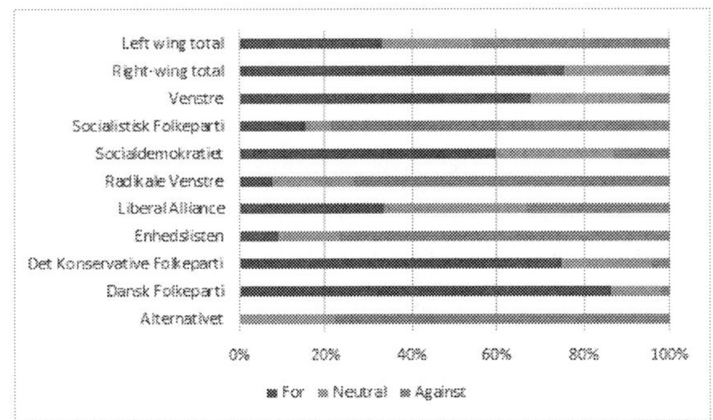

Figure 1: Quote distribution for the subtopic *national policy* between the labels for, against and neutral, for each party, in percentage, totals calculated as sums of quotes

Similarly, a skewness towards the male gender can be observed in the data, shown in Table 4. This is, however, likely to be a reflection of the skewness in the number of male and female politicians included in the party, observed in Table 1.

	Male	Female
For	316	208
Against	124	72
Neutral	98	80
Total	**538**	**360**
%	60	40

Table 4: Quote count divided by gender

The skewness of data, as presented within this section, is likely to constitute a weakness in any classifier built on the dataset, as the classifier will likely be better at recognizing quotes from right-wing than from left-wing parties, and from males than from females.

4.2 Quote Distribution within Parties

Figure 1 shows the distribution of policy quotes on one topic, over parties. Alternativet is the only party univocally against implementing tighter immigration policy. Enhedslisten, Radikale Venstre and Socialistisk Folkeparti are largely *against*, with approximately 80% of quotes within this class. It is worth noting that the quote distributions of both Socialdemokratiet and Liberal Alliance differ significantly from the rest of the parties within their half of the political spectrum, and to a higher degree resembles that of their political opponents. With a *for* distribution of 60%, Socialdemokratiet resides more closely to the right-wing total of 75% than the 32% of the left-wing total, and with a *for* distribution of 32% Liberal Alliance matches that of the left-wing total. However, Liberal Alliance has a lower *against* quote distribution than the left-wing total, and Socialdemokratiet has a larger *against* distribution than the right-wing total. Venstre, Det Konservative Folkeparti and Dansk Folkeparti all have a very low *against* distribution, with Dansk Folkeparti holding the smallest at just a few %.

5 Method

Pretrained fastText word embeddings of size 300 are used as word representations. These are supplemented by what will be denoted as context-based features. These consists of two sets of one-hot embeddings, representing the politicians present in the dataset and the nine parties presently in the Danish parliament respectively. For each quote, a context-based feature vector is generated with a flag raised at the index of the politician behind the quote, and the party affiliation of this politician.

5.1 LSTM Implementation

The initial approach in classifying the stances within the quote dataset was based on a recurrent LSTM-based architecture (Hochreiter and Schmidhuber, 1997), applying forget gate (f_t), input gate (i_t), cell state (C_t), output gate (o_t) and the output vector (h_t) as:

$$H = \begin{bmatrix} h_{t-1} \\ x_t \end{bmatrix}$$
$$f_t = \sigma(W_f \times H + b_f)$$
$$i_t = \sigma(W_i \times H + b_i)$$
$$C_t = f_t \times C_{t-1} + i_t \times tanh(W_c \times H + b_c)$$
$$o_t = \sigma(W_o \times H + b_o)$$
$$h_t = o_t \times tanh(C_t)$$

x_t denotes the input vector at time step t, and h_{t-1} denotes the output of the model at time step t-1. W denotes trainable weight matrices and b denotes trainable biases. By using an LSTM, it was sought to preserve knowledge of long-range dependencies between words, while circumventing the vanishing and exploding gradient problem (Pascanu et al., 2013).

5.1.1 Conditional Encoding

The first model implemented, denoted Conditional LSTM, applies conditionality, inspired by Augenstein et al. (2016), by initializing the LSTM layer

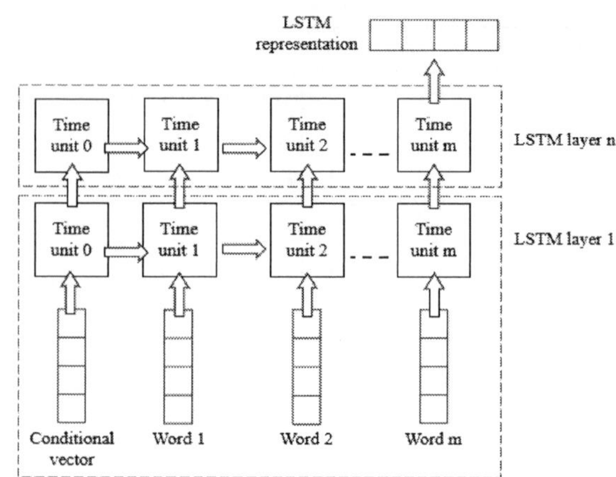

Figure 2: Diagram of Conditional LSTM layer(s)

at time step t_0 on the one-hot embedding representing the quoted politician, and the party of said politician. Thus, the model learns politician and party-dependent quote representations.

The model takes a quote as input, generated as a matrix of word embeddings of the size $E \times L$, E denoting the word embedding size, 300 for the FastText embeddings used within this paper, L denoting the length of the quote. For any value x_i in the quote embedding matrix, it is true that $x_i \in R | -1 \leq x_i \leq 1$. At each time step, the model takes a single word embedding as input. This LSTM layer type is depicted in Figure 2.

5.2 Multi-Layered Perceptron

The second model is a simple multi-layered perceptron (Rosenblatt, 1961), denoted MLP, which applies average quote embeddings, generated as vectors where the value of the vector is the average of all word embeddings in the quote. The vector will be of length 300, when using the FastText word embeddings, and for a quote of length N, average quote embeddings are calculated as:

$$x_i = \frac{\sum_{i=0}^{N} x_{word}}{N}$$

Quote embeddings are concatenated with the one-hot representation of the quoted politician and the politician's party affiliation. See Figure 3.

5.3 Full Model Architecture

The number of deep learning layers are variable, and used as a parameter in hyperparameter search. The output of the deep learning layers are passed

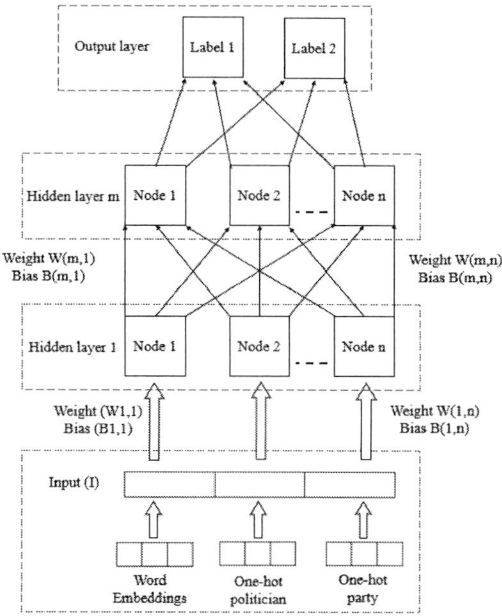

Figure 3: Diagram of Multi-layered perceptron layer(s)

Full Dataset

	GNB	RF	Cond.	MLP
$F1_{macro}$	0.266	0.387	0.375	**0.575**
$F1_{micro}$	0.306	0.461	0.400	**0.717**
F_{acc}	0.442	0.267	0.580	**0.826**
A_{acc}	**0.6**	0.2	0.244	0.120
N_{acc}	0.029	**0.797**	0.440	**0.797**

National Policy dataset

	GNB	RF	Cond.	MLP
$F1_{macro}$	0.254	0.435	0.358	**0.585**
$F1_{micro}$	0.283	0.560	0.372	**0.774**
F_{acc}	0.337	0.525	0.256	**0.963**
A_{acc}	**0.696**	0.435	0.480	0.043
N_{acc}	0.036	0.821	0.478	**0.804**

Table 5: Performance comparison of all models, including benchmark models, using optimized hyperparameters, GNB referring to Gaussian Naïve Bayes, RF referring to Random Forest

to a number of linear layers containing ReLU activation functions (Richard H. R. Hahnloser and Seung, 2000), the number of which are likewise used as a parameter in hyperparameter search, followed by a softmax layer allowing for classification and optimization using categoric cross entropy loss. Both models had the number of deep learning layers and units, number of ReLU layers and units and L2 optimized, using a grid-wise search of the hyperparameter space. A learning rate of 0.001 and dropout of 0.5 is applied to both models.

6 Results and Analysis

The overall evaluation of the three models was performed with the full dataset, as well as with the *national policy* subset, using the optimal hyperparameters. No experiments were made using only the *centralization* dataset, as this was deemed too small at a quote count of just 104. The models were compared on both $F1_{micro}$ and $F1_{macro}$. However, due to the skewed label distribution within the dataset, as pointed out in Section 4, $F1_{macro}$ is the primary metric for model evaluation.

Seeing as the dataset was generated specifically for this piece of research, there exists no prior benchmarks with which to compare the models. For this reason, two benchmark models are built, namely a Gaussian Naive Bayes classifier and Random Forest classifier, both out-of-the-box implementations from the scikit-learn Python library (Pedregosa et al., 2011).

There are three majority-based baselines. The first majority baseline-based model uses the overall majority class of the full dataset to classify quotes. The second applies the majority class for each politician to classify quotes from that politician, and the third model does the same, instead using the majority class for each party.

6.1 Model Comparison

From Table 5 it can be observed that the MLP outperforms all four other models in terms of $F1_{macro}$ on both the full and *national policy* datasets. The MLP also performs best in regards to $F1_{micro}$ on both the full dataset and the *national policy* dataset.

Table 6 show that the MLP model out-performs both majority baseline models in terms of $F1_{macro}$. However, the politician-level baseline outperforms the MLP in terms of $F1_{micro}$.

	$F1_{macro}$	$F1_{micro}$
MLP	**0.575**	0.717
Majority	0.253	0.611
Majority$_{pol}$	0.299	**0.835**
Majority$_{party}$	0.270	0.696

Table 6: Comparison of majority baseline performance to MLP performance

Policy dataset				Full dataset			
	F	A	N		F	A	N
F	77	0	3	F	22	52	1
A	8	15	2	A	5	16	2
N	10	57	2	N	2	52	2

Table 7: Confusion matrices for Multi-layered perceptron, using optimized hyperparameters

6.2 Misclassification Analysis

Table 7 shows the confusion matrix for the MLP, run with optimal hyperparameters on both the full and *national policy* dataset, can be found. For both datasets, the strength of the MLP is its ability to correctly classify *for* and *neutral* quotes. As a function of this, the model more or less ignores the *against* class, in pursuit of correctly classifying the two larger classes instead. A tendency can be observed towards classifying *against*-quotes as *for*, and to some extend also misclassifying some *neutral* quotes as *for*. This is not surprising, *for* being the majority class. Both the *against*-quotes and *neutral*-quotes classified as *for* are generally found to contain a large number of negative words targeting some other topic than immigration. Generally, the quotes within the *for* label apply a large number of negative words, suggesting that the classifiers mis-interpret the target of the negative words. An example of a *neutral*-quote labeled as *for* is:

> *Det er ingen hemmelighed, at vi i Dansk Folkeparti opfatter Dansk Industri som meget manipulerende og utroværdig i diskussionen om udenlandsk arbejdskraft.*

> *It is no secret that we in Dansk Folkeparti perceive Dansk Industri as being very manipulative and untrustworthy in the debate regarding foreign labor.*
> Martin Henriksen, (Ritzau, 2018c)

And an example of an *against* quote:

> *Det er bestemt ikke problemfrit at integrere flygtninge. Men løsningen er da ikke at eksportere problemerne til for eksempel Nordafrika, hvor man i forvejen står med en kæmpemæssig opgave.*

> *Integrating refugees is definitely not without its challenges. But the solution is not to export the problem to, for instance, North Africa, where the region is already faced with a huge task.*
> Johanne Schmidt Nielsen, (Ritzau, 2018e)

6.3 Post-hoc Exploratory Experiments

Additional experiments were performed using the MLP trained on the full dataset, to gain additional insight into the model's performance.

6.3.1 The Effect of Context-based Features

Comparing Table 8 and Table 5, it can be observed that removal of either party or politician from the context-based features significantly reduces the MLP's results. A model applying a feature vector composed only of the two context-based features out-performs models applying combinations of the text-based features and one of the two context-based features, but is in turn out-performed by the model applying all three features. This shows that the inclusion of context-based features significantly improves the model's performance, but that the model still relies on text-based features for optimal performance.

Feature	$F1_{macro}$	$F1_{micro}$
FastText	0.138	0.261
FastText, $Vector_{pol}$	0.405	0.522
FastText, $Vector_{party}$	0.441	0.594
$Vector_{pol}$, $Vector_{party}$	0.439	0.583
FastText, $Vector_{pol}$, $Vector_{party}$	**0.575**	**0.717**

Table 8: Results of experiments on MLP with reduced contextual features

6.3.2 Size of the Dataset

It is assumed that the small size of the quote dataset is a significant factor in preventing the models from achieving better performance, seeing as a smaller dataset size makes generalization to unobserved data points more difficult. To test this hypothesis, experiments were performed on the MLP using the optimal model hyperparameters, but a reduced training set sizes, in the range of 10 - 100% of the total quote dataset, the results of which can be found in Table 9. From this table, it is clear that decreasing the training set size reduces the performance of the model. It is assumed that the opposite is also true, and that a dataset of larger size would thus increase performance of the generated models.

6.3.3 Choice of Optimizer

The models were implemented using a simple stochastic gradient descent optimizer from Py-Torch (Paszke et al., 2017). This decision was made early in the development process, prior to the search of hyperparameter spaces for models. Thus, little testing was performed for the alternative, more advanced, optimizers. To gain insight into whether the use of alternative optimizers would have improved performance, a comparative experiment was performed, the results of which are presented in Table 10.

	Quotes	Optimal epoch	$F1_{micro}$	$F1_{macro}$
10%	72	Any	0.383	0.185
20%	144	Any	0.383	0.185
30%	216	Any	0.383	0.185
40%	288	200	0.5	0.33
50%	360	300	0.478	0.33
60%	432	200	0.567	0.425
70%	504	200	0.583	0.428
80%	576	200	0.656	0.488
90%	648	300	0.727	0.52
100%	720	300	**0.717**	**0.575**

Table 9: Dataset size impact on MLP performance

	Adagrad		Adadelta		Adam	
rate ϵ	0.001	0.01	0.001	0.01	0.001	0.01
Epoch	Any	200	300	30	30	Any
$F1_{micro}$	0.383	0.633	**0.722**	0.622	0.661	0.383
$F1_{macro}$	0.185	0.490	0.518	0.536	**0.547**	0.185

Table 10: Performance of the Adagrad, Adadelta and Adam optimizers in the MLP

Learning Rate	Epoch	$F1_{macro}$	$F1_{micro}$
0.001	30	0.185	0.383
	50	0.185	0.383
	70	0.185	0.383
	100	0.348	0.506
	200	0.525	**0.733**
	300	**0.575**	0.717
0.01	30	**0.526**	**0.733**
	50	0.410	0.606
	70	0.396	0.594
	100	0.454	0.578
	200	0.478	0.633
	300	0.410	0.500
0.1	30	0.423	0.589
	50	**0.504**	**0.706**
	70	0.442	0.617
	100	0.437	0.639
	200	0.397	0.572
	300	0.497	0.667

Table 11: Results of Learning Rate experiments on Quote LSTM using optimal hyperparameters

From this table it can be seen, that the Adam optimizer reaches an $F1_{macro}$ score of 0.547, comparable to the best score of the basic SGD optimizer which was 0.575, despite hyperparameters being trained using the basic SGD optimizer. It is worth noting that this result is achieved after only 30 epochs, whereas the basic SGD optimizer required 300 epochs. This indicates that using an adaptive optimizer would not necessarily lead to higher performance than stochastic gradient descent, for this task, but can be a more efficient choice of optimizer.

6.3.4 Alternative Learning Rates

As can be seen in Table 11, a higher learning rate decreases the convergence time on high F1-scores significantly, however reducing the performance of models for higher numbers of epochs. The fact that the models applying a higher learning rate can not achieve as strong a performance as that using a learning rate of 0.001 is likely to be due to the models skipping some maxima. One solution would be a variable learning rate, reducing the learning rate once the model shows per-epoch diminishing loss reduction, thus achieving both quick convergence and precision.

7 Conclusion

This work created both a dataset and approach for political stance detection in Danish. A dataset of quotes from Danish politicians, including the quoted politician and the quoted politician's party, annotated for use in stance detection was generated, and annotation guidelines for this dataset were defined. Two deep learning-based classifiers were designed, implemented and optimized for the task. The simple MLP model that took an averaged quote embedding as input far outperformed the more advanced LSTM model, which took a single word at each time step. The generated dataset is applicable for use in future research within the field of stance detection in Danish, and the created models can be used as benchmarks when testing stance detection classifiers on this dataset.

Labeled quote data and code for this project is available on GitHub (**link**).

Acknowledgements

We thank the reviewers, whose suggestions proved highly useful, and Victor Petrén Bach Hansen and Jakob Bang Helvind, whose sparring and feedback was invaluable during both the research behind this paper, and the writing of the paper itself. This research was conducted under the NeIC/NordForsk sponsored Nordic Language Processing Laboratory (NLPL) project.

References

Ahmet Aker, Leon Derczynski, and Kalina Bontcheva. 2017. Simple open stance classification for rumour analysis. In *Proc. RANLP*.

Isabelle Augenstein, Tim Rocktäschel, Andreas Vlachos, and Kalina Bontcheva. 2016. Stance Detection with Bidirectional Conditional Encoding. In *Proceedings of the 2016 Conference on Empirical Methods in Natural Language Processing*, pages 876–885.

Emily M. Bender and Batya Friedman. 2018. Data statements for natural language processing: Toward mitigating system bias and enabling better science. *Transactions of the Association for Computational Linguistics*, 6:587–604.

Michael Collins and Nigel Duffy. 2001. Convolutional Kernels for Natural Language. In *Proceedings of the 14th International Conference on Neural Information Processing Systems*, pages 625–632, Vancouver, Canada.

Leon Derczynski, Kalina Bontcheva, Maria Liakata, Rob Procter, Geraldine Wong Sak Hoi, and Arkaitz Zubiaga. 2017. SemEval-2017 Task 8: RumourEval: Determining rumour veracity and support for rumours. In *Proceedings of the 11th International Workshop on Semantic Evaluations (SemEval-2017)*, page 69–76, Vancouver, Canada.

Omar Enayet and Samhaa R. El-Beltagy. 2017. Determining Rumour and Veracity Support for Rumours on Twitter. In *Proceedings of the 11th International Workshop on Semantic Evaluations (SemEval-2017)*, pages 470–474, Vancouver, Canada.

Kenneth C. Enevoldsen and Lasse Hansen. 2017. Analysing political biases in danish newspapers using sentiment analysis. *Journal of Language Works*, 2(2).

Genevieve Gorrell, Elena Kochkina, Maria Liakata, Ahmet Aker, Arkaitz Zubiaga, Kalina Bontcheva, and Leon Derczynski. 2019. SemEval-2019 task 7: RumourEval, determining rumour veracity and support for rumours. In *Proceedings of the 13th International Workshop on Semantic Evaluation*, pages 845–854, Minneapolis, Minnesota, USA. Association for Computational Linguistics.

Sepp Hochreiter and Jürgen Schmidhuber. 1997. Long short-term memory. *Neural Computation*, 9(8):1735–1780.

Mohit Iyyer, Peter Enns, Jordan Boyd-Graber, and Philip Resnik. 2014. Political Ideology Detection Using Recursive Neural Networks. In *Proceedings of the 52nd Annual Meeting of the Association for Computational Linguistics*, pages 1113–1122, Baltimore, Maryland, USA.

Kristen Johnson and Dan Goldwasser. 2016. "All I know about politics is what I read in Twitter": Weakly Supervised Models for Extracting Politicians' Stances From Twitter. In *Proceedings of COLING 2016, the 26th International Conference on Computational Linguistics: Technical Papers*, pages 2966–2977, Osaka, Japan.

Andreas Kirkedal, Barbara Plank, Leon Derczynski, and Natalie Schluter. 2019. The Lacunae of Danish Natural Language Processing. In *Proceedings of the Nordic Conference on Computational Linguistics (NODALIDA)*.

Kristoffer Kvalvik. 2017. Køn, indkomst og geografi: Her er vælgernes vigtigste dagsordener. https://www.altinget.dk/artikel/163051-koen-indkomst-og-geografi-her-er-vaelgernes-vigtigste-dagsordener.

Mirko Lai, Delia Irazu Hernandez Farias, Vivian Patti, and Paolo Rosso. 2016. Friends and Enemies of Clinton and Trump: Using Context for Detecting Stance in Political Tweets. In *Advances in Computational Intelligence: 15th Mexican International Conference on Artificial Intelligence, MICAI 2016*, pages 155–168, Cancun, Mexico.

Anders Edelbo Lillie, Emil Refsgaard Middelboe, and Leon Derczynski. 2019. Joint rumour stance and veracity. In *Proceedings of the Nordic Conference on Computational Linguistics*.

Saif M. Mohammad, Svetlana Kiritchenko, Parinaz Sobhani, Xiodan Zhu, and Colin Cherry. 2016. A Dataset for Detecting Stance in Tweets. In *LREC*, Portoroz, Slovenia.

Saif M. Mohammad, Parinaz Sobhani, and Svetlana Kiritchenko. 2017. Stance and sentiment in tweets. *ACM Transactions on Internet Technology (TOIT) - Special Issue on Argumentation in Social Media and Regular Papers*.

Finn Årup Nielsen. 2011. A new ANEW: evaluation of a word list for sentiment analysis in microblogs. In *Proceedings of the ESWC2011 Workshop on 'Making Sense of Microposts': Big things come in small packages*, pages 93–98.

Razvan Pascanu, Tomas Mikolov, and Yoshua Bengio. 2013. On the difficulty of training recurrent neural networks. In *Proceedings of the 30th International Conference on International Conference on Machine Learning*, pages 1310–1318.

Adam Paszke, Sam Gross, Soumith Chintala, Gregory Chanan, Edward Yang, Zachary DeVito, Zeming Lin, Alban Desmaison, Luca Antiga, and Adam Lerer. 2017. Automatic differentiation in PyTorch. In *NIPS-W*.

F. Pedregosa, G. Varoquaux, A. Gramfort, V. Michel, B. Thirion, O. Grisel, M. Blondel, P. Prettenhofer, R. Weiss, V. Dubourg, J. Vanderplas, A. Passos, D. Cournapeau, M. Brucher, M. Perrot, and E. Duchesnay. 2011. Scikit-learn: Machine learning in Python. *Journal of Machine Learning Research*, 12:2825–2830.

Vahed Qazvinian, Emily Rosengren, Dragomir R. Radev, and Qiaozhu Mei. 2011. Rumor has it: identifying misinformation in microblogs. In *Proceedings of the Conference on Empirical Methods in Natural Language Processing*, pages 1589–1599, Edinburgh, United Kingdom.

Misha A. Mahowald Rodney J. Douglas Richard H. R. Hahnloser, Rahul Sarpeshkar and H. Sebastian Seung. 2000. Digital selection and analogue amplification coexist in a cortex-inspired silicon circuit. *Nature*, 405:947–951.

Ritzau. 2018a. Alternativet vil i EU med fyret græsk finansminister. *Ritzau*.

Ritzau. 2018b. DF siger nej til S-plan om jobcentre i Sydeuropa. *Ritzau*.

Ritzau. 2018c. OVERBLIK: Det siger politikerne om ghettoplanen. *Ritzau*.

Ritzau. 2018d. S vil skabe fem danske jobcentre i sydeuropa. *Ritzau*.

Ritzau. 2018e. Socialdemokratisk asyludspil deler rød blok. *Ritzau*.

Ritzau. 2018f. Støjberg vil have migranter fra dansk skib i land i Italien. *Ritzau*.

Ritzau. 2018g. Tyrkiske kulturformænds sympati for rabiat bevægelse alarmerer politikere. *Ritzau*.

Ritzau. 2019. Ejerskab, bestyrelse og årsregnskab. https://ritzau.com/ejerskab-bestyrelse-og-aarsregnskab/.

Frank Rosenblatt. 1961. *Principles of neurodynamics: Perceptrons and the theory of brain mechanisms.* Cornell Aeronautical Laboratory, Buffallo, New York, USA.

Maria Skeppstedt, Vasiliki Simaki, Carita Paradis, and Andreas Kerren. 2017. Detection of stance and sentiment modifiers in political blogs. In *Proceedings of the International Conference on Speech and Computer, SPECOM*, pages 1589–1599, Hatfield, United Kingdom.

Martin Tutek, Ivan Sekulic, Paula Gombar, Ivan Paljak, Filip Culinovic, Filip Boltuzic, Mladen Karan, Domagoj Alagic, and Jan Snajder. 2016. TakeLab at SemEval-2016 Task 6: Stance Classification in Tweets Using a Genetic Algorithm Based Ensemble. In *Proceedings of the 10th International Workshop on Semantic Evaluation (SemEval-2016)*, pages 464–468.

Wan Wei, Xiao Zhang, Xuqin Liu, Wei Chen, and Tengijao Wang. 2016. pkudblab at SemEval-2016 Task 6 : A Specific Convolutional Neural Network System for Effective Stance Detection. In *Proceedings of the 10th International Workshop on Semantic Evaluation (SemEval-2016)*, pages 384–388.

Guido Zarrella and Amy Marsh. 2016. MITRE at SemEval-2016 Task 6: Transfer Learning for Stance Detection. In *Proceedings of the 10th International Workshop on Semantic Evaluation (SemEval-2016)*, pages 458–463.

Li Zeng, Kate Starbird, and Emma S. Spiro. 2016. Unconfirmed: Classifying Rumor Stance in Crisis-Related Social Media Messages. In *Proceedings of the Tenth International AAAI Conference on Web and Social Media (ICWSM)*, pages 747–750, Cologne, Germany.

Appendix 1: Data Statement

Curation rationale   Quotes from Danish politicians published by the Ritzau news agency.

Language variety   BCP-47: da-DK

Speaker demographic

- Danish politicians.
- Age: approx. 25-70.
- Gender: mixed; see Section 3.1.
- Race/ethnicity: mostly white with Scandinavian background.
- Native language: Danish.
- Socioeconomic status: minimum 56494.17 DKK per month ($8470 USD).
- Different speakers represented: 63.
- Presence of disordered speech: Quotes are mostly curated, so not prevalent.

Annotator demographic

- Age: 20-30.
- Gender: male.
- Race/ethnicity: white northern European.
- Native language: Danish.
- Socioeconomic status: higher education student.

Speech situation   Quotes given by politicians in parliament during debate or discussion, during verbal interviews or in writing, transcribed and then published in edited newswire.

Text characteristics   Danish Newswire.

Provenance   Originally taken from Ritzau.

Joint Rumour Stance and Veracity

Anders Edelbo Lillie[*]
ITU Copenhagen
Denmark
aedl@itu.dk

Emil Refsgaard Middelboe[*]
ITU Copenhagen
Denmark
erem@itu.dk

Leon Derczynski
ITU Copenhagen
Denmark
ld@itu.dk

Abstract

The net is rife with rumours that spread through microblogs and social media. Not all the claims in these can be verified. However, recent work has shown that the stances alone that commenters take toward claims can be sufficiently good indicators of claim veracity, using e.g. an HMM that takes conversational stance sequences as the only input. Existing results are monolingual (English) and mono-platform (Twitter). This paper introduces a stance-annotated Reddit dataset for the Danish language, and describes various implementations of stance classification models. Of these, a Linear SVM provides predicts stance best, with 0.76 accuracy / 0.42 macro F_1. Stance labels are then used to predict veracity across platforms and also across languages, training on conversations held in one language and using the model on conversations held in another. In our experiments, monolinugal scores reach stance-based veracity accuracy of 0.83 (F_1 0.68); applying the model across languages predicts veracity of claims with an accuracy of 0.82 (F_1 0.67). This demonstrates the surprising and powerful viability of transferring stance-based veracity prediction across languages.

1 Introduction

Social media has come to play a big role in our everyday lives as we use it to connect with our social network, but also to connect with the world. It is common to catch up on news through Facebook, or to be alerted with emerging events through Twitter. However these phenomena create a platform for the spread of rumours, that is, stories with unverified claims, which may or may not be true (Huang et al., 2015). This has lead to the concept of *fake news*, or misinformation, where the spreading of a misleading rumour is intentional (Shu et al., 2017). Can we somehow automatically predict the veracity of rumours? Research has tried to tackle this problem (Qazvinian et al., 2011), but automated rumour veracity prediction is still maturing (Gorrell et al., 2019).

This project investigates stance classification as a step for automatically determining the veracity of a rumour. Previous research has shown that the stance of a crowd is a strong indicator for veracity (Dungs et al., 2018), but that it is a difficult task to build a reliable classifier (Derczynski et al., 2017). Moreover a study has shown that careful feature engineering can have substantial influence on the accuracy of a classifier (Aker et al., 2017). A system able to verify or refute rumours is typically made up of four components: rumour detection, rumour tracking, stance classification, and veracity classification (Zubiaga et al., 2018). This project will mainly be concerned with stance classification and rumour veracity classification.

Current research is mostly concerned with the English language, and in particular data from Twitter is used as data source because of its availability and relevant news content (Derczynski et al., 2017; Gorrell et al., 2019). To our knowledge no research within this area has been carried out in a Danish context. To perform automated rumour veracity prediction for the Danish language following the components in Zubiaga et al. (2018), a number of problems must be solved. (1) to facilitate Danish stance classification a Danish dataset must be generated and annotated for stance. (2) developing a good stance classifier is difficult, especially given the unknown domain of the Danish language. Therefore experiments must be per-

---

*: These authors contributed to the paper equally.

formed to investigate what approach to apply to Danish stance classification. (3) given rumourous data, and aided by stance classification, a rumour veracity prediction component should be able to determine whether it is true or false.

2 Background

The attitude that people express towards claims can be used to predict veracity of those claims, and these attitudes can be modelled by stance classifiers. This section will cover some state-of-the-art research for stance classification and rumour veracity resolution. While the introduced classification tasks are related to the work carried out in this project, they differ in a number of ways: (1) this project performs stance classification for the Danish language, (2) the generated dataset is from the Reddit platform, and (3) this project seeks to join stance classification and veracity prediction without external fact verification.

Stance classification: Long-Short Term Memory (LSTM) neural network models are popular, as they have proven to be efficient for working with data within NLP. In particular (Kochkina et al., 2017) introduced a stance classifier based on a "Branch-LSTM" architecture: instead of considering a single tweet in isolation, whole branches are used as input to the classifier, capturing structural information of the conversation. The model is configured with several dense ReLU layers, a 50% dropout layer, and a softmax output layer, scoring a 0.78 in accuracy and 0.43 macro F_1 score. They are however unable to predict the under-represented "denying" class.

Another LSTM approach deals with the problem introduced in the SemEval 2016 task 6 (Mohammad et al., 2016). The LSTM implements a bidirectional conditional structure, which classifies stance towards a target with the labels "positive", "negative", and "neutral" (Augenstein et al., 2016). The approach is unsupervised, i.e. data is not labelled for the test targets in the training set. In this case the system achieves state-of-the-art performance with a macro F_1 score of 0.49, and further 0.58 when applying weak supervision.

A different approach is based on having well-engineered features for stance classification experiments using non-neural networks classifiers instead of Deep Learning (DL) methods (Aker et al., 2017). Common features such as CBOW and POS tagging are implemented, but are extended with problem-specific features, which are designed to capture how users react to tweets and express confidence in them. A Random Forest classifier performed best, with an accuracy of 0.79.

The lack of labelled data is a major challenge for stance classification. One study shows that classification can be improved by transferring knowledge from other datasets (Xu et al., 2019). In particular, a model is implemented with *adversarial domain adaptation* to train on the FEVER dataset (Thorne et al., 2018) and test on the Fake News Challenge dataset.[1] By augmenting the traditional approach for stance classification with a domain adaption component, the model learns to predict which domain features originate from.

RumourEval 2019 is a very recent SemEval task which deals with stance classification and veracity prediction (Gorrell et al., 2019), and a first look at the scoreboard indicates very promising results.[2] With the Branch-LSTM approach as a baseline on the RumourEval 2019 dataset, scoring 0.4930 macro F_1, the "BERT" system scores a macro F_1 of 0.6167 (Fajcik et al., 2019). The implementation employs transfer learning on large English corpora, then an encoding scheme concatenates the embeddings of the source, previous and target post. Finally the output is fed through two dense layers to provide class probabilities. These BERT models are used in several different ensemble methods where the average class distribution is used as the final prediction.

Rumour veracity prediction: Rumour veracity classification is considered a challenging task as one must typically predict a truth value from a single text, being the one that initiates the rumour. The best performing team for that task in RumourEval 2017 (Derczynski et al., 2017) implements a Linear Support Vector Machine (SVM) with only few (useful) features (Enayet and El-Beltagy, 2017). They experiment with several common features such as hashtag existence, URL existence, and sentiment, but also incorporates an interesting feature of capturing whether a text is a question or not. Furthermore the percentage of replying tweets classified as supporting, denying, or querying from stance classification is applied. It is concluded that content and Twitter features were the most useful for the veracity classification task

---

[1]http://www.fakenewschallenge.org
[2]https://competitions.codalab.org/competitions/19938 26-05-2019

and the system scores an accuracy of 0.53.

While the system described above engages in the task of resolving veracity given a single rumour text, another interesting approach is based on the use of crowd/collective stance, which is the set of stances over a conversation (Dungs et al., 2018). This system predicts the veracity of a rumour, based solely on crowd stance as well as tweet times. A Hidden Markov Model (HMM) is implemented, which is utilised such that individual stances over a rumour's lifetime is regarded as an ordered sequence of observations. This is then used to compare sequence occurrence probabilities for true and false rumours respectively. The best scoring model, which include both stance labels and tweet times, scores an F_1 of 0.804, while the HMM with only stance labels scores 0.756 F_1. The use of automatic stance labels from (Aker et al., 2017) is also applied, which does not change performance much, proving the method to have practical applications. It is also shown that using the model for rumour veracity prediction is still useful when limiting the number of tweets to e.g. 5 and 10 tweets respectively.

Danish: While Danish is not a privileged language in terms of resources (Kirkedal et al., 2019), there is stance classification work on political quotes (Lehmann and Derczynski, 2019). However, this is over a different text genre, and does not focus on veracity prediction as its final goal.

Comprehensive reviews of automatic veracity and rumour analysis from an NLP perspective include Zubiaga et al. (2018), Atanasova et al. (2019), and Lillie and Middelboe (2019b).

3 Dataset

Because of various limitations on big social media platforms including Facebook and Twitter, Reddit is used as platform for the dataset.[3] This is a novel approach; prior research has typically relied on Twitter (Mohammad et al., 2016; Derczynski et al., 2017; Gorrell et al., 2019).

Data sampling: The data gathering process consists of two approaches: to manually identify interesting submissions on Reddit, and; to issue queries to the Reddit API[4] on specific topics. An example of a topic could be "Peter Madsen" refer-

ring to the submarine murder case, starting from August 2017.[5] A query would as such be constructed of the topic "Peter Madsen" as search text, a time window and a minimum amount of Reddit upvotes. A minimum-upvotes filter is applied to limit the amount of data returned by the query. Moreover the temporal filters are to ensure a certain amount of relevance to the case, specifically *when* the event initially unfolded. Several submissions prior or subsequent to the given case may match a search term such as "ubåd" (submarine).

Four Danish Subreddits were browsed, including "Denmark, denmark2, DKpol, and Gammel-Dansk",[6] although all relevant data turned out to be from the "Denmark" Subreddit. The submission IDs found manually and returned by the queries are used to download all posts from each submission using the `praw`[7] and `psaw`[8] Python libraries. The submission data is subsequently stored in a JSON format, one JSON file per submission, consisting of submission data and a list of comment data. These files include submission post text and comment text, as well as meta-information about the following: submission post, submitter user, Subreddit, comments, and commenting users.

Annotation: One widely used annotation scheme for stance on Twitter is the SDQC approach from Zubiaga et al. (2016). Twitter differs from Reddit in the way conversations are structured. Each tweet spawns a *conversation* which can have nested replies, and as such creates *branches*. Reddit implements the same mechanism, but a set of conversations are tied to a specific submission, which is initiated by a submission post. The Reddit structure is depicted in Figure 1, illustrating a conversation (in green) and two respective branches (in respectively red and purple). Note that branches share at least one comment. Thus, a way to annotate data from the Reddit platform with the annotation scheme from Zubiaga et al. (2016) is by regarding a submission post as a source, instead of each top-level comment for the conversations.

The stance of the source/submission post is taken into account when annotating the stance for

---

[3]In particular the Danish Subreddit at `www.reddit.com/r/Denmark/`

[4]`www.reddit.com/dev/api/`

[5]`www.dr.dk/nyheder/tema/ubaadssagen`

[6]`www.reddit.com/r/Denmark/wiki/danish-subreddits`

[7]`praw.readthedocs.io/en/latest/` v. 6.0.0.

[8]`github.com/dmarx/psaw` v. 0.0.7.

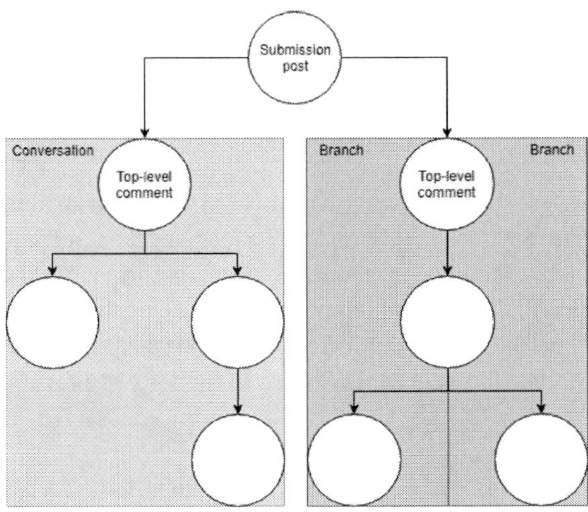

Figure 1: The structure of a Reddit submission

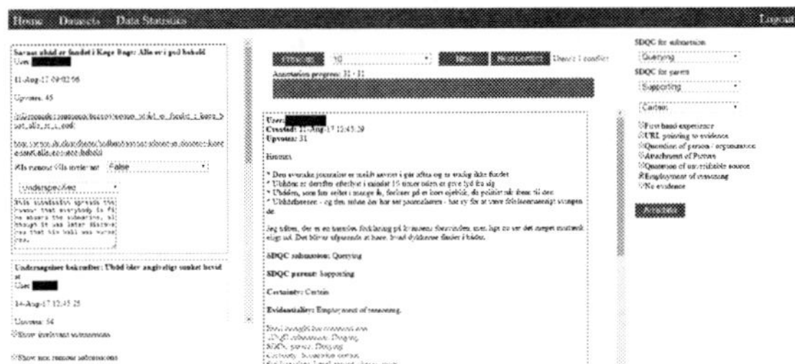

Figure 2: Screenshot of the annotation tool

replying posts of top-level posts. As stance annotations are relative to some target, each post does not have one single stance annotation: each post is annotated for the stance targeted towards the submission and the stance targeted towards the direct parent of the post. The double-annotation should facilitate a way to infer the stance for individual posts. For instance, if the source post supports a rumour, and a nested reply supports its parent post, which in turn denies the source, then the nested reply is implicitly denying the rumour.

Further, a majority of submissions have no text, but a title and a link to an article, image or another website, with content related to the title of the submission. If this is the case and the title of the submission bears no significant stance, it is assumed that the author of the submission takes the same stance as the content which is attached to the submission.

Annotation tool: A custom web-based annotation tool was built to facilitate the annotation process of the data. C# and MySQL technologies were used to build the tool in order to support rapid development. The tool enables annotators to partition datasets into events and upload submissions in the JSON form from the gathering Reddit data to each event. Further the tool allows for a branch view of each submission in the event and facilitates annotation following the SDQC scheme, as well as certainty and evidentiality as presented by Zubiaga et al. (2016). Any annotation conflicts are highlighted by the tool, which will cause the annotators to discuss and re-annotate the post with a conflict. A screenshot of the annotation page for the annotation tool is presented in Figure 2.

During annotation of the first $\sim$ 500 posts, annotators disagreed upon labels for around 40-50% of posts. However after the initial annotation work this rate dropped to around 25%. Annotation conflicts were handled in collaboration between the annotators after annotation of every $\sim$ 100 posts.

DAST: The result of the data sampling and annotation process is the **Da**nish **st**ance-annotated Reddit dataset (DAST). The dataset consists of a total of 11 events with 3,007 stance-annotated Reddit posts across 33 submissions with a total of 1,161 branches. Information on DAST is presented in Table 1 including event names, SDQC distribution and total post counts.

Event \ Label	S	D	Q	C	Total
5G	26	47	7	193	273
Donald Trump	39	17	5	185	246
HPV vaccine	24	4	8	219	255
ISIS	3	40	8	118	169
"Kost"	50	56	4	447	557
MeToo	1	8	3	48	60
"Overvågning"	41	20	13	278	352
Peter Madsen	15	45	19	302	381
"Politik"	43	46	7	227	323
"Togstrejke"	8	6	3	84	101
"Ulve i DK"	23	11	4	252	290
Total	273	300	81	2,353	3,007
%	9.1	10	2.7	78.2	100

Table 1: SDQC stance labels per event

The "querying" label is rare with a total of 81 annotations out of the 3,007 posts. The "supporting" and "denying" labels are almost equally distributed with a total of respectively 273 "supporting" and "300" denying posts. The "commenting" class is the absolute dominant one, with a total of 2,353 annotations.

Table 2 illustrates the relative SDQC distribution for the whole dataset for both response types, being targeted towards respectively submission

Target \ Label	S	D	Q	C
Submission post	273	300	81	2,353
Parent comment	261	632	304	1,810
Submission post %	9.1	10	2.7	78.2
Parent comment %	8.7	21	10.1	60.2

Table 2: SDQC stance label distribution in DAST

(source) and parent posts, i.e. the posts replied to. The distribution is quite skewed towards the "commenting" class label, with a total distribution of S(0.091), D(0.1), Q(0.027) and C(0.782).

Rumour data: The dataset contains 16 rumourous submissions, 3 of which are true, 3 are false and the remaining 10 are unverified. They make up 220 Reddit conversations, or 596 branches, with a total of 1,489 posts, equal to about half of the dataset. The posts are distributed across the nine events as follows: 5G (233), Donald Trump (140), ISIS (169), "Kost" (324), MeToo (60), Peter Madsen (381), "Politik" (49), "Togstrejke" (73), and "Ulve i DK" (56). Thus ISIS, MeToo, and Peter Madsen are the only events which only contain rumourous conversations.

Although rumours with known truth value would be optimal for veracity classification, this might reflect reality as the truth value of rumours may stay unverified. The amount of unverified rumours does however warrant more investigation in order to use all of the rumourous submissions for rumour veracity classification. Further details about the approach to unverified rumours are covered in Section 4.

In total the dataset contains 3,007 Reddit posts distributed across 33 submissions respectively grouped into 16 events.

The tools[9] and annotated corpora (Lillie and Middelboe, 2019a) are openly released with this paper in GDPR-compliant, non-identifying format. See appendix for data statement (Bender and Friedman, 2018).

4 Method

Our veracity prediction approach depends on two components: a stance classifier and a veracity classification component (Zubiaga et al., 2018).

4.1 Stance Classification

For stance classification two different approaches have been used, one being an LSTM classifier inspired by (Kochkina et al., 2017) and the other employing a number of classic machine learning models with a focus on feature engineering as presented in Aker et al. (2017).

LSTM classifier: The LSTM model is widely used for tasks where the sequence of data and earlier elements in sequences are important (Goldberg, 2016). The temporal sequence of tweets was one of the motivations for Kochkina et al. (2017) to use the LSTM model for branches of tweets, as well as for the bidirectional conditional LSTM for Augenstein et al. (2016).

While the results from both the Bi-LSTM in Augenstein et al. (2016) and Branch-LSTM in Kochkina et al. (2017) achieve state-of-the-art performance, they both note that their deep learning approaches suffer from the lack of a larger training dataset. This is not uncommon in this task (Taulé et al., 2017; Zubiaga et al., 2016; Gorrell et al., 2019). We suspect that we would observe the same tendency for the DAST dataset, which is relatively small with its 3,007 Reddit posts. However, as the LSTM approach still manages to achieve state-of-the-art performance, we opted to include an LSTM implementation for the stance classification task.

Specifically, the LSTM classifier used for stance classification here is implemented with PyTorch[10] and consists of a number of LSTM layers and a number of ReLU layers, followed by a dropout layer and a softmax layer to perform classifications. The model is trained with stochastic gradient descent (SGD) and a negative log likelihood loss function. The configurations considered and overall approach is inspired by the Branch-LSTM classifier in (Kochkina et al., 2017), except that we do not input data grouped sequentially by branches, but one by one.

Non-neural network classifiers: It is the intention to use non-neural network models in contrast to the LSTM deep learning approach above, as research shows that this approach can do very well (Derczynski et al., 2017), and particularly Decision Tree and Random Forest classifiers (Aker et al., 2017). Furthermore Support Vector Machine (SVM) and Logistic Regression have proven to be efficient (Enayet and El-Beltagy, 2017; Derczynski et al., 2017). The models are listed below, prefixed with a label, which we will use to denote them throughout the paper:

---

logit *Logistic Regression* classifier

tree *Decision Tree* classifier

svm *Support Vector Machine* (linear kernel)

  rf *Random Forest* classifier

Baselines: A simple majority voter (**MV**) as well as a stratified classifier (**SC**) were implemented. The former predicts only the most frequent class, and the latter generates predictions by respecting the training set's class distribution.

The non-neural networks models and baseline models described above are all implemented with the Scikit Learn (Pedregosa et al., 2011) framework, which provides a wide variety of machine learning implementations.

Preprocessing: As a preprocessing step, all post texts are lower-cased and then tokenised with the NLTK library (Bird et al., 2009), and finally all punctuation is removed, not including cases such as commas and periods in numbers, as well as periods in abbreviations. Furthermore URLs are replaced with the tag "urlurlurl" and quotes with the tag "refrefref".

Features: In order to represent the features of the preprocessed data numerically we employ eight feature categories, which are grouped by how they relate: text, lexicon, sentiment, Reddit, most frequent words, BoW, POS, and word embeddings. Note that only the Reddit specific features are domain-dependent, while the others should apply for the general case. The choices of features are a compilation of select features from various state-of-the-art systems (Aker et al., 2017; Kochkina et al., 2017; Enayet and El-Beltagy, 2017), except for the Reddit specific ones. Most of the features are binary, taking either a 0 or a 1 as value, and those that are not are min-max normalised (Han et al., 2011, p. 114), except for the word embeddings.

Table 3 presents an overview of the total feature vector, including the feature categories and their number of individual features. Note that the word embeddings are actually 300 long, but the extra 3 features are the cosine similarities between different word embeddings with regards to parent, source, and branch word tokens.

Sentiment analysis is performed with the Afinn library (Årup Nielsen, 2011), and POS tagging is performed with the Danish Polyglot library (Al-Rfou et al., 2013). Text features include binary

Category	Length
Text	13
Lexicon	4
Sentiment	1
Reddit	10
Most frequent words	132
BOW	13,663
POS	17
Word embeddings	303
Total	14,143

Table 3: Feature vector overview

features for presence of: '.', '!', '?', 'hv'-words, '...', as well as text length, URL count, maximum length of capital character sequence, and count of: '...', '?', '!', and words. Finally the text features include ratio of capital letters to non-capital letters and average word length.

Lexicon features are extracted by looking up occurrences of items in four predefined lexicon/dictionaries: negation words, swear words, positive smileys, and negative smileys. Negation words are translated from the English list used in Kochkina et al. (2017), as no list could be found for this purpose elsewhere. Beyond ourselves, swear words are taken from various sources: youswear.com, livsstil.tv2.dk, dansk-og-svensk.dk, and dagens.dk. Smiley lists were compiled from Wikipedia using the western style emoticons.[11]

Reddit-specific features include karma, gold status, Reddit employment status (if any), verified e-mail, reply count, upvotes, and whether the user is the submission submitter. Further, based on Reddit commenting syntax, the following features are included: sarcasm ('/s'), edited ('edit:'), and quote count ('>').

Finally, word embeddings are generated with word2vec (Mikolov et al., 2013) using the Gensim framework (Řehůřek and Sojka, 2010). The word vectors are trained on a Danish text corpus acquired from "Det Danske Sprog- og Litteraturselskab" (DSL),[12] consisting of 45 million tokens of written LGP (Language for General Purposes),[13] as well as the preprocessed Reddit text.

4.2 Rumour Veracity Prediction

The rumour veracity classification implemented is inspired by the approach presented in Dungs et al. (2018). This approach is especially interesting

---

[11]en.wikipedia.org/wiki/List_of_emoticons
[12]https://dsl.dk/
[13]https://korpus.dsl.dk/resources.html

as it relinquishes language specific features such as word embeddings and relies on sequences of stance labels and temporal features of the posts. This possibly enables the use of data across languages and platforms. One implemented HMM, λ is alike the model presented in Dungs et al. (2018) receiving sequences of stance labels ordered by their posting time as input. For each label presented in the data, a model is trained with training data for that label. For example in a label space containing the labels "True" and "False", two HMM models λ_{false} and λ_{true} are trained. The predicted label of the model λ will be whichever labelled model presents a higher probability score for the given sequence.

Further a model ω is built, which differs from λ by also containing normalised timestamps for each post. This was done as inclusion of temporal features boosted performance in (Dungs et al., 2018). Note that ω is not the same model as the variably-spaced λ' of Dungs et al. (2018).

As a baseline throughout the experiments, a simple stratified baseline will be used, denoted *VB*. The baseline notes the average distribution of stance labels as a four-tuple for respectively true and false (and unverified where relevant) rumours. When predicting rumour veracity, *VB* calculates the distribution of stance labels in a given sequence in the testing data and chooses the truth value with the most similar class label distribution.

The data used for experiments across languages and platforms include the PHEME dataset (Zubiaga et al., 2016; Derczynski et al., 2015). First, experiments are performed isolated on DAST. Then, the PHEME dataset is used as training data while DAST is used as test set. Further, unverified rumours are approached in two ways: (1) three-way classification is performed on true, false *and* unverified rumours, and (2) two-way classification is performed with unverified rumours treated as True. The results are presented in Section 5.2.

The data from DAST is used in three different ways, given the expected discrepancies between the English Twitter data and the Danish Reddit data. The Reddit conversation structure in Figure 1 differs slightly from the Twitter structure. The submission post is the actual source of conversation, while conversation top level comments are the source for Twitter conversations. Three different representations are tested for DAST:

BAS each branch in a conversation is regarded as a rumour (**branch-as-source**). This causes partial duplication of comments, as branches can share parent comments.

TCAS top level comments are regarded as the source of a rumour and the conversation tree they spawn are the sequences of labels (**top-level comment-as-source**).

SAS the entire submission is regarded as a rumour (**submission-as-source**). The SAS approach means that only 16 instances are available.

4.3 Evaluation Measures

Most of the related work report results with accuracy as scoring metric (Derczynski et al., 2017; Aker et al., 2017), which expresses the ratio of number of correct predictions to the total number of input samples. However, this becomes quite uninteresting if the input samples have imbalanced class distributions, which is the case for our dataset. What *is* interesting to measure is how well the models are at predicting the correct class labels. As such, in addition to reporting accuracy we will also use the F_1 scoring metric. In particular we will use an unweighted macro-averaged F_1 score for the case of multi-class classification.

5 Results and Analysis

This section reports performance at stance classification and rumour veracity prediction.

5.1 Stance Classification Results

First, an ablation study of the feature groups revealed that the Reddit specific features as well as lexicon features contributed negatively to performance for stance classification. Further, it turned out that the Most Frequent Words (MFW) feature category resembled BOW with low variance features removed. Finally the generated MFW list contained stopwords very specific to DAST, such as "B12", "CO2", and "5G". As such all classifiers has the feature categories Reddit, lexicon, and MFW removed.

Second, parameter search was performed through grid-search for three classifiers, being LSTM, Logistic Regression (**logit**), and Support Vector Machine (**svm**). Decision Tree and Random Forest were omitted due to poor performance. Full details of the parameters searched are given in Middelboe and Lillie (2019).

Classifier results are given in Table 4, under 5-fold (stratified) cross validation. Top-level com-

Model	Macro-F_1	σ	Accuracy	σ
MV	0.2195	(+/- 0.00)	0.7825	(+/- 0.00)
SC	0.2544	(+/- 0.04)	0.6255	(+/- 0.01)
logit	0.3778	(+/- 0.06)	0.7812	(+/- 0.02)
svm	0.3982	(+/- 0.04)	0.7496	(+/- 0.02)
logit'	0.4112	(+/- 0.07)	0.7549	(+/- 0.04)
svm'	**0.4212**	(+/- 0.06)	0.7572	(+/- 0.02)
LSTM	0.2802	(+/- 0.04)	0.7605	(+/- 0.03)
LSTM'	0.3060	(+/- 0.05)	0.7163	(+/- 0.16)

Table 4: Stance cross validation results for *logit*, *svm*, LSTM, and baselines with macro F_1 and accuracy, including standard deviation (σ).

Structure	Model	Acc.	F_1
SAS	λ	**0.81**	**0.45**
	ω	0.81	0.45
	VB	0.39	0.36
TCAS	λ	0.73	**0.63**
	ω	**0.79**	0.61
	VB	0.35	0.35
BAS	λ	0.78	0.66
	ω	**0.83**	**0.68**
	VB	0.43	0.42

Table 5: Stance-only veracity prediction, cross-validated over the Danish-language DAST corpus.

ments are not shared across splits. The baselines **MV** and **SC** and the default models for Logistic Regression (*logit*) and Support Vector Machine (*svm*) are included. *logit'* and *svm'* denote parameter-tuned models without Reddit, lexicon, and MFW features. Finally *LSTM* is the parameter-tuned model with all features; *LSTM'* is without Reddit, lexicon, or MFW features.

We see that *svm'* is the best performing model, achieving a macro F_1 score of 0.42, an improvement of 0.02 over the default model. Note that the accuracy is worse than the *MV* baseline, and *logit'* has even decreased its accuracy. The reason for this could be that the models have been tuned specifically for macro F_1. As expected we see that *MV* only predicts "commenting" classes and that *SC* follows the class label distribution of the dataset, while *logit'* and *svm'* are able to predict the under-represented classes. Because of the low-volume of data in DAST we did not expect the LSTM to perform very well, which was reflected in its best macro F_1 score of 0.3060.

5.2 Rumour Veracity Prediction Results

The results for the rumour veracity experiments are presented in this section. For size limitation reasons only the result tables for "Unverified" rumours interpreted as "False" are included, as these are superior. When interpreting "Unverified" as "True" the overall results for the experiments are worse. This indicates that the stance sequences in "Unverified" and "False" rumours are more alike than those in "True" rumours. When performing 3-fold cross validation on DAST, the best results are observed with the ω model on the BAS structure with an accuracy of 0.83 and an F_1 of 0.68.

We hypothesise that stance structures leading to veracity predictions may be similar across languages. To investigate this, we trained HMMs using the PHEME data (mostly English and German)

and evaluated performance of these models over DAST. Results are in Table 6.

Structure	Model	Acc.	F_1
SAS	λ	**0.88**	**0.71**
	ω	0.75	0.67
	VB	0.81	0.45
TCAS	λ	0.77	**0.66**
	ω	**0.81**	0.59
	VB	0.80	0.62
BAS	λ	**0.82**	**0.67**
	ω	0.67	0.57
	VB	0.77	0.53

Table 6: Veracity prediction from stance only, training on English/German PHEME rumour discussions and testing on Danish-language DAST.

The best performance is under the SAS structure. Note that the results when transferring veracity prediction across languages not only match the in-language training, but in fact exceed it. This indicates that cross-lingual stance transfer is possible with advantages, suggesting extra-lingual behaviours present in conversations about true and false claims. The increase in performance is attributed to the larger amount of training size available in the PHEME dataset compared to performing cross-validation within DAST.

There is also an interesting note about the effect of post times. λ performs better than ω when training on PHEME data, but ω performs better when solely training and testing on DAST. This suggests differences in the posting time tendencies, which may be caused by either the platform or language differences between the datasets.

5.3 Joining Stance and Veracity Prediction

To investigate the use of the system on new unseen data, the SVM stance classifier is used to classify stance labels for each of the rumour submissions. This is done by training on all of DAST except the one rumour to classify stance for ("hold one out").

Structure	Model	Acc.	F_1
SAS	λ	0.81	0.64
	ω	0.75	**0.67**
	VB	0.81	0.45
TCAS	λ	0.79	0.56
	ω	0.68	0.55
	VB	0.76	0.43
BAS	λ	**0.82**	0.58
	ω	0.76	0.56
	VB	0.76	0.48

Table 7: Training on the PHEME dataset and testing on automatic stance labels generated for DAST with "Unverified" rumours treated as "False".

This use of predicted instead of gold stance labels evaluates the system's extrinsic performance.

The best results were seen with "Unverified" labels as false, with the λ model on the BAS structure, which is reported in Table 7. A general tendency compared to the gold label results is a marginal drop in F_1, but little to no effect in the veracity prediction performance of the system.

5.4 Unverified as True

In the following experiments the unverified rumours have been interpreted as true rumours. Comparisons between these results and the 'Unverified as false' experiments above, might reveal interesting properties about the data. Switching between interpreting unverified as true or as false should approximately afford either higher rumour detection precision or higher recall, respectively.

Structure	Model	Acc.	F_1
SAS	λ	0.74 (+/- 0.21)	0.49 (+/- 0.13)
	ω	**0.74** (+/- 0.21)	0.53 (+/- 0.33)
	VB	0.19 (+/- 0.03)	0.16 (+/- 0.02)
TCAS	λ	0.67 (+/- 0.09)	0.55 (+/- 0.08)
	ω	0.65 (+/- 0.16)	0.49 (+/- 0.16)
	VB	0.34 (+/- 0.02)	0.34 (+/- 0.02)
BAS	λ	0.61 (+/- 0.05)	0.54 (+/- 0.07)
	ω	0.71 (+/- 0.06)	**0.62** (+/- 0.05)
	VB	0.59 (+/- 0.10)	0.54 (+/- 0.03)

Table 8: Danish veracity results on 3-fold cross validation for unverified being true.

Results are given in Table 8. This framing generally saw lower scores than comparable prior results (i.e. Table 5), with the highest accuracy at 0.74 achieved with the ω and λ models on the SAS structure. The highest F_1 score is achieved by ω on BAS, at 0.62.

To check if this result was specific to Danish, we repeated the experiment, over the English and German conversations in the larger PHEME dataset,

Structure	Model	Acc.	F_1
SAS	λ	0.75	**0.59**
	ω	**0.81**	0.45
	VB	0.69	0.54
TCAS	λ	0.72	0.54
	ω	0.76	0.52
	VB	0.70	0.56
BAS	λ	0.62	0.56
	ω	0.60	0.51
	VB	0.61	0.58

Table 9: Training and testing on PHEME data, with "Unverified" rumours treated as "True".

again using its gold stance labels. Results are in Table 9. The performance level held in this non-Danish setting. The highest accuracy achieved is 0.81 reached by the ω model on the SAS structure. The highest F_1 score is 0.59, achieved on the SAS structure as well by the λ model.

5.5 Usage Implications

The consequences of declaring a claim to be true or false can be serious. As in Derczynski et al. (2019), we intend this technology to be used solely as part of a "human-in-the-loop" system; although stories may be flagged automatically as false (or true), these should be presented to humans as unreliable results for analysis. On the other hand, technology offers potential to assist in the vital task of finding candidate misinformation among vast amounts of web data.

6 Conclusion

Social media has created a platform for the spread of rumours, which are stories with unverified claims. We investigated how to automatically predict the veracity of rumours spread on Danish social media by analysing the stance of conversation participants. Through experiments a Linear SVM gave SDQC stance classification with an accuracy of 0.76 and a macro F_1 of 0.42. An HMM then predicted rumour veracity automatically-labelled stance with up to 81% accuracy.

Interestingly, we find that veracity prediction models that use only stance labels from conversations in one language can be transferred effectively to predict veracity in conversations held in another language, based again on stance. This indicates the presence and utility of cross-lingual conversational behaviours around true and false claims.

Further and extensive experimentation and results can be found in the thesis that led to this work (Middelboe and Lillie, 2019).

References

Ahmet Aker, Leon Derczynski, and Kalina Bontcheva. 2017. Simple Open Stance Classification for Rumour Analysis. In *Proceedings of Recent Advances in Natural Language Processing*, pages 31–39, Varna, Bulgaria.

Rami Al-Rfou, Bryan Perozzi, and Steven Skiena. 2013. Polyglot: Distributed word representations for multilingual nlp. In *Proceedings of the Seventeenth Conference on Computational Natural Language Learning*, pages 183–192, Sofia, Bulgaria. Association for Computational Linguistics.

Pepa Atanasova, Preslav Nakov, Lluís Màrquez, Alberto Barrón-Cedeño, Georgi Karadzhov, Tsvetomila Mihaylova, Mitra Mohtarami, and James Glass. 2019. Automatic fact-checking using context and discourse information. *Journal of Data and Information Quality*, 11(3):12.

Isabelle Augenstein, Tim Rocktäschel, Andreas Vlachos, and Kalina Bontcheva. 2016. Stance Detection with Bidirectional Conditional Encoding. In *Proceedings of the 2016 Conference on Empirical Methods in Natural Language Processing*, pages 876–885, Austin, Texas.

Emily M. Bender and Batya Friedman. 2018. Data statements for natural language processing: Toward mitigating system bias and enabling better science. *Transactions of the Association for Computational Linguistics*, 6:587–604.

Steven Bird, Edward Loper, and Ewan Klein. 2009. Natural language processing with python.

Leon Derczynski, Torben Oskar Albert-Lindqvist, Marius Venø Bendsen, Nanna Inie, Viktor Due Pedersen, and Jens Egholm Pedersen. 2019. Misinformation on twitter during the danish national election. In *Proceedings of the conference for Truth and Trust Online*.

Leon Derczynski, Kalina Bontcheva, Maria Liakata, Rob Procter, Geraldine Wong Sak Hoi, and Arkaitz Zubiaga. 2017. SemEval-2017 Task 8: RumourEval: Determining rumour veracity and support for rumours. In *Proceedings of the 11th International Workshop on Semantic Evaluations (SemEval-2017)*, pages 69–76, Vancouver, Canada.

Leon Derczynski, Kalina Bontcheva, Michal Lukasik, Thierry Declerck, Arno Scharl, Georgi Georgiev, Petya Osenova, Toms Pariente Lobo, Anna Kolliakou, Robert Stewart, et al. 2015. PHEME: Computing Veracity—the Fourth Challenge of Big Social Data. In *Proceedings of the Extended Semantic Web Conference EU Project Networking session*.

Sebastian Dungs, Ahmet Aker, Norbert Fuhr, and Kalina Bontcheva. 2018. Can Rumour Stance Alone Predict Veracity? In *Proceedings of the 27th International Conference on Computational Linguistics*, page 3360–3370, Santa Fe, New Mexico, USA.

Omar Enayet and Samhaa R. El-Beltagy. 2017. NileTMRG at SemEval-2017 Task 8: Determining Rumour and Veracity Support for Rumours on Twitter. In *Proceedings of the 11th International Workshop on Semantic Evaluations (SemEval-2017)*, pages 470–474, Vancouver, Canada.

Martin Fajcik, Pavel Smrz, and Lukas Burget. 2019. BUT-FIT at SemEval-2019 Task 7: Determining the Rumour Stance with Pre-Trained Deep Bidirectional Transformers. In *Proceedings of the 13th International Workshop on Semantic Evaluation*.

Yoav Goldberg. 2016. A primer on neural network models for natural language processing. *Journal of Artificial Intelligence Research 57*, pages 345–420. Chapters 10-11.

Genevieve Gorrell, Elena Kochkina, Maria Liakata, Ahmet Aker, Arkaitz Zubiaga, Kalina Bontcheva, and Leon Derczynski. 2019. SemEval-2019 task 7: RumourEval, determining rumour veracity and support for rumours. In *Proceedings of the 13th International Workshop on Semantic Evaluation*, pages 845–854. Association for Computational Linguistics.

Jiawei Han, Micheline Kamber, and Jian Pei. 2011. *Data Mining, Concepts and Techniques*, 3 edition. Morgan Kaufmann Publishers Inc.

Y. Linlin Huang, Kate Starbird, Mania Orand, Stephanie A. Stanek, and Heather T. Pedersen. 2015. Connected through crisis: Emotional proximity and the spread of misinformation online. In *CSCW '15 Proceedings of the 18th ACM Conference on Computer Supported Cooperative Work & Social Computing*, pages 969–980, Vancouver, BC, Canada. Association for Computing Machinery.

Andreas Kirkedal, Barbara Plank, Leon Derczynski, and Natalie Schluter. 2019. The Lacunae of Danish Natural Language Processing. In *Proceedings of the Nordic Conference on Computational Linguistics (NODALIDA)*. Northern European Association for Language Technology.

Elena Kochkina, Maria Liakata, and Isabelle Augenstein. 2017. Turing at SemEval-2017 Task 8: Sequential Approach to Rumour Stance Classification with Branch-LSTM. In *Proceedings of the 11th International Workshop on Semantic Evaluations (SemEval-2017)*, pages 475–480, Vancouver, Canada.

Rasmus Lehmann and Leon Derczynski. 2019. Political Stance in Danish. In *Proceedings of the Nordic Conference on Computational Linguistics (NODALIDA)*. Northern European Association for Language Technology.

Anders Edelbo Lillie and Emil Refsgaard Middelboe. 2019a. Danish stance-annotated Reddit dataset. doi: 10.6084/m9.figshare.8217137.v1.

Anders Edelbo Lillie and Emil Refsgaard Middelboe. 2019b. Fake news detection using stance classification: A survey. *arXiv preprint arXiv:1907.00181*.

Emil Refsgaard Middelboe and Anders Edelbo Lillie. 2019. Danish Stance Classification and Rumour Resolution. Master's thesis, ITU Copenhagen.

Tomas Mikolov, G.s Corrado, Kai Chen, and Jeffrey Dean. 2013. Efficient estimation of word representations in vector space. In *Proceedings of the International Conference on Learning Representations (ICLR 2013)*, pages 1–12. arXiv preprint arXiv:1301.3781.

Saif M. Mohammad, Svetlana Kiritchenko, Parinaz Sobhani, Xiaodan Zhu, and Colin Cherry. 2016. SemEval-2016 Task 6: Detecting Stance in Tweets. In *Proceedings of SemEval-2016*, pages 31–41, San Diego, California.

Finn Årup Nielsen. 2011. A new ANEW: evaluation of a word list for sentiment analysis in microblogs. In *Proceedings of the ESWC2011 Workshop on 'Making Sense of Microposts': Big things come in small packages. Volume 718 in CEUR Workshop Proceedings*, pages 93–98.

F. Pedregosa, G. Varoquaux, A. Gramfort, V. Michel, B. Thirion, O. Grisel, M. Blondel, P. Prettenhofer, R. Weiss, V. Dubourg, J. Vanderplas, A. Passos, D. Cournapeau, M. Brucher, M. Perrot, and E. Duchesnay. 2011. Scikit-learn: Machine learning in Python. *Journal of Machine Learning Research*, 12:2825–2830.

Vahed Qazvinian, Emily Rosengren, Dragomir R. Radev, and Qiaozhu Mei. 2011. Rumor has it: Identifying Misinformation in Microblogs. In *Proceedings of the 2011 Conference on Empirical Methods in Natural Language Processing*, pages 1589–1599, Edinburgh, Scotland.

Radim Řehůřek and Petr Sojka. 2010. Software Framework for Topic Modelling with Large Corpora. In *Proceedings of the LREC 2010 Workshop on New Challenges for NLP Frameworks*, pages 45–50, Valletta, Malta. ELRA. `http://is.muni.cz/publication/884893/en`.

Kai Shu, Amy Sliva, Suhang Wang, Jiliang Tang, and Huan Liu. 2017. Fake news detection on social media: A data mining perspective. *ACM SIGKDD Explorations Newsletter*, 19(1):22–36.

Mariona Taulé, M. Antónia Martí, Francisco Rangel, Paolo Rosso, Cristina Bosco, and Viviana Patti. 2017. Overview of the Task on Stance and Gender Detection in Tweets on Catalan Independence at IberEval 2017. In *Proceedings of the Second Workshop on Evaluation of Human Language Technologies for Iberian Languages (IberEval 2017)*, pages 157–177.

James Thorne, Andreas Vlachos, Oana Cocarascu, Christos Christodoulopoulos, and Arpit Mittal. 2018. The Fact Extraction and VERification (FEVER) shared task. In *Proceedings of the First Workshop on Fact Extraction and VERification*.

Brian Xu, Mitra Mohtarami, and James Glass. 2019. Adversarial domain adaptation for stance detection. In *Proceedings of the Conference on Neural Information Processing Systems*, Montréal, Canada.

Arkaitz Zubiaga, Ahmet Aker, Kalina Bontcheva, Maria Liakata, and Rob Procter. 2018. Detection and Resolution of Rumours in Social Media: A Survey. *ACM Computing Surveys, Vol. 51, No. 2, Article 32*.

Arkeitz Zubiaga, Maria Liakata, Rob Procter, Geraldine Wong Sak Hoi, and Peter Tolmie. 2016. Analysing How People Orient to and Spread Rumours in Social Media by Looking at Conversational Threads. *PLoS ONE*. 11(3).

A Rumour sources

Event	Submission title	Rumour status
5G	5G-teknologien er en miljøtrussel, som bør stoppes	Unverified
	Det er ikke alle, som glæder sig til 5G.	Unverified
	Uffe Elbæk er bekymret over de "sundhedsmæssige konsekvenser" af 5G-netværket	Unverified
Donald Trump	Hvorfor må DR skrive sådan noget åbenlyst falsk propaganda?	Unverified
	16-årig blev anholdt for at råbe 'fuck Trump' til lovlig demonstration mod Trump	Unverified
ISIS	23-årig dansk pige har en dusør på \$1 million på hendes hovede efter at have dræbt mange ISIS militanter	Unverified
	Danish student 'who killed 100 ISIS militants has \$1million bounty on her head but is treated as terrorist' (The Mirror)	Unverified
Kost	Bjørn Lomborg: Du kan være vegetar af mange gode grunde - men klimaet er ikke en af dem	Unverified
	Professor: Vegansk kost kan skade småbørns vækst	False
MeToo	Björks FB post om Lars Von Trier (#MeToo)	Unverified
Peter Madsen	Savnet ubåd er fundet i Køge Bugt: Alle er i god behold	False
	Undersøgelser bekræfter: Ubåd blev angiveligt sunket bevidst	True
	Peter Madsen: Kim Wall døde i en ulykke på ubåden	False
Politik	KORRUPT	True
Togstrejke	De ansatte i DSB melder om arbejdsnedlæggelse 1. april.	True
Ulve i DK	Den vedholdende konspirationsteori: Har nogen udsat ulve i Nordjylland?	Unverified

Table 10: Overview of the rumour submissions
and their veracity.

B Veracity results

Structure	Model	Acc.	F_1
SAS	λ	0.53 (+/- 0.09)	0.53 (+/- 0.10)
	ω	0.55 (+/- 0.09)	0.55 (+/- 0.10)
	VB	0.37 (+/- 0.03)	0.31 (+/- 0.07)
TCAS	λ	0.60 (+/- 0.07)	0.58 (+/- 0.08)
	ω	0.64 (+/- 0.05)	0.61 (+/- 0.05)
	VB	0.53 (+/- 0.04)	0.38 (+/- 0.03)
BAS	λ	0.60 (+/- 0.05)	0.58 (+/- 0.05)
	ω	**0.67** (+/- 0.03)	**0.62** (+/- 0.04)
	VB	0.49 (+/- 0.10)	0.40 (+/- 0.01)
None	λ	0.55 (+/- 0.05)	0.54 (+/- 0.07)
	ω	0.57 (+/- 0.08)	0.55 (+/- 0.10)
	VB	0.43 (+/- 0.03)	0.33 (+/- 0.08)

Table 11: Training and testing on mix of PHEME data and different DAST structures for unverified false

C   Data statement

Curation rationale Comments around rumourous claims.

Language variety   BCP-47: `da-DK`

Speaker demographic

- Reddit users

- Age: Unknown – mixed.

- Gender: Unknown – mixed.

- Race/ethnicity: Unknown – mixed.

- Native language: Unknown; Danish speakers.

- Socioeconomic status: Unknown – mixed.

- Different speakers represented: Unknown; upper bound is the number of posts.

- Presence of disordered speech: Rare.

Annotator demographic

- Age: 20-30.

- Gender: male.

- Race/ethnicity: white northern European.

- Native language: Danish.

- Socioeconomic status: higher education student.

Speech situation   Discussions held in public on the Reddit platform.

Text characteristics   Danish colloquial web speech.

Provenance   Originally taken from Reddit, 2018.

Named-Entity Recognition for Norwegian

Bjarte Johansen
Digital Centre of Excellence
Equinor ASA
{bjajoh@equinor.com}

Abstract

NER is the task of recognizing and demarcating the segments of a document that are part of a name and which type of name it is. We use 4 different categories of names: Locations (LOC), miscellaneous (MISC), organizations (ORG), and persons (PER). Even though we employ state of the art methods—including sub-word embeddings—that work well for English, we are unable to reproduce the same success for the Norwegian written forms. However, our model performs better than any previous research on Norwegian text. The study also presents the first NER for Nynorsk. Lastly, we find that by combining Nynorsk and Bokmål into one training corpus we improve the performance of our model on both languages.

1 Introduction

NER is the task of recognizing and demarcating the segments of a document that are part of a name and which type of name it is. We use 4 different categories of names: Locations (LOC), miscellaneous (MISC), organizations (ORG), and persons (PER). Even though we employ state of the art methods—including sub-word embeddings—that work well for English, we are unable to reproduce the same success for the Norwegian written forms. However, our model performs better than any previous research on Norwegian text.

We also find that when we train on a combined corpus of Nynorsk and Bokmål, which we call Helnorsk, we get significantly better results (+5 percentage points) than if we train the models separately. We believe that this shows us, together with evidence provided by Velldal et al. (2017) that it is possible to use the similarities in the two written forms to produce better models than we would

otherwise be able to when the models are trained separately. We discuss this further in section 7 and 8.

Previous research on NER for Norwegian has chosen a more granular approach to the categories of names and have included the categories "works" and "events". The reason we chose to exclude these two categories was firstly that international research on English and other languages mainly focus on the same categories as us—that means that it is easier for us to compare our research to what has been done for other languages.

Secondly, previous research on Norwegian NER does not implement the same type of model that we and international researchers have implemented. They focus solely on the task of recognizing what type of name an already segmented name is categorized as. Our research also includes the segmentation of the names as well. This makes it difficult to compare our research directly with theirs.

Using their tools would also prevent us from using the NER directly on new documents if we wanted to build new research on top of such a NER model. We would have to first segment the text through Named-Entity Chunking (NEC) and then run the their recognizer on the result from the NEC. Johansen (2015) does provide a chunker that performs well (>95% $F_{\beta=1}$ score) However, we want to see how well a model that use state-of-the-art algorithms developed for English will perform on Norwegian. These algorithms usually do chunking as an implicit step of the NER process.

In our study we show that our model performs better than all previous attempts at a Bokmål NER (> +5 percentage points). There are no other NER models for Nynorsk that we are aware of. We show that by combining Nynorsk and Bokmål, into what we call Helnorsk in our study, we get better results than if we train separate models for the two written forms. "Helnorsk" translates to "The whole of Norwegian", which is fitting as it combines both of the official written forms.

The steps we take to present our study are to

1. Present related research on NER in section 2.

2. Introduce a new corpus which is tagged with named entities and their types in section 3.

3. Develop a sub-word embedding model for Nynorsk, Bokmål, and Helnorsk and implement a deep learning system designed to train a NER model based on a state-of-the-art English model in section 4.

4. Run experiments on Bokmål, Nynorsk, and Helnorsk to show how the model performs in section 5.

5. Discuss the results of the experiments in section 6.

6. Conclude on what we believe the experiments show us in section 7.

7. Present future research that we believe should be explored to answer some of the questions that we found at the end of this study in section 8.

2   Related research

Bick (2000) developed an early Danish NER base on constraint grammar parsing. They report an error rate of ~5%. It is unclear how their measure relates to the more standard way of reporting accuracy with F-scores. Bick (2004) improved the first model and achieved an $F_{\beta=1}$ score of 93%. It is however unclear how they arrive at this score as they originally report on different error rates of the model and then say that these numbers translate to the given F score. They do not tell us how they translated these numbers.

Derczynski et al. (2014) worked on a NLP toolkit for danish based on the Stanford NER package that includes a NER part. They annotated the Copenhagen Dependency Treebank for person, location and organisation entities. However, they do not report on the performance of their tool.

Jónsdóttir (2003) did some early work on chunking and recognition for Norwegian Bokmål. They used a ruled-based approach through the use of constraint grammar rules. The approach did provide good recall scores (>90%) for NER, but the precision did not reach satisfactory results (<50%).

Jónsdóttir does not provide the corresponding numbers for their NEC.

Nøklestad (2009) and Haaland (2008) also worked on named entities for Norwegian Bokmål texts. Nøklestad uses a Memory-Based Learning approach while Haaland uses Maximum Entropy Models. The main challenge with the approach implemented by Nøklestad and Haaland is that they only categorize names that are already chunked from the text. That means that they are dependent on a named-entity chunker to tell the categories of names in running text. Haaland provide a $F_{\beta=1}$ score of 81.36%, while Nøklestad achieve a score of 82.53%.

Husevåg (2016) explores the role of named entities in automatic indexing based on text in subtitles. They show that the distribution of named entities are not the same for all types of text and that Norwegian text has a significantly lower name density than English for non-fiction text. They also argue that NER is an important tool for indexing as named entities are a common search request.

Kokkinakis (2004) created a NER for Swedish and showed that they could get good results on a test corpus of 45962 tokens. They got a $F_{\beta=1}$ score of 90.50%.

Dalianis and Åström (2001) use a rule-based approach to NER for Swedish and show a $F_{\beta=1}$ score of 61%.

Mickelin (2013) also worked on NER for Swedish. They use SVM to train their model and achieve a $F_{\beta=1}$ score of 20%.

Olsson (2008) developed a tool for annotating NER data an showed that their tool decreases the number of documents an annotator needs to review and still get good results.

Kokkinakis et al. (2014) converted and adapted the NER described by Kokkinakis (2004) to the Helsinki Finite-State Transducer Technology platform (HFST). HFST is a pattern matching tool (Karttunen, 2011). Their NER tags 8 different categories: Person, location, organization, artifact, work, event, measure, and temporal. They report a precision of 79.02%, recall of 70.56%, and a $F_{\beta=1}$ score of 74.55%.

Kapočūtė-Dzikienė et al. (2013) use CRF to train a NER model for Lithuanian. They achieve an $F_{\beta=1}$ score of 89.5%.

Chiu and Nichols (2015) implemented NER for English using LSTM-BiRNNs, and is the research that we have tried to implement for Norwegian, except that we are using sub-word embeddings, represent the character and case information differently, and work with Norwegian text instead of English. We also combine two different written forms of the same language to increase performance.

Rama et al. (2018) present a new corpus consisting of Norwegian clinical trials annotated with entities and relationships. The entities are categorized into 10 different categories, while there are 5 different categories for relationships. They build two different models, one entity extraction model and one model for relationship extraction. The entity extraction model achieves a F_1 score of 84.1%. The relation extraction model achieves a F_1 score of 76.8%. They use SVMs for both models. The entities that they describe are not all fully *named* entities. They are also interested in finding family members addressed as, for example, "bestefar" (translation: grandfather) and nouns that refer to the patient in question, such as "pasienten" (translation: the patient).

Stadsnes (2018) trained and evaluated different word embeddings models for Norwegian and came to the conclusion that while fastText skipgram embeddings performed better when recognizing analogies, word2vec CBOW embeddings were better for synonym extraction. In section 5 we show that skipgrams work better for NER.

Peters et al. (2018) implemented NER for English using a novel approach they call ELMo, which "is a deep contextualized word representation that models both complex characteristics of word use (e.g. syntax and semantics) and how these uses vary across linguistic context (i.e. to model polysemy)." They achieve a $F_{\beta=1}$ score of 92.22% on English text.

3 Corpus

We introduce a newly tagged corpus with named entities for the task of NER of Norwegian text. It is a version of the Universal Dependency (UD) Treebank for both Bokmål and Nynorsk (UDN) where we tagged all proper nouns with their type according to our tagging scheme. UDN is a converted version of the Norwegian Dependency Treebank into the UD scheme (Øvrelid and Hohle, 2016).

Table 1 shows the distribution of the different types of text in the corpus. It consists of 82% newspaper texts, 7% government reports, 6% parliament transcripts, and 5% blogs (Solberg et al., 2014). Table 2 shows the number of names for

Resource	Percentage
Newspaper texts	82
Government reports	7
Parliament transcripts	6
Blogs	5

Table 1: Description of data set.

each of the categories that the corpus has been tagged with. We chose to tag it with the same categories as the CONLL-2003 shared task for language-independent NER (Tjong Kim Sang and Buchholz, 2000): Location (LOC), miscellaneous [1] (MISC), organization (ORG), and person (PER). The corpus along with the source for the project can be found here: `https://github.com/ljos/navnkjenner`.

We chose this scheme despite previous research on NER for Norwegian has chosen a more granular approach (e.g. Haaland (2008); Jónsdóttir (2003); Nøklestad (2009)) This meant that we are to be able to more easily compare our NER tagger to taggers developed for English. Previous research studies on Norwegian text are also not solving the exact same problem as we are investigating for our research. They focus solely on categorizing named entities and do not also delineate them from the text at the same time. Having fewer categories also meant that an annotator could perform the tagging faster as there were fewer choices to make when they decided the category of a name.

There are however some constraints on our corpus. The corpus has only been tagged by one annotator in one pass. This means that there are probably mistakes which will affect the performance of the trained models. The type of deep learning model that is trained for this research can never be better than the input it receives. After some investigation of the UDN data set, we also decided to trust that all named entities were tagged in the original UDN corpus with the PROPN (proper noun) tag. It is entirely possible that some of the entities are tagged as nouns only, further degrading the performance.

During the tagging we noted that—especially for the Nynorsk part of the UDN corpus—not all parts of a name were always tagged as a proper noun. This is not necessarily wrong in a grammatical sense, but it does mean that the two written forms

---

[1] By "michellaneous" we mean a catch-all category where any named entity that does not belong in any of the other categories goes into this category.

Bokmål	Tokens	Sentences	LOC	MISC	ORG	PER	Total
Training	243894	15686	3241	498	3082	4113	10934
Development	36369	2410	409	113	476	617	1615
Test	29966	1939	420	90	317	564	1391
Total	310229	20035	4070	701	3875	5294	13940

Nynorsk	Tokens	Sentences	LOC	MISC	ORG	PER	Total
Training	245330	14174	3482	588	2601	3992	10663
Development	31250	1890	340	67	268	421	1096
Test	24773	1511	300	59	246	362	967
Total	301353	17575	4122	714	3115	4775	12726

Helnorsk	Tokens	Sentences	LOC	MISC	ORG	PER	Total
Training	489224	34170	6723	1086	5683	8105	21597
Development	67619	4300	749	180	744	1038	2711
Test	54739	3450	720	149	563	926	2358
Total	611582	41920	8192	1415	6990	10069	26666

Table 2: Number of names for each data set.

follow a slightly different grammatical UD tagging schema. Since the tagging of named entities was quite time consuming, we did not have time to investigate further or try to figure out how to correct any mistakes that were made in our named-entity tags or the PoS tags of the UDN corpus.

4 Method

For the NER tagger we chose to use the BIOES tagging scheme as other researchers report that the BIOES tagging scheme performs (marginally) better on this type of task (Lample et al., 2016). The BIOES tagging scheme uses 5 different tags, instead of the 3 of the IOB2 scheme. The tags are

B A token at the **beginning** of a sequence.

I A token **inside** a sequence.

O A token **outside** a sequence.

E A token at the **end** of a sequence.

S A **single** token representing a full sequence.

We tagged each of the tokens in our corpus with one of these tags and the corresponding class of that token. There is an example in table 3.

We then trained a CBOW and a skipgram embedding model for each of the language forms: Nynorsk, Bokmål, and Helnorsk. The models were trained on a cleaned and combined corpus consisting of texts from Wikipedia, the Norwegian News Corpus (Andersen and Hofland, 2012), and the Norwegian Dependency Treebank (Solberg et al., 2014). We used fastText to train the sub-word embeddings with a vectors size of 300 components with a minimum n-gram size of 2 and maximum of 5 for the sub-words (Bojanowski et al., 2017).

We created a gazetteer from the NER corpus by extracting all words that appear as part of a name in the corpus. The gazetteer is used as part of the input to the model so the model can tell if a token has been used as part of a given category of names in the past.

The model that we use is a bidirectional Recurrent Neural Network with a Long Short-Term Memory unit (biLSTM) and it is trained on sentences that we treat as sequences of words. Recurrent Neural Networks "are a family of neural networks for processing sequential data" (Goodfellow et al., 2016, Chap. 10).

For each word in the sequence, we create an input vector that consists of the sub-word embedding of the word, membership in the gazetteer, the sequence of the characters of the word, and the part-of-speech of the word.

A biLSTM is a recurrent neural network that walks the sequence in both the forward and backwards directions. Long Short-Term Memory units introduces "self-loops to produce paths where the gradient can flow for long durations" and thereby capturing long-term dependencies (Goodfellow et al., 2016, Chap. 10). Using biLSTMs allows

O		O	O	O		O	B-PER	I-PER	E-PER		O
Folk	er	så	opptatt	av		Karl	Ove	Knausgård	.
People	are	so	occupied	with		Karl	Ove	Knausgård	.

Table 3: Example of tagging a sequence that mentions a person.

us to capture information about each word from both the past and future words in the sentence.

We also train a character embedding as part of the model. The character embeddings for each character in a word is run through a 1-dimensional Convolutional Neural Network layer (CNN), and the output of the convolutional layer is pooled together by selecting the maximum value for each position in the vector from the character embeddings. By 1-dimensional we mean that the CNN operates on a view of the neighbouring characters in each word .

The convolutional layer is activated by a Rectified Linear Unit. It constrains the value its output to be 0 or greater and is used in many types of tasks from image classification to machine translation (Ramachandran et al., 2018).

CNNs are "neural networks that use convolution in place of general matrix multiplication" (Goodfellow et al., 2016) and are used in tasks such as image classification. Using a dense network for these types of tasks would require too many neurons to be possible to train in a reasonable amount of time. Instead of operating on every point of the image, each neuron in a CNN operates on a n-dimensional view of the input.

We use the sub-word embeddings, the part-of-speech, gazetteer information, and the pooled character embeddings as the input to the biLSTM layer.

The output of the biLSTM layer is then fed through a linearly-activated dense layer that reduces the dimensionality of the output from the biLSTM down to the number of tags in our vocabulary.

A dense layer is a neural network where every input to the layer is connected to every output of the layer (Mitchell, 1997). It still has a weight for every connection, an activation function, and a bias for every output in the network. Each node in the neural network calculates the affine transformation of the inputs where the inputs $\vec{x}$ are weighted by the kernel $\vec{w}$ and then summed together with a bias b. The bias makes it possible to improve the fit of the input of the activation function to the prdiction by altering the shape of the function. The bias is either

set to a specific number like 1, or trained as one of the parameters of the network. The sum is then put through an activation function. The activation function acts as a decision boundary for the node.

The output of the dense layer is fed to a Linear-chain Conditional Random Field (CRF), that we use to calculate the log likelihoods of the predicted tags. We then use the CRF to calculate the most likely sequence given the evidence we have seen. The model can be found here: [redacted for review].

A CRF is used to classify sequences where the variables can be dependent on any other part of the sequence (Lafferty et al., 2001) like in a sentence. A CRF needs a takes a parameter vector that it uses for classification and is usually learned through an optimization algorithm, but in our case it is the output of the dense layer that we use as the parameter vector. In other words, the neural network decides the parameter vector for the CRF and then the CRF uses that to classify each token in the input.

Variable	Value
Batch size	100
Char. embed size	25
Conv. kernel	3
Pool size	53
Depth	1
Dropout	0.5
RNN hidden size	256
Learning rate	0.01

Table 4: Hyperparameter configuration of the model training.

We trained the model using the Adam optimizing algorithm on the cross entropy loss given the predicted likelihood for each tag. The cross entropy loss then provides how many bits are needed to represent the difference between the two distributions. Therefore, the smaller the difference, the more similar the distributions are.

We manually tested the training parameters, but because of time constraints we ended up using the hyperparameter configuration in table 4 as those were giving us the best results for the values that were tested.

Adam is an algorithm for "first-order gradient-based optimization of stochastic objective functions" (Kingma and Ba, 2014). It gets its name from the fact that it uses "adaptive moment estimation" to train the weights in the model based on the local moments, instead using the global moments as the estimated error.

The way the algorithm works is by calculating adaptive learning rates for different parameters by estimating the mean (the first moment) and the uncentred variance (the second moment).

In further detail, it first calculates the gradient for the stochastic objective of our loss function. Then it updates the first and second moment estimates based on the current timestep. It then uses the individual moment estimates of each gradient to calculate the updated parameters for the loss function. To update the network, it uses back-propagation of the errors through the network to update all the weights of the network.

To avoid the problem of exploding gradients in biLSTMs as described by Bengio et al. (1994), it is adviced to clip the gradients to the global norm, or to a max value, as suggested by Pascanu et al. (2013). The reason for this problem is that biLSTMs allow the network to keep information about the past for an unspecified amount of time. This results in "an explosion of the long term components, which can grow exponentially more than the short term ones" (Pascanu et al., 2013).

For each model we set a batch size of 100, a character embedding size of 25, the convolution kernel was 3, the max pooling of the convolution run was set to 53 wide and the biLSTM depth–or how many biLSTM layers there are—was 1. The dropout between layers was 50% and the hidden size of the RNN was 256 neurons. The learning rate for the ADAM optimizing algorithm was 0.01.

Dropout is a regularization technique that helps to reduce overfitting by holding out a percentage of the input to a neural network at random (Hinton et al., 2012). This forces each neuron in the network to detect a specific feature that can help the network give the correct prediction.

5   Results

The results from training the different models are displayed in table 5. We trained 4 different models. One for Bokmål, Nynorsk, and Helnorsk using the CBOW embedding model. It shows that the combined Helnorsk model performs better than either of the models trained on a single written form by $\sim$5 percentage points (p.p.) over both forms. We then trained a skipgram model for Helnorsk which performs $\sim$5 p.p. above the CBOW Helnorsk model.

In the end we end up with a $F_{\beta=1}$ score of 86.73%, with a precision of 87.22% and recall of 86.25% for the combined written form. The model performs slightly better on Bokmål with an $F_{\beta=1}$ score of 87.20%, precision of 87.93%, and recall of 86.48%. The same model has an $F_{\beta=1}$ score of 86.06% for Nynorsk, 86.20% precision, and 85.93% recall.

Written form	Precision	Recall	$F_{\beta=1}$
Bokmål, CBOW	80.03	73.47	76.61
Nynorsk, CBOW	77.86	68.04	72.62
Helnorsk, CBOW	84.42	76.33	80.17
H/Bokmål, CBOW	87.06	77.42	81.96
H/Nynorsk, CBOW	80.78	74.76	77.65
Helnorsk, SG	87.22	86.25	86.73
H/Bokmål, SG	87.93	86.48	87.20
II/Nynorsk, SG	86.20	85.93	86.06
Helnorsk, SG-g	86.69	85.96	86.32
H/Bokmål, SG-g	87.74	86.48	87.11
H/Nynorsk, SG-g	85.21	85.21	85.21

Table 5: Results of NER experiments. (CBOW = continous-bag-of-words, SG = skipgram, SG-g = skipgram with smaller gazetteer)

LOC	Nynorsk	Bokmål	Helnorsk
Precision	87.98	89.55	88.89
Recall	90.33	89.76	90.00
$F_{\beta=1}$	89.14	89.65	89.44
ORG			
Precision	81.63	80.06	80.74
Recall	81.30	82.33	81.88
$F_{\beta=1}$	81.46	81.18	81.31
MISC			
Precision	71.88	74.54	73.56
Recall	38.98	45.56	42.95
$F_{\beta=1}$	50.54	56.55	54.23
PER			
Precision	88.91	92.58	91.11
Recall	93.09	92.90	92.98
$F_{\beta=1}$	90.96	92.74	92.04

Table 6: Per name precision, recall, and F_1 score for the best performing Helnorsk model.

In table 6 the pr. name category results are displayed. There, it can be seen that it is especially the miscellaneous (MISC) category that through its recall score is driving the results down with a score of 42.95%. The precision is also low with a score of 73.56%.

The organisation (ORG) category also performs worse than the total score with an $F_{\beta=1}$ score of 81.31%. It is the location (LOC) category, with a $F_{\beta=1}$ score of 89.44%, and especially the person (PER) category with a $F_{\beta=1}$ score of 92.04%, that is pushing the over all score upwards.

During the writing of the paper we discovered a mistake in the experimental setup: We had included the names from the full corpus (the training *and* test data), instead of just the training data. This leaks information between the training and test steps and could in turn lead to overfitting the model to the test data. We were able to rerun the experiment without the names from the test data for the Helnorsk model. The results of that are reported in table 5 with the label "SG-g". With this model, the results reduce slightly over most of the measures (<1 p.p), except on the recall of Bokmål where it stays the same.

It is difficult to tell if the difference between the SG and SG-g experiments are because of some variation in the random initialization of the weights, random dropout between the layers, or some other variant. As we did not have time to control for these variables we still report the results of the model with the full gazetteer with the caveat that it includes data from the whole corpus. It could also be that because we use dropout, the gazetteer becomes an unreliable feature and is not used. In the future, we could test this through feature ablation testing—removing features from a model to see which features contribute the most to the performance of the model.

6   Discussion

When comparing the results from our research with that of other research that has been done on the Norwegian written forms, it is evident that our model performs significantly better than what has been shown before:

Haaland (2008) and Nøklestad (2009) shows a $F_{\beta=1}$ score of 81.36% and 82.53%, respectively, for Bokmål and we have a score of 87.20%; almost 5 p.p improvement over their results. However, the comparison is not completely fair. They only try to categorize already segmented names. Our research segments and categorizes the text as part of the same process.

Jónsdóttir (2003) shows a $F_{\beta=1}$ score of 60%. We cannot boast of the same precision that they have (90%) for Bokmål, but we are close with 87.93%. They do not provide any results for Nynorsk.

(Rama et al., 2018) developed an entity extraction model based on SVMs and got a $F_{\beta=1}$ score of 84.1% on a corpus of clinical texts. They are interested in finding nouns, and not only named entities, such as "bestefaren" (translation: the grandfather), and it is therefore difficult to compare our study with theirs.

Chiu and Nichols (2015) achieves a $F_{\beta=1}$ score of 91.62% on the CoNLL-2003 data set and 86.28% on the OntoNotes data set. Both are English data sets. The CoNLL-2003 data set is somewhat comparable to our data set on the number of entities and tokens. Their corpus has 35089 entities over 302811 tokens (Tjong Kim Sang and De Meulder, 2003), while ours has 26666 entities over 611582 tokens for the Helnorsk data set. The OntoNotes data set is 104151 over 1388955 tokens and is much larger than the data set we have available for Norwegian. We see here that the ratio between tokens and entities in OntoNotes is ∼7%, and in CoNLL-2003 it is ∼12%, while for the Helnorsk data the ratio is ∼4%.

Though the CoNLL-2003 data set uses BIO (or IOB2) tags and we use BIOES, this is not a problem as we are not comparing how well the model is labelling each word, but how well the model finds and categorizes named entities.

This supports the conclusion by Husevåg (2016) that Norwegian has a much lower density of named entities compared to English. Since deep learning models require large amounts of data to generalize effectively over the data set, it is possible that this is a problem for training a model for NER on Norwegian text.

We saw in table 6 that the worst performing name category is the miscellaneous category. This is also the category with the fewest named entities, showing us that lower amounts of data gives us worse performance. If one looks at how many names there are for each category, in table 2, and compare to the performance on each category, it shows that the score is higher if there are more examples of names.

Peters et al. (2018) is the latest state-of-the-art

NER for English, as of writing, and achieves a $F_{\beta=1}$ score of 92.22% on the CoNLL-2003 data set. Though we are not able to reach the same score, we are only trailing by $\sim$5 p.p. Right now, there are many avenues to try out for research on Norwegian text to reduce that gap. In section 8 we discuss the ideas that we believe are the most promising and the most immediate.

7 Conclusion

The results of this research show that it is possible to train a deep learning model to learn how to find named entities in Norwegian text and reach close to ($\sim$5 p.p.) the results of state-of-the-art models for English text. Our model achieves a $F_{\beta=1}$ score of 86.73 on the combined Bokmål and Nynorsk corpus (called Helnorsk).

We also show that it is plausible that Norwegian is harder to train for NER because Norwegian has a lower density of named entities compared to English.

We also show that we can get better performing models for both the written forms, Bokmål and Nynorsk, if we use (sub)word embeddings and train on a combined data set instead of training a separate model for each written form of the language. We do not know if this way of combining Nynorsk and Bokmål into one training set will transfer to other natural language tasks.

We do see some challenges like a worse result for Nynorsk compared to Bokmål, which we cannot immediately explain. However, Velldal et al. (2017) has shown similar results as us when they trained a PoS tagger using a combined corpus instead of treating the two written forms as distinct languages.

8 Future work

There are many possible avenues for improving on this research in the future. The first thing we would like to try would be to do a hyperparameter search to see if there are other parameter settings that could improve the results further. We should also perform ablation testing of the input features to see which of the features are the most important to the network. This could give us information about where we should focus our work to improve the model further.

The comparison between the Helnorsk data set and the Nynorsk/Bokmål data could also be improved. As of this paper, it is difficult to say if the improved scores are caused by having a larger data set that is good enough or if the combined data set is truly better. A way we could do this is to run the training on a selection of the Nynorsk and Bokmål data that has the same size as those data sets.

Next, we should investigate if we can train and use the ELMo embeddings presented by Peters et al. (2018) for Norwegian. They report a relative increase of 21% on NER for English using their new embedding model.

More time should be spent on analyzing and cleaning the corpus. For now, only 1 annotator has gone through and annotated the data set with NER tags.

We would also like to investigate why the miscellaneous category is performing so much worse than the other categories. This could be because we have more mistakes there or that the category is too broad; and it is difficult for the model to find a good delineation between the names in the category and the rest of the corpus.

We would also like to further test the hypothesis that a model trained on both written forms performs better than if we train two separate models. Is it just because we have more training data, and despite introducing noise, it performs better; or is it the model that is able to generalize better over the wider data set? Does the performance increase hold for other natural language processing tasks? Is it just Nynorsk and Bokmål that exhibits this behavior, or can we include other similar languages like Swedish and Danish? How close do the languages have to be to show this type of performance increase?

References

Gisle Andersen and Knut Hofland. 2012. Building a large corpus based on newspapers from the web. *Exploring Newspaper Language: Using the web to create and investigate a large corpus of modern Norwegian*, 49:1.

Yoshua Bengio, Patrice Simard, and Paolo Frasconi. 1994. Learning long-term dependencies with gradient descent is difficult. *IEEE transactions on neural networks*, 5(2):157–166.

Eckhard Bick. 2000. Named entity recognition for danish. *I: Årbog for Nordisk Sprogteknologisk Forskningsprogram*, 2004.

Eckhard Bick. 2004. A named entity recognizer for danish. In *Fourth International Conference on Language Resources and Evaluation*.

Piotr Bojanowski, Edouard Grave, Armand Joulin, and Tomas Mikolov. 2017. Enriching word vectors with subword information. *Transactions of the Association for Computational Linguistics*, 5:135–146.

Jason P. C. Chiu and Eric Nichols. 2015. Named entity recognition with bidirectional lstm-cnns. *arXiv preprint arXiv:1511.08308*.

Hercules Dalianis and Erik Åström. 2001. Swenam—a swedish named entity recognizer. *Technical Report, TRITANA-P0113, IPLab-189, KTH NADA*.

Leon Derczynski, Camilla Vilhelmsen Field, and Kenneth S Bøgh. 2014. Dkie: Open source information extraction for danish. In *Proceedings of the Demonstrations at the 14th Conference of the European Chapter of the Association for Computational Linguistics*, pages 61–64.

Ian Goodfellow, Yoshua Bengio, and Aaron Courville. 2016. *Deep Learning*. MIT Press. http://www.deeplearningbook.org.

Åsne Haaland. 2008. *A Maximum Entropy Approach to Proper Name Classification for Norwegian*. Ph.D. thesis, University of Oslo.

Geoffrey E. Hinton, Nitish Srivastava, Alex Krizhevsky, Ilya Sutskever, and Ruslan R. Salakhutdinov. 2012. Improving neural networks by preventing co-adaptation of feature detectors. *arXiv preprint arXiv:1207.0580*.

Anne-Stine Ruud Husevåg. 2016. Named entities in indexing: A case study of tv subtitles and metadata records. In *Networked Knowledge Organization Systems Workshop*, pages 48–58.

Bjarte Johansen. 2015. Named-entity chunking for norwegian text using support vector machines. *NIK: Norsk Informatikkonferanse*.

Andra Björk Jónsdóttir. 2003. *ARNER, what kind of name is that? - An automatic Rule-based Named Entity Recognizer for Norwegian*. Ph.D. thesis, University of Oslo.

Jurgita Kapočūtė-Dzikienė, Anders Nøklestad, Janne Bondi Johannessen, and Algis Krupavičius. 2013. Exploring features for named entity recognition in lithuanian text corpus. In *Proceedings of the 19th Nordic Conference of Computational Linguistics (NODALIDA 2013); May 22-24; 2013; Oslo University; Norway. NEALT Proceedings Series 16*, pages 73–88. Linköping University Electronic Press.

Lauri Karttunen. 2011. Beyond morphology: Pattern matching with fst. In *International Workshop on Systems and Frameworks for Computational Morphology*, pages 1–13. Springer.

Diederik P. Kingma and Jimmy Ba. 2014. Adam: A method for stochastic optimization. *arXiv preprint arXiv:1412.6980*.

Dimitrios Kokkinakis. 2004. Reducing the effect of name explosion. In *Proceedings of the LREC Workshop: Beyond Named Entity Recognition, Semantic Labelling for NLP tasks*, pages 1–6.

Dimitrios Kokkinakis, Jyrki Niemi, Sam Hardwick, Krister Lindén, and Lars Borin. 2014. Hfst-swener – a new ner resource for swedish. In *Proceedings of the Ninth International Conference on Language Resources and Evaluation (LREC'14)*.

John D. Lafferty, Andrew McCallum, and Fernando C. N. Pereira. 2001. Conditional random fields: Probabilistic models for segmenting and labeling sequence data. In *Proceedings of the Eighteenth International Conference on Machine Learning*, pages 282–289. Morgan Kaufmann Publishers Inc.

Guillaume Lample, Miguel Ballesteros, Sandeep Subramanian, Kazuya Kawakami, and Chris Dyer. 2016. Neural architectures for named entity recognition. *arXiv preprint arXiv:1603.01360*.

Joel Mickelin. 2013. Named entity recognition with support vector machines. Master's thesis, KTH Royal Institute of Technology.

Tom M. Mitchell. 1997. *Machine Learning*. McGraw-Hill.

Anders Nøklestad. 2009. *A machine learning approach to anaphora resolution including named entity recognition, pp attachment disambiguation, and animacy detection*. Ph.D. thesis, University of Oslo.

Fredrik Olsson. 2008. *Bootstrapping named entity annotation by means of active machine learning: a method for creating corpora*. Ph.D. thesis, University of Gothenburg.

Lilja Øvrelid and Petter Hohle. 2016. Universal dependencies for norwegian. *Proceedings of the Ninth International Conference on Language Resources and Evaluation*.

Razvan Pascanu, Tomas Mikolov, and Yoshua Bengio. 2013. On the difficulty of training recurrent neural networks. In *International Conference on Machine Learning*, pages 1310–1318.

Matthew E. Peters, Mark Neumann, Mohit Iyyer, Matt Gardner, Christopher Clark, Kenton Lee, and Luke Zettlemoyer. 2018. Deep contextualized word representations. In *Proc. of NAACL*.

Taraka Rama, Pål Brekke, Øystein Nytrø, and Lilja Øvrelid. 2018. Iterative development of family history annotation guidelines using a synthetic corpus of clinical text. In *Proceedings of the Ninth International Workshop on Health Text Mining and Information Analysis*, pages 111–121.

Prajit Ramachandran, Barret Zoph, and Quoc V. Le. 2018. Searching for activation functions.

Per Erik Solberg, Arne Skjærholt, Lilja Øvrelid, Kristin Hagen, and Janne Bondi Johannessen. 2014. The norwegian dependency treebank. In *Ninth International Conference on Language Resources and Evaluation*.

Cathrine Stadsnes. 2018. Evaluating semantic vectors for norwegian. Master's thesis, University of Oslo.

Erik F. Tjong Kim Sang and Sabine Buchholz. 2000. Introduction to the conll-2000 shared task: Chunking. In *Proceedings of the 2nd Workshop on Learning Language in Logic and the 4th Conference on Computational Natural Language Learning - Volume 7*, ConLL '00, pages 127–132. Association for Computational Linguistics.

Erik F. Tjong Kim Sang and Fien De Meulder. 2003. Introduction to the conll-2003 shared task: Language-independent named entity recognition. In *Proceedings of the seventh conference on Natural language learning at HLT-NAACL 2003-Volume 4*, pages 142–147. Association for Computational Linguistics.

Erik Velldal, Lilja Øvrelid, and Petter Hohle. 2017. Joint ud parsing of norwegian bokmål and nynorsk. In *Proceedings of the 21st Nordic Conference on Computational Linguistics, NoDaLiDa, 22-24 May 2017, Gothenburg, Sweden*, pages 1–10. Linköping University Electronic Press.

Projecting named entity recognizers without annotated or parallel corpora

Jue Hou, Maximilian W. Koppatz,
José María Hoya Quecedo and **Roman Yangarber**
University of Helsinki, Department of Computer Science, Finland
`first.last@helsinki.fi`

Abstract

Named entity recognition (NER) is a task extensively researched in the field of NLP. NER typically requires large annotated corpora for training usable models. This is a problem for languages which lack large annotated corpora, such as Finnish. We propose an approach to create a named entity recognizer for Finnish by leveraging pre-existing strong NER models for English, with no manually annotated data and no parallel corpora. We automatically gather a large amount of *chronologically matched* data in the two languages, then project named entity annotations from the English documents onto the Finnish ones, by resolving the matches with simple linguistic rules. We use this "artificially" annotated data to train a BiLSTM-CRF NER model for Finnish. Our results show that this method can produce annotated instances with high precision, and the resulting model achieves state-of-the-art performance.

1 Introduction

The goal of Named Entity Recognition (NER) is to recognize names and classify them into pre-defined categories, based on their context. The quality of NER is crucial, since it is an important step in modern NLP, e.g., information retrieval (IR) or information extraction (IE) systems. Various approaches have been proposed to tackle the NER task, including (Finkel et al., 2005; Huang et al., 2015; Lample et al., 2016; Ma and Hovy, 2016; Chiu and Nichols, 2016; Reimers and Gurevych, 2017; Peters et al., 2018; Devlin et al., 2018). These approaches require large annotated datasets to train models, and have been shown to be effective for languages with abundant linguistic resources, such as English.

However, not all languages are as resource-rich as English. There are significantly fewer resources for languages such as Finnish. Further, very few NER taggers or corpora are publicly available online. The FiNER tagger from the Language Bank of Finnish[1] is one of the few, but we found no documentation of its performance.

Automatically annotating corpora for training NER models is one solution to this problem. Several approaches have been proposed for building such corpora for NER. Most of these rely on the Wikipedia corpus, (Al-Rfou et al., 2015; Ghaddar and Langlais, 2017; Kim et al., 2012; Richman and Schone, 2008; Kazama and Torisawa, 2007; Toral and Munoz, 2006; Nothman et al., 2013). However, the amount of Wikipedia documents in Finnish is also relatively small.

In this paper, we propose a novel approach for automatically marking Finnish text with NE annotations, for the purpose of training a statistical NER model from these annotated data. This can be viewed as a *projection* of a pre-existing NER model in one language to a NER model in another language. The core idea of our annotation approach is to utilize strong NER available for English and to match automatically annotated English data with Finnish data by resolving the base form of names. Ehrmann et al. (2011) proposed an idea of model projection similar to the one in the this work. However, rather than resolving the base form of named entities in target language internally as we do, they used machine translation as the basis for projection. This allows them to project models between different languages, including in languages with different writing systems, such as Russian and English. However, this assumes the existence of a high-quality *machine translation* system, and token binding between the languages, which determine the quality of the NER training dataset.

Using the resulting annotated data, we train an BiLSTM-CRF model on the basis of (Ma and Hovy,

---

[1] `www.kielipankki.fi`

2016; Reimers and Gurevych, 2017), and evaluate it on a *manually annotated* dataset. Our results show that training models on data annotated in this way achieves improved performance for Finnish NER tagging over models trained on the publicly available data alone. This suggests that our approach works well for annotating a corpus with named entities automatically, and enables using this corpus to learn good-quality NER models for less-resourced languages.

The paper is organized as follows. In section 2 we briefly introduce a few terms and key concepts used throughout the paper. In section 3 we describe the data sources, pre-processing steps and the rule-based annotation pipeline. Section 4 describes our model architecture, as well as the parameters used in training. In section 5 we discuss the results obtained from the experiments. Section 6 concludes with current directions of research.

2 Terminology

Base form: The base form of a word, also is referred as *lemma*, is the canonical, or "dictionary" form of a word. For example, the base form of the English token "was" is "be."

Surface form: The surface form of a token is the form in which the word appears in the actual text. Words in this form may be inflected, such as "was," or be identical with its base form, such as the past participle of "run".

Compound: A compound is a word which consists of multiple root morphemes. For example, "pancake" consists of two parts: "pan" and "cake". Some languages, such as Finnish and German, make extensive use of compounding.

3 Automatic projection pipeline

3.1 Data source

Finnish names and their types are obtained by matching the base forms of English names with Finnish *potential* names. This section details this procedure step by step.

English news gathering and name processing: English news is collected by our business news surveillance system, PULS (Du et al., 2016), from over 3,000 English sources.[2] Over 5,000 documents are gathered daily. Each document collected

---

[2]`http://newsweb.cs.helsinki.fi/`

Source	prec	rec	F1
PULS pattern-based	0.68	0.37	0.30
BiLSTM-CRF-GloVe	0.87	0.85	0.85
BiLSTM-CRF-W2V	0.89	0.90	0.89

Table 1: English NER tagger quality on CoNLL2003 test dataset

by the system is processed by a cascade of pre-processing classifiers, including a pattern-based named entity tagger. Here, we obtain the base forms of names and their types, which are later used for projection.

The performance, especially the *precision*, of the English NER tagger is therefore crucial for the entire pipeline. It is worth pointing out that the precision of the English NER tagger controls the quality of the projected Finnish data. The recall, on the other hand, determines the variety of the projected named entities. Lower recall rate can be compensated by feeding in more news articles. Therefore, in this paper, the precision of English NER tagger is considered to be more essential than the recall or the overall F1 score.

For comparison, we also trained two BiLSTM-CRF models (Ma and Hovy, 2016) from scratch, using Word2Vec and GloVe word embeddings. These models were trained on the CoNLL2003 English dataset. Table 1 shows an evaluation of all three English NER taggers on the CoNLL2003 test dataset.

We should mention that the PULS NLP system has different tokenization compared to the CoNLL dataset, and our pattern-based NER tagger is customized for the *business* news domain. Though the output of our pattern-based tagger is aligned to be comparable with the CoNLL dataset, the content of its test dataset, which is mostly sports news, is still skewed against our tagger. In practice, our tagger achieves higher precision on business news. To confirm this, we evaluate the PULS tagger on 10 randomly selected articles, containing both general and business news. Although this is a simple experiment, the overall precision of the PULS tagger increases to 77%. As for the two BiLSTM-CRF models, the results are different from what was reported in the papers (Ma and Hovy, 2016; Reimers and Gurevych, 2017), since we used a default hyper-parameter setup, rather than using the fine-tuned setup in the papers.

Finnish news gathering and name pre-processing: Finnish news articles are collected

233

from two major Finnish online news agencies. Around 200 news articles are collected daily. The Turku dependency parser (Haverinen et al., 2014) has been applied for sentence splitting and tokenization. Three different problems need to be solved so that all potential names can be extracted in these steps: name identification, base form selection, and name merging.

Name identification: For identifying whether a token is a name or part of a name, we use the rules based on the position of tokens as follows:

- Any capitalized token which appears in the middle of a sentence is definitely a name or part of the name.

- If token A is a name according to previous rule, and token B, having the same base form as token A, appears at the beginning of a sentence, we assume token B is the same name.

- If a token of a potential name appears in the document only at the beginning of sentences, it is not certain and therefore not assumed to be a name.

Base form selection: To determine the base form corresponding to a surface form found in text, we consider all base forms returned by our morphological analyzer, (Moshagen et al., 2013), and a simple rule-based stemmer, and look through the entire article. If there is an intersection between the possible base forms of two name tokens, their true base form can then be resolved. When the intersection has only one base form, it can be confirmed to be the base form of a name directly. Otherwise, all of them will be recorded as potential base form of the name. All potential base forms will be further filtered when matching with English named entities during projection.

Suppose the surface form "Trumpille" (in the allative case) and "Trump" (nominative) both exist in an article. Without any external knowledge, the Finnish surface form "Trumpille" will be assigned two potential lemmas by our stemmer: "Trumpi" and "Trump" (both of these lemmas have the same allative form). For the surface form "Trump", only "Trump" will be returned as a potential lemma. Then, in this case, their intersection, "Trump", will be confirmed to be the lemma of both "Trumpille" and "Trump". However, if instead the article only contains the surface forms "Trumpille" and "Trumpin" (genitive). Then both

lemmas "Trumpi" and "Trump" will be recorded as potential lemmas.

We perform name identification and base form selection jointly, since they are connected, by searching for the common base forms of tokens.

Name merging: We use a set of rules to merge names that consist of more than one token. Potential names can contain only the following kinds of tokens in positions other than the final position:

- Singular common noun or proper noun which must be in the nominative case, for example: "Spring Harbour".[3]

- English function words: e.g., "the", "and", "new", etc. For example: "The New York Times"

- Having no valid analyses returned by the Finnish morphological analyzer, and its surface form can be confirmed to be its own lemma during the base form selection process above.
  One example is the token "Trump" in "Trump Towerin" (genitive: "of the Trump Tower"). Our Finnish morphological analyzer will reject (not recognize) the input token "Trump". We assume that "Trump" can be confirmed as a name or as part of a multi-token name according to the rules. "Trump" can be confirmed to be its own base form, which means its base form happens to be the same as its surface form. In this case, "Trump" will be merged with the following token "Towerin".

We should note that when several potential name tokens are strung together, the true partitioning of names is ambiguous. During name merging, all different partitionings and potential forms of the base forms of names are cached as candidates for the following name resolution step.

Hyphenating between tokens are also a criterion for merging names, such as the Indian surname "Ankalikar-Tikekar".

3.2 Name projection

In the next stage, we annotate Finnish names by utilizing the potential names candidates produced by the previous three steps, namely name identification, base form selection, and name merging.

---

[3]Names such as "Helsingin Sanomat" (name of a major newspaper in Finland), where the first token is in the *genitive* case (of "Helsinki") are currently not handled by these rules, and are handled separately by a list.

The fundamental assumption is that *a name refers to only one entity in a given article*. We expect this assumption to hold for well-edited news articles. This means that if only one instance (surface form) of a particular name has been annotated in an article, the remaining occurrences of the same name in the article—possibly involving other surface forms—can be annotated as well.

We gather two sets of named entities from Finnish document and English documents:

- For a Finnish document, published on day t, we use three steps mentioned above to obtain a set of potential Finnish named entity candidates, including both potential base forms and confirmed base form of names.

- From English news in the time interval ($t \pm 2$ days), using an English NER tagger, a set of English named entities and their corresponding tags are obtained. Each of them has its base form resolved by the pre-processing pipeline in PULS.

Names can naturally be matched according to their base form. The type of the English named entities can therefore be projected to their Finnish counterparts. The remaining Finnish names candidates, for which no type annotation can be inferred, are dropped after this step.

The idea of a time window ($t \pm 2$ days) is to take advantage of the fact that names overlap significantly in different articles due to continuous coverage of important events, and therefore optimize our memory usage and time efficiency.

Again, take "Trump" as an example. Suppose we have a named entity "Donald Trump" from the English news articles and it is recognized as "Person". We may have "Donald Trumpille" in a Finnish article; if the surface form "Trump" is not present in the same Finnish article, as we mentioned already, we can only infer that the base form of "Trumpille" is "Trumpi" or "Trump", using stemming rules. In addition, "Donald Trumpille" has two tokens but we do not yet know whether they belong together as one name. Therefore, "Donald", "Donald Trump", "Donald Trumpi", "Trump" and "Trumpi" are all Finnish name *candidates*. After matching, only "Donald Trump" will be kept and annotated as *Person*, while other candidates, namely "Donald", "Donald Trumpi", "Trump" and "Trumpi", are dropped.

In addition, for the *Person* type only, names will be connected by their partial base form. Once "Donald Trump" gets annotated, all the other "Donald" and "Trump" tokens in the entire article will be annotated as *Person* as well.

3.3 Special cases: rule-based projection

We use extra steps to handle special cases in this process. In Finnish, geo-location names, such as the names of countries, are often different from their English names. For example, France is "Ranska" in Finnish, and the United States is "Yhdysvallat" in Finnish. Some organizations also have the same problem, as UN is "YK" in Finnish, etc. Therefore, we manually build a small database of frequent names, including Finnish geo-locations, and a few of the major and most frequently occurring international companies and organizations, to assure that they are annotated correctly. In addition, this covers some cases which the English tagger fails to catch. We also filter out names that can have multiple types, such as MacLaren, since these are ambiguous.

Additionally, we introduce a list of 1000 common first names and assume that names beginning with these tokens are of type *Person*. However, this practice requires more rules to constrain its outcome:

- A Person name should have at most 2 tokens.

- A Person name should not start with "The".

- No token in a Person name should be fully uppercase.

- We require that a Person name be mentioned using the full name at least once in the article.

These rules are simple, naive and strict. The purpose of these rules is to remove any uncertain instances and make the data as clean as possible. Even if only one name in an article can meet all these rules, all other name instances related to that name instance will be correctly annotated. Also, taking advantage of our enormous amount of data, we can afford to filter out uncertain data without worrying about the amount of remaining data.

Currently, the annotations may be wrong when an article only mentions the last name of a person, which also happens to be the name of a location. For example, "Sipilä" is the last name of the current Prime Minister of Finland, and may therefore be mentioned many times in an article, without mentioning the full name, "Juha Sipilä". Coincidentally, "Sipilä" is a town in Finland. The situation where both the person and the location are mentioned in the same article rarely occurs in practice and can be tackled by filtering out such names.

4 NER model

Next we provide the details of the adapted BiLSTM-CRF model for Finnish NER and the hyperparameter setup for training this model. The basic network structure of the model is inspired by (Ma and Hovy, 2016; Reimers and Gurevych, 2017). The model is implemented in Keras with TensorFlow as its backend. The CRF layer is provided by Keras-contrib.[4] The training process was run on an Nvidia GeForce 1080 Ti GPU. It took around 3 hours to train the model using the setup in this section. The model is shown in Figure 1.

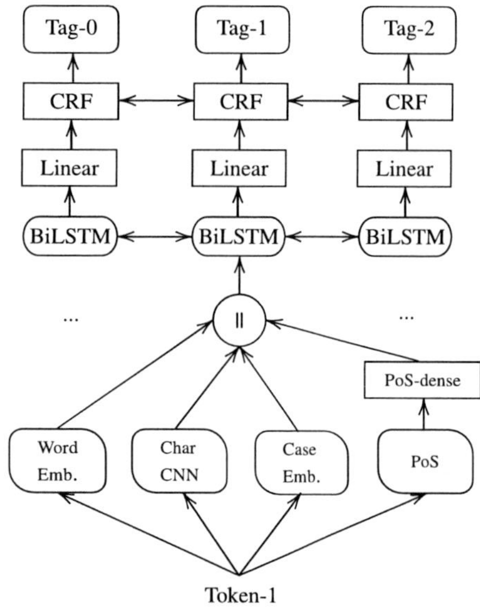

Figure 1: Adapted BiLSTM-CRF network structure for Finnish NER

As seen in Figure 1, Part-of-Speech (PoS) is included as an additional feature, compared to the model of Ma and Hovy (2016). This is because a lemma may be assigned multiple PoS tags by our morphological analyzer (Moshagen et al., 2013). Word embeddings such as Word2Vec (Mikolov et al., 2013) may implicitly contain PoS information but will still be static regardless of context. Using PoS as input feature also compensates for

out-of-vocabulary problem in embeddings. In these cases, not even the implicit PoS information can be detected by the network if PoS is not a part of input features.

4.1 Data encoding

Tokens are encoded into to several features: *word embedding*, *character embedding*, *case embedding* and *Part of Speech* (PoS). Except for PoS, most of the features follow the setup in (Reimers and Gurevych, 2017). Word embeddings are extended with a special mark for ambiguous tokens—tokens, for which our morphological analyzer fails returns more than one base forms and PoS. These tokens are replaced with a special token "AMBIGUOUS". Additionally, we only use the embedding of the last part of a compound word if this word is out-of-vocabulary. This is because the last part is the essential part of compounds in Finnish. Character embeddings are extended with a special value for "unrecognized" character. The PoS feature is encoded as an array of ones and zeros. Each dimension corresponds to one PoS type, including PADDING and UNKNOWN. Integer "1" is assigned to the dimension corresponding to the token's PoS. If a token is a compound word, only the PoS of its last part is used for encoding. If a token has multiple PoS analyses, more than one position in the PoS array is assigned "1". The values of PoS are as follows:

- PADDING
- UNKNOWN
- Noun
- Verb
- Adj
- Adv
- Pron
- Conj
- Interj
- Num
- Punct
- other

These four input features are concatenated before feeding into BiLSTM.

4.2 Parameter initialization

Word embeddings: We use a pre-trained Word2Vec embedding matrix, which is trained by (Laippala and Ginter, 2014). It has been trained on 4.5B words of text. As mentioned previously, we include vectors for "PADDING", "UNKNOWN" and "AMBIGUOUS" tokens. Embeddings for the tokens "UNKNOWN" and "AMBIGUOUS" are randomly initialized with uniform sampling from -0.25 to 0.25, while the "PADDING" embedding is a zero vector.

---

[4]www.github.com/keras-team/keras-contrib

Layer	Hyper-parameter	Number
Char CNN	Number of filters	30
	Filter size	3
PoS-dense	Unit size	30
	Activation	Relu
BiLSTM	Number of layers	2
	State size	200
	Dropout rate	0.25

Table 2: Table of hyper-parameter for experiments

Character embeddings: Character embeddings, including "UNKNOWN" character embedding, are randomly initialized with uniform samples from $-\sqrt{\frac{3}{dim}}$ to $\sqrt{\frac{3}{dim}}$, where $dim = 30$.

Case embedding: Case embeddings are randomly initialized applying a uniform initializer. The dimensionality of the case embeddings is 10.

Weight Matrices and Bias Vectors: Most of weights are initialized as a uniform sample from $[-\sqrt{\frac{6}{N_i+N_o}}, \sqrt{\frac{6}{N_i+N_o}}]$, where N_i and N_o refer to the number of input and output units in the weight tensor. Bias is initialized with zeros.

4.3 Optimization

Optimizer: We used the Adam optimizer, as recommended in (Reimers and Gurevych, 2017). The setup for the Adam optimizer also followed the Keras default setting: $lr = 0.001, \beta_1 = 0.9, \beta_2 = 0.999$. Although Ma and Hovy (2016) used gradient norm clipping of 5.0, we did not.

Early stopping and learning rate decay: We applied early stopping following the categorical accuracy on the training dataset in case of overfitting. On average, the training process stops after 5 epochs. We have also explored reducing the learning rate during the training process if the accuracy stops improving. However, this made the training slower, and did not improve the final result on the validation dataset.

4.4 Hyper-parameter setup

Most of the hyper-parameter values, shown in Table 2, follow the recommendations in (Reimers and Gurevych, 2017). The layer called "PoS-dense" in Figure 1 is a dense layer with a non-linear activation function, rather than an embedding layer, due to the encoding method of the PoS features, as explained in Section 4.1. For the mini-batch

size, the authors recommend using the batch size between 8 and 32, depending on the size of the training dataset. However, that is the result on the CoNLL-2003 dataset, which is an English dataset. We use 50 similarly to the German NER model in (Reimers and Gurevych, 2017).

We should mention that the CRF layer implemented by the *Keras-contrib* package offers two different modes for the training and testing processes: "Join" and "Marginal" for training, "Viterbi" and "Marginal" for testing. The "Join" training mode and "Viterbi" testing mode follows the "vanilla" fitting algorithms for linear chain CRF. "Marginal" training is optimized via composition likelihood (product of marginal likelihood), which is not optimal in this case. "Marginal" testing mode will decode the input sequence according to the training result and compute marginal probabilities. In this mode, it can therefore output a probability prediction of the classes for tokens. According to the documentation, the "Join" training mode can outperform the other training mode, and the "Viterbi" testing mode can achieve better performance than "Marginal" testing mode, but reasonably close. In this work, we evaluate using both "Join-Marginal" and "Join-Viterbi" modes.

5 Performance and evaluation

In this section, we report the performance for the automatic projection pipeline and the NER model. F1-score is used as the evaluation metric. The overall F1-score is the weighted average F1-score of each category.

5.1 Automatic projection pipeline

We currently utilize data only from the beginning of 2017 to July of 2018 for development, model training and validation. The total Finnish data consists of around 83,000 articles.

Our English data, on the other hand, date back 6 years from 2018 to 2012. Only articles from the same time period as the Finnish data can be used for name matching. The amount of usable English articles is around 4,486,000. We consider the NER performance only on "person", "location" and "organization" tags, to make the final outcome comparable to the Polyglot Finnish NER tagger.

To evaluate the performance of the automatic projection, we manually checked 1,000 randomly selected sentences from March 2018 to April 2018. Since our three English NER taggers have different

Tag	Prec	Rec	F1	Support
B-PER	0.97	0.99	0.98	823
I-PER	0.97	0.97	0.97	668
B-LOC	0.99	0.99	0.99	341
I-LOC	1.00	0.67	0.80	3
B-ORG	0.99	0.98	0.98	536
I-ORG	1.00	0.82	0.90	78
Avg / total	0.98	0.98	0.98	2449

Table 3: Quality of Finnish data projected from PULS pattern-based NER: evaluated on 1,000 sentences, annotated manually.

Tag	Prec	Rec	F1	Support
B-PER	0.99	0.97	0.98	776
I-PER	0.99	0.97	0.98	639
B-LOC	0.97	0.97	0.97	376
I-LOC	0.55	0.60	0.57	10
B-ORG	0.95	0.98	0.96	587
I-ORG	0.91	0.87	0.89	92
Avg / total	0.97	0.97	0.97	2478

Table 4: Quality of Finnish data projected from BiLSTM-CRF-W2V model: evaluated on 1,000 sentences, annotated manually.

performance, the manual evaluation is conducted separately, as shown in Table 3, Table 4 and Table 5.

5.2 NER model

For training the NER models, we used data from 2017-01 to 2017-12 (12 months). This period contains 50,009 Finnish documents, for which we found 920,658 matching English documents. We filtered out projected sentences for which the English tagger produced NER tags *other than* Person, Organization, or Location. This data produced approximately 114,000 automatically projected sentences after filtering. For validation, we used two months: 2018-04 to 2018-05. This period contained 11,452 Finnish documents, which had 389,072 English matching documents. This data produced 23,277 automatically projected sentences, after filtering.

Instances are projected from 3 different English NER taggers: the PULS pattern-based tagger, BiLSTM-CRF-GloVe tagger and BiLSTM-CRF-W2V tagger. Two train-test modes, "Join-Marginal" and "Join-Viterbi", are also applied for comparison. Six different Finnish NER models are evaluated.

Tag	Prec	Rec	F1	Support
B-PER	0.96	0.99	0.97	767
I-PER	0.97	0.97	0.97	632
B-LOC	0.97	0.96	0.96	403
I-LOC	0.71	0.53	0.61	19
B-ORG	0.96	0.97	0.96	639
I-ORG	0.97	0.78	0.87	101
Avg / total	0.96	0.96	0.96	2561

Table 5: Quality of Finnish data projected from the BiLSTM-CRF-GloVe model: evaluated on 1,000 sentences, annotated manually.

Table 6 shows the model evaluation on this data.

As expected, upon visual inspection, we noticed instances with incorrect "ground truth" since projection is not entirely clean. Despite its good overall quality, the validation performance may still differ from actual performance.

We conducted further model testing and inspection to obtain better estimates of the true performance. We sampled another set of articles from 2018-08 to 2018-10 (3 months), which is outside our automatic projection time period. For further inspection and error analysis, in Section 5.3, we randomly sampled a total of 36 articles, evenly from the following 6 sections of the newspaper:

- "Talous" (Economics)
- "Politiikka" (Politics)
- "Ulkomaat" (Foreign news)
- "Kotimaa" (Domestic news)
- "Koti" (Home)
- "Kaupunki" (The City)

The first three of these categories are more closely related to the Business domain. Again, articles are **evaluated manually**. The result is shown in Table 7. Polyglot is used as the performance baseline. Two additional Finnish NER models are trained with full FiNER-data (Ruokolainen et al., 2019), including the validation and test dataset, for better comparison.[5]

As shown in Table 7, Polyglot and the model trained with FiNER-data have better precision than most of our Finnish NER taggers, but have a worse recall rate. Overall, most of our Finnish NER taggers achieve better performance. Only one model, projected from BiLSTM-CRF-W2V in Join-Viterbi mode, performs worse than the FiNER-data model

---

[5] www.github.com/mpsilfve/finer-data

Eng-NER Source	Train-test mode	Prec	Rec	F1	Support
PULS pattern-based	Join-Viterbi	0.94	0.92	0.93	28858
PULS pattern-based	Join-Marginal	**0.94**	**0.93**	**0.93**	28858
BiLSTM-CRF-GloVe	Join-Viterbi	0.92	0.89	0.90	34526
BiLSTM-CRF-GloVe	Join-Marginal	0.93	0.91	0.92	34526
BiLSTM-CRF-W2V	Join-Viterbi	0.87	0.83	0.84	37219
BiLSTM-CRF-W2V	Join-Marginal	0.87	0.85	0.85	37219

Table 6: Validation scores on 2018-04 to 2018-05. "PULS pattern-based" and "BiLSTM-CRF-*" refer to the Finnish NER models that are projected from our PULS pattern-based NER tagger and English BiLSTM-CRF NER tagger respectively. "GloVe" and "W2V" indicates the embedding that English NER taggers use.

NER Source	Train-test mode	Prec	Rec	F1	Support
PULS pattern-based	Join-Viterbi	**0.89**	0.77	**0.82**	916
PULS pattern-based	Join-Marginal	0.80	**0.83**	0.81	916
BiLSTM-CRF-GloVe	Join-Viterbi	0.80	0.75	0.76	916
BiLSTM-CRF-GloVe	Join-Marginal	0.79	0.74	0.75	916
BiLSTM-CRF-W2V	Join-Viterbi	0.76	0.72	0.73	916
BiLSTM-CRF-W2V	Join-Marginal	0.78	0.79	0.78	916
FiNER-data	Join-Viterbi	0.83	0.72	0.75	916
FiNER-data	Join-Marginal	0.73	0.68	0.64	916
Polyglot		0.82	0.55	0.64	916

Table 7: Test evaluation. "FiNER-data" refer to the Finnish NER model trained with data from FiNER-data. "Polyglot" entry illustrates the performance of their model on our test dataset

in Join-Viterbi mode. The Finnish NER tagger that is projected from the PULS pattern-based English NER tagger in Join-Viterbi mode achieves the overall best performance. This result also suggests that the dataset produced by our automatic projection pipeline is valid for model training, data of large size and various topics, while FiNER-data only covers technology-related news.

5.3 Error analysis

Despite good overall performance on all automatically projected datasets, the average F1 score of models with the different setups is still around 77%. More work is required to improve performance. To guide future work, we did further visual inspections to examine the predictions in general.

One major problem is that the NER model gets data from automatic projection with **limited pattern diversity**. During the training pipeline, including automatic projection, there are two reasons that may cause this problem.

Firstly, flaws still exist in the automatic projection pipeline. One flaw that shows up often during visual inspection is that the projection currently does not support named entities without any capital letters. Named entities such as "Valkoinen talo" (the White House) cannot be fully recognized at the beginning of the pipeline (because the second token is lowercase). As a result, only the token with a capitalized letter such as "Valkoinen" will be predicted as a named entity by Finnish NER tagger.

Secondly, the English data source is biased in favor of foreign business topics. Within the time period of the training data, our database contains mostly business news. As a consequence, more business-related news and their named entities in Finnish news can be tagged. General news may behave differently than business news, and may contain more patterns for the task of NER. To verify this conjecture, we inspect each category with the model projected from the PULS pattern-based tagger in Join-Viterbi mode. As shown in Table 8, the model can achieve better performance on average on the topics which are related to foreign business or politics news, compared to domestic or local news.

Another major problem is due to a **flaw in**

Category	Prec	Rec	F1	Support
Overall	0.89	0.77	0.82	916
Talous	0.91	0.90	0.90	123
Politiikka	0.89	0.79	0.83	191
Ulkomaat	0.92	0.75	0.83	227
Kotimaa	0.90	0.70	0.78	100
Koti	0.86	0.73	0.77	167
Kaupunki	0.83	0.71	0.74	108

Table 8: Performance of the Finnish NER tagger for each category. The tagger is projected from the pattern-based English NER tagger in Join-Viterbi mode, first line in Table 7.

Tag	Prec	Rec	F1	Support
B-PER	0.88	0.70	0.78	20
I-PER	0.83	1.00	0.91	10
B-LOC	0.85	0.90	0.88	52
I-LOC	0.00	0.00	0.00	5
B-ORG	1.00	0.32	0.48	19
I-ORG	0.00	0.00	0.00	2
avg/total	0.83	0.71	0.74	108

Table 9: Detailed performance of Finnish NER tagger for category "Kaupunki" ("The City") in Table 8.

data encoding. As mentioned previously, out-of-vocabulary compound lemmas are decomposed and assigned the embedding of the last part of the compound lemma. Many ordinary tokens may benefit from this approach, while organization named entities do not. During visual inspection, we noticed that the name of some Finnish national or local governmental departments can be a made-up word or a compound word. Such names will either be assigned the "UNKNOWN" token embedding or the embedding of the last part of the compound word, which is most likely a common noun. For example, "Verohallinto" (Tax Administration) does not have an embedding as a whole. However, "hallinto" ("government") is a common noun within the embedding vocabulary. As a result, these named entities are more likely to be tagged incorrectly. As illustrated in Table 9, the performance of organizations (B-ORG) suffers from severely low recall rates due to this problem, as well as the previously mentioned problem that Finnish domestic named entities are less likely to get projections in the pipeline.[6]

6   Conclusions and future work

In this paper, we propose the idea of building a Finnish NER dataset by leveraging the output of an English NER tagger and projecting the type of recognized named entities from English to Finnish. The contributions of this paper are:

- Our work shows that the Finnish NER dataset produced by only simple rule-based projection can be used for NER model training. No parallel bilingual documents are used, only projected named entities, obtained by several *monolingual* tools.

- We demonstrate the performance of our NER model, and set a new benchmark for Finnish NER.

For future work, we plan to first tackle the problems that we mentioned in the error analysis section and conduct further inspection. Secondly, we plan to combine our pipeline with a disambiguation model, to improve both the pre-processing and the data encoding steps. Thirdly, it would be interesting to experiment and generalize our approach with other languages with limited NER tools, such as Estonian, if corresponding news datasets are easily accessible.

Acknowledgements

This work was supported in part by TEKES, the Finnish Funding Agency for Technology and Innovation, Project "iMEDL—Digital Media Evolution through Deep Learning", number 5933/31/2017.

References

Rami Al-Rfou, Vivek Kulkarni, Bryan Perozzi, and Steven Skiena. 2015. Polyglot-ner: Massive multilingual named entity recognition. In *Proceedings of the 2015 SIAM International Conference on Data Mining*. SIAM, pages 586–594.

Jason P.C. Chiu and Eric Nichols. 2016. Named entity recognition with bidirectional LSTM-CNNs. *Transactions of the Association for Computational Linguistics* 4:357–370.

Jacob Devlin, Ming-Wei Chang, Kenton Lee, and Kristina Toutanova. 2018. BERT: pre-training of deep bidirectional transformers for language understanding. *CoRR* abs/1810.04805.

---

[6]Because they are unlikely to appear in English-language news.

Mian Du, Lidia Pivovarova, and Roman Yangarber. 2016. PULS: natural language processing for business intelligence. In *Proceedings of the 2016 Workshop on Human Language Technology*.

Maud Ehrmann, Marco Turchi, and Ralf Steinberger. 2011. Building a multilingual named entity-annotated corpus using annotation projection. In *Proceedings of the International Conference Recent Advances in Natural Language Processing 2011*. pages 118–124.

Jenny Rose Finkel, Trond Grenager, and Christopher Manning. 2005. Incorporating non-local information into information extraction systems by Gibbs sampling. In *Proceedings of the 43rd Annual Meeting on Association for Computational Linguistics*. Association for Computational Linguistics, Stroudsburg, PA, USA, ACL '05, pages 363–370.

Abbas Ghaddar and Phillippe Langlais. 2017. Winer: A Wikipedia annotated corpus for named entity recognition. In *Proceedings of the Eighth International Joint Conference on Natural Language Processing (Volume 1: Long Papers)*. pages 413–422.

Katri Haverinen, Jenna Nyblom, Timo Viljanen, Veronika Laippala, Samuel Kohonen, Anna Missilä, Stina Ojala, Tapio Salakoski, and Filip Ginter. 2014. Building the essential resources for Finnish: the Turku Dependency Treebank. *Language Resources and Evaluation* 48(3):493–531.

Zhiheng Huang, Wei Xu, and Kai Yu. 2015. Bidirectional LSTM-CRF models for sequence tagging. *CoRR* abs/1508.01991.

Jun'ichi Kazama and Kentaro Torisawa. 2007. Exploiting Wikipedia as external knowledge for named entity recognition. In *Proceedings of the 2007 Joint Conference on Empirical Methods in Natural Language Processing and Computational Natural Language Learning (EMNLP-CoNLL)*.

Sungchul Kim, Kristina Toutanova, and Hwanjo Yu. 2012. Multilingual named entity recognition using parallel data and metadata from Wikipedia. In *Proceedings of the 50th Annual Meeting of the Association for Computational Linguistics: Long Papers-Volume 1*. Association for Computational Linguistics, pages 694–702.

Veronika Laippala and Filip Ginter. 2014. Syntactic N-gram collection from a large-scale corpus of internet Finnish. In *Human Language Technologies-The Baltic Perspective: Proceedings of the Sixth International Conference Baltic HLT 2014*. IOS Press, volume 268, page 184.

Guillaume Lample, Miguel Ballesteros, Sandeep Subramanian, Kazuya Kawakami, and Chris Dyer. 2016. Neural architectures for named entity recognition. In *Proceedings of the 2016 Conference of the North American Chapter of the Association for Computational Linguistics: Human Language Technologies*. Association for Computational Linguistics, San Diego, California, pages 260–270.

Xuezhe Ma and Eduard H. Hovy. 2016. End-to-end sequence labeling via bi-directional LSTM-CNNs-CRF. *CoRR* abs/1603.01354.

Tomas Mikolov, Kai Chen, Greg S Corrado, and Jeffrey Dean. 2013. Efficient estimation of word representations in vector space. In *NIPS*.

Sjur N Moshagen, Tommi Pirinen, and Trond Trosterud. 2013. Building an open-source development infrastructure for language technology projects. In *Proceedings of NODALIDA 2013: the 19th Nordic Conference of Computational Linguistics*. Oslo, Norway.

Joel Nothman, Nicky Ringland, Will Radford, Tara Murphy, and James R Curran. 2013. Learning multilingual named entity recognition from Wikipedia. *Artificial Intelligence* 194:151–175.

Matthew E. Peters, Mark Neumann, Mohit Iyyer, Matt Gardner, Christopher Clark, Kenton Lee, and Luke Zettlemoyer. 2018. Deep contextualized word representations. In *Proc. of NAACL*.

Nils Reimers and Iryna Gurevych. 2017. Optimal hyperparameters for deep lstm-networks for sequence labeling tasks. *CoRR* abs/1707.06799.

Alexander E Richman and Patrick Schone. 2008. Mining wiki resources for multilingual named entity recognition. In *Proceedings of ACL-08: HLT*. pages 1–9.

Teemu Ruokolainen, Pekka Kauppinen, Miikka Silfverberg, and Krister Lindén. 2019. A finnish news corpus for named entity recognition. *Language Resources and Evaluation* pages 1–26.

Antonio Toral and Rafael Munoz. 2006. A proposal to automatically build and maintain gazetteers for Named Entity Recognition by using Wikipedia. In *Proceedings of the Workshop on NEW TEXT Wikis and blogs and other dynamic text sources*.

Template-free Data-to-Text Generation of Finnish Sports News

Jenna Kanerva, **Samuel Rönnqvist**, **Riina Kekki**, **Tapio Salakoski** and **Filip Ginter**
TurkuNLP
Department of Future Technologies
University of Turku, Finland
`{jmnybl,saanro,rieeke,sala,figint}@utu.fi`

Abstract

News articles such as sports game reports are often thought to closely follow the underlying game statistics, but in practice they contain a notable amount of background knowledge, interpretation, insight into the game, and quotes that are not present in the official statistics. This poses a challenge for automated data-to-text news generation with real-world news corpora as training data. We report on the development of a corpus of Finnish ice hockey news, edited to be suitable for training of end-to-end news generation methods, as well as demonstrate generation of text, which was judged by journalists to be relatively close to a viable product. The new dataset and system source code are available for research purposes.[1]

1 Introduction

Automated, or robotic, journalism aims at news generation from structured data sources, either as the final product or as a draft for subsequent post-editing. At present, automated journalism typically focuses on domains such as sports, finance and similar statistics-based reporting, where there is a commercial product potential due to the high volume of news, combined with the expectation of a relatively straightforward task.

News generation systems—especially those deployed in practice—tend to be based on intricate template filling, aiming to give the users the full control of the generated facts, while maintaining a reasonable variability of the resulting text. This comes at the price of having to develop the templates and specify their control logic, neither of which are tasks naturally fitting journalists' work.

Further, this development needs to be repeated for every domain, as the templates are not easily transferred across domains. Examples of the template-based news generation systems for Finnish are Voitto[2] by the Finnish Public Service Broadcasting Company (YLE) used for sports news generation, as well as Vaalibotti (Leppänen et al., 2017), a hybrid machine learning and template-based system used for election news.

Wiseman et al. (2018) suggested a neural template generation, which jointly models latent templates and text generation. Such a system increases interpretability and controllability of the generation, however, recent sequence-to-sequence systems represent the state-of-the-art in data-to-text generation. (Dušek et al., 2018)

In this paper, we report on the development of a news generation system for the Finnish ice hockey news domain, based on sequence-to-sequence methods. In order to train such a system, we compile a corpus of news based on over 2000 game reports from the Finnish News Agency STT. While developing this corpus into a form suitable for training of end-to-end systems naturally requires manual effort, we argue that compiling and refining a set of text examples is a more natural way for journalists to interact with the system, in order for them to codify their knowledge and to adapt it for new domains.

Our aim is to generate reports that give an overview of a game based on information inferrable from the statistics. Such reports can be used either as a basis for further post-editing by a journalist imprinting own insights and background information, or even used directly as a news stream labelled as machine-generated.

In the following, we will introduce the news dataset and the process of its creation, introduce an end-to-end model for news generation, and eval-

---

[1] `https://github.com/scoopmatic/`
`finnish-hockey-news-generation-paper`

[2] `https://github.com/Yleisradio/`
`avoin-voitto`

uate its output respective to the abovementioned objectives.

2   Ice Hockey News Dataset

An ice hockey game is recorded into statistics in terms of different events occurring during play, such as goals and penalties. In order to train a model to generate game reports, we need access to these events, as well as example news articles about the game. Only recently have game statistics become available to the public through a web interface or API, whereas the information has traditionally been recorded as structured text files.

The news corpus from the Finnish News Agency STT[3] includes, among all other news, articles covering ice hockey games in the Finnish leagues during the years 1994–2018. In addition to news articles, the corpus also includes the original game statistics text files. This creates an opportunity to align the game statistics with the corresponding news articles, producing a dataset of over 20 years of ice hockey data with reference news articles for the games. When automatically pairing the game statistics with news articles using date and team names as a heuristic, we obtain a total of 3,454 games with existing statistics and at least one corresponding news article.

Utilizing real journalistic material poses a challenge in that the articles mix information that can be found directly in the game statistics (e.g., scores and names) with information inferable from the statistics (e.g., statements such as *shortly after*), information based on background knowledge (e.g., a team's home city or player's position), game insight and judgement based on viewing the game (e.g., expressions such as *slapshot* or *tipping the puck* describing the character of a shot), and even player interviews.

Therefore, directly using the limited amount of actual news articles for end-to-end system training becomes problematic. In our initial experiments the generation model learns to "hallucinate" facts, as easily occurs when the target text is too loosely related to the conditioning input.[4] In order to ensure that the generation model is able to learn to generate accurate descriptions from game statistics, we clean the news corpus by manually aligning corresponding text spans with game events detailed in the statistics.

For the sake of comparison, let us consider the Rotowire corpus (Wiseman et al., 2017) containing basketball game summaries and statistics, which was recently released and has become a popular data set for training data-to-text generation systems (cf., e.g., Nie et al. (2018); Wiseman et al. (2018); Puduppully et al. (2019)). The Rotowire game summaries are straightforward in their style of reporting, focusing on the game at hand and tend for the most part to reference facts in the statistics. By contrast, our news corpus is more heterogeneous, including both articles focusing on the particular game and articles that take a broader perspective (e.g., describing a player's career). The STT news articles tend to read in the journalist's voice, putting substantial emphasis on the character of the game, often in colorful language, as well as quoting players and coaches.

An example of the events available in the game statistics, the actual news article on the game, and how these align, is shown in Figure 1. Text spans highlighted with blue color are based on information available in the statistics, all other being external information. It illustrates the typical portion of a raw article that is not inferrable from the data. English translations are available for a comparable example in Figure 4.

2.1   Extraction of Game Events

For each event occurring in a game and recorded in statistics, we identify its type and associated features. There are four event types: *end result*, *goal*, *penalty* and *save*. As a general rule, for each game the end result entry specifies total scores, participating teams and additional circumstances of the game such as overtime or shootout. The goal event is the most frequent and includes features such as goal scorer, assists, team, resulting score, time and the current state of the game (e.g., power play, penalty shot). We also derive special features that in many cases require consideration of other events in the context, but pertain to one particular event, e.g., is the goal deciding or final. The penalty event specifies player, team, time in the game and penalty time. The save event summarises the number of saves of a goaltender/team.

We perform information extraction with regular expressions on the statistics in order to structure the game into a chronological sequence of events,

---

[3]A version of the corpus is available at `http://urn.fi/urn:nbn:fi:lb-2019041501` for academic use.

[4]This observation is also supported by Wiseman et al. (2017) mentioning that their generation model occasionally "hallucinates factual statements" that are plausible but false.

Game events:

E1 Lopputulos Blues–HPK 4–0 (1–0, 2–0, 1–0)
E2 Jäähy Jaakko Turtiainen, HPK 2min 11.57
E3 Maali 1–0 Arttu Luttinen, Blues (Jari Sailio) 14.56
E4 Jäähy Petri Lammassaari, Blues 2min 16.31
E5 Jäähy Mathias Porseland, HPK 2min 20.47
E6 Jäähy Janne Kolehmainen, HPK 2min 21.20
E7 Maali 2–0 yv Toni Kähkönen, Blues (Camilo Miettinen) 22.26
E8 Maali 3–0 yv Jere Karalahti, Blues (Stephane Veilleux, Stefan Öhman) 23.01
E9 Jäähy Roope Ranta, Blues 2min 25.57
E10 Jäähy Jere Sallinen, Blues 2min 29.04
E11 Jäähy Oskari Korpikari, Blues 2min 32.41
E12 Maali 4–0 J Sallinen, Blues (Valtteri Virkkunen) 42.11
E13 Jäähy Turtiainen, HPK 2min 44.58
E14 Jäähy Teemu Lassila, HPK 2min 48.47
E15 Jäähy Virkkunen, Blues 2+2min 50.29
E16 Jäähy Jukka Laamanen, HPK 2min 51.30
E17 Jäähy Laamanen, HPK 2min 57.46
E18 Torjunnat Iiro Tarkki, Blues 30 torjuntaa
E19 Torjunnat Teemu Lassila, HPK 34 torjuntaa

Original game report (with alignments):

Espoon Blues kukisti HPK:n jääkiekon SM-liigassa 4–0-numeroin.[E1] Kotijoukkue Blues hankkiutui avauserässä 1–0-johtoon Arttu Luttisen maalilla [E3], mutta ottelun ratkaisut nähtiin toisessa erässä. Blues iski erän alussa vajaassa minuutissa kaksi osumaa [E7,8], ja HPK:n pelihalut karisivat.
– Oikea joukkue voitti. Monessa pelissä olemme onnistuneet kirimään, tänään emme. Ekassa erässä olimme hyvin mukana, mutta selkeät ratkaisut tulivat meidän alivoimissa, joissa emme onnistuneet, HPK-käskijä Harri Rindell harmitteli.
Ensin osui Toni Kähkönen ajassa 22.26 kahden miehen ylivoimalla.[E7] Alle minuutin päästä Jere Karalahti lisäsi kotijoukkueen johdon jo 3–0:aan.[E8] Kokenut puolustaja nousi kulmalta maalille, laukoi ja iski oman paluukiekon ohi HPK-vahti Teemu Lassilan. Osumaan nappasi syöttöpisteen pirteästi pelannut Stephane Veilleux[E8], jolle peli oli ensimmäinen SM-liigassa. Jere Sallinen kaunisteli vielä päätöserässä lukemat 4–0:aan.[E12]
– Pelimme oli kurinalaista, ei kauhean nättiä, mutta pisteet ratkaisevat. Oltiin, hyviä, tehokkaita ja suht tylyjä, Blues-valmentaja Petri Matikainen ynnäsi.

Figure 1: A representative example of events extracted from game statistics and the corresponding report in the news corpus. Events that are mentioned in the article are boldfaced (left) and the aligned text spans are highlighted in blue (right). Event references are indicated at the end of each alignment (e.g., [E1]).

which can then be aligned with the corresponding text spans from the news article, as well as used as input in the text generation. An initial sequence of events after information extraction is shown on the left side in Figure 1. Before text generation, these events are yet enhanced with additional information derived from the event itself, or the game.

2.2 Manual Alignment

The manual alignment of game events and the article text is carried out by a single annotator in approximately 6 weeks as an integral part of the system development work. The annotator receives a sequence of extracted events and aligns these with the corresponding news article, typically but not necessarily a single sentence for every expressed event. All ungrounded parts within the text are removed and if necessary, the text is modified for fluency. We cannot align full sentences with events as, for instance, Barzilay and Lapata (2005) do, as often information not grounded in the statistics is expressed together with statistics-based facts within the same sentences and clauses.

The alignment process therefore frequently requires rephrasing the text, for instance, in order to make it more neutral and avoid generating arbitrary subjective judgements. We find that the news article commonly includes description that is not evident from the data (e.g., subjective characteristics of the player or the shot), and often may reflect the reporter's viewpoint. For instance, the reporter may evaluate an event negatively by writing

Player A did not manage to score more than one goal, reflecting expectation of the player's performance, which we would change into a more objective form such as *Player A scored one goal*. Similarly, word choices based on viewing the game (e.g., *slapshot*) are changed to more neutral counterparts.

After removing the uninferable parts of a sentence, the remainder is often relatively short, in which case we sometimes opt to replace the information that was removed with references to other appropriate information from the game statistics, such as the time of the event or the state of the game. This serves to maintain a similar sentence and clause structure as that of the original corpus.

In the majority of our aligned data one text span refers to one game event. However, in some cases the same indivisible span can describe multiple events, most commonly of the same type (e.g., *Player A scored two goals*, or *Team A received a total of eight penalties*). In such cases, we produce multi-event alignments, where all related events are aligned with a single text span.[5] Multi-event alignments support the development of more advanced generation, which stands to produce more natural-sounding reports in terms of less repetition and more flexible structuring.

---

[5]Cf. Figure 1, alignments of E7 and E8: The events are expressed differently depending on type of alignment, where the 2-to-1 aligned text says that the team scored two goals.

Games	2,134
Events	36,097
Aligned events	12,251
End result	2,092
Goal	6,651
Penalty	2,163
Save	1,345
Aligned spans	8,831
Aligned sentences	9,266
Aligned tokens	84,997

Table 1: Event alignment statistics.

	Original Corpus	Aligned
Sentences	49,496	9,266
Tokens	601,990	84,997
Unique tokens	54,624	7,393
Unique lemmas	24,105	4,724
STTR (words)	0.641	0.525
STTR (lemmas)	0.501	0.424

Table 2: Comparison of the original hockey news and the aligned sentences, including analysis of lexical diversity.

2.3 Corpus Statistics

In Table 1, we summarize the overall size statistics of the final ice hockey corpus after the statistics and news articles have been automatically paired, and events have been manually aligned with the text. In total, 2,307 games were manually checked (66.8% of the paired corpus), of which 2,134 games were correctly paired with the article describing the game. In these games, 12,251 out of 36,097 events (33.9%) were referenced in the text and successfully aligned. *End result* occurs in nearly all news articles as the first event, whereas the *goal* event is by far the most frequent one, each game mentioning on average 3.1 goals. The number of aligned events is greater than the number of aligned text spans due to multi-event alignments. While 82.1% of text spans align with a single event, there is a long tail of multi-event alignments, with 11.2% aligning to two events, 3.4% to three, 1.4% to four, etc.

In Table 2 we measure the lexical diversity of original ice hockey news articles, as well as the resulting dataset after manual alignment, by computing the Standardized Type–Token Ratio (STTR). The measure is defined as the number of unique tokens or lemmas divided by the total number of tokens, calculated on every segment of 1,000 tokens separately and averaged across the corpus. STTR is more meaningful than the standard type–token ratio when comparing corpora of substantially different sizes. Both corpora are tokenized and lemmatized using the Turku Neural Parser pipeline (Kanerva et al., 2018, 2019). STTR of the aligned corpus is lower than in the original hockey news on both word and lemma level, indicating a somewhat—but not substantially so—more restricted vocabulary use in our aligned subset.

3 Event Selection Model

As illustrated previously, any given news article describes only a subset of most noteworthy events of a game. We observe that most reports are concise, referencing on average 5.7 events. The distribution of events/report is: 1st quantile at 3 events (20.9% of events in game), 2nd at 5 (22.2%), 3rd at 7 (38.5%), 4th at 36 (100%).

Our alignment serves as a gold standard reflecting which events the journalists have chosen to mention for each game. In our generation task, we are presented with the problem of selecting appropriate events from the full game statistics. We use the gold standard selection during training and validation of the text generation model, as well as the automatic evaluation. As we deploy our text generation model for manual evaluation, we use a Conditional Random Field (CRF) model to predict which events to mention.

Casting the event selection problem as a sequence labeling task, the CRF model takes as input the full sequence of events in one game together with associated features for each event, and predicts a binary label for each event.[6] We achieve an overall F-score of 67.1% on the test set, which broken down by event type is: end result (98.0%), goal (70.2%), penalty (20.1%), save (47.7%). Penalties are the most difficult to predict, being reported only 7.8% of the time in reality, e.g., compared to 54.1% for goals.

4 Text Generation

Next, we present the model architecture used in text generation, and evaluate the model on a pop-

---

[6]We use label weighting to account for the imbalanced distribution, which we optimize against the validation set to 0.85:1 for the positive class (other optimal hyperparameters are C1=35.0, C2=0.5, as well as defaults). We use CRFsuite (Okazaki, 2007) with label weighting by Sampo Pyysalo: `https://github.com/spyysalo/crfsuite`

ular baseline dataset. After that, we describe the training of the generation model on our ice hockey corpus and use automatic evaluation metrics to compare against existing references.

4.1 Model Architecture

We use a pointer-generation network (Vinyals et al., 2015; Gu et al., 2016; See et al., 2017), where the neural attention mechanism in the encoder-decoder model is adapted to jointly model a probability distribution over words from the known vocabulary, a distribution over words from the input sequence to copy and a probability that controls the copying mechanism. A separate coverage attention vector, a sum of past attention distributions, is maintained to inform the model of its past attention decisions. Such a coverage model is shown to prevent text repetition in generated output (Tu et al., 2016; See et al., 2017).

The model is implemented using the OpenNMT-py library (Klein et al., 2017). The encoder has two bidirectional LSTM layers with 500 hidden units, together with 500-dimensional word embeddings. The decoder has two unidirectional LSTM layers with 500 hidden units. Both encoder and decoder apply a dropout of 0.3 between LSTM layers.

4.2 Baseline Experiments on the E2E Dataset

To demonstrate the performance of our generation model architecture, we report results on a known dataset with published baselines, namely the E2E NLG Challenge (Dušek et al., 2018) on end-to-end natural language generation in spoken dialogue systems. The task is to produce a natural language description of a restaurant based on a given meaning representation (MR)—an unordered set of attributes and their values. The attributes included, among others, the restaurant name, area, food type and rating. We represent the given MR as a sequence of tokens where each attribute value is embedded into XML-style beginning and end attribute markers, and the order of attributes is kept fixed across the whole dataset. The target output is a sequence of tokens. We do not apply any explicit delexicalization steps.

In Table 3 we measure BLEU (Papineni et al., 2002), NIST (Doddington, 2002), METEOR (Lavie and Agarwal, 2007), ROUGE-L (Lin, 2004) and CIDEr (Vedantam et al., 2015) metrics on the 2018 E2E NLG Challenge test data using the evaluation script provided by the orga-

nizers[7]. Our generation system is compared to the official shared task baseline system, TGen (Dušek and Jurčíček, 2016), as well as to the top performing participant system on each score (ST top). Our system outperforms the TGen baseline on 3 out of 5 metrics (BLEU, METEOR and ROUGE-L), which is on par with the official shared task results, where not a single one participant system was able to surpass the baseline on all five metrics. On two metrics, BLEU and METEOR, our system outperforms the best shared task participants.

E2E NLG Challenge evaluation is based on having multiple references for each MR, on average each unique MR in the corpus having 8 reference descriptions. In the evaluation, the output for each unique MR is compared against all references and the maximum score is used, naturally leading to higher scores. To have more comparable numbers to our ice hockey corpus, where we have only one reference for each input event, we also include scores obtained by comparing each MR to each of its reference descriptions separately as if they were individual data points (Ours single ref.).

4.3 Hockey Data Representation

Currently, we concentrate on training the model only with text spans aligning with single events, excluding the less frequent multi-event alignments. Furthermore, we are considering each event as a separate training example, independent of other events in the game.

Given a single event described as a sequence of features and their values, our text generation model is trained to produce the text span aligned with it. Following the data representation used in E2E NLG Challenge experiments, the input events are represented as a linearized sequence of tokens, where XML-style beginning and end tags are used to separate the different features (see Figure 2). This allows the model to directly copy some of the input tokens to the output when necessary. The ability to copy tokens is especially important with player names and exact times, where the vocabulary is sparse, and many of these can even be previously unseen, unknown tokens. In addition, we also include features that are meant to inform generation without being copied themselves, for example, the type of the event. The target of generation is a tokenized sequence of words, where

---

[7]https://github.com/tuetschek/
e2e-metrics

	BLEU	NIST	METEOR	ROUGE-L	CIDEr
Ours	0.6758	8.5588	0.4536	0.6990	2.2007
TGen	0.6593	8.6094	0.4483	0.6850	2.2338
ST top	0.6619*	8.6130*	0.4529**	0.7083†	2.2721‡
Ours single ref.	0.3190	5.1995	0.3574	0.4969	1.7922

Table 3: Performance of our generation model on the E2E test set compared to the shared task baseline (TGen) and winners on each metric (*Juraska et al. (2018), **Puzikov and Gurevych (2018), †Zhang et al. (2018), ‡Gong (2018)), as well as our model in an adapted evaluation setup (Ours single ref.).

also dashes inside scores are separated, allowing the model to swap scores when necessary. The reference text sometimes flips the order of the teams, requiring the score to be inverted as well (*Team A–Team B 0–1* into *Team B won Team A 1–0*).

One particular challenge in our corpus is that the decision of which aspects to focus on, i.e., which particular features from the source event to verbalize, is relatively arbitrary. For example, sometimes a journalist mentions the player or players assisting a goal, but in many cases it is left out. Both options are equally correct, but overlap-based metrics such as BLEU penalize such creative variation. By contrast, in other text generation datasets such as the E2E NLG Challenge, the output text in general describes all input features. To account for this variation, we include a length feature to act as a minimal supervision signal for the model to rely on. We divide output text lengths into three evenly sized categories (*short*, *medium* and *long*) to provide a hint to the model during training of how long and detailed output it is expected to generate for each training example. At test time, we then have the possibility to control the desired approximate length of the generated text. In the experiments throughout this paper, we generate all three length variants for each event and pick the one with the highest average confidence of the generation model.

4.4 Training and Optimization

The model is trained using the Adam optimizer with learning rate of 0.0005 and batch size of 32. The model is trained for a maximum of 8000 steps (ca. 40 epochs), and the final model is chosen based on validation set performance. We use 80% of the aligned games for training, 10% for validation and 10% for testing.

In our initial experiments, we used the RBFOpt library (Costa and Nannicini, 2014) for hyperparameter tuning, maximizing validation set BLEU score. However, when manually inspecting generation results on the validation set, we noticed that models with a higher BLEU score result in more fluent text but generate more factual mistakes. This observation is supported by Wiseman et al. (2017), who note that BLEU score tends to reward fluent text rather than other aspects desirable in generation of sports summaries from data. For this reason, we ultimately decided to use hyperparameters manually tuned on the validation set to give a good perceived balance between fluent and factually correct text.

4.5 Automatic Evaluation of Hockey Generation

In Table 4, we provide evaluation results using the five aforementioned metrics. We evaluate on event level using gold standard event selection, where each generated event description is compared to its existing reference text. As the model is trained to produce a tokenized sequence, we apply a detokenizer to be able to compare against the original untokenized reference text. On the test set, the model achieves a BLEU score of 19.67. To the extent that different datasets allow comparison, the best reported score on the Rotowire basketball news corpus is 16.50 (Puduppully et al., 2019). Compared to our earlier E2E baseline experiment, we score lower than our closest comparable reference of 31.90 (with single references), which is understandable due to the much smaller train set size for the hockey corpus (about 13% in size).

In Figure 3, we plot the learning curve with increasing sizes of training data in order to illustrate how generation performance benefits from more data. The learning curve is still steadily increasing when using 100% of the training data currently available, which indicates that more data would most likely further improve the performance.

```
INPUT:    <length>long</length> <type>result</type> <home> Ässät </home> <guest> Blues </guest>
          <score> 0 - 4 </score> <periods> ( 0 - 3 , 0 - 0 , 0 - 1 ) </periods>
OUTPUT:   Blues vei voiton Ässistä maalein 4 - 0 ( 3 - 0 , 0 - 0 , 1 - 0 ) .
```

Figure 2: An example input–output pair for the text generation model, derived from manual alignment. The original, untokenized output sentence is *Blues vei voiton Ässistä maalein 4–0 (3–0, 0–0, 1–0).* (Literal English translation: *Blues took a win from Ässät with goals 4–0 (3–0, 0–0, 1–0).*)

BLEU	0.1967
NIST	4.4144
METEOR	0.2297
ROUGE-L	0.4159
CIDEr	1.8658

Table 4: Automatic evaluation metrics on hockey corpus test set.

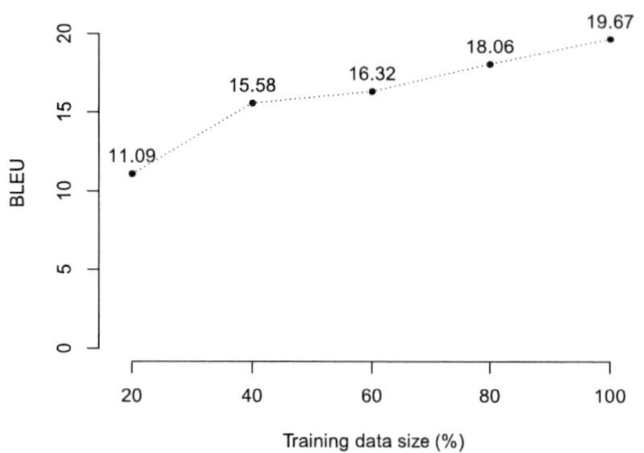

Figure 3: Learning curve demonstrating the effect of training data size on generation performance.

5 Human evaluation

As our objective is practically usable news generation, we carry out a manual evaluation of its output on 59 randomly selected games from the test set, focusing in particular on the corrections that would be necessary to obtain acceptable output. Example corrections are shown in Figure 4. These full game reports are generated by first applying the selection model described in Section 3 to select the events to be included in the report, and then using the text generation model to verbalize each selected event. The generated texts of the events are then detokenized and concatenated in chronological order into a full game report.

5.1 Minimum Edit Evaluation

In the *minimum edit* evaluation, carried out by the annotator who created the news corpus, only factual mistakes and grammatical errors are corrected, resulting in text which may remain awkward or unfluent. The word error rate (WER)

Error type	Count
Team or player name	25
Type or score of goal	24
Time reference	14
Total score	6
Penalty	5
Assist	2
Power play	2

Table 5: Types of factual errors in the generated output for 59 games.

of the generated text compared to its corrected variant as a reference is 5.6% (6.2% disregarding punctuation). The WER measure is defined as the number of insertions, substitutions, and deletions divided by the total length of the reference, in terms of tokens. The measure is the edit distance of the generated text and its corrected variant, directly reflecting the amount of effort needed to correct the generated output.

5.1.1 Factual Correctness

The factual errors and their types are summarized in Table 5. From the total of 510 game events generated by the system, 78 of these contained a factual error, i.e. 84.7% were generated without factual errors.

The most notable errors involved player or team names. The input for a single game event may contain more than one name (e.g. the goal scorer and up to two assisting players). In these cases, the model occasionally paired first name and surname incorrectly. Less frequent errors include wrong team pairings when referring to the end result of the game, e.g., *Team A lost to Team A.*

In sentences where the exact time of a game event is generated as a number (*at time 39.54*) the model copied the time reliably, but when the approximate time of an event is verbalized (*at the end of the second period*) there were occasional errors. Another notable error category is types of goals or their scores (e.g. 3–0, deciding goal, tying goal). In this category, the error similarly occurred in cases when the reference is verbal (*third goal*), but occasionally also in numerical representation (*3–0* instead of *0–3*). The other, less common categories relate to game total scores, power play, assists and penalties.

5.1.2 Fluency

Overall, the generated text is highly grammatical. The most frequent grammatical error in the output is unconjugated player names; commonly names in their Finnish nominative case that should be in genitive. In a few cases, the model makes grammatical errors when it copies an incompatible word from the input, e.g., a name instead of a time reference.

Both error types commonly occur when the model copies from the input. As it operates on the token rather than sub-word level, it is challenging to map between word forms and inflect infrequent words such as player names. The latter error likely occurs when the copy attention is indecisive and fails to recognize the type for infrequent tokens.

Most fluency issues relate to the overall flow and structure of the report. Addressing these issues would require the model to take into account multiple events in a game, and combine the information more flexibly to avoid repetition. For instance, the output may repeatedly mention the period number for all goals in the same period. Likewise, this setup sometimes results in unnatural, yet grammatical, repetition of words across consecutive sentences. Even though the model has learned a selection of verbs meaning *to score a goal*, it is unable to ensure their varied use. While not successful in our initial experiments, generating text based on the multi-event alignments or at document level may eventually overcome these issues.

5.2 Product-Readiness Evaluation

The second human evaluation aimed at judging the acceptability of the output for production use in a news agency. The output is evaluated in terms of its usability for a news channel labelled as being machine-generated, i.e. not aiming at the level of a human journalist equipped with substantial background information. The evaluation was carried out by two journalists from the STT agency, who split the 59 games among themselves approximately evenly. The first journalist edited the games to a form corresponding to a draft for subsequent minor post-editing by a human, simulating the use of the generated output as a product where the final customer is expected to do own post-editing before publication. The second journalist directly edited the news to a state ready for direct publication in a news stream labeled as machine-generated news. In addition to correcting factual errors, the journalists removed excessive repetition, improved text fluency, as well as occasionally included important facts which the system left ungenerated. The WER measured against the output considered ready for post-editing, is 9.9% (11.2% disregarding punctuation), only slightly worse than the evaluation with only the factual and grammatical errors corrected. The WER measured against the output considered ready for direct release, was 22.0% (24.4% disregarding punctuation). In other words, 75–90% of the generated text can be directly used, depending on the expected post-editing effort.

Figure 4 shows two example games along with the generated reports and manual corrections made by the journalist in order to prepare it for publication. Literal translations from the generated, uncorrected Finnish into English are provided for reference.

6 Conclusions and Future Work

We developed and evaluated an end-to-end system for news generation from structured data, using a corpus of news and game statistics in the ice hockey domain. In terms of the data, our primary finding was the level to which professionally produced news contain information that cannot be inferred from the game statistics. This leads to the model learning to "hallucinate" facts and necessitates a manual alignment and editing of the training data. Once we created a suitable training dataset, we were able to generate highly grammatical text which, in terms of word error rate (edit distance), was relatively close to what was judged as a viable product by domain journalists. We found that most factual errors in the generated output fall into a small number of categories, mostly related to copying names from the input, types of events, and time references. Addressing these errors is a matter of future work and can be approached using data augmentation techniques as well as introducing sub-word units which would allow the model to deal with inflections.

Currently, we only generate the news as independent events, with roughly one sentence corresponding to one event. As this leads to a somewhat unnatural text, we have attempted in prelim-

Events (game 1):

E1 Lopputulos Blues–Ilves 3–2 ja (0–1, 1–0, 1–1, 1–0)
E2 Maali 0–1 Linda Välimäki, Ilves (None) 2.07
E3 Jäähy Salla Korhonen, Blues 2min 3.22
E4 Jäähy Annina Rajahuhta, Ilves 2min 6.08
E5 Jäähy Johanna Koivula, Ilves 2min 15.37
E6 Maali 1–1 Essi Hallvar, Blues (None) 27.03
E7 Jäähy Ninni Taskinen, Blues 2min 27.13
E8 Jäähy Anna Kinnunen, Blues 2min 32.43
E9 Jäähy Jenni Hiirikoski, Ilves 2min 37.53
E10 Maali 2–1 Marjo Voutilainen, Blues (Oona Parviainen, Terhi Mertanen) 43.55
E11 Maali 2–2 Annina Rajahuhta, Ilves (Linda Välimäki, Satu Niinimäki) 47.49
E12 Jäähy Ninni Taskinen, Blues 2min 54.03
E13 Jäähy Satu Niinimäki, Ilves 2min 56.04
E14 Jäähy Tea Villilä, Blues 2min 66.55
E15 Jäähy Tiia Reima, Blues 2min 69.07
E16 Jäähy Annina Rajahuhta, Ilves 2min 70.55
E17 Jäähy Linda Välimäki, Ilves 2min 71.16
E18 Maali 3–2 yv Oona Parviainen, Blues (Emma Laaksonen, Terhi Mertanen) 72.34
E19 Torjunnat Anna Vanhatalo, Blues 45 torjuntaa
E20 Torjunnat Linda Selkee, Ilves 30 torjuntaa

Generated game report with manual corrections:
Ilves voitti ~~Ilves~~Bluesin jatkoajalla 3–2 (0–1, 1–0, 1–1, 1-0).
Linda Välimäki vei Ilveksen johtoon 1-0 avauserässä.
Bluesin ~~ainokaisen~~tasoituksen teki Essi Hallvar toisessa erässä.
Kolmannessa erässä Marjo Voutilainen vei Bluesin 2–1 -johtoon.
Ilveksen Linda Rajahuhta viimeisteli 2–2 -tasoituksen.
~~Oona~~ Ottelun ratkaisun teki Oona Parviainen jatkoajalla.
Bluesin maalivahti Anna Vanhatalo torjui 45 laukausta.
Ilveksen maalivahti Linda Selkee torjui 30 laukausta.

Literal English translation of generated report:
Ilves won Ilves on overtime 3–2 (0–1, 1–0, 1–1).
Linda Välimäki took Ilves to a 1-0 lead.
Blues' only goal was made by Essi Hallvar.
In the third period Marjo Voutilainen took to a 2–1 lead.
Linda Rajahuhta finished off with a 2–2 tying goal.
Oona the deciding goal was made by Oona Parviainen.
Blues' goalkeeper Anna Vanhatalo saved 45 shots.
Ilves' goalkeeper Linda Selkee saved 30 shots.

Events (game 2):

E1 Lopputulos HIFK–Jokerit 2–4 (1–1, 1–2, 0–1)
E2 Jäähy Jere Karalahti, Jokerit 2min 3.20
E3 Maali 0–1 Antti Tyrväinen, Jokerit (Nichlas Hardt, Teuvo Teräväinen) 6.12
E4 Maali 1–1 Juuso Puustinen, HIFK (Ville Peltonen, Corey Elkins) 7.12
E5 Jäähy Hardt, Jokerit 2min 17.47
E6 Maali 1–2 Steve Moses, Jokerit (Ossi Väänänen, Teräväinen) 23.36
E7 Maali 1–3 Mikko Kousa, Jokerit (Teräväinen, Hardt) 26.28
E8 Jäähy Braden Birch, HIFK 2min 28.56
E9 Jäähy Trevor Gillies, HIFK 5+20min 32.16
E10 Maali 2–3 av Iiro Pakarinen, HIFK (Eero Somervuori, Peltonen) 34.11
E11 Jäähy Elkins, HIFK 2min 36.02
E12 Jäähy Kousa, Jokerit 2min 37.58
E13 Jäähy Janos Hari, HIFK 2min 39.22
E14 Jäähy Dehner, Jokerit 2min 46.24
E15 Jäähy Toni Söderholm, HIFK 2min 47.21
E16 Jäähy Karalahti, Jokerit 2min 51.53
E17 Jäähy Birch, HIFK 2min 57.40
E18 Jäähy jr, Jokerit 2min 59.21
E19 Jäähy Tomi Mäki, Jokerit 2min 59.33
E20 Maali 2–4 av, tm Jeremy Dehner, Jokerit (None) 59.55
E21 Torjunnat Brad Thiessen, HIFK 27 torjuntaa
E22 Torjunnat Leland Irving, Jokerit 22 torjuntaa

Generated game report with manual corrections:
Jokerit löi HIFK:n 4–2 (1–1, 2–1, 1–0).
Jokerit meni avauserässä 1–0 -johtoon Antti Tyrväi~~nen~~sen osumalla.
HIFK:n Juuso Puustinen iski 1–1 -tasoituksen ajassa 7.12.
Toisessa erässä Jokerien Steve Moses iski 2–1 -johdon.
Toisessa erässä Jokerit meni 3–1 -johtoon.
HIFK:n Trevor Gillies joutui suihkuun.
HIFK:n Iiro Pakarinen kavensi 2–3:een ajassa 34.11 alivoimalla.
2-4 -osuman iski Jokerien Jeremy ~~Dehner~~Dehner.
HIFK:n maalivahti Brad Thiessen torjui 27 kiekkoa.
Jokerien maalivahti Leland Irving torjui 22 kiekkoa.

Literal English translation of generated report:
Jokerit beat HIFK 4–2 (1–1, 2–1, 1–0).
Jokerit went in the opening period to a 1–0 lead due to Antti Tyväinen goal score.
HIFK's Juuso Puustinen scored a 1–1 tie at 7.12.
In the second period Jokerit's Steve Moses scored a 2–1 lead.
In the second period Jokerit went to a 3–1 lead.
HIFK's Trevor Gillies was sent to the shower.
Iiro Pakarinen narrowed to 2–3 at 34.11.
The 2-4 goal was scored by Jokerit's Dehner Dehner.
HIFK's goalkeeper Brad Thiessen saved 27 pucks.
Jokerit's goalkeeper Leland Irving saved 22 pucks.

Figure 4: Generated reports with manual corrections for two example games. Insertions in manual corrections are marked in green and deletions in red and struck through. English translations are based on original, uncorrected generation output. English translations for input events: Lopputulos (End result), Maali (Goal), Jäähy (Penalty), Torjunnat (Saves), ja (overtime), yv (power play), av (short-handed), tm (empty net).

inary experiments to generate whole news texts at once, as well as sentences combining several events, nevertheless with results far from useful. This is likely due to the relatively small number of training examples where a single sentence accounts for several distinct events. We will focus on this problem in our future work, investigating methods which would allow pre-training the generation model so as to be able to successfully accept several events on its input.

The new dataset, the original news corpus and the source code of the model are available for research use. [8]

---

[8] https://github.com/scoopmatic/finnish-hockey-news-generation-paper

Acknowledgments

We gratefully acknowledge the collaboration of Maija Paikkala, Salla Salmela and Pihla Lehmusjoki of the Finnish News Agency STT, as well as the support of the Google Digital News Innovation Fund, Academy of Finland, CSC – IT Center for Science, and the NVIDIA Corporation GPU Grant Program.

References

Regina Barzilay and Mirella Lapata. 2005. https://www.aclweb.org/anthology/H05-1042 Collective content selection for concept-to-text generation. In *Proceedings of Human Language Technology Conference and Conference on Empirical Methods in Natural Language Processing*, pages

331–338, Vancouver, British Columbia, Canada. Association for Computational Linguistics.

Alberto Costa and Giacomo Nannicini. 2014. RBFOpt: an open-source library for black-box optimization with costly function evaluations. *Optimization Online*, 4538.

George Doddington. 2002. http://dl.acm.org/citation.cfm?id=1289189.1289273 Automatic evaluation of machine translation quality using n-gram co-occurrence statistics. In *Proceedings of the Second International Conference on Human Language Technology Research*, pages 138–145. Morgan Kaufmann Publishers Inc.

Ondřej Dušek and Filip Jurčíček. 2016. https://doi.org/10.18653/v1/P16-2008 Sequence-to-sequence generation for spoken dialogue via deep syntax trees and strings. In *Proceedings of the 54th Annual Meeting of the Association for Computational Linguistics (Volume 2: Short Papers)*, pages 45–51, Berlin, Germany. Association for Computational Linguistics.

Ondřej Dušek, Jekaterina Novikova, and Verena Rieser. 2018. https://www.aclweb.org/anthology/W18-6539 Findings of the E2E NLG challenge. In *Proceedings of the 11th International Conference on Natural Language Generation*, pages 322–328. Association for Computational Linguistics.

Heng Gong. 2018. Technical report for e2e nlg challenge. In *Proceedings of the E2E NLG Challenge System Descriptions*.

Jiatao Gu, Zhengdong Lu, Hang Li, and Victor OK Li. 2016. Incorporating copying mechanism in sequence-to-sequence learning. In *Proceedings of the 54th Annual Meeting of the Association for Computational Linguistics (ACL 2016)*.

Juraj Juraska, Panagiotis Karagiannis, Kevin Bowden, and Marilyn Walker. 2018. https://doi.org/10.18653/v1/N18-1014 A deep ensemble model with slot alignment for sequence-to-sequence natural language generation. In *Proceedings of the 2018 Conference of the North American Chapter of the Association for Computational Linguistics: Human Language Technologies, Volume 1 (Long Papers)*, pages 152–162. Association for Computational Linguistics.

Jenna Kanerva, Filip Ginter, Niko Miekka, Akseli Leino, and Tapio Salakoski. 2018. http://www.aclweb.org/anthology/K18-2013 Turku neural parser pipeline: An end-to-end system for the conll 2018 shared task. In *Proceedings of the CoNLL 2018 Shared Task: Multilingual Parsing from Raw Text to Universal Dependencies*. Association for Computational Linguistics.

Jenna Kanerva, Filip Ginter, and Tapio Salakoski. 2019. Universal lemmatizer: A sequence to sequence model for lemmatizing universal dependencies treebanks. *arXiv preprint arXiv:1902.00972*.

Guillaume Klein, Yoon Kim, Yuntian Deng, Jean Senellart, and Alexander M. Rush. 2017. https://doi.org/10.18653/v1/P17-4012 OpenNMT: Open-source toolkit for neural machine translation. In *Proc. ACL*.

Alon Lavie and Abhaya Agarwal. 2007. https://www.aclweb.org/anthology/W07-0734 METEOR: An automatic metric for MT evaluation with high levels of correlation with human judgments. In *Proceedings of the Second Workshop on Statistical Machine Translation*, pages 228–231. Association for Computational Linguistics.

Leo Leppänen, Myriam Munezero, Mark Granroth-Wilding, and Hannu Toivonen. 2017. https://doi.org/10.18653/v1/W17-3528 Data-driven news generation for automated journalism. In *Proceedings of the 10th International Conference on Natural Language Generation*, pages 188–197. Association for Computational Linguistics.

Chin-Yew Lin. 2004. https://www.aclweb.org/anthology/W04-1013 ROUGE: A package for automatic evaluation of summaries. In *Text Summarization Branches Out: Proceedings of the ACL-04 Workshop*, pages 74–81. Association for Computational Linguistics.

Feng Nie, Jinpeng Wang, Jin-Ge Yao, Rong Pan, and Chin-Yew Lin. 2018. https://www.aclweb.org/anthology/D18-1422 Operation-guided neural networks for high fidelity data-to-text generation. In *Proceedings of the 2018 Conference on Empirical Methods in Natural Language Processing*, pages 3879–3889, Brussels, Belgium. Association for Computational Linguistics.

Naoaki Okazaki. 2007. http://www.chokkan.org/software/crfsuite/ Crfsuite: a fast implementation of conditional random fields (crfs).

Kishore Papineni, Salim Roukos, Todd Ward, and Wei-Jing Zhu. 2002. https://doi.org/10.3115/1073083.1073135 Bleu: A method for automatic evaluation of machine translation. In *Proceedings of the 40th Annual Meeting on Association for Computational Linguistics*, pages 311–318. Association for Computational Linguistics.

Ratish Puduppully, Li Dong, and Mirella Lapata. 2019. Data-to-text generation with content selection and planning. In *Proceedings of the of the 33rd AAAI Conference on Artificial Intelligence*, Honolulu, Hawaii. AAAI.

Yevgeniy Puzikov and Iryna Gurevych. 2018. https://www.aclweb.org/anthology/W18-6557 E2E NLG challenge: Neural models vs. templates. In *Proceedings of the 11th International Conference on Natural Language Generation*, pages 463–471, Tilburg University, The Netherlands. Association for Computational Linguistics.

Abigail See, Peter J. Liu, and Christopher D. Manning. 2017. https://doi.org/10.18653/v1/P17-1099 Get to the point: Summarization with pointer-generator networks. In *Proceedings of the 55th Annual Meeting of the Association for Computational Linguistics (ACL 2017)*, pages 1073–1083. Association for Computational Linguistics.

Zhaopeng Tu, Zhengdong Lu, Yang Liu, Xiaohua Liu, and Hang Li. 2016. Modeling coverage for neural machine translation. In *Proceedings of the 54th Annual Meeting of the Association for Computational Linguistics (ACL 2016)*.

Ramakrishna Vedantam, C. Lawrence Zitnick, and Devi Parikh. 2015. Cider: Consensus-based image description evaluation. In *Proceedings of the 2015 IEEE Conference on Computer Vision and Pattern Recognition (CVPR)*, pages 4566–4575.

Oriol Vinyals, Meire Fortunato, and Navdeep Jaitly. 2015. Pointer networks. In *Advances in Neural Information Processing Systems*, pages 2692–2700.

Sam Wiseman, Stuart Shieber, and Alexander Rush. 2017. https://doi.org/10.18653/v1/D17-1239 Challenges in data-to-document generation. In *Proceedings of the 2017 Conference on Empirical Methods in Natural Language Processing*, pages 2253–2263, Copenhagen, Denmark. Association for Computational Linguistics.

Sam Wiseman, Stuart Shieber, and Alexander Rush. 2018. https://www.aclweb.org/anthology/D18-1356 Learning neural templates for text generation. In *Proceedings of the 2018 Conference on Empirical Methods in Natural Language Processing*, pages 3174–3187, Brussels, Belgium. Association for Computational Linguistics.

Biao Zhang, Jing Yang, Qian Lin, and Jinsong Su. 2018. Attention regularized sequence-to-sequence learning for e2e nlg challenge. In *Proceedings of the E2E NLG Challenge System Descriptions*.

Matching Keys and Encrypted Manuscripts

Eva Pettersson and Beáta Megyesi
Department of Linguistics and Philology
Uppsala University
`firstname.lastname@lingfil.uu.se`

Abstract

Historical cryptology is the study of historical encrypted messages aiming at their decryption by analyzing the mathematical, linguistic and other coding patterns and their historical context. In libraries and archives we can find quite a lot of ciphers, as well as keys describing the method used to transform the plaintext message into a ciphertext. In this paper, we present work on automatically mapping keys to ciphers to reconstruct the original plaintext message, and use language models generated from historical texts to guess the underlying plaintext language.

1 Introduction

Hand-written historical records constitute an important source, without which an understanding of our society and culture would be severely limited. A special type of hand-written historical records are encrypted manuscripts, so called ciphers, created with the intention to keep the content of the message hidden from others than the intended receiver(s). Examples of such materials are political, diplomatic or military correspondence and intelligence reports, scientific writings, private letters and diaries, as well as manuscripts related to secret societies.

According to some historians' estimates, one percent of the material in archives and libraries are encrypted sources, either encrypted manuscripts called ciphertexts, decrypted or original plaintext, and/or keys describing how the encryption/decryption is performed. The manuscripts are usually not indexed as encrypted sources (Láng, 2018), which makes it difficult to find them unless you are lucky to know a librarian with extensive knowledge about the selection of the particular library you are digging in. In addition, related ciphertexts, plaintexts and keys are usually

not stored together, as information about how the encrypted sources are related to each other is lost. If the key has not been destroyed over time – unintentionally, or intentionally for security reasons – it is probably kept in a different place than the corresponding ciphertext or plaintext given that these were probably produced in different places by different persons, and eventually ended up in different archives. Information about the origin of the ciphertext and key, such as dating, place, sender and/or receiver, or any cleartext in the manuscript, might give some important clues to the probability that a key and a ciphertext originate from the same time, and persons. However, information about metadata is far from enough to link the related encrypted sources to each other. It is a cumbersome, if not impossible, process for a historian to try to map a bunch of keys to a pile of ciphertexts scattered in the archive in order to try to decrypt these on the basis of the corresponding key. Further, the cryptanalyst might reconstruct a key given a ciphertext, and the reconstructed key might be applicable to other ciphertexts as well thereby providing more decrypted source material.

In this paper, we present work on automatically mapping ciphertext sequences to keys to return the plaintext from the ciphertext based on simple and homophonic substitution from Early Modern times. We measure the output of the mapping by historical language models developed for 14 European languages to make educated guesses about the correct decryption of ciphertexts. The method is implemented in a publicly available online user interface where users can upload a transcribed key and a ciphertext and the tool returns the plaintext output along with a probability measure of how well the decrypted plaintext matches historical language models for these European languages.

In Section 2, we give a brief introduction to historical cryptology with the main focus on en-

253

crypted sources and keys. Section 3 describes the method for mapping ciphers to their corresponding keys. The experimental results are presented in Section 4 and discussed in Section 5. Finally, we conclude the paper in Section 6.

2 Historical Cryptology

Ciphers use a secret method of writing, based on an encryption algorithm to generate a *ciphertext*, which in turn can be used to decrypt the message to retrieve the intended, underlying information, called the *plaintext*. A cipher is usually operated on the basis of a *key*. The key contains information about what output the cipher shall produce given the plaintext characters in some specific language.

Historical cryptology is the study of encoded or encrypted messages from our history aiming at the decryption by analyzing the mathematical, linguistic and other coding patterns and their histories. One of the main and glorious goals is to develop algorithms for decryption of various types of historical ciphers, i.e. to reconstruct the key in order to retrieve the corresponding plaintext from a ciphertext. The main focus for cryptanalysts has been on specific ciphers, see e.g. (Bauer, 2017; Singh, 2000) for nice summaries, while systematic decryption of various cipher types on a larger scale has been paid less attention to (see e.g. Knight et al. (2006); Nuhn and Knight (2014); Ravi and Knight (2008)). Historians, on the other hand, are searching for ciphertexts and keys in libraries to reveal new, important and hitherto hidden information to find new facts and interpretations about our history. Another, less observed goal within historical cryptology is therefore to map the encrypted sources, the original keys and corresponding ciphertexts.

There are many different types of ciphers used throughout our history (Kahn, 1996). In early modern times, when encryption became frequently used in Europe, ciphers were typically based on transposition, where the plaintext characters are reordered in a systematic way, or substitution of plaintext characters to transform each character in the plaintext to another symbol from existing alphabets, digits, special symbols, or a mixture of these (Bauer, 2007). More advanced substitution ciphers include homophonic, polygraphic, and polyalphabetic substitution. In Figure 1, we show a homophonic substitution cipher with a key, a short ciphertext and the corresponding plaintext

generated by the key. Each plaintext character, written in capital letter, has one or several corresponding symbol(s) by which the plaintext characters are substituted to encrypt the message. To make decryption difficult, the most frequently occurring plaintext characters are usually substituted with one of several possible symbols.

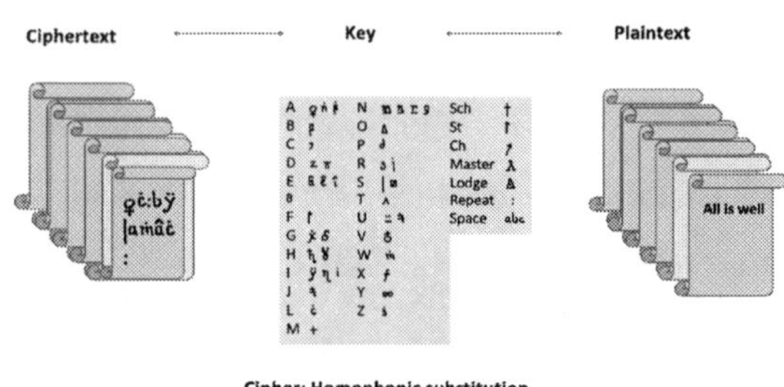

Figure 1: Ciphertext, key, and the corresponding plaintext for a homophonic substitution cipher.

Ciphertexts contain symbol sequences with spaces, or without any space to hide word boundaries. Similar to historical text, punctuation marks are not frequent, sentence boundaries are typically not marked, and capitalized initial characters in the beginning of the sentence are usually missing. We can also find nulls in ciphertexts, i.e. symbols without any corresponding plaintext characters to confuse the cryptanalyst to make decryption even harder.

Keys might contain substitution of not only characters in the plaintext alphabet, but also nomenclatures where bigrams, trigrams, syllables, morphemes, common words, and/or named entities, typically referring to persons, geographic areas, or dates, are substituted with certain symbol(s). Diacritics and double letters are usually not encoded. Each type of entity to be encrypted might be encoded by one symbol only (unigragh), two symbols (digraph), three symbols (trigraph), and so on. For example, the plaintext alphabet characters might be encrypted with codes using two-digit numbers, the nomenclatures with three-digit numbers, space with one-digit numbers, and the nulls with two-digit numbers, etc. Figure 2 illustrates a key based on homophonic substitution with nomenclature from the second half of the 17th century. Each letter in the alphabet has at least one corresponding ciphertext symbol, represented as a two-digit number (digraph), and the vowels and double consonants have one additional graphical sign (unigraph). The key also contains encoded syllables with digraphs consisting of numerals or Latin characters, followed by a nomenclature in the form of a list of Spanish words encoded with three-digit numbers letters or graphical signs.

Figure 2: A key from the second half of the 17th century (Algemeen Rijksarchief, 1647-1698) from the DECODE database (Megyesi et al., 2019).

One of the first steps, apart from digitization of the encrypted source, is the transcription of keys and ciphertext images, before cryptanalysis can be applied, aiming at the decryption of the ciphertext to recover the key. However, there are other challenges that also need attention depending on what document types that are available and what documents that need to be recovered. These are:

1. generate ciphertext given a plaintext and a key (i.e. encryption)

2. reconstruct plaintext from a ciphertext and a key (less trivial due to unknown plaintext language and ambiguous code sequences and nulls)

3. map key and ciphertexts

Next, we will describe our experiments on retrieving plaintext from keys given a ciphertext with the goal to be able to automatically find ciphertexts that belong to a particular key.

3 Mapping Ciphers to Keys

3.1 Data

For our experiments on automatically mapping ciphertext sequences to key-value pairs, we need access to four kinds of input files:

1. a transcribed ciphertext

2. its corresponding key

3. its corresponding plaintext (for evaluation purposes)

4. a set of language models (for language detection)

A collection of several hundreds of ciphers and keys from Early Modern times can be found in the recently developed DECODE database (Megyesi et al., 2019).[1] The database allows anyone to search in the collection, whereas upload of new encrypted manuscripts may be done by registered users only. The collected ciphertexts and keys are annotated with metadata including information about the provenance and location of the manuscript, transcription, possible decryption(s) and translation(s) of the ciphertext, images, and any additional material of relevance to the particular manuscript.

Currently, most of the ciphertexts in the DECODE database are still unsolved. Even though the overall aim of the cipher-key mapping algorithm (CKM) is to automatically try to match these unsolved ciphertexts to existing keys, we need previously solved ciphertexts, connected to a key and a plaintext file, to conduct our experiments. In our experiments, we thus make use of three previously broken keys and their corresponding ciphertexts, written originally during Early Modern times. For all three manuscripts, the transcribed ciphertext as well as the key and a plaintext version of the contents are available through the DECODE database. We also add a fourth decrypted file, the *Copiale* cipher (Knight et al., 2011),[2] for which both the ciphertext and the plaintext are accessible through the DECODE database. This cipher will only be used for evaluation of the language detection part of the algorithm. The data collection used for the experiments is summarized in Table 1, where each manuscript is described with regard to its cipher type and plaintext language.

In our experiments, we will use the *Barb* cipher for initial tests during the development of the CKM algorithm, hence-forth the *training set*. This cipher is based on homophonic substitution with

---

[1]https://cl.lingfil.uu.se/decode/
[2]https://cl.lingfil.uu.se/~bea/
copiale/

Name	Cipher type	Plaintext	Use
Barb.lat.6956	homophonic, nulls, nomenclature	Italian	training
Francia-64	homophonic, nulls, nomenclature	Italian	evaluation
Borg.lat.898	simple substitution	Latin	evaluation
Copiale	homophonic	German	evaluation (lang. detection)

Table 1: Datasets used for training and evaluation of the CKM algorithm.

nomenclatures, and consists of codes with numbers. The codes are 2-digit numbers representing plaintext characters, syllables and some function words, and three-digit codes for place and person names and common words. The cipher also contains two one-digit codes denoting word boundaries. The *evaluation set* on the other hand, consists of two ciphers:

1. the *Francia* cipher, which has the same cipher type (homophonic substitution with nulls and nomenclature) and underlying plaintext language (Italian) as the Barb cipher used during training

2. the more divergent *Borg* cipher, which is instead a simple substitution cipher with Latin as the underlying plaintext language

The transcription of the ciphertexts was also retrieved from the DECODE database. Each transcription file of a particular cipher (which may consist of one or multiple images) starts with comment lines (marked by "#") with information about the name of the file, the image name, the transcriber's id, the date of the transcription, etc. The transcription is carried out symbol by symbol and row by row keeping line breaks, spaces, punctuation marks, dots, underlined symbols, and cleartext words, phrases, sentences, paragraphs, as shown in the original image. In case cleartext is embedded in the ciphertext, the cleartext sequence is clearly marked as such with a language id. For a detailed description of the transcription, we refer to Megyesi et al. (2019).

Original and reconstructed keys also follow a common format, starting with metadata about the key followed by a description of the code groups. Each code is described in a separate line followed by the plaintext entity (character, syllable, word, etc), delimited by at least one space character.

Figure 3 shows a few lines from the key file belonging to the Barb cipher, with codes 1 and 8 denoting a word boundary, codes 00 and 02 denoting the letter *a*, code 03 denoting the letter *o*, code 04

```
#Key
#homophonic with nomenclature
#null = space (word boundary)
1 <null>
8 <null>
00 a
02 a
03 o
04 u/v
...
232 ambasciatore di Spagna
```

Figure 3: Example format for a transcribed key file in the Decode database.

denoting either the letter *u* or the letter *v* (since there was often no distinction between these two letters in historical texts), and code 232 denoting the whole phrase *ambasciatore di Spagna* (ambassador of Spain).

3.2 Storing code-value pairs

In the first step of the CKM algorithm, the key file is processed and the code-value pairs, as well as the length of the longest code, are stored for future reference. The key file is required to be in plain text format, and with one code-value pair on each line. Furthermore, the code and its value should be separated by at least one white space character. If the key file contains values denoting word delimiters, the script will recognise these as such if they are written as "null" (in any combination of upper-case and lower-case characters, so for example "Null" and "NULL" will also be recognised as word delimiters). Any lines initialized with a hashtag sign ("#") will be ignored, as containing comments, in accordance with the format illustrated in Figure 3.

3.3 Mapping ciphertexts to code-value pairs

In the second step, the transcribed ciphertext is processed, and its contents matched against the code-value pairs stored in the previous step, to re-

```
#002r.jpg
<IT De Inenunchi? 14 Maggio 1628.>
6239675017378233236502343051822004623?
```

Figure 4: Example of a ciphertext segment in the Decode database.

veal the underlying plaintext message. In this process, three types of input are ignored:

1. text within angle brackets (presumed to contain cleartext segments)

2. lines starting with a hashtag (presumed to be comments)

3. question marks (presumed to denote the annotator's uncertainty about the transcription)

The first lines from a transcribed ciphertext file in the Decode database is shown in Figure 4, where the name of the image from which the transcription has been made is given as a comment (preceded by a hashtag), cleartext is given within angle brackets, and the annotator's uncertainty about transcribing the last character on the line as the digit "3" is signalled by a question mark.

If the transcribed ciphertext contains word boundaries in the form of space characters, or if the code-value pairs stored in the previous step contain codes for denoting word boundaries, the ciphertext is split into words based on this information, and the remaining mapping process is performed word by word. If no such information exists, the whole ciphertext is treated as a single segment, to be processed character by character.

If word boundaries have been detected, for every word that is shorter than, or equal in length to, the longest code in the key file, we check if the whole word can be matched towards a code. If so, we replace the ciphertext sequence with the value connected to that code. If not, or if the word is longer than the longest code in the key file, we iterate over the sequence, character by character, and try to match each character against the key file. If not successful, we merge the current character(s) with the succeeding character, and try to match the longer sequence against the key file, until we reach a sequence equal in length to the longest code in the key file. If nothing can be matched in the key file for the maximum length sequence, we replace this sequence by a question mark instead, and move on to the next character.

```
If sequence equals a code:
  Replace sequence by matched value
Else:
  While characters in sequence:
    If char(s) equals a code:
      Replace char(s) by matched value
    Else if char length equals
    longest code length:
      Replace char(s) by ? and
      move on to next character
    Else:
      Merge char with next char
      and try again
```

Figure 5: Algorithm for mapping ciphertext sequences to code-value pairs.

This non-greedy search-and-replace mechanism is applied for the whole word, except for the end of the word. Since we know that the key in the training file contains code-value pairs for representing suffixes, the script checks, in each iteration, if the remaining part of the word is equal in length to the longest code in the key file. If so, we try to match the whole sequence, and only if this fails, we fall back to the character-by-character mapping. The whole algorithm for the matching procedure is illustrated in Figure 5.

3.4 Language identification

When the plaintext has been recovered, the next task is to guess what language the decrypted text is written in, and present hypotheses to the user. This is done based on language models for historical text, derived from the HistCorp collection of historical corpora and tools (Pettersson and Megyesi, 2018).[3] We use word-based language models created using the IRSTLM package (Federico et al., 2008), for the 14 languages currently available from the HistCorp webpage: Czech, Dutch, English, French, German, Greek, Hungarian, Icelandic, Italian, Latin, Portuguese, Slovene, Spanish and Swedish. For this particular task, we only make use of the unigram models, i.e. the single words in the historical texts. The plaintext words generated in the previous steps, by matching character sequences in the ciphertext against code-value pairs in the key file, are compared to the words present in the language model for each of these 14 languages. As output, the script produces a ranked list of these languages, presenting the percentage of words in the plaintext file that are also found in the word-based language model

---

[3]https://cl.lingfil.uu.se/histcorp/

for the language in question. The idea is that if a large percentage of the words in the decrypted file are also present in a language model, there is a high chance that the key tested against the cipher-text is actually an appropriate key for this particular text.

3.5 Evaluation

We evaluate our method for cipher-key mapping based on the percentage of words in the evaluation corpus that are identical in the automatically deciphered text and in the manually deciphered gold standard version (taking the position of the word into consideration). Casing is not considered in the comparison, since lower-case and upper-case words are usually not represented by different codes in the key files used in our experiments. Furthermore, some codes may refer to several (related) values, such as in the example given in Figure 3 (see further Section 3.2), where the code 04 could correspond either to the letter *u* or to the letter *v*. This also holds for different inflectional forms of the same lemma, such as the Italian word for 'this', that could be *questo, questa* or *questi*, depending on the gender and number of the head word that it is connected to, and therefore would typically be represented by the same code. In these cases, we consider the automatic decipherment to be correct, if any of the alternative mappings corresponds to the form chosen in the gold standard.

The language identification task is evaluated by investigating at what place in the ranked list of 14 potential languages the target language is presented.

4 Results

4.1 Cipher-Key mapping

In the first experiment, we tested the CKM algorithm on the Francia cipher (see further Section 3.1); a cipher of the same type as the cipher used as a role model during the development of the method. This cipher shares several characteristics with the training text: (i) it is written during the same time period, (ii) it is collected from the Vatican Secret Archives, (iii) it is a numerical cipher with homophonic substitution and nomenclatures, and (iv) word delimiters are represented in the key.

When comparing the automatically decrypted words to the words in the manually deciphered gold standard, approximately 79% of the words are identical. The cases where the words differ could be categorized into four different types:

1. **Incomplete key: Diacritics**
   (36 instances)
   The key only contains plain letters, without diacritics. The human transcriber has however added diacritics in the manually deciphered text, where applicable. For example, the code 9318340841099344 has been interpreted by the script as the word *temerita*. The human transcriber has added a diacritic to the last letter *a*, resulting in the word *temerità* ('boldness'), even though the key states *a* (without accent) as the value for the code "44".

2. **Character not repeated**
   (27 instances)
   In cases where a character should be repeated in order for a word to be spelled correctly (at least according to present-day spelling conventions), the human transcriber has in many cases chosen to repeat the character, even though this is not stated in the key.

3. **Human reinterpretation**
   (2 instances)
   In a few cases where the text contains unexpected inflectional forms, such as a singular ending where a plural ending would be expected, the human transcriber has chosen the grammatically correct form, even though the code in the ciphertext actually is different.

4. **Wrong interpretation by the script**
   (16 instances)
   Due to the non-greedy nature of the algorithm, it will sometimes fail to match longer codes in the key file, when it finds a match for a shorter code. This could be seen for example for prefixes such as buon- in *buonissima* ('very good'), and qual- in *qualche* ('some').

In a second experiment, we tested the script against a cipher of another type, the *Borg* cipher,[4] based on simple substitution with a small nomenclature, encoded by 34 graphical signs with word boundaries marked by space. Since this cipher is based on simple substitution, rather than homophonic substitution, and with word boundaries already marked, it is less ambiguous than the Francia cipher. Accordingly, approximately 97% of the

---

[4]https://cl.lingfil.uu.se/~bea/borg/

words in the output from the cipher-key mapping script are identical to the words in the gold standard. The mismatches are mainly due to some word-initial upper-case letters in the ciphertext being written as the plaintext letter, instead of being encoded. As an example, the Latin word *nucem* (inflectional form of the word 'nut') would normally be enciphered as '9diw1' in the Borg cipher, but in one case it occurs instead as 'Ndiw1'. There are several similar cases for other words throughout the cipher.

4.2 Language identification

For the language identification task, we can see from Table 2 that both the Barb cipher and the Francia cipher are correctly identified as written in Italian by the CKM algorithm, and the Copiale cipher is correctly identified as written in German. These guesses are based on the fact that 79.17% of the tokens in the automatically recovered version of the Barb plaintext, and 80.05% of the tokens in the Francia text, could also be found in the Italian language model, whereas 86.55% of the tokens in the Copiale cipher could be matched in the German language model. As could be expected, the second best guess produced by the algorithm for the Italian manuscripts is for the closely related languages Spanish and Portuguese respectively. More surprisingly, the third best guess for both these texts is German, with a substantial amount of the tokens found in the German language model as well. A closer look at the German language model used in our experiments reveals a possible explanation to this. The German language model is based on data from the time period 1050–1914, where the oldest texts contain a substantial amount of citations and text blocks actually written in Latin, a language closely related to Italian. This might also explain why the Borg text, written in Latin, is identified by the script as written in German. The third guess for the Borg text is Swedish, for which the language model is also based on very old text (from 1350 and onwards), with blocks of Latin text in it. The Latin language model on the other hand is rather small, containing only about 79,000 tokens extracted from the *Ancient Greek and Latin Dependency Treebank*.[5] Due to the small size of this language model as compared to the language models for the other lan-

guages in this study, in combination with the fact that Latin words occur in older texts for many languages, it is hard for the script to correctly identify Latin as the source language.

For the German Copiale cipher, the second best guess is for Slovene, and the third best guess is for Swedish. This could be due to the fact that both Slovene and Swedish were strongly influenced by the German language in historical times, meaning that many German and German-like words would appear in historical Slovene and Swedish texts.

4.2.1 Present-day language models

So far, we have presumed that language models based on historical text would be best suited for the task of language identification in the context of historical cryptology. This is based on the assumption that spelling and vocabulary were different in historical times than in present-day text, meaning that some words and their particular spelling variants would only occur in historical text. It could however be argued that it is easier to find large amounts of present-day text to build language models from. As a small test to indicate whether or not present-day text would be useful in this context, we downloaded the Spacy language models for present day Italian[6] and German,[7] trained on Wikipedia text, and compared the coverage in these language models to the coverage in the historical language models, when applied to the plaintexts of the Barb, Francia and Copiale manuscripts.

As seen from Table 3, the percentage of word forms found in the language models based on present-day data is considerably lower than for the historical language models, even though the present-day data sets are larger. The preliminary conclusion is that language models based on historical text is better suited for the task at hand, but present-day language models could also be useful, in particular in cases where it is hard to find suitable historical data to train a language model. More thorough experiments would however be needed to confirm this.

---

[5]https://perseusdl.github.io/treebank_data/

[6]https://github.com/explosion/spacy-models/releases//tag/it_core_news_sm-2.1.0

[7]https://github.com/explosion/spacy-models/releases//tag/de_core_news_md-2.1.0

Name	Top 3 language models		Gold language
Barb-6956	**Italian**	**79.17%**	Italian
	Spanish	66.77%	
	German	65.73%	
Francia-64	**Italian**	**80.05%**	Italian
	Portuguese	72.40%	
	German	70.22%	
Borg.lat.898	German	56.73%	Latin
	Spanish	55.01%	
	Swedish	51.50%	
Copiale	**German**	86.55%	German
	Slovene	69.95%	
	Swedish	57.76%	

Table 2: Language identification results.

Name	Historical LM	Present-day LM
Barb-6956	79.17%	64.11%
Francia-64	80.05%	66.23%
Copiale	86.55%	81.44%

Table 3: Language identification results, comparing language models based on historical text to language models based on present-day text.

5 Discussion

From our experiments, we can conclude that the implemented algorithm makes it possible to restore the hidden plaintext from ciphertexts and their corresponding key. For one of the ciphers evaluated, 79% of the words were correctly mapped to the gold standard plaintext words, and the mismatches were mainly due to diacritics and repeated characters not being part of the key. This knowledge could easily be taken into consideration in further development of the algorithm, where the script could test to add diacritics in strategic positions and to repeat certain characters in cases where a specific word could not be found in a language model (provided that we already have an educated guess on what language the underlying plaintext is written in). For the other cipher evaluated, being an out-of-domain manuscript of a different cipher type and another underlying language than the manuscript used during training, we got very encouraging results with 97% of the words in the manuscript being correctly matched, and the mismatches in the remaining words mainly being due to plaintext characters occurring as part of ciphertext words.

For the language identification task, the results are mixed. The German and Italian manuscripts are correctly identified as being written in German and Italian respectively, whereas the algorithm assumes the Latin text to be written in German. This indicates that we need to be careful about what texts to put into the language models. In the current experiments, we have simply used the language models at hand for historical texts for different languages, without taking into account differences in time periods and genres covered, nor the size of the text material used as a basis for the language model. Thus, the language models used in the experiments are very different in size, where the Latin language model contains about 79,000 tokens, as compared to approximately 124 million tokens in the German language model. Furthermore, since the language in very old texts is typically quite different from the language in younger texts, language models only containing texts from the time period in which the cipher is assumed to have been created would better suit our purposes. In addition, many old texts contain blocks of Latin words, since this was the Lingua Franca in large parts of the world in historical times. This results in many Latin words being found in language models for other languages as well.

The language detection evaluation also shows that using language models based on historical text has a clear advantage over using state-of-the-art language models based on present-day language.

6 Conclusion

In this paper, we have presented a study within the field of historical cryptology, an area strongly related to digital humanities in general, and digital philology in particular. More specifically, we have introduced an algorithm for automatically mapping encrypted ciphertext sequences to their corresponding key, in order to reconstruct the plaintext describing the underlying message of the cipher. Since ciphertexts and their corresponding keys are often stored in separate archives around the world, without knowledge about which key belongs to which ciphertext, such an algorithm could help in connecting ciphertexts to their corresponding keys, revealing the enciphered information to historians and other researchers with an interest in historical sources.

Acknowledgments

This work has been supported by the Swedish Research Council, grant 2018-06074: DECRYPT - Decryption of historical manuscripts.

References

Belgium Algemeen Rijksarchief, Brussels. 1647-1698. cl.lingfil.uu.se/decode/database/record/960 [link].

Craig Bauer. 2017. *Unsolved! The History and Mystery of the World's Greatest Ciphers from Ancient Egypt to Online Secret Societies*. Princeton University Press, Princeton, USA.

Friedrich Bauer. 2007. *Decrypted Secrets — Methods and Maxims of Cryptology*. 4th edition. Springer.

Marcello Federico, Nicola Bertoldi, and Mauro Cettolo. 2008. IRSTLM: an open source toolkit for handling large scale language models. In *Proceedings of Interspeech 2008*, pages 1618–1621.

David Kahn. 1996. *The Codebreakers: The Comprehensive History of Secret Communication from Ancient Times to the Internet*. New York.

Kevin Knight, Beáta Megyesi, and Christiane Schaefer. 2011. The copiale cipher. In *Invited talk at ACL Workshop on Building and Using Comparable Corpora (BUCC)*. Association for Computational Linguistics.

Kevin Knight, Anish Nair, Nishit Rathod, and Kenji Yamada. 2006. https://www.aclweb.org/anthology/P06-2065 Unsupervised analysis for decipherment problems. In *Proceedings of the COLING/ACL 2006 Main Conference Poster Sessions*, pages 499–506, Sydney, Australia. Association for Computational Linguistics.

Benedek Láng. 2018. *Real Life Cryptology: Ciphers and Secrets in Early Modern Hungary*. Atlantis Press, Amsterdam University Press.

Beáta Megyesi, Nils Blomqvist, and Eva Pettersson. 2019. The DECODE Database: Collection of Ciphers and Keys. In *Proceedings of the 2nd International Conference on Historical Cryptology, HistoCrypt19*, Mons, Belgium.

Malte Nuhn and Kevin Knight. 2014. Cipher type detection. In *Proceedings of the 2014 Conference on Empirical Methods in Natural Language Processing (EMNLP)*, pages 1769–1773. Association for Computational Linguistics.

Eva Pettersson and Beáta Megyesi. 2018. The HistCorp Collection of Historical Corpora and Resources. In *Proceedings of the Digital Humanities in the Nordic Countries 3rd Conference*, Helsinki, Finland.

Sujith Ravi and Kevin Knight. 2008. Attacking decipherment problems optimally with low-order n-gram models. In *Proceedings of the 2008 Conference on Empirical Methods in Natural Language Processing*, pages 812–819. Association for Computational Linguistics.

Simon Singh. 2000. *The Code Book: The Science of Secrecy from Ancient Egypt to Quantum Cryptography*. Anchor Books.

Perceptual and acoustic analysis of voice similarities between parents and young children

Evgeniia Rykova
Université Toulouse Paul Sabatier
rykova.eugenia@gmail.com

Stefan Werner
University of Eastern Finland
stefan.werner@uef.fi

Abstract

Human voice provides the means for verbal communication and forms a part of personal identity. Due to genetic and environmental factors, a voice of a child should resemble the voice of her parent(s), but voice similarities between parents and young children are underresearched. Read-aloud speech of Finnish-speaking and Russian-speaking parent-child pairs was subject to perceptual and multi-step instrumental and statistical analysis. Finnish-speaking listeners could not discriminate family pairs auditorily in an XAB paradigm, but the Russian-speaking listeners' mean accuracy of answers reached 72.5%. On average, in both language groups family-internal f0 similarities were stronger than family-external, with parents showing greater family-internal similarities than children. Auditory similarities did not reflect acoustic similarities in a straightforward way.

1   Introduction

The current paper is based on the research made as a master thesis. An overall inspiration comes from encountering online the company VocaliD Inc., whose aim is to create unique personalized voices for text to speech devices (VocaliD, Inc.). The author asked herself, "How would a (hypothetical) voice of a child, who never had an ability to speak, most likely sound?" Intuitively, it should somehow resemble the voice of the parent(s). However, the up-to-date research does not give a direct answer to the question. In the present paper, the similarity between parents and their young children is also researched from the cross-linguistic perspective, comparing two prosodically different patterns.

2   Background

2.1   Human voice similarities

Human voice, a sound produced by a combination of human organs called vocal apparatus, is used by humans to generate speech and other forms of vocalizations. Each voice is unique due to the physiological factors (e.g., age, body size or hormones) and the manner in which the sounds are articulated (consciously or unconsciously). Due to the same factors, the voice of an individual is subject not only to major changes throughout the lifespan (Decoster and Debruyne, 2000; Stathopolous et al., 2011), but also in everyday communication. Thus, it is a source of biological, psychological and social (Bogdanova, 2001; Bolinger, 1989) information about the speaker. Both related and unrelated people can sound alike. In the blood members of the same family, the reasons for such similarities are both biological (genetic) and environmental. The former are reflected not only in the body parts but also in structural brain organization (Peper et al., 2007; Thompson et al., 2001). The latter include socialization and learning by imitation (Zuo and Mok, 2015; see also Hirvonen, 1970; Bolinger, 1989). Interestingly, the prosody of the native language is acquired earlier than the segmental phonology (Iivonen, 1977) and around two years of age, children are able to produce adult-like intonational contrasts (Bolinger, 1986).

Juslin and Scherer (2008) divide the cues for voice description into four broad groups, as related to 1) fundamental frequency (f0); 2) intensity; 3) temporal aspects; 4) voice quality. Acknowledging the importance of all the voice cues in building voice identity of an individual, for the purposes of the current research, f0 (or its contour, a sequence of f0 values across an utterance) will be the principal feature in focus. F0 analysis is a robust acoustic method of speaker identification (Labutin et al., 2007; Rose, 1999) and the source for prosody generation in speech synthesis. Linguistically, f0 encodes suprasegmental categories of tone, stress and intonation (Rose, 1999). F0 contour is the most important physical correlate of intonation (Iivonen, 2005).

Primarily mean f0 shows significantly high intra-twin correlation in monozygotic twins, (Debruyne et al., 2002; Decoster et al., 2001; Fuchs et al., 2000; Przybyla et al., 1992; Van Lierde et al., 2005). Dizygotic twins show greater discrepancies in f0 than monozygotic twins (Debruyne et al., 2002; Przybyla et al., 1992), but the same f0 variation, which is thus considered to correspond to learnt language behavior (Debruyne et al., 2002). A variety of studies on perceptual similarity also show that twins, followed by same-sex siblings, are the most difficult to differentiate both for human listeners and an automatic system (Decoster et al, 2001; Feiser and Kleber, 2012; Kushner and Bickley, 1995; Nolan et al., 2011; Rose and Duncan, 1995; Rose, 1999; San Segundo and Kunzel, 2015; Sebastian et al., 2013; Weirich and Lancia, 2011). Listeners are also able to identify twin and sibling pairs in different tasks, and in general rate voices of related speakers with higher similarity scores than those of unrelated speakers. In most of the experiments, longer utterances seem to be more suitable stimuli. Albeit one word is enough to distinguish unrelated speakers in the study by Weirich and Lancia (2011); when the voices are knowingly similar-sounding, the task becomes more difficult even for familiar listeners (Rose and Duncan, 1995; Rose, 1999). F0 seems to be one of the most important factors that contribute to detect similarity between speakers, on one hand, and to determine dissimilarity, on the other.

2.2 Finnish and Russian prosody/intonation

A detailed comparison of phonetics, phonology and phonotactics is far beyond the scope of the current paper. In brief, Finnish is a mora-timed language with primary stress is fixed to the initial syllable of the word. Russian is stress-timed with movable word stress. Unlike Finnish, Russian has vowel reduction and no phonological durational contrasts (see, e.g., Suomi et al., 2008 and Zvukovaya forma, 2001-2002, respectively). A typical property of Finnish is falling or rising-falling intonation, steadily and smoothly declining, so that Finnish is often called prosodically monotone (Suomi et al., 2006; 2008). Russian language, on the opposite, presents a variety of f0 falling and rising contrasts with floating intonation center (Bryzgunova, 1977; Nikolaeva, 1970; Volskaya, 2009; see also Ullakonoja et al., 2007 for a comparison). Intonation in Russian plays a distinctive role in structures, where in Finnish, grammatical means are sufficient to express the difference and the difference can be characterized as mostly pragmatical (de Silva and Ullakonoja, 2009).

3 Method

3.1 Audio-data collection

The current paper presents the analysis of data collected from three mother-child pairs, whose native language is Finnish (parents of mean age 43.67 y/o, SD=4.93; two girls of 10 and 12 y/o and one nine-year-old boy), and four pairs, whose native language is Russian (parents of mean age 41.5 y/o, SD=2.65 and 12-year-old girls). The participants had no history of neurological, language or speech deficits, had normal or corrected-to-normal vision and were right-handed. They were monolingual, with some knowledge of foreign languages, but the native language being the only one spoken at home.

The young age of the boy allows to include his voice/f0 into analysis together with the girls. Mutation, or significant f0 lowering ,shows the first signs on average at the age of 10-11 (Hacki and Heitmüller, 1999). Additionally, boys before puberty might speak at a higher f0 with mothers that with fathers (Bolinger, 1989).

The recording of audio-data consisted of reading a text and five short dialogues (20 sentences of different types in total) and producing quasi-spontaneous speech in a picture description task, but only the read-aloud speech was further analyzed acoustically.

The members of the same family were recorded together. The text was first read by the child, then read by the parent in order to promote her own way of reading it and decrease the imitation effect. The dialogues were read in pairs. The recordings were made at 44100 Hz sampling frequency, and 16-bit bit depth. The files were saved in wav-format[1] and later segmented into separate sentences. The Finnish families are coded with letters H, L and P, and the Russian families are coded with letter combinations AL, MA, OO and VN.

3.2 Perceptual experiments

Young (from 20 to 30 y/o, M=26.08, SD=2.68) native speakers of Finnish and Russian (twelve and fifteen, respectively, gender-balanced) were asked to judge the perceptual similarities in the families. They had no history of neurological, language, speech or hearing deficits, and had normal or corrected-to-normal vision.

The perceptual experiments in both languages consisted of two parts. In the first part, a participant first heard an item, pronounced by a child, followed by a beep-signal, and then the same item, pronounced by two adults, one of which was the child's parent (target) and the other served as a distractor. The task was to choose the adult, whose voice sounded more likely to be that of the child's parent. In the second part, the task was the opposite: to choose the child, whose voice sounded more likely to be that of the adult's offspring. There were training trials in each part, and the test trials (36 as 3 families x 6 items x 2 in Finnish, and 40 as 4 families x 10 items in Russian) were randomized and could be repeated three times each. Scoring was binary. The audio was presented binaurally, the experiments were conducted in a quiet environment.

3.3 Instrumental and statistical analysis

First, all the segmented sentences were compared pairwise in the same family in order to find auditory and gross f0 curve similarities. The corresponding recordings were annotated in TextGrid files. All the selected sentences in Finnish resulted to follow a falling pattern (see Iivonen, 1978; Anttila, 2009) and therefore were annotated at syllable and word level only, without distinguishing between sentence types. Annotation of the Russian data included the following: (1) section: (prepeak) – peak – (tail);

---

1   Recording, segmentation, instrumental analysis and perceptual experiment were carried out via Praat (Boersma and Weenink, 2017).

(2) movement: rise/fall/rise-fall; (3) position: non-final/focus (the part containing IC of the sentence)/final; (4) group: subject or predicate; (5) orthographic word; (6) sentence type. Segmenting sentences into positions adapts the principle of additional syntagmatic segmentation (Bryzgunova, 1977). Segmenting into sections adapts the principle of a tone unit structure (see Brazil et al., 1980; Crystal, 2003): a prepeak corresponds to the pre-head and head, and a peak corresponds to the nucleus. After comparing the f0 contours inside each word for the Finnish data, and inside each position for the Russian data, the most similar pairs of sentences were chosen for the following analysis.

The f0 contours of the sentences were described through the following values: maximum f0 of the first syllables, min f0 of the other syllables for the Finnish data; maximum f0 of the peaks, mean and minimum f0 of the prepeaks and tails for the Russian data.

Since the selected Finnish sentences had different number of words and the words had different number of syllables, an equal framework of five three-syllable words was created. Thus, each word was represented by three data points, hereinafter referred to as syllables (1-3), unless otherwise specified. The syllables represent raw initially extracted values or means of the adjacent values that were close to each other. The same principle of "adjacent similarities" was applied to make five-word sentences out of six-word sentences. Missing values of the syllables were added manually following the dependencies shown between the similarly positioned syllables in the speech of the speaker. Such manipulations were applied within identical patterns in family pairs.

Statistical analysis was performed in R (R Core Team, 2017). For the purposes of the current study, analysis of variance (ANOVA) and a posthoc Tukey's Honest Significant Difference (THSD) tests were used. All the tests were carried out at 95% confidence. The graphs were created via ggplot function (Wickham, 2009).

As shown by ANOVA tests, in the Finnish data word position had a statistically significant effect (p-values (p) less than 0.05) on the raw f0 values, while the interaction word*sentence did not (p's greater than 0.1). Therefore, the words from different sentences were compared to each other in accordance with their position (1-5). In the Russian data, the position*sentence interaction was similarly non-significant (p's greater than 0.1), but the effect of the position was significant (p's less than 0.05) for six out of eight speakers. The comparison of the same positions from different sentences was nevertheless applied to all the analyzed data.

The f0 features were scanned for similarities within each family (general speech rhythm comparison). However, each child within a language group was not only compared to their parent, but to all the parents in question (and vice versa) by means of ratios, calculated dividing the f0 values of each word/position from the selected sentences pronounced by an adult by the f0 values of the same words/positions from every selected sentence produced by children, data point by data point. The ratios were selected for the further analysis on the grounds of their homogeneity (0.1 as the maximum difference between the values) within a word/position and, additionally, visual similarity between f0 curves. The exception was made for some individual high peaks in the Russian data. The ratios were considered acceptable if the peak value was more than two standard deviations higher than the adjacent segments in the data from both speakers in question.

Finally, the selected ratios were reviewed word by word or position by position, focusing on the statistical differences in each pair of speakers. The ratios without significant differences were clustered together. The clusters were characterized with a coefficient, which was the mean of the clustered ratios, and strength, which was the number of clustered ratios. The latter was interpreted as the strength of similarity between the speakers. The strongest clusters from each pair of speakers were further compared to each other and used for creation of the "sentence maps", examples of which are presented in the following section.

4 Results

4.1 Perceptual experiments

In the Finnish data, none of the explanatory variables or their interactions show significant effect on the results (p's greater than 0.1 in a series of ANOVA tests). In the parent-matching task, mean accuracy per target ranges from 50% to 61.8%, M=56%, SD=5.9%; and the accuracy of answers per participant ranges from 44.4% to 63.9%, M=56%, SD=6.5%. In the child-matching task, mean accuracy per target ranges from 51.4% to 57.6%, M=53.5%, SD=3.6%; and the accuracy of answers per participant ranges from 33% to 72%, M=53.5%, SD=1.7%.

In the Russian data, the accuracy of answers per participant ranges from 50% to 77.5%, M=65%, SD=8.9% in the parent-matching task; from 50% to 80%, M=66.8%, SD=7% in the child matching task. The ANOVA tests show a significant effect of the target on the answer accuracy in both tasks (p's less than 0.01). In the parent-matching task, mean accuracy of answers for target AL (42%) is significantly lower than for the other targets (range from 68% to 78.7%, M=72%, SD=5.8%). In the child-matching task, mean accuracy of answers for target MA (49.3%) is significantly lower than for the other targets (range from 71.3% to 76.7%, M=73%, SD=2.9%). In the child-matching task, there is also a significant effect of the distractor: mean accuracy of answers with VN distractor is higher than with AL-distractor, adjusted p=0.04. Item and item*target interaction have statistically significant effect in both parts of the experiment: F=3.392, p=0.005, Df=5 and F=9.972, p =2.63e-14, Df=4, respectively, in the parent-matching-task; F=5.082, p=4.96e-04, Df=4 and F=7.448, p=2.44e-10, Df=9, respectively, in the child-matching task. THSD test shows that for every target the distribution of mean accuracy among the items is different. In other words, the same item corresponds to different mean accuracy for different targets.

The effect of language on the results of the perceptual experiment is obvious (F=26.73, p=2.57e-07, Df=1 in the ANOVA test). Task (F value=0.074; p=0.785) and interaction task*language (F=1.549; p=0.213, Df=1) do not show a significant effect on the results

4.2 Family-internal f0 similarities

For each Finnish speaker, ANOVA test shows a significant effect of the syllable and word, but not of their interaction on the f0. The adjacent similarities between the words and syllables inside the words are based on the difference between mean f0 values.

Figure 1 presents the similarities graphically: if the difference between mean f0 values is not statistically significant (adjusted p greater than 0.05 in a THSD test), the adjacent syllables/words are united with a circle. The adjusted p's at the edge of significance are marked with symbols.

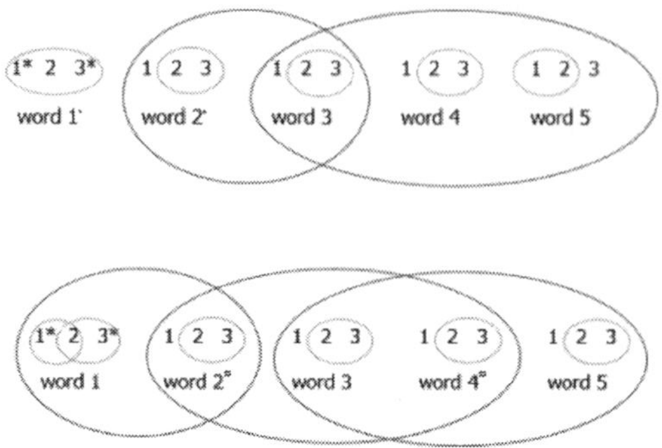

Figure 1. H-child's (above) and H-parent's (below) adjacent syllable and word f0 similarities.

Certain syllable groupings seem to appear mostly as a feature of the language, not showing great differences among all the speakers, while the word groupings seem to be more characteristic of a speaker. The absolute values of the mean f0 differences between syllables do not seem to differ that much from each other; however, the statistical significance of the difference between syllable 2 and syllable 3 varies for every speaker. The strongest child-parent similarity is found in L-family, while in families H and P parents' adjusted p-values are at the edge of significance in comparison to the children's. Majorly, the strongest adjacent similarities in children and their parents resemble each other, while the differences are found in the weakest ones. However, the child-parent dissimilarities manifest themselves differently among the families.

For each Russian speaker, the ANOVA tests do not show a significant effect of the move, so all the curve shapes inside each position are analyzed together. There is a significant effect of the section and position on the f0 values. For some speakers, the ANOVA tests also show effect of the group, but a series of THSD tests reveal that the underlying difference is between the positions. Similarly to the Finnish data, the similarities between the positions and sections inside the positions are based on the difference between mean f0 values. Figure 2 presents the similarities graphically.

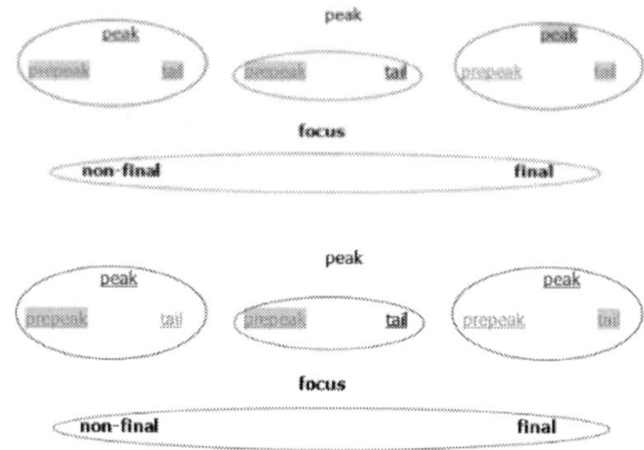

Figure 2. OO-child's (above) and OO-parent's (below) section and position f0 similarities.

Three out of four families show similar patterns of gross similarities among the positions, and each family has its own similarities and differences inside positions and cross-positionally. All of the significant differences have the same direction (sign) in both speakers of each pair.

4.3 Cluster analysis and sentence maps

In the Finnish data, the ANOVA test shows a significant effect of relationship between an adult and a child on the strength of clustered ratios: F=47.15, p=4.03e-11, Df=1. According to a THSD test, the mean strength of the same family-internal clusters is greater than that of the different pairs by 1.43. In fact, family-internal similarities on average are either stronger (H-family members, P-child) or non-significantly different (L-family members, P-parent) in comparison to the respective member's external similarities. The similarities with alien family members can be weaker (importantly, it holds absolutely true for L-parent) or non-significantly different in comparison to the latter's family-internal similarities. In a word-wise comparison, the similarities in families are in total stronger than the similarities of their members with the others in 55%, non-significantly different in 30% and weaker in 15% of the cases.

In the Russian data, The ANOVA test also shows a significant effect of the relationship between an adult and a child on the strength of clustered ratios: F=149.6; p<2e-16, Df=1. According to a THSD test, mean strength of the family-internal clusters is greater than that of the unrelated speakers by 3.47. Family-internal similarities on average are either stronger (AL-family members, VN-family members, OO-parent) or non-significantly different (MA-family members, OO-child) in comparison to the respective member's external similarities. The similarities with alien family members can be weaker (importantly, it holds absolutely true for MA-family members) or non-significantly different in comparison to the latter's family-internal similarities. In a position-wise comparison, the similarities in families in total are stronger than the family-external similarities of their members in 81%, non-significantly different in 8% and weaker in 11% of the cases.

Besides the strength of the clusters (similarities), their coefficients and the homogeneity of the latter through a sentence are an important factor of the parent-child resemblance for both Finnish and Russian speakers. Figure 3 displays the sentence map of H-parent – H-child (HH) clusters.

For HH speaker combination, maximum possible word grouping is five words, clusters [1B + 2A* + 3D + 4C + 5C] with the mean syllable-wise coefficients [0.755; 0.746; 0.745]. The difference of 0.03 between the means of 1B and 2A, however, is at the edge of significance, adjusted p=0.03; while in the rest of the pair-wise comparisons adjusted p's are greater than 0.1. The total strength of the grouped clusters, or the sum of the maximum cluster strengths from each element, equals 28.

Figure 4 displays the sentence map of AL-parent - AL-child (ALAL) clusters. For ALAL speaker combination, maximum possible position grouping is clusters [non-final C, focus A, final A] with the mean section-wise coefficients [0.716; 0.725; 0.733; 0.723; 0.713]. The total strength of the grouped clusters equals 27.

Relation (F=157.17, p-value<2e-16, Df=1; F=144.44, p-value <2e-26, Df=1), language (F=31.49, p=2.95e-08, Df=1; F=6.915, p=0.01), and relation*language interaction (F=33.19, p=1.28e-08, Df=1; F=4.235, p=0.042, Df=1) have a significant effect both on the strength of the clusters (adult-child similarity) and total strength of groupings (statistic values given respectively). For both measures, the strength is greater in pairs of the same family members in general, family-internally greater in Russian, and family-externally greater in Finnish. The (relative) number of grouped elements is also higher in pairs of the same family members in total (adjusted p=0.002), but family-internally is higher in Finnish, and family-externally higher in Russian. It is important to note that a grouping in the Russian data does not correspond to a sentence in the same sense that a grouping in the Finnish data. In Russian, neither the number of data points in positions (three or five), nor the number and the order of the latter are fixed. In Finnish, on the opposite, the framework used in the current study reflects the permanent number and the order of the words and syllables.

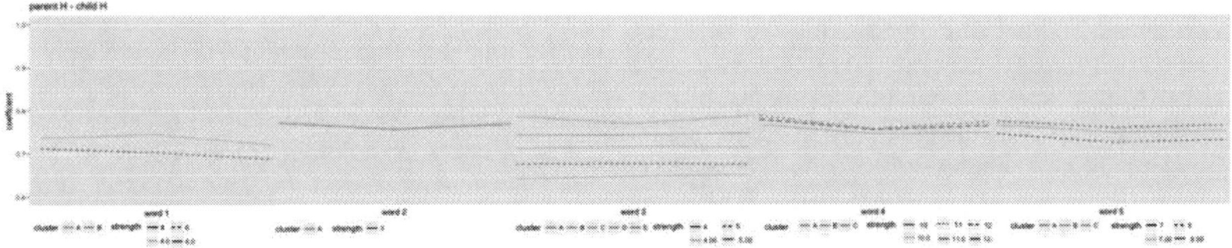

Figure 3. Sentence map of HH-clusters.

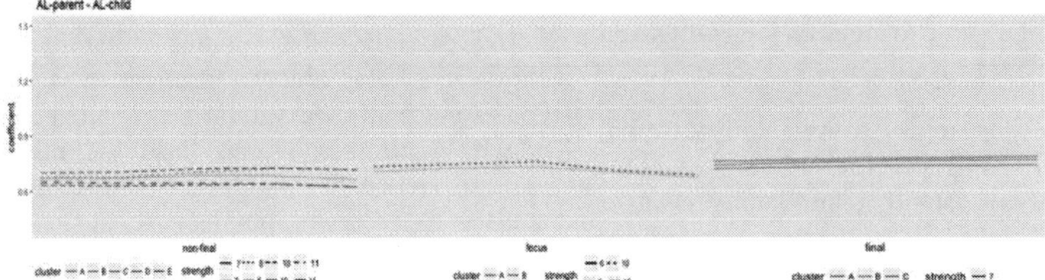

Figure 4. Sentence map of ALAL clusters.

4.4 Relationship between the perceptual experiments and instrumental analysis

ANOVA tests, run with the binary result of the perceptual test as a dependent variable, and the total strength of groupings divided into two explanatory variables, similarity (family-internal) and distracting power (family-external), show the only significant effect of the similarity on the accuracy results in the child-matching task in Russian (F=13.3, p=3.00e-04, Df=1), which reflects that significantly lower accuracy for target MA is associated with its low similarity coefficient.

The only significant correlation found between the total strength of family-internal groupings and mean accuracy in perceptional experiment for the corresponding target is in the subset of the child-matching task in Finnish: r=0.87, r_s=0.87.

5   Discussion

In the current study, the possibility to perceptually distinguish between the members of the same family and unrelated adult-child pairs in an XAB paradigm appears to be language dependent. Finnish naïve unfamiliar listeners do not attribute adults or children to a particular alien family more than to their own one, but rather they cannot draw any conclusions on perceptual (dis)similarity.

In Russian, the accuracy of answers depends on the target family. Interestingly, the families with the chance-level results are different in the two tasks. For the rest of the targets, respectively, the accuracy is above chance (M=72.5%), and comparable to the results of perceptual identification of twin- and same-gender sibling pairs in voice trios (Decoster et al., 2010; Feiser and Kleber, 2012). The same item can correspond to different mean accuracy for different target families. Thus, rephrasing Rose and Duncan's (1995) conclusion, some voices and some tokens of the same utterance may differ in the identification of the adult-child relationship.

In total, despite some strong family-external similarities, family-internal f0 contour similarities are consistently significantly stronger than family-external in both language groups separately and together. The numerical coefficients of family similarity are not language-specific. However, due to the language-conditioned differences in applied frameworks, it might not be reasonable to compare the strengths of pair similarities between language groups.

In Finnish, both the syllable position in a word and the word position in a sentence have a significant effect on f0 in the proposed five-word three-syllable sentence framework. Unlike the adjacent similarities between syllables, which look rather as a language property, adjacent word similarity represents a gross picture of f0 falling in the sentence and therefore to a certain extent reflects the individual's speech rhythm. Two out of three participating families (H and P) demonstrate strong parent-child resemblance in adjacent word similarities and consistently strong internal similarity in the final coefficient groupings. However, the similarity in the final coefficient groupings of the third family (L) also shows a tendency to be stronger or more consistent than its members' external similarities (especially those of L-parent). Whether the reason of this distinction lies in L-child's older age, smaller parent-child age difference, L-parent's hearing disadvantage (self-reported tinnitus) or other, remains unclear.

In Russian, both position and section have a significant effect on f0 in the proposed three-position three-section framework (changeable number and order of positions in a sentence). The similarities of the sections inside and across positions, as well as of the positions among themselves are believed to reflect the individual's speech rhythm. Parent-child resemblance range from nearly identical in two families (OO and VN), slightly less similar in one family (AL) and showing the greatest dissimilarity in the other (MA). The latter family is also characterized by the weakest internal similarity in the final coefficient groupings, which are, however, in five out of six cases stronger than the family-external similarities of its members.

Interestingly, the parents' family-internal similarities are always stronger or/and more consistent than their similarities to alien children, which is not always the case the other way around. Hence, the individual characteristics of adult's f0 contours pervasively appear in the speech of their children, but children can noticeably demonstrate features that are found in other adult speakers of the same language, which is most probably reflecting the classic extremes, biology and socialization (Bolinger, 1989) in parent-child intonation similarities.

The accuracy of the Finnish-speaking listeners' performance in the perceptual experiment shows no dependency on the target, nor on the distractor in a trio of voices, albeit family-internal and external similarities vary. The correlation ($r=0.87$, $r_s=0.87$) found between the similarity strength and mean accuracy of answers in the child-matching (always second) task might signal that the participants get used to the material and are attempting to base the decision, which child sounds more like the adult's offspring, on family-internal f0 similarities. However, it seems that either the similarities, as proposed by the current framework, are not prominent enough or the listeners rely on other voice cues.

The results of the perceptual experiment on Russian seem to interestingly reflect the specificity of an XAB discrimination paradigm. Selecting the answer between A and B, listeners in fact make a decision about X. In the parent-matching task, listeners do not choose the parent (A or B) but attribute the child (X) to one of the adults. Albeit AL-family demonstrates high internal similarity in acoustic analysis, AL-parent's external similarities are also strong. Thus, a listener cannot "learn" within the task to map the features exclusively of AL-child to AL-parent and gives more incorrect answers for target AL. The low internal similarity of MA-family does not bring the accuracy for MA-target down because MA-parent's external similarities are weaker. In the child-matching task, on the opposite, a listener cannot "learn" within the task to map the features exclusively of MA-parent to MA-child due to a combination of low internal similarity strength per se and the differences between it and the average external similarity of MA-child. It is also important to note that proposed explanation concerns only the average results of the perceptual experiment. Not all the sentences from the perceptual experiment were acoustically analyzed, which means that they reflect less f0 contour similarities than the selected ones. Half of the non-selected sentences correspond to quite high accuracy results (median 68.9%). Hence, although the f0 contour similarities between Russian-speaking parents and children contribute to identification of family

pairs in a trio of voices by non-familiar listeners, the relationship is not linear, may have certain thresholds and involve other voice cues.

6   Conclusion

The current paper presents an attempt to find f0 contour similarities between parents and their young children.

The authors fully acknowledge the limitations of the present study. Analyzed data are limited in their amount, on the one hand, and to read-aloud speech, on the other. The recording scripts do not necessarily reflect naturally occurring utterances in terms of pragmatic, which plays an especially important role in Finnish. The f0 contours are analyzed mostly in their static parameters, nor are other voice cues analyzed as possible contributors to perceptual similarity.

However, the presented findings can be used for the further research on perceptual and acoustic voice similarities between parents and young children or, broader, family members of different age (and gender).

References

Hanna Anttila. 2009. Interrogative intonation in spontaneous Finnish. In V. de Silva and R. Ullakonoja (Eds.) *Phonetics of Russian and Finnish, general description of phonetic systems, experimental studies on spontaneous and read-aloud speech,* pages 167-176. Frankfurt am Main: Peter Lang.

Paul Boersma and David Weenink. 2017. *Praat: doing phonetics by computer* [Computer program]. Version 6.0.33, retrieved 29 September 2017 from http://www.praat.org/

Natalya V. Bogdanova. 2001. *Zhivye foneticheskie protsessy russkoi rechi. Posobie po spetskursu [Live phonetical processes in Russian speech. Course manual].* Saint Petersburg: Philological Faculty of Saint Petersburg State University.

Dwight Bolinger. 1986. *Intonation and its parts: Melody in spoken English.* London: Edward Arnold.

Dwight Bolinger. 1989. *Intonation and its uses: Melody in Grammar and Discourse.* Stanford, California: Stanford University Press.

David Brazil, Malcolm Coulthard, and Catherine Johns. 1980. *Discourse intonation and language teaching.* London: Longman.

Elena A. Bryzgunova. 1977. *Zvuki i intonatsiya russkoy rechi [Sounds and intonation of Russian speech]* (3rd ed.). Moscow: Russkiy yazyk.

David Crystal. 2003. *A dictionary of Linguistics and phonetics* (5th ed.). Blackwell Publishing.

Viola de Silva, and Riikka Ullakonoja. 2009. Introduction: Russian and Finnish in Contact. In V. de Silva, and R. Ullakonoja (Eds.), *Phonetics of Russian and Finnish. General Description of Phonetic Systems. Experimental Studies on Spontaneous and Read-aloud Speech,* pages 15-20. Frankfurt am Main: Peter Lang.

Frans Debruyne, Wivine Decoster, Annemie Van Gijsel, Julie Vercammen. 2002. Speaking fundamental frequency in monozygotic and dizygotic twins. *Journal of Voice,* 16(4):466-471.

Wivine Decoster and Frans Debruyne. 2000. Longitudinal voice changes: Facts and interpretation. *Journal of Voice,* 14(2):184-193.

Wivine Decoster, Annemie Van Gijsel, Julie Vercammen, and Frans Debruyne. 2001. Voice similarity in identical twins. *Acta Otorhinolaryngologica Belgica,* 55(1):49-55.

Hanna S. Feiser and Felicitas Kleber. 2012. Voice similarity among brothers: evidence from a perception experiment. In *Proceedings of the 21st Annual Conference of the International Association for Forensic Phonetics and Acoustics (IAFPA).* Santander, Spain.

Michael Fuchs, Jens Oeken, Thomas Hotopp, Roland Täschner, Bettins Hentschel, and Wolf Behrendt. 2000. Similarity of monozygotic twins regarding vocal performance and acoustic markers and possible clinical significance [Abstract]. *HNO,* 48(6):462-469.

Tamas Hacki and S. Heitmüller. 1999. Development of the child's voice. International *Journal of Pediatric Otorhinolaryngology,* 49(1): 141-144.

Pekka Hirvonen. 1970. *Finnish and English communication intonation.* Turku: Publications of the Phonetics Department of the University of Turku 8.

Antti Iivonen. 1977. Lausefonetiikan tutkimuksesta [About the research on phonetics in clauses]. In K. Suomi (Ed.), *Selected papers of the VII Phonetics Symposium Fonetiikan päivät – Turku 1977,* pages 1-14. Turku University, Finland.

Antti Iivonen. 1978. Is there interrogative intonation in Finnish? In E. Gårding, G. Bruce, and R. Bannert (Eds.), *Nordic Prosody: Papers from a Symposium,* pages 43-53. Department of Linguistics, Lund University, Sweden.

Antti Iivonen. 2005. Intonaation käsitteen täsmennystä [Specification of the concept of intonation]. In A. Iivonen (Ed.), *Puheen salaisuudet: Fonetiikan uusia suuntia [Speech secrets: New directions in phonetics],* pages 93-128. Helsinki: Guadeamus.

Patrik N. Juslin and Klaus R. Scherer. 2008. Vocal expression of affect. In J. Harrigan, R. Rosenthal, and K. Scherer (Eds.) *The New Handbook of Methods in Nonverbal Behavior Research,* pages 65-136. Oxford University Press.

Rachel E. Kushner and Corine A. Bickley. 1995. Analysis and perception of voice similarities among family members. *Journal of the Acoustical Society of America 98:* 2936.

Pavel Labutin, Sergey Koval, and Andrey Raev. 2007. Speaker identification based on the statistical analysis of f0. In *Proceedings of IAFPA.* The College of St Mark and St John, Plymouth, UK.

Tatiana M. Nikolaeva. 1970. *Frazovaya intonatsiya slavyansih yazykov [Phrasal intonation of Slavic languages].* Moscow.

Francis Nolan, Kirsty McDougall, and Toby Hudson. 2011. Some acoustic correlates of perceived (dis)similarity between same-accent voices. In *Proceedings of the 17th ICPhS,* pages 1506-1509. Hong Kong.

Jiska S. Peper, Rachel M. Brouwer, Dorret I. Boomsma, René S. Kahn, and Hilleke E. Hulshoff Pol. 2007. Genetic influences on human brain structure: A review of brain imaging studies in twins. *Human Brain Mapping,* 28:464-473.

Beata D. Przybyla, Horii Yoshiyuki, and Michael H. Crawford. 1992. Vocal fundamental frequency in a twin sample: Looking for a genetic effect. *Journal of Voice,* 6(3):261-266.

Phil Rose and Sally Duncan. 1995. Naive auditory identification and discrimination of similar voices by familiar listeners. *Forensic Linguistics,* 2/1:1-17.

Phil Rose. 1999. Differences and distinguishability in the acoustic characteristics of *hello* in voices of similar-sounding speakers: A forensic phonetic investigation. *Australian Review of Applied Linguistics,* 22(1):1-42.

R Core Team. 2017. R: A language and environment for Statistical Computing. R Foundation for Statistical Computing, Vienna, Austria. Retrieved from ttps://www.R-project.org

Eugenia San Segundo and Hermann Künzel. 2015. Automatic speaker recognition of Spanish siblings: (monozygotic and dizygotic) twins and non-twin brothers. *Loquens,* 2(2), e021.

Swapna Sebastian, Anto Suresh Benadict, Geethu K. Sunny, and Achamma Balraj. 2013. An investigation into the voice of identical twins. *Otolaryngology online journal,* 3(2):1-7.

Elaine T. Stathopoulos, Jessica E. Huber, and Joan E. Sussman. 2011. Changes in acoustic characteristics of the voice across the life span: Measures from individuals 4–93 years of age. *Journal of Speech, Language, and Hearing Research,* 54:1011-1021.

Kari Suomi, Juhani Toivanen, and Riikka Ylitalo. 2006. *Fonetiikan ja suomen äänneopin perusteet [The basics of phonetics and Finnish phonology].* Helsinki: Guadeamus.

Kari Suomi, Juhani Toivanen, and Riikka Ylitalo. 2008. *Finnish sound structure: Phonetics, phonology, phonotactics and prosody.* Oulu: Oulu University Press.

Paul M. Thompson, Tyrone D. Cannon, Narr, K.L., Theo G.M. van Erp, Veli-Pekka Poutanen, Matti Huttunen, Jouko Lönnqvist, Carl-Gustav Standertskjöld-Nordenstam, Jaakko Kaprio, Mohammad Khaledy, Rajneesh Dail, Chris I. Zoumalan, and Arthur W. Toga. 2001. Genetic influences on brain structure. *Nature Neuroscience,* 4(12):1253-1258.

Riikka Ullakonoja, Hanna Kärkkäinen, and Viola de Silva. 2007. Havaintoja venäjän kielen lukupuhunnan sävelkulun ja spontaanin puheen jaksottelun oppimisesta [On learning to perceive pitch in read-aloud speech and spontaneous speech segmenting of Russian]. In O.-P. Salo, T. Nikula, and P. Kalaja (Eds.), *Language in Learning – AFinLA Yearbook,* 37(65), pages 215-231. Jyväskylä: Suomen soveltavan kielitieteen yhdistys AfinLA.

Kristiane M. van Lierde, Bart Vinck, Sofia De Ley, Gregory Clement, and Paul Van Cauwenberge. 2005. Genetics of vocal quality characteristics in monozygotic twins: A multiparameter approach. *Journal of Voice,* 19(4):511-518.

VocaliD, Inc. (2015-2017). https://www.vocalid.co

Natalya B. Volskaya. Aspects of Russian Intonation. In V. de Silva and R. Ullakonoja (Eds.), *Phonetics of Russian and Finnish, general description of phonetic systems, experimental studies on spontaneous and read-aloud speech,* pages 37-46. Frankfurt am Main: Peter Lang.

Melanie Weirich and Leonardo Lancia. 2011. Perceived auditory similarity and its acoustic correlates in twins and unrelated speakers. In *The 17th International Congress of Phonetic Sciences (ICPhS XVII): Congress Proceedings,* pages 2118-2121.

Hadley Wickham. 2009. *ggplot2: Elegant graphics for data analysis.* New York: Springer-Verlag.

Donghui Zuo and Peggy Mok. 2015. Formant dynamics of bilingual identical twins. *Journal of Phonetics, 52,* 1-12.

Zvukovaya forma russkoy rechi. Uchebnik po fonetike russkogo yazyka [Sound form of Russian speech. Russian phonetics manual]. 2001-2002. Saint Petersburg: Saint Petersburg State University, Philological Faculty, Department of Phonetics and Experimental Phonetics Lab. Retrieved from www.speech.nw.ru/Manual

Enhancing Natural Language Understanding through Cross-Modal Interaction: Meaning Recovery from Acoustically Noisy Speech

Özge Alaçam

Department of Informatics

University of Hamburg, Hamburg, Germany

alacam@informatik.uni-hamburg.de

Abstract

Cross-modality between vision and language is a key component for effective and efficient communication, and human language processing mechanism successfully integrates information from various modalities to extract the intended meaning. However, incomplete linguistic input, i.e. due to a noisy environment, is one of the challenges for a successful communication. In that case, incompleteness in one channel can be compensated by information from another one (if available). In this paper, by employing a visual-world paradigm experiment, we investigated the dynamics between syntactically possible gap fillers for incomplete German sentences and the visual arrangements and their effect on overall sentence interpretation.

1 Introduction

In recent years, a growing body of literature has investigated how and to what extent cross-modal interaction contributes to natural language understanding. Human language processing system integrates information from various modalities to extract the meaning of the linguistic input accurately, but the contribution of cross-modality to a successful communication goes beyond it. It facilitates early reference resolution while the sentence unfolds and allows disambiguation even without realizing that another (linguistic) interpretation would be possible, e.g. see (Altmann and Mirković, 2009; Knoeferle et al., 2005; Tanenhaus et al., 1995). Furthermore, it also prepares the grounds for the re-construction of the meaning from noisy/missing input. When the environment is noisy, or the communication partner suffers from a motor or cognitive impairment, text

completion/prediction becomes a crucial element of a communication. Instead of waiting for or requesting spoken input, combining the uncertain information from the linguistic channel with information from the visual one increases the fluency and the effectiveness of the communication (Garay-Vitoria and Abascal, 2004).

In this study, by conducting an experiment with human-subjects, we address the problem of compensating the incompleteness of the verbal channel by additional information from visual modality. Investigating how humans reconstruct the meaning from a noisy data provides insights about how to incorporate human-like processing into communication systems. The psycholinguistic experiments help us to understand baseline preferences and the underlying mechanism of gap construction processes for meaning extraction. This capability for multi-modal integration can be a very specific yet crucial feature in resolving references and/or performing commands for i.e. a helper robot that aids people in their daily activities.

2 Meaning Recovery

The task of extracting meaning from a noisy input has been widely addressed by uni-modal approaches. In a uni-modal way, re-construction can be guided by e.g. morphological, syntactic, and semantic properties. In that case, a probability of a syntactic category in a certain context can be obtained from a language model (Asnani et al., 2015; Bickel et al., 2005). For example, using N-grams is a popular method for this task since they provide very robust predictions for local dependencies. However, their power is less when it comes to dealing with long-range dependencies. On the other hand, as several studies (Mirowski and Vlachos, 2015; Gubbins and Vlachos, 2013) show, a language model employing the syntactic dependencies of a sentence brings the relevant contexts closer. Using the Microsoft Research Sentence Completion Challenge (Zweig and Burges, 2012), Gubbins and Vlachos (2013) have showed that incorporating syntactic information leads to grammatically better options for a semantic text completion task. Semantic classification (e.g. ontologies) and clustering can also be used to derive predictions on the semantic level for meaning recovery. However, when it comes to the description of daily activities, contextual information coming from another modality would be more beneficial, since linguistic distributions alone could hardly provide enough clues to distinguish the action of *bringing a pan* from *bringing a mug*, which is a crucial difference for e.g. helper robots.

Cross-modal integration of two modalities can be addressed by various methods in a range from simply putting all features from both modalities together and then train a model to learn the associations, to more complex structures, e.g. relating uni-modal features from several modalities on a conceptual level by using common representations. Considering that the task of meaning extraction may benefit from not only low-level but also high-level knowledge representations, one meaningful method would be to utilize a triplet notation, consisting of $(argument, relation\_type, predicate)$ where $relation\_type$ is one of a predefined set of accepted relations, such as AGENT or THEME while *Predicate* and *Argument* are tokens of the input sentence. Within this framework, the reconstruction of content words can be formalized as recovering/predicting the predicates or argument of a sentence. To put it simply, a sentence like *"the woman carries ...."* can be formulated into two triplets; $(woman_i, \text{AGENT}, carry)$ and $(unknown_i, \text{THEME}, carry)$. Here the task is to determine the unknown entity which has directly related to the *carry* action and indirectly to the agent *woman*. In case the contextual information provided by the visual environment contains additional information (e.g. a scene that depicts a woman with a grocery bag), the missing part can be successfully filled.

Salama et al. (2018) address the problem of incomplete linguistic input referring to daily environment context by utilizing a context-integrating dependency parser. Their focus was to recover content words like nouns, adjectives and verbs given the contextual features (e.g. object properties, spatial relations among the objects or thematic roles). The results indicate that giving a strong influence to contextual information helps to fill a majority of gaps correctly.

While re-construction of content words is mostly about finding out either the argument or the predicate based on the relation between each other, re-construction of grammatical words is to determine the relation between argument and predicate. Furthermore, re-construction of grammatical words could be more challenging since they tend to occur with higher frequencies than the content words, yielding a very small type/token ratio (i.e. weaker a collocational relationship) that makes the reconstruction of them based on only linguistic information more difficult. Although this is beyond the scope of the current paper, it should be noted that a full-fledged cross-modal meaning recovery system is dependent on a success of visual relation extraction component as well. The state-of-art computer vision systems can be considered more effective to extract spatial relations among object and object properties compared to relations between the actors and their actions.

3 Situated Language Comprehension in a Noisy Setting

The noise in communication could be originated from various channels and sources. First of all, it can be a linguistic noise (e.g. spelling mistakes, complex attachments), or visual ambiguities (e.g. clutter of the environment, occlusions) or an acoustic noise.

The issues of how to comprehend noisy linguistic input and reconstruct the intended meaning have been addressed by both psycholinguistic and computational line of research (e.g. (Levy, 2011, 2008)).

According to a noisy-channel account, that mainly focus on linguistic noise, the sentence comprehension mechanism integrates all the information (at the syntactic, semantic and discourse level) from the existing words and use this linguistic evidence to predict the missing parts and infer the possible meaning (Gibson et al., 2013). Several studies have shown that in case of higher degrees of syntactic complexity, humans tend to choose an interpretation which is in line with the concurrent visual information or general world knowledge, even though this interpretation requires to accept grammatically unacceptable syntactic structures (Johnson and Charniak, 2004; Christianson et al., 2001; MacWhinney et al., 1984). Cunnings (2017)'s study on language learners also indicated when the perceiver processes (syntactically) noisy linguistic input, the other linguistic and non-linguistic constraints are prioritized compared to syntactic ones.

Based on noisy-channel framework, Levy (2008) proposes a probabilistic model of language understanding regarding situations where there are uncertainty about word-level representations. He addresses the problem in two different levels; a global inference that can be reached after processing the entire input, and incremental inference that is formed (usually) word-by-word the sentence unfolds. The main contribution of the proposed method is that it takes into account the prior and posterior probabilities calculated based on both linguistic and non-linguistic evidence, including e.g. the expectations about speaker's grammatical competence or about the environmental condition that can hinder the speech signals.

Gibson et al. (2013) describes language understanding as rational integration of noisy evidence and semantic expectations. In their study, they test their predictions by conducting reading experiments, in which mostly the prepositions in the sentences were altered (by deletion or insertion) keeping content-word same across conditions. For example, an ungrammatical sentence *"The mother gave the candle the daughter"* can be easily treated as plausible by inserting *to* before *"the daughter"*. The higher prior probability of the latter version of the sentence compared to that of the former one pulls the sentence meaning towards itself.

4 Negation Processing

One interesting question regarding the task of meaning recovery is how to recover a meaning communicated with a sentence that involves unclear negated statement.

Since negation is considered as a higher order abstract concept, it has its own uniqueness as a grammatical category. Identifying the scope and focus of negation is one of the challenging issues that gets particular attention from the NLP community (e.g. SEM 2012 shared task, Morante and Blanco (2012)). From a psycholinguistic perspective, the core discussion lies around whether both negated and actual situation of content is simu-

lated or only the actual one. However, regardless of how this process happens, the literature agrees on that sentences containing negation are harder to interpret than affirmative sentences (Orenes et al., 2014; Khemlani et al., 2012; Kaup et al., 2006; Lüdtke and Kaup, 2006; Carpenter and Just, 1975; Clark and Chase, 1972).

It has been conclusively shown that a negative sentence is processed by first simulating the positive argument. For example, after reading a negative sentence *"The bird was not in the air"*, a response to image that depicts *a flying bird* was faster than to a image of *a bird at rest*, (Zwaan, 2012). In addition to an overall processing difficulties that negation entails, it has been also shown that it is only integrated into the sentence meaning at a later point (Lüdtke et al., 2008).

On the other hand, there are also some evidence that indicates that when negation is supported by right contextual support, the positive arguments is no longer need to be represented, yielding faster verification compared to no-context situations (Tian et al., 2016; Dale and Duran, 2011; Nieuwland and Kuperberg, 2008).

5 Experiment

This study focuses on humans' preferences for the reconstruction of unclear sentence parts (in German) by using visual-world paradigm. Moreover, the effect of contextual information on situated reference resolution and on gap re-construction has been also manipulated by restricting the affordances of the locative object in one of the visual arrangements.

Gibson et al. (2013) list four different criteria of language processing system that have an impact on meaning recovery; (i) how close the literal sentence is to the plausible alternative, (ii) what kind of change is involved (insertion or deletion), (iii) the expectations about the corruption (noise-rate), and (iv) the plausibility of implausible sentences based on context or speaker-based. Basically by keeping all the criteria described by Gibson et al. (2013) constant, we focus, in this experiment, on obtaining prior probabilities of three types of grammatical words; two common preposition of location (*on* and *next to*) and negation particle (*not*). All sentences are syntactically plausible regardless from which focus-of-interest gap filler is used and their semantic plausibility is dependent on the information coming from the visual-world. Here in this current paper, we focus more on how meaning recovery is affected by negation, instead of detailed discussion into negation processing. Thus we kept the focus of negation constant among conditions, and the scene has been designed to have low referential competition (i.e. there are two tables in the scene, making the decision a binary task instead of a multinomial one).

The task is simply, hearing a sentence that communicates the intended meaning and process it and extract the meaning as close as possible to the intended one (Shannon, 1948). The goals that need to determined are;

- the re-construction of the gap-word

- full-sentence interpretation ("which object needs to be moved, and where to")

5.1 Participants

20 students (native speakers of German) participated in the experiment (*Mean age = 23.8, SD = 3.1*). They were paid or given a course credit to participate. The entire experiment took approximately 45 minutes for each participant including the familiarization and instruction sessions.

5.2 Material

Linguistic Material. In their complete form without a gap, all sentences have the same structure except the negation/preposition part (NEG/PP) as given below. The sentences start with a verb in an imperative form preceding an object (*NP*) and a prepositional phrase that specifies the goal location (*PP*). Then the sentence continues with a disfluency (*umm*) and a repair/complement part consisting of a negation or one of the two preposition of location. Our focus-of-interest gap fillers are (*nicht (not), auf(on), neben (next to)*). These are chosen since they can fill the same position interchangeably.

- Stell den Becher auf den Tisch, umm [auf/nicht/neben] den blauen.
  put the mug on the table, umm [on/not/next to] the blue one.

The choice of filler-word given the visual information determines which object that the repair/complement part is attached to. In this setting, the repair/complement may have three different syntactic roles; referring back to the OBJECT which is the mug (with *not*), referring back to the ADVERBIAL which is the table (with both *on* and *not*) or providing new complementary ADVERBIAL which is an another mug (with *next to*). Due to filling different roles, all possible linguistic interpretations require different parsing results. In all cases, the object referred to in the repair/complement part shares either the property (e.g. blue) or the object class (e.g. mug) with the target object or location.

Pre-prossessing of the spoken material. The sentences were recorded by a male native speaker of German at a normal speech rate. Intonational differences between different linguistic entities have been found to have a significant effect on reference resolution (Coco and Keller, 2015; Snedeker and Trueswell, 2003). Therefore, we avoided unequal intonational breaks that may bias the interpretation. The breaks separating phrases were equalized.

A constant background noise (a sound recording from a restaurant) was added to an entire spoken sentence with the Audacity software [1]. In order to mask the target word completely, the volume of the NEG/PP part starting from the interjection (*umm*) was gradually decreased till the end of the gap-word. Concurrently, the volume of the background noise was increased during this segment.

Scenes. In order to accommodate the intended interpretation(s) and to eliminate others, the object properties and their spatial relations among each other have been systematically manipulated for each scene. Although, other many more different visual arrangements could be possible, for the sake of systematicity, we have narrowed our visual conditions down to five scene arrangements, see Figure 1. Scene-1 conveys all possible interpretations for all the focus-of-interest fillers. Scene-2A and Scene-2B allows only *on* and *not*. However, the availability of the location signaled by *on* is occupied by another object in Scene-2B. The last two visual arrangements allows only one interpretation; signaled by *not* in Scene-3A and by *next to* in Scene-3B. The number of objects in the scenes was limited to eight and one additional object has been used in Scene-2B. For each visual condition, six different visual scene were designed resulting 30 main-trial scene. The 2D visual scenes were

---

created with the SketchUp Make Software [2].

To prevent participants' associating the focus-of-interest gap fillers with a particular visual arrangement, additional slightly changed sentences and scenes were introduced as filler items.

5.3 Procedure

Using the visual-world paradigm, we presented participants visual scenes with accompanying spoken sentences. We employed a simple "look-and-listen" experiment following clicking tasks to get user's preferences. The experiment started with filling out the written consent and demographic data form. Afterwards, the instructions were given in written format, preceding the 3 familiarization trials.

The participants were instructed that multi-modal stimuli always contain some background noise, and at one point, one word will be impossible to hear. Then they are expected to choose the gap-filler word and click on the target object and location communicated in the sentence. It was told that target object is always located on the middle stand and needs to be moved to one of the white trays on the scene located on various places. In order to be able to separate the task of identifying object from identifying location, target objects and locations are presented in a specific layout.

The stimuli were displayed on an SR Eyelink 1000 Plus eye tracker integrated into a 17 monitor with a resolution of 1280 x 1024 pixels. We utilized a total of 53 visual displays with accompanying spoken utterances (3 familiarization, 30 test trials and 20 fillers). Each trial began with a a drift correction and the presentation of a simple fixation cross for 2 sec, located at the middle-bottom of the screen. Afterwards, a 5 sec of visual preview before the onset of the spoken sentence was given. The preview gives a comprehender time to encode the visual information in advance of the linguistic information being presented. So, visual attention is intended to be free of recognizing the objects of the visual context during language processing. Then, the spoken sentence was presented accompanying the visual stimulus. A trial ended 2 sec after the offset of the sentence. Participants were asked to examine the scene carefully and attend the information given in the audio. The order of stimuli was randomized for each participant.

After the sentence is completed, the scene displays appears and the participants are asked to click their preference for the gap position among five options. They were also informed about that the gap could be accurately filled by more than one option. These options are "nicht (*not*)", "neben (*next to*)", "auf (*on*)", "mit (*with*)", and "den/das/die (*the*)[3]". Whereas the focus-of interest gap-fillers are syntactically acceptable for the gap position, two other grammatical words were provided among the options as distractors; *mit (with)* and *den/das/die (the)*. In German, the preposition *mit (with)* requires a dative object, therefore the gender of the following article should be different than the nominative or accusative forms of the article in the repair/complement part. Furthermore, *den/das/die (the)* can be understood in two ways, either as a repetition of the definite article or as a relative pronoun. In the former case, as a gap filler, it does not provide any additional information. On the other hand, the lack of relative clause verb makes the second interpretation unacceptable.

After the preference has been explicitly made, the scene appears again so that the participant can click on the scene to answer two questions respectively; *which object is the target?* and *where is the target location?*.

Although a time-course analysis of fixated items and locations when the sentence unfolds is very relevant in understanding the underlying mechanisms of language processing, in this paper, we narrow down our scope into participants' explicitly made choices after each multi-modal stimulus.

Our hypothesizes are listed as

- Syntactically all gap positions require one insertion to correctly accommodate the intended meaning, however unlike preposition of locations, negation operation is considered as a high-level (abstract) concept. Therefore, the sentences with *on* and *next to* should be more easier to disambiguate, therefore more preferred compared to ones with *not*.

- Conceptual information, i.e. target location's being not available as illustrated in Figure 1e may force to change the interpretation, accordingly the preference, from *on* to *not*.

---

[3]The respective article/relative pronoun was shown among options in accordance with the grammatical gender of the noun it modifies

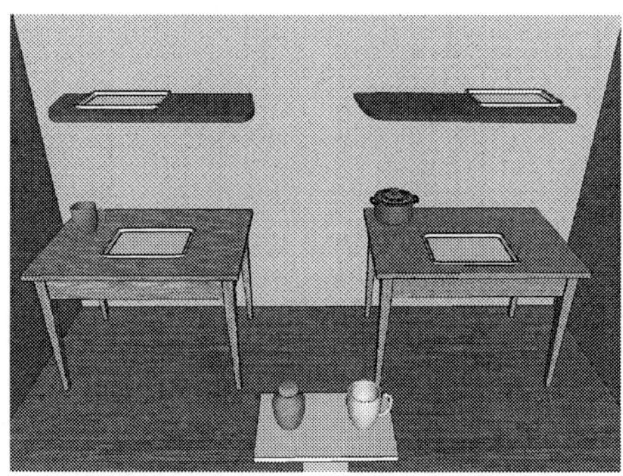

(a) Scene-1: *on, next to, not*

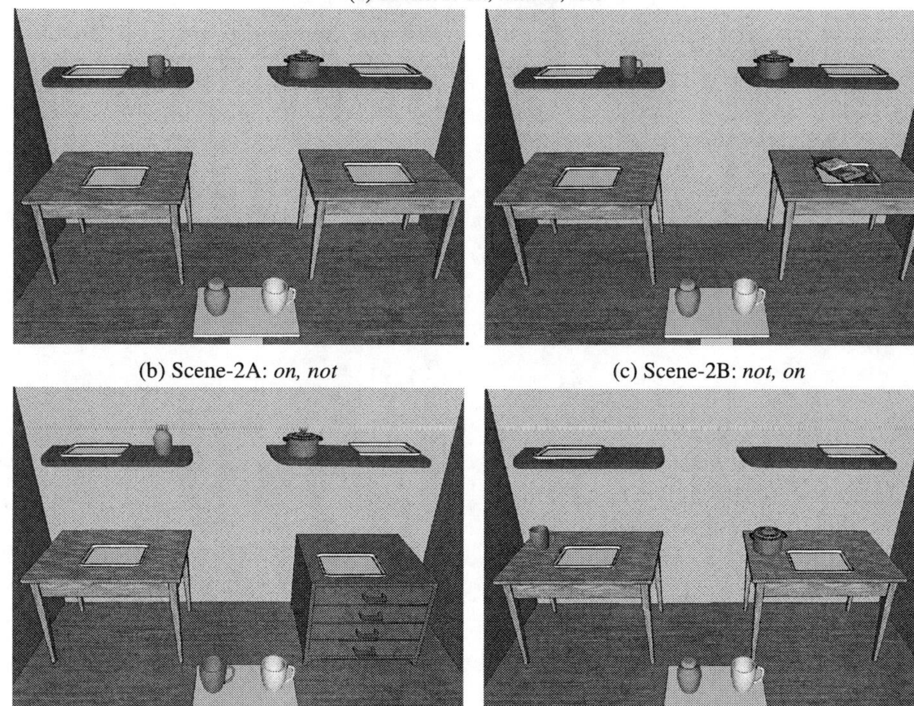

(b) Scene-2A: *on, not*   (c) Scene-2B: *not, on*

(d) Scene-3A: only *not*   (e) Scene-3B:only *next to*

Figure 1: Sample scenes that illustrate five different visual manipulations

6   Results

In this section, the gap-filler preferences and the global sentence interpretation by analyzing accurately chosen object given their preference have been reported. Figure 2 shows the distribution of the preferences for each visual condition. In total, participant preferences for 600 trials (20 participant * 30 scene) were taken into account.

Gap Construction Preferences. The visual condition Scene-1 was designed to analyze user's general tendency among three focus-of interest gap fillers, since all are equally plausible w.r.t. the visual context. In this condition, *next to* was preferred more in 43.9% of the trials compared to *on*

(30.8%) and *not* (20.6%). The other distractor options were preferred only in 3.7% of trials. The results of a Friedmans ANOVA indicated that preference rates for the three focus-of interest gap fillers significantly differs ($\chi^2(2) = 8.95, \; p < .001$). Wilcoxon tests were used to follow up this finding. It seems that this difference among groups is originated by the difference between *not* and *next to* ($z - score = -2.23, \; p < .0167$), *with a Bonferroni correction*.

The analysis on whether the participant could choose the object and the location in line with their explicitly made preference also demonstrated that all target objects are correctly identified. This result is highly expected, considering that the

PP/NEG part does not carry relevant information for the target identification in this visual setting. On the other hand, regarding the location, while 100% of the participants, who chose *next to*, correctly determine the target location, which is in line with their preference, this accuracy score is 90.9% for *on* and it drops drastically to 71.4% for *not*.

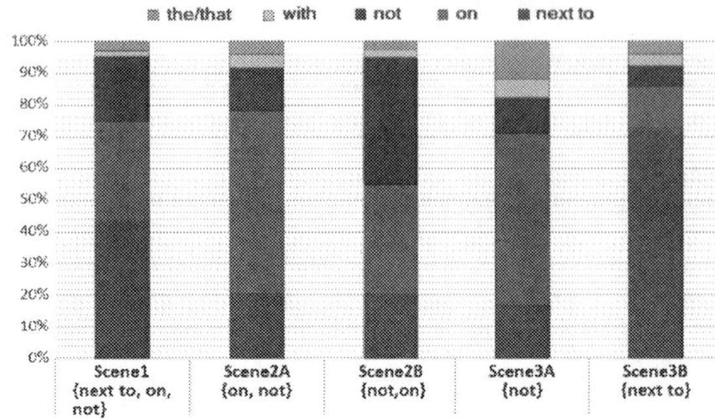

Figure 2: *Preference distributions regarding each visual condition*

The Effect of Contextual Cues. Whether the availability of a location signaled by one of the possible gap fillers has an effect on the preferences has been investigated by a mixed-design ANOVA comparing the number of preferred option across two visual arrangements; Scene-2A and Scene-2B. In these conditions, *on* and *not* are the two only semantically plausible gap fillers. The proportion results indicated that when the two locations are equally available (Scene-2A), participants prefer more *on* as a gap filler (57.5%), and the option *not* was chosen in only almost 13.3% of the trials. On the other hand, while the targeted location referred by the sentence with *on* repair is occupied (Scene 2B), then the participants' tendency to prefer *not* increases considerably by 21%. The preference of *next to* stays almost same across the conditions.

The results of the ANOVA indicated no main effect of the visual condition ($p > .05$). However, the main effect of Preference was significant ($F(2, 38) = 8.642$, $p = .001$). In general, *on* has been preferred more compared to *not* and *neben*; ($F(1, 19) = 10.92$, $p = .004$) and ($F(1, 19) = 11.61$, $p = .003$) respectively. Regarding our research question, the interaction effect between the visual condition and the preference is the relevant one, and it displays a significant interaction ($F(2, 38) = 7.79$, $p = .001$).

This indicates that the preference tendencies significantly differed in Scene-2A and Scene-2B. To break down this interaction, contrasts were performed comparing each level of focus-of-interest preferences across two scene types. These revealed significant interactions when comparing *on* and *not*, ($F(2, 38) = 18.98$, $p < .001$). Looking at the interaction graph in Figure 3, this suggests that when the target location signaled by *on* is occupied, participants looks for alternatives and ending up with only other available interpretation in line with *not*. Moreover, the contrast between *not* and *next to* was significant as well, ($F(2, 38) = 5.30$, $p < .05$).

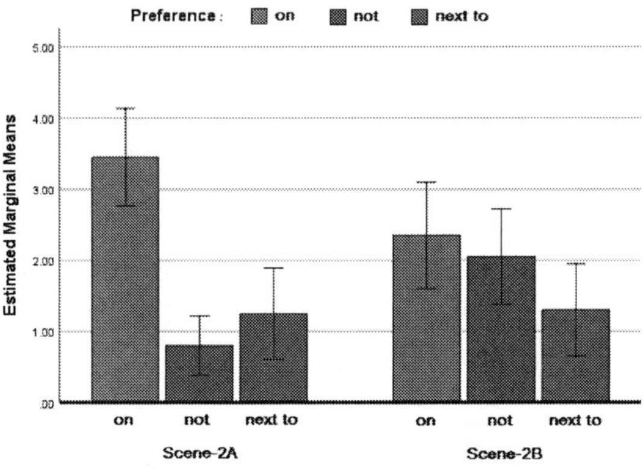

Figure 3: *Mean number of preferred focus-of-interest fillers across Scene-2A and Scene-2B*

Preferences under Restricted Conditions. The last comparison focuses on the cases, in which the visual arrangements and the properties of the objects only allow one interpretation. Scene-3A favors only the interpretation which is in line with the use of *not* as a gap filler. Yet, only in 53.3% of the trials correct option has been chosen as gap filler. Despite their conflict with the visual world, other gap fillers have been chosen in a considerable amount; *next to* (16.7%), *on* (10.8%), *with* (5.8%) and *the/that* (11.7%). On the other hand, Scene-3A syntactically allows only *next-to*. The results showed that in 72.5% of the trials, participants preferred *next to*. The comparison between the number of correct preferences across two visual condition revealed that on average, participants make more correct choices when they see Scene-3B (M = 4.35, SE = 1.72) compared to Scene-3A (M = 3.20, SE = .41), ($t(19) = -2.31$, $p < .05$).

7 Conclusion

In this study, by systematic manipulation of visual scene, we have obtained prior expectations regarding two locative prepositions and negation particle and we have also demonstrated how contextual cues pull an interpretation towards one side.

In order to accommodate different interpretations, five different visual arrangements have been utilized. Although our investigations into this area are still ongoing, the results could be a useful aid for developing models of situated natural language understanding that aims to account noisy data comprehension and meaning recovery. In this study, we particularly tried to put some spotlight into the special case "negation" as well.

The results indicate that when the visual world supports all interpretations, people have tendency to choose *next to* as a gap filler, that entails the repair/complement part referring to another object, which is not mentioned in the sentence before. Their second preference is to attach the repair part to the prepositional phrase (ADVERBIAL) by choosing *on* as gap filler. This selection also inherently assumes that the repair part is an affirmative statement. On the other hand, even in the cases where *not* is the only semantically plausible option as gap filler, the participants showed hesitance to choose it. This results are also in line with noisy-channel framework. A sentence with a gap is more harder to process compared to a complete sentence, since it requires at least two sub-tasks to be performed; predicting the gap-filler given the context and then confirming the inferred meaning. While the spatial relations like *next to* and *on* are easily graspable from an image, a negative statement requires additional operation to account for actual situation, that's why the listeners may prefer to override contextual expectations and stick to more easy-to-process one even it semantically, and sometimes syntactically creates a conflict (Ferreira, 2003). However, this preference (choosing *on* over *not*) still seems to be affected by the contextual cues like the availability of a target location.

It should nonetheless be acknowledged that the systematicity that we had to follow to single out all other effects becomes a limitation for generalization, thus further research is needed to better understand first the dynamics between the preference and the visual arrangements and second the dynamics between negation in detail and contextual cues. Moreover, none of the visual manipulations in this study was designed to address to explain the difference between choosing *next to* and *on*. Another set of experiments with reversed order; the first PP with a *next to* and the complement part with *on* would help us to gain some insights on this issue.

Acknowledgments

This research was funded by the German Research Foundation (DFG) in the project Cross-modal Learning, TRR-169.

References

Gerry TM Altmann and Jelena Mirković. 2009. Incrementality and prediction in human sentence processing. *Cognitive science*, 33(4):583–609.

Kavita Asnani, Douglas Vaz, Tanay PrabhuDesai, Surabhi Borgikar, Megha Bisht, Sharvari Bhosale, and Nikhil Balaji. 2015. Sentence completion using text prediction systems. In *Proceedings of the 3rd International Conference on Frontiers of Intelligent Computing: Theory and Applications (FICTA) 2014*, pages 397–404. Springer.

Steffen Bickel, Peter Haider, and Tobias Scheffer. 2005. Learning to complete sentences. In *European Conference on Machine Learning*, pages 497–504. Springer.

Patricia A Carpenter and Marcel A Just. 1975. Sentence comprehension: a psycholinguistic processing model of verification. *Psychological review*, 82(1):45.

Kiel Christianson, Andrew Hollingworth, John F Halliwell, and Fernanda Ferreira. 2001. Thematic roles assigned along the garden path linger. *Cognitive psychology*, 42(4):368–407.

Herbert H Clark and William G Chase. 1972. On the process of comparing sentences against pictures. *Cognitive psychology*, 3(3):472–517.

Moreno I Coco and Frank Keller. 2015. The interaction of visual and linguistic saliency during syntactic ambiguity resolution. *The Quarterly Journal of Experimental Psychology*, 68(1):46–74.

Ian Cunnings. 2017. Interference in native and non-native sentence processing. *Bilingualism: Language and Cognition*, 20(4):712–721.

Rick Dale and Nicholas D Duran. 2011. The cognitive dynamics of negated sentence verification. *Cognitive science*, 35(5):983–996.

Fernanda Ferreira. 2003. The misinterpretation of noncanonical sentences. *Cognitive psychology*, 47(2):164–203.

Nestor Garay-Vitoria and Julio Abascal. 2004. A comparison of prediction techniques to enhance the communication rate. In *ERCIM Workshop on User Interfaces for All*, pages 400–417. Springer.

Edward Gibson, Leon Bergen, and Steven T Piantadosi. 2013. Rational integration of noisy evidence and prior semantic expectations in sentence interpretation. *Proceedings of the National Academy of Sciences*, 110(20):8051–8056.

Joseph Gubbins and Andreas Vlachos. 2013. Dependency language models for sentence completion. In *Proceedings of the 2013 Conference on Empirical Methods in Natural Language Processing*, pages 1405–1410.

Mark Johnson and Eugene Charniak. 2004. A tag-based noisy channel model of speech repairs. In *Proceedings of the 42Nd Annual Meeting on Association for Computational Linguistics*, ACL '04, Stroudsburg, PA, USA. Association for Computational Linguistics.

Barbara Kaup, Jana Lüdtke, and Rolf A Zwaan. 2006. Processing negated sentences with contradictory predicates: Is a door that is not open mentally closed? *Journal of Pragmatics*, 38(7):1033–1050.

Sangeet Khemlani, Isabel Orenes, and Philip N Johnson-Laird. 2012. Negation: A theory of its meaning, representation, and use. *Journal of Cognitive Psychology*, 24(5):541–559.

Pia Knoeferle, Matthew W Crocker, Christoph Scheepers, and Martin J Pickering. 2005. The influence of the immediate visual context on incremental thematic role-assignment: Evidence from eye-movements in depicted events. *Cognition*, 95(1):95–127.

Roger Levy. 2008. A noisy-channel model of rational human sentence comprehension under uncertain input. In *Proceedings of the Conference on Empirical Methods in Natural Language Processing*, EMNLP '08, pages 234–243, Stroudsburg, PA, USA. Association for Computational Linguistics.

Roger Levy. 2011. Integrating surprisal and uncertain-input models in online sentence comprehension: formal techniques and empirical results. In *Proceedings of the 49th Annual Meeting of the Association for Computational Linguistics: Human Language Technologies-Volume 1*, pages 1055–1065. Association for Computational Linguistics.

Jana Lüdtke, Claudia K Friedrich, Monica De Filippis, and Barbara Kaup. 2008. Event-related potential correlates of negation in a sentence–picture verification paradigm. *Journal of cognitive neuroscience*, 20(8):1355–1370.

Jana Lüdtke and Barbara Kaup. 2006. Context effects when reading negative and affirmative sentences. In *Proceedings of the 28th annual conference of the cognitive science society*, volume 27, pages 1735–1740. Lawrence Erlbaum Associates Mahwah, NJ.

Brian MacWhinney, Elizabeth Bates, and Reinhold Kliegl. 1984. Cue validity and sentence interpretation in English, German, and Italian. *Journal of verbal learning and verbal behavior*, 23(2):127–150.

Piotr Mirowski and Andreas Vlachos. 2015. Dependency recurrent neural language models for sentence completion. *arXiv preprint arXiv:1507.01193*.

Roser Morante and Eduardo Blanco. 2012. * sem 2012 shared task: Resolving the scope and focus of negation. In ** SEM 2012: The First Joint Conference on Lexical and Computational Semantics–Volume 1: Proceedings of the main conference and the shared task, and Volume 2: Proceedings of the Sixth International Workshop on Semantic Evaluation (SemEval 2012)*, volume 1, pages 265–274.

Mante S Nieuwland and Gina R Kuperberg. 2008. When the truth is not too hard to handle: An event-related potential study on the pragmatics of negation. *Psychological Science*, 19(12):1213–1218.

Isabel Orenes, David Beltrán, and Carlos Santamaría. 2014. How negation is understood: Evidence from the visual world paradigm. *Journal of Memory and Language*, 74:36–45.

Amr Rekaby Salama, Özge Alacam, and Wolfgang Menzel. 2018. Text completion using context-integrated dependency parsing. In *Proceedings of The Third Workshop on Representation Learning for NLP*, pages 41–49.

Claude Elwood Shannon. 1948. A mathematical theory of communication. *Bell system technical journal*, 27(3):379–423.

Jesse Snedeker and John Trueswell. 2003. Using prosody to avoid ambiguity: Effects of speaker awareness and referential context. *Journal of Memory and language*, 48(1):103–130.

Michael K Tanenhaus, Michael J Spivey-Knowlton, Kathleen M Eberhard, and Julie C Sedivy. 1995. Integration of visual and linguistic information in spoken language comprehension. *Science*, 268(5217):1632–1634.

Ye Tian, Heather Ferguson, and Richard Breheny. 2016. Processing negation without context–why and when we represent the positive argument. *Language, Cognition and Neuroscience*, 31(5):683–698.

Rolf A Zwaan. 2012. The experiential view of language comprehension: How is negation represented? *Higher level language processes in the brain: Inference and comprehension processes*, page 255.

Geoffrey Zweig and Chris JC Burges. 2012. A challenge set for advancing language modeling. In *Proceedings of the NAACL-HLT 2012 Workshop: Will We Ever Really Replace the N-gram Model? On the Future of Language Modeling for HLT*, pages 29–36. Association for Computational Linguistics.

Predicting Prosodic Prominence from Text with Pre-trained Contextualized Word Representations

Aarne Talman,[*][†] Antti Suni,[*] Hande Celikkanat,[*] Sofoklis Kakouros,[*]
Jörg Tiedemann[*] and Martti Vainio[*]
[*]Department of Digital Humanities, University of Helsinki, Finland
[†]Basement AI, Finland
{name.surname}@helsinki.fi

Abstract

In this paper we introduce a new natural language processing dataset and benchmark for predicting prosodic prominence from written text. To our knowledge this will be the largest publicly available dataset with prosodic labels. We describe the dataset construction and the resulting benchmark dataset in detail and train a number of different models ranging from feature-based classifiers to neural network systems for the prediction of discretized prosodic prominence. We show that pre-trained contextualized word representations from BERT outperform the other models even with less than 10% of the training data. Finally we discuss the dataset in light of the results and point to future research and plans for further improving both the dataset and methods of predicting prosodic prominence from text. The dataset and the code for the models are publicly available.

1 Introduction

Prosodic prominence, i.e., the amount of emphasis that a speaker gives to a word, has been widely studied in phonetics and speech processing. However, the research on text-based natural language processing (NLP) methods for predicting prosodic prominence is somewhat limited. Even in the text-to-speech synthesis domain, with many recent methodological advances, work on symbolic prosody prediction has lagged behind. We believe that this is mainly due to the lack of suitable datasets. Existing, publicly available annotated speech corpora, are very small by current standards.

In this paper we introduce a new NLP dataset and benchmark for predicting prosodic prominence from text which is based on the recently published LibriTTS corpus (Zen et al., 2019), containing automatically generated prosodic prominence labels for over 260 hours or 2.8 million words of English audio books, read by 1230 different speakers. To our knowledge this will be the largest publicly available dataset with prosodic annotations. We first give some background about prosodic prominence and related research in Section 2. We then describe the dataset construction and annotation method in Section 3.

Prosody prediction can be turned into a sequence labeling task by giving each word in a text a discrete prominence value based on the amount of emphasis the speaker gives to the word when reading the text. In Section 4 we explain the experiments and the experimental results using a number of different sequence labeling approaches and show that pre-trained contextualized word representations from BERT (Devlin et al., 2019) outperform our other baselines even with less than 10% of the training data. Although BERT has been previously applied in various sequence labeling tasks, like named entity recognition (Devlin et al., 2019), to the best of our knowledge, this is the first application of BERT in the task of predicting prosodic prominence. We analyse the results in Section 5, comparing BERT to a bidirectional long short-term memory (BiLSTM) model and looking at the types of errors made by these selected models. We find that BERT outperforms the BiLSTM model across all the labels.

Finally in Section 6 we discuss the methods in light of the experimental results and highlight areas that are known to negatively impact the results. We also discuss the relevance of pre-training for the task of predicting prosodic prominence. We conclude by pointing to future research both in developing better methods for predicting prosodic prominence but also to further improve the quality of the dataset. The dataset and the PyTorch code for the models are available on GitHub: `https://github.com/Helsinki-NLP/prosody`.

2 Background

2.1 Prosodic Prominence

Every word and utterance in speech encompasses phonetic and phonological properties that are not resulting from the choice of the underlying lexical items and that encode meaning in addition to that of the individual lexemes. These properties are referred to as prosody and they depend on a variety of factors such as the semantic and syntactic relations between these items, and their rhythmic grouping (Wagner and Watson, 2010). Prosodic variation in speech contributes to a large extend to the perception of natural sounding speech. Prosodic prominence represents one type of prosodic phenomenon that manifests through the subjective impression of emphasis in speech where certain words are interpreted as more salient within their lexical surrounding context (Wagner and Watson, 2010; Terken and Hermes, 2000).

Due to the inherent difficulty in determining prominence — even for human subjects, see, e.g., (Yoon et al., 2004) — the development of automatic tools for the annotation of prominent units has been a difficult task. This is exemplified from the large degree of discrepancy observed between human annotators when labeling prominence where the inter-transcriber agreement can vary substantially based on a multitude of factors such as the choice of annotators or annotation method (Mo et al., 2008; Yoon et al., 2004; Kakouros and Räsänen, 2016). Similarly, in prominence production, certain degree of freedom in prominence placement and large variability between styles and speakers (Yuan et al., 2005), renders the task of prominence prediction from text very difficult compared to most NLP tasks involving text only.

2.2 Generating Prominence Annotations

Throughout the literature a number of methods have been proposed for the labeling of prosodic prominence. These methods can be roughly categorized on the basis of the need for training data (manual prosodic annotations) into supervised and unsupervised, but crucially, on the basis of the information they utilize from speech and language to generate their predictions (prominence labels).

As prominence perception has been found to correlate with acoustic-phonetic features (Lieberman, 1960), with the constituent syntactic structure of an utterance (Gregory and Altun, 2004; Wagner and Watson, 2010; Bresnan, 1973), with the frequency of occurrence of individual lexical items (Nenkova et al., 2007; Jurafsky et al., 2001), and with the probabilities of contiguous lexical sequences (Jurafsky, 1996), automatic methods have been developed utilizing these features either in combination or independently (Nenkova et al., 2007; Kakouros et al., 2016; Ostendorf et al., 1995; Levow, 2008).

Overall, these features can be largely divided into two categories: (i) *acoustic* (derived from the sound pressure waveform of the speech signal) and (ii) *language* (extracted by studying the form of the language; for instance, semantic or syntactic factors in the language). Both acoustic and language-based features have been shown to provide good overall performance in detecting prominence (in both supervised and unsupervised cases), where, however, the methods utilizing acoustic features seem to provide better performance for the unsupervised detection of prominences in speech (Suni et al., 2017; Wang and Narayanan, 2007; Kakouros and Räsänen, 2016), with state-of-the-art results reaching high level of accuracy, close to that of the inter-annotator agreement for the data. While the top-down linguistic information is known to correlate with perceptual prominence, in this paper we want to make a clear distinction between data labelling and text-based prediction. Thus, in this work, we utilize purely acoustic prominence annotations of the speech data using the method developed by Suni et al. (2017) as the prosodic reference.

2.3 Predicting Prosodic Prominence from Text

To what extent prosodic prominence can be predicted from textual input only has been a topic of inquiry in linguistics for a long time. In traditional generative phonology (Chomsky and Halle, 1968), accent placement was considered to be fully determined by linguistic structure, whereas a seminal work by Bolinger (1972) emphasized the importance and relevance of the lexical semantic context as well as the speakers' intention, positing that, in general, a mind reading ability may be necessary to determine prominent words in a sentence.

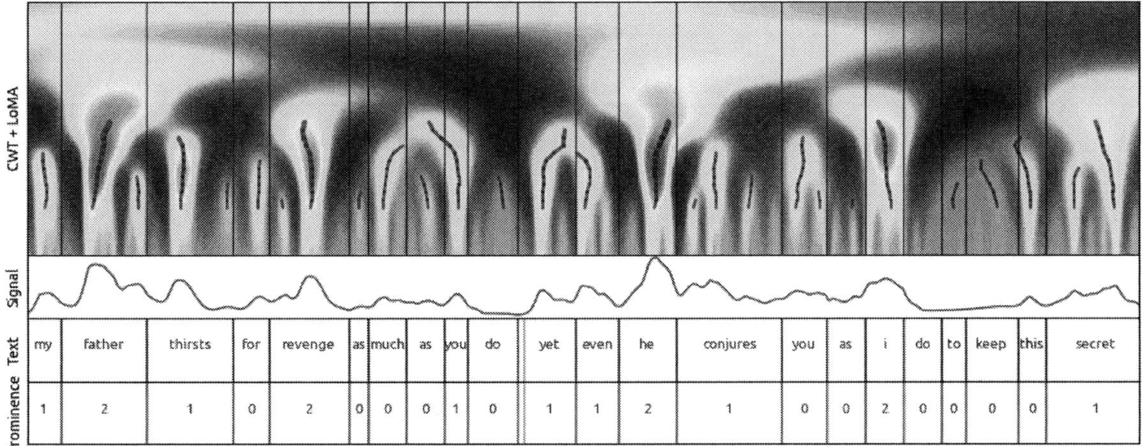

Figure 1: Continuous Wavelet Transform Annotation method.

				non-prominent	**prominent**	
sets (clean)	**speakers**	**sentences**	**words**	**0**	**1**	**2**
train-100	247	33,041	570,592	274,184	155,849	140,559
train-360	904	116,262	2,076,289	1,003,454	569,769	503,066
dev	40	5,726	99,200	47,535	27,454	24,211
test	39	4,821	90,063	43,234	24,543	22,286
total:	1230	159,850	2,836,144	1,368,407	777,615	690,122

Table 1: Dataset statistics

As longstanding inquiries hold, the goal of reliably predicting the placement of prominent entities from information automatically derived from textual resources is still ongoing.

Several efforts have been made towards this direction, especially in text-to-speech (TTS) synthesis research, where generation of appropriate prosody would increase both intelligibility and quality of synthetic speech. Before the deep learning paradigm shift in NLP, several linguistic features were examined for prominence prediction, including function-content word distinction, part-of-speech class, and information status (Hirschberg, 1993). Statistical features like unigrams, bigrams, and TF-IDF have also been frequently used (Marsi et al., 2003). Later, the accent ratio, or simply the average accent status of a word type in the given corpus, was found to be a stronger predictor than linguistic features in the accent prediction task (Nenkova et al., 2007), suggesting that lexical information may be more relevant than linguistic structure for the prominence prediction task.

Recently, continuous representations of words have become commonplace in prosody predic-tion for TTS, though the symbolic level is often omitted and pitch and duration are predicted directly using lexical embeddings (Watts, 2012). Yet, closely related to the proposed method, (Rendel et al., 2016) experimented with various lexical embeddings as an input to a Bi-directional LSTM model, predicting binary prominence labels. Training on a proprietary, manually annotated single speaker corpus of 3730 sentences, they achieved an F-score of 0.71 with Word2Vec (Mikolov et al., 2013) embeddings, with a clear improvement over traditional linguistic features.

3 Dataset

We introduce, automatically generated, high quality prosodic annotations for the recently published LibriTTS corpus (Zen et al., 2019). The LibriTTS corpus is a cleaned subset of LibriSpeech corpus (Panayotov et al., 2015), derived from English audiobooks of the LibriVox project.[1] We selected the 'clean' subsets of LibriTTS for annotation, comprising of 262.5 hours of read speech from 1230 speakers. The transcribed sentences were aligned

---

[1] https://librivox.org

Token	Tell	me	you	rascal	,	where	is	the	pig	?
Discrete label	2	0	0	0	NA	2	0	0	1	NA
Real-valued label	1.473	0.333	0.003	0.167	NA	2.160	0.006	0.037	0.719	NA

Table 2: Example sentence with the annotation from the dataset. Discrete prominence values were used in the experiments of this paper. The real-valued labels are used for generation of the discrete labels, however, they could also be used directly for prominence prediction.

with the Montreal forced aligner (McAuliffe et al., 2017), using a pronunciation lexicon and acoustic models trained on the LibriSpeech dataset. The aligned sentences were then prosodically annotated with word-level acoustic prominence labels. For the annotation, we used the Wavelet Prosody Analyzer toolkit[2], which implements the method described in (Suni et al., 2017). Briefly, the method consists of 1) the extraction of pitch and energy signals from the speech data and duration from the word level alignments, 2) filling the unvoiced gaps in extracted signals by interpolation followed by smoothing and normalizing, 3) combining the normalized signals by summing or multiplication, and 4) performing a continuous wavelet transform (CWT) on the composite signal and extracting continuous prominence values as lines of maximum amplitude across wavelet scales (see Figure 1). Essentially, the method assumes that the louder, the longer, and the higher, the more prominent. On top of this, the wavelet transform provides multi-resolution contextual information; the more the word stands out from its environment in various time scales, the more prominent the word is perceived.

For the current study, continuous prominence values were discretized to two (non-prominent, prominent) or three (non prominent, somewhat prominent, very prominent) classes. The binary case is closely related to the pitch accent detection task, aiming for results comparable with the majority of the literature on the topic. The weights in constructing the composite signal and discretization thresholds were adjusted based on The Boston University radio news corpus (Ostendorf et al., 1995), containing manually annotated pitch accent labels. This corpus is often used in the evaluation of pitch accent annotation and prediction quality, with the current annotation method yielding state-of-the-art accuracy in word level acoustic-based accent detection, 85.3%, us-

ing weights 1.0, 0.5 and 1.0 for F0, energy and duration respectively, and using multiplication of these features in signal composition. For three-way discretization, the non-prominent / prominent cut-off was maintained and the prominent class was split to two classes of roughly equal size. Statistics of the resulting dataset are described in table 1. The full dataset is available for download here: `https://github.com/Helsinki-NLP/prosody`. Although not discussed in this paper, the described acoustic annotation and text-based prediction methods can be applied to prosodic boundaries too, and the boundary labels will be included in the dataset at a later stage.

4 Experiments

In this section we describe the experimental setup and the results from our experiments in predicting discrete prosodic prominence labels from text using the corpus described above.

4.1 Experimental Setup

We performed experiments with the following models:

- BERT-base uncased (Devlin et al., 2019)
- 3-layer 600D Bidirectional Long Short-Term Memory (BiLSTM) (Hochreiter and Schmidhuber, 1997)
- Minitagger (SVM) (Stratos and Collins, 2015) + GloVe (Pennington et al., 2014)
- MarMoT (CRF) (Mueller et al., 2013)
- Majority class per word

The models were selected so that they cover a wide variety of different architectures from feature-based statistical approaches to neural networks and pre-trained language models. The models are described in more detail below.

We use the Huggingface PyTorch implementation of BERT available in the `pytorch_transformers` library,[3] which

---

[2]`https://github.com/asuni/wavelet_prosody_toolkit`

---

[3]`https://github.com/huggingface/`

we further fine-tune during training. We take the last hidden layer of BERT and train a single fully-connected classifier layer on top of it, mapping the representation of each word to the labels. For our experiments we use the smaller BERT-base model using the uncased alternative. We use a batch size of 32 and fine-tune the model for 2 epochs.

For BiLSTM we use pre-trained 300D GloVe 840B word embeddings (Pennington et al., 2014). The initial word embeddings are fine-tuned during training. As with BERT, we add one fully-connected classifier layer on top of the BiLSTM, mapping the representation of each word to the labels. We use a dropout of 0.2 between the layers of the BiLSTM. We use a batch size of 64 and train the model for 5 epochs.

For the SVM we use Minitagger[4] implementation by Stratos and Collins (2015) using each dimension of the pre-trained 300D GloVe 840B word embeddings as features, with context-size 1, i.e. including the previous and the next word in the context.

For the conditional random field (CRF) model we use MarMot[5] by Mueller et al. (2013) with the default configuration. The model applies standard feature templates that are used for part-of-speech tagging such as surrounding words as well as suffix and prefix features. We did not optimize the feature model nor any of the other hyper-parameters.

All systems except the Minitagger and CRF are our implementations using PyTorch and are made available on GitHub: `https://github.com/Helsinki-NLP/prosody`.

For the experiments we used the larger train-360 training set. We report both 2-way and 3-way classification results. In the 2-way classification task we take the three prominence labels and merge labels 1 and 2 into a single prominent class.

4.2 Results

All models reach over 80% in the 2-way classification task while 3-way classification accuracy stays below 70% for all of them. The BERT-based model gets the highest accuracy of 83.2% and 68.6% in the 2-way and 3-way classification tasks, respectively, demonstrating the value of a

pre-trained language model in this task. The 3-layer BiLSTM achieves 82.1% in the 2-way classification and 66.4% in the 3-way classification task.

The traditional feature-based classifiers perform slightly below the neural network models, with the CRF obtaining 81.8% and 66.4% for the two classification tasks, respectively. The Minitagger SVM model's test accuracies are slightly lower than the CRF's with 80.8% and 65.4% test accuracies. Finally taking a simple majority class per word gives 80.2% for the 2-way classification task and 62.4% for the 3-way classification task. The results are listed in Table 3. The fairly low results across the board highlight the difficulty of the task of predicting prosodic prominence from text.

To better understand how much training data is needed in the two classification tasks, we trained selected models with different size subsets of the train-360 training data. The selected subsets were: 1%, 5%, 10%, 50% and 100% of the training examples (token-label pairs). Figures 2 and 3 contain the learning curves for the 2-way and 3-way classification tasks, for all the models except for the majority and random baselines.

For all models and for both of the classification tasks we notice that they achieve quite high test accuracy already with a very small number of training examples. For most of the models the biggest improvement in performance is achieved when moving from 1% of the training examples to 5%. All models have reached close to their full predictive capacity with only 10% of the training examples. For example, BERT achieves 2-way classification test accuracy of 82.6% with 10% of the training data, which is only -0.6% points lower than the accuracy with the full training set. In the 3-way classification task 10% of the training data gives 67.1% for BERT, which is -1.7% points below the accuracy with the full training set.

Interestingly, in the 2-way classification task the BiLSTM model shows a slightly different learning curve, having already quite a high performance with just 1% of the training data, but then making no improvement between 1% and 5%. However, between 5% and 100% the BiLSTM model improvement is almost linear.

As the proposed dataset has been automatically generated as described in Section 3, we also tested the best two models, BERT and BiLSTM, with a manually annotated test set from The Boston University radio news corpus (Ostendorf et al., 1995).

`pytorch-transformers`

[4]`https://github.com/karlstratos/minitagger`

[5]`http://cistern.cis.lmu.de/marmot/`

Model	Test accuracy (2-way)	Test accuracy (3-way)
BERT-base	**83.2%**	**68.6%**
3-layer BiLSTM	82.1%	66.4%
CRF	81.8%	66.4%
SVM+GloVe	80.8%	65.4%
Majority class per word	80.2%	62.4%
Majority class	52.0%	48.0%
Random	49.0%	39.5%

Table 3: Experimental results (%) for the 2 and 3-way classification tasks.

For this experiment we trained the models using the train-360 training set (as above) replacing only the test set. The results of this experiment are shown in Table 4. The good results[6] from this experiment provide further support for the quality of the new dataset. Notice also that the difference between BERT and BiLSTM is much bigger with this test set (+3.9% compared to +1.1%). This difference could be due to the genre difference between the two test sets, with the Boston University news corpus being more contemporary compared to the source for our proposed dataset (pre-1923 books). This point will be further discussed in Section 6.

Model	vs expert	vs acoustic
BERT-base	**82.9%**	**82.1%**
3-layer BiLSTM	79.0%	79.3%

Table 4: Test accuracies (%) for the Boston University radio news corpus (2-way classification). expert = expert annotated perceptual prominence labels, acoustic = our acoustic prominence labels

5 Analysis

The experimental results show that although predicting prosodic prominence is a fairly difficult task, pre-trained contextualized word representations clearly help, as can be seen from the results for BERT. The difference between BERT and the other models is clear if we compare the other models with BERT fine-tuned with a small fraction of the training data. In fact, BERT already outperforms the other models with just 5% of the training examples in the 2-way classification case and with 10% of the training data in the 3-way classification

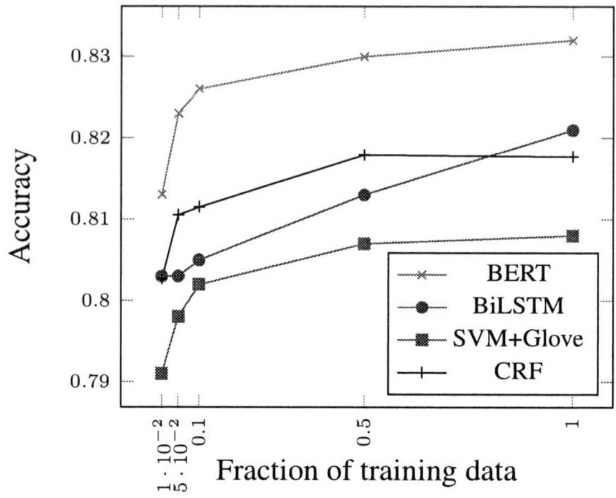

Figure 2: Test accuracy with different size subsets of the training data for the 2-way classification task.

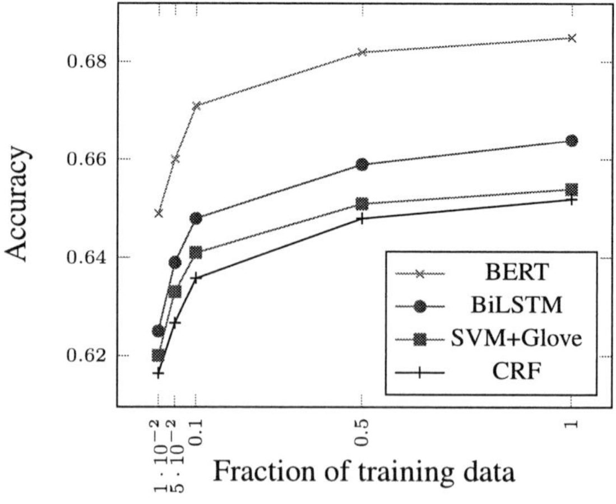

Figure 3: Test accuracy with different size subsets of the training data for the 3-way classification task.

---

[6]Better results have been reported on Boston dataset using lexical features, but there are methodological concerns related to cross-validation training and speakers reading the same text, see discussion on (Rosenberg, 2009).

case. This can be seen as an indication that BERT has acquired implicit semantic or syntactic information during pre-training that is useful in the task of predicting prosodic prominence.

To gain a better understanding of the types of predictive errors BERT makes, we look at the confusion matrices for the two classification tasks and compare those with the confusion matrices for the BiLSTM.

The 3-way classification confusion matrices are more informative as they allow comparison of the two models with respect to the predicted label in cases of error. Figure 4 contains the 3-way classification confusion matrix for BERT and Figure 5 for the BiLSTM model.

		Predicted 0	Predicted 1	Predicted 2	*recall*
Gold	0	35567	5602	2043	**82.3%**
Gold	1	5943	11589	6987	**47.3%**
Gold	2	1661	6208	14374	**64.6%**
	precision	**82.4%**	**49.5%**	**61.4%**	

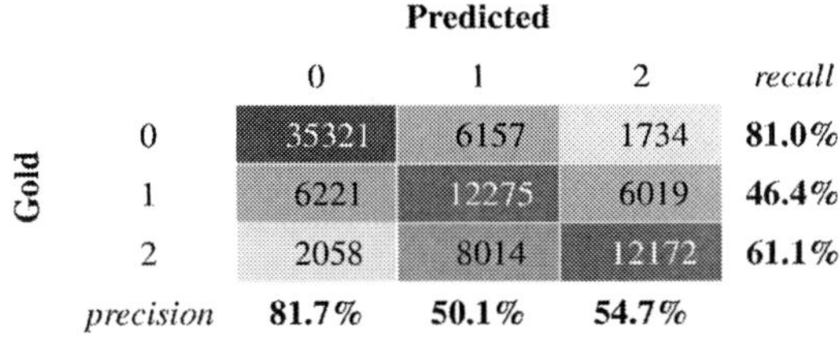

Figure 4: 3-way classification task confusion matrix for BERT.

		Predicted 0	Predicted 1	Predicted 2	*recall*
Gold	0	35321	6157	1734	**81.0%**
Gold	1	6221	12275	6019	**46.4%**
Gold	2	2058	8014	12172	**61.1%**
	precision	**81.7%**	**50.1%**	**54.7%**	

Figure 5: 3-way classification task confusion matrix for BiLSTM.

In the 3-way classification task, when the gold label is 0 (non prominent) BERT makes more errors with prediction being 2 (very prominent) compared to the BiLSTM model. However, when the gold label is 2 (very prominent) BiLSTM makes more predictions with 0 (non prominent) compared to BERT. In general for 0 labels BERT seems to have higher precision and BiLSTM better recall, whereas for label 2 BERT has clearly higher recall and precision. Both models have low precision and recall for the less distinctive prominence (label 1). It seems that the clearest difference between the two models is in their ability to predict high prominence (label 2).

We also provide the confusion matrices for the 2-way classification task for the two models. Figure 6 contains the 2-way classification confusion matrix for BERT and Figure 7 for the BiLSTM model. Here BERT has slightly higher precision and recall across both of the labels.

		Predicted 0	Predicted 1	*recall*
Gold	0	34249	8963	**79.3%**
Gold	1	6186	40579	**86.8%**
	precision	**84.7%**	**81.9%**	

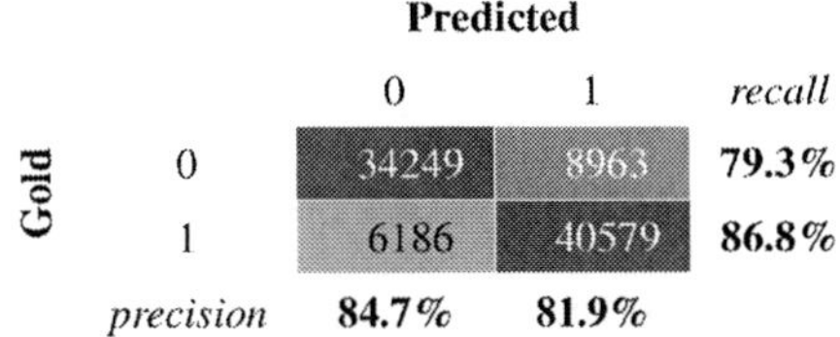

Figure 6: 2-way classification task confusion matrix for BERT.

		Predicted 0	Predicted 1	*recall*
Gold	0	33786	9428	**78.2%**
Gold	1	6670	40090	**85.7%**
	precision	**83.5%**	**81.0%**	

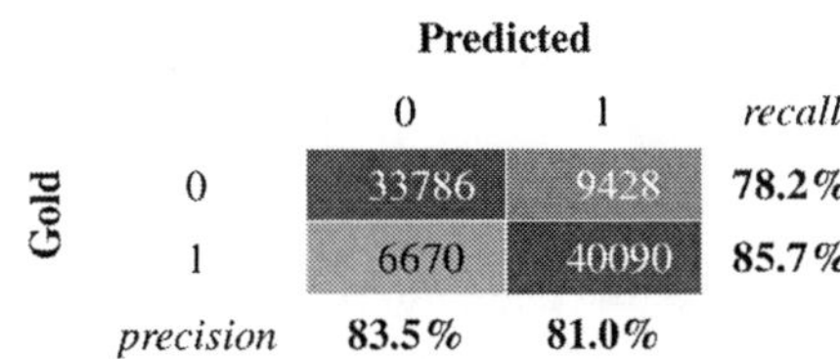

Figure 7: 2-way classification task confusion matrix for BiLSTM.

6 Discussion

We have shown above that prosodic prominence can reasonably well be predicted from text using different sequence-labelling approaches and models. However, the reported performance is still quite low, even for state-of-the-art systems based on large pre-trained language models such as BERT. We list a number of reasons for these shortcomings below and discuss their impact and potential mitigation.

Although the annotation method has been shown to be quite robust, errors in automatic alignment, signal processing, and quantization introduce noise to the labels. This noise might not be detrimental to the training due to dataset size, but the test results are affected. To measure the size of this effect, manual correction of a part of the test set could be beneficial.

It is well known that different speakers have different accents, varying reading proficiency, and reading tempo, which all impact the consistency of the labeling as the source speech data contains in total samples from over 1200 different speakers.

REF:	**One** way _{led} _{to the} left _{and the other} _{to the} right **straight** _{up the} mountain .
BERT:	**One** _{way} led _{to the} **left** _{and the} **other** _{to the} right **straight** _{up the} mountain .
REF:	In _{the} **next** moment _{he was} **concealed** _{by the} leaves .
BERT:	_{In the} **next** moment _{he was} **concealed** _{by the} leaves .
REF:	_I **had** _{to read} _{it over} **carefully** , _{as} _{the} **text** _{must} _{be absolutely} correct .
BERT:	_I **had** _{to} read _{it} over **carefully** , as _{the} **text** must _{be} absolutely **correct** .
REF:	**Where** were _{you when you} **began** _{to} **feel** bad ?
BERT:	Where **were** _{you when you} began _{to} feel **bad** ?
REF:	_{He is} taller than _{the Indian} , **not** _{so} **tall** _{as} **Gilchrist** .
BERT:	_{He is} **taller** _{than} _{the} Indian , **not** so tall _{as} **Gilchrist** .

Table 5: Typical 3-way prominence predictions of BERT compared to reference labels.

Given that inter-speaker agreement on pitch accent placement is somewhere between 80 and 90% (Yuan et al., 2005), we cannot expect large improvements without speaker-specific modelling.

The source speech data contains multitude of genres ranging from non-fiction to metric poems with fixed prominence patterns and children's stories with high proportion of words emphasized. The difference in genres could impact the test results. Moreover, the books included in the source speech data are all from pre-1923, whereas BERT and GloVe are pre-trained with contemporary texts. We expect that the difference between BERT and other models would be higher with a dataset drawn from a more contemporary source. As noted in Section 3, the difference between BERT and BiLSTM is much bigger with the The Boston University radio news corpus test set (+3.9% compared to +1.1% with our test set). This could be due to the genre, with The Boston University radio news corpus being derived from a more contemporary source.

Overall, our results for BERT highlight the importance of pre-training of the word representations. As we noticed, already with as little as 10% of the training data, BERT outperforms the other models when they are trained on the entire training set. This suggests that BERT has implicitly learned syntactic or semantic information relevant for the prosody prediction task. Our results are in line with the earlier results by Stehwien et al. (2018) and Rendel et al. (2016) who showed that pre-trained word embeddings improve model performance in the prominence prediction task. Table 5 lists five randomly selected examples from the test set and shows the prominence predictions

by BERT compared to the reference annotation. These examples indicate that even if the overall accuracy of the model is not high, the predictions still look plausible in isolation.

Finally, the classifiers in this paper are trained on single sentences, losing any discourse-level information and relations to surrounding context. Increasing the context to contain, e.g., also previous sentences could improve the results.

7 Conclusion

In this paper we have introduced a new NLP dataset and benchmark for predicting prosodic prominence from text, which to our knowledge is the largest publicly available dataset with prosodic labels. We described the dataset creation and the resulting benchmark and showed that various sequence labeling methods can be applied to the task of predicting prosodic prominence using the dataset.

Our experimental results show that BERT outperforms the other models with just up to 10% of the training data, highlighting the effectiveness of pre-training for the task. It also highlights that the implicit syntactic or semantic features BERT has learned during pre-training are relevant for the specific task of predicting prosodic prominence.

We also discussed a number of limitations of the automatic annotation system, as well as our current models. Based on this discussion, and more broadly, on the findings of this paper, we want to focus our future research activities in two fronts. Firstly, we will further develop the dataset annotation pipeline, improving the quality of prominence annotation and adding prosodic boundary labels. Secondly, we will further develop methods and models for improved prediction of prosodic prominence. In particular, as our results have shown that pre-training helps in the task, fine-tuning BERT with data involving features that are known to impact prosodic prominence (like part-of-speech tagged data) before training on the prosody dataset could help to improve the model performance. Furthermore, we will look at speaker-aware models, genre adaptation, and models for increased context. And, finally, our ultimate goal is to incorporate these methods into the development of a state-of-the-art text-to-speech synthesizer.

Acknowledgments

 Talman, Celikkanat and Tiedemann are supported by the FoTran project, funded by the European Research Council (ERC) under the European Unions Horizon 2020 research and innovation programme (grant agreement no. 771113).

We also gratefully acknowledges the support of the Academy of Finland through projects no. 314062 from the ICT 2023 call on Computation, Machine Learning and Artificial Intelligence, no. 1293348 from the call on Digital Humanities, and an Academy Fellowship project no. 309575.

References

Dwight Bolinger. 1972. Accent is predictable (if you're a mind-reader). *Language*, pages 633–644.

Joan W Bresnan. 1973. Sentence stress and syntactic transformations. In *Approaches to natural language*, pages 3–47. Springer.

Noam Chomsky and Morris Halle. 1968. The sound pattern of english.

Jacob Devlin, Ming-Wei Chang, Kenton Lee, and Kristina Toutanova. 2019. BERT: Pre-training of deep bidirectional transformers for language understanding. In *Proceedings of the 2019 Conference of the North American Chapter of the Association for Computational Linguistics: Human Language Technologies, Volume 1 (Long and Short Papers)*, pages 4171–4186. Association for Computational Linguistics.

Michelle L Gregory and Yasemin Altun. 2004. Using conditional random fields to predict pitch accents in conversational speech. In *Proceedings of the 42nd Annual Meeting on Association for Computational Linguistics (ACL-2004)*, page 677. Association for Computational Linguistics.

Julia Hirschberg. 1993. Pitch accent in context predicting intonational prominence from text. *Artificial Intelligence*, 63(1-2):305–340.

Sepp Hochreiter and Jürgen Schmidhuber. 1997. Long short-term memory. *Neural Comput.*, 9(8):1735–1780.

Daniel Jurafsky. 1996. A probabilistic model of lexical and syntactic access and disambiguation. *Cognitive science*, 20(2):137–194.

Daniel Jurafsky, Alan Bell, Michelle Gregory, and William D Raymond. 2001. Probabilistic relations between words: Evidence from reduction in lexical production. *Typological studies in language*, 45:229–254.

Sofoklis Kakouros, Joris Pelemans, Lyan Verwimp, Patrick Wambacq, and Okko Räsänen. 2016. Analyzing the contribution of top-down lexical and bottom-up acoustic cues in the detection of sentence prominence. In *INTERSPEECH*, pages 1074–1078.

Sofoklis Kakouros and Okko Räsänen. 2016. 3pro–an unsupervised method for the automatic detection of sentence prominence in speech. *Speech Communication*, 82:67–84.

Gina-Anne Levow. 2008. Automatic prosodic labeling with conditional random fields and rich acoustic features. In *Proceedings of the Third International Joint Conference on Natural Language Processing: Volume-I*.

Philip Lieberman. 1960. Some acoustic correlates of word stress in american english. *The Journal of the Acoustical Society of America*, 32(4):451–454.

Erwin Marsi, Martin Reynaert, Antal van den Bosch, Walter Daelemans, and Veronique Hoste. 2003. Learning to predict pitch accents and prosodic boundaries in dutch. In *41st Annual meeting of the Association for Computational Linguistics : proceedings of the conference*, pages 489–496. Association for Computational Linguistics.

Michael McAuliffe, Michaela Socolof, Sarah Mihuc, Michael Wagner, and Morgan Sonderegger. 2017. Montreal Forced Aligner: Trainable text-speech alignment using kaldi. In *Interspeech*, pages 498–502.

Tomas Mikolov, Kai Chen, Greg S. Corrado, and Jeffrey Dean. 2013. Efficient estimation of word representations in vector space. In *Proceedings of ICLR*.

Yoonsook Mo, Jennifer Cole, and Eun-Kyung Lee. 2008. Naïve listeners prominence and boundary perception. *Proc. Speech Prosody, Campinas, Brazil*, pages 735–738.

Thomas Mueller, Helmut Schmid, and Hinrich Schütze. 2013. Efficient higher-order CRFs for morphological tagging. In *Proceedings of the 2013 Conference on Empirical Methods in Natural Language

Processing, pages 322–332. Association for Computational Linguistics.

Ani Nenkova, Jason Brenier, Anubha Kothari, Sasha Calhoun, Laura Whitton, David Beaver, and Dan Jurafsky. 2007. To memorize or to predict: Prominence labeling in conversational speech. In *Proceedings of the Human Language Technology Conference of the North American chapter of the Association for Computational Linguistics (NAACL-HLT-2007)*, pages 9–16.

Mari Ostendorf, Patti J Price, and Stefanie Shattuck-Hufnagel. 1995. The Boston University radio news corpus. *Linguistic Data Consortium*, pages 1–19.

Vassil Panayotov, Guoguo Chen, Daniel Povey, and Sanjeev Khudanpur. 2015. LibriSpeech: an ASR corpus based on public domain audio books. In *2015 IEEE International Conference on Acoustics, Speech and Signal Processing (ICASSP)*, pages 5206–5210. IEEE.

Jeffrey Pennington, Richard Socher, and Christopher Manning. 2014. GloVe: Global vectors for word representation. In *Proceedings of the 2014 Conference on Empirical Methods in Natural Language Processing (EMNLP)*, pages 1532–1543. Association for Computational Linguistics.

Asaf Rendel, Raul Fernandez, Ron Hoory, and Bhuvana Ramabhadran. 2016. Using continuous lexical embeddings to improve symbolic-prosody prediction in a text-to-speech front-end. In *2016 IEEE International Conference on Acoustics, Speech and Signal Processing (ICASSP)*, pages 5655–5659. IEEE.

Andrew Rosenberg. 2009. *Automatic detection and classification of prosodic events*. Columbia University.

Sabrina Stehwien, Ngoc Thang Vu, and Antje Schweitzer. 2018. Effects of word embeddings on neural network-based pitch accent detection. In *9th International Conference on Speech Prosody*, pages 719–723.

Karl Stratos and Michael Collins. 2015. Simple semi-supervised POS tagging. In *Proceedings of the 1st Workshop on Vector Space Modeling for Natural Language Processing*.

Antti Suni, Juraj Šimko, Daniel Aalto, and Martti Vainio. 2017. Hierarchical representation and estimation of prosody using continuous wavelet transform. *Computer Speech & Language*, 45:123–136.

Jacques Terken and Dik Hermes. 2000. The perception of prosodic prominence. In *Prosody: Theory and experiment*, pages 89–127. Springer.

Michael Wagner and Duane G Watson. 2010. Experimental and theoretical advances in prosody: A review. *Language and cognitive processes*, 25(7-9):905–945.

Dagen Wang and Shrikanth Narayanan. 2007. An acoustic measure for word prominence in spontaneous speech. *IEEE transactions on audio, speech, and language processing*, 15(2):690–701.

Oliver Watts. 2012. *Unsupervised Learning for Text-to-Speech Synthesis*. Ph.D. thesis, University of Edinburgh.

Tae-Jin Yoon, Sandra Chavarria, Jennifer Cole, and Mark Hasegawa-Johnson. 2004. Intertranscriber reliability of prosodic labeling on telephone conversation using tobi. In *Eighth International Conference on Spoken Language Processing*.

Jiahong Yuan, Jason M Brenier, and Daniel Jurafsky. 2005. Pitch accent prediction: Effects of genre and speaker. In *Ninth European Conference on Speech Communication and Technology*.

Heiga Zen, Viet Dang, Rob Clark, Yu Zhang, Ron J Weiss, Ye Jia, Zhifeng Chen, and Yonghui Wu. 2019. LibriTTS: A corpus derived from LibriSpeech for text-to-speech. *arXiv preprint arXiv:1904.02882*.

Short Papers

Toward Multilingual Identification of Online Registers

Veronika Laippala[1], Roosa Kyllönen[1], Jesse Egbert[2], Douglas Biber[2], Sampo Pyysalo[3]

[1] School of Languages and Translation Studies, University of Turku
[2] Applied Linguistics, Northern Arizona University
[3] Department of Future Technologies, University of Turku
[1,3] `first.last@utu.fi`, [2] `first.last@nau.edu`

Abstract

We consider cross- and multilingual text classification approaches to the identification of online registers (genres), i.e. text varieties with specific situational characteristics. Register is arguably the most important predictor of linguistic variation, and register information could improve the potential of online data for many applications. We introduce the Finnish Corpus of Online REgisters (FinCORE), the first manually annotated non-English corpus of online registers featuring the full range of linguistic variation found online. The data set consists of 2,237 Finnish documents and follows the register taxonomy developed for the Corpus of Online Registers of English (CORE), the largest manually annotated language collection of online registers. Using CORE and Fin-CORE data, we demonstrate the feasibility of cross-lingual register identification using a simple approach based on convolutional neural networks and multilingual word embeddings. We further find that register identification results can be improved through multilingual training even when a substantial number of annotations is available in the target language.

1 Introduction

The massive amount of text available online in dozens of languages has created great opportunities for Natural Language Processing (NLP). For instance, methods such as machine translation, automatic syntactic analysis and text generation have benefited from the large-scale data available online (Tiedemann et al., 2016; Zeman et al., 2018; Devlin et al., 2018).

However, the diversity of online data is also a challenge to its use. Documents have little or no information on their communicative purpose or, specifically, on their *register* (*genre*) (Biber, 1988). Register – whether a document is a blog, how-to-page or advertisement – is one of the most important predictors of linguistic variation and affects how we interpret the text (Biber, 2012). Automatic identification of registers could thus improve the potential of online data, in particular for linguistically oriented research (Webber, 2009; Giesbrecht and Evert, 2009).

However, the automatic identification of registers has proven to be difficult. Studies of Web Genre Identification (WGI) have been limited by small and scattered data sets which have resulted in lack of robustness and generalization of the models (Sharoff et al., 2010; Petrenz and Webber, 2011; Pritsos and Stamatatos, 2018; Asheghi et al., 2014). Furthermore, although online data is available in many languages and NLP systems are increasingly focused on multilingual settings (e.g., Zeman et al. (2018)), WGI studies have focused nearly exclusively on English texts. The only large-scale data set representing the full range of online registers is CORE — the Corpus of Online Registers of English — which is based on an unrestricted sample of English documents from the searchable web (Egbert et al., 2015).

In this paper, we extend the scope of modeling online registers to cross- and multilingual settings. We 1) present the first non-English data set of online registers with manual annotations, 2) show that it is possible to identify online registers in a cross-lingual setting, training only on English data while predicting registers also in Finnish, and 3) demonstrate that multilingual training can improve register identification performance even when a substantial number of target language annotations are available. Our approach is based on convolutional neural networks (Kim, 2014) and multilingual word embeddings (Conneau et al., 2018).

2   Previous Work

In WGI, reported performance is often very high due to small and skewed corpora. With six widely used online register corpora composed of 7-70 classes, the best accuracy achieved by Sharoff et al. (2010) was 97% with character n-grams. Similarly, Pritsos and Stamatatos (2018) achieved an F1-score of 79% using two of the same corpora. However, the authors noted that their classifier models identified specific corpus topics rather than generalizable register features. This was further confirmed by Petrenz and Webber (2011) who showed that the applied system performances dropped drastically when the topic distribution of the target data was changed after training.

Using the larger Leeds Web Genre (LWG) corpus (Asheghi et al., 2016) of 3,964 documents, Asheghi et al. (2014) showed that online registers can be identified in a representative collection. Their best accuracy was 78.9% on 15 classes based on plain texts and 90.1% based on a semi-supervised graph-based method. However, as the LWG corpus represents only registers exclusive to the web and is compiled by manually selecting the texts, it does not feature the full range of linguistic variation online. By contrast to LWG, CORE (Egbert et al., 2015) is based on an unrestricted sample of the web. Biber and Egbert (2016) evaluated automatic CORE register detection performance with stepwise discriminant analysis, achieving 34% precision and 40% recall.

In previous studies, crosslingual models have been developed using various methods. Andrade et al. (2015), Shi et al. (2010) and Lambert (2015) applied bilingual dictionaries and machine translation to generate target language models in crosslingual topic detection and sentiment analysis. Many recent neural approaches use multilingual embeddings to build the document representations. Approaches such as that of Klementiev et al. (2012) are based on either the combination of multilingual word embeddings or directly learned sentence embeddings. Schwenk and Li (2018) compared their performance in genre classification of a multilingual Reuters corpus, using word embeddings generated by Ammar et al. (2016) and combined to document representations using a one-layer convolutional network and an LSTM-based system as proposed by Schwenk and Douze (2017), finding out that the system based on word embeddings achieved the best performance.

Register	English	Finnish
Narrative	12,541 (50%)	778 (35%)
Opinion	3,960 (16%)	339 (15%)
D-Informational	3,195 (13%)	379 (17%)
Discussion	2,697 (11%)	140 (6%)
How-to	955 (4%)	144 (7%)
Info-Persuasion	684 (3%)	446 (20%)
Lyrical	576 (2%)	0 (0%)
Spoken	304 (1%)	11 (0%)
Total	24,912	2,237

Table 1: The sizes of the register classes in the two data sets. The proportions of the classes are given in parentheses.

3   Data

The data for our study come from two sources. The English CORE consists of 48,571 documents coded by four annotators, who used a taxonomy developed in a data-driven manner to cover the full range of linguistic variation found in the Internet. The taxonomy is hierarchical and consists of eight main registers divided into 33 subregisters. The *Narrative* main register includes sub-registers such as News, Short stories and Personal blogs. The *Opinion* main register consists of texts expressing opinions, such as Opinion blogs and Reviews. *Informational description (D-Informational)* covers informational registers such as Descriptions of a thing and Research articles. The *Discussion* class includes various discussions such as Discussion forums and Question / answer forums. The *How-to / Instructional* main register consists of sub-registers providing different kinds of instructions, such as actual How-to pages, Recipes and Technical support pages. The *Informational persuasion (Info-Persuasion)* main register covers texts that use facts to persuade, such as Editorials and Descriptions with intent to sell. Finally, the *Lyrical* main register includes, e.g., Song lyrics and Poems, and the *Spoken* main register, e.g., Interviews and Video transcripts. For a detailed description of the CORE annotation process and corpus quality, we refer to Egbert et al. (2015).

The Finnish data is based on a sample of the Finnish Internet Parsebank (Luotolahti et al., 2015), a web-crawled corpus that currently consists of nearly 4 billion words. The annotations were done jointly by a supervisor and a dedicated annotator. The Finnish annotations aim to follow the CORE annotation guidelines as closely as pos-

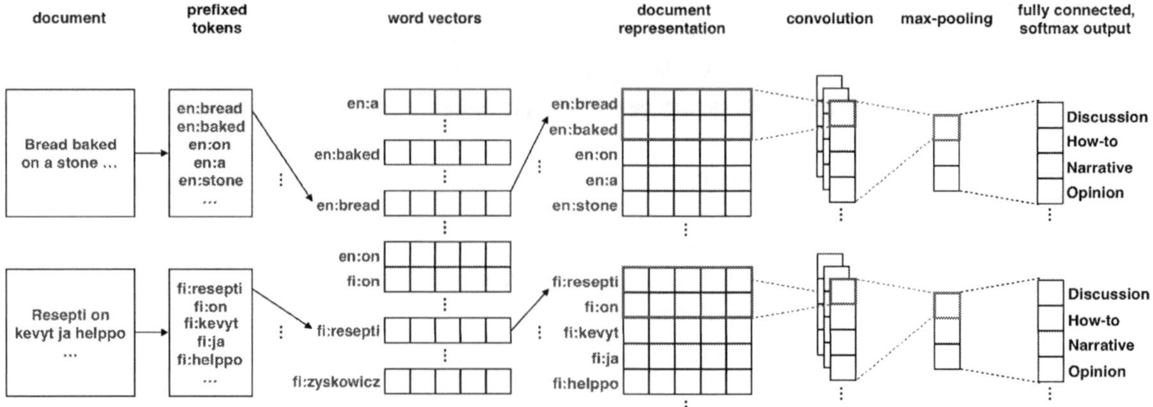

Figure 1: Illustration of text classification approach. Tokens are prefixed with language tags to differentiate e.g. the English word *on* from the Finnish word *on* 'is'. Multilingual word vectors are used and the same network applied regardless of language to allow cross-lingual and multilingual training and classification. (Following in part Kim (2014))

sible. The process advances through a decision tree, where the annotator 1) evaluates the mode of the text (spoken or written), 2) determines whether the text is interactive (multiple authors) or non-interactive (one author) and 3) identifies the general register of the text. Finally, the most accurate sub-register is selected if applicable. If the text appears to have more than one appropriate register, the annotator may choose up to three registers. Texts with several registers are called *hybrid texts*.

In this paper, we focus on the main register level because of the small size of the Finnish data set. Furthermore, to simplify the task setting, we use only the CORE documents for which at least three out of four annotators agreed on the register, thus excluding English hybrid texts, and similarly exclude the Finnish documents that were identified as hybrids. Finally, as the numbers of annotated Finnish texts in the main registers *Spoken* and *Lyrical* were too low for meaningful evaluation (11 and 0, respectively), these registers were excluded from the experiments.

The distribution of documents in the data used in our experiments is shown in Table 1. We note that the classes are very unevenly distributed, and the distributions are quite different in the two languages. In English, Narrative represents half of the data, with Opinion being the second most frequent with 16%. For Finnish, Narrative covers only 35%, and the second most frequent register is Informational persuasion, at 20%. For English, this is one of the least frequent classes, with only 3% of the data.

Both data sets were split into training, development and test sets using a stratified 70%/10%/20% split. The test data was held out during method development and parameter selection and only used for the final experiments.

4 Methods

Our approach is based on a simple convolutional neural network (CNN) architecture following Kim (2014) and illustrated in Figure 1. Documents are first tokenized using the Turku Neural Parser (Kanerva et al., 2018) trained on language-specific Universal Dependencies (Nivre et al., 2016) resources. The input is represented as a word vector sequence to a convolution layer with ReLU activation, followed by max-pooling and a fully-connected output layer. Similarly to Schwenk and Li (2018), we use pretrained multilingual word embeddings for multi- and cross-lingual classification; to differentiate between the same word forms in different languages, we simply prefix a language tag to each token and modify word vector indexing analogously. We use English and Finnish word vectors from the Multilingual Unsupervised and Supervised Embeddings (MUSE) library[1] (Conneau et al., 2018) in all experiments. As MUSE word vectors are uncased, we lowercase text following tokenization.

Based on initial experiments on the development set, we set the maximum number of word vectors to 100000, the number of CNN filters to

---

[1]https://github.com/facebookresearch/MUSE

Setting	Monolingual				Cross-/Multilingual	
Method	fastText		CNN		CNN	
Training data	Finnish	English	Finnish	English	English	En + Fi
Test data	Finnish	English	Finnish	English	Finnish	Finnish
D-Informational	67.1%	93.9%	75.4%	94.1%	69.0%	75.4%
Discussion	86.5%	93.3%	83.1%	96.5%	80.1%	86.5%
How-to	84.6%	94.9%	88.3%	94.8%	82.9%	89.7%
Info-Persuasion	84.5%	93.2%	84.7%	95.2%	74.0%	85.5%
Narrative	76.3%	91.9%	85.2%	92.7%	79.8%	86.3%
Opinion	78.2%	86.6%	86.2%	88.2%	85.8%	88.3%
Average	79.5%	92.3%	83.8%	93.6%	78.6%	85.3%

Table 2: Evaluation results (AUC scores) in mono-, cross-, and multilingual training settings.

128, the filter size to one word, and froze the word vector weights. Wider filters and word vector fine-tuning appeared to give modest benefit in monolingual settings, and reduced performance in cross-lingual settings. The latter results were expected given that wider filters capture aspects of word order that are not consistent cross-lingually, and fine-tuned word vectors may no longer align across languages. Input texts are padded or truncated to 1000 tokens. We train the CNN for 10 epochs using Adam with the default settings suggested by Kingma and Ba (2014). We refer to Kim (2014) and Conneau et al. (2018) for further information on the model and word vectors, and our open-source release[2] for implementation details.

For reference, we also report results using fastText (Joulin et al., 2016), a popular text classification method based on word vector averages that emphasizes computational efficiency. We initialize fastText with the same word vectors and train for the same number of epochs as the CNN, and retain its parameters otherwise at their defaults. As fastText does not support cross-lingual classification, we only use it in the monolingual setting.

The class disbalance and the different class distributions in the two languages represent challenges for cross-lingual generalization and evaluation. We opted to focus on ranking and evaluate performance for each register in a one-versus-rest setting using the distribution-independent area under the receiver operating characteristic curve (AUC) measure. Additionally, to account for random variation from classifier initialization, we repeat each experiment ten times and report averages over these runs.

[2]`https://github.com/TurkuNLP/multiling-cnn`

5 Results

The primary results are summarized in Table 2. First, we briefly note that in a monolingual setting, the CNN and fastText results are broadly comparable, with the CNN achieving slightly higher performance for both English and Finnish overall as well as for most individual classes. This confirms that the somewhat restricted nature of the CNN (e.g. frozen word vector weights) does not critically limit its performance at the task. As expected, performance is notably higher for English, which has more than 10 times the number of annotated examples for Finnish.

In the cross-lingual setting, we find that when trained on English data and tested on Finnish, the CNN clearly outperforms the random baseline (50%) for all classes, confirming the basic feasibility of the approach to cross-lingual register identification. As expected, performance is below the comparable monolingual results (Finnish-Finnish), but the differences are encouragingly small; in particular, the cross-lingual CNN performance is very close to the monolingual fastText baseline.

The best results for Finnish are achieved when training on the combination of English and Finnish data, both overall as well as for most individual classes. Given the different languages and independent development histories of these two corpora, it is far from given that this corpus combination would be successful, and this result is very positive in indicating both the basic compatibility of these specific resources as well as the broader ability to generalize the CORE register classification and annotation strategy to new languages.

To gain further insight into the effectiveness of multilingual training, we evaluated Finnish regis-

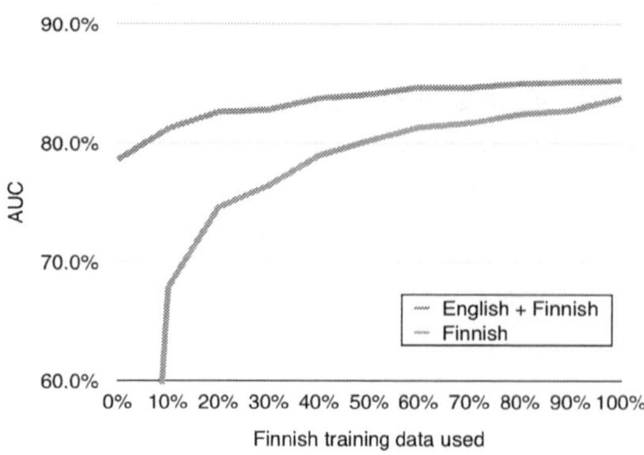

Figure 2: Average AUC for Finnish register prediction when training with varying proportions of Finnish training data, contrasting performance with and without additional English training data.

ter classification performance using subsets (10%, 20%, ...) of the Finnish training data both in the monolingual (Finnish only) and multilingual (English and Finnish) training settings. All of the English training data was used in the latter setting. The results, summarized in Figure 2, show that with these corpora, multilingual training is beneficial regardless of the size of available target language data, and that zero-shot cross-lingual classification (no target language data) outperforms monolingual classification with up to 900 examples of target language data.

6 Discussion and future work

In this paper, we explored the identification of registers in Internet texts in cross- and multilingual settings. We introduced FinCORE, the first non-English corpus annotated following the guidelines of the CORE corpus, the largest online register corpus representing the full range of linguistic variation found online. Evaluation using a simple CNN with multilingual word vectors indicated that cross-lingual register classification is feasible, and that combination of the large CORE corpus data with smaller target language data further benefits classification performance. This positive result also confirmed the compatibility of the English and Finnish corpus annotations.

While our study has only considered a single language pair, we note that the general approach is immediately applicable to any language for which a tokenizer and multilingual word vectors are available, including 30 languages in MUSE at the time of this writing. As the approach avoids many language-specific features (e.g. word order) and is demonstrated on a pair of languages that are not closely related, we are optimistic regarding its ability to generalize to other languages.

This is an early study in a relatively new area and leaves open several avenues to explore. For example, our approach is based on a straightforward application of convolutional neural networks for text classification, and it is likely possible to improve performance through further model development and parameter optimization. Future work should also consider the effectiveness of more advanced deep learning methods, such as multilingual transformer architectures. In current and planned future work, we are building on these initial results to address additional languages as well as the full CORE register hierarchy.

All of the data and methods newly introduced in this work are available under open licenses from `https://github.com/TurkuNLP/FinCORE`.

Acknowledgements

We thank Fulbright Finland, Kone foundation and Emil Aaltonen Foundation for financial support.

References

Waleed Ammar, George Mulcaire, Yulia Tsvetkov, Guillaume Lample, Chris Dyer, and Noah A Smith. 2016. Massively multilingual word embeddings. *arXiv preprint arXiv:1602.01925*.

Daniel Andrade, Kunihiko Sadamasa, Akihiro Tamura, and Masaaki Tsuchida. 2015. Cross-lingual text classification using topic-dependent word probabilities. In *Proceedings of HLT-NAACL*.

Noushin Asheghi, Serge Sharoff, and Katja Markert. 2016. Crowdsourcing for web genre annotation. *Language Resources and Evaluation*, 50(3):603–641.

Rezapour Noushin Asheghi, Katja Markert, and Serge Sharoff. 2014. Semi-supervised graph-based genre classification for web pages. In *Proceedings of TextGraphs-9*, pages 39–47.

Douglas Biber. 1988. *Variation across Speech and Writing*. Cambridge University Press.

Douglas Biber. 2012. Register as a predictor of linguistic variation. *Corpus linguistics and linguistic theory*.

Douglas Biber and Jesse Egbert. 2016. Using grammatical features for automatic register identification in an unrestricted corpus of documents from the open web. *Journal of Research Design and Statistics in Linguistics and Communication Science*, 2:3–36.

Alexis Conneau, Guillaume Lample, Marc'Aurelio Ranzato, Ludovic Denoyer, and Hervé Jégou. 2018. Word translation without parallel data. *CoRR*, abs/1710.04087.

Jacob Devlin, Ming-Wei Chang, Kenton Lee, and Kristina Toutanova. 2018. BERT: Pre-training of deep bidirectional transformers for language understanding. *arXiv preprint arXiv:1810.04805*.

Jesse Egbert, Douglas Biber, and Mark Davies. 2015. Developing a bottomup, userbased method of web register classification. *Journal of the Association for Information Science and Technology*, 66:1817–1831.

Eugenie Giesbrecht and Stefan Evert. 2009. Is part-of-speech tagging a solved task? an evaluation of pos taggers for the german web as corpus. In *Web as Corpus Workshop (WAC5)*, pages 27–36.

Armand Joulin, Edouard Grave, Piotr Bojanowski, and Tomas Mikolov. 2016. Bag of tricks for efficient text classification. *arXiv preprint arXiv:1607.01759*.

Jenna Kanerva, Filip Ginter, Niko Miekka, Akseli Leino, and Tapio Salakoski. 2018. Turku neural parser pipeline: An end-to-end system for the CoNLL 2018 shared task. In *Proceedings of CoNLL 2018 Shared Task*.

Yoon Kim. 2014. Convolutional neural networks for sentence classification. *Proceedings of EMNLP*.

Diederik P Kingma and Jimmy Ba. 2014. Adam: A method for stochastic optimization. *arXiv preprint arXiv:1412.6980*.

Alexandre Klementiev, Ivan Titov, and Binod Bhattarai. 2012. Inducing crosslingual distributed representations of words. In *Proceedings of COLING*.

Patrik Lambert. 2015. Aspect-level cross-lingual sentiment classification with constrained SMT. In *Proceedings of ACL*.

Juhani Luotolahti, Jenna Kanerva, Veronika Laippala, Sampo Pyysalo, and Filip Ginter. 2015. Towards universal web parsebanks. In *Proceedings of Depling'15*, pages 211–220.

Joakim Nivre, Marie-Catherine De Marneffe, Filip Ginter, Yoav Goldberg, Jan Hajic, Christopher D Manning, Ryan McDonald, Slav Petrov, Sampo Pyysalo, Natalia Silveira, et al. 2016. Universal dependencies v1: A multilingual treebank collection. In *Proceedings of LREC 2016*, pages 1659–1666.

Philipp Petrenz and Bonnie Webber. 2011. Stable classification of text genres. *Computational Linguistics*, 37(2):385–393.

Dimitrios Pritsos and Efstathios Stamatatos. 2018. Open set evaluation of web genre identification. *Language Resources and Evaluation*.

Holger Schwenk and Matthijs Douze. 2017. Learning joint multilingual sentence representations with neural machine translation. *Proceedings of the 2nd Workshop on Representation Learning for NLP*.

Holger Schwenk and Xian Li. 2018. A corpus for multilingual document classification in eight languages. In *Proceedings of the 11th Language Resources and Evaluation Conference*.

Serge Sharoff, Zhili Wu, and Katja Markert. 2010. The web library of babel: evaluating genre collections. In *Proceedings of LREC)*.

Lei Shi, Rada Mihalcea, and Mingjun Tian. 2010. Cross language text classification by model translation and semi-supervised learning. In *EMNLP*.

Jörg Tiedemann, Fabienne Cap, Jenna Kanerva, Filip Ginter, Sara Stymne, Robert Östling, and Marion Weller-Di Marco. 2016. Phrase-based SMT for finnish with more data, better models and alternative alignment and translation tools. In *Proceedings of the First Conference on Machine Translation*, volume 2, pages 391–398.

Bonnie Webber. 2009. Genre distinctions for discourse in the Penn treebank. In *Proceedings of ACL-IJCNLP*, pages 674–682.

Daniel Zeman, Jan Hajič, Martin Popel, Martin Potthast, Milan Straka, Filip Ginter, Joakim Nivre, and Slav Petrov. 2018. Conll 2018 shared task: Multilingual parsing from raw text to universal dependencies. In *Proceedings of CoNLL 2018 Shared Task*, pages 1–21.

A Wide-Coverage Symbolic Natural Language Inference System

Jean-Philippe Bernardy
Department of Philosophy, Linguistics
and Theory of Science
University of Gothenburg
jean-philippe.bernardy@gu.se

Stergios Chatzikyriakidis
Department of Philosophy, Linguistics
and Theory of Science
University of Gothenburg
stergios.chatzikyriakidis@gu.se

Abstract

We present a system for Natural Language Inference which uses a dynamic semantics converter from abstract syntax trees to Coq types. It combines the fine-grainedness of a dynamic semantics system with the powerfulness of a state-of-the-art proof assistant. We evaluate the system on all sections of the FraCaS test suite, excluding section 6. This is the first system that does a complete run on the anaphora and ellipsis sections of the FraCaS. It has a better overall accuracy than any previous system.

1 Introduction

Natural Language Inference (NLI) is the task of determining of whether an NL hypothesis H follows from an NL premise(s) P. NLI has received a lot of attention in the Computational Semantics literature and has been approached using a variety of techniques, ranging from logical approaches (Bos, 2008; Mineshima et al., 2015; Abzianidze, 2015; Bernardy and Chatzikyriakidis, 2017), all the way to the recent Deep Learning (DL) models for NLI. The latter approaches, following a general trend in NLP, have been dominating NLI and a number of impressive results have been produced (Kim et al., 2018; Radford et al., 2018; Liu et al., 2019).[1] State-of-the-art DL systems achieve an accuracy of around 0.9 when tested on suitable datasets. However, the datasets that are used are assuming a definition of inference that can be thought to be 'looser' or less precise compared to the definition assumed in platforms based in logical approaches (Bernardy and Chatzikyriakidis, 2019). For example, consider the following example from the SNLI dataset, predominatly used to test DL approaches:

---

[1]These are the three systems with the best results on SNLI in increasing order at the time of writing.

(1) **P** A man selling donuts to a customer during a world exhibition event held in the city of Angeles.
H A woman drinks her coffee in a small cafe.
Label: Contradiction [SNLI]

In (1), a number of non-trivial assumptions have to be made in order to arrive at a contradiction: a) the two situations described have to be taken to refer to the same situation in order to judge that the latter contradicts the former, b) the indefinite article in the premise has to be identified with the indefinite article in the hypothesis. (Additionally considering that a person cannot be a man selling donuts and a woman drinking coffee at the same time.) While this can be part of the reasoning humans perform, it is not the only possibility. More precise, logical reasoning is also a possibility, and will render the above label as unknown. Furthermore, reasoning can get very fine-grained as the Contained Deletion ellipsis example (2) below shows:

(2) **P1** Bill spoke to everyone that John did [elliptic V2].
P2 John spoke to Mary.
Q Did Bill speak to Mary?
H Bill spoke to Mary.
Label: Yes [FraCas 173]

For this reason, and despite the dominance of DL approaches in pretty much all NLP tasks, logical approaches continue to be developed and evaluated on datasets like the FraCaS test suite and the SICK dataset (Marelli et al., 2014). Bernardy and Chatzikyriakidis (2017) define a correspondence between abstract syntax parse trees of the FraCas examples, parsed using the Grammatical Framework (GF, Ranta (2011)), and modern type-theoretic semantics that are output in the Coq proof assistant (the FraCoq system). The accuracy is 0.85 for 5 sections of the FraCaS test suite.

The LANGPRO system presented by Abzianidze (2015) is based on a Natural Logic tableau theorem prover. It achieves an accuracy of .82 on the SICK dataset.

In this paper, we concentrate on this sort of fine-grained, logical reasoning. In particular, we present a logic-based system that deals with many linguistic phenomena *at the same time*. It is the first system covering the sections on ellipsis and anaphora in the FraCaS test suite and has the best coverage and accuracy on the overall test suite.

2 Background

GF In GF, abstract syntax is comprised of: a) a number of syntactic categories, and b) a number of syntactic construction functions. The latter provide the means to compose basic syntactic categories into more complex ones. For example, consider the constructor: $AdjCN : AP \rightarrow CN \rightarrow CN$. This expresses that one can append an adjectival phrase to a common noun and obtain a new common noun. Furthermore, GF is equipped with a library of mappings from abstract syntax to the concrete syntax of various natural languages. These mappings can be inverted by GF, thus offering parsing from natural text into abstract syntax. However, in this project we skip the parsing phase and use the parse trees constructed by Ljunglöf and Siverbo (2011), thereby avoiding any syntactic ambiguity.

Coq Coq is an interactive theorem prover (proof assistant) based on the calculus of inductive constructions (CiC), i.e. a lambda calculus with dependent types. Coq is a very powerful reasoning engine that makes it fit for the task of NLI, when the latter is formalized as a theorem proving task. It supports notably dependent typing and subtyping, which are instrumental in expressing NL semantics.

Dynamic Monadic Semantics Dynamic Monadic Semantics have been proven to be an effective way of dealing with anaphora and ellipsis. There are a number of approaches using monads or other equivalent constructions (e.g. continuations as in the work of de Groote (2006)) for anaphora and ellipsis Shan (2002); Unger (2011); Barker and chieh Shan (2004); Qian et al. (2016); Charlow (2017). In this paper, we follow the approach described in Bernardy et al.. More details are given in the next section.

3 Overview of the system

Our system consists of two main parts.

1. A converter from syntax trees to types. The syntax trees follow the GF formalism, and the types follow the Coq formalism. The converter itself is a Haskell Program, which implements a dynamic semantics and comprises the bulk of our system.
2. A number of type-theoretical combinators, that encode semantical aspects which have no influence on the dynamic part. Such aspects include the treatment of adjectives (intersective, subsective, etc.) and adverbs (veridical or not).

The architecture is represented schematically in Figure 1.

All the underlying systems (GF, Haskell, Coq) are based on lambda calculi with types. We take advantage of typing, ensuring that each translation preserve typing, locally:

1. Every GF syntactic category C is mapped to a type noted $[\![C]\!]$.
2. GF Functional types are mapped compositionally : $[\![A \rightarrow B]\!] = [\![A]\!] \rightarrow [\![B]\!]$
3. Every GF syntactic construction function ($f : X$) is mapped to a function $[\![f]\!]$ such that $[\![f]\!] : [\![X]\!]$.
4. GF function applications are mapped compositionally: $[\![t(u)]\!] = [\![t]\!]([\![u]\!])$.

Because all systems embed the simply-typed lambda calculus, ensuring type-preservation locally means that types are preserved globally. Therefore, we are certain that every GF syntax tree can be mapped to Haskell, and eventually Coq, without error.

The dynamic semantics follows a monadic structure, as pioneered by Shan (2002). There are two kinds of effects carried by the monad. The first one comprises a series of updates and queries of stateful elements. There is one piece of updateable state for every element which can be referred to by anaphoric expressions. These can be the usual ones (like NPs), but also less usual ones (like 2-place verbs, or a quantity — which we illustrate below). The other kind of effects is *non-determinism*. We use non-determinism to model the property that linguistic expressions can have several interpretations. The monadic structure allows to locally express that a given expression has

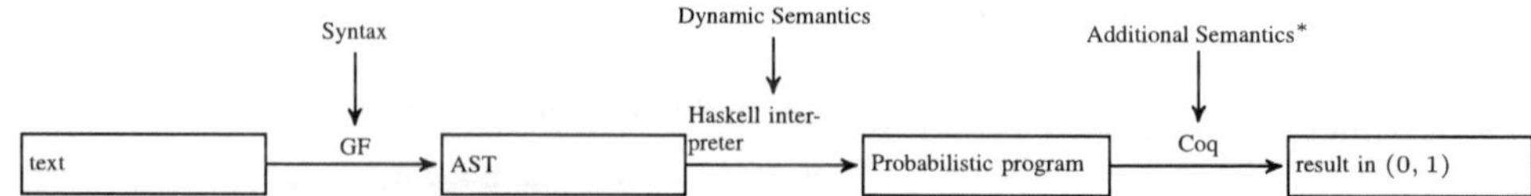

Figure 1: Phases in our system. ($*$) At the level of Coq, we handle the details of the adverbial (veridicality properties) and adjectival semantics (division into subsective, extentional, non-committal, etc. categories.)

several meanings; the monadic bind ensures that all combinations of meanings are considered at the top-level, combinatorially. This dynamic semantics allows us to model many phenomena in a precise way.

Anaphora Thanks to the above system, we can handle many anaphoric cases, including E-Type and Donkey anaphora. Indeed, even objects which have no syntactic representation can be added to the environment. We follow here the general monadic semantics approach as outlined by Unger (2011). However, we use a more general scope-extension mechanism, which allows us to support examples like the following:

(3) **P1** Every committee has a chairman.
P2 He is appointed its members.
H Every committee has a chairman appointed by members of the committee.
Label: YES [FraCaS 122]

In the above example, the pronoun "he" is allowed to refer to the object quantified over by "every", whose scope is extended accordingly. We describe the anaphora resolution system in every detail in a manuscript (Bernardy et al.).

Ellipsis Ellipsis is handled in essentially the same way as anaphora. This method is made especially straightforward thanks to using GF syntax trees, which require an explicit argument for each predicate. Thus, ellipsis are made explicit by the parsing phase. Such ellptic expressions are handled in the same way as anaphora. For example, in (2) repeated below as (4), the argument of "did" is explicitly marked as an elliptic V2, which we resolve to "speak" in that context:

(4) **P1** Bill spoke to everyone that John did [elliptic V2].
P2 John spoke to Mary.
Q Did Bill speak to Mary?
H Bill spoke to Mary.
Label: Yes [FraCas 173]

Definites A naive way to handle definites is using an existential type. However, if the semantics does not feature a dynamic element, then the existential quantification is introduced locally. This means that the quantifier can be introduced in the wrong Context. Consider the phrase "everyone pets the dog". The structure of the interpretation would be $\forall x.person(x) \to \exists y.dog(y) \land pet(x, y)$. Instead, our take is that definites should be treated as an anaphoric expression with an implicit referent. That is, if the referent is not found in the discourse, then it will be forcibly introduced, using an existential type, *at the top-level* of the expression. To be able to do this, we record all definites without referent, using another portion of the environment (using a monadic effect). For the above example, we obtain the desired interpretation: $\exists y.dog(y) \land (\forall x.person(x) \to pet(x, y))$.

Phrasal comparatives Previous attempts to tackle the section of the FraCaS test suite devoted to comparatives showed that handling them is not easy. Our strategy here is to leverage our dynamic semantics, revealing an anaphoric element of comparatives. Indeed, consider the hypothesis of (FraCaS 239): "ITEL won more orders than APCOM lost." We postulate that this sentence is equivalent to the following two separate parts: "APCOM lost zero or more orders. ITEL won more orders [than some elliptic quantity]." A quantity is introduced every time we talk about some quantity (indexed by a CN, in this case "orders"), and it can be referred to by a comparative, later in the discourse. Using this idea, we can go one level deeper in the interpretation of our example: "APCOM lost θ orders. $\theta \geq 0$. ITEL won at least $\theta+1$ orders.". We see here how the quantities are introduced. They are added to the environment so that, they can be referred to as elliptic quantity expressions.[2] Fi-

---

[2]The degree parameter assumption is not new in the formal semantics literature (Cresswell, 1976; Heim, 2000; Kennedy, 2007; Chatzikyriakidis and Luo, 2017) among many others. The specific details and computational imple-

nally, "more" is systematically intepreted as "at least ¡elliptic quantity¿+1". This treatment, which we illustrated here on an example, is systematic in our implementation.

Adjectives We interpret gradable adjectives using a pair of a measure $m : objects \to Z$ and a threshold $\tau : Z$, where Z is treated as an abstract ordered ring by Coq. (This structure has no dynamic aspect in our model, and thus is entirely handled within Coq.) For subsective adjectives, τ will additionally depend on the class of the object in question. This structure has the benefit that opposite adjectives can be easily represented (measures are opposites $\forall x.m_1 x = \neg m_2 x$ and thresholds do not overlap $\tau_1 + \tau_2 > 0$). Formalization aside, this idea is reminiscent of degree-based approaches to gradable adjectives of Cresswell (1976); Kennedy (2007). Additionally adjectival predicates, as present in the FraCaS suite, are interpreted as linear inequations in Z. Solving systems of such inequations is decidable. Indeed, the tactic that Coq offers for this purpose can solve all such problems in the FraCaS suite, automatically.

Adverbs Another point, of minor theoretical importance but major practical one, is our handling of adverbial phrases. We interpret adverbs (and in general all adverbial and prepositional phrases) as VP-modifiers: $Adv = VP \to VP$, where $VP = object \to Prop$. However, applying adverbs to verb-phrases heavily complicates the Coq proofs, because such phrases can contain quantifiers. Therefore, we instead move the adverbs, so that they apply to (atomic) verbs only. Proofs can then be simplify accordingly.

4 Results and evaluation

We evaluated FraCoq against 8 sections of the FraCaS test suite, for a total of 259 cases. We excluded only section 7, "temporal reference". The reason for doing so is that, in our view, it contains too many examples which require *ad-hoc* treatment, and thus makes little sense to include without complementing it with a more thorough suite which captures a more complete landscape of the phenomena that section 7 touches.

FraCaS classifies each problem as either entailment (YES), entailment of the opposite (NO) or no entailment (UNK). In this work, we have amended the FraCaS suite to correct a few problems. First,

test case	new class	comment
005	UNK	missing hypothesis: there are italian tenors
056	Yes	Already identified as such by MacCartney
069	Unk	Mary could have used someone else's workstation
119	Unk	*ibid.*
181	Yes	for the same reason as 180
226	Yes	

Table 1: Overruled FraCaS cases

certain test case are not formed correctly. Those were already identified by MacCartney and Manning (2007) as such (using an "undef" labelling), and we removed those. Second, a few test cases occur twice in the suite, but with two different labellings (one YES and one UNK), with an annotation that those labellings correspond to different readings. However, elsewhere in the suite, if a problem has several readings but only one has entailment, it occurs only once and is marked as YES. To make the test suite consistent, if one reading yields entailment we have always considered it as YES. We have also removed case 199 (which appears to be vacuous). Finally we changed the labelling of 6 cases which appeared to have been misclassified. We note that the majority of the mistaken classifications occur in sections 3 and 4, which have not been previously attempted and thus, we propose, have not been properly scrutinized. In terms of comparison, this only has a minor effect, since our system is the first system to run sections 3 and 4.

Our system classifies a case as YES if a proof can be constructed from the premises to the hypothesis, NO if a proof of the negated hypothesis can be constructed and UNK otherwise. Because we work with a non-decidable logic, one cannot *in general* conclude decisively that no proof exists. Thus, we consider here that no proof exists if it cannot be constructed with reasonable effort. In particular, we test at the minimum that the automatic proof search built in Coq does not succeed before classifying a problem as UNK.[3]

Table 2 shows a considerable improvement over earlier approaches in terms of coverage, with three more sections covered over previous approaches. We thus cover 259 out of 337 cases (77%), compared to at most 174 cases (52%) in previous work. Additionally, our system performs generally the

mentation, however, are.

---

[3]The other way this can be done is by introducing a timeout as Mineshima et al. (2015) have done.

Section	#cases	Ours	FC	MINE	Nut	Langpro
Quantifiers	75	.96 74	.96	.77	.53	.93 44
Plurals	33	.82	.76	.67	.52	.73 24
Anaphora	28	.86	-	-	-	-
Ellipsis	52	.87	-	-	-	-
Adjectives	22	.95 20	.95	.68	.32	.73 12
Comparatives	31	.87	.56	.48	.45	-
Temporal	75	-	-	-	-	-
Verbs	8	.75	-	-	-	-
Attitudes	13	.92	.85	.77	.46	.92 9
Total	337	.89 259	.83 174	.69 174	.50 174	.85 89

Table 2: Accuracy of our system compared to others. "Ours" refers to the approach presented in this paper. When a system does not handle the nominal number of test cases (shown in the second column), the actual number of test cases attempted is shown below the accuracy figure, in smaller font. "FraCoq" refers to the work of Bernardy and Chatzikyriakidis (2017). "MINE" refers to the approach of Mineshima et al. (2015), "NUT" to the CCG system that utilizes the first-order automated theorem prover *nutcracker* (Bos, 2008), and "Langpro" to the system presented by Abzianidze (2015). A dash indicates that no attempt was made for the section.

best in terms of accuracy. In particular, section 6 largely improves in accuracy, which we attribute to our dynamic semantics analysis of comparatives.

error analysis Our system fails to correctly classify 28 cases out of 259. We give here a summary of the missing features which are responsible for the failures. The biggest source of error is incomplete handling of group readings. (FraCaS 013, 014, 046, 084, 111, 124, 126, 127, 137, 171, 172, 191, 193, 195, 243, 250, 333, 346). These are cases where a syntactic conjunction of individuals is treated as a semantic group, or where precise counting of the members of a group is necessary. Other problematic cases include definite plurals with no universal readings (091, 094, 095). Additionally, neither measure phrases (242) nor attributive comparatives (244, 245) are handled.

5   Conclusions and Future Work

We presented a system converting GF trees to Coq types using dynamic semantics. The system outperforms the state of the art in logical approaches when tested on the FraCaS and is the only system to date to perform a run on the FraCaS ellipsis/anaphora section. The system is precise enough to form the start of a precise NL reasoner for controlled domains. In the future, we plan to extend the system to cover the remaining section of the FraCaS (tense/aspect), and also develop a more applied version to perform reasoning on controlled NL domains.

References

Lasha Abzianidze. 2015. A tableau prover for natural logic and language. In *Proceedings of EMNLP15*.

Chris Barker and Chung chieh Shan. 2004. Continuations in natural language. In *in Proceedings of the fourth ACM SIGPLAN workshop on continuations, Hayo Thielecke*, pages 55–64.

Jean-Philippe Bernardy and Stergios Chatzikyriakidis. 2017. A type-theoretical system for the fracas test suite: Grammatical framework meets coq. In *IWCS 2017-12th International Conference on Computational Semantics-Long papers*.

Jean-Philippe Bernardy and Stergios Chatzikyriakidis. 2019. What kind of natural language inference are nlp systems learning: Is this enough? In *Proceedings of ICAART*.

Jean-Philippe Bernardy, Stergios Chatzikyriakidis, and Aleksandre Maskharashvili. A computational treatment of anaphora and its algorithmic implementation. Manuscript available online https://bit.ly/2xQ4G2M.

Johan Bos. 2008. Wide-coverage semantic analysis with boxer. In *Proceedings of the 2008 Conference on Semantics in Text Processing*, pages 277–286. Association for Computational Linguistics.

Simon Charlow. 2017. A modular theory of pronouns and binding. In *Logic and Engineering of Natural Language Semantics (LENLS) 14*. Springer.

Stergios Chatzikyriakidis and Zhaohui Luo. 2017. Adjectival and adverbial modification: The view from modern type theories. *Journal of Logic, Language and Information*, 26(1):45–88.

Max J Cresswell. 1976. The semantics of degree. In *Montague grammar*, pages 261–292. Elsevier.

Philippe de Groote. 2006. Towards a montagovian account of dynamics. In *Semantics and Linguistic Theory*, volume 16, pages 1–16.

I. Heim. 2000. Degree operators and scope. In *Proceedings of SALT*, volume 10, pages 40–64.

Christopher Kennedy. 2007. Vagueness and grammar: The semantics of relative and absolute gradable adjectives. *Linguistics and philosophy*, 30(1):1–45.

Seonhoon Kim, Jin-Hyuk Hong, Inho Kang, and Nojun Kwak. 2018. Semantic sentence matching with densely-connected recurrent and co-attentive information. *arXiv preprint arXiv:1805.11360*.

Xiaodong Liu, Pengcheng He, Weizhu Chen, and Jianfeng Gao. 2019. Multi-task deep neural networks for natural language understanding. *arXiv preprint arXiv:1901.11504*.

P. Ljunglöf and M. Siverbo. 2011. A bilingual treebank for the FraCas test suite. Clt project report, University of Gothenburg.

Bill MacCartney and Christopher D Manning. 2007. Natural logic for textual inference. In *Proceedings of the ACL-PASCAL Workshop on Textual Entailment and Paraphrasing*, pages 193–200. Association for Computational Linguistics.

Marco Marelli, Luisa Bentivogli, Marco Baroni, Raffaella Bernardi, Stefano Menini, and Roberto Zamparelli. 2014. Semeval-2014 task 1: Evaluation of compositional distributional semantic models on full sentences through semantic relatedness and textual entailment. In *Proceedings of the 8th international workshop on semantic evaluation (SemEval 2014)*, pages 1–8.

Koji Mineshima, Yusuke Miyao, and Daisuke Bekki. 2015. Higher-order logical inference with compositional semantics. In *Proceedings of EMNLP*.

Sai Qian, Philippe de Groote, and Maxime Amblard. 2016. Modal subordination in type theoretic dynamic logic. *LiLT (Linguistic Issues in Language Technology)*, 14.

Alec Radford, Karthik Narasimhan, Tim Salimans, and Ilya Sutskever. 2018. Improving language understanding by generative pre-training. *URL https://s3-us-west-2. amazonaws. com/openai-assets/research-covers/languageunsupervised/language understanding paper. pdf*.

Aarne Ranta. 2011. *Grammatical framework: Programming with multilingual grammars*. CSLI Publications.

Chung-chieh Shan. 2002. Monads for natural language semantics. *CoRR*, cs.CL/0205026.

Christina Unger. 2011. Dynamic semantics as monadic computation. In *JSAI International Symposium on Artificial Intelligence*, pages 68–81. Springer.

Ensembles of Neural Morphological Inflection Models

Ilmari Kylliäinen and **Miikka Silfverberg**

Department of Digital Humanities, University of Helsinki, Finland

{ilmari.kylliainen,miikka.silfverberg}@helsinki.fi

Abstract

We investigate different ensemble learning techniques for neural morphological inflection using bidirectional LSTM encoder-decoder models with attention. We experiment with weighted and unweighted majority voting and bagging. We find that all investigated ensemble methods lead to improved accuracy over a baseline of a single model. However, contrary to expectation based on earlier work by Najafi et al. (2018) and Silfverberg et al. (2017), weighting does not deliver clear benefits. Bagging was found to underperform plain voting ensembles in general.

1 Introduction

Natural language processing (NLP) systems for languages which exhibit rich inflectional morphology often suffer from data sparsity. The root cause of this sparsity is a prohibitively high type-token ratio which is typical for morphologically complex languages. A common way to alleviate the problem is to incorporate modeling of inflectional morphology instead of building purely word-based NLP systems—by representing word forms as combinations of a lemma and morphosyntactic description, data sparsity is reduced both in analysis and generation tasks.

Morphology-aware language generation systems usually require a component which generates inflected word forms from lemmas and morphosyntactic descriptions. Such a component is called a morphological inflection (MI)[1] model. For example, given the Italian verb *mangiare* 'to eat' and the morphosyntactic description **V;IND;FUT;1;SG**, an MI system should generate the 1st person singular future indicative form *mangerò* as output.

Traditionally, rule-based methods have been applied in morphological inflection and analysis. Recently, machine learning methods have also gained ground in this task. Especially deep learning methods have delivered strong results in MI (Cotterell et al., 2017, 2018). Starting with the work by Kann and Schütze (2016), the predominant approach has been to use a bidirectional RNN encoder-decoder system with attention. While neural encoder-decoder systems have been successfully applied to the MI task and many papers have investigated simple model ensembles using unweighted majority voting, few studies have fully investigated ensembles of neural systems. Weighted model ensembles for MI are proposed by Najafi et al. (2018) and Silfverberg et al. (2017) but neither provides a detailed analysis of model ensembles. This paper compares the performance of different model ensembles for MI.

We explore methods which use unweighted and weighted voting strategies to combine outputs of different models. We also investigate different ways of training the component models in the ensemble using both random initialization of model parameters and varying the training data using bootstrap aggregation commonly known as bagging (Breiman, 1996). Bagging is a popular ensemble method where new training sets are created by resampling from an existing training set. Both bagging and majority voting are known to reduce the variance of the model. This makes them suitable for neural models which are known to obtain high variance (Denkowski and Neubig, 2017).

Due to practicality concerns, we limit the scope of the paper to methods which can combine existing models without changes to model architecture. Therefore, we do not explore merging model predictions during beam search in decoding or averaging model parameters.

We perform experiments on a selection of ten languages: Arabic, Finnish, Georgian, German,

---

[1]Sometimes also called morphological reinflection (Cotterell et al., 2016)

Hindi, Italian, Khaling, Navajo, Russian, and Turkish. Our experiments on this morphologically and areally diverse set of languages show that model ensembles tend to deliver the best results confirming results presented in earlier work. However, our findings for weighted ensembles and bagging are largely negative. Contrary to expectation based on the work by Najafi et al. (2018) and Silfverberg et al. (2017) weighting did not deliver clear benefits over unweighted model ensembles. Bagging, in general, does deliver improvements in model accuracy compared to a baseline of a single model but does not outperform plain majority voting.

2 Related Work

Following Kann and Schütze (2016) and many others, we explore learning of MI systems in the context of bidirectional LSTM encoder-decoder models with attention. Several papers have employed straightforward majority voting for the task of MI (Kann and Schütze, 2016; Kann et al., 2018; Makarov and Clematide, 2018; Kementchedjhieva et al., 2018; Sharma et al., 2018). However, work on more advanced ensembling methods is scarce for the MI task.

Najafi et al. (2018) and Silfverberg et al. (2017) explored weighted variants of majority voting. Both of these approaches are based on weighting models according to their performance on a held-out development set. Silfverberg et al. (2017) use sampling-based methods for finding good weighting coefficients for the component models in an ensemble. Najafi et al. (2018) instead simply weight models according to their accuracy on the development set. We opt for using the latter weighing scheme in our experiments because Silfverberg et al. (2017) report that the sampling-based method can sometimes overfit the development set which leads to poor performance on the test set. Najafi et al. (2018) combined different types of models, both neural and non-neural, in their ensemble but we apply their technique in a purely neural setting.

Ensemble learning has received more attention in the field of neural machine translation. A common approach is to combine predictions of several models in beam search during decoding (Denkowski and Neubig, 2017). Another approach is to train several models and then distill them into a single model (Denkowski and Neu-

big, 2017). The simplest approach to distillation is to average the parameters of the different models. While these techniques could be applied in MI, the focus of this paper is to explore ensemble methods which do not require any changes to the underlying model architecture. Therefore, such methods fall outside of the scope of our work.

3 Task and Methods

We formulate the MI task as a sequence-to-sequence translation task. The input to our model consists of the characters in the lemma of a word and the grammatical tags in its morphosyntactic description. The output form is the inflected word form represented as a sequence of characters. For example:

Input: m, a, n, g, i, a, r, e, +V, +IND, +FUT, +1, +SG
Output: m, a, n, g, e, r, ò

The remainder of this section describes the neural encoder-decoder models used in our experiments, the ensemble learning methods and our approach to weighting the component models of model ensembles.

3.1 Encoder-Decoder Architecture

We use a standard bidirectional LSTM encoder-decoder with attention. The character embeddings for input and output characters are 100-dimensional. The embeddings are processed by a 1-layer bidirectional LSTM encoder (BRNN) with hidden state size 300. The encoder representations are then fed into a 1-layer LSTM attention decoder with hidden state size 300.

3.2 Ensembles

An ensemble consists of a set of individually trained models whose predictions are combined when classifying novel instances or generating sequences. The aim is to combine the models in a way which delivers better performance than any of the models individually.

Majority Voting Our first ensemble learning technique is majority voting. We train N models on the entire training data with different random initializations of model parameters. During test time, we apply each of the models on a given test input form and then perform voting among model outputs. In case of a tie, the final output is chosen randomly among the most frequent predictions.

		ARA	FIN	GEO	GER	HIN	ITA	KHA	NAV	RUS	TUR
High	Best baseline model	93.40	94.00	99.10	91.60	**100.00**	**98.00**	**99.90**	91.30	91.50	98.00
	Baseline mean	92.74	93.45	98.69	90.78	**100.00**	97.27	99.44	89.63	90.60	97.43
	MV 10.NMV	*94.60	***95.40**	***99.40**	*92.70	100.00	***98.00**	*99.80	*94.00	*92.60	***98.40**
	MV 10.WMV	***94.80**	*94.90	***99.40**	*92.80	100.00	***98.00**	*99.80	***94.20**	*92.80	***98.40**
	Bagging 10.NMV	93.90	95.30	99.10	92.10	**100.00**	97.60	99.70	91.10	92.10	98.00
	Bagging 10.WMV	94.00	95.20	99.10	92.50	**100.00**	97.80	99.60	91.40	91.90	98.00
	Bagging 100.NMV	94.50	95.30	98.90	92.80	**100.00**	97.70	99.50	92.50	92.40	98.00
	Bagging 100.WMV	94.50	**95.40**	98.90	**92.90**	**100.00**	97.70	99.50	92.50	92.40	98.20
Medium	Best baseline model	76.80	75.60	92.50	78.60	98.10	92.10	90.00	47.30	78.00	86.90
	Baseline mean	74.13	71.89	92.14	75.80	96.91	90.21	88.95	43.68	76.60	84.95
	MV 10.NMV	***80.80**	*80.70	***93.50**	*80.30	*98.50	***93.10**	***91.70**	*52.50	***83.00**	***88.70**
	MV 10.WMV	***80.80**	***80.80**	*93.40	***80.70**	***98.60**	*93.00	*91.50	***52.70**	*82.90	*88.60
	Bagging 10.NMV	74.40	72.90	**93.50**	77.70	97.80	91.50	84.00	46.50	76.50	86.80
	Bagging 10.WMV	75.60	74.00	93.40	78.00	97.80	92.00	84.10	47.30	76.60	87.10
	Bagging 100.NMV	78.90	74.50	93.20	79.00	97.70	91.50	85.20	51.80	78.50	88.40
	Bagging 100.WMV	79.10	74.50	93.20	79.10	97.70	91.40	85.50	52.10	78.50	88.40
Low	Best baseline model	**0.40**	1.30	40.26	21.38	21.78	13.29	**6.59**	1.70	8.29	7.29
	Baseline mean	0.23	0.80	33.18	15.92	15.81	8.72	3.16	1.39	5.93	2.77
	MV 10.NMV	0.20	*1.40	***49.80**	*25.67	*22.58	*15.00	*4.30	*1.80	10.30	*5.20
	MV 10.WMV	0.20	***1.50**	*49.50	***26.07**	***22.98**	***17.38**	*5.59	***1.80**	***11.30**	***7.39**
	Bagging 10.NMV	0.09	0.00	9.79	1.30	8.49	0.30	0.80	0.70	0.80	0.00
	Bagging 10.WMV	0.01	0.00	13.89	2.50	8.99	1.10	0.30	0.80	0.90	0.20
	Bagging 100.NMV	0.00	0.00	17.18	2.30	10.59	0.80	1.10	0.60	2.60	0.20
	Bagging 100.WMV	0.00	0.00	19.20	4.00	12.29	1.40	1.30	0.80	2.90	0.60

Table 1: Accuracies (%) of bagging and majority voting ensembles and best baseline models, and baseline model means for Arabic (ARA), Finnish (FIN), Georgian (GEO), German (GER), Hindi (HIN), Italian (ITA), Khaling (KHA), Navajo (NAV), Russian (RUS) and Turkish (TUR). Ensemble size (10 or 100) and majority voting type (NMV or WMV) are marked after the ensemble type (Majority voting (MV) or Bagging). Significant improvements over the baseline mean at the 95% confidence level as measured by a two-sided t-test are indicated by asterisk (*).

Bagging Our second ensemble learning technique is bagging. Here we resample N new training sets from our existing training set and use those to train N models. The aim is to create a more diverse collection of models than can be accomplished simply by varying model initialization. After training the N models, we then apply majority voting on their output during test time.

A standard way to create a bagging ensemble is to generate each of the new training sets by drawing $|D|$ samples with replacement from the original training set D. It can be shown that this gives on average $0.63|D|$ different examples in each of the new data sets (Efron and Tibshirani, 1993).

Weighting Models We compare straightforward majority voting and bagging to weighted voting. The key difference here is that models now get a fractional vote in the interval $[0, 1]$ based on the model weight. The model weight is determined by the accuracy of the model on a held-out set. For example, if a model's accuracy is 87%, its weight in voting is 0.87. Regular majority voting corresponds to assigning the weight 1 to each model. We denote the two different voting strategies by NMV for naive majority voting and WMV for weighted majority voting.

4 Experiments

4.1 Data

We use data for 10 different languages from CoNLL-SIGMORPHON 2017 Task 1 dataset (Cotterell et al., 2017) to train and evaluate models. The languages are Arabic (ARA), Finnish (FIN), Georgian (GEO), German (GER), Hindi (HIN), Italian (ITA), Khaling (KHA), Navajo (NAV), Russian (RUS) and Turkish (TUR). The language set is diverse in terms of morphological structure and encompasses diverse morphological properties and inflection processes.

The shared task data sets are tab separated files with three columns: lemma, inflected form, and morphosyntactic description. For example,

```
überbewerten überbewerteten V;IND;PST;3;PL
```

The data sets are sparse in the sense that they include only a few inflected forms for each lemma instead of complete inflectional paradigms.

For all languages, we perform experiments using the official shared task data splits. We train for the high training data setting (10,000 training examples), medium setting (1,000 training examples) and low setting (100 training examples). Additionally, we use the official shared task development set to tune models and the test sets for final evaluation.

4.2 Experimental Setup

Baseline For baseline experiments, 10 inflection models were trained for each language with different random initial values for the model parameters. We trained models both for the high and medium training data settings. Model parameters were optimized using the Adam optimization algorithm (Kingma and Ba, 2014) and we used minibatches of 64 examples during training.

According to preliminary experiments, the development accuracy and perplexity for each language converged around 6,000-10,000 training steps for each dataset, where one training step corresponds to updating on model parameters for a single minibatch (64 items). To ensure convergence for all languages, we therefore trained all models for 12,500 training steps. We do not employ character dropout. All our models are implemented using the OpenNMT neural machine translation toolkit (Klein et al., 2017).

Ensembles The 10 baseline models of each language and training data setting were used to form voting ensembles. We applied both naive majority voting and weighted majority voting.

For bagging, two experiments are conducted on the high, medium and low training data setting. In the first experiment, we form 10 training sets by resampling from the original training sets. In the second one, we form 100 new training sets by resampling. Each of the sampled training sets has the same size as the original training set for the high, medium and low setting, respectively. Subsequently, we train models on each of the newly formed training sets. In addition to using different data for training, diversity between the ensemble members is ensured by different random initialization of model parameters. In each experiment, both naive majority voting and weighted majority voting are applied to outputs of each model to form two ensembles for each language.

4.3 Results

Table 1 shows results for all experiments. On the whole, ensembles delivered improvements with regard to the baseline of a single model. This holds true both when comparing to the mean accuracy of the 10 individual baseline models and when comparing to the best individual baseline

model. In general, the best accuracies were obtained by naive and weighted majority voting ensembles. For the high, medium and low settings, we obtain small improvements by weighting both majority voting and bagging ensembles. However, in most cases these improvements are not statistically significant at the 95% confidence level.

In most cases, the results of the bagging experiments were worse than results for both naive and weighted majority voting ensembles. For the high training data setting, accuracies delivered by bagging ensembles were similar or slightly worse than results for plain naive and weighted majority voting ensembles. However, in the medium data setting, differences in accuracy between majority voting and bagging ensembles are larger. For example, the difference between the best bagging model and best plain voting model is greater than 2%-points for three languages (KHA, NAV, RUS). For the medium data setting, bagging did not deliver consistent improvements over the baseline of a single model although we do get an improvement for 5 languages (ARA, GEO, GER, NAV, RUS and TUR). For the low training data setting, the bagging ensembles clearly underperform weighted and unweighted majority voting and the baselines for all languages. In general, bagging ensembles consisting of 100 models did deliver improvements upon ensembles consisting of 10 models.

5 Discussion and Conclusions

Our results demonstrate that an ensemble of models trained in parallel nearly always outperforms a single model. Contrary to earlier findings by Najafi et al. (2018) and Silfverberg et al. (2017), we do not see clear improvements from weighting models in ensembles. One reason for this discrepancy may be that Najafi et al. (2018) trained a diverse ensemble of both non-neural and neural models, whereas, all of our models have the same underlying architecture.

Bagging does not deliver clear improvements over majority voting in the high and medium training data setting. Instead it often underperforms the baseline of a single model on medium training sets of 1,000 training examples. For larger training sets of 10,000 examples, bagging typically outperforms the baseline models but its performance still lags behind weighted and unweighted majority voting ensembles. This can partly be explained by the fact that each individual model in a bagging ensemble is trained on a subset containing approximately 60% of all training examples. Therefore, individual models in the ensemble are likely to be weaker than models trained on the entire training set because even our largest training set of 10,000 examples is still relatively small.

In the low training data setting of 100 training examples, bagging substantially underperforms the baselines. Here overfitting becomes a severe problem. Each of the component models in the ensemble, therefore, delivers very poor performance compared to the baselines resulting in poor performance for the entire ensemble.

We observe moderate improvements when the number of models in the bagging ensemble was increased from 10 to 100. Therefore, we believe that bagging could eventually outperform majority voting in the high and medium data setting when the number of models in the ensemble is increased. However, the moderate gains suggest that the number of models that is required may be quite large.

References

Leo Breiman. 1996. Bagging Predictors. *Machine Learning*, 24(2):123–140.

Ryan Cotterell, Christo Kirov, John Sylak-Glassman, Géraldine Walther, Ekaterina Vylomova, Arya D. McCarthy, Katharina Kann, Sebastian J. Mielke, Garrett Nicolai, Miikka Silfverberg, David Yarowsky, Jason Eisner, and Mans Hulden. 2018. The CoNLL-SIGMORPHON 2018 Shared Task: Universal Morphological Reinflection. *CoRR*, abs/1810.07125.

Ryan Cotterell, Christo Kirov, John Sylak-Glassman, Gèraldine Walther, Ekaterina Vylomova, Patrick Xia, Manaal Faruqui, Sandra Kübler, David Yarowsky, Jason Eisner, and Mans Hulden. 2017. CoNLL-SIGMORPHON 2017 Shared Task: Universal Morphological Reinflection in 52 Languages. In *Proceedings of the CoNLL SIGMORPHON 2017 Shared Task: Universal Morphological Reinflection*, pages 1–30. Association for Computational Linguistics.

Ryan Cotterell, Christo Kirov, John Sylak-Glassman, David Yarowsky, Jason Eisner, and Mans Hulden. 2016. The SIGMORPHON 2016 Shared Task—Morphological Reinflection. In *Proceedings of the 2016 Meeting of SIGMORPHON*, Berlin, Germany. Association for Computational Linguistics.

Michael Denkowski and Graham Neubig. 2017. Stronger baselines for trustable results in neural machine translation. In *Proceedings of the First Workshop on Neural Machine Translation*, pages 18–27, Vancouver. Association for Computational Linguistics.

Bradley Efron and Robert J. Tibshirani. 1993. *An Introduction to the Bootstrap*. Number 57 in Monographs on Statistics and Applied Probability. Chapman & Hall/CRC, Boca Raton, Florida, USA.

Katharina Kann, Stanislas Lauly, and Kyunghyun Cho. 2018. The NYU system for the CoNLL–SIGMORPHON 2018 shared task on universal morphological reinflection. In *Proceedings of the CoNLL–SIGMORPHON 2018 Shared Task: Universal Morphological Reinflection*, pages 58–63, Brussels. Association for Computational Linguistics.

Katharina Kann and Hinrich Schütze. 2016. MED: The LMU System for the SIGMORPHON 2016 Shared Task on Morphological Reinflection. In *Proceedings of the 14th SIGMORPHON Workshop on Computational Research in Phonetics, Phonology, and Morphology*, pages 62–70. Association for Computational Linguistics.

Yova Kementchedjhieva, Johannes Bjerva, and Isabelle Augenstein. 2018. Copenhagen at CoNLL–SIGMORPHON 2018: Multilingual inflection in context with explicit morphosyntactic decoding. In *Proceedings of the CoNLL–SIGMORPHON 2018 Shared Task: Universal Morphological Reinflection*, pages 93–98, Brussels. Association for Computational Linguistics.

Diederik P. Kingma and Jimmy Ba. 2014. Adam: A Method for Stochastic Optimization. *CoRR*, abs/1412.6980.

Guillaume Klein, Yoon Kim, Yuntian Deng, Jean Senellart, and Alexander M. Rush. 2017. OpenNMT: Open-Source Toolkit for Neural Machine Translation. In *Proc. ACL*.

Peter Makarov and Simon Clematide. 2018. UZH at CoNLL–SIGMORPHON 2018 shared task on universal morphological reinflection. In *Proceedings of the CoNLL–SIGMORPHON 2018 Shared Task: Universal Morphological Reinflection*, pages 69–75, Brussels. Association for Computational Linguistics.

Saeed Najafi, Bradley Hauer, Rashed Rubby Riyadh, Leyuan Yu, and Grzegorz Kondrak. 2018. Combining neural and non-neural methods for low-resource morphological reinflection. In *Proceedings of the CoNLL–SIGMORPHON 2018 Shared Task: Universal Morphological Reinflection*, pages 116–120, Brussels. Association for Computational Linguistics.

Abhishek Sharma, Ganesh Katrapati, and Dipti Misra Sharma. 2018. IIT(BHU)–IIITH at CoNLL–SIGMORPHON 2018 shared task on universal morphological reinflection. In *Proceedings of the*

CoNLL–SIGMORPHON 2018 Shared Task: Universal Morphological Reinflection, pages 105–111, Brussels. Association for Computational Linguistics.

Miikka Silfverberg, Adam Wiemerslage, Ling Liu, and Lingshuang Jack Mao. 2017. Data augmentation for morphological reinflection. *Proceedings of the CoNLL SIGMORPHON 2017 Shared Task: Universal Morphological Reinflection*, pages 90–99.

Nefnir: A high accuracy lemmatizer for Icelandic

Svanhvít Ingólfsdóttir, Hrafn Loftsson
Department of Computer Science

Reykjavik University
{svanhviti16, hrafn}@ru.is

Jón Daðason, Kristín Bjarnadóttir
The Árni Magnússon Institute
for Icelandic Studies
University of Iceland
{jfd1, kristinb}@hi.is

Abstract

Lemmatization, finding the basic morphological form of a word in a corpus, is an important step in many natural language processing tasks when working with morphologically rich languages. We describe and evaluate *Nefnir*, a new open source lemmatizer for Icelandic. Nefnir uses suffix substitution rules, derived from a large morphological database, to lemmatize tagged text. Evaluation shows that for correctly tagged text, Nefnir obtains an accuracy of 99.55%, and for text tagged with a PoS tagger, the accuracy obtained is 96.88%.

1 Introduction

In text mining and Natural Language Processing (NLP), a *lemmatizer* is a tool used to determine the basic form of a word (*lemma*). Lemmatization differs from *stemming* in the way this base form is determined. While stemmers chop off word endings to reach the common stem of words, lemmatizers take into account the morphology of the words in order to produce the common morphological base form, i.e., the form of the word found in a dictionary. This type of text normalization is an important step in pre-processing morphologically complex languages, like Icelandic, before conducting various tasks, such as machine translation, text mining and information retrieval.

To give an example from the Icelandic language, lemmatization helps find all instances of the personal pronoun *ég* "I" in a text corpus, taking into account all inflectional forms (*ég*, *mig*, *mér*, *mín*, *við*, *okkur*, and *okkar*). These variations of each word can be up to 16 for nouns and over a hundred for adjectives and verbs. The value of being able to reduce the number of different surface forms that appear for each word is therefore evident, as otherwise it is hard or even impossible to correctly determine word frequency in a corpus, or to look up all instances of a particular term.

In this paper, we describe and evaluate *Nefnir* (Daðason, 2018), a new open source lemmatizer for Icelandic. Nefnir uses suffix substitution rules derived (learned) from the Database of Modern Icelandic Inflection (DMII) (Bjarnadóttir, 2012), which contains over 5.8 million inflectional forms.

This new lemmatizer was used for large-scale lemmatization of the *Icelandic Gigaword Corpus* (Steingrímsson et al., 2018) with promising results, but a formal evaluation had not been carried out. Our evaluation of Nefnir indicates that, compared to previously published results, it obtains the highest lemmatization accuracy of Icelandic, with 99.55% accuracy given correct part-of-speech (PoS) tags, and 96.88% accuracy given text tagged with a PoS tagger.

2 Related work

The most basic approach to lemmatization is a simple look-up in a lexicon. This method has the obvious drawback that words that are not in the lexicon cannot be processed. To solve this, word transformation rules have been used to analyze the surface form of the word (the token) in order to produce the base form. These rules can either be hand-crafted or learned automatically using machine learning.

When hand-crafting the rules that are used to determine the lemmas, a thorough knowledge of the morphological features of the language is needed. This is a time-consuming task, further complicated in Icelandic by the extensive inflectional system (Bjarnadóttir, 2012). An example of a hand-crafted lemmatizer is the morphological analyzer that is part of the Czech Dependency Treebank (Hajič et al., 2018).

Machine learning methods emerged to make the rule-learning process more effective, and various algorithms have been developed. These methods rely on training data, which can be a corpus of words and their lemmas or a large morphological lexicon (Jongejan and Dalianis, 2009). By analyzing the training data, transformation rules are formed, which can subsequently be used to find lemmas in new texts, given the word forms.

In addition, maching learning lemmatizers based on deep neural networks (DNNs) have recently emerged (see for example *finnlem* (Myrberg, 2017) for Finnish and *LemmaTag* (Kondratyuk et al., 2018) for German, Czech and Arabic). Along with the best rule-derived machine learning methods, these are now the state-of-the-art approaches to lemmatizers for morphologically complex languages.

The biggest problem in lemmatization is the issue of unknown words, i.e. words not found in the training corpus or the underlying lexicon of the lemmatizer. This has been handled in various ways, such as by only looking at the suffix of a word to determine the lemma, thereby lemmatizing unseen words that (hopefully) share the same morphological rules as a known word (Dalianis and Jongejan, 2006). DNN-based lemmatizers may prove useful in solving this issue, as they have their own inherent ways of handling these out-of-vocabulary (OOV) words, such as by using character-level context (Bergmanis and Goldwater, 2018).

Previous to Nefnir, two lemmatization tools had been developed for Icelandic. We will now briefly mention these lemmatizers, before describing Nefnir further.

2.1 CST Lemmatizer

The CST Lemmatizer (Jongejan and Dalianis, 2009) is a rule-based lemmatizer that has been trained for Icelandic on the Icelandic Frequency Dictionary (IFD) corpus, consisting of about 590,000 tokens (Pind et al., 1991). This is a language-independent lemmatizer that only looks at the suffix of the word as a way of lemmatizing OOV words, and can be used on both tagged and untagged input.

The authors of Lemmald (see Section 2.2) trained and evaluated the CST Lemmatizer on the IFD and observed a 98.99% accuracy on correctly tagged text and 93.15% accuracy on untagged text, in a 10-fold cross-validation, where each test set contained about 60,000 tokens. Another evaluation of this lemmatizer for Icelandic (Cassata,

2007) reports around 90% accuracy on a random sample of 600 words from the IFD, when the input has been PoS tagged automatically (with a tagging accuracy of 91.5%). The PoS tagger used was *IceTagger* (Loftsson, 2008), which is part of the IceNLP natural language processing toolkit (Loftsson and Rögnvaldsson, 2007). These results indicate that the accuracy of this lemmatizer is very dependent upon the tags it is given. To our knowledge, the Icelandic CST Lemmatizer model is not openly available.

2.2 Lemmald

The second tool is Lemmald (Ingason et al., 2008), which is part of the IceNLP toolkit. It uses a mixed method of data-driven machine learning (using the IFD as a training corpus) and linguistic rules, as well as providing the option of looking up word forms in the DMII. Given correct PoS tagging of the input, Lemmald's accuracy measures at 98.54%, in a 10-fold cross-validation. The authors note that the CST Lemmatizer performs better than Lemmald when trained on the same data, without the added DMII lookup. The DMII lookup for Lemmald delivers a statistically significant improvement on the accuracy (99.55%), but it is not provided with the IceNLP distribution, so this enhancement is not available for public use. When used for lemmatization of the Icelandic Tagged Corpus (MÍM) (Helgadóttir et al., 2012), the lemmatization accuracy of Lemmald was roughly estimated at around 90%.[1]

3   System Description

The main difference between Nefnir and the two previously described lemmatizers for Icelandic, CST Lemmatizer and Lemmald, is that Nefnir derives its rules from a morphological database, the DMII, whereas the other two are trained on a corpus, the IFD. Note that the IFD only consists of about 590,000 tokens, while the DMII contains over 5.8 million inflectional forms.

Nefnir uses suffix substitution rules, derived from the DMII to lemmatize tagged text. An example of such a rule is (*ngar*, nkfn, *ar→ur*), which can be applied to any word form with the suffix *ngar* that has the PoS tag nkfn (a masculine plural noun in the nominative case), transforming the suffix from *ar* to *ur*. This rule could, for example,

---

[1]See `https://www.malfong.is/index.php?lang=en&pg=mim`

be applied to the word form *kettlingar* "kittens" to obtain the corresponding lemma, *kettlingur*. Words are lemmatized using the rule with the longest shared suffix and the same tag.

Each inflectional form in the DMII is annotated with a grammatical tag and lemma. As the DMII is limited to inflected words, the training data is supplemented with a hand-curated list of approximately 4,500 uninflected words (such as adverbs, conjunctions and prepositions) and abbreviations.

To account for subtle differences between the tagsets used in the DMII and by the Icelandic PoS taggers, Nefnir translates all tags to an intermediate tagset which is a subset of both.

Rules are successively generated and applied to the training set, with each new rule minimizing the number of remaining errors. Rules continue to be generated until the number of errors cannot be reduced. The process is as follows:

1. Initially, assume that each word form is identical to its lemma.
2. Generate a list of rules for all remaining errors.
3. Choose the rule which minimizes the number of remaining errors and apply it to the training set, or stop if no improvement can be made.
4. Repeat from step 2.

Rules are only generated if they can correctly lemmatize at least two examples in the training set. A dictionary is created for words which are incorrectly lemmatized by the rules, for example because they require a unique transformation, such as from *við* "we" to *ég* "I". Once trained, Nefnir lemmatizes words using the dictionary if they are present, or else with the most specific applicable rule.

A rule is generated for every suffix in a word form, with some restrictions. For base words, Nefnir considers all suffixes, from the empty string to the full word. For *skó* "shoes", an inflected form of the word *skór* "shoe", rules are generated for the suffixes *ε*, *ó*, *kó* and *skó*. However, Nefnir does not create rules for suffixes that are shorter than the transformation required to lemmatize the word. For example, for *bækur* "books", which requires the transformation *ækur→ók* (the lemma for *bækur* is *bók*), only the suffixes *ækur* and *bækur* are considered.

Compounding is highly productive in Icelandic and compound words comprise a very large portion of the vocabulary. This is reflected in the DMII, where over 88% of all words are compounds (Bjarnadóttir, 2017). Any of the open word classes can be combined to form a compound, and there is no theoretical limit to how many words they can consist of. Due to the abundance of compounds in the training data, and the freedom with which they can be formed, Nefnir places additional restrictions on which suffixes to consider when generating rules for them. Suffixes for the final part of a compound are generated in the same manner as for base words, growing part by part thereafter. For example, the compound word *fjall+göngu+skó* "hiking boots" would yield rules for the suffixes *ε*, *ó*, *kó*, *skó*, *gönguskó* and *fjallgönguskó*. Allowing suffixes to grow freely past the final part of the compound may result in overfitting as the rules adapt to incidental patterns in the training data.

4 Evaluation

We have evaluated the output of Nefnir against a reference corpus of 21,093 tokens and their correct lemmas.

Samples for the reference corpus were extracted from two larger corpora, in order to obtain a diverse vocabulary:

- The IFD corpus mostly contains literary texts (Pind et al., 1991). It was first published in book form and is now available online. This corpus has been manually PoS tagged and lemmatized.
- The Icelandic Gold Standard (GOLD) is a PoS tagged and manually corrected corpus of around 1,000,000 tokens, containing a balanced sample of contemporary texts from 13 sources, including news texts, laws and adjucations, as well as various web content such as blog texts (Loftsson et al., 2010).

Samples were extracted at random from these two corpora, roughly 10,000 tokens from each, and the lemmas manually reviewed, following the criteria laid out in the preface of the IFD (Pind et al., 1991).

The incentive when performing the evaluation was to create a diverse corpus of text samples containing foreign words, misspellings and other OOV words. Such words are likely to appear in real-world NLP tasks, and pose special problems for lemmatizers. In the proofread and literature-heavy IFD corpus, which was used for training and

Gold tags		IceTagger tags	
Accuracy (%)	Errors	Accuracy (%)	Errors
99.55	94	96.88	658

Table 1: Results of the evaluation, with the accuracy and the total number of errors found.

evaluating the previous two lemmatizers, these OOV words are less prevalent. Consequently, the test corpus used here is not directly comparable with the corpus used to evaluate Lemmald and the CST Lemmatizer for Icelandic. On the other hand, it is more diverse and offers more challenging problems for the lemmatizer.

One of the motivations of this work was to determine how well Nefnir performs when lemmatizing text which has been PoS tagged automatically, without any manual review, as such manual labour is usually not feasible in large-scale NLP tasks. For this purpose, we created two versions of the test corpus, one with the correct PoS tags, and another tagged using IceTagger (Loftsson, 2008). The accuracy of IceTagger is further enhanced using data from the DMII. Measured against the correct PoS tags, the accuracy of the PoS tags in the reference corpus is 95.47%.

Accuracy of the lemmatizaton was measured by comparing the reference corpus lemmas with the obtained lemmas from Nefnir. This was done for both the correctly tagged corpus (gold tags) and the automatically tagged one (IceTagger tags). As seen in Table 1, the accuracy for the test file with the correct PoS tags is 99.55%, with 94 errors in 21,093 tokens. For the text tagged automatically with IceTagger, the accuracy is 96.88%, with 658 errors.

These results indicate that given correct PoS tags, Nefnir obtains high accuracy, with under a hundred errors in the whole corpus sample. This is comparable to the score reported for Lemmald, when DMII lookup has been added (99.55%). In fact, it can be argued that a higher score is hard to come by, as natural language always contains some unforeseen issues that are hard to accommodate for, such as OOV words, misspellings, colloquialisms, etc. When Nefnir bases its lemmas on the automatically PoS tagged text, the accuracy decreases, from 99.55% to 96.88%, resulting in six times as many errors.

We can classify the errors made by Nefnir into the following main categories:

1. Foreign words
2. Proper names
3. Two valid lemmas for word form
4. Typos
5. Incorrect capitalization, abbreviations, hyphenation, etc.
6. Unknown Icelandic words
7. Wrong PoS tag leads to wrong lemma

The most prevalent error categories when the PoS tags are correct are foreign words and proper names, such as foreign names of people, products and companies. A special issue that often came up is the cliticized definite article in Icelandic proper names. This is quite common in organization names (*Síminn*, *Samfylkingin*), titles of works of art (*Svanurinn*), names of ships (*Vonin*), buildings (*Kringlan*), etc. Ultimately, it depends on the aim of the lemmatization how these should be handled, but in this evaluation we assume as a general rule that they should be lemmatized with the definite article (*Síminn*, and not *sími* or *Sími*). The same applies to the plural, in names such as *Hjálmar* "helmets" (band) and *Katlar* (place name).

In the automatically tagged data, tagging errors are the most common source of lemmatization errors, such as when *læknum* (referring to the plural dative of the masculine noun *læknir* "doctor") is tagged as being in the singular, which leads to it being incorrectly lemmatized as *lækur* "brook". This was to be expected, as the rules learned from the DMII rely on the correct tagging of the input. However, as the authors of Lemmald comment, as long as the word class is correct, the lemmatizer can usually still find the correct lemma (Ingason et al., 2008).

The main reason for the high accuracy in our view lies in the richness of the DMII data. No lexicon can ever include all words of a particular language, as new words appear every day, but most often, new words in Icelandic are compounds, created from words already present in the DMII. This explains how rare or unknown words such as the adjective *fuglglaður* "bird-happy", which appears in the corpus data, can be correctly lemmatized using the suffix rule for *glaður* "happy".

As mentioned above, Nefnir, the CST Lemmatizer for Icelandic, and Lemmald have not been evaluated using the same reference corpus. The accuracy of the three lemmatizers are, therefore, not directly comparable, but our results indicate that Nefnir obtains the highest accuracy.

5   Conclusion

We described and evaluated Nefnir, a new open source lemmatizer for Icelandic. It uses suffix substitution rules, derived from a large morphological database, to lemmatize tagged text. Evaluation shows that Nefnir obtains high accuracy for both correctly and automatically PoS-tagged input.

As taggers for Icelandic gradually get better, we can expect to see the lemmatization accuracy go up as well. Expanding the morphological database with more proper names may also help to achieve even higher accuracy.

References

Toms Bergmanis and Sharon Goldwater. 2018. Context sensitive neural lemmatization with Lematus. In *Proceedings of the 2018 Conference of the North American Chapter of the Association for Computational Linguistics: Human Language Technologies, Volume 1 (Long Papers)*, New Orleans, Louisiana.

Kristín Bjarnadóttir. 2012. The Database of Modern Icelandic Inflection. In *Proceedings of the Workshop on Language Technology for Normalisation of Less-Resourced Languages (SaLTMiL 8 – AfLaT2012)*, LREC 2012, Istanbul, Turkey.

Kristín Bjarnadóttir. 2017. Phrasal compounds in Modern Icelandic with reference to Icelandic word formation in general. In Carola Trips and Jaklin Kornfilt, editors, *Further investigations into the nature of phrasal compounding*. Language Science Press, Berlin, Germany.

Frank Cassata. 2007. Automatic thesaurus extraction for Icelandic. *BSc Final Project, Department of Computer Science, Reykjavik University*.

Hercules Dalianis and Bart Jongejan. 2006. Handcrafted versus Machine-learned Inflectional Rules: The Euroling-SiteSeeker Stemmer and CST's Lemmatiser. In *Proceedings of the 5th International Conference on Language Resources and Evaluation*, LREC 2006, Genoa, Italy.

Jón F. Daðason. 2018. Nefnir. https://github.com/jonfd/nefnir.

Jan Hajič, Eduard Bejček, Alevtina Bémová, Eva Buráňová, Eva Hajičová, Jiří Havelka, Petr Homola, Jiří Kárník, Václava Kettnerová, Natalia Klyueva, Veronika Kolářová, Lucie Kučová, Markéta Lopatková, Marie Mikulová, Jiří Mírovský, Anna Nedoluzhko, Petr Pajas, Jarmila Panevová, Lucie Poláková, Magdaléna Rysová, Petr Sgall, Johanka Spoustová, Pavel Straňák, Pavlína Synková, Magda Ševčíková, Jan Štěpánek, Zdeňka Urešová, Barbora Vidová Hladká, Daniel Zeman, Šárka Zikánová, and Zdeněk Žabokrtský. 2018. Prague dependency treebank 3.5. LINDAT/CLARIN digital library at the Institute of Formal and Applied Linguistics (ÚFAL), Faculty of Mathematics and Physics, Charles University.

Sigrún Helgadóttir, Ásta Svavarsdóttir, Eiríkur Rögnvaldsson, Kristín Bjarnadóttir, and Hrafn Loftsson. 2012. The Tagged Icelandic Corpus (MÍM). In *Proceedings of the Workshop on Language Technology for Normalisation of Less-Resourced Languages (SaLTMiL 8 – AfLaT2012)*, LREC 2012, Istanbul, Turkey.

Anton Karl Ingason, Sigrún Helgadóttir, Hrafn Loftsson, and Eiríkur Rögnvaldsson. 2008. A Mixed Method Lemmatization Algorithm Using a Hierarchy of Linguistic Identities (HOLI). In *Advances in Natural Language Processing, 6th International Conference on NLP, GoTAL 2008, Proceedings*, Gothenburg, Sweden.

Bart Jongejan and Hercules Dalianis. 2009. Automatic Training of Lemmatization Rules That Handle Morphological Changes in Pre-, In- and Suffixes Alike. In *Proceedings of the Joint Conference of the 47th Annual Meeting of the ACL and the 4th International Joint Conference on Natural Language Processing of the AFNLP*, ACL '09, Suntec, Singapore.

Daniel Kondratyuk, Tomáš Gavenčiak, Milan Straka, and Jan Hajič. 2018. LemmaTag: Jointly tagging and lemmatizing for morphologically rich languages with BRNNs. In *Proceedings of the 2018 Conference on Empirical Methods in Natural Language Processing*, Brussels, Belgium.

Hrafn Loftsson. 2008. Tagging Icelandic text: A linguistic rule-based approach. *Nordic Journal of Linguistics*, 31(1):47–72.

Hrafn Loftsson and Eiríkur Rögnvaldsson. 2007. IceNLP: A Natural Language Processing Toolkit For Icelandic. In *Proceedings of InterSpeech 2007, Special session: Speech and language technology for less-resourced languages*, Antwerp, Belgium.

Hrafn Loftsson, Jökull H. Yngvason, Sigrún Helgadóttir, and Eiríkur Rögnvaldsson. 2010. Developing a PoS-tagged corpus using existing tools. In *Proceedings of 7th SaLTMiL Workshop on Creation and Use of Basic Lexical Resources for Less-Resourced Languages*, LREC 2010, Valetta, Malta.

Jesse Myrberg. 2017. finnlem. https://github.com/jmyrberg/finnlem.

Jörgen Pind, Friðrik Magnússon, and Stefán Briem. 1991. *Íslensk orðtíðnibók [The Icelandic Frequency Dictionary]*. The Institute of Lexicography, University of Iceland, Reykjavik, Iceland.

Steinþór Steingrímsson, Sigrún Helgadóttir, Eiríkur Rögnvaldsson, Starkaður Barkarson, and Jon Gudnason. 2018. Risamálheild: A Very Large Icelandic

Text Corpus. In *Proceedings of the Eleventh International Conference on Language Resources and Evaluation*, LREC 2018, Miyazaki, Japan.

Natural Language Processing in Policy Evaluation: Extracting Policy Conditions from IMF Loan Agreements

Joakim Åkerström[1]   Adel Daoud[2,3,4]   Richard Johansson[1]

[1]Department of Computer Science and Engineering, University of Gothenburg, Sweden
[2]Centre for Business Research, Cambridge Judge Business School, University of Cambridge, UK
[3]Harvard Center for Population and Development Studies, Harvard University, USA
[4]The Alan Turing Institute, London, UK
gusjoake@student.gu.se, adaoud@hsph.harvard.edu,
richard.johansson@gu.se

Abstract

Social science researchers often use text as the raw data in investigations: for instance, when investigating the effects of IMF policies on the development of countries under IMF programs, researchers typically encode structured descriptions of the programs using a time-consuming manual effort. Making this process automatic may open up new opportunities in scaling up such investigations.

As a first step towards automatizing this coding process, we describe an experiment where we apply a sentence classifier that automatically detects mentions of *policy conditions* in IMF loan agreements written in English and divides them into different types. The results show that the classifier is generally able to detect the policy conditions, although some types are hard to distinguish.

1 Introduction

In the social sciences, evaluating policies often relies on text. What is the effect of a high-ranking politician's tweet on Wall Street? What is the impact of a new economic treaty on trade between nations? What part of the treaty or the tweet induced the relevant effect? These types of policy evaluation questions often require that researchers identify the relevant text passages in large corpora.

Currently, many researchers in these fields devote considerable amounts of resources to hand-coding the relevant passages of the entire corpus of interest (King et al., 2017). For example, social scientists have recently devoted much attention to identifying the impact of macroeconomic policies. These policies affect a population's living conditions both in the short and the long term.

The International Monetary Fund (IMF) has since the 1980s been involved in setting the macroeconomic policy space for many countries. IMF's programs contain many different policies, where some might be considered more effective than others. Researchers have therefore sought to compile structured databases identifying what policies each IMF program contains. However, this requires that researches sift all these IMF policies by going through the documents of about 880 programs, between 1980 and 2014, that have been implemented in about 130 countries, and qualitatively hand-coding them (Daoud et al., 2019; Kentikelenis et al., 2016; Vreeland, 2007).

Accordingly, combining qualitative coding to guide a machine-learning powered natural language processing (NLP) tool to operate on large textual data will likely produce large benefits for the social science community. In this paper, we carry out an experiment that investigates the feasibility of developing such a system. We use the IMF research domain as a case study to evaluate the efficacy of our method.

2 Background and Related Work

Textual datasets are often used in investigations in the social sciences, but such investigations typically rely on manual qualitative coding, which is not only labor-intensive but also has the risk of introducing a methodological bias. The principles of grounded-theory has spurred ethnographic and other qualitative research. These principles aim to guide in building social science explanations from the meaning of a corpus (Strauss and Corbin, 1998). Often, this approach does not aim to build systematic coding procedures that are meant to be used in quantitative research. A spin-off of this qualitative methodology, however, called *content analysis*, addresses this gap (Evans and Aceves,

2016). A variety of content analysis has been used to produce databases. Two or more researchers are set to the task of implementing a coding schema interpreting the text and coding it up by hand. Using multiple coders help in estimating inter-coder reliability metrics for qualitative validation. Because it is labor-intensive, content analysis suits smaller-sized corpora.

However, with the rise of larger corpora, the need for automatic content analysis has emerged. This has led to a number of methodological innovations in the overlap between computer science and social science. For example, unsupervised machine learning methods such as topic modeling are often used for various social science problems (Daoud and Kohl, 2016; DiMaggio et al., 2013; Meeks and Weingart, 2012). These unsupervised methods help reduce the dimensionality of the data, but they are unsuitable when there is a clear outcome target – policy text – the researchers desire to code. For these task a number of supervised machine learning methods have been proposed (Grimmer and Stewart, 2013; King et al., 2017). Yet, although a combination of NLP and machine learning are on the rise in computer science, they have yet to fully reach their potential within a social science audience. One way of demonstrating the potential of applying NLP techniques in the social sciences is to evaluate these methods in a real application: extracting policy conditions from IMF reports.

So far, we are aware of no previous work where automated NLP methods have been applied to compile IMF policies from program documents. Most of the research uses qualitative content analysis (Kentikelenis et al., 2016). Recent approaches have been based on a combination of content analysis and a dictionary method to identify IMF food and agricultural policies (Daoud et al., 2019). Some unsupervised methods, mainly different types of topic models, have been applied to the sister organization of the IMF, namely to World Bank, to identify overarching topic changes over time (Moretti and Pestre, 2015).

3 Data and Implementation

3.1 IMF reports

The corpus used in this investigation consists of loan agreements between countries and the IMF, all written in English. These agreements form the policy foundation for the IMF and the recip-

ient government. These agreements outline the macroeconomic problems that the country is facing as well as what the IMF expects from the recipient government. These expectations are defined as a set of policy conditions. The conditions are typically outlined at the end of the loan document.

3.2 Annotation

A team of researchers have coded the policy conditions qualitatively using content analysis principles (Kentikelenis et al., 2016). Two researchers coded all of these policy documents resulting in over 54,000 individual conditions in about 880 programs over the 1978–2016 period. When they assigned conflicting codes, these issues were discussed and resolved by consensus. After all the polices were coded, the next step was to categorize all these individual conditions into overarching policy categories. The categories we consider here are *policy area*, such as finance or environment, and *policy type*, such as benchmarks, performance criteria, etc. This qualitative hand-annotated data provides the input to our supervised training.

3.3 Preprocessing

The IMF documents are stored as PDF documents, some of which required scanning and OCR. The documents go back to the late 1970s, and the quality of the OCR'd text is slightly lower in the earlier documents. Finally, all the documents were converted into plain text using the `pdftotext` tool.

The documents were then scanned to extract the text pieces that matched exactly with the hand-annotated instances. When a text piece consisted of two or more sentences, it was split up to create multiple examples of exactly one sentence each. We did not consider text pieces below the sentence level. Furthermore, all tokens were lowercased and all numeric and punctuation symbols were removed. Stop words were not removed.

3.4 Building the Classifiers

We formalized the extraction of policy conditions as a classification problem on sentences. In the simplest case, the classifier just spots the mentions of policy conditions among a document's sentences. We also extended this basic approach to two different multiclass scenarios, where the policy conditions are subdivided in different ways.

We implemented the classifiers using the scikit-learn library (Pedregosa et al., 2011). The classifiers use a tfidf-weighted feature representation based on n-grams of size one and two, without any feature selection. The classifier is a linear support vector machine with L_2 regularization and a regularization term of 1.0. A one-versus-rest approach was used for multiclass classification. Preliminary experiments using a classifier based on BERT (Devlin et al., 2019) were less successful.

4 Experiments

We carried out a number of experiments to see how well the classifier retrieves policy conditions from the IMF loan agreements, and how well different types of policy areas and policy types can be distinguished.

4.1 Finding Policy Conditions

In the first experiment, we investigated the model's capability of finding mentions of the policy conditions in the documents. This task was framed as a binary classification task where annotated text pieces were treated as a positive set while non-annotated pieces constituted a negative set. The negative examples were subsampled in a random fashion to create a balance of 20% positive examples.

We partitioned the data into training sets and test sets in two different ways. In the first case, we wanted to see how well the classifier generalizes between different countries. We assigned the documents corresponding to 80% of the countries into the training set while the remaining documents were placed in the test set. In the second case, we instead considered the question how well the classifier generalizes to newer documents; in this case, we used the oldest 80% of the documents as the training set.

The classifiers were evaluated using precision–recall curves and average precision scores (AP) to see how well they perform for different classification thresholds. Figure 1 shows the curves and AP scores obtained for the country-based and time-based partition schemes, respectively. It is readily apparent that in both cases the model outperforms a random-guess baseline, which would give an AP score of about 0.20. Furthermore, while the classifier is slightly less accurate when the test set consists of the newer documents, the difference in performance appears to be quite small as indicated by the similar AP scores.

4.2 Classifying the Policy Area

Next, we considered how well the model can classify a text piece as one of several *policy areas*. The data sampling scheme employed in this experiment was similar to the one described in 5.1, with the main difference that the policy area for each example was treated as a target attribute to create a multiclass classification task. Furthermore, the partitioning of the data into training and test sets was performed in a random fashion.

Table 1 shows the precision and recall scores obtained for each individual policy area. The precision scores are consistently higher than the corresponding recall scores. One probable cause for this tendency is the imbalance between positive and negative examples in the training set. Table 1 also shows that the results obtained for some policy areas are remarkably low, with redistributive policies being the most obvious example. The most likely explanation for this phenomenon is the imbalance in the number of training instances per class. Figure 2 compares the F_1 scores for the different policy areas to the number of training examples. While the curve is not perfectly smooth, it is clearly visible that the F_1 score increases quite rapidly with the number of training examples, especially in the lower range of the domain.

Policy area	Precision	Recall
Debt	1.000	0.280
Environment	0.750	0.353
External	0.875	0.491
Finance	0.824	0.618
Fiscal	0.880	0.523
Institutional	0.958	0.354
Labor	0.864	0.520
Redistributive	0.000	0.000
Privatization	0.745	0.522
Revenues	0.863	0.548
SOE	0.918	0.421
Social	0.833	0.469
Other	1.000	0.158

Table 1: Policy area classification scores.

4.3 Classifying the Type of Condition

In the final experiment, we evaluated how well the model distinguishes policy conditions by the *policy type*: indicative benchmark (IB), prior action (PA), quantitative performance criterion (QPC), structural benchmark (SB), or structural perfor-

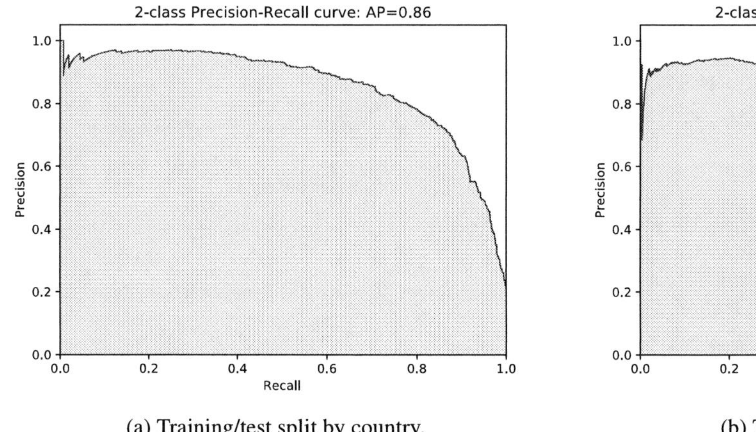
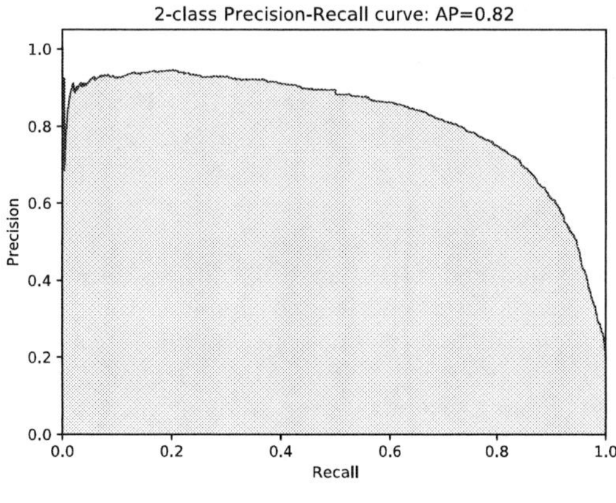

(a) Training/test split by country.   (b) Training/test split by date.

Figure 1: Precision–recall curves for detecting policy conditions.

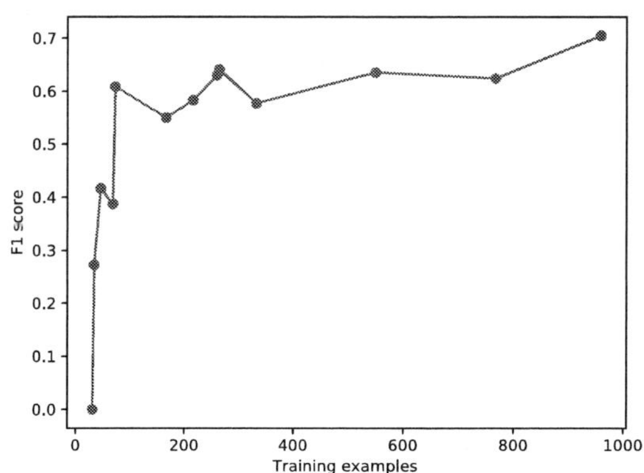

Figure 2: Classification F_1 scores for policy areas as a function of the number of training examples.

Policy type	Precision	Recall
IB	0.955	0.963
PA	0.762	0.535
QPC	0.833	0.269
SB	0.720	0.420
SPC	0.913	0.583

Table 2: Policy type classification scores.

mance criterion (SPC). The partitioning of the data was done in a similar way as in §4.2, with the only difference that policy type was designated as the target attribute. Table 2 shows the precision and recall scores obtained for each individual policy type. As in the experiment on classifying examples according to policy area, the precision scores are consistently higher than the corresponding recall scores and we propose the same explanation for this phenomenon as in §4.2.

5   Conclusions

We have evaluated a sentence classification approach as a supporting technology in a social science research scenario. Our results are promising and show that a straightforward sentence classifier is quite successful in detecting mentions of policy conditions in IMF loan agreements, as well as distinguishing different policy areas and policy types, although the rarer classes are more difficult for our system. This work can be seen as a preparatory effort for the main goal of automatizing coding-based methods in social science, and a more ambitious goal will be to actually apply the classifier in a research scenario and see how the conclusions are affected by the use of an automatic system.

Our use case is just one of many where text processing methods open up new opportunities for changing the way social scientists work with text as research data. Another example is to identify what policies exist around the world: UCLA's WORLD Policy Analysis Center continuously sifts through all the legislation of the world's governments to identify the variation of social, environmental, and economic policies. This includes identifying policies concerning the level of minimum wage, anti-poverty policies, gender inequality, and maternal and child health. These coding procedures require a considerably large team and training to conduct, and this is another scenario where NLP techniques could probably facilitate text-based research in social science.

319

Acknowledgments

Richard Johansson was supported by the Swedish Research Council under grant 2013–4944.

References

Adel Daoud and Sebastian Kohl. 2016. How much do sociologists write about economic topics? Using big-data to test some conventional views in economic sociology, 1890 to 2014. Technical report, Max Planck Institute for the Study of Societies. Discussion Paper.

Adel Daoud, Bernhard Reinsberg, Alexander E. Kentikelenis, Thomas H. Stubbs, and Lawrence P. King. 2019. The international monetary fund's interventions in food and agriculture: An analysis of loans and conditions. *Food Policy*.

Jacob Devlin, Ming-Wei Chang, Kenton Lee, and Kristina Toutanova. 2019. BERT: Pre-training of deep bidirectional transformers for language understanding. In *Proceedings of the 2019 Annual Conference of the North American Chapter of the Association for Computational Linguistics (NAACL)*.

Paul DiMaggio, Manish Nag, and David Blei. 2013. Exploiting affinities between topic modeling and the sociological perspective on culture: Application to newspaper coverage of u.s. government arts funding. *Poetics*, 41(6):570–606.

James A. Evans and Pedro Aceves. 2016. Machine translation: Mining text for social theory. *Annual Review of Sociology*, 42(1):21–50.

Justin Grimmer and Brandon Stewart. 2013. Text as data: The promise and pitfalls of automatic content analysis methods for political texts. *Political Analysis*, 21(3):267–297.

Alexander E. Kentikelenis, Thomas H. Stubbs, and Lawrence P. King. 2016. Imf conditionality and development policy space, 1985-2014. *Review of International Political Economy*, (Online first).

Gary King, Patrick Lam, and Margaret E. Roberts. 2017. Computer-assisted keyword and document set discovery from unstructured text. *American Journal of Political Science*.

Elijah Meeks and Scott Weingart. 2012. The digital humanities contribution to topic modeling. *Journal of Digital Humanities*, 2(1).

Franco Moretti and Dominique Pestre. 2015. Bankspeak. *New Left Review*, (92):75–99.

Fabian Pedregosa, Gaël Varoquaux, Alexandre Gramfort, Vincent Michel, Bertrand Thirion, Olivier Grisel, Mathieu Blondel, Peter Prettenhofer, Ron Weiss, Vincent Dubourg, Jake VanderPlas, Alexandre Passos, David Cournapeau, Matthieu Brucher, Matthieu Perrot, and Edouard Duchesnay. 2011. Scikit-learn: Machine learning in Python. *Journal of Machine Learning Research*, 12:2825–2830.

Anselm L. Strauss and Juliet M. Corbin. 1998. *Basics of qualitative research: techniques and procedures for developing grounded theory*, 2nd edition. SAGE, London and New Delhi.

James Raymond Vreeland. 2007. *The International Monetary Fund: politics of conditional lending*. Routledge, Taylor & Francis Group, New York, NY.

Interconnecting lexical resources and word alignment:
How do learners get on with particle verbs?

David Alfter[1] **& Johannes Graën**[1,2]

[1]Språkbanken, Department of Swedish, University of Gothenburg

[2]Grael, Department of Translation and Language Sciences, Pompeu Fabra University

Abstract

In this paper, we present a prototype for an online exercise aimed at learners of English and Swedish that serves multiple purposes. The exercise allows learners of these languages to train their knowledge of particle verbs receiving clues from the exercise application. At the same time, we collect information which will help us judge the accuracy of our graded word lists. As resources, we use lists with annotated levels from the proficiency scale defined by the Common European Frame work of Reference (CEFR) and a multilingual corpus with syntactic dependency relations and word alignments for all language pairs. From the latter resource, we extract translation equivalents for particle verb constructions together with a list of parallel corpus examples that are used as clues in the exercise.

1 Introduction

Combinations of verbs and particles have been studied extensively in various aspects, e.g. particle placement with regard to cognitive processes (Gries, 2003), the relation between syntactical and semantic structure (Roßdeutscher, 2011) and their compositionality with respect to syntactic argument structure (Bott and Schulte im Walde, 2015). In the field of language learning, verb-particle combinations have been investigated in matters of their use of language learners of English (EFL) (Gilquin, 2015; Liao and Fukuya, 2004), also in comparison to native language speakers (Schneider and Gilquin, 2016) and with regard to pedagogical suggestions for language learning and teaching (Gardner and Davies, 2007).

The term 'phrasal verb' is used in most publications to refer to an English verb-particle combination that "behaves as a semantic unit" (Gilquin, 2015), while for other (mostly Germanic) languages term such as 'verb-particle constructions', 'verb-particle expressions' (Toivonen, 2002) or simply 'particle verbs' prevail (Zeller, 2001). Dehé (2015) compares particle verbs in Germanic languages and regards these terms as synonyms. We will thus refer to construction of verb and particle as particle verbs.

Particle verbs are especially difficult for learners since they present no discernible pattern in the selection of the particle. Gardner and Davies (2007) observe that "many nonnative English speakers actually avoid using phrasal verbs altogether, especially those learners at the beginning and intermediate levels of proficiency." Not all verbs and particles are equally likely to take part in particle verbs. In English, "a number of lexical verbs such as take, get, come, put and go are particularly productive and frequent when they combine with adverbial particles" (Deshors, 2016). Gardner and Davies (2007) recommend learners to memorize those verbs and particles that occur frequently in verb-particle combinations.

Recently, so-called Games With A Purpose (GWAPs) (Lafourcade et al., 2015) have been used to collect information from players while offering a ludic interface that promotes participation. For example, JeuxDeMots (Lafourcade and Joubert, 2008; Lafourcade, 2007) has been used to find lexico-semantic relations between words, ZombiLingo (Fort et al., 2014) for the annotation of dependency syntax in French corpora, RigorMortis (Fort et al., 2018) for the identification of multiword expression by (untrained) learners, relying on their subjective opinion.

With the six reference levels of the Common European Framework of Reference (CEFR) (Council of Europe, 2001), henceforth CEFR levels, we can classify learners according to their level of proficiency. In Section 2.1, we introduce two resources that we build upon, which provide lists of vocabulary units together with their estimated distribution over CEFR levels. In Section 2.2, we explain how we look up translation equivalents in several languages in a word-aligned multiparallel corpus, followed by a manual re-assessment step described in Section 2.4.

In continuation, we present an application that implements a gamified exercise based on particle verbs in English and Swedish, their translation equivalents and corpus examples that demonstrate their use in authentic translations (Section 3). Learners playing the game try to not lose while the game automatically adapts to their current predicted knowledge level. The application keeps track of decisions taken by the user during the course of the game to provide them with feedback regarding their language skills, and points to potential weaknesses and (language-specific) factors for confusions. At the same time, we expect that a sufficiently large collection of decisions will help us assess the CEFR levels of our lexical resources and provide insights for future extensions.

2 Data Preparation

We extract particle verbs for CEFR levels from A1 to C1 from two lexical resources, one for English and one for Swedish.[1] For each particle verb that we find in these resources, we look up potential translation variants for several other languages, from a large multilingual word-aligned corpus. Since word alignment is less reliable when it comes to function words, we need to review the lists of translation variants and adjust word order and missing function words in multiword variants manually.

2.1 Lexical Resources

The CEFRLex project[2] offers lists of expressions extracted from graded textbook corpora for different languages. The languages currently available are French, Swedish and English. For this project, we use the Swedish list SVALex (François et al., 2016) and the English list EFLLex (Dürlich and François, 2018) from the CEFRLex project. Each resource lists single-word and multi-word expressions, as recognized by a syntactic parser, and their frequency in textbooks of different CEFR levels. Table 1 shows examples from the EFLLex list.

We extract particle verbs from both lists. For EFLLex, we use regular expressions to match all two-word expressions that are tagged as verbs. Manual inspection of the results shows that most expressions extracted this way are indeed particle verbs; we only had to exclude four expressions.[3]

For SVALex, we consider the subset of expressions tagged as verbal multi-word expressions. Since not all verbal multi-word expressions are particle verbs, we cross-check for the existence of each expression in the upcoming version of Saldo,[4] which includes particle verbs. Upon manual inspection of the resulting list we removed two reflexive particle verbs.[5] In total, we extracted 221 English and 362 Swedish particle verbs. As we are, among other things, interested in seeing how CEFR levels correlate with self-proclaimed proficiency, we assign each particle verb the CEFR level at which it first occurs in the respective resource, as has been previously done in various other experiments (Gala et al., 2013, 2014; Alfter et al., 2016; Alfter and Volodina, 2018).

2.2 Translation Equivalents from Parallel Corpus Data

The exercise is based on finding the correct particle for a particle verb in the target language based on translations in the source language. In other words, it means that, for example, learners of Swedish (target language) with knowledge of English (source language) will have to guess Swedish particle verbs based on English translations. For identifying translation equivalents in multiple languages, we use the Sparcling corpus (Graën, 2018; Graën et al., 2019), which, in addition to standard annotation such as part-of-speech tagging, features dependency relations from syntactic parsing in a number of languages (including English and Swedish) and bilingual word alignment for all language pairs. We use dependency relations to identify pairs of particles and their head verb matching the list that we extracted from EFLLex and SVALex.

For each occurrence of those pairs in the corpus, we look up aligned tokens in all other languages available to spot corresponding translation equivalents. We then filter the aligned tokens for content

---

[1]No particle verb has been classified as C2.
[2]http://cental.uclouvain.be/cefrlex/

[3]Those are 'finger count', 'deep fry', 'go lame' and 'tap dance', which use other part of speech than particles.
[4]https://spraakbanken.gu.se/eng/resource/saldo
[5]To wit 'ge sig ut' *'go out'* and 'klamra sig fast' *'cling to'*.

Expression	PoS	A1	A2	B1	B2	C1	C2
video	noun	65.19	0	67.87	81.76	111.06	90.93
write	verb	758.66	1421.51	1064.47	682.26	1104.72	1053.96
empty	adjective	0	28.83	28.65	102.29	37.84	61.88
shopping center	noun	0	45.12	9.80	0	15.50	11.45
dream up	verb	0	0	0	0	0.82	0.24

Table 1: Example entries from EFLLex.

words, that is, in terms of universal part-of-speech tags (Petrov et al., 2012), verbs, nouns, adjectives or adverbs. Functional parts of multi-word expressions are notoriously misaligned if the syntactic patterns of the corresponding expressions differ. For instance, English 'to cry out (for sth.)' can be expressed in Spanish with the fixed expression 'pedir (algo) a gritos'. In this case, we often see 'cry' aligned with 'pedir' and 'gritos', and the particle 'out' with the preposition 'a'. A similar expression is 'llevar (algo) a cabo' *'get through (sth.)'*, where 'carry' is aligned with 'llevar' and 'out' with 'cabo'; the preposition 'a' often remains unaligned in this case.

By filtering out function words, we systematically miss any preposition, determiner or particle that forms part of the equivalent expression. Not filtering them out, on the other hand, leads to considerably noisier lists. The missing functional parts need to be added back later and the set of lemmas needs be put in the preferred lexical order (see Section 2.4). We retrieve lemmas of the aligned tokens as a set, disregarding their relative position in the text, and calculate frequencies for each translation equivalent. Translation equivalents are most frequently single verbs. The Swedish particle verb 'ha kvar' (literally *'have left'*), for instance, is aligned to the English verbs 'retain' 49 times, to 'maintain' 31 times and to 'remain' 26 times.

2.3 Example Sentence Selection

Alongside other options (see Section 3), we want to provide learners with authentic examples where the given particle verb is used as translation of a particular expression in another language. We typically find several example sentences per translation correspondence in the Sparcling corpus. The question now is how to select the most adequate one for the respective learner. In previous works, we have used the length of the candidate sentence pair as ranking criterion, downgrad-

ing those pairs that showed a substantial deviation in length (Schneider and Graën, 2018; Clematide et al., 2016).

While there is a substantial amount of previous work on finding good example sentences for use in dictionaries (e.g. GDEX (Kilgarriff et al., 2008)) or for language learners (e.g. HitEx (Pilán et al., 2017)), most of the features they use are language-specific, such as blacklists, 'difficult' vocabulary, or recognizing and excluding anaphoric expressions without referent in the same sentence.

For the purpose of this study, we have thus opted for a simple heuristics which works well across a number of different languages. We use sentence length and a weighted measure for lexical proficiency required to understand the target language sentence (since we do not have gradings for most of the source languages).

2.4 Manual Revision

Manual correction involves the removal of irrelevant translations, the re-ordering of words, in case a particle verb has been aligned to multiple other words, and the insertion of missing words into the translation variants (as in 'llevar *a* cabo'). In addition, we judge example sentences with regard to adequacy.

While the translation candidate extraction could be restricted to allow only verbal translations for particle verbs, this is a constraint that we do not want to impose. Indeed, certain languages tend towards more nominal ways of expression while other languages tend towards more verbal ways of expression (Azpiazu Torres, 2006). Thus, imposing such a constraint could possibly induce non-idiomatic or unnatural translation candidates.

Having multiple part-of-speech possibilities for translation variants also allows us to potentially control the difficulty of the exercise by only giving verbal translation variants to beginners while, as the learner progresses and improves, other part-of-speech variants could be included.

3   Crowdsourcing and Gamification

We use our gamified system to assess knowledge of language learners in their L2 (English or Swedish), and to judge the accuracy of the automatically assigned CEFR labels. The game presents one base verb each round, together with a list of particles to choose from and one initial clue in form of a translation variant for the particle verb that the player is supposed to guess. The player can gain points by choosing the right particle and loose points by choosing a wrong one. Additional clues can be traded off against points. These clues can also be example sentences in the target language or the elimination of several of the non-fitting particles.

The learner assessment is achieved by monitoring how players of certain self-proclaimed proficiency levels deal with expressions that they are supposed to master, according to the automatic CEFR level assignment method. If learners systematically struggle with expressions of their self-chosen proficiency level, we assume that they overvalued their level and provide feedback accordingly. If they show little or no difficulties in dealing with expressions deemed of their current self-proclaimed proficiency level, we assume that their actual proficiency is higher, and gradually increase the challenge by using particle verbs of higher levels and more difficult clues (e.g. less frequent translation variants).

The accuracy of the automatically assigned CEFR labels is measured by aggregating results over all players. We also take into account response times for individual exercises. Significantly large deviance from the average answering time or the average number of points used for 'trading' clues for particle verbs of the supposedly same proficiency level suggests that the particle verb in question could belong to a different level.

Before the actual game starts, learners have to choose the language that they want to train. They are also asked to indicate their mother tongue and any other languages they know, including a self-assessment of their proficiency in the respective languages (beginner, intermediate, advanced). This rough scale is translated to the levels A1 and A2, B1 and B2 and C1 respectively.

Having finished the self assessment, the learner gets a predefined amount of points, as a virtual currency. More points can be gained each round by finding the right particle for the given verb with as few clues as possible. A wrong answer is worth an equally negative amount of points that could have been gained by choosing the right answer. We employ a function to calculate the reward based on hints used and difficulty of the hints in terms of language knowledge, i.e. a clue in a lower-rated language will cost the learner less points than, for instance, in his mother tongue. The game ends when the player is out of points or the game is out of particle verbs. The final score is used to create an entry on a leaderboard.

4   Discussion and Future Work

With the development of new CEFR graded multi-word expression lists, including a wider range of expressions, the exercise can be extended to other types of expressions. With the advent of CEFR graded multi-word lists in other languages, the exercise can also be extended to encompass a more diverse set of languages.

One aspect that is not specifically addressed in this study is the issue of polysemy. Indeed, a particle verb can have multiple meanings, and thus multiple different translations. This aspect will prove problematic when the particle verbs are shown in context, as one has to ensure that both the original as well as the translation pertain to the same sense of the expression.

Another question concerns the accuracy of the automatic assignment of CEFR levels based on the method used. While we surmise that we can gain insights about the accuracy of the assigned levels through the proposed prototype, a separate investigation should be carried out. One could possibly compare the automatically assigned levels from EFLLex to the levels given in English Vocabulary Profile.[6]

Acknowledgements

The authors would like to express their gratitude towards Lars Borin for making available the upcoming version of the Saldo lexical resource. This research is partly supported by the Swiss National Science Foundation under grant P2ZHP1_184212 through the project "From parallel corpora to multilingual exercises – Making use of large text collections and crowdsourcing techniques for innovative autonomous language learning applications".

---

[6]http://www.englishprofile.org

References

David Alfter, Yuri Bizzoni, Anders Agebjörn, Elena Volodina, and Ildikó Pilán. 2016. From Distributions to Labels: A Lexical Proficiency Analysis using Learner Corpora. In *Proceedings of the joint workshop on NLP for Computer Assisted Language Learning and NLP for Language Acquisition*, 130, pages 1–7. Linköping University Electronic Press.

David Alfter and Elena Volodina. 2018. Towards Single Word Lexical Complexity Prediction. In *Proceedings of the 13th Workshop on Innovative Use of NLP for Building Educational Applications (BEA)*.

Susana Azpiazu Torres. 2006. Stylistic-contrastive analysis of nominality and verbality in languages. In *Studies in Contrastive Linguistics: Proceedings of the 4th International Contrastive Linguistics Conference*, 170, pages 69–77. Universidade de Santiago de Compostela.

Stefan Bott and Sabine Schulte im Walde. 2015. Exploiting Fine-grained Syntactic Transfer Features to Predict the Compositionality of German Particle Verbs. In *Proceedings of the 11th International Conference on Computational Semantics (IWCS)*, pages 34–39.

Simon Clematide, Johannes Graën, and Martin Volk. 2016. Multilingwis – A Multilingual Search Tool for Multi-Word Units in Multiparallel Corpora. In Gloria Corpas Pastor, editor, *Computerised and Corpus-based Approaches to Phraseology: Monolingual and Multilingual Perspectives – Fraseologia computacional y basada en corpus: perspectivas monolingües y multilingües*, pages 447–455. Tradulex.

Council of Europe. 2001. *Common European Framework of Reference for Languages: Learning, Teaching, Assessment*. Press Syndicate of the University of Cambridge.

Nicole Dehé. 2015. Particle verbs in Germanic. In Peter O. Müller, Ingeborg Ohnheiser, Susan Olsen, and Franz Rainer, editors, *Word-formation: an international handbook of the languages of Europe*, 40 edition, volume 1 of *Handbücher zur Sprach- und Kommunikationswissenschaft*, chapter 35, pages 611–626. De Gruyter Mouton.

Sandra C. Deshors. 2016. Inside phrasal verb constructions: A co-varying collexeme analysis of verb-particle combinations in EFL and their semantic associations. *International Journal of Learner Corpus Research*, 2(1):1–30.

Luise Dürlich and Thomas François. 2018. EFLLex: A Graded Lexical Resource for Learners of English as a Foreign Language. In *11th International Conference on Language Resources and Evaluation (LREC)*.

Karën Fort, Bruno Guillaume, and Hadrien Chastant. 2014. Creating Zombilingo, a Game With A Purpose for dependency syntax annotation. In *Gamification for Information Retrieval Workshop (GamifIR)*.

Karën Fort, Bruno Guillaume, Mathieu Constant, Nicolas Lefebvre, and Yann-Alan Pilatte. 2018. "Fingers in the Nose": Evaluating Speakers' Identification of Multi-Word Expressions Using a Slightly Gamified Crowdsourcing Platform. In *Joint Workshop on Linguistic Annotation, Multiword Expressions and Constructions*, pages 207–213.

Thomas François, Elena Volodina, Ildikó Pilán, and Anaïs Tack. 2016. SVALex: a CEFR-graded Lexical Resource for Swedish Foreign and Second Language Learners. In *10th International Conference on Language Resources and Evaluation (LREC)*.

Núria Gala, Thomas François, Delphine Bernhard, and Cédrick Fairon. 2014. Un modèle pour prédire la complexité lexicale et graduer les mots. In *21ème Traitement Automatique des Langues Naturelles*, pages 91–102.

Núria Gala, Thomas François, and Cédrick Fairon. 2013. Towards a French lexicon with difficulty measures: NLP helping to bridge the gap between traditional dictionaries and specialized lexicons. *E-lexicography in the 21st century: thinking outside the paper*.

Dee Gardner and Mark Davies. 2007. Pointing Out Frequent Phrasal Verbs: A Corpus-Based Analysis. *TESOL quarterly*, 41(2):339–359.

Gaëtanelle Gilquin. 2015. The use of phrasal verbs by French-speaking EFL learners. A constructional and collostructional corpus-based approach. *Corpus Linguistics and Linguistic Theory*, 11(1):51–88.

Johannes Graën. 2018. *Exploiting Alignment in Multiparallel Corpora for Applications in Linguistics and Language Learning*. Ph.D. thesis, University of Zurich.

Johannes Graën, Tannon Kew, Anastassia Shaitarova, and Martin Volk. 2019. Modelling large parallel corpora:the zurich parallel corpus collection. In *Proceedings of the 7th Workshop on Challenges in the Management of Large Corpora (CMLC)*.

Stefan Thomas Gries. 2003. *Multifactorial analysis in corpus linguistics: A study of particle placement*. Open Linguistics. A&C Black.

Adam Kilgarriff, Milos Husák, Katy McAdam, Michael Rundell, and Pavel Rychlỳ. 2008. GDEX: Automatically finding good dictionary examples in a corpus. In *Proceedings of the XIII EURALEX International Congress*.

Mathieu Lafourcade. 2007. Making people play for Lexical Acquisition with the JeuxDeMots prototype. In *7th International Symposium on Natural Language Processing (snlp)*, page 7.

Mathieu Lafourcade and Alain Joubert. 2008. JeuxDe-Mots: un prototype ludique pour l'émergence de relations entre termes. In *Journées internationales d'Analyse statistiques des Données Textuelles (JADT)*, pages 657–666.

Mathieu Lafourcade, Alain Joubert, and Nathalie Le Brun. 2015. *Games with a Purpose (GWAPS)*. John Wiley & Sons.

Yan Liao and Yoshinori J. Fukuya. 2004. Avoidance of phrasal verbs: The case of Chinese learners of english. *Language learning*, 54(2):193–226.

Slav Petrov, Dipanjan Das, and Ryan McDonald. 2012. A universal part-of-speech tagset. In *Proceedings of the 8th International Conference on Language Resources and Evaluation (LREC)*. European Language Resources Association (ELRA).

Ildikó Pilán, Elena Volodina, and Lars Borin. 2017. Candidate sentence selection for language learning exercises: from a comprehensive framework to an empirical evaluation. *TAL*, 57(3/2016):67–91.

Antje Roßdeutscher. 2011. Particle Verbs and Prefix Verbs in German: Linking Theory versus Word-syntax. *Leuvense Bijdragen*, 97:1–53.

Gerold Schneider and Gaëtanelle Gilquin. 2016. Detecting innovations in a parsed corpus of learner English. *International Journal of Learner Corpus Research*, 2(2):177–204.

Gerold Schneider and Johannes Graën. 2018. NLP Corpus Observatory – Looking for Constellations in Parallel Corpora to Improve Learners' Collocational Skills. In *Proceedings of the 7th workshop on NLP for Computer Assisted Language Learning (NLP4CALL)*, pages 69–78. Linköping Electronic Conference Proceedings.

Ida Toivonen. 2002. Verbal particles and results in swedish and english. In *Proceedings of the West Coast Conference in Formal Linguistics*, volume 21, pages 457–470.

Jochen Zeller. 2001. *Particle verbs and local domains*, volume 41. John Benjamins Publishing.

May I Check Again? — A simple but efficient way to generate and use contextual dictionaries for Named Entity Recognition. Application to French Legal Texts.

Valentin Barriere
Cour de Cassation
Palais de Justice
5 quai de l'horloge
75001 PARIS
valentin.barriere@justice.fr

Amaury Fouret
Cour de Cassation
Palais de Justice
5 quai de l'horloge
75001 PARIS
amaury.fouret@justice.fr

Abstract

In this paper we present a new method to learn a model robust to typos for a Named Entity Recognition task. Our improvement over existing methods helps the model to take into account the context of the sentence inside a court decision in order to recognize an entity with a typo. We used state-of-the-art models and enriched the last layer of the neural network with high-level information linked with the potential of the word to be a certain type of entity. More precisely, we utilized the similarities between the word and the potential entity candidates in the tagged sentence context. The experiments on a dataset of French court decisions show a reduction of the relative F1-score error of 32%, upgrading the score obtained with the most competitive fine-tuned state-of-the-art system from 94.85% to 96.52%.

1 Introduction

Automatic Named Entity Recognition (NER) is a task that has been tackled and tackled over the years, because of the multitude of possible applications that flow from it. It can be useful for entity information extraction (Ferré et al., 2018), for the creation of Knowledge Bases like DBPedia or for purposes of pseudonymisation (identification and replacement) in sensitive documents from the medical or the legal domain (Neamatullah et al., 2008).

In our application, the French Courts of Justice release 3800k court decisions each year. The size of this number makes the manual de-identification of each court decision helpless. Hence it is mandatory to use natural language processing NER tools to automatize the operation.

The domain of NER has considerably evolved in the last several years. The NER models can be rule-based systems using expert knowledge (Neamatullah et al., 2008), hybrid models using linguistics and domain specific cues as features of a learning method (Sutton and McCallum, 2011; Bodnari et al., 2013) or end-to-end deep learning models using distributed learned representations of words and characters (Peters et al., 2018; Lample et al., 2016).

Each method has its own advantages and drawbacks. The rule-based ones allow high precision but are nonetheless domain-specific, nor robust to noisy data and costly to design. Hybrid methods combine the robustness and the high accuracy of Machine Learning algorithms with the fine-grained information of external dictionaries or linguistic rules (Cohen and Sarawagi, 2004; Barriere, 2017). The deep learning approaches that achieve high performances relying on a big amount of training data are the most efficient nowadays (Devlin et al., 2018).

Nevertheless, even the most efficient systems struggle to manage with some kind of noise: the typos and misspelling (Kukich, 1992) are common in real-world tasks, up to 15% of the search queries (Cucerzan and Brill, 2004), and lower the performances of the NER systems (Lai et al., 2015).

In this paper, we propose a new method called MICA (May I Check Again) that improves the performances of a state-of-the-art NER model using contextual information by automatically generating contextual dictionaries of entities. We use a two-learning-step method that: learns a first NER neural network model, then uses the first network to create a list of potential entities that will be used to create new features for each word in the last layer of the second NER neural network model. We chose last layer since those new features contain high-level information regarding our task and the level of complexity increases with the depth of neural network (Sanh et al., 2019). Nevertheless, this method can also be used with a simple NER system like Conditional Random Fields, and it shows interesting results although not state-of-the-art.

The use of language-specific knowledge-source, dictionaries or gazetteers is very common for this type of task. Neelakantan and Collins (2015) also proposed to learn dictionaries of entities for NER and we distinguish our work from theirs by several points. Our method does not aim to create a dictionary of entities but instead use the entities detected in the context of each sentence in order to enhance the NER model.

Finally, we also worked on the language model embeddings in order to adapt the language models and embeddings from general domain to the legal domain. For that, we refined the BiLM Flair embeddings (Akbik et al., 2018) and trained the Fastext embeddings (Grave et al., 2018) on a dataset of 660,000 court decisions in order to adapt the language models and embeddings from general domain to the legal domain.

2   Sequence Labeling models

The method we are presenting :

1. Learn a Vanilla model for NER

2. For each sentence, create a list of potential entities using a context window

3. Create a vector of similarity values for each word between the word and each type of entities

4. Use this vector as a new feature in the last layer of the new NER neural network

As Vanilla sequence tagger model, we chose to use the work of Akbik et al. (2018) which obtained state-of-the-art results for NER, part-of-speech-tagging and chunking. This method is not specific to the use of deep learning, though adding high-level information on the last layer is perfectly adapted to our problem, but can apply to any sequence tagger model.

In order to verify this hypothesis, we also used MICA with a basic NER model composed of a Conditional Random Fields using hand-crafted features as input (Peng and Koborov, 2014).

2.1   Vanilla Model

The Vanilla model consists of a Bidirectional Long Short Term Memory coupled with a Conditional Random Field output layer (BLSTM-CRF)

(Huang et al., 2015) at the word level. The input of the BLSTM-CRF is a global vector composed of the concatenation of three different embedding vectors (see Equation 1).

Vector Stacking This global vector counts a contextualized word embedding vector obtained with a Bidirectional character-level Language Model and a word embedding vector learned independently of the NER task, and a character-level word embeddings learned jointly with the NER task, as shown below:

$$\mathbf{w}_i = \begin{bmatrix} \mathbf{w}_i^{FastText} \\ \mathbf{w}_i^{CharBiLM} \\ \mathbf{w}_i^{Char} \end{bmatrix} \tag{1}$$

where $\mathbf{w}_i^{CharBiLM}$ is the precomputed Bidirectional character-level Language Model from Akbik et al. (2018), $\mathbf{w}_i^{FastText}$ is the precomputed FastText from Grave et al. (2018) and $\mathbf{w}_i^{Char}$ the character-level word embedding learned during the task (Ma and Hovy, 2016).

BLSTM-CRF For each word, we'll obtain as output of the BLSTM a vector $\mathbf{r}_i$ (see Equation 2 where $\mathbf{r}_i^f$ and $\mathbf{r}_i^b$ are respectively the forward and backward output states).

$$\mathbf{r}_i = \begin{bmatrix} \mathbf{r}_i^f \\ \mathbf{r}_i^b \end{bmatrix} \tag{2}$$

The sequence of $\mathbf{r}_i$ vectors is used as observations for the CRF (Lafferty et al., 2001).

More details on the model can be found in (Akbik et al., 2018).

2.2   MICA

Vanilla model Once the training of the Vanilla NER model over, we create a new model with the same architecture and initialize its weights with the ones of the trained Vanilla except for the CRF last layer.

Similarity Vector For every sentence *sent* the new model sees, the Vanilla model sees a bunch of sentences from its neighborhood and create a dictionary of local entity candidates D_{sent} (see Equation 3).

$$D_{sent} = \begin{bmatrix} \text{PER} : [c_{\text{PER}}^1, ..., c_{\text{PER}}^{L_{\text{PER}}}] \\ \text{PRO} : [c_{\text{PRO}}^1, ..., c_{\text{PRO}}^{L_{\text{PRO}}}] \\ \text{LOC} : [c_{\text{LOC}}^1, ..., c_{\text{LOC}}^{L_{\text{LOC}}}] \\ \text{DATE} : [c_{\text{DATE}}^1, ..., c_{\text{DATE}}^{L_{\text{DATE}}}] \end{bmatrix} \quad (3)$$

We can create for each word $w_i \in sent$ a vector $\mathbf{s}_i$ containing the potentiality of a word being an entity of each type, computing similarity with the Damerau-Levenshtein distance d_L (Damerau, 1964; Levenshtein, 1966), and the longest common string LCS. The Damerau-Levenshtein distance is a derivative of the Levenshtein one known to be useful for misspellings detection. For each entity type, we compute the Damerau-Levenshtein similarity between the word w_i and the entity candidates, and take the maximum value. We also used a similarity based on the longest common string between the word and the most similar entity candidate c_{ENT}^*.

$$\mathbf{s}_i = \begin{bmatrix} \max_l(\text{Lev}(w_i, c_{\text{PER}}^l)) + \text{LCS}(w_i, c_{\text{PER}}^*) \\ \max_l(\text{Lev}(w_i, c_{\text{PRO}}^l)) + \text{LCS}(w_i, c_{\text{PRO}}^*) \\ \max_l(\text{Lev}(w_i, c_{\text{LOC}}^l)) + \text{LCS}(w_i, c_{\text{LOC}}^*) \\ \max_l(\text{Lev}(w_i, c_{\text{DATE}}^l)) + \text{LCS}(w_i, c_{\text{DATE}}^*) \end{bmatrix}$$
$$(4)$$

Enriched CRF Then we stack the vector s_i to the previous r_i vector which is the input of the CRF (see Equation 5).

$$\mathbf{r}_i^{\text{enhanced}} = \begin{bmatrix} \mathbf{r}_i^f \\ \mathbf{r}_i^b \\ \mathbf{s}_i \end{bmatrix} \quad (5)$$

2.3 Simple CRF

The MICA method does not necessarily need to be used with a neural network although it is appropriate, so we also experimented MICA with a simple NER model. We tested it using a simple baseline model: a Conditional Random Fields using classical hand-crafted features as input. We used all the features of the CONLL 2002 NER Tutorial of Peng and Koborov (2014) except the parts of speech that are not given in our dataset.

The configuration stays the same, with the handcrafted features vector $\mathbf{r}_i$ concatenated with the similarity vector $\mathbf{s}_i$ as input of the CRF.

3 Experiments

We tested three kind of models, that were all build upon a state-of-the-art performing system for Named Entity Recognition (Akbik et al., 2018) that we call Vanilla for reasons of simplicity. The Vanilla model is a BiLSTM-CRF taking as input different kinds of embeddings learned on general text data. We compared the Vanilla model with a model using embeddings that were fine-tuned or learned on legal text from the same domain that the text in our NER dataset. Eventually, we compare those baseline models to our models with the CRF layer enhanced with high-level similarity information.

All the models were compared on the same dataset, with the same split between the train, validation and test datasets. Each set constitutes respectively approximately 80%, 10% and 10% of the full dataset.

All the models have been implemented using Pytorch (Paszke et al., 2017) and based on the Flair toolbox (Akbik et al., 2018). The simple CRF had been implemented using pycrfsuite (Peng and Koborov, 2014).

3.1 Dataset

Our dataset is composed of 94 of real court decisions for a total of 11,209 sentences and 276,705 tokens. It has been manually annotated by a unique law expert regarding the following 4 types of entities:

1. **PER**: first and last name of the individuals,

2. **PRO**: first and last name of the court members and attorneys,

3. **LOC**: addresses concerning birthplaces and residences,

4. **DATE**: dates of birth.

Following the protocol of CONLL-2003 (Tjong et al., 2003), the dataset has been annotated with the BIO scheme (Ramshaw and Marcus, 1995) and separated into a train, a development and a test dataset. The statistics of the subdivided sets are shown in Table 1.

Examples of decision after anonymization of the PER, LOC and DATE classes can be found on the Internet website of Légifrance.

Due to the facts that a second annotation pass would be costly and that the court decisions follow a writing protocol familiar to the annotator (expert

Dataset		Train	Dev	Test	Total
# of cases		57	20	17	94
# of sentences		6,989	1,963	2,257	11,209
# of tokens		173,448	42,964	60,293	276,705
Ent	PER	1799	447	629	2875
	LOC	468	115	139	722
	PRO	750	215	243	1208
	DATE	57	9	18	84

Table 1: Description of the dataset of French court decisions with the associated entities

in law), there is no validation of the expert's annotations with an inter-agreement score.

Finally, it is important to note that it is a classical NER problem with four classes, nevertheless only the PER, LOC and DATE classes are useful for the de-identification problem.

3.2 Results

Regarding the metrics, we use the ratio of the true positives over the sums of the: true positives and false positives (precision), true positives and false negatives (recall), true positives and false positives and negatives (accuracy). The F1 is the weighted harmonic mean of the precision and the recall.

Table 2 reports the models' performances. First of all, our MICA enhanced CRF models obtain the best performances compared to their respective baselines.

Regarding the *CRF-Baseline*, the results are still far from a state-of-the-art system like the Vanilla model of (Akbik et al., 2018). Nevertheless we can see that the MICA method is improving the results, even when applied on a *CRF-Baseline*. We can note that for both the *CRF-Baseline* and the BLSTM-CRF, when the context window is too wide, the precision of the system is dropping. For a window wider than 128, the gain in recall is not sufficient anymore to counter drop of precision in order to keep a high F1.

The Vanilla model of (Akbik et al., 2018) obtains the poorest performances, but we can notice that using embeddings learned on legal domain rather than general domain helps significantly the system.

Regarding our proposed models, we can notice difference of performances regarding the size of the context used to create the dictionary of entity candidates (see Equation 3). The best model is obtained with a context size of 128.

High Recall In the case of de-identification, we need our systems to reach a high recall in order to remove any sensible information. As a matter of fact, our best model allows a reduction of the relative recall error of 40,90% compared with the fine-tuned Vanilla model.

3.3 Analysis

When analyzing our models, we witnessed several cases in which the systems we proposed improved the results over classical methods. To be more precise, we present in the subsequent few prediction divergences between the model using a context of size 0 and our best model.

Typos Obviously, our system allows to detect the entities with typos, as shown by the results highlighted in Table 2. We noticed some relevant examples of missing spaces like the one below that were not detected by the model using no context:

Whereas [MS.LAVERGNE]$_{PER}$ does not justify her situation ...

Register We noticed that when the register changes, the system can make mistakes. Especially when it happens that the entities to detect are children, they just use the first name to describe them, which is pretty uncommon for this kind of formal text. Our system can detect the name when it is presented for the first time in the text since there is the formality helping the system to detect the entity (Example 1), but struggle to detect the entity when it is in a long sentence without context (Example 2) :

(1) [Jérémy]$_{PER}$, born on February 19th, 1990.

(2) She states that [Jérémy]$_{PER}$ and [Léo]$_{PER}$ have expressed the will to ....

One drawback of this method is that if the first model is predicting a false positive, it is likely that the new model will also predict that false positive. Nevertheless, the results do not show that behavior and the rate of false positive is stable. Another drawback of our system is its inefficiency against the same words that were detected by the first models as different types of entities.

4   Conclusion and Future Works

In this paper, we introduced a new model for Named Entity Recognition. When tagging a sen-

Model	Context	Rec	Prec	F1	Acc
CRF-Baseline (Peng and Koborov, 2014)	0	79.06	92.77	85.37	74.47
MICA + *CRF-Baseline*	8	80.31	94.28	86.74	76.58
MICA + *CRF-Baseline*	128	**86.30**	**93.83**	**89.91**	**81.67**
MICA + *CRF-Baseline*	512	87.39	92.30	89.78	81.45
Vanilla (Akbik et al., 2018)	0	92.18	96.52	94.30	89.21
Vanilla + $LM_{finetuned}$	0	93.62	96.11	94.85	90.20
MICA + $LM_{finetuned}$	0	93.68	97.03	95.33	91.07
MICA + $LM_{finetuned}$	1	93.87	97.04	95.43	91.26
MICA + $LM_{finetuned}$	8	94.36	96.95	95.64	91.64
MICA + $LM_{finetuned}$	32	95.94	96.90	96.42	93.08
MICA + $LM_{finetuned}$	128	**96.23**	**96.81**	**96.52**	**93.28**
MICA + $LM_{finetuned}$	256-512	96.34	96.62	96.48	93.20

Table 2: Results with the different models on the test dataset. The Context is in number of sentences.

tence, It uses context elements in order to create a dictionary of entity candidates. This dictionary allows to compute a value corresponding to the potentiality of a word to be an entity of a certain type using the Damerau-Levenshtein distance and the longest common string distance to calculate a similarity coefficient. We tested our model on a dataset of French court decisions. Our results show a diminution of the relative recall error of more than 40% compared to a fine-tuned state-of-the-art system while also slightly augmenting the precision.

We have in mind several improvements of our system, regarding the creation of the entities dictionary, the similarity function and the embeddings used.

A possible improvement of our system to obtain a more accurate dictionary of entity candidates could be to use the full document instead of a document-blind context window to create the dictionary of the entity candidates. We can see that a window size larger than 128 reduces the performance.

Regarding the similarity function, it could be interesting to use the word embeddings generated by the character embeddings neural network with a cosine similarity. This would be an improvement over using only string-based similarities and take advantage of the robustness to noise of the character embeddings.

Recently, (Edizel et al., 2019) proposed a new method to upgrade the Fastext embeddings in order to make them robust to misspelled words. It could be interesting to improve our system by replacing the classical Fastext embeddings into the vector of stacked embeddings with the ones of (Edizel et al., 2019). We leave this improvement for future work.

Finally, since our system is domain-agnostic and language-agnostic we strongly want to compare it on other classical open-domain NER datasets with different languages (Tjong et al., 2003).

Acknowledgments

We would like to thank Pavel Soriano and Cédric Malherbe for the insighful discussions and helpful comments. The authors of this work have been funded by the EIG program of the State in the context of the OpenJustice project.

References

Alan Akbik, Duncan Blythe, and Roland Vollgraf. 2018. Contextual String Embeddings for Sequence Labeling.

Valentin Barriere. 2017. Hybrid Models for Opinion Analysis in Speech Interactions. In *ICMI*, pages 647–651.

Andreea Bodnari, Louise Deléger, Thomas Lavergne, Aurélie Névéol, and Pierre Zweigenbaum. 2013. A supervised named-entity extraction system for medical text. *CEUR Workshop Proceedings*, 1179:1–8.

William W. Cohen and Sunita Sarawagi. 2004. Exploiting dictionaries in named entity extraction. page 89.

Silviu Cucerzan and Eric Brill. 2004. Spelling correction as an iterative process that exploits the collective knowledge of web users. In *Proceedings of the 2004 Conference on Empirical Methods in Natural Language Processing.*

Fred J. Damerau. 1964. A technique for computer detection and correction of spelling errors. *Communications of the ACM*, 7(3):171–176.

Jacob Devlin, Ming-wei Chang, Kenton Lee, and Kristina Toutanova. 2018. BERT: Pre-training of Deep Bidirectional Transformers for Language Understanding.

Bora Edizel, Aleksandra Piktus, Piotr Bojanowski, Rui Ferreira, Edouard Grave, and Fabrizio Silvestri. 2019. Misspelling Oblivious Word Embeddings.

Arnaud Ferré, Louise Deléger, Pierre Zweigenbaum, and Claire Nédellec. 2018. Combining rule-based and embedding-based approaches to normalize textual entities with an ontology. *11th edition of Language Resources and Evaluation Conference, LREC'18*, pages 3443–3447.

Edouard Grave, Piotr Bojanowski, Prakhar Gupta, Armand Joulin, and Tomas Mikolov. 2018. Learning Word Vectors for 157 Languages. pages 1–5.

Zhiheng Huang, Wei Xu, and Kai Yu. 2015. Bidirectional LSTM-CRF Models for Sequence Tagging.

Karen Kukich. 1992. Technique for automatically correcting words in text. *ACM Computing Surveys*, 24(4):377–439.

John D Lafferty, Andrew McCallum, and Fernando C N Pereira. 2001. Conditional Random Fields: Probabilistic Models for Segmenting and Labeling Sequence Data. *Proceedings of the Eighteenth International Conference on Machine Learning*, pages 282–289.

Kenneth Lai, Maxim Topaz, Foster Goss, and Li Zhou. 2015. Automated misspelling detection and correction in clinical free-text records. *Journal of Biomedical Informatics*.

Guillaume Lample, Miguel Ballesteros, Sandeep Subramanian, Kazuya Kawakami, and Chris Dyer. 2016. Neural Architectures for Named Entity Recognition.

Vladimir I. Levenshtein. 1966. Binary codes capable of correcting deletions, insertions, and reversals. *Soviet Physics Doklady*.

Xuezhe Ma and Eduard Hovy. 2016. End-to-end Sequence Labeling via Bi-directional LSTM-CNNs-CRF. In *ACL*.

Ishna Neamatullah, Margaret M. Douglass, Li Wei H. Lehman, Andrew Reisner, Mauricio Villarroel, William J. Long, Peter Szolovits, George B. Moody, Roger G. Mark, and Gari D. Clifford. 2008. Automated de-identification of free-text medical records. *BMC Medical Informatics and Decision Making*, 8(September 2014).

Arvind Neelakantan and Michael Collins. 2015. Learning Dictionaries for Named Entity Recognition using Minimal Supervision. In *EACL*, pages 452–461.

Adam Paszke, Sam Gross, Soumith Chintala, and G Chanan. 2017. Pytorch: Tensors and dynamic neural networks in python with strong gpu acceleration.

Terry Peng and Mikhail Koborov. 2014. Pycrfsuite.

Matthew E. Peters, Mark Neumann, Luke Zettlemoyer, and Wen-tau Yih. 2018. Dissecting Contextual Word Embeddings: Architecture and Representation. pages 1499–1509.

Lance Ramshaw and Mitchell Marcus. 1995. Text Chunking Using Transformation-Based Learning. In *ACL Workshop on Very Large Corpora*.

Victor Sanh, Thomas Wolf, and Sebastian Ruder. 2019. A Hierarchical Multi-task Approach for Learning Embeddings from Semantic Tasks. In *AAAI Conference on Artificial Intelligence (AAAI-19)*.

Charles Sutton and Andrew McCallum. 2011. An Introduction to Conditional Random Fields. *Machine Learning*, 4(4):267–373.

Erik F. Tjong, Kim Sang, and Fien De Meulder. 2003. Introduction to the CoNLL-2003 Shared Task: Language-Independent Named Entity Recognition. In *CoNLL*.

Predicates as Boxes in Bayesian Semantics for Natural Language

Jean-Philippe Bernardy, Rasmus Blanck, Stergios Chatzikyriakidis, Shalom Lappin,
and **Aleksandre Maskharashvili**
Gothenburg University, Department of philosophy,
linguistics and theory of science,
Centre for linguistics and studies in probability

`firstname.lastname@gu.se`

Abstract

In this paper, we present a Bayesian approach to natural language semantics. Our main focus is on the inference task in an environment where judgments require probabilistic reasoning. We treat nouns, verbs, adjectives, etc. as unary predicates, and we model them as boxes in a bounded domain. We apply Bayesian learning to satisfy constraints expressed as premises. In this way we construct a model, by specifying boxes for the predicates. The probability of the hypothesis (the conclusion) is evaluated against the model that incorporates the premises as constraints.

1 Introduction

Goodman et al. (2008) interpret natural language expressions as probabilistic programs, which are evaluated through Markov chain Monte Carlo (MCMC) methods. This technique assigns meanings to various phenomena, including graded adjectives (Lassiter and Goodman, 2017). Bernardy et al. (2019, 2018) combine this approach with the idea (present in much recent computational linguistic literature (Mikolov et al., 2013, 2018; Pennington et al., 2014) (but which can be traced back to Gärdenfors (1990)) that individuals are encoded as points in a multidimensional space. Using this approach they construct Bayesian models of inference for natural language. While these models work well for many cases, they generate serious complexity problems for others.

In this paper we propose a simplified geometric model that allows us to reduce the need for sampling, and the complexity that it can create. In certain cases we eliminate sampling altogether. We model properties as (unions of) boxes, and we identify individuals as points. To estimate the probability of a predication being true, we determine the likelihood that an individual, a set of individuals, or another property is contained in a box corresponding to a predicate. This framework gives us a more tractable procedure for evaluating the probability of sentences exhibiting the same syntactic and semantic constructions that the approaches proposed by Bernardy et al. (2019, 2018) cover, but it extends to all representations of predicates in a probabilistic language.

The alternative system for evaluating arguments that we propose brings us closer to the prospect of a wide coverage probabilistic natural language inference system. Such a system will be useful for the Recognising Textual Entailment task (Dagan et al., 2009), which encompasses non-logical arguments based on real world knowledge and lexical semantics. It can also be applied in other NLP tasks that rely on probabilistic assessment of inference.

2 Interpretation of predicates as boxes

An underlying assumption of a Bayesian interpretation of natural language is that one has an (immanent) space of all (relevant) individuals, and predicates are represented as measurable subspaces of this space.

We treat every linguistic predicate as a box in an n-dimensional euclidean space. (A scaled n-cube whose faces are orthogonal to the axes.) To simplify computing the volume of a box, we also take the underlying space of individuals itself to be a box of a uniform density. Without loss of generality, we can assume that this box is of dimension 1 in all directions, and it is centred at the origin. We denote this unit box by U.

Formally, with each predicate P we associate two vectors of dimension n, P^c and P^d, where P^c is the centre of the box and P_i^d is the (positive) width of the box in dimension i. Hence, the subspace associated with P is the subspace $S(P)$

given by

$$P(x) = \forall i.||x_i - P_i^c|| < P_i^d$$

Note that $S(P)$ itself never extends past the complete space:

$$S(P) = U \cap \left\{ x \middle| \forall i.||x_i - P_i^c|| < P_i^d \right\}$$

(A box could isomorphically be defined using lower and higher bounds P^l and P^h with $P^c = 0.5(P^h + P^l)$ and $P^d = 0.5(P^h - P^l)$).

Typically, P^c and P^d will be themselves sampled. In our experiments, P_i^c is taken in the uniform distribution on $[0, 1]$, while $1/P_i^d$ is taken in a beta distribution with parameters $a = 2, b = 8$.

2.1 Relative clauses

Boxes are closed under intersections. Thus if we use the expression $P \wedge Q$ to denote the intersection of the predicates P and Q, we have $(P \wedge Q)_i^l = \max(P_i^l, Q_i^l)$ and $(P \wedge Q)_i^h = \min(P_i^h, Q_i^h)$. The centre and the width of the box ($(P \wedge Q)^c$ and $(P \wedge Q)^d$ respectively) are recovered using the habitual formula.

2.2 Quantifiers

With this in place, we can interpret quantifiers. In classical formal semantics the phrase "every P is Q" is interpreted by

$$\forall x.P(x) \rightarrow Q(x)$$

A naive translation of this formula yields:

$$\forall x.(\forall i.||x_i - P_i^c|| < P_i^d) \rightarrow (\forall i.||x_i - Q_i^c|| < Q_i^d)$$

Enforcing this condition *as such* in a probabilistic programming language is expensive. It requires:

1. Sampling an individual x.

2. Verifying if x satisfies the hypothesis ($P(x)$). If not, go back to point 1.

3. Check if x satisfies the conclusion ($Q(x)$). If not, stop, otherwise loop back to point 1.

Typically this loop is iterated thousands of times, in order to ensure that we do not miss (too many) points x where P holds but Q does not. Even though optimisations are possible in the general case, the above algorithm is inefficient. The condition that it tests is really intended to check the

inclusion of $S(Q)$ in $S(P)$. Because both spaces are boxes, this test can be done without sampling by checking the following geometric constraint:

$$\forall i.P_i^l \leq Q_i^l \wedge P_i^h \leq Q_i^h$$

where $P^l = P^c - P^d$ and $P^h = P^c + P^d$.

2.3 Generalised quantifiers

Generalised quantifiers can also be efficiently implemented with box models. Consider the phrase "most P are Q." Following Bernardy et al. (2019, 2018), "most P are Q" can be interpreted as

$$V(P \wedge Q) \geq \theta V(P)$$

for a suitable proportion θ matching the semantics of "most" in the context. Here, $V(P)$ stands for the measure of $S(P)$ in the space of individuals. In general, this measure is given by

$$V(P) = \int \mathbf{1}(P(x)) \, \mathsf{PDF}_{Ind}(x) \, dx$$

with $\mathbf{1}(c)$ being 1 if the condition c is true and 0 otherwise. Considering that individuals are elements in a high-dimensional space, if either the density of individuals PDF_{Ind} or $P(x)$ is non-trivial, the above integral is often non-computable symbolically. (This is the case, for example, if PDF_{Ind} is a Gaussian distribution). Instead it must be approximated numerically, often using a Monte Carlo method.

By contrast, if $S(P)$ is a box in a uniform space, then we have

$$V(P) = \prod_i (P \wedge U)_i^d$$

Thus, "most P are Q" is interpreted as follows:

$$\prod_i (P \wedge Q)_i^d \geq \theta \prod_i P_i^d$$

2.4 Graded predicates

We want our models to support predicates that correspond to comparative degree properties. To accommodate these properties we associate a degree function with predicates.

The degree to which an individual x satisfies a property P is

$$s(P, x) = 1 - \max \left\{ \frac{||x_i - P_i^c||}{P_i^d} \middle| i \in [1..n] \right\}$$

This definition entails that the subspace corresponding to a predicate coincides with the space where its degree of satisfaction is positive. Formally:

$$x \in S(P) \text{ iff. } s(P, x) > 0$$

Additionally, the maximal degree of satisfaction is 1.

The phrase "x is taller then y" is interpreted as x satisfying the $Tall$ predicate to a larger degree than y:

$$s(Tall, x) > s(Tall, y).$$

Predicates formed from positive comparatives are also boxes. For example, the predicate $P(x) = [\![\text{"$x$ is taller than k"}]\!]$ for some constant individual k is a box centered at $Tall^c$ and whose widths is given by

$$Tall^d = (1 - s(Q, y))P^d$$

2.5 Negation and union

Boxes are closed under intersection, but not under negation nor union. Thus, in general, a predicate is represented by a union of disjoint boxes. If a predicate can be represented by a *single* box, we call it a *box-predicate*. Measuring the volume and checking intersection of general predicates is a straightforward combinatorial extension of the corresponding box-predicate algorithms.

However, general predicates cannot be associated with a degree, in the sense of the previous section – only box-predicates can. This limitation is in fact a welcome result. It correctly rules out phrases like "John is more not-tall than Mary" or "John is more tall or happy than Mary" as infelicitous, but sustains "John is shorter than Mary". Traditional formal semantic approaches to gradable predicates (e.g. Klein, 1980; Kennedy, 2007) have a problem excluding cases like "John is more not-tall than Mary."

3 Comparison with bisected multivariate Gaussian model

We highlight a few important differences between the present box model and the bisected multivariate Gaussian model proposed by Bernardy et al. (2018).

In the Gaussian model, individuals are represented as vectors, sampled in a multivariate Gaussian distribution of dimension k, with a zero mean and a unit covariance matrix. A (unary) linguistic predicate is represented as a pair of a bias b and a vector d: d is obtained by normalising a vector sampled in the same distribution as individuals, while b is sampled in a standard normal distribution. The interpretation of a predicate can be understood as a hyperplane orthogonal to d with b being the shortest distance from the origin to the hyperplane. An individual satisfies a predicate P if it lies on the far side of the hyperplane, as measured from the origin. Hence, every predicate partitions the vector space into two parts: one of individuals satisfying P, and one of individuals satisfying not-P.[1]

In the box model, a linguistic predicate is represented as a box, and individuals satisfy the predicate if they lie inside the boundary of the box. Here, individuals are sampled in a uniform distribution. For gradable predicates, we see here an important difference: in the Gaussian model, an individual has a higher degree of P if and only if it lies further from the origin, while in the box model, having a higher degree of P means lying closer to the center of the box.

Priors differ between the Gaussian model and the box model. In the Gaussian model, an arbitrary individual has a 0.5 chance of satisfying an arbitrary predicate when no additional information is given. In contrast, in the box model, the same situation has a 0.15 chance of holding. While these priors are somewhat arbitrarily chosen, they reflect the different geometric structures of the two models. If, in the box model, an arbitrary predicate corresponded to a box covering half the space, any additional predicate would force intuitively very non-probable configurations of the space. In particular, each additional predicate would have a lower probability of holding for an arbitrary individual.

The Gaussian model evaluates the size of a predicate by estimating the volume of the space beyond the corresponding hyperplane using MCMC sampling. Similarly, degrees of predicate inclusion (used for the interpretation of generalised quantifiers) are calculated by estimating the volume of the overlapping space. Approximation of the volumes by sampling is required since the density of individuals in the space is non-trivial. By contrast, in the box model, the volume of a predicate extension can be calculated by symbolic

---

[1] In a recent work, Bernardy et al. (2019) propose a Gaussian model in which a predicate divides the space into three disjoint sections, but we set aside a detailed comparison with that model.

means, since every such extension is a box, the surrounding space is bounded, and individuals are distributed uniformly in this space.

The evaluation of inclusion differs between the two models. In the Gaussian model, a predicate P is fully contained in a predicate Q if and only if the corresponding hyperplanes are parallel and the distance of P from the origin is greater than the distance of Q from the origin. This configuration is stochastically impossible to obtain, meaning that the system would fail to evaluate any argument with "every P is Q" among its premises. This condition can be relaxed in several ways to make it satisfiable. Bernardy et al. (2019, 2018) sample elements from P and check if all satisfy Q. The issue with this approach is that if the predicate P is far from the origin, then the density of individuals is so low that sampling does not converge in a reasonable time. Another possibility is to check that the angle between the planes defining P and Q is less than a certain threshold α. But this raises another issue: implication is no longer transitive (even if the angle between P and Q is less α and the angle between Q and R is also, it does not follow that P and R are also separated by an angle less than α.)

By contrast, the box model interprets inclusion of P in Q by placing the box for P strictly inside the boundaries of Q. This is easier to obtain, by sampling the dimensions for the box P within the box Q. As a consequence, any predicate contained in another predicate has a strictly lower chance of holding for an arbitrary individual than any arbitrary predicate has.

We did a preliminary evaluation of our model using the testsuite for probabilistic inference developed by Bernardy et al. (2019). While there is no gold standard to evaluate against, the results obtained by our model are more stable than the ones obtained from the Gaussian model. This is likely to depend on the indeterminacy introduced by sampling in the Gaussian model: increasing the number of samples would improve stability, but also lead to longer computation times.

4   Related Work

Boxes in Euclidean spaces are simple objects, and as such they have already been considered as geometric representations of predicates. Vilnis et al. (2018) use boxes to encode WordNet lexical entries (unary predicates) in order to predict hyper-

nyms. Like us, they take the distribution in the vector space to be uniform, and the probability of a predicate is defined as the volume of the corresponding box. In our work, we use a Bayesian model. It is best suited to represent a small number of predicates, and to fully model the uncertainty of the boundary for each box. Vilnis et al. (2018) opt for a neural network to learn a large number of box positions. This is appropriate, given that their data set is the complete WordNet hypernym hierarchy. Their model converges on a single mapping of predicates to precise box boundaries, rather than to a distribution of such mappings.

We have not yet tested the box representation of words by Vilnis et al. (2018) for our task, but we plan to do so in future work. As our approach applies Bayesian sampling, we will need to modify the sizes of certain boxes to deal with a data set of this kind. It is important to recall that because their representations are learned for the purpose of detecting the WordNet hypernymy, they do not need to contain any additional lexical information not required for this task.

5   Future Work and Conclusion

We present an approach to natural language inference based on Bayesian probabilistic semantics for natural language. It differs from the work of Bernardy et al. (2019, 2018) in several respects. The main distinction is that we model predicates as boxes contained in a unit box, while they use (infinite) subsets of a vector space equipped with a Gaussian density. The density of the distribution in the current approach is uniform, which allows us to construct a more computationally efficient system for estimating the probability of the conclusion of an argument, given its premises. Our system is more stable than the one described by Bernardy et al. (2019) when tested against their test suite.

We have been relying on expert subjects for judgments on the strength of probabilistic inferences. In future work, we plan to collect crowdsourced data to ground these estimates or try to crowd source existing categorically annotated datasets like the FraCas test suite (Cooper et al., 1996), and use the mean judgments that we obtain as the target values for our system. Another way of testing our system would be to evaluate against the categorically annotated datasets, e.g. the FraCaS test suite. Success in this case would consist in assigning high probability to yes cases, low probability to no cases, and intermediate values to unknown instances.

Instead of boxes, one could use arbitrary convex polytopes. This would give a more precise, but more computationally expensive model. We leave further evaluation of this trade-off to future work.

Acknowledgements

The research reported in this paper was supported by grant 2014-39 from the Swedish Research Council, which funds the Centre for Linguistic Theory and Studies in Probability (CLASP) in the Department of Philosophy, Linguistics, and Theory of Science at the University of Gothenburg. We are grateful to our colleagues in CLASP for helpful discussion of some of the ideas presented here. We also thank three anonymous reviewers for their useful comments on an earlier draft of the paper.

References

Jean-Philippe Bernardy, Rasmus Blanck, Stergios Chatzikyriakidis, and Shalom Lappin. 2018. A compositional Bayesian semantics for natural language. In *Proceedings of the International Workshop on Language, Cognition and Computational Models, COLING 2018, Santa Fe, New Mexico*, pages 1–11.

Jean-Philippe Bernardy, Rasmus Blanck, Stergios Chatzikyriakidis, Shalom Lappin, and Aleksandre Maskharashvili. 2019. Bayesian inference semantics: A modelling system and a test suite. In *Proceedings of the Eighth Joint Conference on Lexical and Computational Semantics (*SEM), Minneapolis*, pages 263–272. Association for Computational Linguistics.

R. Cooper, D. Crouch, J. van Eijck, C. Fox, J. van Genabith, J. Jaspars, H. Kamp, D. Milward, M. Pinkal, M. Poesio, and S. Pulman. 1996. Using the framework. Technical report LRE 62-051r, The FraCaS consortium. `ftp://ftp.cogsci.ed.ac.uk/pub/FRACAS/del16.ps.gz`.

Ido Dagan, Bill Dolan, Bernado Magnini, and Dan Roth. 2009. Recognizing textual entailment: Rational, evaluation and approaches. *Natural Language Engineering*, 15:1–17.

Peter Gärdenfors. 1990. Induction, conceptual spaces and AI. *Philosophy of Science*, 57(1):78–95.

N. Goodman, V. K. Mansinghka, D. Roy, K. Bonawitz, and J. Tenenbaum. 2008. Church: a language for generative models. In *Proceedings of the 24th Conference Uncertainty in Artificial Intelligence (UAI)*, pages 220–229.

Christopher Kennedy. 2007. Vagueness and grammar: The semantics of relative and absolute gradable adjectives. *Linguistics and philosophy*, 30(1):1–45.

Ewan Klein. 1980. A semantics for positive and comparative adjectives. *Linguistics and Philosophy*, 4(1):1–45.

Daniel Lassiter and Noah Goodman. 2017. Adjectival vagueness in a Bayesian model of interpretation. *Synthese*, 194:3801–3836.

Tomas Mikolov, Edouard Grave, Piotr Bojanowski, Christian Puhrsch, and Armand Joulin. 2018. Advances in pre-training distributed word representations. In *Proceedings of the International Conference on Language Resources and Evaluation (LREC 2018)*.

Tomas Mikolov, Ilya Sutskever, Kai Chen, Greg Corrado, and Jeffrey Dean. 2013. Distributed representations of words and phrases and their compositionality. In *Proceedings of the 26th International Conference on Neural Information Processing Systems - Volume 2*, NIPS'13, pages 3111–3119.

Jeffrey Pennington, Richard Socher, and Christopher D Manning. 2014. Glove: Global vectors for word representation. In *EMNLP*, volume 14, pages 1532–1543.

Luke Vilnis, Xiang Li, Shikhar Murty, and Andrew McCallum. 2018. Probabilistic embedding of knowledge graphs with box lattice measures. In *Proceedings of the 56th Annual Meeting of the Association for Computational Linguistics (Volume 1: Long Papers)*, pages 263–272. Association for Computational Linguistics.

Bornholmsk Natural Language Processing: Resources and Tools

Leon Strømberg Derczynski
ITU Copenhagen
Denmark
`ld@itu.dk`

Alex Speed Kjeldsen
University of Copenhagen
Denmark
`alex@hum.ku.dk`

Abstract

This paper introduces language processing resources and tools for Bornholmsk, a language spoken on the island of Bornholm, with roots in Danish and closely related to Scanian. This presents an overview of the language and available data, and the first NLP models for this living, minority Nordic language.

Sammenfattnijng på borrijnholmst: Dæjnna artikkelijn introduserer natursprågsresurser å varktoi for borrijnholmst, ed språg a dær snakkes på ön Borrijnholm me rødder i danst å i nær familia me skånst. Artikkelijn gjer ed âuersyn âuer språged å di datan som fijnnes, å di fosste NLP modællarna for dætta læwenes nordiska minnretâlsspråged.

1 Introduction

Bornholmsk is a language spoken on Bornholm, an island in the Baltic Sea, the easternmost land mass of Denmark.[1] Bornholmsk is an endangered language. Inhabitants of Bornholm have been changing to using standard Danish over the past century – a development that has escalated within the last 20 years or so; cf. Larsen (2019). In total the island has around 40.000 residents, though there is notable migration to and from the other Danish islands and the mainland, leading to a Bornholmer diaspora.

Given the endangered status of the language, it is important to capture knowledge about it now. One way of doing this is to create tools for working with the language. In particular, we attempt to

---

[1]Following the most common usage on Bornholm we refer to Bornholmsk as a separate language and not a variant of Danish. Although Bornholmsk is normally described as a Danish dialect (the language code for Bornholmsk under IETF BCP-47 is `da-bornholm`), this shouldn't pose any problems in the context of this paper.

(1) *Fârijn kjöre te böjn å fikkj âu ejn*
Faren kørte til byen og fik også en
fæzelia nætter kjâul kjefter te 'na
utrolig pæn kjole købt til hende
'The father drove to town and got her a really beautiful dress'

(2) *Horrana hâ løvved ætte dæjn piblijn hela*
Drengene har løbet efter den pige hele
dâjn
dagen
'The boys have run after that girl the entire day'

Figure 1: Sentences in Bornholmsk

build machine translation support for Bornholmsk, to not only assist with understanding the language, but also to enable users of it to stick with Bornholmsk instead of being forced to switch to standard Danish – a factor in language erosion – while helping open access to Bornholmsk to those who use standard Danish. Additionally the development of such tools could give higher linguistic status to Bornholmsk among its potential users.

Code switching between Danish and Bornholmsk remains common and has been for some time (Baumann-Larsen, 1973).

Historically Bornholmsk is categorised as East Danish (along with the language spoken in Skåne, Halland and (part of) Blekinge) of which it is the only representative in present-day Denmark. Examples of distinctive linguistic features are: 1) the existence of three grammatical genders (the gender inflection is not limited to the definite article, but is also manifested in adjectives, past participles and possessive pronouns). 2) An enclitic form of the third person personal pronoun, namely masculine *-(i)jn* "him" and feminine *-na* "her". 3) The occurrence of *a* in unstressed syllables along with *e* (as well as *i* and *u* in certain contexts). 4) So-called "double definiteness" like in Norwegian and

Swedish. Of other, perhaps less distinctive features, one could mention: 5) A special intonation (neither glottal stop nor pitch-accent is used). 6) Two (long) *a* variants. 7) Palatal variants of *g*, *k*, *l* and *n*. 8) A voiced variant of *s* (*z*). 9) A more archaic verbal inflectional system. 10) Different usage of the reflexive *sig/dem* compared to standard Danish. 11) Many lexical differences compared to standard Danish (including very common words). Examples of Bornholmsk are given in Figure 1.

A detailed description of Bornholmsk phonology (*Lautlehre*) and morphology is given by Thomsen and Wimmer in their introduction to Espersen et al. (1908). Shorter, general introductions and descriptions, some of which are of more popular nature, are found in Møller (1918, 25–70), Prince (1924) (many errors and misunderstandings), Rohmann (1928), Koefoed (1944, 1969) Sonne (1957), and Pedersen (2018). An exploration of the syntax of Bornholmsk can be found in Pedersen (2009). See also Pedersen (2013, 31–32) on the *s*-passive in Bornholmsk.

Compared to other Danish dialects Bornholmsk has been utilised much more frequently in writing. The 1920s–1940s is considered the Golden Age for written Bornholmsk, but the tradition dates back to the 19th century, and writings in Bornholmsk have continued to be published until this day, e.g. in local newspapers. In recent years the language has also found its way to social media (generally in a less canonical form). In spite of the lack of normative (spelling) dictionaries and formal training most speakers of Bornholmsk find it reasonably easy to read Bornholmsk. The reason for this is at least fourfold: 1) familiarity/tradition (users have been exposed to the language in its written form in newspapers etc.). 2) there is generally a fairly straightforward mapping between spoken and written Bornholmsk, presumably also to a greater extent than for other Danish dialects.[2] 3) Regional variation is very limited (when excluding the so-called "Rønna-fint"). 4) Until very recently the language has changed quite slowly compared to most other Danish dialects (the sound system is e.g. still more or less identical to the system described in Espersen et al. 1908). For the same reasons most of the orthographic variation found in actual examples of written Bornholmsk is of a

Name	Genre	Tokens
Otto J. Lund:		
"Brâfolk" å Stommene	Fiction	35K
"Lyngblomster"	Fiction (poetry)	5.6K
"Vår Larkan ryggar"	Fiction	55K
Crawled and scraped text	Web & social media	2K

Table 1: Monolingual Bornholmsk data

kind that can be normalised fairly easily without losing any actual linguistic information.

In this paper, we outline efforts to digitise and capture Bornholmsk resources, and see what can be done with the scarce resources currently available, leading to embeddings, a part-of-speech tagger, and a prototype machine translation system.

2 Corpora

Bornholmsk digital text is generally absent. It has no data in the UD treebank, nor in CLARIN-DK, nor the LDC repository. Collection thus proceeded ad-hoc. Via the web, we compiled an informal corpus of texts including illustrative examples of the language (from e.g. Wikipedia pages), poems, song lyrics, social media comments, and stories. Additionally, some websites include small introductions to phrases in Bornholmsk for Danish speakers;[3] these serve multiple functions, providing sentences in the target language, as well as word:word translations, and finally acting as sentence-level parallel text data. In addition to material collected via the web, we use resources that have been digitised within the recently resumed *Bornholmsk Ordbog* (BO) dictionary project.[4]

A dictionary in digital format, primarily based upon Espersen et al. (1908), but supplied with various other lexicographic resources, has been compiled by Olav Terkelsen and is available from `http://onpweb.nfi.sc.ku.dk/espersen/index.html`. This material has not been used in this paper, but since the citations and phrases are translated into modern standard Danish, they represent a good candidate for future parallel text.

Other lexical resources have also been digitised, e.g. LærOrdb (1873), Adler (1856) and the glossary found in Skougaard (1804). Together with two very large, lexically ordered records of Bornholmsk,[5] primarily composed between 1923 and

---

[2]If other Danish dialects were to be transcribed using somewhat similar principles the result would deviate to a greater or lesser extent from both Bornholmsk and Standard Danish, depending on the dialect in question.

[3]See e.g. Allan B. Hansen's gubbana.dk.

[4]For a description of this project, see Kjeldsen (2019).

[5]These records contain about twice as many lemmata as

1931 by the three original editors of BO, and the part of BO which was edited before work on the project came to a halt in the 1940s, these resources will be published as a fully searchable meta dictionary in August 2020. For this reason, apart from a smaller part of the edited part of BO which is used for training of the MT models (about 3000 sentence pairs), these sources have not been used in the present project.

Some prose and poems have been digitised, namely three longer prose texts written by Otto J. Lund (*Mâgârsfolken*, Lund 1935b, *Enj Galnerojs*, Lund 1935a, and *Brâfolk â Stommene*, Lund 1941), a number of poems by the same author, *Lyngblomster* (Lund, 1930), as well as a collection of folk stories published by J. P. Kuhre in 1938 under the title *Borrinjholmska Sansâger* has been used. The latter text collection is of special value: it is in many respects the best written representative of canonical Bornholmsk, the orthography used is unusually consistent and each story is translated to (somewhat old fashioned) standard Danish, more or less sentence by sentence. Although not identical, the orthographic principles used by Kuhre are very similar to those used in the BO dictionary project.

A data statement (Bender and Friedman, 2018) for these resources is given in the appendices. The data used in and produced by the dictionary project will be published under CC BY-SA.

3 Embeddings and Alignment

Given some text in Bornholmsk, we attempted to induce distributional word embeddings. For this, we chose FastText (Bojanowski et al., 2017). As Bornholmsk is a low-resource language, it is important to be able to connect it to other languages easily. Standard FastText embeddings are available for many languages. FastText supports subword embeddings, which are likely to be useful in a language like Bornholmsk that has a relatively small alphabet, and also have some chance of compensating for the high data sparsity.

Embeddings are induced with 300 dimensions, in order to be compatible with the public Common Crawl-based FastText embeddings. Having induced these embeddings for Bornholmsk $e_{bornholmsk}$, they are then aligned into the embedded space of Danish from FastText e_{danish}. We try three alignment methods: (1) unsupervised align-

Espersen's dictionary.

da-bo 'hvid'	bo-da 'vid'	da-bo 'morgen'	bo-da 'mârn'
vid	hvid	mârn	morgen
vidd	sort	Imârn	aften
vid-	rød	mârnmål	eftermiddag
vidt	gul	mârnijn	majmorgen
vida	hvidfarvet	mârna	formiddag

Table 2: Closest words after supervised alignment

ment, where matching surface forms are used as anchor points for the two embedded spaces; (2) alignment augmented with the 1:1 word dictionaries captured earlier, where these translations are used as anchor points; (3) a mixed alignment, using both unsupervised and supervised points. Dictionary words missing from just one language are inserted into the dictionary using the embedding of anchor point in the other language, post-alignment. We choose Danish (e_{danish}) as the target space for Bornholmsk as the two languages are likely to have some lexical overlap, and there is vastly more data for Danish.

To align vectors, a transformation is built from the singular value decomposition of the product of the target space and the transpose of the source space (Smith et al., 2017). This orthogonal transformation aligns the source language to the target, thus mapping Bornholmsk embeddings into e_{danish}. A test set of 10 % of the bilingual mappings was held out for evaluation. In this case, the mean similarity was 0.3469 for unsupervised (i.e. lexical match) anchoring, 0.4238 for supervised anchoring over translated word pairs, and 0.3959 for the union of unsupervised and supervised anchor pairs. We can see that while the unsupervised alignment is helpful, when supervised pairs are available, it detracts from performance. Table 2 shows closest pairs for sample words.

4 Part-of-speech Tagging

Because there is no part-of-speech (PoS)-tagged data, we must look to resources from other languages. Using aligned embeddings, it is possible to train a PoS tagger for one language l_{source} where the words are represented in embeddings space e. By mapping words in sentences in a target language l_{target} into e, these sentences can be posed to the tagger as if they were in l_{source}. This requires that embeddings for both languages, e_{source} and e_{target}, are aligned to the general embeddings space e. There is also an assumption that l_{source} and l_{target} will be sufficiently distributionally and grammatically similar.

One is more likely to encounter new words during tagging when training data is limited, so a PoS tagger that tolerates previously-unseen words is preferable. The `structbilty` tagger[6] uses a bidirectional LSTM with language modelling as auxiliary loss function and achieves good accuracy on unknown words (Plank et al., 2016).

The source language evaluated is Danish and training and validation data is taken from the Universal Dependencies corpus (Nivre et al., 2016). Sans PoS-annotated Bornholmsk, we give example tagged sentences. Many structures and words picked up correctly, despite absent training data and a very small monolingual dataset for embedding induction. However, basic structures are occasionally missing (cf. #3).

   1)   *Hanj/PROPN   fijk/VERB   dask/NOUN på/ADP sinj/ADJ luzagâda/NOUN*

   2)   *de/PRON   ska/VERB   varra/X   så/ADV galed/ADJ ,/PUNCT sa/SCONJ de/PRON ammar/VERB ijkkje/ADV ./PUNCT*

   2)   *Hon/PROPN   ve/X   hâ/X   ham/PRON som/ADP kjærest/NOUN*

5   Danish-Bornholmsk Translation

Despite the low-resource situation, there is some useful data for developing Bornholmsk-Danish translation. These vary in term: Full translations of a few songs and poems can be found, which are parallel line-by-line. Snippets of words giving example uses in various informal 1:1 word-level dictionaries are also available – as well as the word mappings themselves.

We used Kuhre's folk stories as parallel Danish-Bornholmsk text. Further, we used entries from the nascent *Bornholmsk Ordbog*, which includes a number of genuine examples of how the language might be used. Noisier and non-canonical web data were included, to improve vocabulary coverage. The monolingual corpora is the basis for word embeddings, in this case with GloVe (Pennington et al., 2014) in 50 dimensions.

The Kuhre text is in an older form of Danish, some spelling reforms ago. Specifically, vowels are annotated differently (aa and ee vs. å and é),

and nouns have a capital initial. This data is copied with case removed, and with the vowels converted to the modern format, so that the resulting model is not too surprised by modern Danish.

The *Bornholmsk Ordbog* is a work in progress, i.a. containing usage examples such as:

<*bællana hadde âgebakka hærudanforr i vijnters {børnene havde kælkebakke herudenfor (huset) i vinters}*>

These are converted into plaintext and used as supporting parallel examples. Table 3 gives an overview of the parallel text used.

5.1   Experimental Setup

We trained a translation model with Open-NMT (Klein et al., 2017) using all parallel text. The Bornholmsk side of this was combined with the Bornholmsk monolingual texts to build a language model and embeddings. Test and validation data were both 500 pairs taken from the input data. Parameters included: Glorot initialization, locked to the encoding vectors, dropout at 0.4, an average decay of 1e-4, and validation every 4000 steps.

5.2   Pilot Results

The translation performed reasonably, given the very small training data size. Examples:

Danish: *der stod en lys sky på en mørk baggrund .*
Output: *dær sto en art sjy på ejn âzstæl .*
Reference: *dær sto et lyst sjy på ejn morkjer bâggrujnn .*

Danish: *Vil du have lidt brød*
Output: *Vil du hâ lid brø*
Reference: *Ve du hâ lid brø*

Danish: *bliver der så at de alle kan komme op og køre?*
Output: *bler dær så a di ajle ver opp å kjöra ?*
Reference: *bler dær sa dı ajle kajn komma opp å aga ?*

Danish: *hesten satte bagkoden så hårdt i stenen , at der er mærke efter det endnu .*
Output: *hæstijn satte bâgkodan så hårt i stenijn , at dær e mærke ætte dæjn len .*
Reference: *hæstijn satte bâgkodan så hårt i stenijn , at dær e mærke ætte 'd inu .*

Danish: *Hvor står mit klapbord*
Output: *Vor fâr minj dâuestola*
Reference: *Vor står mit flojbor*

Due to the relatively small size of the datasets involved today, we do not report an evaluation metric score. However, we do provide a qualitative evaluation with examples.

There are many unknown words, also in the reference data. These words are mostly a factor of the limited corpus size, and will become rarer as the amount of digitised Bornholmsk increases.

---

[6]`https://github.com/bplank/bilstm-aux.`

[7]These entries contain optional terms that are both expanded & omitted to create additional training data.

Name	Genre	Sentence pairs	Tokens (da)	Tokens (da-bornholm)
Borrinjholmska Sansåger (Kuhre)	Fiction	1K	29.1K	30.2K
Bornholmsk Ordbog: citations	Dictionary	3.6K[7]	41.9K	34.2K
Gubbana.dk	Web data	1.4K	8.3K	8.0K
Web scrape	Web data	<1K	<1K	<1K

Table 3: Parallel corpora for Bornholmsk-Danish

Another result of the low volume of training data is that there are few points in the embeddings. This means that the nearest neighbour may actually have a quite different meaning to the target. Thus, qualitatively, when the model gets things wrong, it will tend to get them really wrong.

Despite its small size and different training genre, the model was also capable of producing tolerable output given colloquial modern Danish. Some Danish spellings creep through and the phrasing is imprecise, but nevertheless, a rough mapping is available between the two languages:

Danish: *Hej , hvad hedder du ?*
Model output: *Te , va heder du ?*
Correct Bornholmsk: *Hai , va heder du ?*

Danish: *Det er Mads og han er en god dreng.*
Model output: *Ded e slæføre å hajn e en go majn.*
Correct Bornholmsk: *De(d) e Mads å hajn e ejn goer horra.*

Danish: *København er en af de større byer – faktisk den største .*
Model output: *København e en majed råganat !*
Correct Bornholmsk: *Kjøvvenhawn e ejn å di storre byana – fakta dæjn storsta .*

6   Related Work

There is no former work that we are aware of on NLP for Bornholmsk. The closest resource is an openly-available toolkit for Danish, DKIE (Derczynski et al., 2014), which is designed for the GATE platform (Cunningham et al., 2012), though even for Danish work is scarce (Kirkedal et al., 2019). Written Bornholmsk corpora are also rare; these exist almost entirely in smaller collections, some of which have been built with great care.

Two other Scandinavian tongues as small as Bornholmsk have had quite different stories. Faroese (ISO639: `fao`; BCP-47: `fo-FO`) is spoken by about 72000 people, many of whom live in the Faroes; it has a fairly long written tradition and is actively published in. It has some NLP visibility, being present in the Universal Dependencies treebanks, and a steady if slow stream of NLP research includes the language (e.g. Richter et al. (2018)). In contrast, Scandoromani (ISO639: `rmg/rmu`) has many fewer speakers than Bornholmsk; its original grammar has been overtaken by that of the dominant languages in the regions where it is spoken and is thus lost. There are nevertheless efforts to document the remnants of this tongue (Carling et al., 2014).

No machine translation is available for Scandoromani or Faroese. The Faroes built an innovative solution to this where phrases to be translated are distributed to citizens, who film themselves saying the translation, making essentially a translation memory (Kay, 1997) for Faroese.[8]

7   Conclusion

This work introduced resources and tools for doing natural language processing for Bornholmsk, an endangered Nordic language. Contributions included corpus creation, corpus collection, basic NLP resources, and a pilot translation model. The corpora are licensed separately; the NLP embeddings and models are available openly via ITU Copenhagen's NLP group page, `https://nlp.itu.dk/resources/`, and the public domain texts are available from this paper's authors. Future work should focus on digitising more text (incl. lexicographic resources); on making the best use possible out of the available corpora; on tuning models to perform better on the existing data; on increasing awareness around Bornholmsk; on helping learn Bornholmsk; and on making it possible for Bornholmsk-speakers to work digitally in Bornholmsk instead of Danish.

Acknowledgments

This research was carried out with support from the *Bornholmsk Ordbog* project sponsored by Sparekassen Bornholms Fond, Brødrene E., S. & A. Larsens Legat, Kunst- og Kulturhistorisk Råd under Bornholms Regionskommune and Bornholms Brandforsikring, and with thanks to the NEIC/NordForsk NLPL project. Titan X GPUs used in this research were donated by the NVIDIA Corporation. We are grateful to those who have gathered and published resources on Bornholmsk. Thanks to Emily M. Bender for helpful feedback.

---

[8]See https://www.faroeislandstranslate.com/ .

References

A. P. Adler. 1856. *Pröve paa et bornholmsk Dialekt-Lexikon, 1. og 2. Samling.* C. A. Reitzels Bo og Arvinger, København.

M. Baumann-Larsen. 1973. The function of dialects in the religious life of the bornholm inhabitants. In *Zur Theorie der Religion/Sociological Theories of Religion*, pages 236–242. Springer.

Emily M. Bender and Batya Friedman. 2018. Data statements for natural language processing: Toward mitigating system bias and enabling better science. *Transactions of the Association for Computational Linguistics*, 6:587–604.

Piotr Bojanowski, Edouard Grave, Armand Joulin, and Tomas Mikolov. 2017. Enriching word vectors with subword information. *Transactions of the Association for Computational Linguistics*, 5:135–146.

Gerd Carling, Lenny Lindell, and Gilbert Ambrazaitis. 2014. *Scandoromani: Remnants of a mixed language.* Brill.

Hamish Cunningham, Diana Maynard, Kalina Bontcheva, Valentin Tablan, Niraj Aswani, Ian Roberts, Genevieve Gorrell, Adam Funk, Angus Roberts, Danica Damljanovic, Thomas Heitz, Mark A. Greenwood, Horacio Saggion, Johann Petrak, Yaoyong Li, Wim Peters, Leon Derczynski, et al. 2012. *Developing Language Processing Components with GATE Version 8 (a User Guide).* University of Sheffield.

Leon Derczynski, C. Vilhelmsen, and Kenneth S Bøgh. 2014. DKIE: Open source information extraction for Danish. In *Proceedings of the Demonstrations at the 14th Conference of the European Chapter of the Association for Computational Linguistics*, pages 61–64.

Johan Christian Subcleff Espersen, Vilhelm Thomsen, Ludvig Frands Adalbert Wimmer, and Viggo Holm. 1908. *Bornholmsk Ordbog.* Bianco Lunos Bogtrykkeri.

Martin Kay. 1997. The proper place of men and machines in language translation. *machine translation*, 12(1-2):3–23.

Andreas Kirkedal, Barbara Plank, Leon Derczynski, and Natalie Schluter. 2019. The Lacunae of Danish Natural Language Processing. In *Proceedings of the Nordic Conference on Computational Linguistics (NODALIDA)*. Northern European Association for Language Technology.

Alex Speed Kjeldsen. 2019. Bornholmsk Ordbog, version 2.0, forthcoming. *Mål og Mæle*, 40. årgang:22–31. [expected medio 2019].

Guillaume Klein, Yoon Kim, Yuntian Deng, Jean Senellart, and Alexander M. Rush. 2017. Open-NMT: Open-source toolkit for neural machine translation. In *Proc. ACL.*

H. A. Koefoed. 1944. Sproget – Bornholmsk. In Hans Hjorth, editor, *Bornholmernes Land*, volume 2, pages 267–282. Bornholms Tidendes Forlag, Rønne.

H. A. Koefoed. 1969. Folkemål. In Bent Rying, editor, *Gyldendals egnsbeskrivelser. Bornholm*, pages 99–109. Gyldendal, København.

J. P. Kuhre. 1938. *Borrinjholmska Sansåger. Bornholmske folkeæventyr og dyrefabler*, volume 45 of *Danmarks Folkeminder*. Schønberg, København.

LærOrdb. 1873. *Bornholmsk Ordbog. Udgivet af Lærere.* Colbergs Boghandel, Rønne.

Anne Larsen. 2019. Dialekt på tværs af steder og generationer. Available online at https://dialekt.ku.dk/maanedens_emne/dialekt-i-periferien/.

Otto J. Lund. 1930. *Lyngblomster. Borrinjholmska Dækt.* Henry Andersen, Aakirkeby.

Otto J. Lund. 1935a. Enj Galnerojs. In *Vår Larkan ryggar. To borrinjholmska Fortællinjer*, pages 69–139. Eget Forlag, Aakirkeby.

Otto J. Lund. 1935b. Mågårsfolken. In *Vår Larkan ryggar. To borrinjholmska Fortællinjer*, pages 5–68. Eget Forlag, Aakirkeby.

Otto J. Lund. 1941. *Bråfolk å Stommene, Fortælling.* Eget Forlag, Aakirkeby.

Peter Møller. 1918. *Det bornholmske Sprog.* Fritz Sørensens Boghandels Forlag, Rønne.

Joakim Nivre, Marie-Catherine De Marneffe, Filip Ginter, Yoav Goldberg, Jan Hajic, Christopher D Manning, Ryan McDonald, Slav Petrov, Sampo Pyysalo, Natalia Silveira, et al. 2016. Universal dependencies v1: A multilingual treebank collection. In *Proceedings of the Tenth International Conference on Language Resources and Evaluation (LREC)*, pages 1659–1666.

Karen Margrethe Pedersen. 2009. Bornholmsk dialektsyntaks. In *I mund og bog*, pages 249–262. Museum Tusculanum Press.

Karen Margrethe Pedersen. 2013. Refleksivt *sig/dem* – varianter gennem 800 år. *Danske talesprog*, 17:1–37.

Karen Margrethe Pedersen. 2018. Bornholmsk dialekt – i historisk og geografisk belysning. *Mål og Mæle*, 39. årgang:12–17.

Jeffrey Pennington, Richard Socher, and Christopher Manning. 2014. Glove: Global vectors for word representation. In *Proceedings of the 2014 conference on empirical methods in natural language processing (EMNLP)*, pages 1532–1543.

Barbara Plank, Anders Søgaard, and Yoav Goldberg. 2016. Multilingual Part-of-Speech Tagging with Bidirectional Long Short-Term Memory Models and Auxiliary Loss. In *Proc. ACL.*

John Prince. 1924. The Danish Dialect of Bornholm. *Proceedings of the American Philosophical Society*, 63:190–207.

Caitlin Richter, Matthew Wickes, Deniz Beser, and Mitch Marcus. 2018. Low-resource post processing of noisy OCR output for historical corpus digitisation. In *Proceedings of the Eleventh International Conference on Language Resources and Evaluation (LREC)*, Miyazaki, Japan. European Languages Resources Association (ELRA).

Aage Rohmann. 1928. Det bornholmske sprog. *Bornholmske Samlinger*, 1. Række, 19:153–166.

Peder Nikolai Skougaard. 1804. *Beskrivelse over Bornholm, 1. Del*. København.

Samuel L. Smith, David H. P. Turban, Steven Hamblin, and Nils Y. Hammerla. 2017. Offline bilingual word vectors, orthogonal transformations and the inverted softmax. In *Proc. ICLR (conference track)*.

H. P. Sonne. 1957. Sproget. In R. Nielsen and Th. Sørensen, editors, *Bogen om Bornholm*, pages 520–544. Danskernes Forlag, Aabenraa.

Appendix 1: Data Statement

Curation rationale   Collection of Bornholmsk documents and parallel texts from speakers who have had Bornholmsk as their (dominant) L1.

Language variety   BCP-47: `da-DK-bornholm`

Speaker demographic

- Speakers of Bornholmsk

- Age: mostly 60+

- Gender: male and female.

- Race/ethnicity: mostly of Scandinavian descent.

- Native language: Danish (Bornholmsk).

- Socioeconomic status: various.

- Different speakers represented: unknown.

- Presence of disordered speech: Generally not prevalent.

Annotator demographic

- Age: 30+

- Gender: male and female.

- Race/ethnicity: white northern European.

- Native language: Danish (Bornholmsk).

- Socioeconomic status: unknown.

Speech situation   Literary works, with some ad-hoc collections and samples of the language.

Text characteristics   Mostly literary works.

Provenance   Original authors are credited in this work.

Morphosyntactic Disambiguation in an Endangered Language Setting

Jeff Ens♠ **Mika Hämäläinen**◇ **Jack Rueter**◇ **Philippe Pasquier**♠
♠ School of Interactive Arts & Technology, Simon Fraser University
◇ Department of Digital Humanities, University of Helsinki
`jeffe@sfu.ca, mika.hamalainen@helsinki.fi,`
`jack.rueter@helsinki.fi, ppa12@sfu.ca`

Abstract

Endangered Uralic languages present a high variety of inflectional forms in their morphology. This results in a high number of homonyms in inflections, which introduces a lot of morphological ambiguity in sentences. Previous research has employed constraint grammars to address this problem, however CGs are often unable to fully disambiguate a sentence, and their development is labour intensive. We present an LSTM based model for automatically ranking morphological readings of sentences based on their quality. This ranking can be used to evaluate the existing CG disambiguators or to directly morphologically disambiguate sentences. Our approach works on a morphological abstraction and it can be trained with a very small dataset.

1 Introduction

Most of the languages in the Uralic language family are endangered. The low number of speakers, limited linguistic resources and the vast complexity in morphology typical to these languages makes their computational processing quite a challenge. Over the past years, a great deal of work related to language technology for endangered Uralic languages has been released openly on the Giellatekno infrastructure (Moshagen et al., 2014). This includes lexicographic resources, FST (finite-state transducer) based morphological analyzers and CG (constraint grammar) disambiguators.

Despite being a great resource, the Giellatekno infrastructure has tools and data originating from different sources by different authors. Recent research conducted with the resources for Komi-Zyrian, Skolt Sami, Erzya and Moksha has identified a need for proper evaluation of the resources

available in the infrastructure, as they are not free of errors (Hämäläinen et al., 2018; Hämäläinen, 2018).

This paper presents a method to learn the morphosyntax of a language on an abstract level by learning patterns of possible morphologies within sentences. The resulting models can be used to evaluate the existing rule-based disambiguators, as well as to directly disambiguate sentences. Our work focuses on the languages belonging to the Finno-Permic language family: Finnish (fin), Northern Sami (sme), Erzya (myv) and Komi-Zyrian (kpv). The vitality classification of the three latter languages is definitely endangered (Moseley, 2010).

2 Motivation

There are two main factors motivating this research. First of all, data is often very scarce when dealing with endangered Uralic langauges. Apart from Northern Sami, other endangered Uralic languages may have a very small set of annotated samples at best, and no gold standard data at worst. As a result, evaluating disambiguated sentences can often only be conducted by consulting native speakers of the language or by relying on the researcher's own linguistic intuition.

Secondly, canonical approaches involving Part-of-Speech (POS) tagging will not suffice in this context due to the rich morphology of Uralic languages. For example the Finnish word form *voita* can be lemmatized as *voi* (the singular partitive of butter), *vuo* (the plural partitive of fjord), *voittaa* (the imperative of win) or *voitaa*[1] (the connegative form of spread butter).

The approach described in this paper, addresses these two issues, as we use a generalized sentence representation based on morphological tags to capture morphological patterns. Moreover, our

---

[1] A non-standard form produced by the Finnish analyzer

models can be trained on low resource langauges, and models that have been trained on high resource languages can be applied to low or no resource languages with reasonable success.

3 Related Work

The problem of morphological tagging in the context of low-resource languages has been approached using parallel text (Buys and Botha, 2016). From the aligned parallel sentences, their Wsabie-based model can learn to tag the low-resource language based on the morphological tags of the high-resource language sentences in the training data. A limitation of this approach is the morphological relatedness of the high-resource and low-resource languages.

A method for POS tagging of low-resource languages has been proposed by Andrews et al. (2017). They use a bi-lingual dictionary between a low and high-resource language together with monolingual data to build cross-lingual word embeddings. The POS tagger is trained on an LSTM neural network, and their approach performs consistently better than the other benchmarks they report.

Lim et al. (2018) present work conducted on syntactically parsing Komi-Zyrian and Northern Sami using multilingual word-embeddings. They use pretrained word-embeddings for Finnish and Russian, and train word-embeddings for the low-resource languages from small corpora. These individual word-embeddings are then projected into a single space by using bilingual dictionaries. The parser was implemented as an LSTM model and it performed better in a POS tagging task than in predicting syntactic relations. The key finding for our purposes is that including a related high-resource language (Finnish in this case) improved the accuracy.

DsDs (Plank and Agić, 2018) is a neural network based POS tagger for low-resource languages. The idea is to use a bi-LSTM model to project POS tags from one language to another with the help of word-embeddings and lexical information. In a low-resource setting, they find that adding word-embeddings boosts the model, but lexical information can also help to a smaller degree.

Much of the related work deals with POS tagging. However, as the Uralic languages are morphologically rich, a full morphological disam-

biguation is needed in order to improve the performance of higher-level NLP tools. In addition, we do not want to assume bi-lingual parallel data or access to word embeddings as we want our approach to be applicable for truly endangered languages with extremely limited resources.

4 The Rule-based Tools and Data

We use the morphological FST analyzers in the Gieallatekno infrastructure to produce morphological readings with UralicNLP (Hämäläinen, 2019). They operate on a word level. This means that for an input word form, they produce all the possible lemmas together with their parts-of-speech and morphological readings, without any weights to indicate which reading is the most probable one.

The existing CG disambiguators get the morphological readings produced by the FST for each word in a sentence and apply their rules to remove the non-possible readings. In some cases, a CG disambiguator might produce a fully disambiguated sentence, however these models are often unable to resolve all morphological ambiguity.

In this paper, we use the UD Treebanks for our languages of interest. For Finnish, we use Turku Dependency Treebank (Haverinen et al., 2014) with 202K tokens (14K sentences). The Northern Sami Treebank (Sheyanova and Tyers, 2017) is the largest one for the endangered languages with 26K tokens (3K sentences). For Komi-Zyrian, we use the Komi-Zyrian Lattice Treebank (Partanen et al., 2018) of 2K tokens (189 sentences) representing the standard written Komi. The Erzya Treebank (Rueter and Tyers, 2018) is the second largest endangered language one we use in our research with 15k tokens (1,500 sentences).

5 Sentence Representation

We represent each word as a non-empty set of morphological tags. This representation does not contain the word form itself nor its lemma, as we aim for a more abstract level morphological representation. This representation is meant to capture the possible morphologies following each other in a sentence to learn morphosyntactic inter-dependencies such as agreement rules. This level of abstraction makes it possible to apply the learned structures for other morphosyntactically similar languages.

As we are looking into morphosyntax, we train our model only with the morphosyntactically relevant morphological tags. These are case, number, voice, mood, person, tense, connegative and verb form. This means that morphological tags such as clitics and derivational morphology are not taken into account. We are also ignoring the dependency information in the UD Treebanks as dependencies are not available for text and languages outside of the Treebanks due to the fact that there are no robust dependency parsers available for many of the endangered Uralic language.

Each sentence is simply a sequence of morphological tag sets, represented as a sequence of integers with a special token SP demarcating spaces between words. For example the sentence "Nyt on lungisti ottamisen aika." (now it is time to relax), is encoded as $[150, \text{SP}, 121, 138, 168, 178, 205, 214, 221, \text{SP}$ $150, \text{SP}, 25, 138, 158, \text{SP}, 31, 138, 158, \text{SP}, 165]$.

Equation 1 is used to measure the distance between two sentences containing n words, where x_i denotes set of morphological tags associated with the ith word in x, $|| \cdot ||$ denotes the number of elements in a set, and $\triangle$ denotes the symmetric difference of two sets. This distance measure is used to approximate the quality of different readings, based on the assumption that the quality of a reading decreases as its distance from the gold standard sentence increases.

$$\texttt{distance}(a, b) = \sum_{i=1}^{n} ||a_i \triangle b_i|| \qquad (1)$$

6 Model

We implement our models using Keras (Chollet et al., 2015), which are trained to rank two sentences encoded as described in Section 5. The model is comprised of a Long Short Term Memory (LSTM) (Hochreiter and Schmidhuber, 1997) layer π and a feed-forward layer ϕ. Given two sentences a and b, the LSTM layer is used to produce the n-dimensional vectors $\pi(a)$ and $\pi(b)$, which are concatenated and passed through the feed-forward layer to produce a single scalar value $\phi(\pi(a), \pi(b))$ indicating the preferred sentence. We train each model with early stopping based on the validation accuracy with a patience of 10 epochs. We use the Adam optimizer (Kingma and Ba, 2014), train the model with batches of size 32, and set $n = 128$.

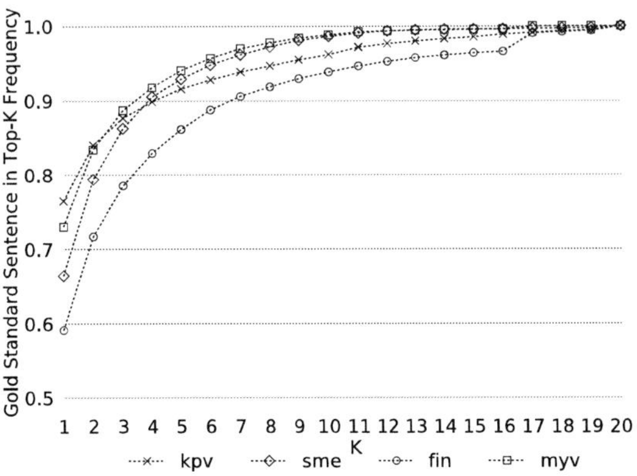

Figure 1: The frequency with which the gold standard sentence is ranked in the top-k with 1000 trials per model averaged over 10 data splits.

7 Evaluation

We produce all the morphological readings for each word in a gold standard sentence (GSS) using FST analyzers, and construct incorrect sentences (INS) of varying quality by randomly selecting a reading for each word. In order to provide a detailed evaluation, we categorize each sentence based on their distance from the GSS using the ranges $[[0, 1), [1, 10), [10, 20), [20, +\infty)]$, which we will refer to as categories G,1,2, and 3. By construction, category G only contains GSS. These ranges were chosen so that each bin contains approximately the same number of sentences. We measure the accuracy of the model for each of the $\binom{4}{2} = 6$ possible types of comparisons between sentence categories. To create training, validation and testing data, the set of GSS are randomly split before generating INS. In cases where two languages are used to train the model, the training data consists of an even number of comparisons from each language to ensure that a larger language does not dominate a smaller language.

Since we are interested in exploring the viability of using high resource to disambiguate low resource languages, we evaluate the models by training on each language and each possible combination of languages, resulting in $4 + \binom{4}{2} = 10$ distinct models.

8 Results

In order to ensure that our results are not the artifact of a particular data split, we train each model on 10 random splits of the data. The average ac-

model	kpv						sme						fin						myv					
	Gv1	Gv2	Gv3	1v2	1v3	2v3	Gv1	Gv2	Gv3	1v2	1v3	2v3	Gv1	Gv2	Gv3	1v2	1v3	2v3	Gv1	Gv2	Gv3	1v2	1v3	2v3
kpv	**.93**	**.97**	.97	**.79**	.95	.77	.53	.62	.66	.56	.60	.54	.62	.65	.68	.59	.64	.58	.65	.72	.77	.64	.71	.62
myv	.59	.68	.68	.66	.76	.62	.18	.13	.10	.40	.32	.40	.66	.65	.68	.56	.61	.56	**.95**	**.99**	**.99**	.78	.92	.76
sme	.65	.70	.70	.55	.56	.52	**.93**	**.98**	**.99**	**.73**	**.89**	**.71**	.57	.59	.61	.56	.58	.56	.22	.14	.10	.39	.31	.40
fin	.49	.60	.66	.60	.70	.60	.44	.58	.68	.58	.67	.57	**.88**	**.95**	**.98**	.72	**.85**	.70	.70	.74	.74	.62	.67	.59
kpv+myv	.92	**.97**	**.99**	**.79**	**.96**	**.79**	-	-	-	-	-	-	-	-	-	-	-	-	.92	.98	**.99**	**.80**	**.93**	**.77**
kpv+fin	.90	.95	**.99**	.77	.95	.78	-	-	-	-	-	-	.87	.94	.97	.72	**.85**	.69	-	-	-	-	-	-
kpv+sme	.91	.95	**.97**	.73	.89	.69	.91	.97	**.99**	**.73**	.86	.69	-	-	-	-	-	-	-	-	-	-	-	-
myv+fin	-	-	-	-	-	-	-	-	-	-	-	-	.83	.90	.94	.69	.82	.69	.93	.98	**.99**	.79	.91	.75
myv+sme	-	-	-	-	-	-	.89	.95	.97	**.73**	.86	.70	-	-	-	-	-	-	.86	.94	.96	.75	.87	.72
sme+fin	-	-	-	-	-	-	.90	.96	.98	**.73**	.88	**.71**	.86	.93	.97	**.73**	**.85**	**.71**	-	-	-	-	-	-

Table 1: Model accuracy averaged over 10 data splits with 1000 trials per model.

curacy across data splits is shown in in Table 1, where the accuracy of a single model with respect to a single comparison type is calculated based on 1000 comparisons. The mean standard error was 0.008, and the maximum standard error was 0.054 for these measurements. Figure 1 shows the percentage of times the GSS is ranked in the top-k sentences, given a set of 20 sentences containing 19 randomly selected INS. The $\binom{20}{2} = 190$ pairwise rankings are aggregated using iterative Luce Spectral Ranking algorithm (Maystre and Grossglauser, 2015).

9 Discussion and Future Work

The results in Table 1 demonstrate that our models are as effective for extremely low resource languages like Komi-Zyrian (kpv) as they are for high resource languages like Finnish (fin). Furthermore, there is evidence that training on a higher resource langauge that is genealogically related to a low resource langauge is a viable option. For example, the models trained on Finnish (fin) data performed relatively well when tested on the Erzya (myv) data. In cases where languages are not genealogically close to each other, such as Northern Sami (sme) and Erzya (myv), models perform very poorly when trained on one of these langauges and tested on another.

According to the results, the most difficult comparisons are 1v2 and 2v3. Since Equation 1 is only a proxy for sentence quality, it is possible that for some number of comparisons category 1 sentences are actually lower quality than category 2 sentences. In contrast, Gv1, Gv2, and Gv3 are comparisons against GSS, which are guaranteed to be correct. Consequently, it seems reasonable to conclude that this decrease in performance is partially due to deficiencies in measuring sentence quality.

Figure 1 demonstrates that pairwise rankings can be aggregated to reliably rank sentences based on their quality, as the GSS was frequently in the top-k sentences for small values of k. For example, the kpv, myv and sme models ranked the GSS in the top 3 roughly 86 percent of the time.

Future work may involve experiments with very closely related languages. For instance, out of 9 Sami languages, North Sami is the only one with a UD Treebank. Testing the performance of our system on the other Sami languages while training on North Sami is one of our goals for the future research. However, as due to the lack of gold annotated data, we need to recruit nearly native or native speakers with linguistic knowledge to evaluate our system. This is a time consuming task and it is outside of the scope of this paper.

10 Conclusion

Uralic languages exhibit a high degree of morphological ambiguity, and resources for these languages are often limited, posing difficulties for traditional methods that have been employed successfully on other languages. In order to mitigate these issues, we proposed a representation based on the morphological tags associated with each word in a sentence.

Our experimental results demonstrate that an LSTM based model can accurately rank alternate readings of a single sentence, even when the model is trained on an extremely low-resource language. This technique requires much less effort than developing complex rule-based grammar models for an endangered languages, as our model can be trained on a small set of gold-standard examples. Furthermore, a trained model can be used to disambiguate morphological readings produced by an FST analyzer or to evaluate the output of a CG model.

References

Nicholas Andrews, Mark Dredze, Benjamin Van Durme, and Jason Eisner. 2017. https://doi.org/10.18653/v1/P17-1095 Bayesian modeling of lexical resources for low-resource settings. In *Proceedings of the 55th Annual Meeting of the Association for Computational Linguistics (Volume 1: Long Papers)*, pages 1029–1039. Association for Computational Linguistics.

Jan Buys and Jan A. Botha. 2016. https://doi.org/10.18653/v1/P16-1184 Cross-lingual morphological tagging for low-resource languages. In *Proceedings of the 54th Annual Meeting of the Association for Computational Linguistics (Volume 1: Long Papers)*, pages 1954–1964. Association for Computational Linguistics.

François Chollet et al. 2015. Keras. `https:// keras.io`.

Mika Hämäläinen. 2018. Extracting a Semantic Database with Syntactic Relations for Finnish to Boost Resources for Endangered Uralic Languages. In *Proceedings of the Logic and Engineering of Natural Language Semantics 15 (LENLS15)*.

Mika Hämäläinen. 2019. UralicNLP: An NLP library for Uralic languages. *Journal of Open Source Software*, 4(37):1345. 10.21105/joss.01345.

Mika Hämäläinen, Liisa Lotta Tarvainen, and Jack Rueter. 2018. Combining Concepts and Their Translations from Structured Dictionaries of Uralic Minority Languages. In *Proceedings of the Eleventh International Conference on Language Resources and Evaluation (LREC 2018)*. European Language Resources Association (ELRA).

Katri Haverinen, Jenna Nyblom, Timo Viljanen, Veronika Laippala, Samuel Kohonen, Anna Missilä, Stina Ojala, Tapio Salakoski, and Filip Ginter. 2014. https://doi.org/10.1007/s10579-013-9244-1 Building the essential resources for finnish: the turku dependency treebank. *Language Resources and Evaluation*, 48(3):493–531.

Sepp Hochreiter and Jürgen Schmidhuber. 1997. https://doi.org/10.1162/neco.1997.9.8.1735 Long short-term memory. *Neural Comput.*, 9(8):1735–1780.

Diederik P Kingma and Jimmy Ba. 2014. Adam: A method for stochastic optimization. *arXiv preprint arXiv:1412.6980*.

KyungTae Lim, Niko Partanen, and Thierry Poibeau. 2018. Multilingual dependency parsing for low-resource languages: Case studies on north saami and komi-zyrian. In *Proceedings of the Eleventh International Conference on Language Resources and Evaluation (LREC 2018)*.

Lucas Maystre and Matthias Grossglauser. 2015. http://dl.acm.org/citation.cfm?id=2969239.2969259 Fast and accurate inference of plackett-luce models. In *Proceedings of the 28th International Conference on Neural Information Processing Systems - Volume 1*, NIPS'15, pages 172–180, Cambridge, MA, USA. MIT Press.

Christopher Moseley, editor. 2010. *Atlas of the World's Languages in Danger*, 3rd edition. UNESCO Publishing. Online version: http://www.unesco.org/languages-atlas/.

Sjur Moshagen, Jack Rueter, Tommi Pirinen, Trond Trosterud, and Francis M. Tyers. 2014. http://www.lrec-conf.org/proceedings/lrec2014/workshops/LREC2014-Workshop-CCURL2014-Proceedings.pdf Open-Source Infrastructures for Collaborative Work on Under-Resourced Languages. The LREC 2014 Workshop "CCURL 2014 - Collaboration and Computing for Under-Resourced Languages in the Linked Open Data Era".

Niko Partanen, Rogier Blokland, KyungTae Lim, Thierry Poibeau, and Michael Rießler. 2018. The first komi-zyrian universal dependencies treebanks. In *Proceedings of the Second Workshop on Universal Dependencies (UDW 2018)*, pages 126–132.

Barbara Plank and Željko Agić. 2018. http://aclweb.org/anthology/D18-1061 Distant supervision from disparate sources for low-resource part-of-speech tagging. In *Proceedings of the 2018 Conference on Empirical Methods in Natural Language Processing*, pages 614–620. Association for Computational Linguistics.

Jack Rueter and Francis Tyers. 2018. Towards an Open-Source Universal-Dependency Treebank for Erzya. In *Proceedings of the Fourth International Workshop on Computatinal Linguistics of Uralic Languages*, pages 106–118.

Mariya Sheyanova and Francis M. Tyers. 2017. Annotation schemes in north sámi dependency parsing. In *Proceedings of the 3rd International Workshop for Computational Linguistics of Uralic Languages*, pages 66–75.

Tagging a Norwegian Dialect Corpus

Andre Kåsen
Department of Informatics
University of Oslo
andrekaa@ifi.uio.no

Kristin Hagen
The Text Laboratory
University of Oslo

Anders Nøklestad
The Text Laboratory
University of Oslo

Joel Priestley
The Text Laboratory
University of Oslo

{kristin.hagen, anders.noklestad, joel.priestley}@iln.uio.no

Abstract

This paper describes an evaluation of five data-driven Part-of-Speech (PoS) taggers for spoken Norwegian. The taggers all rely on different machine learning mechanisms: decision trees, hidden Markov models (HMMs), conditional random fields (CRFs), long-short term memory networks (LSTMs), and convolutional neural networks (CNNs). We go into some of the challenges posed by the task of tagging spoken, as opposed to written, language, and in particular a wide range of dialects as is found in the recordings of the LIA (Language Infrastructure made Accessible) project. The results show that the taggers based on either conditional random fields or neural networks perform much better than the rest, with the LSTM tagger getting the highest score.

1 Introduction

The most commonly used PoS tagger for Norwegian is the the Oslo-Bergen tagger (OBT); a Constraint Grammar tagger for Bokmål and Nynorsk (Johannessen et al., 2012), the two written standards that exist for written Norwegian. For spoken language transcribed into Bokmål, the statistical NoTa tagger was developed and trained on Bokmål transcriptions from Oslo and the surrounding area (Nøklestad and Søfteland, 2007). A recent infrastructure project, LIA (Language Infrastructure made Accessible) has produced a large number of dialect transcriptions in Nynorsk, the other written standard. This creates a need for a new tagger that works on this written standard and that can also handle a diverse data set containing a wide range of dialects.

In this paper we will first describe the LIA dialect transcriptions and then the manually annotated training material for Nynorsk as well as some challenges in annotating spoken language. Afterwards we will describe a number of experiments with five different open source taggers.

2 Dialect transcriptions

The audio files were recorded between 1950 and 1990 in order to explore and survey the many different dialects in Norway. Most of the informants are older people and native speakers of their dialect. Typically, the recordings are interviews about old trades such as agriculture, fishing, logging and life at the summer farm. Other topics are weaving, knitting, baking or dialects. Sometimes the research questions also concern person or place names. The recordings are semi-formal to informal and often take place in an informant's home.

The original LIA transcriptions are semi-phonetically transcribed (Hagen et al., 2015). Example (1) below shows the semi-phonetic and normalized transcription. To make the transcriptions searchable and suitable for automatic tagging, they are semi-automatically transliterated to Nynorsk by the Oslo Transliterator, which is trained on more than 200 Norwegian dialects.

(1)   *hann e flinngke te driva garen*
      han   er   flink   å   drive garden
      'He is good at running the farm.'

Øvrelid et al. (2018) note that the segmentation heuristic in this material is such that segments do not necessarily correspond to sentences, but rather to (conversational) meaningful units.

3 The Training Corpus, Dialects and Spoken language PoS

The starting point was the annotation scheme of the Norwegian Dependency Treebank (NDT) described by Solberg et al. (2014). This is an extension of the OBT scheme (which is based on

(Faarlund et al., 1997)) with additions necessary for NDT. Table 1 shows the PoS tag set of the training corpus.

PoS tag	Description
adj	Adjective
adv	Adverb
det	Determiner
inf-merke	Infinitive marker
interj	Interjection
konj	Conjunction
nol	Hesitation
pause	Pause
prep	Preposition
pron	Pronoun
sbu	Subordinate conjunction
subst	Noun
ufullst	False start
verb	Verb

Table 1: The PoS tag set of the training corpus.

In addition to the traditional PoS classes, there is one for hesitations *nol*, one for pauses *pause* and one for false starts *ufullst*. Unlike the classification in British National Corpus where all these unclassified words seem to be classified as UNC (Burnard (2007))[1] this solutions gives us the possibility to experiment with the different types of pauses, hesitations etc., see the result chapter and the description of the different categories further below.

The manually corrected training corpus contains 163,687 tokens from 37 transcriptions and 29 dialects as listed in table 2, whereas the geographical distribution of the data is shown in figure 1.

---

[1] See in particular chap. 6 *Wordclass Tagging in BNC XML*

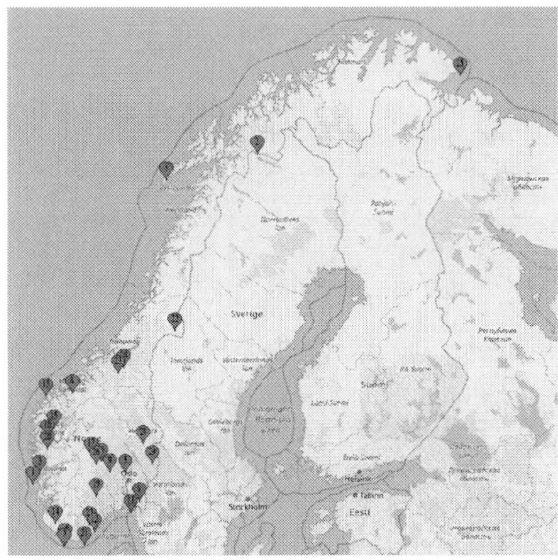

Figure 1: The map shows the locations of the 29 dialects in the training corpus.

Next we discuss some challenges encountered in spoken language when moving from an annotation scheme primarily developed for written language. Or as Miller and Weinert (1998) put it: "The terms 'spoken language' and 'written language' do not refer merely to different mediums but relate to partially different systems of morphology, syntax, vocabulary, and the organization of texts."

Transcription was conducted in accordance with transcription guidelines (Hagen et al., 2015) that stipulate a strict, verbatim representation of speech, regardless of fluency or perceived correctness. Some frequent categories of phenomenon in speech have to be considered in this respect:

Disfluency (as described in Shriberg (1996)) is a category that goes beyond PoS tags, but has some relevance at the word level. For example, incomplete or interrupted words, i.e. false starts of different kinds, have to be tagged, and while such words are transcribed as far as possible, interruption and incompleteness are marked with a hyphen - (see example 2). False starts are marked with the tag *ufullst* 'incomplete'. Pauses, which we transcribe with the '#' symbol, are stops or interruptions in the speech flow of the speaker. We have marked them with the tag *pause*. Filled pauses or hesitations are standardized as *ee* and tagged *nol*.

Dialect area	# segments	# tokens
Austevoll	1193	11191
Bardu	560	4205
Bergen	993	10416
Bolsøy	645	6669
Brandbu	404	6112
Eidsberg	679	5880
Farsund	351	3707
Flakstad	1201	11080
Flå	149	2808
Førde	332	3175
Fredrikstad	554	7676
Froland	378	6660
Giske	874	10821
Gjesdal	415	4101
Gloppen	526	5724
Gol	158	2414
Hemsedal	244	4436
Herad	214	2186
Hjartdal	354	4032
Høyanger	330	4357
Kristiansand	259	3713
Lierne	365	3867
Skaun	482	4661
Trondheim	216	3392
Vardø	481	6055
Ål	542	8685
Åmli	212	3128
Åmot	423	5123
Åsnes	466	7413
Total	14000	163687

Table 2: The manually corrected training corpus contains tokens from 37 transcriptions and 29 dialects.

(2)   *så det var ganske m- # ee*
     so it was very ufullst pause nol
     mange der
     many there
     'There were a lot of people there.'

Another challenge is frequent and form-identical words. For example, sentential connectives or conjunctions are a well delimited group of words in written Norwegian. In spoken Norwegian, however, the usage patterns of certain words have yet to be examined, and the difference between certain conjunctions and pragmatic markers/particles is somewhat unclear.[2]. For instance, *så* seems to take on multiple functions:

(3)   *så Kari løp fort*
     so Kari ran fast.
     'so Kari ran fast.'

The next two examples illustrate another challenge. Adverbs, interjections and particles are far more common in spoken language than in written text. The pragmatic particle *lell* probably has a function like the adverb *heller* ('just as well'), or some sort of particle. Then in example (5) we see a somewhat similar use pattern, but with a token that is form-identical with the conjunction *eller* ('or'). In both cases, we have chosen to tag the words as adverbs.

(4)   *men huttetu eg greidde nå ikkje å*
     but my I could PART not TO
     sjå på det lell
     see on it PART
     'oh my I couldn't look at it.'

(5)   *er det langt for deg å reise til #*
     is it long for you TO travel to pause
     til jobben da eller?
     to work then or?
     'do you have a long travel to work?'

Håberg (2010) describes and analyzes what is known as the preproprial article, which is form-identical with the third person pronoun:

(6)   *så dæ skræiv hu F1 en særåppgave*
     so then wrote she F1 a paper
     omm dæ
     about you
     'Then F1 wrote a paper about you.'

The analysis given by Håberg (2010) states that the function of the preproprial article is more akin to that of a determiner, and therefore constitutes an ambiguity between the tags *det* and *pron*. In both of the cases above a heuristic that only considered form was employed, i.e. the preproprial article is tagged *pron*. Note also that the preproprial article is close to non-existent in written language.

Other problems that can be considered are variable word order in embedded structures (Rognes, 2011) or form-identical subjunctions and prepositions (Huus, 2018). To draw an intermediate conclusion, we can say that an investigation like that of Hohle (2016) is called for with regard to spoken language.

---

[2]Several case studies can be found in the special issue on pragmatic particles of The Norwegian Linguistic Journal http://ojs.novus.no/index.php/NLT/issue/view/196/showToc

4 Taggers

In order to find the most suitable tagger, an array of different taggers from different paradigms were tested. In the following, we give a short description of the systems in use in the present paper, along with references to them.

TreeTagger[3] In order to keep some continuity with the aforementioned NoTa tagger, new models were induced for the TreeTagger. TreeTagger is based on the decision tree paradigm (Schmid, 1999), and was shown by (Nøklestad and Søfteland, 2007) to be the best performing system for the NoTa data set.

TnT[4] is a second order HMM tagger (Brants, 2000). It has been used on multiple occasions (see Hohle et al. (2017), Velldal et al. (2017)) to tag Norwegian. It is therefore natural to include it among the systems in the present paper.

MarMoT[5] is a generic CRF tagger (Müller et al., 2013), and is widely used as a baseline tagger. It can with relative ease be extended to include morphological tags as well which is a natural next step for the present work.

Bilstm-aux[6] is a bidirectional LSTM tagger with auxiliary loss that has been shown to work well for Norwegian (Plank et al., 2016). Plank et al. (2016) report a tagging accuracy of 98.06% for the Norwegian part of the Universal Dependency Treebanks v1.2 (Nivre et al., 2015). The Norwegian UD part is the NDT mentioned earlier, converted to the UD standard (see (Øvrelid and Hohle, 2016; Øvrelid et al., 2018)).

Sclem2017-tagger[7] is a general purpose tagger utilizing a CNN with a character composition component and a context encoder (Yu et al., 2017). Yu et. al (2017) report a accuracy of 97.65% for Norwegian UD.

5 Results

In the current work, we only tested the performance of the taggers on the entire corpus, not on individual dialects, for several reasons:

First, there is considerable variation in the amount of material we have for the different dialects, preventing a balanced comparison between dialects. Furthermore, for many of the dialects the size of the material is too small to yield a reliable evaluation. Finally, the transcription into standard orthography by necessity removes parts of what distinguishes the dialects, in particular with respect to morphological features, and the amount of normalization is highest for those dialects that differ the most from standard written Nynorsk, again preventing a fair comparison of dialects.

All systems were evaluated intrinsically using 10-fold cross validation and reported with accuracy. Care has been taken to ensure that each fold has the relative equal distribution of dialects as the whole data set to prevent skewed folds. After splitting the whole data set (80-10-10) evenly w.r.t. dialects and distributing the 80% portion into 10 folds each with a hold out portion, the data was randomized. Table 3 shows the calculated accuracy for all the systems with the respective standard deviation for the ten folds. As is evident, the top performing taggers have relatively similar scores, but according to McNemars test, Bilstm-aux performs significantly better than the next best tagger, MarMoT ($p < 0.05$), and it also shows a somewhat smaller standard deviation. For the best system we also add a table for each PoS tags precision and recall (Table 4).

System	Accuracy (std.)
TreeTagger	95.16 (0.0020)
TnT	93.18 (0.18)
MarMoT	97.25 (0.14)
Sclem2017	97.16 (0.15)
Bilstm-aux	**97.33** (0.11)

Table 3: The PoS accuracy and standard deviation for the 10-fold cross validation for each system.

Both Sclem2017 and Bilstm-aux are evaluated with their integrated test function, whereas MarMot and TreeTagger are evaluated with an ad hoc python script. What sets these systems apart is the fact that the neural networks are given a development set at training time for early stopping purposes, while MarMot demands brown-like clusters induced with Marlin [8][9]

---

[3]https://www.cis.uni-muenchen.de/ schmid/tools/TreeTagger/

[4]http://www.coli.uni-saarland.de/ thorsten/tnt/

[5]https://github.com/muelletm/cistern/tree/master/marmot

[6]https://github.com/bplank/bilstm-aux

[7]https://github.com/EggplantElf/sclem2017-tagger

[8]https://github.com/muelletm/cistern/tree/master/marlin

[9]Marlin was trained with the Nynorsk part of the Habit corpus and the Norwegian Newspaper Corpus.

(Martin et al., 1998; Müller and Schütze, 2015). This is most likely one of the reasons it performs so well compared to the neural taggers, and call for an investigation of neural taggers with pre-training as well, i.e. neither of the neural taggers was trained with pre-trained word embeddings.

PoS tag	Presicion	Recall
adj	89.45	90.87
adv	96.64	94.90
det	94.03	92.95
inf-merke	97.07	98.17
interj	99.32	99.08
konj	96.42	97.95
nol	100	100
pause	100	100
prep	97.77	98.11
pron	98.53	98.65
sbu	92.05	91.97
subst	95.85	96.86
ufullst	97.81	99.06
verb	98.20	98.20

Table 4: The precision and recall (averaged across all 10 folds) for the best performing system: Bilstm-aux (Plank et al., 2016)

5.1 Removal of pauses, hesitations and pauses+hesitations

In the style of Nøklestad and Søfteland (2007), evaluations where different speech specific tokens were removed were also carried out. Nøklestad and Søfteland (2007) report that this in fact lowered the performance of the systems they tested. The results that were obtained from the two best performing systems in the present paper are found in Table 5.

System	Accuracy (std.)
MarMoT$_{hesitations}$	97.19 (0.001)
Bilstm-aux$_{hesitations}$	97.27 (0.1)
MarMoT$_{pauses}$	97.08 (0.001)
Bilstm-aux$_{pauses}$	97.17 (0.14)
MarMoT$_{hesitations+pauses}$	97.03 (0.001)
Bilstm-aux$_{hesitations+pauses}$	97.07 (0.18)

Table 5: The PoS accuracy and standard deviation for the 10-fold cross validation with speech specific tokens removed. The subscripts indicate what kinds of tokens are removed in each case.

The accuracy deteriorates as speech specific to-

kens are removed, and for both systems removal of pauses have a greater impact on the accuracy than hesitations. This supports the findings by (Strangert et al., 1993) that pauses tend to occur at important positions in an utterance, including syntactic boundaries, and hence may provide important clues about the syntactic structure.

6 Conclusions and Further Work

The present paper has reported on new results for PoS tagging of Norwegian dialect data. It has also shown that, among the tagger technologies tested, the ones based on CRFs or neural networks show the best performance on this task.

A subset of the training material in this paper constitutes the LIA Treebank of Spoken Norwegian Dialects and it would be interesting to investigate whether removal of other phrasal disfluencies than the ones already tested would have an impact on the final accuracy score (see Dobrovoljc and Martinc (2018) and references therein). It would also be worth the effort to see whether neural taggers respond better if the input is semi-phonetic rather than normalized. Finally, if we are able to produce a considerable amount of material for a set of dialects, transcribed in a way that is more faithful to the peculiarities of each dialect, it would be interesting to test and compare the performance of the taggers on individual dialects.

References

Thorsten Brants. 2000. Tnt: a statistical part-of-speech tagger. In *Proceedings of the sixth conference on Applied natural language processing*, pages 224–231.

Lou Burnard. 2007. Reference guide for the british national corpus. Technical report.

Kaja Dobrovoljc and Matej Martinc. 2018. Er ... well, it matters, right? on the role of data representations in spoken language dependency parsing. In *Proceedings of the Second Workshop on Universal Dependencies*, pages 37–46.

Jan Terje Faarlund, Svein Lie, and Kjell Ivar Vannebo. 1997. *Norsk referansegrammatikk*. Universitetsforlaget.

Live Håberg. 2010. Den preproprielle artikkelen i norsk: ei undersøking av namneartiklar i kvæfjord, gausdal og voss. Master's thesis.

Kristin Hagen, Live Håberg, Eirik Olsen, and Åshild Søfteland. 2015. Transkripsjonsrettleiing for lia. Technical report.

Petter Hohle. 2016. Optimizing a pos tag set for norwegian dependency parsing. Master's thesis.

Petter Hohle, Lilja Øvrelid, and Erik Velldal. 2017. Optimizing a pos tagset for norwegian dependency parsing. In *Proceedings of the 21st Nordic Conference on Computational Linguistics*, pages 142–151.

Andrea Myklebust Huus. 2018. Distribusjonen av te som infinitivsmerke i norsk: En korpusbasert undersøkelse av utbredelsen av te som infinitivsmerke i norsk. Master's thesis.

Janne Bondi Johannessen, Kristin Hagen, André Lynum, and Anders Nøklestad. 2012. Obt+ stat. a combined rule-based and statistical tagger. In *Exploring Newspaper Language. Corpus compilation and research based on the Norwegian Newspaper Corpus*.

Sven Martin, Jörg Liermann, and Hermann Ney. 1998. Algorithms for bigram and trigram word clustering. *Speech communication*.

James Edward Miller and Regina Weinert. 1998. *Spontaneous spoken language: Syntax and discourse*. Oxford University Press.

Thomas Müller, Helmut Schmid, and Hinrich Schütze. 2013. Efficient higher-order crfs for morphological tagging. In *Proceedings of the 2013 Conference on Empirical Methods in Natural Language Processing*, pages 322–332.

Thomas Müller and Hinrich Schütze. 2015. Robust morphological tagging with word representations. In *Proceedings of the 2015 Conference of the North American Chapter of the Association for Computational Linguistics: Human Language Technologies*, pages 526–536.

Joakim Nivre, Željko Agić, Maria Jesus Aranzabe, Masayuki Asahara, Aitziber Atutxa, Miguel Ballesteros, John Bauer, Kepa Bengoetxea, Riyaz Ahmad Bhat, Cristina Bosco, et al. 2015. Universal dependencies 1.2.

Anders Nøklestad and Åshild Søfteland. 2007. Tagging a norwegian speech corpus. In *Proceedings of the 16th Nordic Conference of Computational Linguistics*, pages 245–248.

Lilja Øvrelid and Petter Hohle. 2016. Universal dependencies for norwegian. In *Proceedings of the Tenth International Conference on Language Resources and Evaluation*, pages 1579–1585.

Lilja Øvrelid, Andre Kåsen, Kristin Hagen, Anders Nøklestad, Per Erik Solberg, and Janne Bondi Johannessen. 2018. The lia treebank of spoken norwegian dialects. In *Proceedings of the Eleventh International Conference on Language Resources and Evaluation*, pages 4482–4488.

Barbara Plank, Anders Søgaard, and Yoav Goldberg. 2016. Multilingual Part-of-Speech Tagging with Bidirectional Long Short-Term Memory Models and Auxiliary Loss. In *Proceedings of the 54th Annual Meeting of the Association for Computational Linguistics*, pages 412–418.

Stig Rognes. 2011. V2, v3, v4 (and maybe even more): The syntax of questions in the rogaland dialects of norway. Master's thesis.

Helmut Schmid. 1999. Improvements in part-of-speech tagging with an application to german. In *Natural language processing using very large corpora*, pages 13–25. Springer.

Elizabeth Shriberg. 1996. Disfluencies in switchboard. In *Proceedings of International Conference on Spoken Language Processing*, volume 96, pages 11–14.

Per Erik Solberg, Arne Skjærholt, Lilja Øvrelid, Kristin Hagen, and Janne Bondi Johannessen. 2014. The norwegian dependency treebank. In *Proceedings of the Ninth International Conference on Language Resources and Evaluation*, pages 789–795.

E. Strangert, E. Ejerhed, and D. Huber. 1993. Clause structure and prosodic segmentation. In *FONETIK-93 Papers from the 7th Swedish Phonetics Conference*.

Erik Velldal, Lilja Øvrelid, and Petter Hohle. 2017. Joint ud parsing of norwegian bokmål and nynorsk. In *Proceedings of the 21st Nordic Conference on Computational Linguistics*, pages 1–10.

Xiang Yu, Agnieszka Falenska, and Ngoc Thang Vu. 2017. A general-purpose tagger with convolutional neural networks. In *Proceedings of the First Workshop on Subword and Character Level Models in NLP*, pages 124–129.

The Lacunae of Danish Natural Language Processing

Andreas Kirkedal[†] ▦
ITU Copenhagen & Interactions LLC
Denmark
anki@itu.dk

Barbara Plank ▦
ITU Copenhagen
Denmark
bplank@itu.dk

Leon Derczynski ▦
ITU Copenhagen
Denmark
ld@itu.dk

Natalie Schluter ▦
ITU Copenhagen
Denmark
natschluter@itu.dk

Abstract

Danish is a North Germanic language spoken principally in Denmark, a country with a long tradition of technological and scientific innovation. However, the language has received relatively little attention from a technological perspective. In this paper, we review Natural Language Processing (NLP) research, digital resources and tools which have been developed for Danish. We find that availability of models and tools is limited, which calls for work that lifts Danish NLP a step closer to the privileged languages.

Dansk abstrakt: Dansk er et nordgermansk sprog, talt primært i kongeriget Danmark, et land med stærk tradition for teknologisk og videnskabelig innovation. Det danske sprog har imidlertid været genstand for relativt begrænset opmærksomhed, teknologisk set. I denne artikel gennemgår vi sprogteknologi-forskning, -ressourcer og -værktøjer udviklet for dansk. Vi konkluderer at der eksisterer et fåtal af modeller og værktøjer, hvilket indbyder til forskning som løfter dansk sprogteknologi i niveau med mere priviligerede sprog.

1 Introduction

Danish is the majority language of the Kingdom of Denmark, a country of around six million people, with five written languages across its many islands (others including Færøysk, Kalaallisut, Tunumiit oraasiat, and Borrinjholmsk (Der-

czynski and Kjeldsen, 2019)). Despite its privileged place in the world, Denmark has not kept up pace with comparable countries in developing language technology. Few systems are designed explicitly for Danish; rather, general-purpose systems might be run on Danish and results produced for it as a by-product of larger studies. This supposes having adequate developed datasets. As a result, language technology does not have as prominent a place in Denmark as it might in other countries. This paper gives an overview of NLP models, tasks and datasets for Danish.

Traditionally, the country has created corpora, lexicographic resources, and other symbolic knowledge through government sponsorship. This has led to excellent research at the Dansk Sprognævn (dsn.dk) and by CLARIN DK (clarin.dk), who have both consistently produced volumes of quality Danish data within their remit. This paper examines NLP from perhaps the opposite direction: our study is task-driven instead of corpus-driven, meaning we pragmatically consider what NLP technology exists, how it is represented in the scope of Danish, and, where appropriate, what might help improve the situation.

While Denmark has multiple languages (as above), Danish also has multiple language variants – for example ømålsdansk, which encompasses all from the absence of stød (Hansen, 1943; Basbøll, 2005) in fynsk, to københavnsk, with its quirks, like the use of *forrasten* in place of standard Danish *forræsten* (Institut for Dansk Dialektforskning, 1992-). This study ignores these variants, focusing on standard Danish. We recognise that this choice perpetuates the erosion of other tongues within Denmark but, at the same time, we are aware of how the high prevalence of English in the country similarly erodes access to good NLP for Danish users – and addressing the lacunae of latter is the primary concern for this paper.

---

† : Research Scientist at Interactions LLC.
▦ : These authors contributed to the paper equally.

We present an overview of the status of Danish on a sample of NLP tasks drawn from the "NLP Progress" list,[1] automatic speech recognition and speech synthesis, organized thematically. This work considers speech to be natural language and applications such as automatic speech recognition and speech synthesis as NLP tasks.

2 Syntactic Tasks

Starting at the most basic linguistic hierarchy is often to identify the syntactic structure of a sentence.

2.1 Part-of-speech tagging

PoS tagging is the task of assigning abstract basic syntactic categories to every token. PoS tagging is one of the cornerstone NLP tasks and typically one of the first to be addressed for a new language. Consequently, PoS tagging schemes and corpora have emerged for a variety of languages, including Danish (Bilgram and Keson, 1998).

Typically, each annotation effort developed their own annotation guidelines. Early work on Danish included over 100 fine-grained PoS tags (Bilgram and Keson, 1998). A recent initiative, the Universal Dependencies (UD) (Nivre et al., 2016), initiated a new broadly-adopted model to homogenize prior diverging efforts. By sacrificing detail for standardisation, UD proposes a unified annotation scheme for syntactic annotation of dependency trees including PoS tags and morphological features, which maximizes parallelism between languages while still allowing for language-specific annotations. For PoS, the UD scheme consists of 17 universal PoS tags.[2] The latest UD release (v2.4) covers 83 languages. UD has been widely adopted in both academia and industry (Nivre et al., 2016; Bohnet et al., 2018).

Two existing Danish-specific PoS taggers exist under restricted access (Asmussen, 2015). They include mostly rule-based systems accessible via an online interface: the Brill PoS tagger developed by the Centre for Language Technology[3] and a tagger developed by GrammarSoft. In contrast, many general purpose tagging tools are widely available as open-source taggers.[4] The current best systems rely on deep learning implementing bidirectional LSTM architectures (Plank et al.,

2016; Bohnet et al., 2018). They reach accuracies in the high 90s for Danish, i.e 96% on UD Danish (Plank et al., 2016). Contrary to major languages such as English, there is a lack of data for PoS annotated data for non-canonical domains like social media or specialized medical data.

2.2 Dependency Parsing

Dependency parsing is the task of identifying the syntactic structure of a sentence. In dependency parsing, the syntactic structure is expressed as a set of bilexical head-modifier relationships called *dependencies*, e.g., $subj(Anna, sings)$. The set of dependencies forms a tree structure, thereby yielding a structured prediction problem.

The first Danish treebank is the Copenhagen Dependency Treebank (CDT) (Kromann et al., 2003). It consists of 100k tokens of syntactially-annotated data from the Parole corpus (Bilgram and Keson, 1998). The Danish UD treebank (Danish-DDT) is a conversion of the Copenhagen Dependency Treebank to UD (Johannsen et al., 2015). In recent evaluations, labeling accuracies of 86% were reported for Danish UD dependency parsing (Zeman et al., 2018), mainly over news articles. Overall, Danish dependency parsing has received the most attention.

3 Semantic Tasks

The processing tasks that depend on the meanings of a target text are gathered in this section. While a broad area of NLP, including meaning representation, commonsense reasoning, automatic summarization, spatial and temporal information extraction, and linguistic inference, we focus areas where some work on Danish exists: recognising name mentions and supersenses, handling clinical text, and sentiment extraction.

3.1 Named Entity Recognition and Senses

Picking up on specifically named items, like names of people, places and organizations, can lead to useful analyses; this is called Named Entity Recognition (NER). For some genres and languages, NER has advanced to high accuracies (e.g. English Newswire). For others, the technology is less advanced. It is a more coarse-grained task than sense tagging which has received attention in Danish (Alonso et al., 2015; Pedersen et al., 2015).

Many NER results for Danish are outdated and based on closed, systems. E.g., Bick (2004) offers

---

[1] https://nlpprogress.com/
[2] universaldependencies.org/u/overview/morphology.html
[3] https://cst.dk/online/pos_tagger/
[4] https://github.com/bplank/bilstm-aux/

details of a system trained on 43K tokens but reports no F1. One has to pay for this tool and the data is not open. Johannessen et al. (2005) mention efforts in Danish NER but the research lies behind a paywall that the authors do not have access through, and we failed to find other artefacts of this research. More recently, Derczynski et al. (2014) describe a dataset used to train a recognizer that is openly available in GATE (Cunningham et al., 2012). Current efforts focus on addressing the problem of data sparsity and on providing accessible tools (Plank, 2019; Derczynski, 2019), including as part of the ITU Copenhagen open tool set for Danish NLP.[5]

In contrast, for English, F1 scores are in the mid-90s (e.g., 94.03 from Chiu and Nichols (2016)). Researchers have since moved on to more exotic challenges, such as nested entities, emerging entities, and clinical information extraction (Katiyar and Cardie, 2018; Derczynski et al., 2017; Wang et al., 2018).

To improve Danish NER seems simple: we need open tools and annotated data. Fortunately, the landscape for Danish NER is somewhat barren, and so first movers have an advantage. Openly contributing such a dataset to a shared resource would mean that Danish NER would be included in multilingual NER exercises, thus enabling the rest of the world to also work on improving entity recognition for Danish.

3.2 Clinical IE

The language used in biomedical and clinical applications has its own nuance. Technical terms abound, and dialects vary between specialisations and even from institution to institution. Patient record notes have the potential for particularly broad variations: they are uncurated, they are not designed for publication, and the target audience tends to be quite similar to the target author, thus permitting greater use of idiosyncratic language. These factors make text in this domain hard to deal with for standard tools. They also make it difficult to use transfer approaches from other languages. For example, while one might reasonably be able to use belles lettres in English to better process belles lettres in Danish, the idiosyncrasies in clinical notes mean that one language's clinical note data is unlikely to hugely help understanding clinical notes in other languages.

Danish clinical NLP lags behind that for other languages, even when English is taken out of the picture, with for example four times as many Pubmed references to Swedish clinical processing, and twice as many to Finnish, than exist for Danish clinical NLP (Névéol et al., 2018). Work relies on older technology, not exploiting the higher performance of deep learning (Eriksson et al., 2013). Efforts to improve on this situation are hampered by the data being tightly closed to NLP researchers, compared to the situation in Sweden and Finland – this despite Denmark having an unusually rich archive of clinical data, which is "gathering dust" (Reiermann and Andersen, 2018).

There is limited Danish clinical data (Pantazos et al., 2011), but basic tasks such as entity recognition are not yet in place. Adverse drug reaction extraction tools have been built (Eriksson et al., 2013), achieving an F1 of 0.81 on psychiatric hostpial patient records, compared to an F1 of 0.87 for English on the more difficult task of multi-genre records (Huynh et al., 2016). Clinical timeline extraction (Sun et al., 2013; Bethard et al., 2016) is absent for Danish.

To improve the situation for people whose medical data is stored in Danish, both the institutional access problem and the technology development problems need to be addressed. Fortunately, research into clinical NLP for other languages is quite advanced, making it easier to catch up.

3.3 Sentiment Extraction

Sentiment analysis is a long-standing NLP task for predicting the sentiment of an utterance, in general or related to a target (Liu, 2012). It has been investigated for non-formal text, which presents its own hurdles (Balahur and Jacquet, 2015), leading to a series of shared tasks (Rosenthal et al., 2015).

The `afinn` tool (Nielsen, 2011) performs sentiment analysis using a lexicon consisting of 3552 words, labelled with a value between -5 (very negative) and 5 (very positive). This approach only considers the individual words in the input, and therefore the context is lost.

Full-text annotations for sentiment in Danish have appeared in previous multilingual work, including systems reaching F-scores of 0.924 on same-domain Trustpilot reviews and 0.462 going across domains (Elming et al., 2014). Alexandra Institute offer a model[6] based on Facebook's

---

LASER multilingual sentiment tool.[7] This is total of Danish sentiment text tools, and all are included incidentally as part of multilingual efforts.

4 Machine Translation

Machine translation (MT) is the automatic translation from one language to another. MT typically thrives on sentence-aligned data, where sentences in the source language are paired with their translation in the target language. Tools specifically designed in Denmark for Danish are not open and often only translate one way;[8] this makes them impossible to benchmark.

On the other hand, it is rare that translation tools include Danish in evaluations. Popular pairs are en-fr, en-de, en-zh and en-ja, which tend to be present in most large-scale research exercises (Johnson et al., 2017; Chen et al., 2018). When Danish does appear, it is typically in order to make a linguistic point, rather than improve MT for Danish-speakers (Vanmassenhove et al., 2018). However, even given that, there is a relatively large amount of Danish parallel text (that MT relies on): Opus[9] reports 63M sentences for English-Danish, 70M for English-Swedish, 117M for English-German, and 242M for English-French. A large amount of the Danish data comes from colloquial, crowdsourced sites like Open-Subtitles.net and Tatoeba. Just as it's incidental that Danish is included in these (i.e. their translations is not purpose-created for Danish, which is a signal of quality), there are also no dedicated Danish parallel texts listed on CLARIN.eu.[10] The result is thus that Danish MT is missing focused technology, and focused corpora, specifically designed to give correct Danish translations.

5 Speech Technology

Automatic speech recognition (ASR) converts spoken utterances to text. Converting text to spoken utterances is known as speech synthesis or text-to-speech (TTS) systems.

5.1 Automatic speech recognition

Danish ASR has received limited attention from a research perspective. In terms of data, Danish should be considered a medium-resource language largely due to the access to the open-domain speech corpus known as Språkbanken,[11] which contains 300 hours of phonetically-balanced ASR training data and 50 hours of test data – as well as data for telephony and dictation. The data is read-aloud speech which assures a good correspondence between text and speech. However, this genre does not contain examples of many issues in realistic speech like dysfluencies, restarts, repairs and foreign accents. ELRA hosts the Speech-Dat/Aurora, EUROM1 and Collins data collections behind a paywall, but these do not contain a substantial amount of spontaneous speech; access to realistic spontaneous speech is extremely limited for Danish languages. This is a barrier to research and development for Danish ASR. Creating these resources from scratch is expensive and cannot be undertaken by start-ups, SMEs or single research groups without substantial backing.

In terms of available software or systems, a speech recogniser training recipe based on the Kaldi toolkit (Povey et al., 2011) is available online.[12] This is a hybrid DNN-HMM system that requires a phonetic transcription, but if we desire to train end-2-end ASR systems, phonetic transcription is not necessary and we can take an off-the-shelf toolkit like OpenSeq2Seq (Kuchaiev et al., 2018) and train an off-line system.[13] Google, Nuance, IBM and Danish companies like MIRSK, Dictus and Corti develop Danish ASR; Dictus and Mikroværkstedet also have TTS solutions. Dictus recently released Dictus Sun[14] which will be used at the Danish parliament to draft speech transcriptions.

ASR system performance depends on language models. As speech genre is important for acoustic model performance, so language models trained on newswire, Wikipedia, Twitter data or similar will not work as well as language models trained on speech transcriptions. Dictus Sun has access to 11 years of transcribed speeches and so may work well for monologues in that domain, but we have not been able to test the system and cannot know its performance on spontaneous speech.

A lot of medium quality transcribed data is better than a little perfectly transcribed data and creating more data rather than correcting existing transcriptions provides better performance (Sperber et al., 2016; Novotney and Callison-Burch,

---

[7] See https://github.com/facebookresearch/LASER

[8] See https://visl.sdu.dk/visl/da/tools/

[9] See http://opus.nlpl.eu/

[10] See www.clarin.eu/resource-families /parallel-corpora

[11] See github.com/fnielsen/awesome-danish for links.

[12] github.com/kaldi-asr/kaldi/tree/master/egs/sprakbanken.

[13] *Offline* means it cannot recognise speech in real-time.

[14] https://www.dictus.dk

2010). This was used to create the Fisher corpus, a standard benchmark (Cieri et al., 2004). We recommend this approach, coupled with release of publicly-owned parallel data (e.g. subtitles & audio from Danmarks Radio archives; Danish parliament speeches with transcriptions).

5.2 Speech synthesis.

The synthesisers available online are eSpeak and Responsive Voice.[15] Språkbanken contains a section of data that can be used to train a speech synthesiser. Recently, toolkits to train DNN-based speech synthesisers have become available online[16] because they can be trained on aligned speech and text data like ASR systems, but we are not aware of any systems or recipes to train Danish speech synthesisers. A first step would be to develop a synthesiser on the TTS part of Språkbanken and then the ASR part.

6 Discussion and Conclusion

This paper discussed a range of NLP tasks and available technologies. It is a not an exhaustive survey of Danish NLP tools: good resources and resource lists can be found out on the web. Rather, we focus on academic research and pressing tasks.

Danish language technology remains nascent. Corpora are somewhat available, but not guided by modern technological advances. The argument of a national report on language technology, parallel to and independent of this paper, was that more data is needed (DSN, 2019). In the era of deep learning, which a major part of contemporary NLP relies upon, we need huge datasets. These do not exist on the same scale as in privileged languages. Danish language text needs to be annotated, but because in the Danish context annotation is very expensive and doesn't scale (cf. e.g. annotation for the world's second language, English), one must be careful about where effort is allocated. The exact kinds of annotation must be led by modern NLP research to have the most impact, listening to advances in the field. We recommend a top-down approach, basing choices for development on those where they are found to be lacking for a certain specific applied goals. For example, modern and colloquial parallel corpora will serve to improve the standard of machine translations that Danish speakers experience daily; sentiment

and NER datasets and benchmarks for Danish will enable the innovation and technology projects that often serve to spark local industrial interest in NLP; high-vocabulary-coverage contextual embeddings for Danish will enhance performance of contemporary machine learning approaches in both research and in innovation; including Danish in NLI datasets will drive forward progress on Danish as the NLP world works on multilingual reasoning and inference. A bottom-up approach, constructing a set of resources with the eventual goal of assembling a large, complex system, risks failing to match opportunities in Denmark and the broader NLP community. We draw an analogy between these approaches and the choice of being market-led or product-led. Product-led organisations specialise in producing one kind of product and do it very well. In contrast, market-led businesses learn their market and provide what their market wants. The bottom-up approach to structuring and funding NLP research is similar to being product-led. The resources are good, but there can be a disconnect with important parts of the community, making it a risky strategy. The present lacunae are a symptom of this strategy.

We propose that Danish language technology is steered in directions that directly support and engage with the global frontier in NLP. Danish syntactic tools, Danish semantic processing, and applied Danish NLP comprise the core pillars of such a strategy. As this paper shows, much existing Danish NLP is included incidentally as part of multilingual efforts. This means that Denmark has lost ownership and control of important parts of Danish NLP, and Danish speakers risk experiencing substandard technology as a result.

In the mean time, Danish NLP – intrinsically interdisciplinary – remains absent from local research agendae and so continues to languish; it is really this technology that we need if Danish users are to enjoy the benefits that NLP can deliver.

Acknowledgments

This work was conducted under Carlsberg Infrastructure Grant no. CF18-0996 on Danish Language Inclusion. This work was also conducted under the NeIC/NordForsk NLPL project. We gratefully acknowledge the support of NVIDIA Corporation with the donation of Titan X GPUs used for this research. We thank the anonymous reviewers for their comments.

---

[15]See `https://responsivevoice.org/`

[16]For example `github.com/NVIDIA/tacotron2`, `github.com/r9y9/deepvoice3_pytorch`, `github.com/CSTR-Edinburgh/merlin`.

References

Héctor Martínez Alonso, Anders Johannsen, Sussi Olsen, Sanni Nimb, Nicolai Hartvig Sørensen, Anna Braasch, Anders Søgaard, and Bolette Sandford Pedersen. 2015. Supersense tagging for Danish. In *Proceedings of the Nordic Conference of Computational Linguistics (NODALIDA)*, 109, pages 21–29. Northern European Association for Language Technology.

Jørg Asmussen. 2015. Survey of POS taggers. Technical report, DK-CLARIN WP 2.1 Technical Report, DSL.

Alexandra Balahur and Guillaume Jacquet. 2015. Sentiment analysis meets social media–Challenges and solutions of the field in view of the current information sharing context. *Information Processing & Management*, 51:428–432.

Hans Basbøll. 2005. *The phonology of Danish*. Oxford University Press.

Steven Bethard, Guergana Savova, Wei-Te Chen, Leon Derczynski, James Pustejovsky, and Marc Verhagen. 2016. SemEval-2016 task 12: Clinical TempEval. In *Proceedings of the 10th International Workshop on Semantic Evaluation (SemEval-2016)*, pages 1052–1062.

Eckhard Bick. 2004. A named entity recognizer for Danish. In *Proc. LREC*. European Language Resources Association.

Thomas Bilgram and Britt Keson. 1998. The construction of a tagged Danish corpus. In *Proceedings of the Nordic Conference on Computational Linguistics (NODALIDA)*, pages 129–139. Northern European Association for Language Technology.

Bernd Bohnet, Ryan McDonald, Goncalo Simoes, Daniel Andor, Emily Pitler, and Joshua Maynez. 2018. Morphosyntactic tagging with a meta-BiLSTM model over context sensitive token encodings. In *Proc. EMNLP*. Association for Computational Linguistics.

Mia Xu Chen, Orhan Firat, Ankur Bapna, Melvin Johnson, Wolfgang Macherey, George Foster, Llion Jones, Niki Parmar, Mike Schuster, Zhifeng Chen, et al. 2018. The best of both worlds: Combining recent advances in neural machine translation. *arXiv preprint arXiv:1804.09849*.

Jason PC Chiu and Eric Nichols. 2016. Named entity recognition with bidirectional LSTM-CNNs. *Transactions of the Association for Computational Linguistics*, 4:357–370.

Christopher Cieri, David Miller, and Kevin Walker. 2004. The Fisher Corpus: a resource for the next generations of speech-to-text. In *Proc. LREC*, pages 69–71. European Language Resources Association.

Hamish Cunningham, Diana Maynard, Kalina Bontcheva, Valentin Tablan, Cristian Ursu, Marin Dimitrov, Mike Dowman, Niraj Aswani, Ian Roberts, Yaoyong Li, et al. 2012. *Developing Language Processing Components with GATE Version 8.0: A User Guide*. University of Sheffield.

Leon Derczynski. 2019. Simple Natural Language Processing Tools for Danish. *arXiv*, abs/1906.11608.

Leon Derczynski and Alex Speed Kjeldsen. 2019. Bornholmsk Natural Language Processing: Resources and Tools. In *Proceedings of the Nordic Conference on Computational Linguistics (NODALIDA)*. Northern European Association for Language Technology.

Leon Derczynski, Eric Nichols, Marieke van Erp, and Nut Limsopatham. 2017. Results of the WNUT2017 shared task on novel and emerging entity recognition. In *Proceedings of the 3rd Workshop on Noisy User-generated Text*, pages 140–147.

Leon Derczynski, C. Vilhelmsen, and Kenneth S Bøgh. 2014. DKIE: Open source information extraction for Danish. In *Proceedings of the Demonstrations at the Conference of the European Chapter of the Association for Computational Linguistics*, pages 61–64.

DSN. 2019. Dansk sprogteknologi i verdensklasse. Technical report, Dansk Sprognævn.

Jakob Elming, Barbara Plank, and Dirk Hovy. 2014. Robust cross-domain sentiment analysis for low-resource languages. In *Proceedings of the 5th Workshop on Computational Approaches to Subjectivity, Sentiment and Social Media Analysis*, pages 2–7.

Robert Eriksson, Peter Bjødstrup Jensen, Sune Frankild, Lars Juhl Jensen, and Søren Brunak. 2013. Dictionary construction and identification of possible adverse drug events in Danish clinical narrative text. *Journal of the American Medical Informatics Association*, 20(5):947–953.

Aage Hansen. 1943. Stødet i dansk. *Det Kongelige Danske Videnskabernes Selskab. Historisk-Filologiske Meddelelser*, 29.

Trung Huynh, Yulan He, Alistair Willis, and Stefan Rüger. 2016. Adverse drug reaction classification with deep neural networks. In *Proc. COLING*.

Institut for Dansk Dialektforskning. 1992-. *Ømålsordbogen*. C. A. Reitzels Forlag.

Janne Bondi Johannessen, Kristin Hagen, Åsne Haaland, Andra Björk Jónsdottir, Anders Nøklestad, Dimitris Kokkinakis, Paul Meurer, Eckhard Bick, and Dorte Haltrup. 2005. Named entity recognition for the mainland Scandinavian languages. *Literary and Linguistic Computing*, 20(1):91–102.

Anders Johannsen, Héctor Martínez Alonso, and Barbara Plank. 2015. Universal dependencies for Danish. In *Proc. International Workshop on Treebanks and Linguistic Theories (TLT)*, page 157.

Melvin Johnson, Mike Schuster, Quoc V Le, Maxim Krikun, Yonghui Wu, Zhifeng Chen, Nikhil Thorat, Fernanda Viégas, Martin Wattenberg, Greg Corrado, et al. 2017. Google's multilingual neural machine translation system: Enabling zero-shot translation. *Transactions of the Association for Computational Linguistics*, 5:339–351.

Arzoo Katiyar and Claire Cardie. 2018. Nested named entity recognition revisited. In *Proceedings of the Conference of the North American Chapter of the Association for Computational Linguistics: Human Language Technologies, Volume 1 (Long Papers)*, pages 861–871.

Matthias T Kromann, Line Mikkelsen, and Stine Kern Lynge. 2003. Danish dependency treebank. In *Proc. International Workshop on Treebanks and Linguistic Theories (TLT)*, pages 217–220.

Oleksii Kuchaiev, Boris Ginsburg, Igor Gitman, Vitaly Lavrukhin, Jason Li, Huyen Nguyen, Carl Case, and Paulius Micikevicius. 2018. Mixed-Precision Training for NLP and Speech Recognition with OpenSeq2Seq. *arXiv preprint arXiv:1805.10387*.

Bing Liu. 2012. Sentiment analysis and opinion mining. *Synthesis Lectures on Human Language Technologies*, 5(1):1–167.

Aurélie Névéol, Hercules Dalianis, Sumithra Velupillai, Guergana Savova, and Pierre Zweigenbaum. 2018. Clinical natural language processing in languages other than English: Opportunities and challenges. *Journal of Biomedical Semantics*, 9(1):12.

Finn Årup Nielsen. 2011. A new ANEW: Evaluation of a word list for sentiment analysis in microblogs. In *Proceedings of the ESWC2011 Workshop on 'Making Sense of Microposts': Big things come in small packages*, volume 718, pages 93–98. CEUR-WS.

Joakim Nivre, Marie-Catherine De Marneffe, Filip Ginter, Yoav Goldberg, Jan Hajic, Christopher D Manning, Ryan McDonald, Slav Petrov, Sampo Pyysalo, Natalia Silveira, et al. 2016. Universal dependencies v1: A multilingual treebank collection. In *Proc. LREC*, pages 1659–1666. European Language Resources Association.

Scott Novotney and Chris Callison-Burch. 2010. Cheap, fast and good enough: Automatic speech recognition with non-expert transcription. In *TheAnnual Conference of the North American Chapter of the Association for Computational Linguistics*, pages 207–215. Association for Computational Linguistics.

Kostas Pantazos, Søren Lauesen, and Søren Lippert. 2011. De-identifying an EHR database-anonymity, correctness and readability of the medical record. In *MIE*, pages 862–866.

Bolette Sandford Pedersen, Sanni Nimb, and Sussi Olsen. 2015. Eksperimenter med et skalérbart betydningsinventar til semantisk opmærkning af dansk. In *Rette Ord*, pages 247–261. Dansk Sprognævns skrifter.

Barbara Plank. 2019. Cross-Lingual Transfer and Very Little Labeled Data for Named Entity Recognition in Danish. In *Proceedings of the Nordic Conference on Computational Linguistics (NODALIDA)*. Northern European Association for Language Technology.

Barbara Plank, Anders Søgaard, and Yoav Goldberg. 2016. Multilingual part-of-speech tagging with bidirectional long short-term memory models and auxiliary loss. In *Proceedings of the 54th Annual Meeting of the Association for Computational Linguistics (Volume 2: Short Papers)*, pages 412–418. Association for Computational Linguistics.

Daniel Povey, Arnab Ghoshal, Gilles Boulianne, Lukas Burget, Ondrej Glembek, Nagendra Goel, Mirko Hannemann, Petr Motlicek, Yanmin Qian, Petr Schwarz, et al. 2011. The Kaldi speech recognition toolkit. Technical report, IEEE Signal Processing Society.

Jens Reiermann and Torben K. Andersen. 2018. Guldgrube af sundhedsdata samler støv. *Mandag Morgen*.

Sara Rosenthal, Preslav Nakov, Svetlana Kiritchenko, Saif Mohammad, Alan Ritter, and Veselin Stoyanov. 2015. Semeval-2015 task 10: Sentiment analysis in twitter. In *Proceedings of the 9th international workshop on semantic evaluation (SemEval 2015)*, pages 451–463.

Matthias Sperber, Graham Neubig, Satoshi Nakamura, and Alex Waibel. 2016. Optimizing computer-assisted transcription quality with iterative user interfaces. In *Proc. LREC*, pages 1986–1992. European Language Resources Association.

Weiyi Sun, Anna Rumshisky, and Ozlem Uzuner. 2013. Evaluating temporal relations in clinical text: 2012 i2b2 Challenge. *Journal of the American Medical Informatics Association*, 20(5):806–813.

Eva Vanmassenhove, Christian Hardmeier, and Andy Way. 2018. Getting gender right in neural machine translation. In *Proceedings of the Conference on Empirical Methods in Natural Language Processing*, pages 3003–3008.

Xu Wang, Chen Yang, and Renchu Guan. 2018. A comparative study for biomedical named entity recognition. *International Journal of Machine Learning and Cybernetics*, 9(3):373–382.

Daniel Zeman, Jan Hajič, Martin Popel, Martin Potthast, Milan Straka, Filip Ginter, Joakim Nivre, and Slav Petrov. 2018. Conll 2018 shared task: Multilingual parsing from raw text to universal dependencies. In *Proceedings of the CoNLL 2018 Shared Task: Multilingual Parsing from Raw Text to Universal Dependencies*, pages 1–21.

Docria: Processing and Storing Linguistic Data with Wikipedia

Marcus Klang
marcus.klang@cs.lth.se
Lund University
Department of Computer Science
S-221 00 Lund, Sweden

Pierre Nugues
pierre.nugues@cs.lth.se
Lund University
Department of Computer Science
S-221 00 Lund, Sweden

Abstract

The availability of user-generated content has increased significantly over time. Wikipedia is one example of a corpus, which spans a huge range of topics and is freely available. Storing and processing such corpora requires flexible document models as they may contain malicious or incorrect data. Docria is a library which attempts to address this issue with a model using typed property hypergraphs. Docria can be used with small to large corpora, from laptops using Python interactively in a Jupyter notebook to clusters running mapreduce frameworks with optimized compiled code. Docria is available as opensource code at `https://github.com/marcusklang/docria`.

1   Introduction

The availability of user-generated content has increased significantly over time. Wikipedia is one example of a corpus, which spans a huge range of topics and is freely available. User-generated content tests the robustness of most tools as it may contain malicious or incorrect data. In addition, data often comes with valuable metadata, which might be semi-structured and/or incomplete. These kinds of resources require a flexible and robust data model capable of representing a diverse set of generic and domain-specific linguistic structures.

In this paper, we describe a document model which tries to fill the gap between fully structured and verifiable data models and domain-specific data structures. This model, called Docria, aims at finding a tradeoff between the rigidity of the former and the specificity of the latter. To show its merits, we contrast the application of fully structured data models to practical noisy datasets with the simplicity of Docria.

2   Related Work

Linguistically annotated data have been stored in many different formats, often developed to solve practical problems. We can group prior work into three categories:

Formats – the technical formats which are used to serialize the data;

Document models – conceptual descriptions of how the data is connected, often mapped to concrete software implementations;

Applications and tooling – user-facing applications for annotation, search, etc.

in this section, we will focus on the low-level formats and libraries to parse and access the data contained within.

Pustylnikov et al. (2008), in their work on unifying 11 treebanks, made a summary of formats typically used, which shows a dominance of XML variants and CoNLL-like formats. We examine some of them here.

Tabular annotation.   The tabular annotation in plain text is one of the simplest formats: One token per line and white space separation for the data fields connected to the token followed by a double line separation to mark a sentence. This kind of format was used first in the CoNLL99 task on chunking (Osborne, 1999) and then on subsequent tasks. Its main merits are the ease of use with regards to writing parsers and its readability without documentation.

Universal Dependencies (Nivre et al., 2019) is an example of a recent project for multilingual corpora using this format. It defines a variant called CoNLL-U, an adaption of the format used in CoNLL-X shared task on multilingual dependency parsing (Buchholz and Marsi, 2006). CoNLL-U includes field descriptions at the start of a document using hashtag (#) comments, adds subword support, and a field, if used, would allow for untokenization by including information about spacing between tokens.

CoNLL-* formats are tightly connected to data used in the shared tasks. Variations of these plaintext formats in the wild have no real standard and are mostly ad-hoc development. The field separation is a practical aspect, which may vary: spaces or tabulations. Depending on the corpus, these are not interchangeable as the token field might include ordinary spaces as part of the data field.

Semi-structured formats. Semi-structured formats specify stricter rules and a frequent choice is to follow the XML syntax to implement them (Bray et al., 2008). XML is hierarchical and can support higher-order structures such as sections, paragraphs, etc. XML has been used successfully in the development of the TIGER Corpus (TIGER XML) (Brants et al., 2002) and the Prague Dependency Treebank (PML) (Hajič et al., 2018).

The XML annotation relies on a schema defining its content on which programs and users must agree. Aside from TIGER XML and PML, the Text Encoding Initiative (TEI) and FoLiA XML (van Gompel and Reynaert, 2013) are general purpose XML schema definitions focused on linguistic and text annotation. TEI and FoLiA provide extensive documentation and guidelines on how data should be represented in XML.

Graph formats. From primarily hierarchical formats, the NLP Interchange Format (NIF) provides a graph-oriented way of connecting information which builds on existing standards such as LAF/GrAF, RFC 5147, and RDF. The main innovation in NIF is a standardized way of referring to text with offsets also known as a stand-off annotation. NIF is similar to WIKIPARQ (Klang and Nugues, 2016).

3 Docria

Docria is a document model based on typed property hypergraphs. We designed it to solve scalability and tooling problems we faced with the automatic processing and annotation of Wikipedia. This corresponds notably to:

- The lack of document models and storage solutions that could fit small and large corpora

and that could be compatible with research practices;

- The impossibility to use the same document model with potentially costly large-scale extraction algorithms on a cluster with a mapreduce computing framework such as Apache Spark.

Motivation. These aspects were dominant in the construction of Docria, for which we set a list of requirements:

Openness – release the library as open source[1]; share processed corpora such as Wikipedia in formats used by this library; invite others to use the library for various tasks;

Scalability – from small corpora using a few lines of code to show a concept on a laptop to large-scale information extraction running on multiple computers in a cluster with optimized code;

Low barrier – progressive learning curve, sensible defaults, no major installations of services or configurations. Specifically, we wanted to reduce barriers when we shared larger corpora with students for use in project courses;

Flexibility – capable of representing a diverse set of linguistic structures, adding information and structures progressively, changing structure as needed;

Storage – reducing disk-space and bandwidth requirements when distributing larger corpora.

Design. To meet these goals, we implemented Docria in both Python and Java with a shared conceptual model and storage format. One of the user groups we had in mind in the design step was students in computer science carrying a course project. As our students have programming skills, we elected a programmer-first approach with a focus on common tasks and algorithms and a tooling through an API.

Python with Jupyter notebooks provides an interactive Read-Evaluate-Print-Loop (REPL) with rich presentation possibilities. We created extensions for it to reduce the need for external tooling and so that with a few lines of code, a programmer can inspect the contents of any Docria

---

[1] `https://www.github.com/marcusklang/docria`

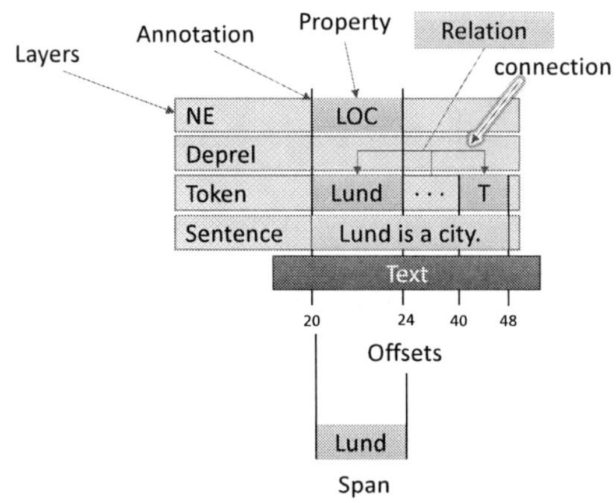

Figure 1: Docria data model

document. Through a matching implementation in Java, Docria provides a path to scale up when needed, as specific tasks can be orders of magnitudes faster than with a CPython implementation.

Docria documents consist of text collections and layers, shown in Figure 1. Text collections allow for multiple representations of a single text. A layer is a collection of nodes. These nodes can have fields which refer to the text collections. One particular restriction we impose is that a user must define a schema per layer. This is essential for introspection and verification of the data contained in documents. The schema defines the available fields and their data type with support for metadata.

Datatypes. The datatypes include basic types such as Boolean, integer, float, and string. Advanced types include text spans, node spans, node references, and node array references, which enable a programmer to represent graph structures. Field types, which are node references, must specify a target layer. In addition, this restriction results in well-defined dependencies between layers, which can be used in the future for partial document reconstruction when reading.

Using a relational database analogy, layers correspond to tables; they contain nodes which are equivalent to rows with fields, which are typed columns with specialized support for references to other nodes in other layers.

Stand-off references. Docria uses stand-off references in which we separate text from linguistic layers. These layers refer to ranges in the original text. To simplify the implementation and re-

duce sources of common bugs, the text string is split into pieces according to the offsets and stores text as a list of substrings, which is reconstructed without a loss by a join. Offsets, when serialized, only refer to spans of substrings. Software implementations can reconstruct offsets by computing the actual substring length and creating a lookup table. This will generate correct offsets even if the in-memory representation of a string differs, which is the case with standard strings in Java and Python 3.

Binary format. For the binary format, we selected MessagePack. MessagePack is self-describing, has an open well-defined specification, and has multiple open-source implementations in a diverse set of programming languages. The binary format can be used on a per document basis or in an included collection container, which writes multiple binary documents in sequence. This binary format was also designed to allow for a quicker content listing by separating content into compartments which can be read independently: document properties, schema, text, and layer data.

The Wikipedia corpus. We used the official REST API provided by Wikimedia and a page listing from the official dump page to collect the Wikipedia corpus. We downloaded all the pages in HTML format from this page listing in October 2018. This HTML format was processed and converted into a DOM using JSoup. Using recursive rules, we transformed the DOM into a flat text representation with structural layers referring to ranges such as section, paragraph, and anchors. Furthermore, we linked anchors to Wikidata by translating page targets to Q-numbers where available. We also retained formatting, such as bold and italics. We stored all this information using Docria.

In this dump, there are 5,405,075 pages excluding redirections.

4 Evaluation

We applied the spaCy library[2] to annotate all the English Wikipedia pages with parts of speech, entities, and dependency graphs, and we made the result available at http://fileadmin.cs.lth.se/papers/nodalida2019/. On average, each page of the corpus, after annotation,

---

[2]https://spacy.io/

contains 72.2 sentences, 901.8 tokens, 144.8 entities, and 4,383 characters.

We used this annotated corpus to evaluate the technical aspects of Docria and compare them to XML. We chose XML as it is pervasive in the literature and capable of representing all the structures present in Wikipedia.

We selected FoLiA as the XML format. FoLiA is well-defined, has good tooling, defines a diverse set of structural annotations which covers most, if not all, aspects of Wikipedia. FoLiA also has an official Python library, which we used to read documents.

Millions of XML files can be stored uncompressed in a file system. However, this often results in considerable overhead in terms of access times and reading and is therefore not practical for efficient processing. In addition, XML is verbose and contains redundant information. All this makes compression and streaming a necessity when storing and processing millions of documents.

To compare FoLiA XML with Docria, we chose to use a sequential tarball format with a bzip2 compression. We chose this format as it provided the most similar way to store documents in sequence applicable to both FoLiA XML and Docria. We created one XML file per article in-memory and saved them in a sequence using the tarfile API of Python. The structures we included for the comparison were section, paragraph, entities, tokens with their part of speech and lemma, and dependency relations.

5   Benchmark

We stored the Wikipedia corpus in 432 parts, containing on average 12,512 pages per part. Due to time constraints, the metrics below are computed using only 64 of the 432 parts.

First, we measured the difference in size when compressed: FoLiA XML files are on average 2.47 times larger than the matching Docria files. The compressed Docria parts have a mean size of 85.0 MB[3] compared to 209.8 MB for the compressed FoLiA XML parts. This translates to a compressed size of 6.8 kB resp. 16.8 kB on average per page.

Secondly, we measured the cost of decompressing the files in memory. Reading a single bzip2 Docria compressed file without any processing and a 1 MB buffer requires, on an Intel Xeon at

---

[3]1 MB = 1,000,000 bytes

3.40 GHz, 16.3 sec $\pm$ 18.9 ms compared to 104 seconds $\pm$ 136 ms to read FoLiA XML, both averaged over 7 runs. Reading compressed FoLiA XML over binary Docria tar-files is on average 6.4 times slower.

Uncompressed Folia XML documents are on average 9.5 times larger per document with a mean size of a page of 314.5 kB vs. 32.1 kB for Docria. For comparison, the mean average size of raw UTF-8 encoded text is of 4.4 kB per page. Put another way, using the plain text as starting point, Docria has an annotation overhead of 7.6 times vs. 69.6 times for XML.

6   Programming Examples

In this section, we show programs for three basic operations:

1. Create a new document and add a token with part-of-speech annotation.

2. Read a sequential tarball and print all the tokens of all the sentences of the corpus;

3. Read a sequential tarball and extract the entities of type person.

Create a document and add a part of speech. We first create a document from a string and we add a token layer. We then add a node to this layer, spanning the 0..4 range and we annotate it with a part of speech using the add() method as this:

```
# Initial include
from docria import Document, \
    DataTypes as T

# Create a document
doc = Document()

# Add main text
doc.maintext = "Lund University"

# Create a token layer with two fields
doc.add_layer("token",
    pos=T.string, text=T.span)

# The token layer, when displayed
# in a Jupyter notebook, will be
# rendered as a HTML table.
tokens = doc["token"]

# Adding a token node
# referencing range 0:4
token = tokens.add(
    pos="PROPN",
    text=doc.maintext[0:4]
)
```

Print the tokens. We assume we have a tarball of documents segmented into sentences and tokens, and annotated with the parts of speech. We read the tarball with `TarMsgpackReader` and we access and print the sentences, tokens, and parts of speech using the Python dictionary syntax.

```
from docria.storage \
    import TarMsgpackReader

with TarMsgpackReader(
    "enwiki00001.tar.bz2",
    mode="r|bz2") as reader:
  for rawdoc in reader:
    # Materialize document
    doc = rawdoc.document()

    # Lists all layers with field
    # types and metadata
    doc.printschema()

    # Print the original text
    # Equivalent to doc.text["main"]
    print(doc.maintext)

    for sentence in doc["sentence"]:
      # Print the full sentence
      print(sentence["tokens"].text())

      for tok in sent["tokens"]:
        # Form <TAB> part-of-speech
        print("%s\t%s" %
            (tok["text"], tok["pos"]))
```

Extract entities of a certain type. We assume here that the tarball is annotated with entities stored in an `ENTITY` layer. We read the tarball and access the entities. We then extract all the entities of category `PERSON`:

```
with TarMsgpackReader(
    "enwiki00001.tar.bz2",
    mode="r|bz2") as reader:
  for rawdoc in reader:
    # Materialize document
    doc = rawdoc.document()

    # Get the entity layer
    entities = doc["entity"]

    # Filter out PERSON in entity
    # layer having field label
    # equal to PERSON
    query = (entities["label"]
            == "PERSON")

    for person in entities[query]:
      # Tokens represents potentially
      # many tokens, text()
      # transforming it to a string
      # from the leftmost
      # to the rightmost token.
      print(person["tokens"].text())
```

7 Discussion

When converting the Wikipedia corpora to fit the FoLiA XML format, we had issues identifying a suitable span annotation for the Wikipedia anchor link. We decided to associate it with the FoLiA XML entity type.

In addition, when using stand-off annotations, some documents did not pass validation with offset errors, possibly due to normalization issues common to Wikipedia text. This gives an argument that these kinds of formats do not work reliably with noisy datasets. We instead included the sentences as text and used the nospace attribute to allow untokenization, which does increase verbosity slightly.

Initially, we used the official foliapy library, but we were unable to get a decent performance with it, potentially addressed in the future. We resorted to using the LXML DOM matching example documents with Folia. To ensure correctness, we verified samples of our XMLs using foliavalidator.

Acknowledgments

This research was supported by Vetenskapsrådet, the Swedish research council, under the *Det digitaliserade samhället* program, grant number 340-2012-5738.

References

Sabine Brants, Stefanie Dipper, Silvia Hansen, Wolfgang Lezius, and George Smith. 2002. The tiger treebank. In *Proceedings of the workshop on treebanks and linguistic theories*, volume 168.

Tim Bray, Eve Maler, François Yergeau, Michael Sperberg-McQueen, and Jean Paoli. 2008. Extensible markup language (XML) 1.0 (fifth edition). W3C recommendation, W3C. Http://www.w3.org/TR/2008/REC-xml-20081126/.

Sabine Buchholz and Erwin Marsi. 2006. Conll-x shared task on multilingual dependency parsing. In *Proceedings of the Tenth Conference on Computational Natural Language Learning*, CoNLL-X '06, pages 149–164, Stroudsburg, PA, USA. Association for Computational Linguistics.

Maarten van Gompel and Martin Reynaert. 2013. Folia: A practical xml format for linguistic annotation — a descriptive and comparative study. *Computational Linguistics in the Netherlands Journal*, 3:63–81.

Jan Hajič, Eduard Bejček, Alevtina Bémová, Eva Buráňová, Eva Hajičová, Jiří Havelka, Petr Homola, Jiří Kárník, Václava Kettnerová, Natalia Klyueva, Veronika Kolářová, Lucie Kučová, Markéta Lopatková, Marie Mikulová, Jiří Mírovský, Anna Nedoluzhko, Petr Pajas, Jarmila Panevová, Lucie Poláková, Magdaléna Rysová, Petr Sgall, Johanka Spoustová, Pavel Straňák, Pavlína Synková, Magda Ševčíková, Jan Štěpánek, Zdeňka Urešová, Barbora Vidová Hladká, Daniel Zeman, Šárka Zikánová, and Zdeněk Žabokrtský. 2018. Prague dependency treebank 3.5. LINDAT/CLARIN digital library at the Institute of Formal and Applied Linguistics (ÚFAL), Faculty of Mathematics and Physics, Charles University.

Marcus Klang and Pierre Nugues. 2016. WIKIPARQ: A tabulated Wikipedia resource using the Parquet format. In *Proceedings of the Ninth International Conference on Language Resources and Evaluation (LREC 2016)*, pages 4141–4148, Portorož, Slovenia.

Joakim Nivre, Mitchell Abrams, Željko Agić, Lars Ahrenberg, Gabrielė Aleksandravičiūtė, et al. 2019. Universal dependencies 2.4. LINDAT/CLARIN digital library at the Institute of Formal and Applied Linguistics (ÚFAL), Faculty of Mathematics and Physics, Charles University.

M. Osborne. 1999. *CoNLL-99. Computational Natural Language Learning. Proceedings of a Workshop Sponsored by The Association for Computational Linguistics.* Association for Computational Linguistics (ACL).

Olga Pustylnikov, Alexander Mehler, and Rüdiger Gleim. 2008. A unified database of dependency treebanks: Integrating, quantifying & evaluating dependency data. In *LREC 2008*.

Towards High Accuracy Named Entity Recognition for Icelandic

Svanhvít Ingólfsdóttir, Sigurjón Þorsteinsson, Hrafn Loftsson
Department of Computer Science
Reykjavik University
{svanhviti16, sigurjont, hrafn}@ru.is

Abstract

We report on work in progress which consists of annotating an Icelandic corpus for named entities (NEs) and using it for training a named entity recognizer based on a Bidirectional Long Short-Term Memory model. Currently, we have annotated 7,538 NEs appearing in the first 200,000 tokens of a 1 million token corpus, MIM-GOLD, originally developed for serving as a gold standard for part-of-speech tagging. Our best performing model, trained on this subset of MIM-GOLD, and enriched with external word embeddings, obtains an overall F_1 score of 81.3% when categorizing NEs into the following four categories: persons, locations, organizations and miscellaneous. Our preliminary results are promising, especially given the fact that 80% of MIM-GOLD has not yet been used for training.

1 Introduction

Named Entity Recognition (NER) is the task of identifying named entities (NEs) in text and labeling them by category. Before the work presented in this paper, no labeled data sets for NER existed for Icelandic. On the other hand, NER data sets exist for various other languages, e.g. for Spanish and Dutch (Tjong Kim Sang, 2002), for English and German (Tjong Kim Sang and De Meulder, 2003), and for seven Slavic languages (Piskorski et al., 2017). In all these data sets, NEs have been categorized into the following four categories: PER (person), LOC (location), ORG (organization), and MISC (miscellaneous), according to the CoNLL shared task conventions (Tjong Kim Sang, 2002).

The work in progress described in this paper is twofold. The first part consists of categorizing NEs in an Icelandic corpus, MIM-GOLD, containing about 1 million tokens, that has been developed to serve as a gold standard for training and evaluating part-of-speech (PoS) taggers (Loftsson et al., 2010). In the second part, MIM-GOLD is used to train and evaluate a named entity recognizer by applying a Bidirectional Long Short-Term Memory (BiLSTM) model (Hochreiter and Schmidhuber, 1997; Schuster and Paliwal, 1997). Our work will result in the first annotated Icelandic training corpus for NER and the first named entity recognizer for Icelandic based on machine learning (ML).

Currently, we have categorized 7,538 NEs appearing in the first 200,000 (200K) tokens of MIM-GOLD with the commonly used four NE categories: PER, LOC, ORG and MISC. Our best performing BiLSTM model, trained on this subset of MIM-GOLD, and enriched with external word embeddings (representations of words in n-dimensional space), obtains an overall F_1 score of 81.3%. Given the fact that 80% of MIM-GOLD has not yet been used for training, this preliminary result is promising and indicates that we may be able to develop a high accuracy named entity recognizer for Icelandic.

2 Background

In the last few years, neural network methods and deep learning have become the prevalent ML method in NER (Collobert et al., 2011; Yadav and Bethard, 2018). The main advantage of these methods is that they typically do not need domain-specific resources like lexicons or gazetteers (lists containing names of known entities) and features are normally inferred automatically as opposed to being learned with the help of hand-crafted feature templates as in feature-engineered systems.

Commonly used neural network architectures for NER include convolutional neural networks and recurrent neural networks (RNNs), along with other ML methods, such as conditional random fields (Lafferty et al., 2001), which have been implemented as layers in neural network architectures (Lample et al., 2016) and used for NER tasks in under-resourced languages such as Persian (Poostchi et al., 2018).

Various studies show that pre-trained character and word embeddings are beneficial for NER tasks (Demir and Özgür, 2014; Wu et al., 2015; Dernoncourt et al., 2017). This is especially relevant for morphologically rich languages without large annotated datasets, such as Icelandic, since they offer a way to obtain subword information that cannot be inferred from the training corpus alone (Lafferty et al., 2001). Word embeddings have also been used to construct multilingual NER systems with minimal human supervision (Al-Rfou et al., 2014).

2.1 NeuroNER

Neural networks can be complicated and challenging to use, even for experts. *NeuroNER* (Dernoncourt et al., 2017) is an easy-to-use tool for NER based on a bidirectional RNN. An RNN is a neural network that is specialized for processing a sequence of values. A bidirectional RNN combines an RNN that moves forward in a sequence with another RNN that moves backward. The specific type of a bidirectional RNN used in NeuroNER is a BiLSTM model, which is capable of learning long-term dependencies.

The BiLSTM model in NeuroNER contains three layers: 1) a character-enhanced word-embedding layer, 2) a label prediction layer, and 3) a label sequence optimization layer (Dernoncourt et al., 2016). The first layer maps each token to a vector representation using two types of embeddings: a word embedding and a character-level token embedding. The resulting embeddings are then fed into the second layer which outputs the sequence of vectors containing the probability of each label for each corresponding token. Finally, the last layer outputs the most likely sequence of predicted labels based on the output from the previous label prediction layer.

Instead of implicitly learning the word embeddings, NeuroNER allows users to provide their own external (pre-trained) word embeddings (see Section 4).

NeuroNER enables users to annotate a corpus for NEs by interfacing with the web-based annotation tool *BRAT* (Stenetorp et al., 2012), and use the annotated corpus to train a named entity recognizer.

2.2 NER for Icelandic

As mentioned in Section 1, no labeled Icelandic data set for NER existed before our work started. Annotating a training corpus of a viable size for NER can be time-consuming task even if semi-automatic methods are used (Lample et al., 2016; Piskorski et al., 2017). Presumably, this is why no NER tools based on ML had been developed for Icelandic.

A rule-based named entity recognizer for Icelandic, *IceNER*, is part of the IceNLP toolkit (Loftsson and Rögnvaldsson, 2007). It has been reported to reach F_1 score of 71.5% without querying gazetteers, and 79.3% using a gazetteer (Tryggvason, 2009).

Greynir is an open-source NLP tool and website that parses sentences and extracts information from Icelandic news sites (Þorsteinsson et al., 2019). One of the features of Greynir is a rule-based named entity recognizer used to find and label person names in the news texts. The accuracy of this named entity recognizer has not been evaluated.

3 Developing the Training Corpus

The MIM-GOLD corpus is a balanced corpus of 1 million tokens of Icelandic texts, written in 2000-2010, from 13 different sources, including news texts, speeches from the Icelandic Parliament, laws and adjucations, student essays, and various web content such as blogs and texts from websites (Loftsson et al., 2010).[1] The texts have been tokenized and automatically PoS-tagged using the tagset developed for the Icelandic Frequency Dictionary corpus (Pind et al., 1991), with subsequent manual corrections (Helgadóttir et al., 2014). Note that MIM-GOLD is tagged for proper nouns, but does not contain any categorization of the proper nouns.

In order to reduce the work of categorizing Icelandic proper nouns in MIM-GOLD, we gathered official gazetteers of persons, organizations and place names, and used them as input to an automatic pre-classification program. Thereafter, we manually reviewed and corrected the results.

---

[1]Available for download from `http://malfong.is`

Category	Count	%
PER	3,045	40.4
LOC	1,748	23.2
ORG	1,768	23.4
MISC	977	13.0
Total	**7,538**	100.0

Table 1: Number of NEs in the 200K token training corpus.

| W. embeddings | Implicit | | External | |
Corpus size	100K	200K	100K	200K
PER	71.8	76.1	95.2	93.3
LOC	61.8	65.6	81.8	85.6
ORG	23.5	40.5	62.7	69.2
MISC	3.2	28.3	14.8	41.5
Overall	**55.5**	**61.8**	**80.6**	**81.3**

Table 2: F_1 scores (%) of four different training configurations.

Foreign tokens in the MIM-GOLD are all assigned the same tag with no further distinction, and since a large portion of them are NEs, they were reviewed and classified manually.

To make the review and correction process more efficient, we used the BRAT annotation tool (see Section 2). We use the IOB (inside, outside, beginning) format as used in the CoNLL data sets (Tjong Kim Sang, 2002).

At the time of writing, we have categorized 7,538 NEs appearing in the first 200K tokens of MIM-GOLD with the commonly used four categories: PER, LOC, ORG and MISC (see Table 1).

The annotated corpus was reviewed by a single linguist (first author), using the following definitions for each of the four categories:

- **Persons**: Names of humans and other beings, real or fictional, deities, pet names.

- **Locations**: Names of locations, real or fictional, i.e. buildings, street and place names, both real and fictional. All geographical and geopolitical entities such as cities, countries, counties and regions, as well as planet names and other outer space entities.

- **Organizations**: Icelandic and foreign companies and other organizations, public or private, real or fictional. Schools, churches, swimming pools, community centers, musical groups, other affiliations.

- **Miscellaneous**: All other capitalized nouns and noun phrases, such as works of art, products, events, printed materials, vessels and other named means of transportation, etc.

4   Training and Evaluation

The training corpus was arranged into two sets of different sizes, 100K and 200K tokens, each split into training (80%), validation (10%) and test

(10%) sets. Four different models were trained and evaluated, for the two different training set sizes and for both implicitly and externally trained word embeddings.

We pre-trained our own word embeddings of 200 dimensions using about 543 million tokens from a large unlabelled corpus, the Icelandic Gigaword Corpus (Steingrímsson et al., 2018), using a Word2Vec architecture (Mikolov et al., 2013).

All the parameters in NeuroNER's configuration file, controlling the structure of the model, along with the hyperparameters directed towards the learning process, were left at their default values. The only exception to this is the *token_embedding_dimension* parameter, controlling the length of the word vectors. This value was increased from 100 to 200 for the external word embeddings.

In the training, early stop was applied by default when no improvement had been seen on the validation set for ten consecutive epochs. The model used is based on the network weights taken from the epoch where the F_1 score last peaked for the validation set.

Evaluation was done automatically by NeuroNER according to CoNLL practices, which means that to score a true positive, both the NE category and the token boundaries need to be correct.

The F_1 scores for the models of the four training configurations, i.e. for the two training corpora sizes, with implicit and external word embeddings, are shown in Table 2. The best performing model is the one trained on 200K tokens and using external pre-trained word embeddings, achieving an overall F_1 score of 81.3%.

5   Discussion

The results presented in Section 4 are promising, especially given the few NEs found in the 200K tokens of the training corpus (see Table 1).

Table 2 shows that, using implicitly trained word embeddings, the F_1 score increases considerably when doubling the corpus size, i.e. from 55.5% to 61.8%. This was to be expected, as the training set in the 100K token corpus only contains around 80K tokens, and has thus a very limited number of NE examples to learn from. When further increasing the training corpus, we expect this trend to continue.

However, a more effective approach to increase the accuracy proved to be incorporating pre-trained word embeddings. In that case, the F_1 score increases to 81.3% when using the 200K corpus. In what follows, we refer to this best performing model as *200K_External*.

Most studies on the benefits of word embeddings in NER tasks do not report more than a few percent points increase in F_1 score by introducing pre-trained word embeddings. Intuitively, we deduce that the main reason we are experiencing this huge benefit of pre-trained word embeddings is the small size of our training corpus. For a small training set, the model will more often encounter unseen words in the test set. In our 200K corpus, 60% of the incorrectly labeled words had not been seen in the training set. When the large collection of word embeddings is added to the pool, the chances that a word is known increase substantially.

Another reason as to why word embeddings from a large external corpus are so beneficial for our model may be the underlying language. Icelandic, a morphologically rich language, presents special challenges for various NLP tasks, such as NER. Nouns, generally the building blocks of NEs, have up to 16 unique inflectional forms, and verbs and adjectives can have over a hundred different forms. This greatly increases the vocabulary size of a corpus, and causes a problem with data sparsity, as pointed out by Demir and Özgür (2014), for the case of Turkish and Czech. The implication is that a NER system may not recognize a NE in the test set even if it has seen it in a different form in the training set.[2] We could try to lemmatize the tokens in the training corpus and use the normalized output for building the NER model, but then we would lose important contextual information about the NEs and their neighbors. The

pre-trained word embeddings contribute many examples to the model of different word forms that do not appear in the training set, and the likelihood of correctly labeling them increases as a result.

With a larger corpus, say by doubling it once again, we believe, from the trend, that the F_1 score without external embeddings might end up between the earlier score (61.8%) and the one obtained by 200K_External (81.3%). On the other hand, the results with pre-trained embeddings indicate a much slower increase in F_1 score when increasing the size of the corpus (from 80.6% to 81.3% when increasing the corpus size from 100K to 200K). This might indicate that we are approaching the upper limit with regard to the F_1 score.

NeuroNER has achieved 90.5% F_1 score for English on the CoNLL data set (Dernoncourt et al., 2017). This English data set contains 35,089 NEs (Tjong Kim Sang and De Meulder, 2003) whereas our 200K Icelandic training corpus contains only 7,538 NEs. Therefore, we are optimistic that increasing the training corpus size for Icelandic will further increase the overall F_1 score, albeit we do not expect getting close to the score for English, which is a morphologically simple language compared to Icelandic.

5.1 Accuracy for Different Categories

Table 2 shows a considerable difference in the accuracy of different categories. Especially promising are the results for the PER category, with F_1 score of 93.3% for 200K_External. The recall for PER is high, 94.85%, which means that only about 5% of the person names in the test set were not identified. Several factors may explain the top performance in this category. Most importantly, person names are by far the most frequent entity type in the training corpus, almost double that of the LOC and ORG categories (see Table 1). Person names are often constructed in a similar manner, with Icelandic full names usually composed of one or two given names and a surname ending in *-son* or *-dóttir* "daughter". Furthermore, they are almost always capitalized, and since they are not unique (many people can have the same name), each person name is bound to appear more often than, for example, each organization name.

200K_External also performs quite well on the LOC category (85.6%). It is the nature of a corpus sampled from any geographic area that some lo-

<hr>

[2]For example, the Icelandic person name "Egill" (nominative) may be tagged as such in the training set and then appear as "Egil" (accusative), "Agli" (dative), or "Egils" (genitive) in the test set.

372

	Predicted categories				
	LOC	MISC	ORG	PER	O
LOC	161	3	11	8	5
MISC	7	87	26	14	68
ORG	19	6	174	4	21
PER	0	3	1	568	16
O	1	46	33	12	19,245

Table 3: Confusion matrix for the classification of the test set in 200K_External. True categories are shown vertically, predicted categories horizontally. The *O* category denotes "outside", i.e. that the corresponding token is not a part of a NE.

cations appear more often than others, in this case *Ísland* "Iceland" and *Reykjavík*, to name two of the most common. This means that during testing, the system is much more likely to label them correctly, because they are likely to have been found during training. Another property of place names is that they tend to be single word entities, and are capitalized, with a few exceptions. As a result, detecting word boundaries becomes less of a challenge.

The LOC and ORG categories are equally common in the corpus, but the accuracy for ORG (69.2%) is significantly worse. In the ORG category, word boundaries are a problem, as organizations are often composed of more than one word, not necessarily capitalized, e.g. *Samband lífeyrisþega ríkis og bæja* "Organization (of) pensioners (of) state and towns". Furthermore, sometimes it can be hard to decide whether an entity is an organization name or a product, which may cause overlap with the MISC category.

The MISC category was the most problematic one for 200K_External, with F_1 score of only 41.5%. Recall is particularly low (33.6%), meaning many MISC entities are not found, and precision is not particularly high either (54.17%), thus many entities are mislabeled.

The confusion matrix (see Table 3) from the classification of the test set in 200K_External shows how many of the tokens in the test set were correctly labeled (the diagonal line running from the top left corner to the bottom right), and where mislabeling occurs. The MISC category contains the most outliers, with a total of 115 NEs mislabeled out of 202 in total. In the PER category only 20 NEs out of 588 are mislabeled. There are only around 1000 MISC entities in the whole 200K corpus, and a lot of variation in how they are

constructed, which makes detecting them harder, even for human annotators. Some are long book or movie titles, some are complicated product names with numbers and hyphens, and there is no correlation within the category. This is the category that tends to score lowest in most NER models, but a substantially larger corpus should lead to some improvement.

6 Conclusion

We have described work in progress consisting of annotating the MIM-GOLD corpus for NEs and using it to train a named entity recognizer based on a BiLSTM model. By only categorizing about 20% of the NEs found in MIM-GOLD, the best resulting model, enriched with external word embeddings, achieves an overall F_1 score of 81.3%. We are optimistic that we can further increase the F_1 score for Icelandic by increasing the training corpus size. Currently, the number of NEs found in our training corpus (7,538) is only about 1/5 of the training examples provided in the English CoNLL data set.

In future work, we will continue categorizing NEs in MIM-GOLD, such that we will be able to use 100% of the corpus to train NER models for Icelandic. We are also working on adding categories for numerical units, such as dates and prices. The annotated corpus will be publicly released, in order to serve as a valuable asset for further research on NER for Icelandic. The resulting NER models will also be made available for public use.

In addition to further developing our BiLSTM model and testing different configurations, we intend to develop models based on other ML techniques, for the sake of comparison, as well as being able to combine various different classifiers.

As mentioned in Section 2, different word and character representations have shown promise when developing NER models. In this preliminary work we used the Word2Vec architecture, which resulted in a large improvement, but in the future we intend to measure how some of the other word and character representation methods compare, e.g. contextual word embeddings such as ELMo (Peters et al., 2018) and flair (Akbik et al., 2018).

References

Alan Akbik, Duncan Blythe, and Roland Vollgraf. 2018. Contextual String Embeddings for Sequence Labeling. In *Proceedings of the 27th International Conference on Computational Linguistics*, COLING 2018, Santa Fe, New Mexico, USA.

Rami Al-Rfou, Vivek Kulkarni, Bryan Perozzi, and Steven Skiena. 2014. POLYGLOT-NER: Massive Multilingual Named Entity Recognition. *CoRR*, abs/1410.3791.

Ronan Collobert, Jason Weston, Léon Bottou, Michael Karlen, Koray Kavukcuoglu, and Pavel Kuksa. 2011. Natural language processing (almost) from scratch. *CoRR*, abs/1103.0398.

Hakan Demir and Arzucan Özgür. 2014. Improving Named Entity Recognition for Morphologically Rich Languages Using Word Embeddings. In *13th International Conference on Machine Learning and Applications*, Detroit, MI, USA.

Franck Dernoncourt, Ji Young Lee, and Peter Szolovits. 2017. NeuroNER: an easy-to-use program for named-entity recognition based on neural networks. In *Proceedings of the 2017 Conference on Empirical Methods in Natural Language Processing: System Demonstrations*, Copenhagen, Denmark.

Franck Dernoncourt, Ji Young Lee, Ozlem Uzuner, and Peter Szolovits. 2016. De-identification of patient notes with recurrent neural networks. *CoRR*, abs/1606.03475.

Sigrún Helgadóttir, Hrafn Loftsson, and Eiríkur Rögnvaldsson. 2014. Correcting Errors in a New Gold Standard for Tagging Icelandic Text. In *Proceedings of the Ninth International Conference on Language Resources and Evaluation*, LREC 2014, Reykjavik, Iceland.

Sepp Hochreiter and Jürgen Schmidhuber. 1997. Long Short-Term Memory. *Neural computation*, 9(8):1735–1780.

John D. Lafferty, Andrew McCallum, and Fernando C. N. Pereira. 2001. Conditional Random Fields: Probabilistic Models for Segmenting and Labeling Sequence Data. In *Proceedings of the Eighteenth International Conference on Machine Learning*, ICML 2001, Williamstown, MA, USA.

Guillaume Lample, Miguel Ballesteros, Sandeep Subramanian, Kazuya Kawakami, and Chris Dyer. 2016. Neural Architectures for Named Entity Recognition. In *Proceedings of the 2016 Conference of the North American Chapter of the Association for Computational Linguistics: Human Language Technologies*, San Diego, California, USA.

Hrafn Loftsson and Eiríkur Rögnvaldsson. 2007. IceNLP: A Natural Language Processing Toolkit for Icelandic. In *Proceedings of InterSpeech, Special Session: Speech and language technology for less-resourced languages*, Antwerp, Belgium.

Hrafn Loftsson, Jökull H. Yngvason, Sigrún Helgadóttir, and Eiríkur Rögnvaldsson. 2010. Developing a PoS-tagged corpus using existing tools. In *Proceedings of 7th SaLTMiL Workshop on Creation and Use of Basic Lexical Resources for Less-Resourced Languages*, LREC 2010, Valetta, Malta.

Tomas Mikolov, Kai Chen, Greg Corrado, and Jeffrey Dean. 2013. Efficient Estimation of Word Representations in Vector Space. *CoRR*, abs/1301.3781.

Matthew E. Peters, Mark Neumann, Mohit Iyyer, Matt Gardner, Christopher Clark, Kenton Lee, and Luke Zettlemoyer. 2018. Deep contextualized word representations. In *Proceedings of the 2018 Conference of the North American Chapter of the Association for Computational Linguistics: Human Language Technologies, Volume 1 (Long Papers)*, New Orleans, Louisiana, USA.

Jörgen Pind, Friðrik Magnússon, and Stefán Briem. 1991. *Íslensk orðtíðnibók [The Icelandic Frequency Dictionary]*. The Institute of Lexicography, University of Iceland, Reykjavik, Iceland.

Jakub Piskorski, Lidia Pivovarova, Jan Šnajder, Josef Steinberger, and Roman Yangarber. 2017. The First Cross-Lingual Challenge on Recognition, Normalization, and Matching of Named Entities in Slavic Languages. In *Proceedings of the 6th Workshop on Balto-Slavic Natural Language Processing*, Valencia, Spain.

Hanieh Poostchi, Ehsan Zare Borzeshi, and Massimo Piccardi. 2018. BiLSTM-CRF for Persian Named-Entity Recognition ArmanPersoNERCorpus: the First Entity-Annotated Persian Dataset. In *Proceedings of the Eleventh International Conference on Language Resources and Evaluation*, LREC 2018, Miyazaki, Japan.

Mike Schuster and Kuldip. K. Paliwal. 1997. Bidirectional Recurrent Neural Networks. *IEEE Transactions on Signal Processing*, 45(11):2673–2681.

Steinþór Steingrímsson, Sigrún Helgadóttir, Eiríkur Rögnvaldsson, Starkaður Barkarson, and Jón Guðnason. 2018. Risamálheild: A Very Large Icelandic Text Corpus. In *Proceedings of the Eleventh International Conference on Language Resources and Evaluation*, LREC 2018, Miyazaki, Japan.

Pontus Stenetorp, Sampo Pyysalo, Goran Topić, Tomoko Ohta, Sophia Ananiadou, and Jun'ichi Tsujii. 2012. brat: a Web-based Tool for NLP-Assisted Text Annotation. In *Proceedings of the Demonstrations at the 13th Conference of the European Chapter of the Association for Computational Linguistics*, Avignon, France.

Erik F. Tjong Kim Sang. 2002. Introduction to the CoNLL-2002 Shared Task: Language-Independent

Named Entity Recognition. In *Proceedings of CoNLL-2002*, Taipei, Taiwan.

Erik F. Tjong Kim Sang and Fien De Meulder. 2003. Introduction to the CoNLL-2003 Shared Task: Language-Independent Named Entity Recognition. In *Proceedings of CoNLL-2003*, Edmonton, Canada.

Aðalsteinn Tryggvason. 2009. Named Entity Recognition for Icelandic. Research report – Reykjavik University.

Yonghui Wu, Jun Xu, Min Jiang, Yaoyun Zhang, and Hua Xu. 2015. A Study of Neural Word Embeddings for Named Entity Recognition in Clinical Text. *AMIA Annual Symposium Proceedings*, 2015:1326–33.

Vikas Yadav and Steven Bethard. 2018. A Survey on Recent Advances in Named Entity Recognition from Deep Learning models. In *Proceedings of the 27th International Conference on Computational Linguistics*, COLING 2018, Santa Fe, New Mexico, USA.

Vilhjálmur Þorsteinsson, Hulda Óladóttir, and Hrafn Loftsson. 2019. A Wide-Coverage Context-Free Grammar for Icelandic and an Accompanying Parsing System. In *Proceedings of Recent Advances in Natural Language Processing (to appear)*, RANLP 2019, Varna, Bulgaria.

Neural Cross-Lingual Transfer and Limited Annotated Data for Named Entity Recognition in Danish

Barbara Plank
Department of Computer Science
ITU, IT University of Copenhagen
Denmark
bplank@itu.dk

Abstract

Named Entity Recognition (NER) has greatly advanced by the introduction of deep neural architectures. However, the success of these methods depends on large amounts of training data. The scarcity of publicly-available human-labeled datasets has resulted in limited evaluation of existing NER systems, as is the case for Danish. This paper studies the effectiveness of cross-lingual transfer for Danish, evaluates its complementarity to limited gold data, and sheds light on performance of Danish NER.

1 Introduction

Named entity recognition is a key step for natural language understanding (NLU), and important for information extraction, relation extraction, question answering and even privacy protection. However, the scarcity of publicly-available human annotated datasets has resulted in a lack of evaluation for languages beyond a selected set (e.g., those covered in early shared tasks like Dutch, German, English, Spanish), despite the fact that NER tools exists or recently emerged for other languages. One such case is Danish, for which NER dates back as early as (Bick, 2004) and tools exist (Bick, 2004; Derczynski et al., 2014; Johannessen et al., 2005; Al-Rfou et al.,

2013) but lack empirical evaluation.

Contemporarily, there exists a surge of interest in porting NLU components quickly and cheaply to new languages. This includes cross-lingual transfer methods that exploit resources from existing high-resource languages for zero-shot or few-shot learning. This line of research is blooming, particularly since the advent of neural NER, which holds the state of the art (Yadav and Bethard, 2018). However, neither neural tagging nor cross-lingual transfer has been explored for Danish NER, a gap we seek to fill in this paper.

Contributions We present a) publicly-available evaluation data to encourage research on Danish NER; b) an empirical comparison of two existing NER systems for Danish to a neural model; c) an empirical evaluation of learning an effective NER tagger for Danish via cross-lingual transfer paired with very little labeled data.

2 Approach

We investigate the following questions: **RQ1:** To what extent can we transfer a NER tagger to Danish from existing English resources? **RQ2:** How does cross-lingual transfer compare to annotating a very small amount of in-language data (zero-shot vs few-shot learning)? **RQ3:** How accurate are existing NER systems for Danish?

2.1 NER annotation

To answer these questions, we need gold annotated data. Access to existing resources is limited as they are not available online or behind a paywall. Therefore, we annotate NERs on top of publicly available data.[1]

In line with limited budget for annotation (Garrette and Baldridge, 2013), we add an annotation layer for Named Entities to the development and test sets of the Danish section of the Universal Dependencies (UD) treebank (Nivre et al., 2016; Johannsen et al., 2015). To answer RQ2, we further annotate a very small portion of the training data, i.e., the first 5,000 and 10,000 tokens. Examples are shown in Figure 1. Dataset statistics are provided in Table 2.

The Danish UD treebank (`Danish-DDT`) is a conversion of the Copenhagen Dependency Treebank (CDT). CDT (Kromann et al., 2003) consists of 5,512 sentences and 100k tokens, originating from the PAROLE-DK project (Bilgram and Keson, 1998). In contrast to original CDT and the PAROLE tokenization scheme, starting from the Danish UD has the advantage that it is closer to everyday language, as it splits tokens which were originally joined (such as 'i_alt').

We follow the CoNLL 2003 annotation guidelines (Tjong Kim Sang and De Meulder, 2003) and annotate proper names of four types: person (PER), location (LOC), organization (ORG) and miscellaneous (MISC). MISC contains for example names of products, drinks or film titles.

2.2 Cross-lingual transfer

We train a model on English (a medium and high resource setup, see details in Section 3) and transfer it to Danish, examining the following setups.

B-LOC	O	O	O	O	O	O	O
Rom	blev	ikke	bygget	på	èn	dag	.
O	O	O	B-PER	O	O	B-MISC	I-MISC
vinyl	,	som	Elvis	indspillede	i	Sun	Records

Table 1: Example annotations.

	Evaluation		Training	
	DEV	TEST	TINY	SMALL
Sentences	564	565	272	604
Tokens	10,332	10,023	4,669	10,069
Types	3,640	3,424	1,918	3,525
TTR	0.35	0.34	0.41	0.35
Sent.w/ NE	220	226	96	206
Sent.w/ NE%	39%	34%	35%	34%
Entities	348	393	153	341

Table 2: Overview of the annotated Danish NER data. Around 35%-39% of the sentences contain NEs. TTR: type-token ratio.

- **Zero-shot**: Direct transfer of the English model via aligned bilingual embeddings.
- **In-Language**: Training the neural model on very small amounts of in-language Danish training data only. We test two setups, training on the tiny data alone; or with unsupervised transfer via word embedding initialization (+Poly).
- **Few-shot direct transfer**: Training the neural model on English and Danish jointly, including bilingual embeddings.
- **Few-shot fine-tuning**: Training the neural model first on English, and fine-tuning it on Danish. This examines whether fine-tuning is better than training the model from scratch on both.

3 Experiments

As source data, we use the English CoNLL 2003 NER dataset (Tjong Kim Sang and De Meulder, 2003) with BIO tagging.

We study two setups for the source side: a MEDIUM and LARGE source data setup. For LARGE we use the entire CoNLL 2003

---

[1] `https://github.com/`
`UniversalDependencies/UD_Danish-DDT`

| | TnT | neural in-lang. | | neural transfer | | FineTune |
		plain	+Poly	+Medium src	+Large src	
zero-shot	—	—	—	58.29	61.18	—
Tiny	37.48	36.17	56.05	67.14	67.49	62.07
Small	44.30	51.90	67.18	**70.82**	70.01	65.63

Table 3: F_1 score on the development set for low-resource training setups (none, tiny 5k or small 10k labeled Danish sentences). Transfer via multilingual embeddings from Medium (3.2k sentences, 51k tokens) or Large English source data (14k sentences/203k tokens).

training data as starting point, which contains around 14,000 sentences and 200,000 tokens. To emulate a lower-resource setup, we consider a Medium setup, for which we employ the development data from CoNLL 2003 as training data (3,250 sentences and 51,000 tokens). The CoNLL data contains a high density of entities (79-80% of the sentences) but is lexically less rich (TTR of 0.11-0.19), compared to our Danish annotated data (Table 2), which is orders of magnitudes smaller, lexical richer but less dense on entities.

Model and Evaluation We train a bilstm-CRF similar to (Xie et al., 2018; Johnson et al., 2019). As pre-trained word embeddings we use the Polyglot embeddings (Al-Rfou et al., 2013). The word embeddings dimensionality is 64. The remaining hyperparameters were determined on the English CoNLL data. The word LSTM size was set to 50. Character embeddings are 50-dimensional. The character LSTM is 50 dimensions. Dropout was set to 0.25. We use Stochastic Gradient Descent with a learning rate of 0.1 and early stopping. We use the evaluation script from the CoNLL shared task and report mean F1 score over three runs.

Cross-lingual mapping We map the existing Danish Polyglot embeddings to the English embedding space by using an unsupervised alignment method which does not require parallel data. In particular, we use character-identical words as seeds for the Procrustes rotation method introduced in MUSE (Conneau et al., 2017).

4 Results

Table 3 presents the main results. There are several take-aways.

Cross-lingual transfer is powerful (RQ1). Zero-shot learning reaches an F1 score of 58% in the Medium setup, which outperforms training the neural tagger on very limited gold data (plain). Neural NER is better than traditional HMM-based tagging (TnT) (Brants, 2000) and greatly improves by unsupervised word embedding initialization (+Poly). It is noteworthy that zero-shot transfer benefits only to a limiting degree from more source data (F1 increases by 3% when training on all English CoNLL data).

To compare cross-lingual transfer to limited gold data (RQ2), we observe that training the neural system on the small amount of data together with Polyglot embeddings is close to the tiny-shot transfer setup. Few-shot learning greatly improves over zero-shot learning. The most beneficial way is to *add* the target data to the source, in comparison to fine-tuning. This shows that access to a tiny or small amount of training data is effective. Adding gold data with cross-lingual transfer is the best setup.

DEV	All	PER	LOC	ORG	MISC
Majority	44.8	61.8	0.0	0.0	—
DKIE	55.4	65.7	58.5	20.3	—
DKIE July 23	58.9	68.9	63.6	23.3	
Polyglot	64.5	73.7	**73.4**	36.8	—
Ours	**70.8**	**83.3**	71.8	**60.0**	23.9
TEST	All	PER	LOC	ORG	MISC
Polyglot	61.6	78.4	**69.7**	24.7	—
Ours	**66.0**	**86.6**	63.6	**42.5**	24.8

Table 4: F_1 score on the Danish dev set.

In both MEDIUM and LARGE setups are further gains obtained by adding TINY or SMALL amounts of Danish gold data. Interestingly, a) fine-tuning is less effective; b) it is better to transfer from a medium-sized setup than from the entire CoNLL source data.

Existing systems (RQ3) perform poorly (Table 4). Polyglot (Al-Rfou et al., 2013) is better than DKIE (Derczynski et al., 2014). Our best system is a cross-lingual transfer NER from MEDIUM source data paired with SMALL amounts of gold data. Per-Entity evaluation shows that ours outperforms Polyglot except for Location, which is consistent across evaluation data (Table 4). Overall we find that very little data paired with dense representations yields an effective NER quickly.

5   Related Work

Named Entity Recognition has a long history in NLP research. While interest in NER originally arose mostly from a question answering perspective, it developed into an independent task through the pioneering shared task organized by the Message Understanding Conference (MUC) (Grishman and Sundheim, 1996; Grishman, 1998). Since then, many shared task for NER have been organized, including CoNLL (Tjong Kim Sang and De Meulder, 2003) for newswire and WNUT for social media data (Baldwin et al., 2015). While

Danish NER tools and data exists (Bick, 2004; Derczynski et al., 2014; Johannessen et al., 2005; Al-Rfou et al., 2013), there was a lack of reporting F1 scores. Supersense tagging, a task close to NER has received attention (Martínez Alonso et al., 2015).

The range of methods that have been proposed for NER is broad. Early methods focused on hand-crated rule-based methods with lexicons and orthographic features. They were followed by feature-engineering rich statistical approaches (Nadeau and Sekine, 2007). Since the advent of deep learning and the seminal work by (Collobert et al., 2011), state-of-the-art NER systems typically rely on feature-inferring encoder-decoder models that extract dense embeddings from word and sub-word embeddings, including affixes (Yadav and Bethard, 2018), often outperforming neural architectures that include lexicon information such as gazetteers.

Recently, there has been a surge of interest in cross-lingual transfer of NER models (Xie et al., 2018). This includes work on transfer between distant languages (Rahimi et al., 2019) and work on projecting from multiple source languages (Johnson et al., 2019).

6   Conclusions

We contribute to the transfer learning literature by providing a first study on the effectiveness of exploiting English NER data to boost Danish NER performance.[2] We presented a publicly-available evaluation dataset and compare our neural cross-lingual Danish NER tagger to existing systems. Our experiments show that a very small amount of in-language NER data pushes cross-lingual transfer, resulting in an effective Danish NER system.

---

[2]Available at: `https://github.com/ITUnlp/transfer_ner`

Acknowledgements

We kindly acknowledge the support of NVIDIA Corporation for the donation of the GPUs and Amazon for an Amazon Research Award.

References

Rami Al-Rfou, Bryan Perozzi, and Steven Skiena. 2013. Polyglot: Distributed word representations for multilingual NLP. In *ACL*.

Timothy Baldwin, Marie-Catherine de Marneffe, Bo Han, Young-Bum Kim, Alan Ritter, and Wei Xu. 2015. Shared tasks of the 2015 workshop on noisy user-generated text: Twitter lexical normalization and named entity recognition. In *Proceedings of the Workshop on Noisy User-generated Text*, pages 126–135.

Eckhard Bick. 2004. A named entity recognizer for danish. In *LREC*.

Thomas Bilgram and Britt Keson. 1998. The construction of a tagged danish corpus. In *Proceedings of the 11th Nordic Conference of Computational Linguistics (NODALIDA 1998)*, pages 129–139.

Thorsten Brants. 2000. Tnt: a statistical part-of-speech tagger. In *Proceedings of the sixth conference on Applied natural language processing*, pages 224–231. Association for Computational Linguistics.

Ronan Collobert, Jason Weston, Léon Bottou, Michael Karlen, Koray Kavukcuoglu, and Pavel Kuksa. 2011. Natural language processing (almost) from scratch. *Journal of machine learning research*, 12(Aug):2493–2537.

Alexis Conneau, Guillaume Lample, Marc'Aurelio Ranzato, Ludovic Denoyer, and Hervé Jégou. 2017. Word translation without parallel data. *arXiv preprint arXiv:1710.04087*.

Leon Derczynski, Camilla Vilhelmsen Field, and Kenneth S Bøgh. 2014. Dkie: Open source information extraction for danish. In *Proceedings of the Demonstrations at the 14th Conference of the European Chapter of the Association for Computational Linguistics*, pages 61–64.

Dan Garrette and Jason Baldridge. 2013. Learning a part-of-speech tagger from two hours of annotation. In *Proceedings of the 2013 Conference of the North American Chapter of the Association for Computational Linguistics: Human Language Technologies*, pages 138–147.

Ralph Grishman. 1998. Research in information extraction: 1996-98. In *Proceedings of the TIPSTER Text Program: Phase III*, pages 57–60, Baltimore, Maryland, USA. Association for Computational Linguistics.

Ralph Grishman and Beth Sundheim. 1996. Message understanding conference- 6: A brief history. In *COLING 1996 Volume 1: The 16th International Conference on Computational Linguistics*.

Janne Bondi Johannessen, Kristin Hagen, Åsne Haaland, Andra Björk Jónsdottir, Anders Nøklestad, Dimitris Kokkinakis, Paul Meurer, Eckhard Bick, and Dorte Haltrup. 2005. Named entity recognition for the mainland scandinavian languages. *Literary and Linguistic Computing*, 20(1):91–102.

Anders Johannsen, Héctor Martínez Alonso, and Barbara Plank. 2015. Universal dependencies for danish. In *International Workshop on Treebanks and Linguistic Theories (TLT14)*, page 157.

Andrew Johnson, Penny Karanasou, Judith Gaspers, and Dietrich Klakow. 2019. Crosslingual transfer learning for Japanese named entity recognition. In *Proceedings of the 2019 Conference of the North American Chapter of the Association for Computational Linguistics: Human Language Technologies, Volume 2 (Industry Papers)*, Minneapolis - Minnesota. Association for Computational Linguistics.

Matthias T Kromann, Line Mikkelsen, and Stine Kern Lynge. 2003. Danish dependency treebank. In *Proc. TLT*, pages 217–220. Citeseer.

Héctor Martínez Alonso, Anders Johannsen, Sussi Olsen, Sanni Nimb, Nicolai Hartvig Sørensen, Anna Braasch, Anders Søgaard, and Bolette Sandford Pedersen. 2015. Supersense tagging for Danish. In *Proceedings of the 20th Nordic Conference of Computational Linguistics (NODALIDA 2015)*, Vilnius, Lithuania.

Linköping University Electronic Press, Sweden.

David Nadeau and Satoshi Sekine. 2007. A survey of named entity recognition and classification. *Lingvisticae Investigationes*, 30(1):3–26.

Joakim Nivre, Marie-Catherine De Marneffe, Filip Ginter, Yoav Goldberg, Jan Hajic, Christopher D Manning, Ryan McDonald, Slav Petrov, Sampo Pyysalo, Natalia Silveira, et al. 2016. Universal dependencies v1: A multilingual treebank collection. In *Proceedings of the Tenth International Conference on Language Resources and Evaluation (LREC 2016)*, pages 1659–1666.

Afshin Rahimi, Yuan Li, and Trevor Cohn. 2019. Multilingual ner transfer for low-resource languages. In *Proceedings of the 2019 Conference of the Chapter of the Association for Computational Linguistics*.

Erik F Tjong Kim Sang and Fien De Meulder. 2003. Introduction to the conll-2003 shared task: Language-independent named entity recognition. *arXiv preprint cs/0306050*.

Jiateng Xie, Zhilin Yang, Graham Neubig, Noah A Smith, and Jaime Carbonell. 2018. Neural cross-lingual named entity recognition with minimal resources. *arXiv preprint arXiv:1808.09861*.

Vikas Yadav and Steven Bethard. 2018. A survey on recent advances in named entity recognition from deep learning models. In *Proceedings of the 27th International Conference on Computational Linguistics*, pages 2145–2158.

The Seemingly (Un)systematic Linking Element in Danish

Sidsel Boldsen and **Manex Agirrezabal**
Centre for Language Technology
University of Copenhagen
{sbol,manex.aguirrezabal}@hum.ku.dk

Abstract

The use of a linking element between compound members is a common phenomenon in Germanic languages. Still, the exact use and conditioning of such elements is a disputed topic in linguistics. In this paper we address the issue of predicting the use of linking elements in Danish. Following previous research that shows how the choice of linking element might be conditioned by phonology, we frame the problem as a language modeling task: Considering the linking elements *-s/-∅* the problem becomes predicting what is most probable to encounter next, a syllable boundary or the joining element, *s*. We show that training a language model on this task reaches an accuracy of 94 %, and in the case of an unsupervised model, the accuracy reaches 80 %.

1 Introduction

In Danish, Norwegian and Swedish, as well as in other Germanic languages, a common way of forming new words is by compounding. Here, novel words can be formed by combining already known words with an addition of a linking element between the components. Within linguistic research this linking element is somewhat of a puzzle: First of all, several languages within the Germanic family seem to share similar linking elements (Fuhrhop and Kürschner, 2014). The origin of these elements are however disputed (Nübling and Szczepaniak, 2013). Even if we assume a common origin, the use and distribution of single elements have changed among daughter languages, and we often find contradicting examples e.g., when comparing Ge. *Volk-s-musik* and Da. *folk-e-musik* 'folk music' (Fuhrhop and

Kürschner, 2014). Secondly, even though the choice of a linking element may be clear to the individual speaker, linguists still struggle to establish rules for when the individual elements occur. In Danish, the linking element is decided from the first member of a compound. But when looking for rules that systematize what words take which element, only few guidelines are given (Hansen and Heltoft, 2011). Interestingly, recent studies on linking elements in German suggest that the choice of linking element is at least partially phonological, determined by features such as stress (Nübling and Szczepaniak, 2013).

Compounding has received attention in language technology as well, since it is the essence of one of the main challenges within this field: that language is productive. Within the area of statistical machine translation, segmentation of compounds into units is an important task, e.g., when translating compound words from German to English where compounding is not productive (Sag et al., 2002). Similarly, when translating English multiword expressions (MWE) into German, methods for synthesis or generation of compounds are called for (Stymne et al., 2013). Here the choice of a correct linking element becomes an issue. In the work by Cap and Fraser (2014) they rely on a rule-based morphological analyzer for German to generate the correct compounding form. Here they report that on a reference set of 283 correctly identified compounds 44 had an incorrect linking element. Recent work by Matthews et al. (2016) proposes a translation model from English MWE to German compounds that allows for modeling linking elements. In their work, they report a high recall score when generating novel compounds. Their error analysis show that their model has issues when choosing linking elements (e.g., when generating *Kirchen*türme instead of the correct *Kirch*türme 'church towers'), but they do not further provide any metrics on this subtask.

In this paper we wish to see how well a simple character-based language model is able to predict the usage of linking elements in Danish. More specifically we will look at the case of predicting occurrence of two elements *-s* and *-∅* (traditionally referred to as a *nulfuge* 'zero link') in Danish noun-noun compounds.

2   The linking element in Danish

In Danish, a compound is formed by attaching a linking element to the stem of its first member. Table 1 shows a list of the most common linking elements. The choice of linking element in a compound is determined by the first member. While most nouns only have one possible linking element, we do find alternation: First of all, a noun may have more competing elements that are used in connection with certain second members. An example is the noun *båd* 'boat' to which different elements can be attached depending on the compound (*båd-skat* 'boat tax', but *båd-e-byggeri* 'boat building'). Secondly, some nouns have alternating linking elements that can be used interchangeably as in *aluminium(s)rør* 'aluminum tube'.

Hansen & Heltoft (2011) present rules only for cases where the linking element *-s* is used: Usually an *-s* occurs when the first member is a compound, but many exceptions can be added to this rule. Moreover, words derived with the suffixes *-(n)ing*, *-ion*, and *-tek* always get an *-s*.

LE	Example	
-s	*idræt*	*idrætsdag* 'sports day'
-∅	*ankel*	*ankelled* 'ancle joint'
-e	*mælk*	*mælkepulver* 'milk powder'
-er	*student*	*studenterhue* 'graduation hat'
-n	*rose*	*rosenbed* 'rose bed'

Table 1: Linking elements (LE) in Danish. The elements above the separator are considered productive while the elements below are only found in isolated forms (Hansen and Heltoft, 2011).

In some dialects the use of *-s* is preferred instead of the unmarked *-∅* in some cases. This could suggest that phonology does play a role in the choice of linking element as was also proposed by Nübling and Szczepaniak (2013) in the case of German. Following this suggestion, we focus on the two linking elements *-s* and *-∅* in order to explore how well the choice between these elements can be predicted using a character-based language model.

3   The task

We formulate the problem of determining the correct linking element of a noun as a language modeling task over the characters of a word: Given a word as a sequence of characters, what is the most probable element to come next, assuming that the word continues? Thus, when trying to determine whether a noun should take *-s* or *-∅*, the problem becomes to estimate what would be most probable to observe next: an *s* or a *syllable boundary*?

The intuition behind this approach is, assuming that some underlying phonological process governs the choice of linking elements, then, learning the distribution over the sounds or characters of a word (including the two linking elements—the sound s and a syllable boundary), will help us to predict what element will occur as the linking element of the first member of a compound.

Data The dataset that we use for the task is *Retskrivningsordbogen* (RO) (Jervelund, 2012), which is the main source for official orthography in Danish with over $61,000$ entries in total. In RO, all words are marked with syllable boundaries (indicated by a $+$ in the text string) and information on what linking element(s) the word takes as a first member of a compound. From RO we extract the syllabified forms of nouns with linking element *-s*/*-∅* (excluding nouns with alternate linking elements), providing us with a dataset of 6,880 instances of nouns and linking elements.

4   Experiments

We introduce two models to approach the problem and two baselines from which we make our conclusions. First, we investigated whether character-based language models would be able to estimate the correct linking element of a word. To this end, we trained a language model on syllabified words together with their linking element (s/+). Second, we approached the problem in an unsupervised manner, training a general language model on syllabified words, without providing any specific information on linking elements.

In both experiments the models are evaluated as a prediction task on how well they are able to predict the correct linking element of a word by weighing the estimated probabilities of observing an *s* or a syllable boundary (+) in the end of

Training objective	Input	Training signal	Prediction task	Correct answer
Language model, unsupervised	ˆi+dræt		$P(s) > P(+)$?	True
Language model, unsupervised	ˆan+kel		$P(s) > P(+)$?	False
Language model, supervised	ˆi+dræt$	s	$P(s) > P(+)$?	True
Language model, supervised	ˆan+kel$	+	$P(s) > P(+)$?	False

Table 2: Examples of input, training signals and prediction task for the supervised and unsupervised approaches. Adapted from (Linzen et al., 2016).

a word. In order to validate the performance of our models, we employ 5-Fold Cross-Validation on the set of *-s/-∅* nouns from RO. For each iteration, we train a model with four folds and we divide the remaining fold equally for development and test.

4.1 Experiment 1: Supervised approach

In the first experiment, we train a character-based Recurrent Neural Network (RNN) language model on the entire set of *-s/-∅* nouns from RO, including the linking element at the end of each instance.

We use a two-layer RNN with LSTM that receives an embedded representation of the characters with 128 dimensions, which are learned while training. Each LSTM layer has 64 dimensions and predictions are made using a softmax over the vocabulary of characters. We train the model using Stochastic Gradient Descent with cyclical learning rate (Smith, 2015) using the DyNet framework (Neubig et al., 2017).

As Table 2 shows, besides a beginning-of-word symbol (ˆ), we also add an end-of-word symbol (EOW) ($) to the input. We expect that this addition will improve the performance of the model, as it helps to supervise the training signal more clearly by restricting the distribution of s and $+$ as compounding elements to occur only after the EOW symbol. However, this approach also adds noise to the signal as the original sequence of characters is altered.

4.2 Experiment 2: Unsupervised approach

In the second experiment, we train an RNN identical to that in the first experiment, but without including any specific information on linking elements. Thus, at test time, this model has not been trained on nouns and linking elements, but would estimate the probabilities, $P(s)$ and $P(+)$, from the distribution of s and $+$ word-internally. The model is trained on the words from RO that are not included within the set of *-s/-∅* nouns. The

difference between the two models is summarized in Table 2.

4.3 Baseline

For each of the experiments we create two baselines. The first baseline common to both experiments chooses the most frequent linking element from the dataset. In the supervised approach, this means choosing the most frequent label from the training set. In the unsupervised case, this corresponds to the most frequent character (as it does not have access to labeled examples). In the second baseline we create an iterative back-off model that attempts to match the input word with already observed sequences of syllables from the training set.

For the supervised model, the reason that we create this baseline is because we know the rime of a word may be predictive for the choice of linking element. Thus, the back-off model starts by trying to retrieve the whole word in order to test if this was observed during training. If not, it will try to match iteratively shorter sequences of syllables until a matching rime is found. If a match is found the most frequent case of linking element is predicted. If no match is encountered, the model will back-off to the most frequent strategy.

The back-off model in the unsupervised case is similar. Here, the only difference is that we do not look for rimes, but all of the possible continuous subsequences of syllables. This is done in order to test how well a model performs in determining the joining element by remembering exact sequences of possible syllables word internally.

5 Results

The results from the two experiments are presented in Table 3. Starting with the results from Experiment 1 using the supervised approach, we see that the supervised LM reaches 0.94 for both accuracy and f1, which is higher than both of the baselines we provided. Looking more closely

	Set	Support	Supervised LM		Baseline I		Baseline II	
			avg	std	avg	std	avg	std
accuracy	all	3440	**0.94**	0.009	0.56	0.023	0.83	0.023
f1			**0.94**	0.009	0.36	0.009	0.81	0.023
accuracy	seen	2977	**0.95**	0.009	0.62	0.019	0.93	0.013
f1			**0.94**	0.009	0.38	0.007	0.92	0.014
accuracy	unseen	463	**0.90**	0.024	0.17	0.028	0.17	0.028
f1			**0.82**	0.050	0.15	0.021	0.15	0.021
f1 $(-\varnothing)$	unseen	383	**0.94**	0.014	0.00	0.000	0.00	0.000
f1 $(-s)$		80	**0.71**	0.088	0.29	0.042	0.29	0.042

	Set	Support	Unsupervised LM		Baseline I		Baseline II	
			avg	std	avg	std	avg	std
accuracy	all	3440	0.80	0.011	0.44	0.023	**0.82**	0.001
f1			0.80	0.011	0.30	0.011	**0.82**	0.001
accuracy	seen	3287	0.80	0.010	0.41	0.022	**0.82**	0.001
f1			0.80	0.010	0.29	0.011	**0.82**	0.001
accuracy	unseen	153	0.87	0.061	**0.88**	0.035	**0.88**	0.035
f1			**0.66**	0.126	0.47	0.010	0.47	0.010
f1 $(-\varnothing)$	unseen	135	**0.96**	0.035	0.94	0.020	0.94	0.020
f1 $(-s)$		18	**0.39**	0.219	0.00	0.000	0.00	0.000

Table 3: Results for the supervised and unsupervised approaches and their baselines.

into the results, we divide the test instances into two subsets, seen and unseen words, indicating whether words with the same rime were found during training. Considering the seen words, the LM only has a small gain compared to Baseline II, which was the baseline that used observed rimes to determine the linking element of a word. Contrarily, if we observe the set of unseen words, the gain is much higher. However, this set of words is imbalanced with respect to what linking elements are represented. This is reflected in the low accuracy score of 0.17 of both baselines, that in these cases choose the most frequent linking element observed in the training set (s). If we compare the f1 score for this set of words to the f1 score of the seen, the performance is lower. This is due to the model being worse at predicting the occurrence of -s in the unseen examples where it only reaches an f1 score of 0.71.

Turning to the results of the second experiment, Baseline II clearly outperforms Baseline I except for in the unseen cases, where the two baselines have the same strategy of choosing the most frequent of the characters in the training data. Furthermore, we observe that the unsupervised LM performs similarly to Baseline II overall. In the specific case of the unseen words, we can observe

that the f1 score is moderately higher. Here the model does find a strategy of predicting a joining element (in contrast to the two baselines that always choose -$\varnothing$), however, the f1 score of -s is still quite low. This is similar to the behavior of the supervised model on its unseen test instances. However, the individual results for -s in these cases are supported by relatively few instances (80 and 18 examples in the supervised and unsupervised experiments respectively) which is also reflected in high standard deviations.

6 Discussion

By providing a character-based language model with tagged data consisting of words and their joining elements, the model performs well on the test set. This is the case for words that are similar to the ones observed during training. But also, the model is able to generalize to words with previously unseen structure.

In the unsupervised approach, in which we did not provide any information on joining elements, the model still performs well. However, it does not outperform the baseline that retrieves sequences observed while training. This means that we cannot say that the representations learned by this model are more powerful than simply recalling observed sequences. Nevertheless, the model is able to predict the joining element in some cases of unseen rimes.

7 Conclusion & future work

In this paper we approached the issue of predicting the linking element of Danish -s/-∅ compounds using a character-based language model. When using a language model trained of examples of words and linking elements, we reach an accuracy of 94 %. Using a language model that has never seen tagged examples reaches an accuracy of 80 % on the same task. These are promising results, but we need further error analysis to better understand the examples in which language modeling is struggling to identify the correct elements.

To pursue the approach of language modeling further, one future line of work would be to add more information to the training signal. As mentioned in the introduction, features such as stress may be an important factor in the phonological processes determining what linking element is chosen. Such information is not immediately apparent using the orthographic representation of a word as was used in this experiment. In this respect, it would be interesting to see how the models perform using phonetic transcriptions instead. Since such transcription is expensive, one could try to construct this level using grapheme-to-phoneme conversion software. As an alternative one could also attempt to reproduce the experiment using speech data.

In this paper we used a dictionary of words as training corpus. An alternative would be to use a collection of text in which information about word frequency would be included. This, in turn, might result in a different model that would be interesting to compare to the one presented above.

Furthermore, it would be interesting to see how well this approach is able to predict other linking elements in Danish, as well as in other languages.

Acknowledgments

The first author is supported by the project *Script and Text in Time and Space*, a core group project supported by the Velux Foundations. We are grateful to Patrizia Paggio for her support and comments regarding this paper. We would also like to acknowledge the anonymous reviewers for their suggestions and comments.

References

Fabienne Cap, Alexander Fraser, Marion Weller, and Aoife Cahill. 2014. How to produce unseen teddy bears: Improved morphological processing of compounds in SMT. In *Proceedings of the 14th Conference of the European Chapter of the Association for Computational Linguistics*, pages 579–587, Gothenburg, Sweden. Association for Computational Linguistics.

Nanna Fuhrhop and Sebastian Kürschner. 2014. Linking elements in Germanic. In Susan Olsen Franz Rainer Peter O. Müller, Ingeborg Ohnheiser, editor, *Word formation. An international handbook of the languages of Europe*, HSK 40/1, page 568–582. de Gruyter Mouton, Berlin/New York.

Erik Hansen and Lars Heltoft. 2011. *Grammatik over det Danske Sprog*, 1 edition, volume 1-3. Syddansk Universitetsforlag.

Anita Ågerup Jervelund. 2012. *Retskrivningsordbogen*, 4. udg. edition. Alinea, København.

Tal Linzen, Emmanuel Dupoux, and Yoav Goldberg. 2016. Assessing the ability of LSTMs to learn syntax-sensitive dependencies. *Transactions of the Association for Computational Linguistics*, 4:521–535.

Austin Matthews, Eva Schlinger, Alon Lavie, and Chris Dyer. 2016. Synthesizing compound words for machine translation. In *Proceedings of the 54th Annual Meeting of the Association for Computational Linguistics (Volume 1: Long Papers)*, pages 1085–1094, Berlin, Germany. Association for Computational Linguistics.

Graham Neubig, Chris Dyer, Yoav Goldberg, Austin Matthews, Waleed Ammar, Antonios Anastasopoulos, Miguel Ballesteros, David Chiang, Daniel Clothiaux, Trevor Cohn, et al. 2017. Dynet: The dynamic neural network toolkit. *arXiv preprint arXiv:1701.03980*.

Damaris Nübling and Renata Szczepaniak. 2013. Linking elements in german origin, change, functionalization. *Morphology*, 23(1):67–89.

Ivan A. Sag, Timothy Baldwin, Francis Bond, Ann Copestake, and Dan Flickinger. 2002. Multiword expressions: A pain in the neck for nlp. In *Computational Linguistics and Intelligent Text Processing*, pages 1–15, Berlin, Heidelberg. Springer Berlin Heidelberg.

Leslie N Smith. 2015. 'cyclical learning rates for training neural networks', cite. *arXiv preprint arxiv:1506.01186*.

Sara Stymne, Nicola Cancedda, and Lars Ahrenberg. 2013. Generation of compound words in statistical machine translation into compounding languages. *Computational Linguistics*, 39(4):1067–1108.

Demo Papers

LEGATO: A flexible lexicographic annotation tool

David Alfter
Språkbanken
Department of Swedish
University of Gothenburg
Sweden
david.alfter@gu.se

Therese Lindström Tiedemann
Department of Finnish, Finno-Ugrian
and Scandinavian Studies
University of Helsinki
Finland
therese.lindstromtiedemann@helsinki.fi

Elena Volodina
Språkbanken
Department of Swedish
University of Gothenburg
Sweden
elena.volodina@gu.se

Abstract

This article reports an ongoing project aimed at analyzing lexical and grammatical competences of Swedish as a Second language (L2). To facilitate lexical analysis, we need access to linguistic information about relevant vocabulary that L2 learners can use and understand. The focus of the current article is on the lexical annotation of the vocabulary scope for a range of lexicographical aspects, such as morphological analysis, valency, types of multi-word units, etc. We perform parts of the analysis automatically, and other parts manually. The rationale behind this is that where there is no possibility to add information automatically, manual effort needs to be added. To facilitate the latter, a tool LEGATO has been designed, implemented and currently put to active testing.

1 Introduction

Lexical competence has been acknowledged as one of the most important aspects of language learning (e.g. Singleton, 1995; Milton, 2013; Laufer and Sim, 1985). Some claim that we need to understand 95–98% of the words in a text to manage reading comprehension tasks (cf. Laufer and Ravenhorst-Kalovski, 2010; Nation, 2006; Hsueh-Chao and Nation, 2000). It has also been observed that vocabulary is actively taught at all levels of L2 proficiency courses with a tendency to be dominating at more advanced levels in comparison to other linguistic skills, see for example findings from a course book corpus COCTAILL (Volodina et al., 2014, p.140). Lexical features have also been found to be one of the best predictors in text classification studies (e.g. Pilán and Volodina, 2018; Xia et al., 2016; Vajjala and Meurers, 2012) with important implications to the

area of educational NLP. Deciding on which vocabulary to use and include is thus an important part of teaching a foreign language, in designing course materials and tests. In theoretical descriptions of L2 acquisition, lexical knowledge was previously "side-lined" according to Milton, but within academic circles its place has been "significantly revised" and received an increasing amount of interest over recent decades (Milton, 2013).

There are multiple characteristics of vocabulary that are interesting from the point of view of both theoretical analyses, as well as for pedagogical and NLP-based applications. Such characteristics include, among others, vocabulary size & breadth (e.g. Nation and Meara, 2010; Milton, 2013), corpus frequency (Dürlich and François, 2018; François et al., 2016), word family relations (Bauer and Nation, 1993), syllable structure, morphological characteristics, semantic relations, topical domain categorization (Alfter and Volodina, 2018), and many others (e.g. Capel, 2010, 2012).

While frequency information comes from corpora, most linguistic characteristics are non-trivial to acquire by automatic methods and require either manual effort or access to manually prepared resources – lexicons being the most extensive and reliable sources for that. However, dictionaries and lexicons are often proprietary resources (e.g. Sköldberg et al., 2019), which complicates automatic lexicon enrichment. Among freely available lexicons for Swedish, we can name Saldo (Borin et al., 2013), Swesaurus (Borin and Forsberg, 2014), Lexin (Hult et al., 2010) and a few other resources provided through Språkbanken's infrastructure Karp (Borin et al., 2012), although, even there many aspects of vocabulary are not documented, e.g. the transitivity of verbs, the morphological structure of the words (root, prefix, suffix) or the topical domain of the words.

To circumvent the problem of access to the information that may prove crucial in the context of the current project for the three outlined areas of application (theoretical studies, pedagogical studies/applied linguistics and educational NLP), we have initiated semi-automatic annotation of learner-relevant vocabulary interlinking available resources with manual controls of those, and adding missing aspects manually. The work is ongoing, and below we present the reasoning around this annotation process and the main components of the system that facilitate that.

2 Second language profiles project

In the current project, *Development of lexical and grammatical competences in immigrant Swedish* funded by Riksbankens Jubileumsfond, the main aim is to provide an extensive description of the lexical and grammatical competence learners of L2 Swedish possess at each CEFR[1] level, and to explore the relation between the receptive and productive scopes. The exploration of the grammatical and lexical aspects of L2 proficiency is performed based on two corpora, COCTAILL (Volodina et al., 2014), a corpus of course books used in teaching L2 Swedish and the SweLL-pilot (Volodina et al., 2016a), a corpus of L2 Swedish essays. The corpora are automatically processed using the SPARV pipeline (Borin et al., 2016), and include, e.g., tokenization, lemmatization, POS-tagging, dependency parsing, and word sense disambiguation.

3 LEGATO tool

LEGATO[2] - **LE**xico**G**raphic **A**nnotation **TO**ol - is a web-based graphical user interface that allows for manual annotation of different lexicographic levels, e.g. morphological structure (root, affix etc), topic, transitivity, type of verb (e.g. auxiliary, motion verb), etc. The interface shows a lemgram for a given word sense, the part of speech and the CEFR level, as well as the Saldo sense and the primary and secondary sense descriptors used in Saldo (Borin et al., 2013), and up to three example sentences taken from the COCTAILL corpus. If there are fewer than three sentences available at the target CEFR level, the maximum number of sentences found is shown. It also features search, filter and skip functionalities as well as ex-

ternal links to other information sources such as Karp (Ahlberg et al., 2016); SAOL, SO & SAOB via svenska.se (Malmgren, 2014; Petzell, 2017); and the Swedish Academy's Grammar (SAG, the main grammar of the Swedish language) (Teleman et al., 1999). Figure 1 shows the user interface for the annotation of *nominal type* category.

3.1 Data for lexicographic annotation

For lexical analysis, we generate word lists (SenSVALex and SenSweLLex) based on senses from the two linguistically annotated corpora, both lists being successors of the lemgram-based ones from the same corpora (François et al., 2016; Volodina et al., 2016b). The lists contain accompanying frequency information per CEFR level according to the level assigned to the texts/essays where they first appear. In practical terms, the task of preparing a resource for lexical studies involves:

1. labeling all items for their "target" level of proficiency – that is, the level at which the item is expected to be understood (receptive list) or actively used (productive list). The CEFR level of each item is approximated as the first level at which the item appears, i.e. the level would be B2 for entry X if it was first observed at level B2 (cf. Gala et al., 2013, 2014; Alfter and Volodina, 2018).

2. interlinking items with other resources for enrichment, e.g. adding information on adjective declension

3. manually controlling the previous step for a subset of items to estimate the quality

4. setting up an annotation environment for adding missing information.

While (1) above has been partially addressed by Alfter et al. (2016) and Alfter and Volodina (2018), steps (2–4) are described shortly in the sections below.

3.2 Automatic enrichment

An overview of linguistic aspects annotated using LEGATO is provided in Table 1. All aspects are kept as close as possible to the terminology and the description of Swedish grammar in SAG (Teleman et al., 1999). A subset of those aspects, marked as *A* or *A-M* in Table 1 (column "Mode") are annotated automatically using a range of available resources mentioned in the column "Resources for auto-enrichment". Other aspects are added manually (*M*) following guidelines[3] explaining choices

---

[1]CEFR = Common European Framework of Reference (Council of Europe, 2001)

[2]https://spraakbanken.gu.se/larkalabb/ legato; user "test" for testing purposes

[3]https://urlzs.com/PZoRm

Aspect	Explanation / choices	Mode	Resources for auto-enrichment
1 Adj/adv structure	comparisons: periphr.: *(mer/mest) en-tusiastisk*; morph.: *vacker-vackrare-vackrast*; irreg.: *god-bra-bäst*	A-M[2]	Saldo-Morphology
2 Adj declension	decl. 1 & 2, irregular, indeclinable	A-M	Saldo-Morphology
3 Morphology 1	word analysis for morphemes: *oändlig*: prefix:*o-*; root:*-änd-*; suffix:*-lig*	M[3]	
4 Morphology 2	word-building: root, compound, derivation, suppletion, lexicalized, MWE[1]	M	
5 MWE type	taxonomy under development	M	
6 Nom declension	decl. 1-6, extra	A[4]	Saldo-Morphology
7 Nom gender	common, neuter, both, N/A	A	Saldo-Morphology
8 Nom type	abstract–concrete, (un)countable, (non)collective, (in)animate, proper name, unit of measurement	M	
9 Register	neutral, formal, informal, sensitive	M	
10 Synonyms	free input, same word class	A-M	Swesaurus
11 Topics/domains	general + 40 CEFR-related topics[5]	A-M	Lexin, COCTAILL
12 Transitivity	(in-, di-)transitive, N/A	A-M	SAOL (under negotiation)
13 Verb category	lexical, modal, auxiliary, copula, reciprocal, deponent	M	
14 Verb conjugation	conjugations 1-4, irregular, N/A	A	Saldo-Morphology
15 Verb action type	motion, state, punctual, process[6]	M	

Table 1: Linguistic aspects added to SenSVALex and SenSweLLex items
[1]MWE = Multi-Word Entity; [2]Manual based on automatically enriched input; [3]Manual; [4]Automatic; [5]Topics come from the CEFR document (Council of Europe, 2001), COCTAILL corpus (Volodina et al., 2014), and some other resources; [6]Incl. limited and unlimited process verbs

and argumentation based on SAG and other work on the Swedish language and linguistic description in general.

To augment SenSVALex & SenSweLLex, we use different resources. Besides the information already present in these lists (word senses, Saldo descriptors, automatically derived CEFR level, part-of-speech), we use Saldo / Saldo morphology (Borin et al., 2013), Swesaurus (Borin and Forsberg, 2014), Lexin (Hult et al., 2010) and potentially SAOL (Malmgren, 2014) to enrich the lists.

Saldo morphology is used to add nominal gender, nominal declension and verbal conjugation. Adjectival declension and adjectival (and adverbial) structure are derived from the comparative and superlative forms given in Saldo morphology and checked manually. Synonyms are added using Swesaurus. Other named resources are planned for enriching topics and transitivity patterns. The remaining categories are left to be manually annotated.

3.3 Tool functionality

LEGATO offers a range of useful functionalities. It allows moving forward as well as backwards through the list; to search through the list of word senses to be annotated and to filter by certain criteria; to skip words you are uncertain about. Items that are skipped are added to a dedicated 'skip list' which makes it is easy to come back to these items. It also keeps track of your progress, allowing the annotator to close the interface, come back at a later time and continue where they left. Finally, it includes (automatically generated) links to different external resources such as Saldo (through Karp), Wiktionary, svenska.se, Lexin, synonymer.se, Korp and SAG.

For user friendliness, we keep guidelines, issue-reporting and lookup/reference materials linked to the front page of the tool. It is possible to leave comments, start issues/discussion threads, as well as see an overview of all completed tasks and tasks that are remaining.

3.4 Piloting the tool

To test LEGATO's functionality as well as to control that the automatic linking of items is sufficiently reliable, we carried out an experiment with 100 SenSVALex items, divided equally between nouns, verbs, adjectives and adverbs. The selected words represent all the CEFR levels available in the COCTAILL corpus, various morphological paradigms and other types of linguistically relevant patterns as shown in Table 1.

In order to test the tool, two of the authors volunteered as annotators. After gathering data from the intial test phase, we calculated inter-annotator agreement (IAA) between the automatic analysis and annotator one (IAA 1), as well as the inter-annotator agreement between annotator one and annotator two (IAA 2). Table 2 shows Cohen's κ^4 for the various categories. For IAA 1, only categories where annotator one had completed all tasks, and where automatic enrichment was used, were taken into account. For IAA 2, only categories where both of the annotators had completed all tasks were taken into account. This explains why some of the values are missing in the Table.

As can be gathered from Table 2, categories with closed answers, e.g. only one possible answer value, lead to higher agreement (nominal declension, nominal gender, verbal conjugation), while categories that allow multiple answers or free-text input show less agreement (nominal type, adjectival adverbial structure, morphology 1). For example, for nominal type, if one annotator selects

Category	IAA 1	IAA 2
nominal declension (6)	0.85	0.80
nominal gender (7)	0.82	0.73
nominal type (5)		0.20
verbal conjugation (14)	0.82	0.94
adjectival declension (2)	0.49	
adjectival adverbial structure (1)	0.39	
morphology 1 (3)		0.48
Overall κ	0.73	0.60

Table 2: Inter-annotator agreement. Numbers in brackets (Column 1) refer to the numbering of categories in Table 1

"abstract, countable, inanimate" and another annotator select "concrete, countable, inanimate", this would be counted as disagreement. In order to address such problems, one would have to calculate partial agreement. One notable exception is adjectival declension, which only allows one value, but has low agreement between the automatic analysis and annotator one. This discrepancy could stem from the fact that all forms in Saldo morphology are automatically expanded, according to regular morphology, thus potentially producing forms that are incorrect.

As a result of the IAA calculations, a subset of categories has been deemed reliable enough to be added automatically (categories 6, 7, 14 in Table 1), and another subset will be offered in a semi-automatic way, where a manual control check will be performed (categories 1, 2, 10, 11, 12 in Table 1).

The experiment with the 100 items has also helped us set up and refine guidelines for more extensive annotation by project assistants, as well as improve the functionality of the tool.

3.5 Technical details

LEGATO is a module integrated with the Lärka-Labb[5] platform. Like its parent platform, the LEGATO front-end is written in TypeScript and HTML using the Angular (previously called *Angular 2*) framework[6]. The back-end is written in Python 2. Data is stored in MySQL format.

Data preparation (i.e. automatic enrichment, see Section 3.2) is done outside of the LEGATO platform using a set of dedicated scripts. In a multi-

---

[4]While values between 0.40 and 0.60 are generally considered borderline, values of 0.75 and above are seen as good to excellent.

[5]https://spraakbanken.gu.se/larkalabb
[6]https://angular.io

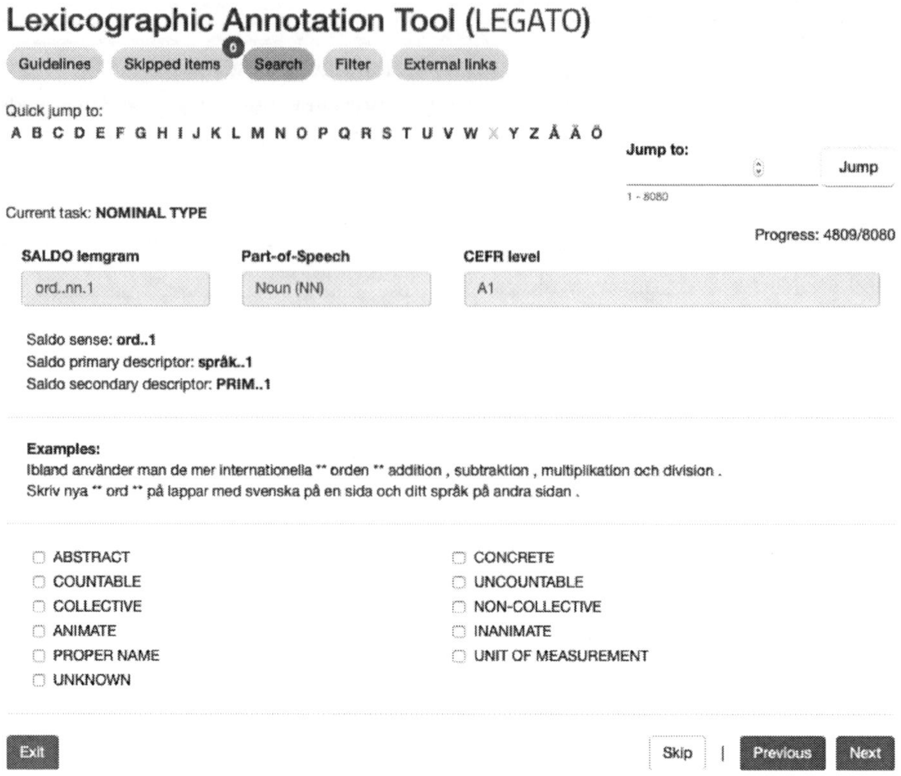

Figure 1: LEGATO graphical user interface

step process, these scripts (1) create the sense-based word list, (2) add Saldo primary and secondary descriptors, (3) add further information such as synonyms and nominal gender by linking lexical resources based on lemgram, sense and part-of-speech tuples and (4) add example sentences. The resulting data is played into the databases on the server side to reduce the number of API calls and reduce runtime. As some of these scripts have a rather long runtime (the average time per entry for example selection is 0.66 seconds on an Intel Core i5-5200U processor, resulting in about 3 hours total for the whole list), they are not distributed as an integrated part of LEGATO and we do not consider advisable to integrate them into the LEGATO platform. However, the code for running interlinking can be made available for reuse.

4   Concluding remarks

We are currently exploring a possibility of using Lexin (Hult et al., 2010) and COCTAILL (Volodina et al., 2014) to automatically derive topical domains for vocabulary items. Furthermore, fruitful negotiations are ongoing on a potential access to parts of the SAOL database (Malmgren, 2014) for semi-automatic support of annotation of transitivity patterns.

A full-scale annotation of the two lists is planned for the near future, with the results (i.e. a full resource) expected by the end of 2019. Once the resources are richly annotated, we expect to perform both quantitative and qualitative analysis of L2 lexical competence. The LEGATO tool will have a thorough testing during that time and we hope this will lead to further improvements of the tool.

Since Legato is a module in a highly intricate and interlinked system Lärka, we do not deem it reasonable to release the code for this module only. However, in the future, we would like to make the platform available to other users by allowing them to upload their own data and define what they want to annotate.

5   Acknowledgements

This work has been supported by a grant from the Swedish Riksbankens Jubileumsfond (Development of lexical and grammatical competences in immigrant Swedish, project P17-0716:1).

References

Malin Ahlberg, Lars Borin, Markus Forsberg, Olof Olsson, Anne Schumacher, and Jonatan Uppström. 2016. Språkbanken's open lexical infrastructure. *SLTC 2016*.

David Alfter, Yuri Bizzoni, Anders Agebjórn, Elena Volodina, and Ildikó Pilán. 2016. From distributions to labels: A lexical proficiency analysis using learner corpora. In *Proceedings of the joint workshop on NLP for Computer Assisted Language Learning and NLP for Language Acquisition at SLTC, Umeå, 16th November 2016*, 130, pages 1–7. Linköping University Electronic Press.

David Alfter and Elena Volodina. 2018. Towards Single Word Lexical Complexity Prediction. In *Proceedings of the 13th Workshop on Innovative Use of NLP for Building Educational Applications*.

Laurie Bauer and Paul Nation. 1993. Word families. *International journal of Lexicography*, 6(4):253–279.

Lars Borin and Markus Forsberg. 2014. Swesaurus; or, The Frankenstein approach to Wordnet construction. In *Proceedings of the Seventh Global Wordnet Conference*, pages 215–223.

Lars Borin, Markus Forsberg, Martin Hammarstedt, Dan Rosén, Roland Schäfer, and Anne Schumacher. 2016. Sparv: Språkbanken's corpus annotation pipeline infrastructure. In *The Sixth Swedish Language Technology Conference (SLTC), Umeå University*, pages 17–18.

Lars Borin, Markus Forsberg, and Lennart Lönngren. 2013. SALDO: a touch of yin to WordNet's yang. *Language resources and evaluation*, 47(4):1191–1211.

Lars Borin, Markus Forsberg, Leif-Jöran Olsson, and Jonatan Uppström. 2012. The open lexical infrastructure of Spräkbanken. In *LREC*, pages 3598–3602.

Annette Capel. 2010. A1–B2 vocabulary: insights and issues arising from the English Profile Wordlists project. *English Profile Journal*, 1.

Annette Capel. 2012. Completing the English vocabulary profile: C1 and C2 vocabulary. *English Profile Journal*, 3.

Council of Europe. 2001. *Common European Framework of Reference for Languages: Learning, Teaching, Assessment*. Press Syndicate of the University of Cambridge.

Luise Dürlich and Thomas François. 2018. EFLLex: A Graded Lexical Resource for Learners of English as a Foreign Language. In *Proceedings of the Eleventh International Conference on Language Resources and Evaluation (LREC-2018)*.

Thomas François, Elena Volodina, Ildikó Pilán, and Anaïs Tack. 2016. SVALex: a CEFR-graded Lexical Resource for Swedish Foreign and Second Language Learners. In *LREC*.

Núria Gala, Thomas François, Delphine Bernhard, and Cédrick Fairon. 2014. Un modèle pour prédire la complexité lexicale et graduer les mots. In *TALN 2014*, pages 91–102.

Núria Gala, Thomas François, and Cédrick Fairon. 2013. Towards a French lexicon with difficulty measures: NLP helping to bridge the gap between traditional dictionaries and specialized lexicons. *E-lexicography in the 21st century: thinking outside the paper., Tallin, Estonia*.

Marcella Hu Hsueh-Chao and Paul Nation. 2000. Unknown vocabulary density and reading comprehension. *Reading in a foreign language*, 13(1):403–30.

Ann-Kristin Hult, Sven-Göran Malmgren, and Emma Sköldberg. 2010. Lexin-a report from a recycling lexicographic project in the North. In *Proceedings of the XIV Euralex International Congress (Leeuwarden, 6-10 July 2010)*.

Batia Laufer and Geke C Ravenhorst-Kalovski. 2010. Lexical threshold revisited: Lexical text coverage, learners' vocabulary size and reading comprehension. *Reading in a foreign language*, 22(1):15–30.

Batia Laufer and Donald D Sim. 1985. Measuring and explaining the reading threshold needed for english for academic purposes texts. *Foreign language annals*, 18(5):405–411.

Sven-Göran Malmgren. 2014. Svenska akademiens ordlista genom 140 år: mot fjortonde upplagan. *LexicoNordica*, (21).

James Milton. 2013. Measuring the contribution of vocabulary knowledge to proficiency in the four skills. In Camilla Bardel, Lindqvist Christina, and Batia Laufer, editors, *L2 vocabulary acquisition, knowledge and use. New perspectives on assessment and corpus analysis*, pages 57–78. EuroSLA monograph series 2.

I Nation. 2006. How large a vocabulary is needed for reading and listening? *Canadian modern language review*, 63(1):59–82.

Paul Nation and Paul Meara. 2010. Vocabulary. *An introduction to applied linguistics*, pages 34–52.

Erik M Petzell. 2017. Svenska akademiens ordbok på nätet. *LexicoNordica*, (24).

Ildikó Pilán and Elena Volodina. 2018. Investigating the importance of linguistic complexity features across different datasets related to language learning. In *Proceedings of the Workshop on Linguistic Complexity and Natural Language Processing*, pages 49–58.

David Singleton. 1995. Introduction: A critical look at the critical period hypothesis in second language acquisition research. *The age factor in second language acquisition*, pages 1–29.

Emma Sköldberg, Louise Holmer, Elena Volodina, and Ildikó Pilán. 2019. State-of-the-art on monolingual lexicography for Sweden. *Slovenščina 2.0: empirical, applied and interdisciplinary research*, 7(1):13–24.

Ulf Teleman, Staffan Hellberg, and Erik Andersson. 1999. *Svenska akademiens grammatik*. Svenska akademien.

Sowmya Vajjala and Detmar Meurers. 2012. On improving the accuracy of readability classification using insights from second language acquisition. In *Proceedings of the seventh workshop on building educational applications using NLP*, pages 163–173. Association for Computational Linguistics.

Elena Volodina, Ildikó Pilán, Stian Rødven Eide, and Hannes Heidarsson. 2014. You get what you annotate: a pedagogically annotated corpus of coursebooks for Swedish as a Second Language. In *Proceedings of the third workshop on NLP for computer-assisted language learning at SLTC 2014, Uppsala University*, 107. Linköping University Electronic Press.

Elena Volodina, Ildikó Pilán, Ingegerd Enström, Lorena Llozhi, Peter Lundkvist, Gunlög Sundberg, and Monica Sandell. 2016a. Swell on the rise: Swedish learner language corpus for European reference level studies. *LREC 2016*.

Elena Volodina, Ildikó Pilán, Lorena Llozhi, Baptiste Degryse, and Thomas François. 2016b. SweLLex: second language learners' productive vocabulary. In *Proceedings of the joint workshop on NLP for Computer Assisted Language Learning and NLP for Language Acquisition at SLTC, Umeå, 16th November 2016*, 130, pages 76–84. Linköping University Electronic Press.

Menglin Xia, Ekaterina Kochmar, and Ted Briscoe. 2016. Text readability assessment for second language learners. In *Proceedings of the 11th Workshop on Innovative Use of NLP for Building Educational Applications*, pages 12–22.

The OPUS Resource Repository: An Open Package for Creating Parallel Corpora and Machine Translation Services

Mikko Aulamo, Jörg Tiedemann
Department of Digital Humanities / HELDIG
University of Helsinki, Finland
{name.surname}@helsinki.fi

Abstract

This paper presents a flexible and powerful system for creating parallel corpora and for running neural machine translation services. Our package provides a scalable data repository backend that offers transparent data pre-processing pipelines and automatic alignment procedures that facilitate the compilation of extensive parallel data sets from a variety of sources. Moreover, we develop a web-based interface that constitutes an intuitive frontend for end-users of the platform. The whole system can easily be distributed over virtual machines and implements a sophisticated permission system with secure connections and a flexible database for storing arbitrary metadata. Furthermore, we also provide an interface for neural machine translation that can run as a service on virtual machines, which also incorporates a connection to the data repository software.

1 Introduction

Parallel corpora are tremendously useful for a variety of tasks. Their natural home is the development of machine translation (MT) where data-driven approaches such as neural MT are data-hungry and still most language pairs and textual domains are under-resourced. Besides MT, there is also plenty of other work that exploits parallel corpora for, e.g., annotation projection (Tiedemann and Agić, 2016), representation learning (Artetxe and Schwenk, 2018), word sense disambiguation (Lefever, 2012), discovery of idiomatic expressions (Villada Moirón and Tiedemann, 2006) and automatic paraphrase detection (Sjöblom et al., 2018). Finally, we should not forget translation studies (Doval and Sánchez Nieto, 2019) and computer-aided language learning

(Frankenberg-Garcia, 2005) as additional application areas.

We have a long tradition in collecting and providing parallel corpora for the public use. OPUS[1] has become the major hub for such data sets and we are now in the process of developing software that makes it easier for external collaborators to contribute to the collection. For this purpose, we have created the OPUS resource repository toolkit that we introduce in this paper. The purpose of this software package is to implement a scalable data processing pipeline that can be accessed via intuitive interfaces and powerful and secure APIs.

Figure 1 illustrates the overall architecture of the repository software. The package is divided into a distributed backend that combines storage servers, metadata databases, a cluster of pre-processing nodes, and a frontend that provides the interface to the backend via secure HTTPS connections. More details about both parts will be given further down.

Finally, we also implement a translation tool that connects to the repository software. The main purpose of that tool is to serve translation engines that can be trained on parallel data from the repository or other sources via a clean web-interface with options for donating data to the project. More details are given in section 3.2.

The software itself is available as open source from github[2] and we provide a public instance of the toolkit from `http://opus-repository.ling.helsinki.fi/`. The implementation of the online translator is also available[3] and currently we run an instance for the translation between Scandinavian languages (Swedish, Danish, Norwegian) and Finnish.[4]

---

[1] http://opus.nlpl.eu
[2] https://github.com/Helsinki-NLP/OPUS-repository
[3] https://github.com/Helsinki-NLP/OPUS-translator
[4] https://translate.ling.helsinki.fi

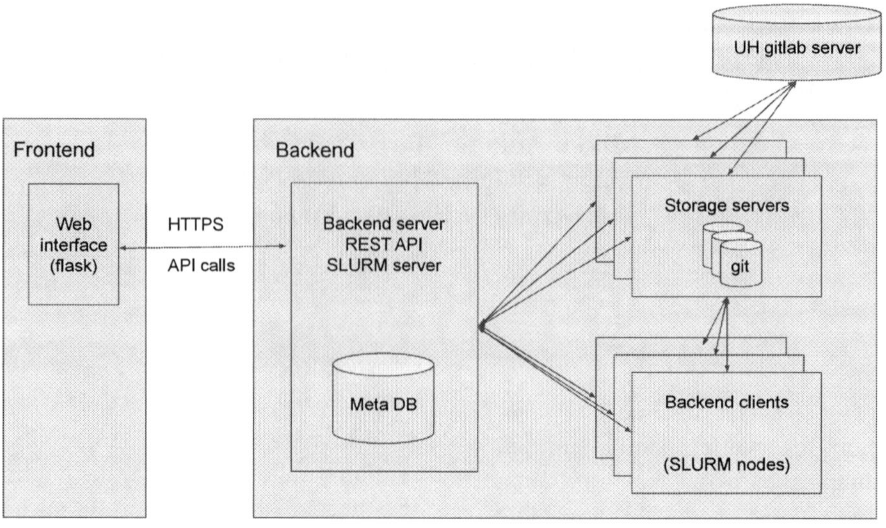

Figure 1: Overall architecture of the OPUS resource repository software.

2 Resource Repository Backend

The backend of the resource repository is based on software development for LetsMT! (Vasiļjevs et al., 2012), a project within the ICT Policy Support Programme of the European Commission.[5] The basic architecture of the OPUS resource repository is the same as in the package developed in that project but the software has been updated and extended in various ways:

- The job scheduler now uses SLURM[6] for workload management and the distribution of jobs over connected nodes in the cluster.

- The storage servers rely on git as their default data repository backend. Other backends are also still supported such as SVN repositories and plain file systems without revision control. We also support the connection to a remote git server for automatic replication and backups of the data.

- The software has been updated to run on Ubuntu servers with the current versions of software libraries and tools. This update included numerous bug fixes and performance optimizations to reduce bottlenecks and memory leaks in the backend.

- The data processing pipeline has been improved in various ways, e.g. integrating modern language identifiers (langid.py (Lui and

Baldwin, 2012) and CLD2[7]) and robust document conversion tools such as ApacheTika[8] running in server mode.

- The APIs have been extended with many additional functionalities. This includes changes to the job control API, metadata search and the storage API. We now also support the creation of translation memories for better interoperability. More details can be found in the online documentation of the repository software at `https://github.com/Helsinki-NLP/OPUS-repository/tree/master/doc`

- New sentence alignment modes have been added, word alignment using eflomal[9] (Östling and Tiedemann, 2016) has been integrated and an experimental call for setting up interactive sentence alignment has been added.

An important feature for the backend is scalability. The system has been designed in a modular way to ensure that additional servers can be connected to the network to adjust for increasing workloads. Figure 1 shows the overall picture of the backend architecture. The main server provides the REST API that can be accessed from the outside for the different actions and requests

---

[5] http://project.letsmt.eu
[6] https://slurm.schedmd.com
[7] https://github.com/CLD2Owners/cld2
[8] https://tika.apache.org
[9] https://github.com/robertostling/eflomal

to be send to the system. It also serves the meta-data DB that stores the essential information for all data records, users and permissions. The actual data sets can be distributed over several storage servers. In the basic setup, they will also be placed on the main backend server with local git repository on mounted file systems. Communication between all nodes in the backend and from the frontend to the backend is done via secure HTTPS connections with signed certificates and private keys. The main bottleneck for the repository is data pre-processing and alignment. For scalability and robustness we, therefore, implement a workload manager based on SLURM that can distribute data processing tasks to various worker clients in the backend cluster. Those workers communicate with the SLURM server and with the storage and metadata servers via the repository API.

The metadata DB is based on a flexible key-value store using TokyoTyrant and TokyoCabinet[10]. It enables fast access and complex queries about data records and configurations. It scales well to large numbers of data records and provides the essential functionality that we require in a system, which will be further enhanced in the future and that requires extensive meta-information, which is not pre-defined and strictly categorical. The key-value store allows arbitrary data records to be connected with any data record in the repository. It is also used to control jobs and process configurations.

Each backend client includes the software necessary for converting and processing data including language identification, data validation, text extraction, sentence boundary detection, tokenization and sentence alignment. The result of this conversion process is a unified format for parallel corpora based on XCES Align for the standoff sentence alignment and a standalone XML format for encoding the textual documents. With this, we follow the structure of OPUS to be immediately compatible with that data source.

The repository software and pre-processing pipelines received substantial improvements. The system now runs ApacheTika servers for robust document conversion, another server for language identification based on langid.py and CLD2 and the system supports pre-processing with UD-compatible models using UDpipe (Straka and Straková, 2017) with pre-trained models from

the universaldependencies project.[11] In the basic setup, this includes sentence boundary detection and tokenisation but even full parsing is supported. Alternative pre-processing tools are also available such as the Moses tokenizers (Koehn et al., 2007) and OpenNLP pre-processing modules.[12] Additional tools may be added later on.

A final feature is the automatic word aligner based on eflomal and pre-trained models from the OPUS project. The system can use model priors derived from existing OPUS data to reliably align even the smallest document pair that arrives in the repository. This is, however, an experimental feature and not enabled by default.

The backend provides a number of complex APIs that control the system. Those APIs are only accessible via verified connections. The frontend implements the public interface that allows external users to communicate with the system. This interface supports the essential functionality of the system. Details will be given in the following section.

3 Interfaces

The project includes open source online interfaces for the resource repository backend[13] and for a translation system.[14] Both of the interfaces are written in Python using the Flask web framework[15] and our running instances are accessible via any common web browser. Users can register on either website and the same account may be used to login to both of these services. Using the translator is possible without a user account, but gaining access to the repository requires being logged in as a registered user.

3.1 Online repository

The online repository website is a graphical user interface for the resource repository API. With the API, one can upload documents, that are translations of each other, and the backend aligns them on the sentence level. The interface enables the use of the API without certification and command line operations. In practice, whenever a user takes an action on the repository website, a command line request is sent to the API. The API sends a response, which is parsed and displayed on the web-

---

[10]https://fallabs.com/tokyotyrant/

[11]https://universaldependencies.org

[12]https://opennlp.apache.org

[13]https://github.com/Helsinki-NLP/OPUS-interface

[14]https://github.com/Helsinki-NLP/OPUS-translator

[15]http://flask.pocoo.org/

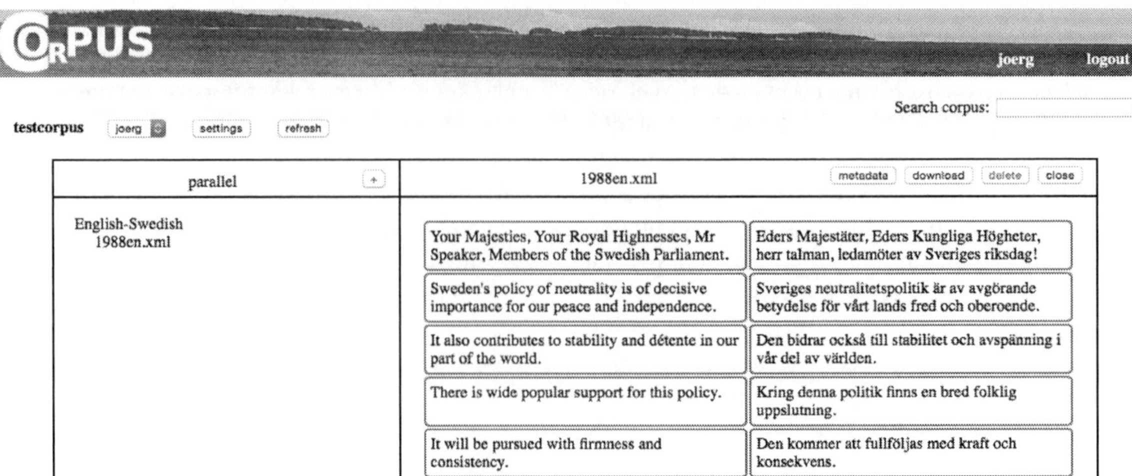

Figure 2: A screenshot of the OPUS resource repository interface.

site in an appropriate way depending on the type of request. Anytime a web page or a part of a web page is generated, all the data, that is presented, is received from the API, e.g. lists of corpora, documents, jobs or users.

In order to use the interface, one must first register to the website and login. Once logged in, users may create new corpora with metadata and settings, which can be edited later. User groups can also be created, and a corpus may be set to be accessible to only a specific group. Users can upload translated documents to a corpus, which are then aligned in the backend. Currently, the allowed document formats are PDF, DOC, TXT, XML, HTML and EPUB. Multiple files may be uploaded at once using TAR, TAR.GZ, or ZIP archives. All uploaded documents and the resulting alignment files are browsable using the tree file system on the interface. Figure 2 shows an example. The website also has a function to search for public corpora and to clone them for further use.

3.2 Online translator

The current translation application runs two multilingual translation models: Finnish to Danish/Norwegian/Swedish (fi-da/no/sv) and Danish/Norwegian/Swedish to Finnish (da/no/sv-fi). The models are trained using the Marian Neural Machine Translation framework (Junczys-Dowmunt et al., 2018) and they run using the framework's web-socket server feature. To translate a text, a source language is first selected from two options: Finnish or Danish/Norwegian/Swedish. The source language can

also be automatically detected. Language detection is performed using pycld2 Python bindings[16] for Google Chromium's Compact Language Detector 2.[17] The target language is chosen from Finnish, Danish, Norwegian, or Swedish. Once the source and target languages are selected and an input text is entered, the text can be translated. If the source language is Finnish and the target language is either Danish, Norwegian or Swedish, the source sentence is translated with fi-da/no/sv model. If the source language is Danish/Norwegian/Swedish and the target language is Finnish, da/no/sv-fi model is used. The resulting translation is represented on the web page. A screenshot of the interface is shown in Figure 3.

The online translator includes a feature to donate more training data. There are three different options to upload data. The first option is to upload translation memories, which can be either TMX or XLIFF files. The second option is to upload documents that are translations of each other and the files must be in XML, HTML, TXT, PDF, DOC, SRT, RTF or EPUB format. In the third option, the user enters two URLs, which point to two web pages that are translations of each other. When uploading translated files or entering translated web pages, the user has an option to receive a TMX file created from their contributed data.

4 Conclusions

This paper presents a new public resource repository for creating and managing parallel corpora

---

[16]https://pypi.org/project/pycld2/
[17]https://github.com/CLD2Owners/cld2

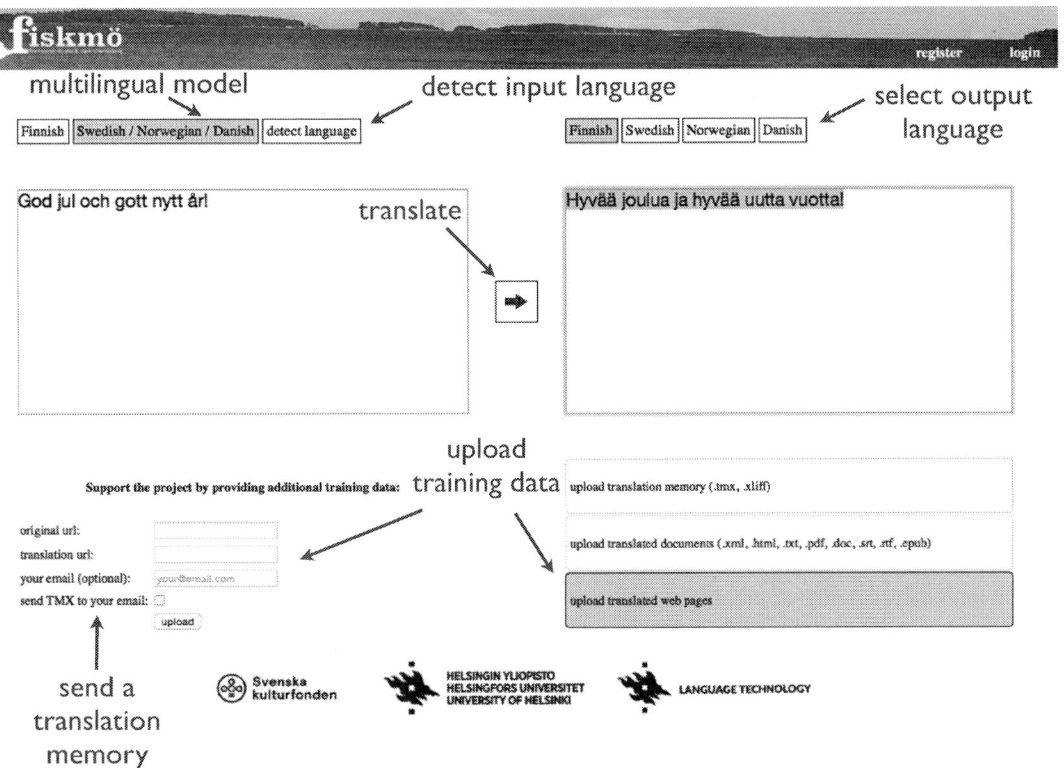

Figure 3: A screenshot of the translator interface.

with a scalable backend and intuitive interfaces. A translation demonstrator is also provided and the software is released as open source.

Acknowledgments

The work was supported by the Swedish Culture Foundation and we are grateful for the resources provided by the Finnish IT Center for Science, CSC.

References

Mikel Artetxe and Holger Schwenk. 2018. http://arxiv.org/abs/1812.10464 Massively multilingual sentence embeddings for zero-shot cross-lingual transfer and beyond. *CoRR*, abs/1812.10464.

Irene Doval and M. Teresa Sánchez Nieto. 2019. https://doi.org/https://doi.org/10.1075/scl.90 *Parallel Corpora for Contrastive and Translation Studies – New resources and applications*. John Benjamins.

Ana Frankenberg-Garcia. 2005. Pedagogical uses of monolingual and parallel concordances. *ELT journal*, 59(3):189–198.

Marcin Junczys-Dowmunt, Roman Grundkiewicz, Tomasz Dwojak, Hieu Hoang, Kenneth Heafield, Tom Neckermann, Frank Seide, Ulrich Germann, Alham Fikri Aji, Nikolay Bogoychev, André F. T. Martins, and Alexandra Birch. 2018. http://www.aclweb.org/anthology/P18-4020 Marian: Fast neural machine translation in C++. In *Proceedings of ACL 2018, System Demonstrations*, pages 116–121, Melbourne, Australia. Association for Computational Linguistics.

Philipp Koehn, Hieu Hoang, Alexandra Birch, Chris Callison-Burch, Marcello Federico, Nicola Bertoldi, Brooke Cowan, Wade Shen, Christine Moran, Richard Zens, Chris Dyer, Ondřej Bojar, Alexandra Constantin, and Evan Herbst. 2007. http://dl.acm.org/citation.cfm?id=1557769.1557821 Moses: Open source toolkit for statistical machine translation. In *Proceedings of the 45th Annual Meeting of the ACL on Interactive Poster and Demonstration Sessions*, ACL '07, pages 177–180, Stroudsburg, PA, USA. Association for Computational Linguistics.

Els Lefever. 2012. *ParaSense: parallel corpora for word sense disambiguation*. Ph.D. thesis, Ghent University.

Marco Lui and Timothy Baldwin. 2012. https://www.aclweb.org/anthology/P12-3005 langid.py: An off-the-shelf language identification tool. In *Proceedings of the ACL 2012 System Demonstrations*, pages 25–30, Jeju Island, Korea. Association for Computational Linguistics.

Eetu Sjöblom, Mathias Creutz, and Mikko Aulamo. 2018. http://arxiv.org/abs/1809.07978 Paraphrase detection on noisy subtitles in six languages. *CoRR*, abs/1809.07978.

Milan Straka and Jana Straková. 2017. http://www.aclweb.org/anthology/K/K17/K17-3009.pdf Tokenizing, pos tagging, lemmatizing and parsing ud 2.0 with udpipe. In *Proceedings of the CoNLL 2017 Shared Task: Multilingual Parsing from Raw Text to Universal Dependencies*, pages 88–99, Vancouver, Canada. Association for Computational Linguistics.

Jörg Tiedemann and Željko Agić. 2016. https://doi.org/doi:10.1613/jair.4785 Synthetic treebanking for cross-lingual dependency parsing. *Journal of Artificial Intelligence Research*, 55:209–248.

Andrejs Vasiļjevs, Raivis Skadiņš, and Jörg Tiedemann. 2012. http://www.aclweb.org/anthology/P12-3008 LetsMT!: Cloud-based platform for do-it-yourself machine translation. In *Proceedings of the ACL 2012 System Demonstrations*, pages 43–48, Jeju Island, Korea. Association for Computational Linguistics.

Begoña Villada Moirón and Jörg Tiedemann. 2006. http://aclweb.org/anthology//W/W06/W06-2405.pdf Identifying idiomatic expressions using automatic word-alignment. In *Proceedings of the EACL 2006 Workshop on Multiword Expressions in a Multilingual Context*, Trento, Italy.

Robert Östling and Jörg Tiedemann. 2016. http://ufal.mff.cuni.cz/pbml/106/art-ostling-tiedemann.pdf Efficient word alignment with markov chain monte carlo. *The Prague Bulletin of Mathematical Linguistics (PBML)*, (106):125—-146.

Garnishing a phonetic dictionary for ASR intake

Iben Nyholm Debess
Sandra Saxov Lamhauge
Grunnurin Føroysk Teldutala
ibendebess@gmail.com
sandralamhauge@gmail.com

Peter Juel Henrichsen
Danish Language Council
pjh@dsn.dk

Abstract

We present a new method for preparing a lexical-phonetic database as a resource for acoustic model training. The research is an offshoot of the ongoing Project Ravnur (Speech Recognition for Faroese), but the method is language-independent. At NODALIDA 2019 we demonstrate the method (called SHARP) online, showing how a traditional lexical-phonetic dictionary (with a very rich phone inventory) is transformed into an ASR-friendly database (with reduced phonetics, preventing data sparseness). The mapping procedure is informed by a corpus of speech transcripts. We conclude with a discussion on the benefits of a well-thought-out BLARK design (Basic Language Resource Kit), making tools like SHARP possible.

1   Introduction

We introduce a new method for pre-processing phonetic databases for use in ASR development. Our research, to be presented at NODALIDA 2019, is an offshoot of the ongoing Faroese ASR project (automatic speech recognition) called Ravnur. After giving some background on the project proper, we turn to the main focus of the present paper: the algorithm SHARP.

We first introduce the Ravnur components and the principles behind them (section 2), and then go into details with SHARP (section 3). In conclusion we offer some remarks on the challenges and advantages of developing an 'eco-system' of inter-dependent language technology resources.

Project Ravnur was initiated in January 2019 with the purpose of creating all the necessary constituents for developing high quality ASR for Faroese. One of the challenges of ASR for small languages is the sparsity of language resources, making the development of such resources a vital

part of the project (Nikulasdóttir et al., 2018). Existing speech and language materials for Faroese have been developed for other purposes (Helgason et al., 2005; Johannesen et al., 2009; Hansen, 2014; Bugge, 2018; Debess, 2019), but these alone are insufficient in size, quality and/or availability. Beginning almost from scratch allowed us the advantage of establishing rational and explicit principles for all aspects of data collection, annotation, and processing.

2   The Faroese BLARK

A BLARK (Basic Language Resource Kit) is defined as the minimal set of language resources necessary for developing language technology for a particular language (Krauwer, 2003; Maegaard et al., 2006). Although the BLARK is not the main theme of this paper, it is detailed below as a prerequisite to the following section on SHARP.

2.1   Inter-dependent language resources

Only non-proprietary file formats are used (txt, csv, html, rtf, textGrid, wav, flac).

- SAMPA: the phonetic inventory is inspired by the SAMPA initiative providing computer-readable phonetic alphabets [1]. Following the tradition within Faroese phonetic research and description, our SAMPA includes the most common, salient, and distinctive phones and diacritics (Rischel, 1964; Helgason, 2003; Árnason, 2011; Thráinsson et al., 2012; Knooihuizen, 2014; Petersen and Adams, 2014; Weyhe,

---

[1]   According to John Wells, the founding father of the international SAMPA initiative, the project is long closed, the website no longer maintained. As recommended by Wells (p.c.), we hereby put our suggestion for a Faroese SAMPA definition forward, inviting future projects to use it as a reference. The phone table (and documentation) is available at https://lab.homunculus.dk/Ravnshornid

2014). Our work is closely coordinated with the (now completed) Faroese TTS project (Helgason and Gullbein, 2002; Helgason et al., 2005).

- PoS: the tagset for Faroese complies with the Pan-European PAROLE meta-tagset (Bilgram and Keson, 1998).
- Dictionary: the dictionary encompasses largely all function words and irregular content words, and a substantial part of highly frequent content words. Each entry includes pronunciation, PoS, and frequency information. The dictionary is versatile by design and can be used for many purposes including traditional lexicographic editions, teaching materials (e.g. CALL and CAPT), TTS development, interactive voice-response systems, and more. The dictionary currently holds about 3,000 entries, aiming at 25,000 by January 2021.
- Speaker sessions: transcripts of speech recordings documenting the phonetic and prosodic variation of modern Faroese. Reading materials comprise a word list, a closed vocabulary reading (numerals 1-100, calculator commands), a phrase list (eliciting prosodic variation, intonation patterns, etc.), and a few samples of connected text (2-5 minutes each). Each session produces roughly 20 min. of speech. The speech corpus currently holds 8 hours of speech (26 speakers), aiming at 200 hours by January 2021 (project end). All acknowledged contemporary dialects of Faroese (Thráinsson et al., 2012) are covered.
- Transcript Corpus: the recordings are transcribed manually by multiple transcribers (orthography and SAMPA) and time coded according to the Ravnur conventions (https://lab.homunculus.dk/Ravnshornid). Phonetic transcription of speech production is carried out by trained phoneticians.
- Background Text Corpus: at present, the background corpus holds 13M words (formal and informal styles). Some of the material is collected in collaboration with Sjúrður Gullbein from the TTS project and Hjalmar P. Petersen from the University of the Faroe Islands.
- Background Speech Corpus: the background speech corpus consists of audiobooks and material from UiO (Johannesen, 2009; Johannesen et al., 2009) and elsewhere.

- Tools: the text and speech tools developed in Project Ravnur can be accessed at (https://lab.homunculus.dk/Ravnshornid).

2.2 Consistency Principle

All BLARK components relate to and depend on each other: each word appearing in a transcript must correspond to a lexical entry. Each manuscript (for recording sessions) must represent all SAMPA phones, and so forth. The Consistency Principle allows the BLARK to develop like an eco-system where the individual components feed off and grow from each other in an iterative process.

3 Garnishing the dictionary

We are now in a position to discuss the SHARP algorithm for optimizing lexical-phonetic information prior to the training of ASR acoustic models.

3.1 Phone inventories

When phoneticians need to represent pronunciation phenomena in symbolic form, they largely follow one of two strategies, either abstracting over speakers and contexts (the lexical approach) or sampling actual speech productions (the descriptive approach). ASR projects typically apply the lexical strategy only, shying away from the burden of phonetic transcription. Since classical phonetic dictionaries (complying with structuralist minimal-pair tests) are usually considered too rich for ASR purposes, lexical-phonetic forms are reduced prior to acoustic training, deleting certain phone types and collapsing others. To the best of our knowledge, the concrete reduction procedure is most often based on technological considerations or gut feeling rather than linguistic principle.

By way of an example, most popular commercial ASR applications for Danish allow users to supply phonetics for new lexical insertions, but in impoverished form without symbols for stød, accent, prolongations, assimilations, and only a subset (not a very rational one) of the Danish vowel inventory. Such linguistically unwarranted restrictions limit the general usability of the users' accumulated lexical contribution, in effect tying it to a particular ASR product.

Thus, in keeping with the Consistency Principle, we needed to devise a principle-based procedure allowing us to maintain the versatility of the dictionary and yet provide the reduced phonetic forms required for acoustic training. Our solution, called SHARP, utilizes the transcript corpus for deriving a reduced SAMPA in a non-destructive way.

Lex	*Trsc*	
X	$\rightarrow X$	opposed phones MATCH
$X\,Y$	$\rightarrow Y\,X$	adjacent phones 'swapped'
$X\,Y$	$\rightarrow Y$	1 phone skipped
$X\,Y\,Z$	$\rightarrow Z$	2 phones skipped
$X\,Y\,Z$	$\rightarrow W\,Z$	2+1 phones skipped
$X\,Y\,V\,Z$	$\rightarrow Z$	3 phones skipped
$X\,Y\,V\,Z$	$\rightarrow W\,Z$	3+1 phones skipped
X	$\rightarrow Y$	two opposed phones skipped
X	$\rightarrow \_$	fallback rule: IGNORE

Table 1. Transduction rules. Lex = lexical-phonetic tier, Trsc = transcript tier. Rules also apply in mirrored versions (e.g. $Y \rightarrow X\,Y$). Transduction of identical strings uses the MATCH rule only. The IGNORE rule ensures completion (_ is the empty string). The term 'skipped' is used for symbols only occurring in one tier.

3.2 The phonetic mapping

As mentioned above, each word appearing in the Transcript Corpus is also represented in the Dictionary. We can therefore align the phonetic representation of any phrase appearing in a transcript with its corresponding lexical projection. For alignment of phone strings, we employ a finite state transducer (FST) with limited look-ahead. Pairs of phone strings are traversed left-to-right applying the transduction rules in table 1.

Consider the alignment of two phonetic renderings of "vónandi er hann ikki koyrdur útav" *hopefully he hasn't driven off (the road)*, one lexical and one descriptive.

Lex: `[vOWnandIerhanIHdZIkOrdurOWdEAv]`
Trsc: `[vOWnandIer anIS   kORDIRU dEAv]`

Observe that this alignment corresponds to the FST transitions (h→_), (H→S), (dZI→_), (r→R), (d→D), (u→I), (r→R), and (OW→U).

Repeating the alignment procedure for all phrases in the Transcription Corpus, a list of rule instances develops. A sample from the rule list (excluding instances of the MATCH rule) is shown below, with the number of instances.

128	(j → _)
96	(I → _)
80	(U → I) *
68	(r → _)
58	(I → 3)
58	(r → R)
43	(U → _) *
36	(U → 3) *
32	(d → _)
32	(i → I)
25	(d → D)
22	(E A → a)
21	(E A d → a)

Consider the three starred rules, all concerning the lexical phone [U], in 80 cases pronounced as [I], in 36 cases as [3], and in 43 cases not pronounced at all. There are several (less frequent) (U→X) rules for (X≠U). In comparison, the MATCH rule (U→U) has only 63 occurrences, contributing to the general impression that [U] is an unstable phone exposed to pronunciation variation.[2]

Several other phones are shown to be unstable in this sense, evident in rules such as ('→_), (5→_), (j→_), (4→E), (w→_), (u→o). Such rules we shall call *skewed*. Formally, skewed rules are determined by

$$count(X \rightarrow X) < \textstyle\sum count(X \rightarrow Y) \text{ for all } (Y \neq X).$$

3.3 Generations

Skewed rules are interpreted in SHARP as transformation rules and are applied everywhere in the Dictionary and Transcription Corpus (in size-order), creating new tiers of phonetic forms. In some cases, phone symbols are cut out of the SAMPA renderings (like (5→_)), in other cases two phones are collapsed into one (e.g. (u→o)), effectively reducing the cardinality of the phone inventory. We call this new lexical tier of transformed phonetic forms the Generation-1 tier (or simply G1).

The transduction procedure is repeated using G1 as lexical forms, producing a G2 tier, and so forth. With each new generation, the cardinality of the phone table decreases (often by 1-3 items) while the average inhabitation (number of exemplars) in the remaining types increases.

---

[2]   Observe that rule types (X→_) outnumber the mirror form (_→X), as a sign of a general fact: phonetic dictionaries aim at a high degree of articulatory explicitness while speech production show exactly the opposite tendency.

At G12 the iteration stops naturally as no more skewed transduction rules can be found. At this point, 24 out of the original 45 SAMPA symbols are still present. It is an important observation, though, that the meaning of each remaining symbol at this point has changed. The symbols can therefore no longer be expected to represent the usual phonetic flavours.

3.4 Turning to ASR

Acoustic models for ASR are trained on sound samples, phonetically labeled. Two complementary factors affect the training efficiency, *parsimony* (a smaller set of labels provides more robust training) and *discrimination* (a larger set preserves more phonetic distinctions).

Since we now have a procedure for gradually reducing the phonetic richness as controlled by (the transcription of) actually occurring speech production, the next step is to evaluate the G0, G1, … G12 phonetic forms for training acoustic models. We use the sphinxtrain engine (ver. 5prealpha, cf. https://github.com/cmusphinx/), employing a standard ten-fold cross validation regime to yield statistically valid test figures.[3]

3.5 Preliminary results

Our initial results are encouraging if preliminary. Using our current smallish dictionary of 2990 entries and 1366 spoken phrases only, our acoustic models do not reach impressive results in terms of absolute WER figures (word-error rate). However, as our performance measures are reasonably consistent (cf. the narrow error bars in fig.1) it still makes sense to compare learning sessions across SHARP-generations.

From an initial WER at 50.2%, error rates improve rapidly: WER_{G1}=41.2%, WER_{G2}=31.6%, WER_{G3}=25.6%, …, WER_{G7}=13.8%. Of course, this impressive recovery is owed to the very poor outset, and also to an atypical ASR setup based on small linguistic databases. We do not know yet to what extent the SHARP algorithm will remain relevant in more realistic scenarios. However, it seems safe to conclude that SHARP may offer a relief to very small ASR projects in distress.

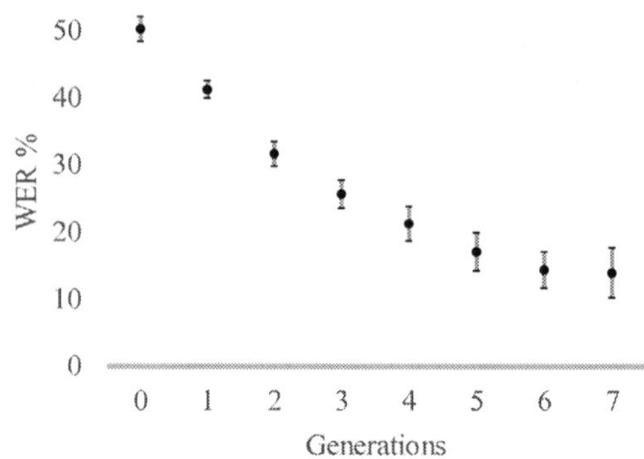

Figure 1. ASR results trained on SHARPened lexical-phonetic forms. The graph shows Word-error rates (WER) for each SHARP generation. Error bars: standard deviation for data sets after ten-fold cross validation. Average WER keeps improving somewhat in generations >7, however less significantly so as error margins increase.

Our work is clearly in progress, and the specifics of the SHARP implementation are bound to change as our BLARK matures. Among many new features we would like to test context sensitive transformation rules ($X\ A\ Y{\rightarrow}X\ B\ Y$) as used by phonologists. However, this step (and many others) make sense only for much larger pools of phonetic samples.

4   Concluding remarks

Much R&D in speech technology has been hampered by implicit or explicit obligations to recycle existing, often inadequate, databases. One example is the government-supported Danish ASR project in the mid-2000s leaning on mediocre speech data from NST, lexical data from the Danish TTS project and various sources unrelated to the project objectives (cf. Kirchmeier et al 2019). Recognition rates never met international standards, much labour was wasted on smartening up poor data, and yet the delivered modules could not, for legal reasons, be shared publicly.

In contrast, the Faroese ASR project, starting afresh, could adopt strict consistency principles to be followed by all, from lexicographers to field workers. Carefully synchronized lexical and descriptive procedures paved the way for the SHARP tool presented in this paper, exploiting the complementarity of theory-driven and data-driven phonetics and getting the most out of our smallish, but undefiled databases.

"More data will solve any problem", "Principles are for sissies", "Fire your

---

3   For the sake of reproducibility, we use a flat language model with minimum likelihood (0%) for all n-grams (n>1) and equal likelihood for individual words.

linguists!". Such fresh attitudes are currently shared by many developers. We invite the serious ASR manufacturer to rediscover the power of linguistic precision.

Acknowledgments

Project Ravnur wishes to personally thank Karin Kass for her never-failing entrepreneurship and diligence. We also wish to thank a number of investors from the Faroese society.

References

Anna Björk Nikulasdóttir, Inga Rún Helgadóttir, Matthías Pétursson and Jón Guðnason. 2018. Open ASR for Icelandic: Resources and a Baseline System. In *Proceedings of the 11th International Conference on Language Resources and Evaluation*, pages 3137-3142.

Bente Maegaard, Steven Krauwer, Khalid Choukri and Lise Damsgaard Jørgensen. 2006. The BLARK concept and BLARK for Arabic. In *Proceedings of the 5th International Conference on Language Resources and Evaluation*, pages 773-778.

Edit Bugge. 2018. Attitudes to variation in spoken Faroese. *Journal of Sociolinguistics* 22(3):312-330.

Eivind Weyhe. 2014. Variatión av i og u í herðingarveikari støðu í føroyskum. *Fróðskaparrit*, 61:116-136. Fróðskapur, Tórshavn, Faroe Islands.

Höskuldur Thráinsson, Hjalmar P. Petersen, Jógvan í Lon Jacobsen and Zakaris Hansen. 2012. *Faroese, an overview and reference grammar*, 2nd edition. Fróðskapur, Tórshavn, Faroe Islands, and Linguistic Institute, University of Iceland, Reykjavík, Iceland.

Iben Nyholm Debess. 2019. *FADAC Hamburg 1.0. Guide to the Faroese Danish Corpus Hamburg.* Kieler Arbeiten zur skandinavistischen Linguistik 6. Institut für Skandinavistik, Frisistik und Allgemeine Sprachwissenschaft (ISFAS), FID Northern Europe https://macau.uni-kiel.de/receive/macau_publ_00002318

Janne Bondi Johannesen. 2009. A corpus of spoken Faroese. *Nordlyd*, 36(2):25-35.

Janne Bondi Johannesen, Joel Priestly, Kristin Hagen, Tor Anders Åfarli and Øystein Alexander Vangsnes. 2009. The Nordic Dialect Corpus - an Advanced Research Tool. In Kristiina Jokinen and Eckhard Bick (eds.). 2009. *NEALT Proceedings Series*, 4:73-80.

Jonathan Adams and Hjalmar P. Petersen. 2014. *A Language Course for Beginners*, 3rd edition. Stiðin, Tórshavn, Faroe Islands.

Jørgen Rischel. 1964. Toward the Phonetic description of Faroese vowels. *Fróðskaparrit*, 13:99-113.

Kirsti Dee Hansen. 2004. FTS - Føroyskt TekstaSavn/færøsk talekorpus. In Henrik Holmboe (ed.). 2005. *Nordisk sprogteknologi 2004 - Årbog for Nordisk Sprogteknologisk Forskningsprogram 2000-2004*, pages 47-50.

Kristján Árnason. 2011. *The Phonology of Icelandic and Faroese.* Oxford University Press, Oxford, UK.

Pétur Helgason. 2003. Faroese Preaspiration. In *Proceedings of the 15th International Congress of Phonetic Sciences*, pages 2517-2520. Universidad Autònoma de Barcelona, Barcelona, Spain.

Pétur Helgason and Sjúrður Gullbein. 2002. Phonological norms in Faroese speesch synthesis. In *Proceedings of the International Conference on Spoken Language Processing*, pages 2269-2272, Denver, Colorado.

Pétur Helgason, Sjúrður Gullbein and Karin Kass. 2005. Færøsk talesyntese: Rapport marts 2005. In Henrik Holmboe (ed.). 2005. *Nordisk sprogteknologi 2005 - Årbog for Nordisk Sprogteknologisk Forskningsprogram 2000-2004*, pages 51-58.

Remco Knooihuizen. 2014. Variation in Faroese and the development of a spoken standard: In search of corpus evidence. *Nordic Journal of Linguistics*, 37(1):87-105.

Sabine Kirchmeier, Peter Juel Henrichsen, Philip Diderichsen and Nanna Bøgebjerg Hansen. 2019. *Dansk Sprogteknologi i Verdensklasse.*

Steven Krauwer. 2003. The Basic Language Resource Kit (BLARK) as the First Milestone for the Language Resources Roadmap. In *Proceedings of the International Workshop "Speech and Computer", SPECOM 2003*, Moscow, Russia.

Thomas Bilgram and Britt Keson. 1998. The Construction of a Tagged Danish Corpus. *Proceedings of the 11th Nordic Conference of Computational Linguistics, NODALIDA 1998*, pages 129-139.

UniParse: A universal graph-based parsing toolkit

Daniel Varab
IT University
Copenhagen, Denmark
`djam@itu.dk`

Natalie Schluter
IT University
Copenhagen, Denmark
`natschluter@itu.dk`

Abstract

This paper describes the design and use of the graph-based parsing framework and toolkit UniParse, released as an open-source python software package developed at the IT University, Copenhagen Denmark. UniParse as a framework novelly streamlines research prototyping, development and evaluation of graph-based dependency parsing architectures. The system does this by enabling highly efficient, sufficiently independent, readable, and easily extensible implementations for all dependency parser components. We distribute the toolkit with ready-made pre-configured re-implementations of recent state-of-the-art first-order graph-based parsers, including highly efficient Cython implementations of feature encoders and decoding algorithms, as well as off-the-shelf functions for computing loss from graph scores.

1 Introduction

Motivation. While graph-based dependency parsers are theoretically simple models, extensible and modular implementations for sustainable parser research and development have to date been severely lacking in the research community. Contributions to parsing research generally centres around particular components of parsers in isolation, such as novel decoding algorithms, novel arc encodings, or novel learning architectures. However, due to perceived gains in performance or due to the lack of foresight in writing sustainable code, these components are rarely implemented modularly or with extensibility in mind. This applies to prior sparse-feature dependency parsers (McDonald and Pereira (2006)'s MST parser), as well as recent state-of-the-art neural parsers (Kiperwasser and Goldberg, 2016; Dozat and Manning, 2017). Implementations of parser components are generally tightly coupled to one another which heavily hinders their usefulness in future research.

With UniParse, we provide a flexible, highly expressive, scientific framework for easy, low-barrier of entry, highly modular, efficient development and fair benchmarking of graph-based dependency parsing architectures. With the framework we distribute pre-configured state-of-the-art first-order sparse and neural graph-based parser implementations to provide strong baselines for future research on graph based dependency parsers.

Novel contributions

- We align sparse feature and neural research in graph-based dependency parsing to a **common terminology**. With this shared terminology we develop a unified framework for the UniParse toolkit to rapidly prototype new parsers and easily compare performance to previous work.
- Prototyping is now rapid due to **modularity**: parser components may now be developed in isolation, with no resulting loss in efficiency. Measuring the empirical performance of a new decoder no longer require implementing an encoder, and investigating the synergy between a learning strategy and a decoder no longer requires more than a flag or calling a library function.
- **Preprocessing is now made explicit** within its own component and is thereby adequately isolated and portable.
- **The evaluation module is now easy to read and fully specified.** We specify the subtle differences in computing unlabeled and labeled arc scores (UAS, LAS) from previous

literature and have implemented these in Uni-Parse in an explicit manner.

- To the best of our knowledge, UniParse is the first attempt at **unifying existing dependency parsers to the same code base**. Moreover, UniParse is to our knowledge the first attempt to enable first-order sparse-feature dependency parsing in a *shared* python codebase.

We make the parser freely available under a GNU General Public License[1].

2 Terminology of a unified dependency parser

Traditionally, a graph-based dependency parser consists of three components. An *encoder* Γ, a set of *parameters* λ, and a *decoder* h. The possible dependency relations between all words of a sentence S are modeled as a complete directed graph G_S where words are nodes and arcs are the relations. An arc in G_S is called a factor which Γ associates with a d-dimensional feature vector, its *encoding*. The set of parameters λ are then used to produce scores from the constructed feature vectors according to some learning procedure. These parameters are optimized over treebanks. Lastly a decoder h is some maximum spanning tree algorithm with input G_S and scores for factors of G_S given by λ; it outputs a well-formed dependency tree, which is the raw output of a dependency model.

Recent work on neural dependency parsers learns factor embeddings discriminatively alongside the parameters used for scoring. The result is that Γ and λ of dependency parsers fuse together into a union of parameters. Thus, in this work we fold the notion of encoding into the parameter space. Now, for the neural models, all parameters are trainable, whereas for sparse-feature models, the encodings of sub-sets of arcs are non-trainable. So the unified terminology addresses only parameters λ and a decoder h.

3 API and the joint model architecture

We provide two levels of abstraction for implementing graph-based dependency parsers. First, our descriptive high-level approach focuses on expressiveness, enabling models to be described in

just a few lines of code by providing an interface where the required code is minimal, only a means to configure design choices. Second, as an alternative to the high-level abstraction we emphasise that parser definition is nothing more than a composition of pre-configured low-level modular implementations. With this we invite cherry picking of the included implementations of optimised decoders, data preprocessors, evaluation module and more. We now briefly overview the basic use of the joint API and list the central low-level module implementations included with the UniParse toolkit.

Elementary usage (high level). For ease of use we provide a high-level class to encapsulate neural training. Its use results in a significant reduction in the amount of code required to implement a parser and counters unwanted boilerplate code. It provides default configurations for all included components, while enabling custom implementation whenever needed. Custom implementations are only required to be callable and adheres to the framework's function definition. The minimum requirement with the use of this interface is a parameter configuration, loss function, optimizer, and batch strategy. In Listing 1 we show an example implementation of Kiperwasser and Goldberg (2016)'s neural parser in only a few lines. The full list of possible arguments along with their interfaces can be found in the toolkit documentation.

Vocabulary. This class facilitates preprocessing of CoNLL-U formatted files with support for out-of vocabulary management and alignment with pre-trained word embeddings. Text preprocessing strategies have significant impact on NLP model performance. Despite this, little effort has put into describing such techniques in recent literature. Without these details preprocessing becomes yet another hyper-parameter of a model, and obfuscates research contribution. In the UniParse toolkit, we include a simple implementation for recently employed techniques in parsing for token cleaning and mapping.

Batching. UniParse provides functionality to organise tokens into batches for efficient computation and learning. We provide several configurable implementations for different batching strategies. This includes 1. batching by sentence length (bucketing), 2. fixed-length batching with padding, and 3. clustered-length batching as seen

---

[1]`github.com/danielvarab/uniparse`

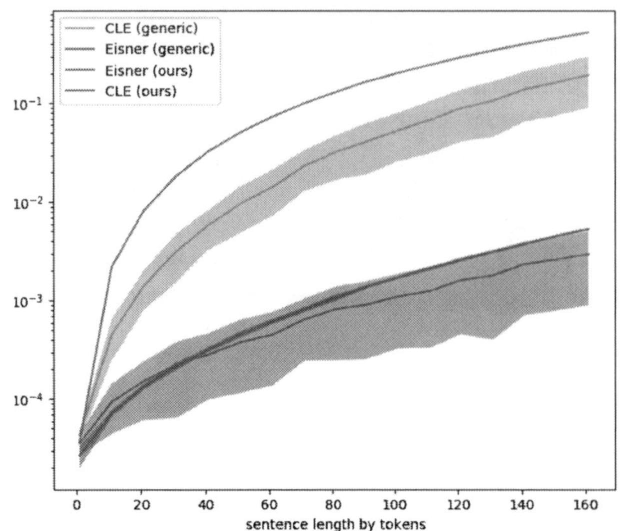


```python
from uniparse import *
from uniparse.models import *

vocab = Vocabulary().fit(train)
params = KiperwasserGoldberg()
model = Model(params,
              decoder="eisner",
              loss="hinge",
              optimizer="adam",
              vocab=vocab)
metrics = model.train(train, dev,
                      epochs=30)
test_metrics = model.evaluate(test)
```

Algorithm	en_ud	en_ptb	sents/s
Eisner (generic)	96.35	479.1	~ 80
Eisner (ours)	1.49	6.31	~ 6009
CLE (generic)	19.12	93.8	~ 404
CLE (ours)	1.764	6.98	~ 5436

Figure 1: (Right code snippet) Implementation of Kiperwasser and Goldberg (2016)'s neural parser in only a few lines using UniParse.
(Right table and left figure) Number of seconds a decoder takes to decode an entire dataset. Score matrices are generated uniformly in the range $[0, 1]$. The random generated data has an impact on CLE due to its greedy nature; The figure demonstrates this by the increasingly broad standard deviation band. Experiments are run on an Ubuntu machine with an Intel Xeon E5-2660, 2.60GHz CPU.

in the codebase for Dozat and Manning (2017)[2] (this is not described in the published work). With unobtrusive design in mind any alternative custom batching strategy may be employed directly, no interaction with the framework is needed.

Decoders We include optimised Cython implementations of first-order decoder algorithms with the toolkit. This includes Eisner's algorithm (Eisner, 1996) and Chu-Liu-Edmonds (Chu and Liu, 1965; Edmonds, 1967; Zwick, 2013). In Figure 1 we compare the performance of our decoder implementations against pure python implementations[3] on randomised score input. Our implementations outperform a pure python implementations by a order of several magnitudes.

Evaluation. UAS and LAS are central dependency parser performance metrics, measuring unlabeled and labeled arc accuracy respectively with $\text{UAS} = \frac{\#\text{correct arcs}}{\#\text{arcs}}$ and $\text{LAS} = \frac{\#\text{correctly labeled arcs}}{\#\text{arcs}}$. Unfortunately, there are also a number unreported preprocessing choices preceding the application of these metrics, which renders direct comparison of parser performance in the literature futile, regardless of how well-motivated these preprocessing choices are. These are generally discovered by manually screening the code implementations when these implementations are made available to the research community. Two important variations found in state-of-the-art parser evaluation are the following.

1. **Punctuation removal.** Arcs incoming to any punctuation are somtimes removed for evaluation. Moreover, the definition of punctuation is not universally shared. We provide a clear python implementation for these metrics with and without punctuation arc deletion before application, where the definition of punctuation is clear: punctuation refers to tokens that consist of characters complying to the Unicode punctuation standard.[4] This is the strategy employed by the widely used Perl evaluation script, which to our knowledge, originates from the CoNLL 2006 and

---

[2] https://github.com/tdozat/Parser-v1
[3] https://github.com/
LxMLS/lxmls-toolkit/blob/
1bdc382e509d24b24f581c1e1d78728c9e739169/
lxmls/parsing/dependency_decoder.py

[4] https://www.compart.com/en/unicode/
category

Parser configurations	Dataset	UAS wo.p.. original	LAS wo.p. original	UAS wo.p.	LAS wo.p.	UAS w.p.	LAS w.p.
Kiperwasser and Goldberg	en_ud	—	—	87.71	84.83	86.80	85.12
(2016)	en_ptb	93.32	91.2	93.14	91.57	92.56	91.17
	da	—	—	83.72	79.49	83.24	79.62
Dozat and Manning	en_ud	—	—	91.47	89.38	90.74	89.01
(2017)	en_ptb	95.74	95.74	95.43	94.06	94.91	93.70
	da	—	—	87.84	84.99	87.42	84.98
MSTparser	en_ud	—	—	75.55	66.25	73.47	65.20
(2006) + extensions	en_ptb	—	—	76.07	64.67	74.00	63.60
	da	—	—	68.80	55.30	67.17	55.52

Table 1: UAS/LAS for included parser configurations. We provide results with (w.p.) and without (wo.p.) punctuation. For the English universal dependencies (UD) dataset we exclude the github repository suffix *EWT*. Regarding (Dozat and Manning, 2017), despite having access to the published TensorFlow code of we never observed scores exceed 95.58.

2007 shared tasks.[5] We infer this from references in (Buchholz and Marsi, 2006).

2. **Label prefixing.** Some arc labels are "composite", their components separated by a colon. An example from the English Universal Dependencies data set is the label `obl:tmod`. The official CoNLL 2017 shared-task evaluation script[6] allows partial matching of labels based on prefix matches for components, for example matching to `obl` of `obl:tmod` giving full points. We include this variant in the distributed UniParse evaluation module.

Loss Functions. Common loss functions apply to scalar values, or predictions vectors representing either real values or probabilities. However loss functions for dependency parsers are unorthodox in that they operate on graphs, which has been dealt with in various creative ways over the years. We include a set of functions that apply to first-order parser graphs which are represented as square matrices. In the future we hope to expand this set for first-order, as well as explore higher-order structures.

Callbacks. While we have done our uttermost to design UniParse in a unobtrusive manner, few limitations may occur when developing, and especially during exploration of model configurations when using the high-level model class. This could be the likes of manual updating of optimisers learning rates during training, or logging granulated loss and accuracy. To accommodate this we include callback functionality which hooks into the training procedure enabling users to do the last few things perhaps inhibited by the framework. We include a number of useful pre-implemented callback utilities, such as a Tensorboard logger[7], model saver, and a patience mechanism for early stopping.

Included parsers. We include three state-of-the-art first-order dependency parser implementations as example configurations of UniParse: McDonald and Pereira (2006)'s MST sparse-feature parser [8], Kiperwasser and Goldberg (2016) and Dozat and Manning (2017)'s graph-based neural parsers. Experiments are carried out on English and Danish: the Penn Treebank (Marcus et al., 1994) (en_ptb, training on sections 2-21, development on section 22 and testing on section 23), converted to dependency format following the default configuration of the Stanford Dependency Converter (version $\geq$ 3.5.2), and the English (en_ud), and Danish (da) datasets from Version 2.1 of the Universal Dependencies project (Nivre et al., 2017). Table 1 shows how our parser configurations perform compared with the originally reported parser performance.

<hr>

[5] `https://depparse.uvt.nl/SoftwarePage.html#eval07.pl`

[6] `https://universaldependencies.org/conll17/baseline.html`

[7] `github.com/tensorflow/tensorboard`

[8] Note that this MST parser implementation consists of a restricted feature set and is only a first-order parser, as proof of concept.

4 Concluding remarks

In this paper, we have described the design and usage of UniParse, a high-level un-opinionated framework and toolkit that supports both feature-based models with on-line learning techniques, as well as recent neural architectures trained through backpropagation. We have presented the framework as answer to a long-standing need for highly efficient, easily extensible, and, most of all, directly comparable graph-based dependency parsing research.

The goal of UniParse is to ease development and evaluation of graph-based syntatic parsers. Future work includes extending UniParse to a general parsing pipeline from raw text.

References

Sabine Buchholz and Erwin Marsi. 2006. Conll-x shared task on multilingual dependency parsing. In *In Proceedings of CoNLL*, pages 149–164. Association for Computational Linguistics.

Y.J. Chu and T.H. Liu. 1965. On the shortest arborescence of a directed graph. *Sci. Sinica*, 14:13961400.

Timothy Dozat and Christopher M. Manning. 2017. Deep biaffine attention for neural dependency parsing. In *Proceedings of ICLR*.

J. Edmonds. 1967. Optimum branchings. *J. Res. Nat. Bur. Standards*, 71B:233240.

Jason M. Eisner. 1996. https://doi.org/10.3115/992628.992688 Three new probabilistic models for dependency parsing: An exploration. In *Proceedings of the 16th Conference on Computational Linguistics - Volume 1*, COLING '96, pages 340–345, Stroudsburg, PA, USA. Association for Computational Linguistics.

Eliyahu Kiperwasser and Yoav Goldberg. 2016. Simple and accurate dependency parsing using bidirectional lstm feature representations. *Transactions of the ACL*, 4:313–327.

Mitchell Marcus, Grace Kim, Mary Ann Marcinkiewicz, Robert MacIntyre, Ann Bies, Mark Ferguson, Karen Katz, and Britta Schasberger. 1994. The penn treebank: Annotating predicate argument structure. In *Proceedings of the Workshop on Human Language Technology*, HLT '94, pages 114–119, Stroudsburg, PA, USA. Association for Computational Linguistics.

Ryan McDonald and Fernando Pereira. 2006. Online learning of approximate dependency parsing algorithms. In *Proceedings of EACL*. Association for Computational Linguistics.

Joakim Nivre et al. 2017. http://hdl.handle.net/11234/1-2515 Universal dependencies 2.1. LINDAT/CLARIN digital library at the Institute of Formal and Applied Linguistics (ÚFAL), Faculty of Mathematics and Physics, Charles University.

Uri Zwick. 2013. http://www.cs.tau.ac.il/ zwick/grad-algo-13/directed-mst.pdf Lecture notes on "analysis of algorithms": Directed minimum spanning trees.

Association for Computational Linguistics
209 N. Eighth Street
Stroudsburg, Pennsylvania 18360

ISBN 978-1-5108-9444-0